G000115684

The Ravenstonedale Parish Registers, 1571-[1812]

With the Editor's Compliments.

Ravenstonedale.
27th Novr. 1895.

THE

RAVENSTONEDALE

PARISH REGISTERS.

TRANSCRIBED AND EDITED BY

THE REV. R. W. METCALFE, M.A.,

VICAR OF RAVENSTONEDALE.

VOL. I.—1571 TO 1710.

KENDAL:
T. WILSON, PRINTER, 28, HIGHGATE.
1893.

INTRODUCTION.

A LONG narrow volume, measuring 15¼ by 7½ inches and containing 186 pages of parchment rudely bound together, forms the earliest "Register Booke of yᵉ Church of Rayvinstondall." Like most of its kind it has suffered from neglect and ill-usage, which have combined to render portions almost illegible. The last pages, in particular, recording the Burials from 1648 to 1655, are so much discoloured from the effects of damp or some other cause as to add considerably to a transcriber's difficulties.

These Registers are, it is believed, the oldest records extant in the original which the Parish possesses. It seems very desirable, therefore, that they should in some form or other be preserved in perpetuity; and not merely preserved but at the same time made more accessible to all who may wish to consult them. With this object in view, I have ventured to undertake their publication.

In order that it may be as faithful a reproduction of the original as is possible, this first volume is an exact copy, page for page, line for line, letter for letter; nothing has been added by way of suggestion where the reading was doubtful, nothing has been omitted.

The registration of deaths, and perhaps of burials, dates from very ancient times; that of baptisms appears to have been of later origin. The keeping of Church Registers by the Clergy was instituted by law in 1538; subsequently, in 1597, these Registers were to be of parchment: the Canon Law of 1603 further required that the Churchwardens should forward to the Bishop or his Chancellor, annually, a true copy of each year's entries. This duty of registration was discharged only very indifferently by the majority of the Clergy, the work being generally entrusted to the parish clerk; and the forwarding of the Ravenstonedale duplicates does not seem to have been commenced until the year 1667, at least none of an older date are in existence. From this year, however, the Transcripts are, with but few exceptions, continuous, and have proved invaluable in supplying gaps caused presumably by the corresponding page of the Register having first become loose and then lost.

Of the Ravenstonedale Transcripts kept in the Carlisle Diocesan Registry, it may be remarked that the only missing years from 1667 to 1710 are those of 1682, 1684, 1686, 1688, 1693, 1703, 1707, 1708, and 1709. It is quite possible that even these may be recovered eventually, if, as is most probable, they have strayed into the bundle of some other parish.

"Henery Shawe, clerk of ye parish," signs the Transcript for 1667; "Tho. Dodson," that for 1668, while all the rest from 1670 to 1720 are subscribed by "Wm. Balife, parish clerk." The Transcript for 1673 is signed by "Anth: Prockter, minister, Tho: Dennis, Anthony ffothergill, Thomas Parkin," and the same incumbent examines that for 1677 as "curate." There is only one presentment, viz., in 1710, by "Tho. Tolmin, minister of Ravenstonedale. William Parkin, John Hunter, Churchwardens." This is all the information as to the church officials that can be gathered from these duplicates.

In the Ravenstonedale Registers little will be found beyond a plain matter-of-fact record of Baptisms, Weddings, and Burials,—here and there, however, it is possible to read between the lines.

During the religious anarchy of the Cromwellian usurpation the disturbed state of the parish as regards matters ecclesiastical may be deduced from the variations in the writing of the Marriage entries,—seeming to point to a frequent change of minister. The "Bare Bones" Parliament of 1653 enacted a law to secularize the marriage rite by making it a civil contract. This accounts for there having been no weddings in the parish from 1653 to 1657, parties being obliged to journey to "Appellbye" or "Kendall" to be married by "ye maire" or some other "Justiss" of the Peace.

It seems strange that no mention is anywhere made of that dread visitant,—the Plague. Yet it is very evident that our parish did not escape its ravages. In 1579, 1588, and again in 1597—during the whole of which period the pestilence was more or less prevalent throughout the northern counties—the mortality in Ravenstonedale was abnormally high. But it was not until the spring of 1623 that the storm burst in its full fury. The entries for that year, though obviously incomplete, three months being omitted, give a death-roll of 48, or 33 above the average for that period. The scribe himself appears to have fallen a victim to the epidemic, for, after the gap following the entry of February 22nd the handwriting is changed. The great London outbreak of 1665 does not appear to have reached Ravenstonedale.

It may here be noted that another epidemic, no less deadly than the Plague, swept over the parish in 1730. In that year 53 deaths occurred, at a time when the average was only 17. The mortality was highest in June, in which month 16 burials are recorded. It is somewhat curious that there is, I believe, no evidence of this visitation having been prevalent in the neighbouring parishes; nor am I aware of any local tradition defining its nature. Perhaps now some light may be thrown upon it.

It will be seen that in the year 1678 the "Woollen" Act was enforced in Ravenstonedale as also in other parishes in the vicinity. The object of the enactment was, no doubt, to give a stimulus to the home manufacture of woollen goods.

Of the old sixteenth century names few are left. The Adamthwaites, Bovells, Cawtleys, Chamberlaines, Dents, Greens, Halls, Murthwaites, Peares, Pinders, and Rogersons have all disappeared: the Bousfields, Fawcetts and Shaws, once so numerous, have now only one or two representatives; the Fothergills alone remain unaffected by the lapse of three centuries.

As of names, so of places: many of the old homesteads are gone. "Keldhead," "Howkeld," "Galehead," "Mires," "Askgill," "Breckfoot," "Crog" (?) and others seem to be unknown to the present inhabitants of the Dale, and their sites are only of doubtful identification.

As the proceeds derived from the sale of "Parish Registers" seldom cover the cost of publication, I take this opportunity of tendering my acknowledgments to the forty-one Subscribers, whose names are appended to this volume, for the support they have accorded to my undertaking.

I have also to express my indebtedness to our Diocesan Registrar (A. N. Bowman, Esq.) for affording me every facility for examining the Transcripts and other old documents preserved in the Bishop's Registry.

Ravenstonedale.

A register booke of
all wedings Chrestnings
and Buryalles Begining
the xiith of June Ano/Dni/1577
and so Contenewing untill the xth
of Janewarye Ano/Dni/1598 wth
as maynye more Chrestneings Wedings and Buryalles
as Cowld be fownde in the sayme
Church of Rayvinstondall Before the
Sayde day wch Christnengs and
wedings and Buryalles ar wryttne
in the foremost partt of this booke
wth both the day and year of the
sayme in the first partt of this
Booke is wryttne Christneings in
the Second partt wedings and
in the thred partt Buryalles
wth the day and yeare

Henery Shawe clericus
nostræ parochiæ 1633 & post hac quam diu
anti

1571.		CHRISTENYNGS.
DECEMBAR.	15	Was chrestned Giles sonn to henrye garethwat
	16	Was chrest Maybell Bovell dawghter to Bartle Bovell
	19	Was chrest herrye sonn to myghell murthwat
JANEWARYE.	18	Was xpest Janat dawghter to John pindar
	21	Was xpest hew sonn to John handlaye
	22	Was margeret dawghter to willm grene
	23	Was xpestned Janatt dawghter to Robartt Chambarlaine
	26	Was xpestned Richard sonn to Anthonye ffothrgill
MARCH.	10	Was xpestned Janat dawghtr to John grene
	19	Was baptest margerett dawghter to Jenkin grene
	23	Was baptysed Essaybell dawghter to maythew Dentt
	26	Was baptysed margerett dawghter to Richard pindar
APPRELL. ano dni 1572	3	Was baptest Robartt sonn to myghell shaw
MAY.	11	Was babtist Maybell dawghter to xpofor Busfeld
JUNE.	19	Was baptist John sonn to Edward grene
JULII.	6	Was baptest hew sonn to gilbartt ffothrgill
	19	Was baptest Thomas sonn to John hayswhittle
	23	Was bapt Essaybell dawghter to Raynold todd
SEPTEMBAR.	19	Was baptest John sonn to xpofor ffothrgill
DECEMBAR.	2	Was baptysed Lanc sonn to Abraham tayler
JANEWARYE.	24	Was baptysed xpobell dawghter to John ffothergill and Raynold sonn to John*

* Corner of page gone.

1572. CHRISTNEYNGS.

FFAYBrEWAry. 3 Was baptysed Jeffaray sonn
to gilbartt heblethwat
21 Was baptysed Janatt dawghter
to Richard wilson
and ffrancis dawghter
to Richard ffawcitt
MARCH. 2 Was bap margarytt dawghtr
to henrye Adamthwat
20 Was bap henrye sonn to
Ano Dni Richard Bovell
1573. 26 Was bap Essaybell dawghter
to Edward Dentt
APPRELL. 5 Was bap Issaybell dawghter
to Miles Busfeld
MAY. 1 Was bap margerett dawghtr
to Thomas Adamthwat
7 Was bap Willm sonn to
Robartt ffothrgill
8 Was bap margerett dawghtr
to Willm Adamthwat
15 Was bap Lanc sonn to willm grene
JULI. 14 Was bap xpobell dawghter
to Richard Rogrson
AUGUST. 6 Was bap margerett dawghtr
to John Ewbank
24 Was bap Thomas sonn to
Rowland holme
SEPTEBr. 8 Was bap Janatt dawghter
to gilbartt ffothrgill
DECEMBAr. 15 Was bap Ellin dawghter
to Rowland Raykstro
28 Was bap margayrett dawghtr
to John hawle
JANEWARY. 6 Ellin dawghter to willm shaw
MARCH. 14 Bap John sonn to myghell
Ano Dni shaw
1574.
26 Was baptysed margerett
dawghter fo John grene
APRELL. 1 Was baptysed Phillip sonn
to Jenkin grene
2 was baptysed John sonn
to James tayler

1574. CHRISTNEYNGS.

MAY. 17 Was baptised Janatt dawghter to henrye Swinbanke

JULI. 5 Was baptysed Elizabeth dawghter to Rawff melnear

25 Was bap maythew sonn to Roger pindar

1575.

(Is not to be fownd in this book) 28 Was bap margerett dawghter to myles ffoth^r^gill

An^o^ Dn^i^, 1576.

DECEMB^r^. 2 Was baptysed mayrye dawghter to Cuthbartt Chambarlaine

9 Was bap John dawghter to xpofor hawle

16 Was bap willm sonn to pettar grene

21 Was bap John dawghter to Edward ffawcit

JANEWARY. 1 Was bap John son to John grene

13 Was bap Alic daught^r^ to symond busfeld & ellin daughter to John ewbanke

FAB^r^EWARY. 3 Was bap myghell sonn to Raynold todd, of Asfell

24 Was bap pettar Sonn to Richard pindar

24 Was baptysed henrye Sonn to Roger pindar

These ar all the xpestneyngs
that Cowld be fownd in the
Church of Rayvinstondall
before the XIIth of maye An^o^/1577
whare the booke begineth heare
in the next leaff.

1577. CHRISTNEYNGS.

MAY. 12 Was baptysed george sonn
to myles Busfeld
26 Was baptest John sonn to
Rowland holme
JULI. 21 Was bap xpofor Sonn to
Steven Busfeld
21 Anthonye sonn to John ffoth^r^gill
28 Was bap Elizabeth dawghter
to John Smeth a poore man
AUGUST 4 Was bap Sibell the dawghter
to Lanc ffawcitt
4 And Elic dawghter to herry ffawcit
11 Elin the dawghter to myghell
shaw baptyzed
18 Was bap Elic the dawghter
to Bartle Bovell
SEPTEBAR. 22 Was bap Annas dawghter
to giles tayler
OCTOBAR. 6 Was bap margerett the dawghter
to James boone
18 Was bap xpobell the dawghter
to Abraam tayler
NOVEMBA^r^. 17 Was bap mawdlaine the dawght^r^
to Richard ffawcit
24 Was bap Alic the dawghter
to Richard ffoth^r^gill
DECEMBAR. 1 Was bap Ellin the dawghter
to Richard Busfeld
3 Was bap Joan dawghter to
Rawff Melner
26 Was bap Annas the dawghter
to xpofor Busfeld
JANEWARY. 12 Was bap margerett dawghter
to Richard Wilson
19 Was bap John sonn to willm
Adamthwat
19 Was also bap John sonn to
maythew Dentt

1577. CHRISTNEYNGS.

FAYBREWA^r^Y. 2 Was baptyzed henrye sonn to John handlay yong^r^
16 Was baptyst george sonne to Anthony blertt

MARCH. 2 Was bap willm the Sonn to henrye peares
15 Was bap Robartt the Sonn to James ffawcit of murthwat
15 Also was Essaybell the dawght^r^ to Thomas Rogerson

An^o^ Dn^i^ 1578.

APPRELL. 1 Was bap Richard sonn to Thomas Adamthwat
6 Was bap xpofor sonn to John ffoth^r^gill

MAY. 8 Was bap pettar the sonn to xpofor powson
18 Was bap Robartt the sonn to Anthonye shaw

JUNE. 1 Was bap margarett the dawght^r^ to Willm grene

JULI. 20 Was bap Ellin the dawghter to John ffawcit
27 Was bap Elizabeth the dawght^r^ to Edward grene

AUGUST. 3 Was bap Elizabeth dawght^r^ to Robartt gowldinton gottne in adultre
24 Was bap hew sonn to John shaw
31 Was bap margerett the dawght^r^ to John ffawcit

SEPTEMBAR. 21 Was bap Rowland the Sonn to Cuthbartt Swinbank
21 Was bap maybell the dawght^r^ to Rainold Busfeld

OCTOBA^r^. 12 Was bap Joan the dawghter to willm heblethwat
12 Was baptysed Elic dawght^r^ to Thomas grene

1578. CHRISTNEINGS.

OCTOBER. 26 Was baptysed John the Sonn
to Anthonye Swinbanke
26 Also was bap Cuthbartt sonn of
the sayd Anthonye being twenes
26 Was also bap Edmond sonn to
John handlay of the strett
28 Was bap Richard sonn to Thomas
ffawcit of grenesyd
DECEMBAR. 7 Was bap willm sonn to
Richard Rogerson
7 Also was bap Essaybell daught[r]
to maythew paycok
21 Was bap willm sonn to Raynold
grene of Ristnedall
21 Also was bap Elin dawghter
Ano Dni to Richard ffawcit
1579.
APP[r]ELL. 12 Was bap Robartt the sonn to
Richard Bovell
MAY. 17 Was bap maybell the dawghter
to Anthonye ffoth[r]gill
28 Was bap willm the sonn to
xpofor Adamthwat
JUNE. 14 Was bap John the sonn to
willm Chambarlaine
21 Was bap Richard the sonn to
herrye ffawcit
JULI. 12 Was bap Essaybell dawghter
to James tayler
26 Was bap James the sonn to
John Ewbanke
AUGUST. 2 Was bap margerett dawghter
to Rawff Awdarson
30 Was bap Elin the dawghter
to John ffawcit
SEPTEBA[r]. 20 Was baptysed Joan dawghter
to steven Busfeld

1579.		CHRISTNEINGS.
SEPTEMBAR.	24	Was baptysed Ann dawghter to John parkin
OCTOBAR.	4	Was bap Essaybell dawghte[r] to John Coatlaye
	11	Was bap Richard the sonn to Anthonye tayler
	28	Was bap Alic the dawghter to miles Busfeld
NOVEMBAR.	8	Was bap Robartt the sonn to Rainold Todd
	8	Also was Robartt the sonn to myghell Chambarlaine
	22	Was bap Elin the dawghter to xpofor Busfeld
DECEMBAR.	6	Was bap willm the sonn to herrye ffawcit
	6	Also was bap margarett the dawghter to Thomas grene
JANEWARY.	1	Was bap margarett the dawghter to giles hawle
	6	Was bap Richard the sonn to giles parkin
ffAYBREWARYE	14	Was bap xpobell the dawghte[r] to Thomas Adamthwat
	21	Was bap margarett dawghter to John ffawcit of nayth[r]ings and Robartt sonn to lanc shaw
	25	Was bap John the sonn to Rowland Raykstro The same day was Anthonye the son to Rawff mellner
An[o] Dn[i] 1580.		
APPRELL.	24	Was bap margarett dawghter to Bartholmew Bovell
MAY.	21	Was bap James Sonn to lanc ffawcit
JULI.	10	Was bap Janatt dawghter to Rowland ffoth[r]gill & to maybell Cook begottne in advltarrye

1580.		CHRISTNEINGS.
JULI.	17	Was baptysed Essaybell the dawghter to Richard pindar
AUGUST.	14	Was bap Lanard sonn to John grene
	21	Was bap Elizabeth dawghter to Richard Busfeld
OCTOBAR.	9	Was bap hellin dawghter to Richard gowldinton
	28	Was bap John sonn to Thomas shaw
NOVEMBAR.	13	Was pap Richard sonn to xpofor hawle
	17	Was pap Essaybell the dawghter to symond busfeld
DECEMBA[r].	4	Was bap Rainold the Sonn to James ffawcit
	11	Was bap Anthonye sonn to Richard ffawcit
JUNE.	19	And Robartt Sonn to willm Cowpar
	26	Was bap willm the sonn to Roger ffawcit
JANEWA[r]Y.	22	Was bap Essaybell the dawghter to John parkin
ffAYB[r]EWA[r]Y.	5	Was bap margarett the dawght[r] to John ffawcit of murthwat
MARCH.	5	Was bap Elizabeth dawghter to Roger pindar
		And the same day margarett dawghter to Edward Dent
An[o] Dn[i] 1581.		
MARCH.	25	Was bap margarett dawghter to John Ewbanke
	26	Was bap margarett dawght[r] to myles paycok
APP[r]ELL.	9	Was bap sebell the dawght[r] to Rowland holme
	16	Was baptysed Annas dawght[r] to Thomas ffawcit

1581. CHRISTNEINGS.

MAY.	4	Was baptysed John Sonn to Richard Wilson
	14	Was bap Joan the dawghter to Willm Chambarlaine
	28	Was bap xpobell dawghter to Willm Cooke
JUNE.	11	Was bap Elizabeth dawghter to herrye shaw
	29	Was bap Issaybell dawghter to John handlaye eld[r]
JULI.	9	Was bap John Sonn to Rawff melner
	9	and margarett the dawghter Xpofor busfeld
	16	Was bap willm the sonne to myghell chambarlaine
AUGUST.	6	Was bap Ann the dawghter to willm Shaw
	13	Was bap xpofor the sonn to Raynold grene
SEPTEMB[r].	10	Was bap Issaybell dawghter to Richard ffawcit
	10	and Joan dawghter to willm adamthwat
	10	and the same day margarett Supposed dawghter to willm ffawcit in advltry
	17	Was bap willm sonn to anthonye ffothergill and Elizabeth dawghter to John Adamthwat
OCTOBAR.	15	Was bap Richard Sonn to Thomas ffoth[r]gill yong[r] also the same day Ellin the dawghter to herry peres

1581. CHRISTNEINGS.

OCTOBAR.	15	Was baptysed James Sonn to Olever paycok
	22	Was bap george the sonn to herrye Dentt and the same day Issaybell dawghter to Robartt ffoth[r]gill
NOVEMB[r].	19	Was bap margarett dawghter to Robartt handlaye
	30	Was bap Joane dawghter to maythew paycok
DECEMB[r].	3	Was bap Elizabeth dawghter to Anthonye Swinbanke
	17	Was bap Joane dawghter to Pettar grene and margarett dawghter to a pore man Called pettar Carr
	21	Was bab margarett dawght[r] to John ffawcit
	24	Was bap James sonn to Steven ffawcit of Ristnedall and Margarett dawghter to Lanc shaw
JANEWA[r]Y.	1	Was bap Elizabeth dawghter to Rainold grene of Rystnedall
	21	Was bap mayrye dawghter to John handlaye
ffAYB[r]EWA[r]Y.	22	Was bap John dawghter to xpofor adamthwat
MARCH.	4	Was baptest Elizabeth dawghter to gilles hawle
	11	Was bap Raynold sonn to giles parkin
	18	Was bap willm the Sonn to Thomas Adamthwat

1582. CHRISTENINGS.

MARCH. 25 Was baptysed Annas dawght^{r}
to Thomas walkar

APPRELL. 1 Was bap xpofor sonne to Thomas
ffawcit of murthwat

13 Was bap Essaybell dawghter
to willm heblethwat

15 Was bap Annas dawghter to
herrye ffawcit

MARCH. 16 Was bap VinCentt sonn to John
Coatlaye of newbegin

28 Was bap James sonn to
edward grene

JUNE. 10 Was bap Edward the Sonn
to John ffawcit of nayth^{r}ings

24 Was bap Ann the dawghter
to Richard Bovell

AUGUST. 19 Was bap Ann dawghter to
Raynold ffoth^{r}gill
and niColas sonn to the sayd
Rainold ffoth^{r}gill twenes

24 Was bap John sonn to xpofor
ffawcit of murthwat

SEPTEMBAR. 9 Was bap maybell dawghter
to John Robinson

21 Was bap Richard sonne to
willm Rogerson
and the same day Thomas
the Sonne to Rawffe melner

NOVEMBAR. 11 Was bap xpofor the Sonn
to myles busfeld
and also that day Ann the
dawghter to Willm Cook
and John the Sonn to John
mayson of patarryg Brutton

DECEMBAR. 9 Was bap Elizabeth dawghter
to Anthony ffoth^{r}gill

25 Was bap Richard the Sonn to
steven Busfeld

1582.		CHRISTNEINGS.
DECEMBAR.	27	Was baptysed Thomas the sonn to Rogar ffawcit
		Was bap Symond the Sonn to Roger pindar
JANEWARYE.	27	Was bap margarett the dawght[r] to Lanc murthwat and margarett hewatson fornicatores
FAYBREWARY.	9	Was bap maybell the dawght[r] to John medCalff fornicator
MARCH.	17	Was bap VinCentt Sonne to henrye garethwat
An° Dni. 1583.		
MARCH.	29	Was bap Roba[r]tt shaw Sonn to herrye shaw of Devingill
		tho Same day was bap georg sonn to xpobell ffawcit gottne in forniCation by a pedler
APP[r]ELL.	29	Was bap Issaybell dawghter to Richard ffawcit
	28	Was bap Olever Sonn to george whithead and Thomas Sonn to george grene of nayth[r]garthes
MAY.	5	Was bap xpofor sonn to Steven Robinson eld[r]
	20	Was bap Raynold sonne to gilles hawle and also Ellin the dawghter to xpofor busfeld welsdall
JUNE.	9	Was bap Annas the dawghter to Thomas shaw
	9	and the same day Elizabeth dawghter to Anthony tayler
JULI.	7	Was bap Richard Sonn to James ffawcit murthwat
	14	Was baptyzed Elin the dawght[r] to herrye shaw

1583. CHRISTNEINGS.

JULI. 18 Was baptysed Thomas sonn to VinCentt murthwat

28 Was bap margarett dawghtr to John Coattlaye

SEPTEMBAR. 1 Was bap willm sonn to Robartt ffawcitt

8 Was bap myghell sonn to henrye Dentt

21 Was bap Ellin dawghter to John Adamthwat, yongr

OCTOBAR. 11 Was bap Agness the dawghtr to willm huntar

13 Was bap Essaybell dawghtr to Robartt handlay

20 Was bap John sonn to Raynold ffothrgill of Ristnedall

NOVEMBAR. 3 Was bap Anthonye the sonn to Robartt ffothrgill

3 and Edmond Sonn to myghell shaw

10 Was bap mayrye dawghtr to John Chappylow and the same day margarett the dawghter to thomas ffothrgill

17 Was bap Essaybell dawghter to Richard wilson

24 Was bap Issaybell dawghter to georg hawle

DECEMBAR. 28 Was bap helin dawghter to Lanc ffawcit

ffAYBREWARY. 2 Was bap Issabell dawghtr to Janatt gowldinton and Supposed willm ffawcit of murthwat to be the ffayther begottne in fornication

1583.		CHRISTNEINGS.
FAYYREW ARYE.	2	Was baptysed Issaybell the dawghter to Alexsandar Steward a pore man
	6	Was bap John the Sonn to John parkin
	23	Was bap margarett dawghtr to John ward
MARCH.	4	Was bap Raynold the sonn to bartlemew Bovell
	8	Was bap Essaybell dawghtr to Steven ffawcit
	15	Was bap Sebell dawghter of John ffawcit murthwat
Ano Dni. 1584.		
MARCH.	26	Was bap John the sonne of willm Chambarlaine
APPrELL.	26	Was bap John the sonn to Rawff melner
MAY.	10	Was bap lanard the Sonn to henrye peares
JUNE.	14	Was bap John sonn to Thomas Adamthwat
JULI.	16	Was bab Richard the Sonn to myghell chambarlaine and lanclott Sonn to Robartt bayle
	23	maybell dawghter to John Robinson
AUGUST.	23	margarett dawghter to Richard ffawcit
	30	sybell dawghtr to xpofor busfeld
SEPTBr.	13	Was bap hew the sonn to Anthonye ffothrgill & willm the sonn to Raynold grene the same day Edward sonn to Lanc shaw
	20	Was bap margarett dawghter to John Bovell
	26	Was baptest henrye sonne to Raynold ffothrgill

1584.		CHRISTNEINGS.
SEPTEMBAR.	27	Was baptysed Bartholmew the Sonn to Willm heblethwat
OCTOBAR.	4	Was bap margarett dawghter to Thomas walkar
	25	Was pap Abrayam sonne to John handlay eld[r] and Joane the dawghter to Anthonye Swinbanke
NOVEMBAR.	25	Was bap Elizabeth dawghter to Thomas grene clergill
JANEWARY.	8	Was bap giles the sonn to willm Cooke
	31	Was bap Thomas the sonn to herrye shaw and the same day Robartt sonn to the sayd herry twenes
FAYBEREWARY.	7	Was bap James the Sonn to Roger ffawcit blayflat
	14	Was bap margarett dawghter to Richard wharton and the same day mayrye dawghter to Symond Coatlay
	21	Was bap maythew the sonn to John ffawcit welsdall
	24	Wat bap henrye the Sonne to John Coatlay
MARCH.	21	Was bap mayrye dawghter to Richard ffawcit
An[o] Dni. 1585.		
APP[r]ELL.	4	Was bap Richard the sonn to Robartt Rogerson
	18	Was bap Alic the dawghter to John ffawcit
MAYE.	9	Was bap Joan the dawghter to Richard Bovell
	9	and Robartt the sonn to willm Rogerson and Thomas sonn to herry shaw devengill

1585. CHRISTNEINGS.

MAY.	9	Was baptysed Edward the Sonn to myles holme and Angnes the dawghter to the sayd myles holme
JUNE.	13	Was bap John the Sonn to willm shaw
JULI.	20	Was bap Thomas sonn to willm Smartt
AUGUST.	22	Was bap Robartt Chappilow Sonn to John Chappylow
	22	and Ellin the dawghter to James tayler Caldbec
	22	and also Elizabeth the dawghtr to James tayler Cawdbeck
	29	Was bap george the sonn to John Wine of Vldall and Alic the dawghter to John walkar of nathwat
SEPTBAR.	7	Was bap margarett the dawghtr to Steven Robinson
	8	Was bap John the Sonn to george whythead newbygin
	12	Was bap margarett the dawghtr to John berkhead of devingill
OCTOBAR.	3	Was bap margarett dawghtr to willm huntar
	11	Was bap willm the Sonn of Thomas Shaw
	11	and Edmond Sonn to Willm Adamthwat of Adamthwat
	17	Was bap Johne dawghter to herrye garethwat
	17	and margarett the dawghtr to maythew paycok
	17	Was baptysed also Raynold the Sonn to John parkin of Rystndall towne

1585.		CHRISTNEINGS.
NOVEMBAR.	16	Was baptysed Anne the dawghter to Robart handlay
DECEMBAR.	2	Was bap John the sonne to James ffawcit blayflat and James the sonn to Steven Dent of Devingill
	23	Was Issaybell the dawghter to gilles hawle
JANEWARY.	1	Was bap Ann dawghter to myles bownes of welsdall
	8	Was bap george the Sonn to herrye Dentt welsdall
	21	Was bap Elizabeth dawght^r to Robartt ffothergill of
FAYBREWARY.	3	Was bap John the Sonn to Steven busfeld
An^o Dni. 1586.		
MARCH.	31	Was baptysed hellin the dawghter to Raynold grene
APP^rELL.	17	Was bap george the Sonn to Rawffe melner of Asfell And xpofor the Sonn to Richard busfeld Also the same day Annas the dawghter of John Bovell
	22	Was bap Edward the sonn of Thomas ffawcit of grensyd
MAY.	1	Was bap Joan the dawghter to Thomas Adamthwat
	8	Was bap Charles the sonn to myles Busfeld
JUNE.	19	Was bap margarett the dawghter of george hawle and the same day also was bap myghell sonn to Rainold tod of Ristnedall
SEPTEMBAR.	11	Was bap Elizabeth the dawghter to willm Cooke

1586.		CHRISTNEINGS.
SEPTBA^r^.	11	Was bap margarett the dawght^r^ to Willm heblethwat
OCTOBAR.	3	Was bap Richard the Sonn to John Robinson yong^r^
	3	Was bap Janatt the dawghter to myles ffoth^r^gill of Adamthat and she was gottne in adulterry and the same day was bap Joan the dawghter to James ffawcit
NOVEMB^r^.	20	Was bap hellin the dawghter of Thomas ffoth^r^gill yong^r^
DECEMBAR.	1	Was bap hellin the dawghter to Richard ffawcit of Ristnedall and Alic the dawghter of Anthonye tayler
JANEWARY.	8	Was bap pettar the sonn to John handlay of Devingill
ffAYB^r^EWA^r^Y.	5	Was Bap Angnas the dawght^r^ of gilles hawle
	12	Was bap george the sonne of herrye peares
	26	Was bap Alic the dawghter of Anthony ffoth^r^gill of Adamthwat
An^o^ Dni. 1587.		
MARCH.	25	Was baptysed maybell the dawghtar of myles holme
APP^r^ELL.	2	Was bap hellin the dawght^r^ of Robartt ffawcit ellergill
MAY.	7	Was pap herrye the sonn of John Ewbanke & Alic the dawg^r^ to willm Dentt begottne in adultry
MAY.	14	Was bap Alic the dawghter to John berkhead
JUNE.	11	Was bap hew the sonn of Lanc shaw of trannay hill

1587. CHRISTNEINGS.

JUNE. 18 Was baptysed maythew the
Sonn of Rowland Dentt
and also the same day was
bap margarett the dawghter
of Raynold ffothergill

24 Was bap John the Sonn off
Janatt gowldinton in adultrye

JUNE. 29 Was bap VinCentt the Sonn
of Rawffe melner of Asfell
And the same day Richard
the sonn of willm weste

AUGUST. 6 Was bap willm the sonn of
Lanc ffawcit of tarne

24 Was bap Richard the sonn
of willm Chambarlaine

OCTOBAR. 8 Was bap Dorryty the dawght
of Symond Coatlay

NOVEMBAR. 5 Was bap John the Sonn
of george hawle

12 Was bap marye the dawght[r]
of Steven Dentt

19 Was bap margarett the dawght[r]
to John Chapylow

26 Was bap xpobell dawght[r]
to xpofor husfeld

30 Was bap gilbartt sonn of
m[r] Richard wharton

FAYBREWARY. 4 Was bap willm the Sonn
of Robartt Rogerson

MARCH. 10 Was bap myghell the
Sonn of herrye shaw

17 Was bap Joan the dawght[r]
of myles bowness

An° Dni.
1588.

MARCH. 31 Was bap pettar the sonn
of John Coatlay

MAY. 12 Was bap Joan the dawght[r]
of willm Rogarson

An° Dni 1588. CHRISTNEINGS.

May. 16 Was baptysed John sonn of
Robartt handlaye
allso willm sonn of John
bovell of newbygin

August. 4 Was bap george the sonn
of myghell chambarlaine

Septemb^{r}. 1 Was bap ellin dawghter
of Lanc towneson in fornication

8 Was bap Sybell dawghter
to James ffawcitt

15 Was bap John sonn to Thomas
walkar of newbygin
the same day Issaybell
dawghtar to John ffawcit

Octobar. 7 Was bap Angnes dawght^{r}
to Thomas peres

14 Was bap Lanard sonn of
the sayd Thomas peres
And xpofor sonn of John
ffawcit of murthwat
And also Steven sonne
of the sayd John ffawcit
that day Also was bap
pettar sonn of Steven Robinson

28 Was bap willm sonn of willm
shaw of the tarne howse
And Joan the dawghter
of John Adamthwat yong^{r}

Novembar. 10 Was bap alic the dawght^{r}
of Roger ffawcit blayflatt

16 Was bap Issaybell dawght^{r}
to Thomas ffawcitt

Decemb^{r}. 25 Was bap Issaybell the
dawghter of Anthony tayler

Janewa^{r}y. 1 Was bap george sonn of
Robartt ffoth^{r}gill

5 Was baptysed willm sonn of
willm holand

1588. CHRISTNEINGS.

JANEWARYE.	5	Was baptysed Issaybell the dawght[r] of Robartt ffawcit
	5	Was bap Joan the Supposed dawghter of John Atkinson
	6	Was bap hellin the dawght[r] of Thomas shaw Ristnedall
	12	Was bap Elizabeth dawght[r] to willm heblethwat
	19	Was bap was bap Joan dawght[r] of Rawffe shaw
FAYB[r]EWARY.	2	Was bap george the son of Richard Busfeld
	9	Was baptysed Anthonye sonn of James tayler welsdall And Joan the dawghter of Richard ffawcit Rystndall
	23	Was bap Cuthbartt sonn of Robartt hunttar
MARCH.	9	Was bap Thomas sonn to giles hawle of Sprenttgill
Ano Dni 1589.		
APP[r]ELL.	3	Was bap Robartt the Sonn of Anthonye Swinbank
MAY.	1	Was bap margarett dawght[r] to herry garethwatt
	20	Was bap Ann the dawghter to Richard gowldinton
JUNE.	29	Was bap george the sonn of Jenkin ffawcit
JULY.	18	Was bap margarett dawght[r] to willm Cooke of Lockholme
AUGUST.	7	Was bap Ellin the dawght[r] of Steven Busfeld
	14	Was bap Elin the dawght[r] of John ffawcitt
	21	Was baptysed Elizabeth the dawghter of Richard wharton stoneaskew

CHRISTNEINGS 1592.

MARCH. 1 Was baptysed margarett
dawghtar of Richard Busfeld
15 Robartt sonn off xpofor busfeld
And Issaybell dawghtar of
xpofor pkin Locholme
22 Was bap Janatt dawghter
of James tayler

1593.

25 And phillipp Sonn of Steven
Busfeld
And Dorryty dawghtar
to Anthonye ffoth[r]gill
28 Was bap John Sonn of Oswold
Robinson of newbegin

JUNE. 3 Was bap Essaybell dawght[r]
to Robartt wallar
10 Was bap george sonn of gilbartt
blertt
17 Was bap Janat dawghtar of
Lanc pacoke
24 Was bap Elizabeth dawghter
of Lanc paycok

JULI. 6 Was bap Steven sonn of Lanc
ffawcitt of tarne

AWGUST. 8 Was bap Elizabeth dawghtar of
VinCentt ffothergill
15 Was bap Elizabeth dawghtar of
george ffoth[r]gill tarne howse
22 Was bap Elin dawghtar of
Robartt Rogerson

SEPTEMB[r]. 7 Was bap Ann dawghtar of
george ffawcitt of waingarthes
15 maybell dawghtar of James
ffawcit was bap

OCTOBAR. 16 Was bap xpofor Sonn of
Thomas Adamthwat
29 Was bap Elizabeth dawghter
of edward Adamthwat

NOVEBA[r]. 11 Was bap ellin dawghter of
Steven ffawcit Ristnedall
And Richard sonn of willm ffoth[r]gill
gottne in fornication

1593.		CHRISTNEINGS.
DECE'BAR.	14	Was baptysed hew sonne of Thomas shaw
	21	Was bap Richard sonn of Thomas ffawcit of murthwat
JANEWARY.	15	Was bap John sonn of VinCentt tayler
	22	Was bap willm Sonn of xpofor Rogerson
ffAYB^r^EWARYE	16	Was bap Robartt sonn of george hawle welssdall
An° Dni 1594		
	28	Was bap Ann dawghtar off myghell ffothergill bowd^r^dall ffaybrewary was Jeffarray Sonn of VinCentt Dentt & margarett dawghtar of myghell Chambarlaine
APP^r^ELL.	14	Was bap James sonn of James Atkinson gottne in fornication
	21	Was bap Edmond sonn of m^r^ Robartt Calvertt
	29	Was bap Ann dawghtar off willm Cooke of Locholme
MAY.	29	Was bap John sonn of Lance towneson And ellin dawghter of Thomas peares
JUNE.	8	Thomas sonn of John Coatlay & John sonn of myles ffoth^r^gill
JULI.	15	Was bap Thomas sonn of george ffawcit wainegares
AWGUST.	10	Was bap James sonn of Richard tayler Rystnedall
	28	Was bap Elizabeth dawght^r^ of Rainold todd
SEPTBAR.	15	Was bap John sonn of James ward
	24	Was bap maybell dawghter to george grene Anthonye Sonn of herrye ffawcit
	29	Was bap Thomas sonn off Robartt ffoth^r^gill

1594. CHRISTNEINGS.

OCTOBAR.	13	Was baptysed Alic dawghter of herrye shaw
	27	Was bap maybell dawghtar of herrye shaw
	29	Was bap Elin dawght[r] of
NOVEBAR.	3	Was bap henrye sonn of Richard wharton of stoneaskew
	10	Was bap mayrye dawght[r] of Robartt shaw of towne the same day Issaybell dawght[r] of Rawffe melner
	24	Was bap george Sonn of Rogar pindar
DECEMB[r].	15	Issaybell dawghtar of giles hawle
	26	Was John sonn of xpofor pkin
JANEWA[r]Y.	5	Was bap Elizabeth dawght[r] of Steven pindar
ffAYB[r]EWA[r]Y.	9	Was bap Ann dawghter of george ffoth[r]gill
	16	Was bap Janatt dawghtar of Rogar ffawcitt and Ann dawghtar of John ffawcit
	23	Was bap margarett dawghter of John Robinson
MARCH.	16	Was bap Janatt dawghtar of Richard ffawcit Devingill
	23	Was bap Elizabeth dawght[r]
An[o] Dni 1595.		of Edward Adamthwat
	30	Was bap Adam Sonn of myghell tayler murthwat and the same day Elizabeth dawghter of John walkar
APP[r]ELL.	6	Was bap John Sonn of Rawff shaw and margarett dawght[r] of James ffawcit
	21	Was bap Annas dawghter of Lanc shaw
	28	Was baptysed Richard sonn of george ffoth[r]gill

1595. CHRISTNEINGS.

MAYE. 25 Was baptysed Elizabeth dawght^{r}
of VinCentt tayler

26 Was bap willm sonne of
Robartt huntar

AWGUST. 20 Was bap myghell sonn of
Robartt waller

SEPTB^{r}. 7 Was bap Thomas sonn of willm
holand of Locholme

28 Was bap margarett dawght^{r}
of Thomas ffawcit

OCTOBAR. 7 Was bap george sonn of Robartt
Rogerson

19 Was bap Anthonye Sonn of
Anthonye tayler

26 Was was bap John sonn of george
Ewbanke of bowdardall

27 Was bap Richard sonn of willm
ffothergill
And the same day maybell
the dawghtar of John Berkhead .

NOVEBAR. 6 Was Elizabeth dawghtar of
Roland Dentt nedlehowse

8 Was bap maybell dawght^{r}
of Richard Busfeld

26 Was bap Sybell dawghtar of
george ffawcit

27 Was bap henrye sonn of
george ffothergill Locholme

DECEMBAR. 6 Was bap Ann dawghtar of
James tayler

22 Was bap xpofor Sonn of
myghell ffoth^{r}gill

26 Was bap John sonn of xpofor
parkin Locholme

FAYBREWARYE 11 Was bap willm sonn of
John ffawcit

MARCH. 14 Was baptysed James sonn
of John walkar

1596. CHRISTNEINGS.

MARCH.	25	Was baptysed John sonn of herrye shaw of westardall
APPrELL.	19	Was bap Elin dawghter of VinCentt Dentt bowdrdall
MAY.	5	Was bap Roger sonn of hew shaw of naythrgares
	25	Was ellin dawghtar of Anthonye ffothrgill brownebar
JULI.	6	Was bap Adam sonn of Steven Bell bowdrdall .
AWGUST.	15	Was bap Thomas sonn of James ffawcit of blayflatt And margarett dawghter of Steven busfeld of bowdrdall wath
SEPTBr.	19	Was bap Thomas sonn of xpofor Rogrson of stoneaskew the same day was margarett haystwytle dawghtr of hew
OCTOBr.	24	Was bap John sonn of Jenkin ffawcitt of murthwat
	28	Was bap Cuthbartt Cmpstone Sonn of John gottne in adulterry
NOVEBr.	14	Was bap Issaybell dawghter of John grene
	21	Was bap John Sonne of Richard tayler of Ristnedall towne and the same day was george hewatson son to John hewatson
	28	Was bap xpobell dawghter to John hewatson yonger
JANEWARYE.	13	Was baptysed margarett dawghter of Anthony wharton
FAYBrEWARY.	19	Was baptysed margarett dawghter of Robartt ffawcit
MARCH.	18	Was baptyzed Annas dawghtr of willm Chambarlaine

1597. CHRISTNEINGS.

MARCH.	28	Was baptysed Janatt dawght[r] of Steven Busfeld
	29	Was Bap willm Sonne of Lanc grene Crosbanke
MAYE.	28	Was bap willm sonn of Richard whythead of Locholme And mayrye the dawghter of Steven pindar
JUNE.	6	Was bap Janat the dawght[r] of Raynold ffoth[r]gill
	13	Was bap bartle sonn of Richard Bovell newbygin
	20	Was bap Rainold sonn of george ffawcit of Devingill And Issaybell dawghter of Thomas ffawcitt
JULI.	18	Was bap Issaybell dawght[r] of Robartt wilkinson
	25	Was bap Ann dawghtar of Robartt wallerr nedlehowse And Ann dawghtar of Thomas Chesborne of Ristnedall
	26	Was bap ellin dawghtar of henrye Dentt welsdall
	30	Was bap Issaybell dawghtar of John ffawcit
AWGUST.	27	Was bap Ann dawghter off hew shaw of nayth[r]garthes
SEPTB[r].	3	Was bap James sonn of Lanc pacok
	23	Was bap maybell dawghtar of herrye garethwat of Ellergill
OCTOBAR.	29	Was bap John son of VinCentt ffoth[r]gill of Stoneaskew
NOVEBAR.	12	Was bap henrye Sonn of Robartt shaw of Rystnedall
DECEMBAR.	3	Was baptysed margarett dawghtar of myghell tayler

1597.		CHRISTNEINGS.
DECEBAR.	17	Was baptysed george & elizabeth Sonne And dawghtar off myghell Chambarlaine twenes
	24	Was bap Ann dawghtar of george ffawcit
JANEWARYE.	15	Was bap myles sonn of george Ewbanke of bowdardall
	22	Was bap Janatt dawghter off george ffoth^{r}gill
	29	Was bap Elizabeth dawghtar of willm shaw at Locholme
FAYB^{r}EWARY.	12	Was pap margarett dawght^{r} off
An^{o} Dni 1598.		Edward Adamthwatt of Adamthwat
APPRELL.	12	Was pap Elizabeth dawghter of Oswald Robinson of newbygin
	26	Was bap margarett dawghtar of Robartt ffothergill of brownebar
MAY.	7	Was bap Annas dawghtar off Cuthbartt ffawcit of Cawldbeck
JULI.	16	Was bap Thomas sonn of willm Robinson of newbygine
SEPTEB^{r}.	17	Was bap Joan dawghtar of myghell ffoth^{r}gill of bowdardall And the same day Ann dawghter of Richard Bovell of newbygin
OCTOBAR.	15	Was bap Richard sonn of John hewatson
NOVEB^{r}.	16	Was bap John sonn of Thomas ffawcitt
	26	Was bap Issaybell dawghter off Richard whythead of Locholme
	30	Was bap Ann dawght^{r} of herrye pindar Was bap Ann dawght^{r} of Anthonye wharton of nathwat
	24	Was bap Richard sonn of Roger ffawcit
JANEWARY.	6	Was bap John sonn of hew hayswytle
	21	Was baptysed John sonn of Lance shawe of trannay hill

1598.		CHRISTNEINGS.
JANEWARYE.	28	Was baptysed Robartt and Thomas sonne to willm ffawcit And the same day Also was bap Richard sonn to willm ffoth^{r}gill
ffAYB^{r}EWARY.	4	Was bap Issaybell dawght^{r} to Anthonye ffoth^{r}gill
	23	Was bap Anthonye Sonn to Steven pindar
MARCH.	10	Was bab Thomas sonn
An^{o} 1599		to John ffawcit nayth^{r}ings
APPRELL.	22	Was babtysed Richard sonn to herrye ffothe^{r}gill and margarett dawght^{r} to Thomas Wilson
	28	Was Ann dawghter to Rowland Dentt
MAY.	20	Was Chrestned margarett dawghter to georg ffoth^{r}gill
JUNE.	10	Was bap Rowland sonn to VinCentt Tayler
	30	Was bap Richard sonn to edward pindar
JULII.	1	Was bap xpofor sonn to John walkar
	8	Was bap Thomas sonn to willm chambarlaine
	22	Was bap Issaybell dawghter to Lanc grene the same day Also was baptysed margarett dawghter to John hewattson

1599.		CHRISTNENGS.
AWGUST.	xii	Was baptysed Elizabeth Dawghter to John Tood
	26	Was bap : Anthonye sonn to James Ward
SEPTEMBr.	2	Was bap : Thomas sonn to Steven Dent and myghell sonn to Steven Busfeld
	9	Was bap : Edward sonn to John Grene &
	9	Was bap Janatt dawghter to willm holme
	16	Was bap : John sonn to Robert Shawe
OCTOBER.	7	Was bap : Thomas sonn to giles hawle
	14	Was bap : Margarett Dawghter to george ffawcitt
NOVEMBER.	8	Was bap : Sebell Dawghter to Rowlad sponar
DECEMBER.	3	Was bap : Richard sonn to Thomas ffawcitt
	17	Was bap : Ann Dawghter to James ffawcitt
JANEWARY.	10	Was bap : Richard sonn to Willm hunter
	17	Was bap : Elizabeth Dawghter to xpofor Rogersonn
ffAYBrEWARY.	24	Was bap : Richard sonn to willm holand
MARCH.	4	Was bap : margarett Dawghter to xpofor parkin
	11	Was bap : Janatt Dawghter to Richard Tayler
Ann Dn 1600	18	Was bap : margarett Dawghter to Roger pinder
MARCH.	25	Was bap : margarett Dawghter to Vincentt powsonn
	27	Was bap : Richard sonn to Vincentt ffothergill
APPRELL.	8	Was bap : willm sonn to oswold Robinson
MAY.	4	Was bap : Ann Dawghter to Steuen busfeld
	13	Was bap : John sonn to Thomas Chese borne
		CHRISTNINGES 1600
MAY.	24	Was christnid henery sonne to Robartt Wilkingsonne
JUNE.	28	Was bap : George sonne to Thomas Dennysonne
eadem di		Was bap : Ann Dawghter to Stephe Bousfelde
eadem di		Was bap : Richard sonne to A pedlar
JULY.	12	Was bap : Gilbertt sonne to Lennclot ffawcitt
	19	w bap : henery sonne to Anthony Whartan

1600. CHRISTNINGES.

	26	Was bap: Mabell Dawghter to Robartt Handley
AWGUST.	16	Was bap: Ellis Dawghter to Phillip Grene
	29	Was bap: Richarde sonne to Henery ffothergill
SEPTEBER.	13	Was bap: Margaritt Dawght^{r} to Cuthbertt ffawcitt
	20	Was bap: Margaritt Dawght^{r} to Edwarde Hunter
OCTOBER.	15	Was bap: John sonne to Richard Bouell
	22	Was bap: John sonne Christoper Todde
	29	Was bap: Ellis Dawght^{r} to John ffawcitt basse gotten
NOVEMBER.	15	Was bap: Ellinge Dawghter to George Ubannke
DECEMBER.	27	Was bap: Richard sonne to Stephen Robinson *
OCTOBER.	8	Was bap: Ellinge Dawghter to Hewghe Hastwhitle
JANWARIE.	31	Was bap: Margaritt Dawghter to Stephen Pinder
FABRUARIE.	28	Was bap: Mabell Dawghter to Henery ffothergill
MARCH.	2	Was bap: Margaritt Dawght^{r}
Ano Dni		to Anthony ffothergill
1601	21	Was bap Sibbell Dawghter to Edwarde Addamthwaite
APRRELL.	2	Was baptysed Ellin dawght^{r} to Robartt ffoth^{r}gill
MAYE.	10	Was baptysed margarett
1601		Daght^{r} to John Adamthwat
MAY.	24	Was bap Christopher & Robertt sonnes to Tohomas Wilsonn
JUNE.	14	Was bap Annas dawghter to Stephen Dentt
JULI.	5	Was bap Margarett Dawghter to Richard Haule
	19	Was bap Richarde sonn to Thomas ffawcitt
	26	Was bap James sonn to Roger Baliffe
AWGUST.	9	Was bap John sonn to Rowland sponer
	23	Was bap Annas dawghter to George ffothergill
eadem di	23	Was bap Alce dawghter to Richarde whitheade
SEPTEBER.	6	Was bap margarett dawghter to willm ffothergill
	27	Was bap w^{m} sonn to John Walker
	29	Was bap steuen sonn to Ranold ffoth^{r}gill
OCTOBER.	13	Was bap Elizabeth dawghter to Rouland dent
	28	Was bap Elin dawghter to Henery dent
NOVEMBER.	1	Was bap Anas dawghter to Thomas ffawcitt & Elizabeth dawghter to John Huatsonn
	15	Was bap Richard sonn to vincentt Powson

1600
gyles fothergill
son to henry
fothergill

* Bousfelde erased, Robinson substituted.

1601	1601	CHRISTNENGS. 1601
DECEBER.	25	Was baptized Issabell dawghter to John gray
	27	Was bap. Richarde sonn to John Walker
JANUARY.	24	Was bap. Mychell sonn to John Tode
MARCH.	10	Was bap. John sonn to George ffothergill
APRILL.	6	Was bap. Margaret daughter to Vincent
1602		ffothergill
	24	Was bap margarett dawghter
		to Lanc grene
MAY.	9	Was bap Richard sonn
		to John ffawcit
JULI.	11	Was bap Janatt dawghter
		to willm chambarlaine
	28	Was bap mawd dawghter
		to willm ffawcit
AWGUST.	2	Was bap ellin dawghter
		to John ffawcit
	15	Was bap maybell dawght^{r}
		to Anthonye Wilson
	22	Elizabeth & Annas dawghteres
		to John Adamthwat
SEPT.	18	Was bap Symond sonn to
		Rawff Awd^{r}son
	25	Was essaybell dawghter
		to Richard Rog^{r}son
OCTOB^{r}.	8	Was bap mabell dawght^{r}
		to steven busfeld
	15	Was bap margarett dawghter
		to James ffawcit
NOVEM.	13	Was bop xpoffor sonn
		to Richard hawle
DECEM.	6	Was bap Gyles sonn to
		oswold Robinson
	27	Was bap Annas dawght^{r}
		to Thomas denyson
		And Essaybell dawghter
		to Rowland Tayler
JANEW.	9	Was bap myghell sonn
		to Thomas proctor

CHRISTNENGS.

ffAYBREW	9	Was bap myghell sonn to willm chambarlin
ARY.	15	Was bap Maythew and Issaybell sonn and dawghter to Rainold ffothergill of Locholme
MARCH.	2	Was bap Ann daw to Anthoni ffoth^{r}gill
	16	Was bap John sonn to Rawff Awd^{r}son
An^{o} Dni 1606	23	Was bap elizabeth daw to Vincentt dent March 25 was bap mayry dawghter to giles swinbanke
	30	Was margarett daw to Edward Cooke
AP^{r}ELL.	27	Was bap symond sonn to John busfeld
MAY.	11	Was bap Janatt daw to oswold Robinson
	25	Was bap Thomas sonn to steven ffawcyth Rainold sonn to xpofor pkin and Ellic dawghter to myghell Tayler
JUNE.	8	Was xpofor sonn to Thomas proctar Anthony sonn to James pereson
JULLII.	25	Was bap georg son to w^{m} ffothergill
AWGUST.	3	Was bap John sonn to xpofor grene and w^{m} sonn to Thomas dennyson
SEPT	21	Was bap Issaybell daw to Ranold pkin & John sonn to george ffothergill & margerett daw to Richard Tayler and Issaybell daw to Anthoin foth^{r}gi
OCTOB^{r}.	5	Was Richard sonn to hew shaw
	12	John sonn to John hewatson & margarett dawghter to edward Adamthwat
	19	Was bap xpofor son to Roger baylay and Richard sonn to steven bell
NOVEM.	23	Was bap Richard sonn to Phillip grene
	29	Was Robartt sonn to Rowland dentt
DECEM.	10	Was Issaybell daw to Anthoni Wha^{r}ton and Jane daw to Thomaa ffawcyth
JANEW.	27	Was bap willm sonn to Robartt Rog^{r}son and maybell dawghter to VinCentt ffoth^{r}gill

CHRISTNEINGS An° dni 1606

JANEWA^{r}Y.	24	Was bap Ann dawghter to
		Anthonye Wilson
		and margat * dawghter to hery bovell
	28	Was bap willm sonn to mathew ffoth^{r}gill
ffAYB^{r}EW.	4	Was bap John sonn to John ffawcyt
		and margarett daw to Richard whithed
	11	Was bap margarett dawghter
		to Cuthbartt ffawcyth
		and Ellin dawghter
		to herry ffoth^{r}gill
	21	Was bap george sonn to
		Robartt waller
	28	herry and John ** sonnes
		to steven dentt was baptysed
MARCH.	21	Was bap John sonn to Thomas shaw
An° Dni		and Edward sonn to John Admthwat
1607		
MAY.	10	Was bap Elizabeth dawghter
		to Rowland sponor
JUNE.	14	Was bap Ellin dawghtar to
		John whartton
JULLII.	26	Was bap myghell sonn to
		Edward darbye
AWGUST.	16	Was bap Elizabeth dawght^{r}
		to Willm grene Cawldbeck
SEPTEM.	27	Was baptysed steven sonn to Anthony grene
OCTOBAR.	4	Was baptysed henry sonn to georg ewbank
NOVEMBAR.	29	Was baptysed george ffoth^{r}gill sonn
		to Anthonye ffoth^{r}gill
DECEMBAR.	6	Was baptysed Issaybell Adamthwat
		dawghter to John Adamthwat
		that day Also was baptysed sebell
		powson dawghter to VinCentt powson
JANEWARY.	6	Was bap John sonn to Richard hawll
	12	Was bap george sonn to w^{m} chambarlin
		and Issaybell dawgh^{r} to John busfeld
		and Sebell dawght^{r} to Rog^{r} shaw
	24	Was bap willm sonn to Thomas ffawcytt
ffAYBREW	7	Was bap Roger sonn to Symond pindar
ARY.	21	Was bap Rawff sonn to James melner
MARCH.	6	Was bap margaritt dawght^{r} to John hewatson

* Mayry crossed out.
** Maythew crossed out.

CHRISTNEINGS.

MARCH. 25 Was bap hew Cheseburgh sonn
to Thomas Chesburgh •

1608 28 Was bap Robartt sonn to xpofor Todd

29 Was bap margarytt dawghter to
giles Swinbanke

APRELL. 17 Was bap. Annas dawghter to
Steven ffawcyt

24 Was bap Lance sonn to Thomas shaw
Was bap William sonne to Robart shawe

MAY. 8 Was bap Annas dawght^r to Richard bell

22 Was bap maythew sonn to george ffawcyth
and Robartt sonn to willm whytlock

JUNE. 12 Was bap henrrye sonn to myghell ffoth^rgill

JULY. 11 Was bap John sonn to Anthonye ffoth^rgill

AWGUST. 21 Was bap margarytt dawght^r to Thomas
denyson & Janatt dawghter to Robartt Rogerson

SEPTEM. 4 Was bap Ellic dawghter to John ffawcyt

11 Was bap John sonn to Anthony ffoth^rgill

OCTOBA^r. 10 Was bap Alic dawghter to
John ffawcyth

18 Was pap Ellin dawghtar to
Robartt ffawcyth

NOVEM. 6 Was bap John sonn to
herry busfeld

15 Was

20 Was bap Issaybell dawghter
to Edward ffawcyth
And also ffrancys Richardson
dawghter to a pore man off w^m
hearesons xyff

DECEM. 6 Was bap Thomas sonn to Anthony dentt

20 Was bap Thomas sonn to John Adamthwat
off Artlegarth

JANEWARY. 15 Was bap Elizabeth dawghter
Steven pindar off wath

22 Was bap Edward sonn to pettar pindar
and Ellin dawghtar to Rainold pkin

ffAYBREW-ARY. 19 Was bap John sonn to Thomas tayler
and willm sonn to Richard ffawcyt

CHRESTNEINGS An° Dni 1608

ffAYB^{r}EW ARY. 21 Was baptysed Robartt sonn to Mighell Tayler

An° Dni 1609

MARCH. 26 Was bap James sonn to xpoffor pkin

APRELL. 2 Was bap Ellin dawghter to Oswold Robinson off newbygin

10 Was bap margaritt dawghter to to John grene

17 Was bap margarytt dawghter to maythew ffoth^{r}gill of brownebar

23 Was bap xpobell dawghter to John Beck at blaywflatt and Elizabeth dawghter to Willm ffothe^{r}gill of Lyth

30 Was bap mawde dawghtar to James ffawcyth of tarne

MAY. 14 Was bap Thomas sonn to herry ffoth^{r}gill

21 Was bap Willm sonn to Rog^{r} baylay the same day was bap willm sonn to herry bovell of newbygin

28 Was bap margarit dawghtar to xpoffor grene and Ann dawght^{r} to Rainold ffoth^{r}gill

JUNE. 5 Was bap George sonn to nicolas murthwat

JULLII. 5 Was bap Issaybell dawghter to VinCentt ffoth^{r}gill

18 Was bap Ellin dawghter to Anthony Wilson

AWGUST. 15 Was bap Issaybell dawghter to edward Adamthwat

SEP. 9 Was bap xpoffor sonn to Richard Rogerson

OCTOBAR. 12 Was bap george sonn to Rawff Awdarson

CHRISTNEINGS Anº Dni 1611

MAY.	28	Was baptysed Elizabeth dawghter to VinCentt powson
JUNE.	2	Was bap Ellin dawghter to Anthony dentt
	9	Was bap willm and sebell sonn & dawghter to Cuthbertt ffawcyt
	16	Was bap Ellin dawghter to myghell ffothergill and Ann dawghter to Robartt waller
JULII.	7	Was bap Ann dawghter to herry bovell
	14	Was bap willm sonn to Edward holme
AWGUST.	25	Was bap Anthony * sonn to Rawff shaw
SEPT.	1	Was bap steven sonn to oswold Robinson
	15	Was bap Thomas sonn to Richard ffawcyt
OCTOBr.	8	Was bap Issaybell dawgh to mighell waller
	24	Was bap willm sonn to Rainold ffothrgill
NOVEM.	18	Was bap Richard sonn to VinCent ffothrgill
	27	Was bap Elic dawghter to edmand shaw
DECEM.	10	Was bap Elizabeth daw to Willm grene
	17	Thomas sonn to Rowland Adamthat
	24	Was bap Issaybell to Robartt ffawcyt
		Was bap margarit daw to Roger shaw
	25	Was bap Richard sonn to edward ffawcyt
		James sonn to Richard Tayler novem 8
		Ann dawghter to xpoffor Todd
JANEW	7	Was bap mayry daw to steven ffawcyt
ARY.	15	Was bap Anthony sonn to Richard ffawcyt
	24	Was margaritt daw to wm ffothrgill baptysed
	&	was bap Janatt dawghtar to wm grene
1612		and mayry dawghter to xpoffor grene
JANEW	28	Was bap dorryty daw to maythew ffothrgill
ARYE.	15	Was bap Ellin dawghter to oswold ewbanke
	13	Was bap Giles sonn to xpoffor pkin and John sonn to John gowldinton
MARCH.	14	Was bap willm sonn to george ffawcyt &
1612		Was bap Thomas sonn to george ffawcyt
MARCH.	29	Was bap myghell sonn to John hewatson and herry sonn to herry ffothrgill

* Lanc crossed out.

CHRESTNEENGS 1612

JULI.	8	Was bap Janatt dawghter to Richard Rog^{r}son
AWGUST.	2	Was bap maythew son to steven pindar
		and Thomas sonn to willm grene
		and mayry dawghter to Anthony wilson
	9	Was bap John sonn to edward adamthat
	16	Was bap Anthony sonn to Rawff shaw
		and Ellin dawghter to Rog^{r} murthat
SEPT.	9	Was bap Janatt dawghter to Richard
		sonn dawghter Rogerson *
	02	Was bap John sonn to Thomas pkin
		and Elin dawghtar to Rich ffawcyt
OCTOBAR.	8	Was bap Issaybell daw to bartle waller
	15	Was bap margaryt daw to Thomas ffawcyt
NOVEMB^{r}.	10	Was bap willm sonn to myles ffoth^{r}gill
	17	Was bap Issaybell daw to Thomas mu^{r}that
DECEMBR.	7	was bap harry sonn to Johu wharton
JANEW^{a}ry.	8	Was bap Elizabeth daw to maythew pindr
MARCH.	18	Was bap Robartt sonn to Thomas Tayler
1613		and herry sonn to John shaw
APPRELL.	18	Was bap James sonn to Thomas bland
	27	Was bap Jane daw to pettar pindar
MAY.	8	Was bap willm sonn to John gowldinton
	14	Was bap Janat dawght^{r} to xpofor busfeld
JUNE.	7	Was bap Thomas sonn to Richard hawle
	14	Was bap Robartt sonn to willm ffoth^{r}gill
JULL.	11	Was bap Richard sonn to Robartt Rog^{r}son
	28	Was bap John sonn to herry Coatlay
AWGUST.	10	Was bap george sonn to James ffawcyt
SEPT.	4	Was bap Thomas sonn to Myghel waller
	26	willm sonn to myles ffothergill
	28	Was bap VinCnt son to Anthony Wharton
OCTOBAR.	8	Was bap sebell daw to herry bovell
	18	Was bap Ellin daw to steven ffawcyt
NOVEM.	9	Was bap Richard sonn to Richard tayler

* This line has been subsequently struck out.

CHRESTNEINGS 1613

NOVEBA^r. 14 Was bap John sonn to Richard whythead
DECEM^r. 12 Was bap Janatt daw to Edward holme
JANEW. 2 Was bap John sonn to Oswold ewbank
26 Was bap (1) to steven ffawcyt
ffAYB^rEW. 6 Was bap elizabeth (2) daw to John Adamthat
13 Was bap Issaybell daw to Anthony ffoth^rgill
27 Was bap willm sonn to Anthony grene
MARCH. 6 Was bap Ann daw to Richard Rogerson
Ano Dni 1614 March 27 was bap Elizabeth dawght^r to Edward ffawcyt
and Janatt daw to Anthony Robinson
AP^rELL. 3 Was bap Janatt daw to John tompson
10 Was bap steven sonn to Roba^rt ffawcyt
and Edward sonn to John hewatson (3)
JUNE. 13 Was bap magerye dawght^r to John ffawcyt
JULI. 6 Was bap John sonn to pettar handlay
31 Was bap herry sonn to hew ffoth^rgill
and Ann daw to Willm grene
AWGUST. 21 Was bap margaryt daw to John shaw (4)
SEPT. 4 Was bap Robartt sonn to steven busfeld
12 Was bap James sonn to Richard ffawcyt
OCTOBA^r. 16 Was bap xpofor sonn to steven dentt
23 Was bap willm sonn to Lanc shaw
NOVBA^r. 27 Was bap herry sonn to Edward ffawcyt
DECEMB^r. 25 Was bap John sonn to symond pind^r
and Issaybell dawghter to herry Coatlay
26 Was Elizabeth dawght^r to georg payCok
27 Was bap margarit daw to James ffawcyt
JANEWARY. 2 Was bap John sonn to Richard busfeld
4 Was bap Issaybell daw to steven Robinson dawgh^r
ffAYB^rEWARY. 26 Was bap Janatt daw to Anthony Wilson
MARCH. 19 Was bap John sonn to Thomas denyson
and John sonn to willm ffoth^rgill
Ano Dni 1615
APRELL. 2 Was bap Ellin daw to Rainold ffoth^rgill
and myghell sonn to Thomas Tayler
13 Was bap Richard sonn to John gowldinton
and Willm son to John Chambarlin
MAY. 7 Was bp george sonn to maythew dentt
21 Was bap John sonn to Robartt shaw
29 Was bap Thomas sonn to Wyllm holland
JUNE. 11 Was bap Anthonye sonn to xpofor pkin
and xpofor sonn to Richard powson
and Richard sonn to Thomas murthwat

(1) Space left blank.
(2) Margaritt crossed out.
(3) Ewbank crossed out
(4) ffawcyt crossed out.

1615. CHRESTNEINGS.

JUNE. 25 Was bap Rainowld sonn to willm grene
and Ellin d. to Thomas niColson
JULLI. 9 Was bap Anthony sonn to hew ffoth^{r}gill
and Sayray dawgh^{r} to pettar handlay
AWGUST. 6 Was bap herry sonn to Richard hawle
and Ann d. to xpoffor grene
20 Was willm sonn to John adamthat
SEPTEM. 3 Was bap Issaybell daw to xpoffor todd
14 Was bap mawd daw to Roger shaw
OCTOBAR. 15 Was bap Annas daw to edward Adamthat
28 Was bap Elizabeth daw to herry handlay
and Issaybell daw to Anthony ffoth^{r}gill
NOVEMB^{r}. 8 Was John sonn to willm chamb^{r}lin
DECEMB^{r}. 10 herry sonn to Anthony dentt
17 Was bap Ellin daw to W^{m} fioth^{r}gill
24 Was bap sebell daw to willm grene
JANEWARY. 8 Was bap Anthony sonn to Anthony tayler
22 Was bap Janatt daw to Thomas ffawcyt
ffAYBREW. 4 Was bap pettar sonn to John wharton
and Janatt daw to georg Robinson
An^{o} Dni MAR
1616 CH 26 Was bap Ann daw to hew hayswytle
APRELL. 3 Was bap sebell daw to edward ffawcyt
and sebell daw to Richard Robinson
16 Was bap Richard sonn to John Adamthat
and Richard sonn to maythew pind^{r}
and John sonn to Richard ffawcyt
MAY. 3 Was baptysed Janatt dawghter
to Anthonye Robinson
10 Was baptysed steven sonn to
philipp busfeld
JUNE. 23 Was bap Richard sonn to edward ffawcyt
JULII 28 Janatt daw to Vincent ffothrgill & herry sonn to Lanard peares
& elizabeth daw to James ffawcyth
SEPTEM. 22 Was bap John sonn to Willm Adamthat
OCTOBAR. 5 Was bap ellin daw to willm holland
20 Was bap xpofor sonn to Richard Rog^{r}son
& Roger sonn to symond pindar
& margaritt dawght^{r} pettar Carr
AWGUST. 28 Was Sayra daw to steven pindar
NOVEMB^{r}.

CHRISTNEINGS.

NOVEMB^r^.	4	Was bap Issaybell dawghter to Thomas denison
DECEMB.	15	Was margaritt daw to Anthony Wilson
	24	Was margaritt daw to Anthony grene
	28	Was steven sonn to Rainold bell
JANEWARY.	6	Was ellin and Issaybell dawghteres to pettar powson
	13	Was bap Robartt sonn to John handlay
	21	Ann dawg. to Anthony wharton
ffAYB^r^Y.	7	Was bap elizabeth daw to Thomas hawle
	26	Was bap mary (1) daw to herry (2) coatlay
MARCH.	1	Was bap Richard sonn to Rawf Shaw
	18	Was bap maybell dawghter to edmond handla
1617		May 24 Was bap James sonn to Rich skayf and dorryty dawght^r^ to steven ffawcyt
MAY.	15	Was bap Thomas sonn to herry ffoth^r^gill
JULLII.	6	Was bap marye daw to Abram handlay
AWGUST.	4	Was bap margarett daw to Lanc shaw
SEPTEM.	15	Was bap Thomas sonn to phillipp grene
	24	Was bap ellin daw to hew ffoth^r^gill
OCTOBAR.	8	Was bap John sonn to Thomas murthwat
	26	Was bap Richard sonn to phillip busfeld
NOVEM.	6	Was bap Ann daw to John Tayler
	14	Was bap John sonn to steven busfeld
	24	Was bap Annas daw to Richard murthwat
DECEMB^r^.	7	Was Ann daw to Rainowld ffawcyt bap
	14	Was bap Edward sonn to steven dentt & John sonn to willm ffawcyt was bap george and elizabeth sonn and daw to maythew ffothergill
	24	Was bap John sonn to James ffawcyt
JANEWARY.	7	Was bap ellin dawghter to Thomas Wilkinson and Sayray daw to Lanard peres & Elizabeth dawghter to Thomas Tayler
	23	Was bap george sonn to Richard busfeld
ffAYB^r^EY.	1	Was bap margaritt daw to John shaw
	4	Was bap John sonn to Richard Tayler
	11	Was bap Abraam sonn to John gowldinton
	24	Was bap xpofor sonn to xpofor powson
MARCH.	6	Was bap georg sonn to Richard willon
	11	Was bap Gyles sonn to Raynold pkin
An^o^ Dni 1618	24	Was bap John sonn to John ffawcyt and ellic dawghtar to Rainold ffoth^r^gill
APRELL.	4	Was bap John sonn to Richard ffawcyth
	26	Was bap willm sonn to willm ffothergill of brownebar

(1) xpobell crossed out.
(2) John crossed out.

CHRESTNEINGS 1618

MAY. 4 Was baptysed James son to Rainold ffawcyt
JUNE. 28 Was bap xpofor sonn to John handlay
and margaryt daw to herry Wharton
and mary daw to maythew pindar
JULLI. 5 Was bap Issaybell daw to wm ffoth'gill
19 Was bap myghell sonn to georg Chamb'lin
AWGUST. 16 Was bap maybell daw to edwa'd Adamthat
23 was margarit d to wm holland
SEPTEM. 3 Was bap Jane daw to Thomas ffawcyt
13 Was Elizabeth daw to Wm ffawcyt
OCTOBAR. 6 Was bap Richard sonn to maythew breaks
NOVEMBr. 8 Was ellin daw to Richard Rog'son
and Elizabeth to edward ffawcyt
18 Was bap sebell da to Anthony ffoth'gill
JANEWARY. 10 Was bap margarit to symond pindar
30 Was bap Sebell daw to John bovell
MARCH. 20 Was bap margarit to mathew murthat
1619 Aprell 11 was bap willm sonn
to edward ffawcyt
APRELL. 25 Was bap ellic to John Rogerson
MAY. 23 Was wm sonn to James ffawcyt
28 Was bap Robartt sonn edward waller
JUNE. 6 Was baptysed Issaybell dawghter
to John hegdayll
14 Was bap John sonn to wm grene
JULII. 4 Was bap Ann daw to Roger shaw
14 Was bap margarit daw to Thomas hawle
25 Was bap Sayray daw to Abraam handlay
AWGUST. 8 Was bap Ellin daw to willm Adamthat
SEPTEM. 8 Was bap Issaybell daw to (1) ffawcyt
12 Was bap Ellin daw to g (1) Cooke
19 Was bap Robartt sonn to Thomas bland
OCTOBAR. 4 Was bap Ellizabeth daw to Thomas
denyson
10 Was bap Ellin daw to Rainowld pkin
22 Was bap pettar sonn to Richard powson
NOVEMBAR. 14 Was bap margarit daw to georg paycok
21 Was bap peter (2) sonn to herry coatlay
28 Was bap Issaybell daw to Roger murthat
DECEM. 25 Was bap Ellin daw to gilbart ffawcyt

(1) Illegible
(2) Robartt crossed out.

CHRESTNEINGS 1619

DECEMBr.	26	Was bap John sonn to Anthony hegdayll
	28	Was bap pettar sonn to Richard ffawcyt
JANEWARY.	9	Was bap hannay daw to mr benson
		and mayry daw to Thomas murthwat
Ano 1620	22	Was bap Lanc sonn to herry Towneson
MARCH.	28	Was bap Ann daw to Thomas Tayler
APRELL.	23	Was bap John sonn to John gowldinton
		and Richard sonn to Anthony wharton
		and margaritt daw to Steven ffawcyt
MAY.	7	Was bap Ann daw to Robartt Clarke
		and Thomas sonn to Richard ffawcyt
	14	Was bap margaritt daw to herry ffothrgill
	15	Was bap myghell sonn to edward shaw
	22	Was baptysed Richard sonn to harry Wharton
JUNE.	2	Was bap James sonn to pettar powson
	25	Was bap James sonn to John ffawcyt
AWGUST.	1	Was bap Iseack sonn to Rainold bell
	7	Was bap maythew sonn to myghell murthat
	14	Was bap mayry Daw to Thomys Wilkinson
SEPT.	10	Was bap margarit daw to Willm shaw
	14	Was bap Thomas sonn to Anthony ffothrgill
OCTOBAR.	8	Was bap ellin (1) dawghtar to Robartt Todd
	14	Was bap Richard sonn to Anthony wilson
NOVEMBr.	6	Was bap John sonn to Anthony grene
		and Sebell dawghtar to wyllm hollann
		and Elizabeth dawghr to Thomas ffawcyt
DECEMBr.		14 Was bap Thomas sonn to John handlay
	10	Was bap John sonn to pettar handlay
	17	Was bap steven sonn to willm chambarlin
fEB.	2	Was bap steven sonn to heugh ffothergill
ffAYBREW	28	Was bap Richard sonn to John parke
ARY.	14	Was bap Elizabeth dawghtar to John tayler
MARCH.	10	Was bap Thomas sonn to herry ffothrgill
1621	22	Was bap Josya sonn to mr Benson
		hic meum nomen est
APRELL.	8	Was bap Robartt sonn to henrye shaw of towne
	28	Was bap pettar sonn to maythew pindr
MAY.	4	Was bp Robartt sonn to herry shaw
	14	Was bap Tbomas sonn to John shaw
JUNE.	4	Was bap Ellin daw to Richard Rogerson
JULLII.	29	Was bap Richard sonn to edward waller
		and Issaybell daw to Robart Rogr (2)

(1) Ann crossed out.
(2) Corner of page gone.

CHRESTNEINGS An° Dni 1622
MAY 23 Was bap Anthony sonn
to herry ffoth[r]gill
JULLII 10 Was bap mawd dagh[r]
to Robartt ffawcyt
AWGUST 18 Was bap xpoffor
sonn to herry wharton
SEPTEM 10 Was bap John sonn
to herry shaw
OCTOBAR 10 Was bap Richard
sonn to John parke
18 Was bap Ann daw to Anthony shaw
22 NOVEMBAR Thomas son (1) to
maythew breaks
JANEWARY 14 Was bap
george sonn to herry Towneson
MARCH 22 Was bap Issaybell
dawght[r] to herry Robinson

1621
Robert son to Henery Shaw was bap the 8 of Aprill
1621
John shaw son to Henery shaw was bap y[e]
10 of Septem 1622
william son to Henery Shaw was bap the
6 of March 1624
was bap Thomas son (2) shaw
the 2 of March 1628
Samewell shaw was bap the 2 of decem
1632
Henry shaw was bap ye 1 of Janeway 1635

[*The following is amongst the Marriages on p.* 81 *of the Register.*]

1622 ffEBREWARIE 24 was Baptysed Mathew
Sonn to Richard fawcet of sandbed

(1) Maybell da crossed out.
(2) Illegible.

1621 CHRESTNEINGS Ano Dni 1621

AWGUST. 8 Was bap Sayrya dawghtar
to herry handlay
17 Was bap mayry dawghtar
to Anthony ffothrgill
SEPT. 8 Was bap steven sonn to John Chambrlin
OCTOBr. 9 Was bap Annas daw to Abram handlay
27 Was bap Robartt sonn to willm ffawcyth
NOVEM. 6 Was bap Richard sonn to Thomas ffawcyth
18 Was bap Robartt sonn to Gilbartt ffawcyt
DECEM. 4 Was bap Robartt sonn to Richard Tayler
24 Was bap Elizabeth daw to John hegdall
30 Was bap John sonn to herrye Robinson
JANEWARY. 10 Was bap ellin daw to John bovell
18 Was bap Willm sonn to giles Cook
27 Was bap Thomas sonn to Willm Adamthat
ffAY 7 Was bap george sonn to Thomas boneson
BREWrY. 18 Was bap ellin dawghtr to John gowldinton
29 Was bap myghell sonn to philip busfeld
28 Was bap John sonn to Thomas hawle
MARCH. 6 Was bap John sonn to willm ffawcyt
12 Was bap steven sonn to Symond pindr
1622 28 Was bap Isack sonn to mr Richard benson
and myghell sonn to Roger shaw
and Richard sonn to wyllm grene
APrELL. 6 Was bap Issaybell daw to Richard ffawcyt
and Issaybell daw to willm grene
13 Was bap Issaybell daw to James ffawcyt
17 Was baptised Abraham son to Rychat bell

1623 CHRISTNINGS.

MAY. 20 Was baptised margret dawghter of georg chambrlain
26 Was baptised John son to georg handlowe
JUN. 6 Was baptised John son to Abraham handlow
JULI. 13 Was baptised william son to Raynold pkin
20 Was baptised george son to henrie townson
AGUST. 8 Was baptised thomas son to wil (1) hollan
15 Was baptised Robart son to w (1) shawe
28 Was baptised An dowghtr to (1) futhergill
SEPTr. 7 Was baptised sibell dowghter to Rychard bell
14 Was baptised Rebeckae dowghtr to henri handlow
OCTOBER. 1 Was baptised An dowghter to John handlow
NOVBr. 7 Was baptised marie dowghter to Roger murthwait
fEBRUARI. 8 Was baptised Annas(2) margret dotr to henri cawtle

(1) Illegible.
(2) sibell erased.

1624		1624
MARCH.	29	Was baptised marie the dowghter of peter handlow
APRELL.	25	Was baptised Thomas sonn to william fawcet neth[r]ings
MAY.	13	Was baptised An the dowght[r] of thomas fawcet
JULY.	18	Was baptised Thomas son to John fawcet of blafflat
SEPT[r].	12	Was baptised Steven sonn to Thomas Robinson
	26	Was baptised henrie son to wylliam dennyson
OCTOBR.	3	Was baptised mayre dowghter to Anthony futhergill
	17	Was baptised mayre dowghter to henrie Bousfell
DECEMB[r].	5	Was baptised mychaell the sonn of phillipe bousfell of greneside And the same day was baptised Ellise the dowghter of Rychard fawcet of murthwait
JANNARI.	2	Was baptised John son to Richard hunter and the same day was baptised Annes dowghter to henrie townson
fEBRUARI.	6	Was baptised wylliam sonn to Edward waller & marie the dowghter of henrie handlowe
MARCH.	6	Was baptised wylliam sonn to henrie shaw
1625		1625
APRILL.	10	Was Baptised Robart sonn to henrie futhergill
MAY.	22	Was Baptised John son to mychaell haull
MAY.	29	Was Baptised Gylles sonn to Thomas haull
JUN.	19	Was baptised Georg sonn to John Chamberlain
JUN.	26	Was Baptised marie the dowghter of John Rogerson the same day was baptised An the dowghter of John Shaw of stenerskewe
JULY.	3	Was Baptised Georg sonn to william Clemeson
	17	Was baptised Robart son to James fawcet town
	24	Was baptised Thomas son to henry Wharton
	30	Was baptised Rowland son to Rychard taylor
AGUST.	7	Was baptised margret dowghter to Robart todd also Issabell dowghter to Thomas wilkenson
SEPTEMB[r].	21	Was baptised Richard son to Ralfe Alderson
OCTOB[r].	9	Was baptised Rychard sonn to wylliam fawcet Rothebrigg
	26	Was Baptised Rychard Sonn to John Bovell
NOVEMB[r].	6	Was Baptised marie dowght[r] to peter Cawtle
	12	Was Baptised Georg son to edward thornbrowe
dECEB[r].	4	Was baptised Ann dowghter to hewgh Shawe
	18	Was baptised Robart son to Gilbart fawcet the same day Rychard son to Anthony Robinson
JANNARI.	22	Was baptised John son to Thomas haistwhitle the same day margret dowght[r] to henrie Robinson
fEBRUARI.	12	Was baptised Robart sonn to Anthony gren of Rissendaill towne

1628 CHRISNINGS.

APRELL. 13 Was baptised An dowghter to John shaw of Ryssendaill town
20 Was baptised Jacob son to Raynold bell
MAY. 1 Was baptised Leonard son to Robart dowthwait a pour man of kirbysteven
4 Was baptised Ann dowghtr to Thomas garthwait
JUNE. 1 Was baptised Georg son to Phillip bousfell
8 Was baptised doritie dowghter to edward ffawcet of dovengill
15 Was baptised wylliam son to Rychard hunter
22 Was baptised Annes dowghter to georg fawcet
JULY. 13 Was baptysed Thomas son to John tomson
20 Was baptised elizabeth dowghtr to thomas wilkenson
AGUST. 3 Was baptised william son to georg fawcet of murthwait
10 Was baptised Thomas son to mychaell murthwait
SEPTEBr. 21 Was baptised An dowghter to Rychard bousfell
28 Was baptised An dowghter to John handlow of weelsdaill
OCTOBr. 5 Was baptised Vincent son to henrie Wharton
12 Was baptised Elizabeth dowghter to Rychard porter
26 Was baptised Jane dowghter to mychael haull
NOVEMBr. 9 Was baptised Essabell dowghter to Rychard taylor
23 Was baptised Steven son to Thomas dent
the same day was baptised Grace dowghtr to mr Dodsonn
DECEMB. 7 Was baptised An dowghtr to Robart Shawe of Asfell
15 Was baptised Robart son to Anthonye futhergill of tranwath hill
27 Was baptised marie dowghter to Rychard Gren of Greneside
JANNARI. 18 Was baptised ellin dowghter to william Gren crossbank
25 Was baptised ezabell dowghtr to Georg bousfell
fEBRUARI. 1 Was baptised John sonn to Symond bousfell
MARCH. 1 Was baptised Thomas son to henry Shaw
1629
APRELL.* 12 Was baptised Robart son to Cuthbart hunter
the sam day Thomas son to Rychard fawcet of wandell banck
MAY.* 31 Was baptised margrat dow to Edward thorbro

* These entries have been crossed out and repeated on the next page.

CHRISNINGS.

1629.		
APRELL.	12	Was baptised Robart Son to Cuthbart hunter
		the sam day Thomas son to Rychard fawcet wadil
	19	Was baptised John son to Jeffray fawcet
		the sam day * dowghter to Thomas Robinson
MAY.	31	Was baptised margret dowghtr to edward thornbrow
JUNE.	8	Was baptised John son to Essabel lam begoten in advltri
	14	Was baptised ezabell dowghter to peter handlowe
JULY.	12	Was baptised william Son to Thomas futhergill of tarn house
		the same day was baptised margret dowghter to Cuthbart Robinson
AGUST.	2	Was baptysed Rychard son to henry Cawtle
	23	Was baptised georg son to John ewbanke
SEPTEBr.	6	Was baptised elin dowghtr to mychael prockter
	13	Was baptised Ann dowghter to Edward Adamthwait
OCTOBR.	11	Was baptised Thomas son to henry townson
	25	Was baptised John sonn to henry futhergill carsikes
		the sam day william sonn to Georg handlowe
NOV.	8	Was Baptised mary Daughter to Richard ffaucet murthwt
	15	Was baptised margret Daughter to Tho: Shawe bleaflat
	22	Was baptised mary daughter to lenored adamthwait
FEB.	7	Was baptised margat daughter to simond alldersonn
	24	Was baptised Anthony son to John Robinsson
		was baptised elsabeth daughter to georg fothergill of wandell
MARCH.	1	Was baptised Richard son to william faucet of netherings
MARCH.	7	Was baptised John son to vinson shawe
1630		Was baptised John son to william addamthwat
	21	Was baptised Renold sonn to John bouell
APRELL.	11	Was baptised John son to Thomas haull
	25	Was Baptysed Rychard son to Thomas haistwitle
MAY.	9	Was baptysed mary Daughter to Heugh shaw of trannow hill
JUNE.	20	Was baptysed Thomas sonn to Jeffrey dent
	20	Was baptysed margatt daughter to Robert todd of Rissendaile toown
JULIE.	25	Was baptised John son to Abram bousfeild
		the same day was baptised An daughter to Jaymes faucet of Rissendaill town
AGUST.	29	Was baptised Isack son to Richard bell
OCTOBER.	10	Was baptised elsabeth daughter to george faucet of stowphill yaet
	17	Was baptysed John son to Richard pousson
		the same day was John son to Robart green
	24	Was baptised John son to edward faucet of sandbed

* Space left blank.

CRISSNINGS 1630

Novem. 7 Was Crissned george son to John Ubank

Decem. 27 Was baptised margrat daughter to milles Townsonn

Janewarie. 16 Was baptised An daughter to william shaw of hye stenescae

Jan. 30 Was baptised Thomas son to kerstofer ffaucet the same day was baptised william sonn to John Shawe

feb. 6 Was baptised Phillip sonn to Renold bell

6 Was baptised Vinson sonn to John ffothergill

feb. 27 Was baptised Heugh sonn to Robert shaw of Asfell allso margat daughter to edward adamthwait of artlegarth

March. 6 Was baptysed George sonn to George fawcet of murthwait

March. 13 Was baptized John son to John Roggersonn the same day was baptized stephen sonn to John pinder : and marye daughter to Thomas Perkin

March. 20 Was baptized william sonn to william green of crossbank

Ano Dni 1631

Aprill. 3 Was baptized Jaymes sonn to Thomas dent the same day michell sonn to henery ffothergill

10 Was baptized Richard son to Thomas garthwat

May. 26 Was baptised John sonn to mr dodson

July. 3 Was Baptised Vinson sonn to simond bousfeild Was baptised Richard sonn to Thomas fothergill of tarn house

Agust. 21 Was Baptised Ealse daughter to Michaiell Procter

Sept. 4 Was Baptised Thomas sonn to Cuthbert Hunter

12 Was Baptized John sonn to Michaiell murthwaite

12 the same day was Saraih daughter to Anthony Pinder

Sep. 18 Was Baptised william sonn to Anthony ffothergill of trannow hill

Sep. 24 Was Baptized Vinson sonn to william shaw

Octo. 23 Was Baptized Ezabell daughter to edward waller

Nov. 20 Was Baptized Ezabell daughter to Richard fawcet of wandell

Nov. 27 Was Baptized John son to Michaell todd the same day Ellen daughter to Jaymes dent

CHRISSINGS Anno Dom 1632

Novem.	30	Was Baptized Margat daughter to Thomas Robinsone
Decem.	25	Was Baptized Ezabell daughter to Henery Wharton
Janew.	29	Was Babtized Robart sonn to John Hodgshon the same day was Annas daughter to Richard Birkitt
ffeb.	12	Was baptised Ralfe son to simond Alderson
March.	19	Was Baptized Jaymes sonn to Jaymes wetherhead
Aprell.	8	Was Baptized Lanclot sonn to Vinson shaw the same day was baptized Anthony sonn to John Pinder
Apr.	22	Was Baptyzed Abraham sone to Peter Handley
June.	26	Was Baptized Ann daughter to Michaell Haull
July.	1	Was Baptized Maubell daughter to Edward thornbrough
July.	29	Was baptized Margrat daughter to Richard Hunter The same day was baptized Margat daughter to william Adamthwait
Septem.	4	Was baptised Margrat daughter to Jeffray dent
Octob.	6	Was Baptized Izabell daughter to Christofer ffawcet of wandell
Octobr.	14	Was Baptized William sone to Edmond shawe
Octobr.	21	Was Baptized Williame sonn to Henery* Robinson of Newbigin the same day was Baptized William son to George ffawcet of stouphilyeat
Novem.	6	Was baptized Marye daughter to John pinder the same day was Baptized Margat daughter to John Robinsone
Novem.	13	Was Baptized William son to George ffothergill of wandell
	25	Was Baptized James son to william faucet of netherings
Decem.	2	Was Baptized samewell sonn to Henery shaw
Jen.	13	Was babtized Margret daughter to Thomas Perkin
Jen.	27	Was babptized Margat daughter to william shaw of hye stenesku
ffeb.	3	Was baptized mary daugh to Anthony pinder Likwise John sonn to Richard birkitt

* John erased.

1633

fEB.	10	Was baptysed Christofer sonn
1633		to Thomas dent
MARCH.	24	Was baptized Elin daughter to Henery wilkinson
APR.	14	Was baptized william sonn to Thomas Robinson
	21	Was baptized John sonn to Thomas shawe of uldall
MAY.	1	Was bap Ellen daughter to Henere Adamthwait
MAY.	25	Was baptised Mary daughter to Thomas Hall
JUNE.	15	Was baptysed Margat daughter to Gilbert fawcet
JUNE.	23	Was Baptyzed Robart (1) sonn to Heugh Shaw of trannow hill
JULY.	7	Was Baptised Richard sonne to Richard Pouson
SEPTEM.	25	Was Baptized Margat and Marie daughters to John Ubank
OCTOBR.	6	Was Baptyzed John sonn to Cuthbert Robinson
		the same day was baptyzsed Mary daughter to Richard Pinder
DECEM.	8	Was baptized Isack sonn to simond bousfeld
DECEM.	8	Was baptized Jaymes sonn to Michaell Prockter
DECEM.	15	Was baptysed John sonn to Anthony ffothergill of trannow hill
DEC.	22	Was baptysed Marie daughter to Henery ffothergill of Crooksbeck
ffEB.	23	Was Baptysed Ann daughter to Thomas ffothergill of tarnhouse
MARCH.	2	Was Baptysed Mary daughter to Myles Holm
MARCH.	9	Was Baptysed mary daughter to
1634		Jaymes wethereld
APRIL.	6	Was Baptysed Ellsabeth daughter to Georg ffawcet of murthat
		Gorge s hnery Shaw
APR.	02	Was Bapt Mathew son to Richard fothergil of Brounbar
MAY.	1	Was bapt An daughter to a poore man and no dews
MAY.	4	Was bap Robert sonn to Jaymes fawcet of murthat
MAY.	11	Was bapt Anthony sonn to John ffothergill of brounbar
	11	allso mary daughter to Robart green
MAY.	27	Was Bap mary daughter to Henery Shaw
JUNE.	14	Was bap Ezabell daughter to thomas Perkin
JULY.	6	Was bap William son to Jaymes Pacock

(1) John erased.

CHRISSINGS 1634

JULY.	20	Was Baptized John sonn to John ffothergill
JULY.	27	Was Bap John sonn to wiliam wharton
AGUST.	3	Was Bap mary daughter to John Handley
	11	Was Bap Elsabeth daughter to John Rodgerson
AGUST.	17	Was Bap Robert sonn to William Rodgerson
	17	Was Bap Maudlen daughter to Michel Bousfeild
SEP.	14	Was Bap Richard Sonn to John Pinder
SEP.	21	Was Bap Ezabell daughter to Robert shaw
SEP.	28	Was bap Margat daughter to Michall tod
		Was bap Ellen daugh to Heney ffothergil
OCTOBER.	12	Was bap George ssonn to George ffawcet of stouphillyat
		as allso Thomas sonn to John Perkin
		Was bap margatt daughter to Anthony Pinder
NOVEMBr.	23	Was bap Robart and John Sonns to Robart Todd
NOVEM.	27	Was bap Rodger sonn to Michal murthat
NOVEM.	30	Was bap Ėlsabeth daughter to Richard birkit
DECEM.	6	Was bap Marye daughter to John shaw
DEEEM.	21	Was bap Marye daughter to Michell Haul
	24	Was bap Marye daughter to mr dodson
	25	Was bap Thomas sonn to Jarrerd Elyetson
JANEWARY.	11	Was bap Ann daughter to Vinsent shaw
ffEB.	8	Was bap Ralfe sonn to John aldersone
1635		
MAY.	17	Was bap John Sonn to Edward Adamthwait
MAY.	24	Was bap Izabell daughter to william shaw
JUNE.	1	Was bap Margat daughter to James ffawcet
JULY.	12	Was bap Jacob and Anna sonn and daughter to peter Handly ꝥhalf dews
	12	Was bap Ezabell daughter to william green
JULY.	27	Was bap Ezabell daughter to Thomas Robinson
AGUST.	2	Was bap margat daugter to Richard todd

AGUST. 29 Was baptizsed Sibbell and Anas daughters
to John Lademan half dews
SEPT. 27 Was bapt George sonn to Richard half ds
ffawcett of wandell
OCTO. 12 Was bap John sonn to Thomas Robinson | half
18 Was bap Margat Daughter to
Christofer ffothergill
NOV. 10 Was Bap Ezabell supposed daughter
to John ffothergill begotten In adulltry
NO. 23 Was Bap marie daughter to
Richard ffothergil of lith side half dews
NO. 29 Was bap Ezabell daughter to william Adamthat
JAN. 1 Was bap Henery sonn to Henery shaw
JAN. 10 Was Bap John son to Thomas Adamthat
17 Was Bap Abram son to Anthony ffothergill half
JAN. 31 Was Bapt Margat daughter to Richard
ffothergill of Brounbar
ffEB. 6 Was bap william and Margat sonn and
daughter to John Ubank half dews
ffEB. 27 Was bap John sonn to Heugh shaw
MARCH. 3 Was bap mary daughter to John heutson
MARCH. 12 Was bap Elsabeth daughter to mr
Richard Branthwait
as allso Richard sonn to Georg Murthait
and Elles daughter to Christofer ffawcet
of wandall
MARCH. 19 Was bapt Christofer son to william fawcet | half ds
APRIL. 10 Was Bap Robart sonn to Michaell Jaikson
1636
APR. 18 Was Bap Mary daughter to Richard powson
JUNE. 5 Was Bap Ellen daughter to Jarerd Elyetson
Was Bapt Elsabeth daughter to simond alderson
JULY. 10 Was bap Hewgh sonn to vincent shaw
JULY. 13 Was bapt Vinson son to simond Bosfeild
AGUST. 14 Was bap stephn sonn to Michaell Bousfeild
SEPT. 4 Was bap Robert sonn to John Perkin
SEP. 12 Was bap Elles daughter to George ffawcet
of Stouphill yeat
SEP. 18 Was bap John sonn to thomas ffothergill
Was bapt maubell daughter to heney pearson
NOVEM. 16 Was bap John sonn to william Rodgerson
27 Was bapt Ellsabeth daughter to Jaymes pacok
DECEM. 4 Was bap Mathew sonn to John pinder
allso Ellen daughter to Henery willkinson
22 Was bap Joseph sonn to Peter Handley

JAN.	29	Was Bap Ann daughter to Jeffray dent
JAN.	29	Was Bap Annas daughter to Anthony pinder
FEB.	5	Was Bap mary daughter to Richard ffawcett
fEB.	12	Was Bap Thomas Sonn to John ffothergill of brownbar
MARCH.	12	Was bap Ellen daghter to a pore man
MARCH.	26	Was bap Johnathan sonn to Michaell Todd
1637		
APRILL.	16	Was bap Abram son to Thomas dent
		Was bap Richard sonn to Cuthbert hunter as allso Sarah daughter to Thomas perkin
APRILL.	23	Was bap Eles daughter to Richard birket
	30	Was bap Abram sonn to Anthony ffothergill
SEPTEM.	15	Was bap John sonn to Christofer ffawcet
SEPT.	15	Was bap Dorathy daughter to Henery shawe
OCTOBER.	21	Was bap Annas daughter to william
JANEWARY.	14	Was bap Margat daughter to Anthony Shaw of Mallestang
ffEB.	25	Was bap Jean daughter to Myles bousfeild
MARCH.	23	Was bap Jaymes son to John Rodgersone
MARCH.	25	Was bap william sonn to Richard ffothergill of Brounbar
Anno dom 1638		
APRELL.	29	Was Bapt John sonn to John heutson all Thomas sonn to Henery wharton
MAY.	6	Was Bap George son to Richard ffawcet
MAY.	20	Was bap Ellen daughter to Michaell murthat
JUNE.	3	Was bap Henery sonn to Thomas Robinson as allso Margat daughter to Thomas garthat
JULY.	15	Was bap Richard sonn to Christofer Bousfeild
AGUST.	12	Was bap Phillip sonn to Thomas Green as allso william sonn to Robart shawe and Jaymes sonn to william Adamthwait
AGUST.	26	Was bap Ellen daughter to Henery Robinson
SEP.	2	Was bap Thomas sonn to Jaymes ffawcet of newbigin
SEP.	16	Was Bap Margat daughter to Georg ffothergill
	30	Was bap Sibbell daughter to Hewgh shaw
OCTOB^r^.	14	Was bap Christofer son to John Alderson
	21	Was bap Margat daughtr to William Grene of Crossbank
	28	Was bap Edward son to Richard ffawcet of Sandbed
NOVEM.	4	Was bap Ellen daughter to Michaell Bousfeild
	18	Was bap mary daughter to simond Alderson
NOVEM.	25	Was bap Ellen daughter to Jaymes ffawcet of murthatt

GENEW.	13	Was bap Robart sonn to Henery Willkyson
GEN.	13	allso Ann daughter to Robart Green
GEN.	20	Was bap Robart sonn to John Ridden
GEN.	20	Was bap margatt daughter to Thomas Perkin
	27	Was bap mary daughter to Simond Bousfeilld
MARCH.	3	Was bap william sonn to Vincon Shaw
	20	Was bap margat daughter to Thom ffothergill
MARCH.	17	Was bap mary daughter to Jaret Elyetson
	24	Was bap Thomas sonn to Thomas Robinson
MARCH.	24	allso was bap mary daughter to Anthony
1639		pinder of wath
	30	Was bap Mary daughter to Thom Saule
APR.	14	Was bapt Elsabeth daughter to Michell Chamberlai
MAY.	12	Was baptiz Margat & dorathy daughters
		to william ffothergill of Adamthwait
MAY.	23	Was baptized Henery sonn to Michall Jackson
	26	Was bap Margat daughter to George ffawcet
		of stoup hill yeat
JUNE.	9	Was bap william sonn to Robart Baliff
JULY.	21	Was bap william son to Anthony Shawe
AGUST.	25	Was bap Richard son to William Rodgerson
SEP.	8	Was bap Henery son to John Bousfeild
	21	Was bap Gyles son to Thom dent
OCTO.	02	Was bap John son to Will Emerson
NOV.	24	Was bap Ann daughter to Jaymes Pacok
DEC.	25	Was bap william son to Thomas Johnson
		as also Richard son to John ffothergill of brounbar
JAN.	12	Was bap Elles daughter to Lenard ffothergill
fEB.	2	Was bap Sibbell daughter to Cuthbert Hunter
	9	Was bap Isabell daughter to Rodger medcalf
fEB.	23	Was bap Ezabell daughter to
MARCH.	1	Was bap Richard sonn to Henery Haull
1604		
MAY.	16	Was bap Jaymes sone to Richard ffothergill of brounbar
JUNE.	22	Was bap Sarah daughter to Michaell Tod
JULY.	19	Was bap Ezabell daughter to John Heutson
	26	Was bap Elsabeth daughter to Richard tod
AGUST.	23	Was bap Thomas sone to Richard birkett
OCTOB.	11	Was bap Ezabel daugh^t to steuen Bousfeild
		Was bap Jaymes(1) son to michaell Haul
		Was bap will^m son to Jarard Elyetson
OCTO.	28	Was bap John sonn to Gyles ffothergill
No.	29	Was bap Jaymes sonn to Richard Powson
		Was bap michaell son to Thomas ffothergill
DEC.	13	Was bap Margatt daughter to Richard ffawcet
		of sandbed
JAN.	31	Was bap Thomas son to Richard willson

(1) William erased.

ffEB. 16 Was bap stephn sone to Robert Baliff
ffEB. 21 Was bap Henery sone to Richard Gooslen
MARCH. 3 Was bap Ellen daughter to Richard Shaw
MARCH. 7 Was bap Ann daughter to Ralfe millner
as all Margratt daughter to Thomas Green
MARCH. 21 Was bap William sonn to Robert Whitelock
1641 28 Was bap John son to Thomas Robinson
APRILL. 4 Was bap Philip sonn to michaell Bousfeild
APRILL. 18 Was bap Margatt daughter to John Allderson
APRIL. 26 Was bap Peter son to Edward Pinder
MAY. 8 Was bap Sarah daughter to Chrystofer Bousfeild
and Elles daughter to John lambert
MAY. 16 Was Bap William son to Will shaw of
hye stenesku
MAY. 23 Was bap Nickalas Sonn to William
Adamthwait of Lowcome heade
MAY. 23 also Jannatt daughter to Simond
Bousfeild of skarsikes
JULY. 4 Was bap Richard sonn to John
Laidman of Sandbed
JULY. 7 Was bap Ezabell daughter to
Anthony Pinder of moreowslack
JULY. 11 Was bap Jaine daughter to
Jaymes Robinson Smith
SEP. 19 Was bap Ezabell daughter to
John ffothergill of stenersku
OCTOBr. 3 Was bap ffrances daughr to
william ffothergill of Adamthwait
OCTOBr. 24 Was bap william Sonn to Heugh
Shaw of trannow hill
Allso Jaine daughter to Lancelott
Hodshon
OBTOBr. 30 Was bap Richard sonn to Christofer
Rodgerson
NOVEMBr. 14 Was bap mary daughter to John Bousfeild
25 Was bap Thomas son to Thomas
Parkin of greenside
also Robart son to Georg ffawcet
of stouphill yayt
DECEMBr. 5 Was bap Thomas sonn to Richard
ffothergill of brounbar
JANEW. 16 Was bap william sonn to Jarred Elyetson
16 Was bap Elles daughter to John Tayler
ffEB. 5 Was bap Richard sonn to stephn Bousfeild
ffEBR. 20 Was bap Thomas sonn to Gyles ffothergill
MARCH. 6 Was bapt Anthony sonn to Richard willson
MARCH. 26 Was bap Ellsabeth daughter to Thomas Jonson

Anno dom 1642

APRILL.	10	Was bap Edward sonn to William Emerson as allso Elsabeth daughter to Michaell Chamb'laine
MAY.	1	Was bap Elsabeth daughter to Jaymes Pacok
MAY.	8	Was bap Stephn Sonn to Anthony Pinder of wath
MAY.	15	Was bap Ellsabeth daughter to George Chamberlaine
JUNE.	5	Was bap Robart sone to Anthony Shawe as allso margarat daughter to John Pinder
JUNE.	12	Was bapt william sonn to thomas Robinson
JUNE.	26	Was bap Richard sonn to Henery wilkinson
JULY.	17	Was bap Ann daughter to John Shaw of wath
JULY.	25	Was bap marye daughter to John Hewetsonn
JULY.	31	Was bap Thomas sonn to Thomas ffothergil of beck
JULY.	31	Was bap Margarat daughter to John Perkin
SEP.	11	Was bap John Sonn to John Pearson
	25	Was bap Thomas sonn to william Green of cbank
OCTOBr.	2	Was bap marye daughter to Robart Shaw of asfel
OCTOBr.	23	Was bap Thomas sonn to Henery Haull
DEC.	4	Was bap Issabell daughter to Jaymes Perkin
	18	Was bap Ann daughter to Richard Powson
DEC.	25	Was bap Thomas son to Thomas Green allso An daughter to Anthony Pinder of morowslack
JANEW.	1	Was bap Annas daughter to william Huthisson
	8	Was bap Ann daughter to Michell Tod
	22	Was bap Thomas Son to John ffawcet of stret
	22	Was bap Annas daughter to John Green of Caudbeck
ffEB.	5	Was bap Issabell daughter to Ralfe millner
ffEB.	12	Was bap Ellsabeth daughter to Thomas Johnson
MARCH.	19	Was bap maubell daughter to Jaymes Robinson Was bap Sibbell daughter to Edward Adamthwait
Anno dom 1643		Was bap Thomas sonn to Thomas ffothergill Was bap dorathy daughter to Richard ffawcet of sandbed
APRILL.	3	Was bap Margat daughter to Robart Baliffe
	23	Was bap Marye daughter to Thomas dent as allso Ellsabeth daughter to Jeffray dent
	30	Was bap margarat daughter to William Adamthwait of artellgarth
MAY.	14	Was bap michaell Sonn to John Taylor of waingars
JUNE.	12	Was bap Robart sonn to Lance Hodshon
JULY.	2	Was bap margat daughter to Cuthbert Hunter
JULY.	9	Was bap Ann daughter to Robart Tod of weesdall
JULY.	16	Was bap Issabell daughter to Jaymes ffawcet of murthat
JULY.	30	Was bap Richard Sonn to William whitehead
	30	Was bap stephn sonn to William ffothergill
AGUST.	13	Was bap John sonn to John ffothergil of brounbar
	20	Was bap Richard sonn to George ffothergill of wandall
AGUST.	24	Was bap Thomas sonn to Robart Taylor
AGUST.	27	Was bap Richard sonn to John Lambert
SEP.	10	Was bap John sonn to Christofer Rodgerson
	17	Was bap Richard sonn to Thomas Robinson
	24	Was bap Peter sonn to Christofer powson
OCTOB.	1	Was bap Ann daughter to Christofer whorton
	8	Was bap mathew & margrat sonn and daughter to Henery Pinder of weesdail
OCTO.	8	Was bap Anthony son to Henry Robinson
OCTO.	8	Was bap Richard son to Richard shawe of Ellergill

OCTOBER.	22	Was baptized Edward sonn to John Heutson
	29	Was bapt Ellen daughter to Robart Green
NOVEM.	5	Was bap Ellen daughter to Michell Bousfell
		allso Jaymes sonn to Georg fawcet of stophilyat
NOVEM.	22	Was bap Ellsabeth daughter to William
		Adamthwait of Lowcom head
	19	Wap bap Thomas sonn to Richard Willson
DEC.	3	Was bap marye daughter to ffrances Willson
		of Longg'll
	21	Was bap mary daughter to Anthony Parkin
	21	Was bap William son to Richard Gouldingtonn
		allso Izabell daughter to Christofer ffawcet
		of tarn
DEC.	28	Was bap margatt daughter to Michell Chamberlaine
		as allso margatt daughter to Richard ffothergill of brounbar
ffEB.	4	Was bap Ellen daughter to Christofer Bousfeild
MARCH.	3	Was bap william sonn to John ffawcet of murthatt
Anno dom		as allso marye daughter to Cuthbert Robinson
1644		
MARCH.	31	Was bapt william son to Jerrard Ellyetson
APRIL.	7	Was bap william sonn to william Rodgerson
	14	Was bap marye daughter to John Pinder
		as allso Ellen daughter to vinson murthat
	21	Was bap Jaymes sonn to Thomas Parkine
		—— below alowed ——
MAY.	12	Was bap Izabell daughter to Simond Bousfeild
MAY.	19	Was bap Janatt daughter to Richard Hayton
JUNE.	30	Was baptized william sonn to George Chamberlaine
JULY.	7	Was bap marye daughter to Will ffothergill
AGUST.	26	Was bap John sonn to John Ridden
		allso mary daught to John Lademan
		and marye daughter to Richard Tod
SEP.	1	Was bap margat daughter to Robart Tod
	22	Was bap Elsabeth daughter to Anthony pinder
OCTOB.	26	Was bap Izabell daughter to John Bousfeild
DEC.	8	Was bap Ralfe sonn to John Shaw of street
	29	Was bap George sonn to Rodger Mecka
JANE.	12	Was bap Jaymes sonn to Gyles ffothergill
		and Issabell daughter to Robart Baliffe
		as allso bap marye daughter to John shawe
	26	Was bap margatt daughter to william ffothergill
ffEB.	9	Was bap Lanslott sonn to Anthony shaw
		all was bap Ann daughter to Jaymes ffawcett
MARCH.	9	Was bap George* sonn to Jaymes Parkin
		Was bap John* sonn to Symonde alldersone
		as also George sonn to stephn Bousfeild
MARCH.	23	Was bap william son to Ralfe millner
APRILL.	6	Was bap marye daughter to Thomas Green
1645		as allso Ann daughter to Robart Tayler
	27	Was bap Margratt daughter to Jaynes ffawcet
MAY.	4	Was bap Richard sonn to Thomas Robinson
	5	Was bap George sonn to Lanclot hodhon
MAY.	11	Was bap Sibbell daughter to Will Adamthwatt
JUNE.	8	Was bap John Sonn to Robart whitelock
		as all John sonn to William Huthison
	22	Was bap Richard sone to Jaymes Pacoke
JULY.	20	Was bap Ellen daughter to Abram Gouldinton

* These two names originally written in inverse order.

AGUST. 24 Was baptized Margatt daughter to William
Whitehead of Lowcome
SEPTr. 7 Was bap stephn Sonn to Tho Robinson
SEP. 14 Was bap Ellsabeth daughter to Jaymes Robinson
22 Was bap Adam sonn to John Taylor of garrs
allso John sonn to Thomas Adamthwait
OCTOBER. 19 Was bap Richard son to Michaell Tod
26 Was bap Janet* daughter to Jaymes ffawcet
Was bap Ellen daughter to Edard Bland
NOVEMBr. 16 Was bap margatt daughter to Tho Johnson
23 Was bap Richard sonn to Michell Bousfeild
DECEMB. 29 Was bap Richard sonn to John Heutson
Was bap Ann daughter to Anthony Pinder
Was bap Jennat daughter to John perkin
ffEBREW. 1 Was bap Anthony son to Richard ffawcet of sandbed
ffEBRE. 15 Was bap Annas daughter to Vinson murthwait
22 Was bap Richard sonn to Richard Willson
MARCH. 8 Was bap Stephn sonn to Christofer ffawcet
Anno dom 15 Was bap John sonn to John Pinder
1646 Was bap John sonn to John ffawcet of strete
APRIL. 12 Was bap Richard sonn to Christofer Powson
MAY. 3 Was bap Ann daughter to Robart Tod
JUNE. 21 Was bap marye daughter to michell Chamberlin
7 Was bap margatt daughter to Anthony ffothrgill
JUNE. 19 Was bap Thomas son to Will Rodgerson
also Ellsabeth daughtr to Richard ffothergill
JULY. 10 Was bap William sonn to Henry Haule
allso Margatt daughter to George Alderson
JULY. 19 Was bap Richard son to Robart Whitelock
23 Was bap John sonn to Jarerd Ellyetson
AGUST. 11 Was bap margat daughtr to Christofer Rodgerson
SEPT. 02 Was bap Christofer son to John hymmore
OCTOB. 11 Was bap margat daughter to
Christofer wharton
OCTOBr. 22 Was bap william son to Christofer Powson
allso elsabeth daughter to simond Bousfeild
NOVEMB. 15 Was bap John sonn to Richard Gouldinton
allso George son to Richard Hayton
DECEM. 11 Was bap stephn son to Robart Bayliff
allso Ellsabeth daughtr to Willm Perkin
20 Was bap John sonn to Jaymes ffawcet
allso Sibbell daughter to John shaw of street
JANEW. 10 Was bap George sonn to Anthony parkin
10 allso marye daughter to Thomas Green
10 allso Izabell daughter to Will ffothergill
JANEW. 24 Was bap John sonn to Stephn Bousfeild
allso Abram sonn to John Bousfeild of town
ffEBREW. 21 Was bap maubell daughter to Anthony Shaw
24 Was bap Richard sonn to william ffawcet of newbigin
MARCH. 11 Was bap margaratt daughter to Ralfe millner
1647 14 Was bap Ann daughter to George fothergill
of back of wandall
APRILL. 10 Was bap william sonn to Jaymes parkin
15 Was bap mary daughter to John Redin
MAY. 9 Was bap margrat daughter to
Rodger mecay of studfould
15 Was bap Ellen daughter
to Abram Gouldinton

* Ellen erased.

Anno dom 1647

MAY. 22 Was bap Annas daughter to Richard birkat
MAY. 26 Was bap Thomas sonn to John Taylor
JUNE. 20 Was bap Margat daughter to Georg Chambel
27 Was bap Jaymes sonn to Thomas Robinson
JULY. 19 Was bap Richard sonn to Christofer Powson
AGUST. 14 Was bap Margat daughter to John pearson
22 Was bap John sonn to John Laidman
SEP. 5 Was bap George sonn to Michaell Chamberlain
SEP. 13 Was bap marye daughter to Lanclot Hodshon
SEP. 17 Was bap margat daugh to Richard powson
29 Was bap Michall sonn to Michaell Bousfeild
OCTOBr. 24 Was bap John sonn to George ffawcet of yeat
NOVEM. 21 Was bap Thomas sonn to John Taylor
also Ellen daughter to william Adamthwait
28 Was bap Robart sonn to Jaymes ffawcet
DECEMB. 12 Was bap Robart sonn to Robart whitlock
DECEM. 19 Was bap stephn sonn to John ffawcet of murthwat
Was bap Joseph sonn to Richard willson
Was bap John sonn to Jaymes ffawcet of blaaflat
Was bap Thomas sonn to william whiithead
DECEM. 26 Was bap Elsabeth daughter to william Adamthwait
JANEW. 23 Was bap Ellen daughter to Jayms ffawcet
of murthwait yonger (of brounbar
ffEB. 6 Was bap marye daughter to John ffothergill
Was bap marye daughter to Jaymes Robinson
13 Was bap Thomas sonn to Thomas
Robinson of Newbigin
20 Was bap Richard son to Thomas Rigg
MARCH. 7 Was bap faith daughter to Anthony pinder
9 Was bap Jaymes sonn to Robart wardell
1648 of sourbye
26 Was bap Robert sonn to Thomas ffothergill
APRILL. 16 Was bap William sonn to Thomas Adamthwait
as allso Ann daughter to Jaymes ffawcett
MAY. 21 Was bap margarat daughter to John
ffawcet of town
JUNE. 6 Was bap Gyles and Henry sonns
to Gyles ffothergill
JUNE. 10 Was bapt William sonn to Richard
ffawcet of Uldall
allso Elles daughter to simond Alderson
JUNE. 18 Was bap Isabell daughter to Will huthison
25 Was bap John sonn to Richard tod
JULY. 2 Was bap Saray daughter to John Shaw of wath
JULY. 9 Was bap Ellsabeth daughter to John Hegdail
SEP. 3 Was bap Peter and Ann sonn and daughter
to Henry pinder of weesdaill
Was bap simond son to Rodger Pinder
SEP. 10 Was bap Thomas sonn to Will Green of crosbank
OCTOBr. 1 Was bap John sonn to Richard Shaw of elergill
OCTOB. 8 Was bap William sonn to John Green of Caudbeck
15 Was bap marye dawghter to Robart taylor
allso Saray daughter to Jaret Elyetson
NONEMBr. 29 Was bap Izabell daughter to Tho Johnson
DECEM. 8 Was bap Izabell daughter
to Richard Hunter

Anno Dom. 1648

DECEMBER. 24 Was bap : Christopher son to Robart Todd
on the same day was Bap: Isabell daughter to John ffawcet of street

JANEWARY. 14 Was bap maubell daughter to
Richard ffothergill of brounbar

JAN. 20 Was bap Jaymes son to John Hinemour
as allso Elles daughter to Thomas green

ffEBRUARY. 4 Was Baptised Mary daughter to Richard Willson
18 was Bap marye daughter to Anthony ffothergill
of Causie end

ffEB. 25 Was bap Jaymes sonn to Christofer Shaw

ffEB. 28 Was bap marye daughter to John parkin

MARCH. 18 Was bap marye daughter to John Pinder

Anno dom. 1649 25 Was bap william son to michaell Chamberlain

MARCH. 27 Was bap Richard son to Christofer Rodgerson

APRILL. 1 Was bap Margat daughter to Lanclot hodson
8 Was bap Ellsabeth daugh to John ffawcet

APRILL. 22 Was bap Thomas sonn to John ffawcet of Murthat

JULY. 1 Was bap Ann daughter to simond bousfell
Bousfeild of Scarsikes

JULY. 22 Was bap Robart sonn to Michall tod
as allso sarah daughtr to Ralfe millner

SEPTEM. 16 Was bap Elsabeth daughter to John Hunter

OCTOBER. 1 Was bap marye daughtr to Will ffawcet

NOVEM. 18 Was bap Auther sonn to John Bousfeild

DECEM. 2 Was bap Ellsabeth daughter to Thomas
ffothergill of tarnhouse

JANEW. 26 Was bap margat daugter to Thomas
ffothergill of Nubegine

ffEB. 10 Was bap marye daughtr to stephn bouell

ffEB. 24 Was bap Richard sonn to Henry Haull

MARCH. 3 Was bap Henry sonn to Christofer Wharton

MARCH. 31 Was bap Annas daughter to John Hegdaill

Anno dom 1650 Aprill 14 was bap Christofer sonn
to Stephn Bousfeild

APRILL. 28 Was baptised John son to Roger Pinder

MAY. 5 Was bap Marye daughter to simond Alderson
12 Was bap Thomas son to John Shaw
19 Was bap mary daughter to Thomas deny

JUNE. 11 Was baptised margret daughter to Robart whitelocke
31 Was bap william son to Richard shaw of elergill
allso John son to Richard powson of moss

AGUST. 19 Was bap Robart son to John Laidman

SEPT. 1 Was bapt Ezabell daughter
to Anthony ffothergill of Adamthwat

SEPT. 15 Was bap marye daughtr to Lanclot Townso

SEP. 29 Was bap mary daughter to Roger medcalfe

OCTO. 6 Was bap James son to Jahnes ffawcet
of murthwaite
on the same day was bap Elsabeth dauther
to willyam ffothergill
And henry son to Thomas Johnson

OCTOB^r. 13 Was bap Marye daughtr to Anthony ffothergill

Anno Dom. 1605

OCTOBER.	20	Was bap Jaymes sonn to John ffawcet of town
NOVEM.	3	Was bap John son to George Thorneborrow
NOVEM.	10	Was baptised mary daughter to michaell Chamber laine younger
NOVE.	17	Was Bap Richard son to Henery Wilkinson the same day was Bap Thomas son to Edward Bland
DECEMB.	29	Was bap marye daughter to Michell Bousfeild
JANUARY.	12	Was bap Thomas son to James ffawcett of Blafleat
JAN.	19	Was Bap: Thomas son to James Robinson & Thomas son to John ffawcett of Dubbs
JAN.	30	Was Bap John son to Christopher ffawcett Was Bap An daughter to Richard shaw on the same day was bap Elsabeth daug. to Richard ffawcet of sandbed
MARCH.	9	Was Bap willyam Son to Thomas Greene
1651		Was Bap the same day Sara daughter to Richard willson
APRILL.	6	Was bap margatt daugter to John Bousfell as allso Elles daughter to Richard Powson
APRILL.	28	Was bap John sonn to George Chamberlaine
JUNE.	14	Was Baptised Christopher son to Robert Taylor
JULY.	27	Was Baptised James son to willya Adamthwaite
AGUST.	23	Was bap Phillip sonn to William Rodgerson allso Ellen daughter to william whitehead
AGUST.	5	Was bap Ann daughter to Jayms ffawcet of murthat yonger
SEP.	14	Was Bap Thomas son to Jayms parkin Allso Mary daughter to Henry pinder
OCTOB.	20	Was bap Richard sonn to Jarrard elyetson
OCTOB.	4	Was bap Ezabell daugter to John ffawcet of murthatt
OCTOB.	24	Was bap Izabell daughtr. to John Robinson of neubygin
DECEMBr.	14	Was bap ffrances daughter to Ralf millner
DECEMBER.	28	Was Baptized margrett daughter to John Hunter
JANEWARY.	1	Was bap Ellsabeth daughtr to Tho fothergill
ffEB.	8	Was bap George sonn to Rodger pinder
ffEB.	22	Was bap Ellsabeth daughter to Thomas Adamththwat
MARCH.	16	Was bap Richard son to stephn bouell
	13	Was bap Jaymes sonn to Christofer Powson
1652		Was bap marie daught to michaell Todd
APRILL.	5	Was bap Annas daughter to Christofer Rodgerson

Anno domini 1652

MAY. 2nd Was baptised Richard son to Henrie garethwait
9 of May was baptised Elise daughter to John ffawcett
JUNE. 6 Was bap Henry sonn to Christofer wharton
JUNE. 16 Was bap George son to John spooner of grenside
allso margatt daugter to William ffawcet
JULY. 4 Was bap Ellsabeth daughtr
to Thomas ffawcet
AGUST. 24 Was Bap margat daughter to Robart Taylor
SEP. 19 Was Bap Thomas son to Thomas denye
OCTOBr. 10 Was bap Mary daughter to Tho Rigg
NOV. 14 Was bap Stephn son to Tho fawcett
NOV. 29 Was Bap George Sonne to Anthony Shaw
Was Bap Richard Sonne to Michaell Chamblaine
Was Bap Willyam Sonne to Roger Medcalfe
Was Bap Phillip Sonne to Stephen Bousfeild
Was Bap John & An son & daughter to Antho : Pindr of wath
Pinder of wath
DECEMBr. 14 Was bap Edmond sonn to Richard Adamson
DECEMBr. 20 Was bap Richard son to George huetson
allso marie daughter to Abram Gouldinton
JANEWARY. 9 Was Bap Issabell daugher
to John Heuetson
JAN. 16 Was bap Ellen daughtr to
John Bousfeilld Hatter
ffEBRU. 6 Was Baptised Stephen Sone to John ffawcett of Towne
allso Heugh Sonne to Anthonie ffothergill causeyend
MARCH. 13 Was baptized Richard son to John ffawcett of Dubbs
27 Was bap mary daughtr to Anthony
1653 ffothergill of Adamthatt
APRILL. 3 Was bapt John sonn to Renold bouell
APRILL. 24 Was bap Ellen daught to Jaymes fawcet of tarn
MAY. 8 Was bap Ellen daughtr to John Robinson
JUNE. 12 Was bap Christofer soen to Thomas ward
JUNE. 26 Was bap Vinson son to Richard
Shawe of Ellergill
JULY. 10 Was bap Richard son to Tho Green
24 Was bap Margatt daugh to Richard wilson
AGUST. 6 Was bap Jaine daugtr to will Rodgerson
AGUST. 14 Was bap Lanclot son to Jaymes pacoke
28 Was bap Thomas sonn to steuen dent
SEPTEM. 11 Was bap Thomas sonn to Jarratt close
OCTOBER. 2 Was Baptised Issabell daughtr to Michaell Busfield
NOVEM. 16 Was bap Henry sonn to Lanclot Townson
Was bap Henry sonn to Tho fothergil gre
DECEM. 11 Was bap Saraih daughter to John Bousfell
allso ezabell daughtr to will whitehead

(110)

JANEWARY.		1653
FEB.	11	Was bap william sonn to Jaymes ffawcet of blafflat
	22	Was bap Anthony sonn to Rodger Pinder
ffEB.	22	Was bap Thomas sonn to Ralfe millner
	26	Was bap marye daugtr to wil fothergil loucom
MARCH.	1	Was bap Ann daugter to Tho fawcet of blaflat
MARCH.	19	Was Bap Richard son to Richard Powson of howkeld
MARCH.	26	Was Bap Issabell daughter to John Lademan
1654		
APRILL.	26	Was bap Sibbell daughter to John Hunter
JUNE.	4	Was bap Margat daug to Richard hayton
JUNE.	8	Was Bap Dorothie daughter to Thomas
JUNE.	22	Was bp mary dautr to Thomas Atkinson * ffothergill of Tarnehouse
JULY.	16	Was bap Thomas sonn to Henry Garthwait
SEPTEMBR.	22	Was Baptized Edmond sonn to Tho: Adamthwait
SEPTEMBR.	27	Was Baptized Mary Daughter to James parkin
OCTOBER.	15	Was Bap: Robert sonne to Robert Whitelocke
		Was Baptized John sonne to Stephen Chamberlaine and Annas Daughter to Thomas Denny
NOVEMBR.	26	Was bap dorathy daughtr to John hegdall
DECEMB.	4	Was bap Phillip sonn to Stephn bousfell
DECEMBR.	12	Was bp George sonn to Thomas ffawcet of hole
DEC.	20	Was bap Richard sonn to Richard Adamson
DEC[r].	20	allso stephn son to John ffothergill of brounb
DECEMBER.	30	Was bap Saraih daugtr to Rodger meccay
JANEWARY.	1	Was bap Sarah daugtr to Johnathan dodson
JEN.	7	Was bap Saraih daughter to Isak Handlay
GENEWARY.	27	Was bap Isabell daughtr to John Bousfeild
FEB.	7	Was bap margat daughter to Philip bell
ffEB.	10	Was bap George son to Tho ffawcet
	15	Was bap mary daugter to Tho Green
ffEB.	17	Was bap Thomas sonn to Christofer wharton
		Was bap Richard sonn to Phillip bousfeild
		allso Isabell daughtr te Christofer powson
MARCH.	4	Was bap Ann daughter to John ffawcet of dubs
APRILL.	29	Was bap Thomas son to michell chamberlain
Anno dom 1655	MAY 16	Was bap Issabell daugh[tr] to Thomas ffawcet of blaflat
JUNE.	24	Was bap Isabell daugter to John Cautlay
JULY.	1	Was bap Jane daughter to Rodger ellwood
JULY.	22	Was bap Richard sonn to Anthony shaw
AGUST.	2	Was bap Anna daughter to Richard willson
SEP.	23	Was bap Anns daughter to John spooner
		Was bap John sonn to Anthony ffothergill of causyend
NOVEMB.	15	Was bap Richard son to John fawet of street
		Was bap Ann daugtr to Georg Huetson
		Was bap Ellen daughter to John ffawcet of town

* An after insertion, and in the wrong place.

Anno dom 1655

Novembr.	23	Was Bap Jone daughter to Richard dent of Adamthat
December.	20	Was bap Henry sonn to John ffawcet of brakinbar
Janew.	10	Was bap stephn sonn to Rodger pinder
Janew.	19	Was bap John sonn to Thomas dent of bouderdall foot
ffeb.	8	Was bap Grace daughter to James willson
Anno Dom 1656		Aprill 1 Was bap Henry sonn to Thomas ffothergill of brounbar
		Ap. 6 Was bap Ann daughter to william ffothergill allso Saraih daugtr to Robart Tayler of town
Aprill.	19	Was bap Thomas sonn to Anthony ffothergill
May.	4	Was bap Thomas sonn to Ralf millner allso mary daughter to Jarett close
May.	27	Was bap Anthony sonn to Thomas ffawcet of grensid allso dorathy daughter to John moreland
June.	8	Was bap John sonn to Henry Garthat as allso Thomas sonn to Christofer Rodgerson
June.	24	Was bap thomas sonn to steuen dent
Agust.	1	Was bap peter son to Isack handlay* allso was bap Annas daughter to John Gouldinton
Agust.	8	Was bap Thomas sonn to Lanclot Townson
Agust.	24	Was bap Richard sonn to John Hunter
October.	4	Was bp Anthony sonn to John Hegdall
	19	Was bap margat daughter to Thom Denye
December.	16	Was bap Author sonn to John bousfeild of town head
Janewary.	8	Was bap marye daugtr to Thomas ffawcet of blaflat
Febrewary	28	Was bap Annas daugtr to Peter fawcet
March.	7	Was bap margrat daugtr to John knustop of caudbeck
March.	10	Was bap stephen sonn to John spooner
March.	19	Was bap Richard sonn to Christofer wharton of stenercu
1657 April.	5	Was bap Ellsabeth daughter to Willian Whitehead
Aprill.	18	Was bap William and Edward sonns to John ffawcet of dubs
May.	9	Was bap saraih daughter to Thomas Adamthwait
May.	17	Was bap John sonn to Rodger meccay
May.	22	Was bap Agnas daughter to Rodger pinder

* An after insertion; should have been written below the entry following.

1657

14 of June Was bap Phillip sonn to John Bousfeild
June. 20 Was Bap Robart sonn to
Jaymes ffawcet of blaflatt
July. 03 Was bap marye daughter to
Richard shaw of Ellergill
September. 27 Was bap marye daughter
to Phillip Bousfeild of bouderdail
October. 24 Was bap John sonn to Abram gouldinton
Novemb. 17 Was bap Joseph sonn to
Richard Willson of town
November. 19 Was Baptiz Thomas sonn
to Thomas ffawcet of yeat
Decemb. 5 Was bap Margatt daughter
to Thomas dent of Bouderdaill
Decemb[r]. 17 } Was bap marye daugter to
} John Cautlay of newbigin
Janewary. 02 Was bap George sonn to
Thomas ffothergill of greenside
Janew. 28 Was bap Heugh sonn to Robart
shaw of trannow hill
ffebr. 9 Was bap dorathi daugter
to George ffothergill of Lowcom
ffeb. 18 Was bap John sonn to michaell
Chamberlaine of nauthatt
ffeb. 28 Was bap Elsabeth daughter
to John ffawcet oth dikes
March. 4 Was bap Jaymes sonn to
Robart ffawcet of greenside
March. 16 Was bap mathew sonn to
1658 Richard breaks of greenside
May. 6 Was bap saraih daughtr toJayms Parkin
May. 26 Was bap georg sonn to
stephn Chamberlain
July. 3 Was bap Grace daughter Johnathan dodson
July. 4 Was Bap Sarah daughtr
to Anthony ffothergill of trannohill
July. 12 Was bap Georg sonn to Thomas ffawcet
of Greenside
July. 24 Was bap Saraih daughter to John
Robinson of newbygin
Agust. 5 Was bap margrat daughter
to Robert Hunter
Agust. 6 Was bap michaell sonn to Robart
tayler

Sept. 26 Was bap Sibbell daughter
to Anthony ffothergill of Adamthwat
October. 19 Was bap Ellen daughter to
John ffawcet of town head
Novem. 3 Was bap Ellen daughter
to George Ubank of bouderdail
Novem. 23 Was bap Vinson sonn to Christofer wharton
Decemb. 21 Was bap william son to John Hunter
Was bap Richard son to peter fawcet
Janewary. 14 Was bap Godfraye son to Ralfe Millner
ffebre. 24 Was bap John sonn to John Hegdall
1659 March. 24 Was bap Robart sonn to stephen futhergill
Aprill. 8 Was bap margat daughter to Rodger pinder
Julye. 26 Was bap Annas daughter to Thomas ffothergill of tarnhous
July. 31 Was bap Thomas sonn to
Rodger meccay of studfould
Agust. 2 Was bap Ann daughter to John fawcet
Sep. 3 Was bap Ellen daughter to John sponer
October. 4 Was bap marye daughter to william whitehead
November. 3 Was bap Thomas son to Thomas Tayler of bent
November. 10 } Was bap Jaymes sonn to Lanclot Townson
} as allso Elen daughter to Richard breaks
November. 18 Was bap William son to Stephn Chamberlain
No. 29 Was bap John sonn to Thomas ffawcet of blaflat
Decem. 29 Was bap Sarah daughter to Robart Shaw of tranohill
Janewary. 12 Was bap margrat daughter to Thomas fawcet of stoup
Jan. 18 Was bap Sarah daughter to Anthony ffothergill of trannow
Feb. 8 Was bap Jaymes son to James ffawce of blaf
Feb. 19 Was bap zaraih daughter to John
Bosfeild of town hatter
March. 5 Was bap Ealse daugter to John Moreland
166
Aprill. 15 Was bap Eallse daughter to
John Knoustubb
May. 29 Was bap Ezabell daughter
to John shaw of towne
July. 6 Was baptized stephn sonn to steuen dent
July. 22 Was bap Richard son to
vinson powson
allso Henry son to John Cawtley
July. 29 Was bap John son to Phillip
Bousfeild of wath yonger
Agust. 19 Was bap marye daughter to Thomas
Adamthwait of Artelgarth
Agust. 22 Was bap Ann daughter
to Edward Bland
September. 03 Was bap Ellen and ffrances daughters
to Thomas dennye of stenercue
October. 6 Was bap Richard sonn to Thomas ffawcet
allso Anthony sonn to John Hegdaill
October. 21 Was bap margrat daughter to George
ffothergill of LowCom

DEC. 6 Was bap marie daughter to Willm ffothergill of town
DECEMB. 25 Was bap Richard sonn to
Thomas Breaks begotte in fornecat[n]
JAN. 10 Was bap Simond sonn to Rodger pinder
JAN. 26 Was bap Richard sonn to Robart Hunter
allso Annas daughter to michell ffothergill of wandall
ffEB. 7 Was bap margat Daughter
to vinson ffothergill of stenerscu
allso marie daughter to John Hunter
FEB. 10 Was bap Izabell daughter to John fawcet of town
FEB. 19 Was bap George sonn to Johnathan dodson
1661 APRILL 1 Was bap John son to Christofer powson
APRILL 7 Was bap Sibbell daughter
to John Adamthwait of Adamthat
APRILL. 26 Was bap George sonn to Richard Murthat
APRILL. 28 Was bap Thomas sonn to John Adamth
thwait yongger of Adamthwat
JUNE. 6 Was bap marie daughter to giles haull
JUNE. 7 Was bap Elsabeth daughtor to J[o]hn haiswhitle
JUNE. 9 Was bap stephen son to stephen chamberlane
JUNE. 11 Was bap Richard son to Christopher fawcett
JUNE. 21 Was bp Ezabell daughter to George Clemison
AGUST. 14 Was bap marie daughter to Robart shaw
of trannow hill
SEPT. 14 Was bap John sonn to Ralf Alderson
OCTOB[r]. 3 Was bap Thomas sonn to Richard Breaks
OCTOB[r]. 6th Was bap Anthony sonn to Thomas Knoustop
OCTOB[r]. 13 Was bap dorathy daughter to Thomas ffothergill
NOV. 13 Was bap John sonn to Robert whitlock
DECEMB. 1 Was bap Ann daughtr to John swainson
DECEMBR. 19 Was bap Isabell daughter to John Clark
DECEM. 24 Was bap Thomas sonn to John sponr
JANEWARY. 3 Was bap marye daug[r] to Thomas ffawcet
JANEWARY. 10 Was bap Robart sonn to Robart ffawcet
JANEWARY. 19 Was bap John sonn to John ffawcet of Dikes
ffEB. 6 Was bap John sonn to Christofer waller
ffEB. 21 Was bap John sonn to George Ubank
MARCH. 9 Was bap Thomas son to Thomas
1662 ffawcet of blaflatt
APRILL. 2 Was bap margatt daughter to lanclot Richardson
of crossbygarett
APRILL. 17 Was bap margat daughter to stephn ffothergill
APRILL. 19 Was bap Phillip sonn to Michell Bousfeild
of Greenside
MAY. 18 Was bap Richard sonn to Richard Alderson
JUNE. 1 Was bap Robert sonn to Rodger Meccy
JULYE. 8 Was bapt Johnathan sonn to Richard Willson
AGUST. 6 Was bap John sonn to Thomas Breaks
AGUST. 24 Was bap Ellen daughter to John Knoustob
OCTOBER. 6 Was bap Isabell daughter to John pinder
as allso Isabell daugtr to Thomas Thomson
OCTOBER. 20 Was bap Robart son to Anthony ffothergill of tranow
NOVEMBR. 2 Was bap George sonn to Johnathan dodso

NOUEM. 23 Was baptized Elsabeth daughter
to william whithead
DECEMBER. 12 Was bap mary daugter to Roba^rt
JANEW. 3 shawe of trannow hill
JAN. 22 Was bap william sonn to
Anthony fothergill of adamthatt
ffEBR. 3 Was bapt John sonn to
John Hunter of bouberhead
MARCH. 4 Was bap Robert sonn to
Rodger pinder
MARCH. 11 Was bap Phillip sonn
to Thomas Adamthwait
MARCH. 20 Was bap william
1663 sonn to George Clemison
APRILL. 5 Was bap George sonn to John
swainson of wandall
APRILL. 8 Was bap John sonn to John
Blackburne
APRILL. 15 Was bap william sonn to James
ffawcet
and Ann daughter to Phillip
Bousfeild of bouderdaill
allso Ellen daughter to Richard
murthwat of wath
APRILL. 28 Was bap Izabell daughter to
Thomas ffawcet of greenside
JUNE. 8 Was bap Thomas sonn to John Bousfeild
JUNE. 13 Was bap simond sonn to Ralfe Allderson
JUNE. 24 Was bap stephn sonn to John fawcet
JULY. 18 Was bap John sonn to Christofer Allderson
AGUST. 5 Was bap George sonn to lanclot Townson
as all Richard sonn to stepn Chamberlain
SEPT. 23 Was bap Thomas sonn to John C *
OCTOBR. 8 Was bap Ezabell daughter to Thom
fothergill of neubigin
OCTOB. 28 Was bap Robart sonn to
Edward bland
NOVEMB^r 19 Was bap marye daughter
to william shawe of crooksbeck
NOV. 29 Was bap Ellen daughter
to Thomas dent of bouderdail
DECEM. 18 Was bap Thomas sonn to
John sponner
DECEMB. 20 Was bap John sonn to Thomas tomson
MARCH. 18 Was bap marye daughter to Richard Breaks
MARCH. 23 Was bap mary daughter
1664 to Robart perkine
APRILL. 11 Was bap Ellen daughter to michael
Bossfell
as all John sonn to a pour woman
MAY. 16 Was bap William sonn to
Thomas ffawcet of greensid
MAY. 29 Was bap Izabell daughter to
Robart Hunter

* Name illegible, probably Close, or Clark.

1664		
May.	20	Was bap Robart sonn to Gyles Haull
Agust.	4	Was Baptized Isabell daughter to stephn Robinson In fornecaton
Agust.	20	Was bap Mary daughter to John Barber
Agust.	23	Was bap John sonn to Thomas hastwitle of wandall
Agust.	31	Was bap mary daughter to Henry ffothergill
Sept.	13	Was bap Annas daughter to John Birket
Sept.	29	Was bap william sonn to Thomas ffawwcet of blaflat
Octobbr.	2	Was bap Mary daugtr to John Adamthwat
November.	1	Was bap Thomas sonn to Thomas breaks
Nevembr	19	Was bap John sonn to Jaymes ffawcet of dubbs
Decembr.	21	Was bap Thomas sonn to Richard Alderson of tarnhous
Decemb.	25	Was bap Thomas son to John fawcet of howkeld
Janewary.	12	Was bap Robart sonn to John hunter
Janewary.	26	Was bap John sonn to william whitehead of lowcom
Febr.	16	Was bap Anthony sonn to Anthony ffothergill of tranoh
March.	19	Was bap Jayms sonn to Thomas ffawcet o th yeat
1665		
Aprill.	19	Was bap Henry sonn to John Knoustobb
Aprill.	23	Was bap John sonn to Georg Clemison
May.	5	Was bap John sonn to John sponner
June.	25	Was bap Richard sonn to Rodger pinder
July.	2	Was bap Thomas sonn to Christofer Allderson
July.	7	Was bap Thomas sonn to Robart shawe
July.	25	Was bap Abram sonn to steuen dent
Julye.	03	Was bap John son to william Robinson of Neubigin
Agust.	3	Was bap Ann daughter to steuen Chamberlaine
Agust.	16	Was baptised peter sonn to peter Billbowe
Agust.	30	Was bap margrat daught william blenkarn

SEPT.	01	Was bapt Robarte sonn to John ffawcet of town
SEPTEMB.	21	Was bap John son to Robart parkin
OCTOBER.	3	Was bap Isabell daughter to Robart Riden
OCTOBER.	15	Was bap Ann daughter to Robart Hunter
NOVEMB.	19	Was bap Ellen daughter to Richard murthat sandbed
DECEMB.	3	Was bap mary daughter to william fawcet
DECEMB.	6	Was bap mary daughter to John Bousfeld
DECEM.	17	Was bap George sonn to Thomas ffothergill of Neubigin
DECEMBR.	28	Was bapt william sonn to mary fawcet born in fornicaton at lunns
JANEW[r]AY.	1	Was bap John sonn to John meason
JANEWARY.	6	Was bap John sonn to phillip Bousfell as allso Ezabell daughter to Georg Ubank
JANARY.	8	Was bapt Heugh and Annas sonn and daugter to william shaw of Crooksbeck
FEBREWARY.	12	Was baptiz william sonn Anthonye fothergill of Adamthat
FEBRE.	18	Was bap frances daughter to Thomas Adamthwat of artellgarth
ffEB.	27	Was bap Robart sonn to Richard breaks
MARCH.	4	Was bap John sonn to Robart Handly allso Henry sonn to Jaymes stanklaye
MARCH.	11	Was bap Thomas sonn to John Hunter
MARCH.	18	Was bap Jaine daughter to Thomas Robinson of greenside
MARCH.	23	Was Bap Rodger sonn to John Barber
1666		
MAY.	6	Was bap Phillip sonn to michell bousfell
MAY.	18	Was bap mary daugter to John · · · · · · *
JUNE.	2	Was bap Annas daughter to Phillip Tayler
SEPTEMBR.	25	Was bap Isabell daughter to Lanclot Townson of Artellgarth
OCTOBER.	12	Was bap mary daughtr to george Clemison
OCTOBER.	14	Was bap margat daughtr to John swainsone
NOVEMBR.	11	Was bap Jaymes the sonn of Thomas fawcet of blaflat
1667		
MARCH.	30	Was bap william sonn to John Heutson
APRILL.	11	Was bap Isabell daughter to steuen Chamberlaine allso mary daughter to Rodger barber
APRILL.	21	Was bap John sonn to Thomas fawcet
APRILL.	28	Was baptized Robart sonn to Thomas ffawcet of greenside
MAY.	2	Was babtized John sonn to Gyles hall of sprintgill

* Illegible; transcripts give "blackburn."

1667

MAY.	9	Was baptised marye daughter to George ffothergill of tarnhouse
JUNE.	19	Was Bap Anthony sonn to Anthony ffothergill of Causie end
JULY.	21	Was bap william sonn to Robart handlay
JULY.	25	Was bap John sonn to Robart shawe of tranow hill
JULY.	28	Was bap Elsabeth daughter to Richard ffothergill of grensid
AGUST.	23	Was baptiz John sonn to John haistw[il]te
SEPT.	6	Was bap william sonn to Thomas breaks
NOUEMBER.	16	Was bap marye daughter to Thomas simson
DECEMBER.	8	Was bap Isabell daughter to Robart Hunter
DECEMBER.	21	Was bap margrat daughter to John broune.
DECEMBER.	26	Was bapt margat daughter to Richard Alderson of needlous
JANEWARI.	1	Was bap Thomas sonn to John Knoustob allso margrat daughter to Ralfe Alderson
ffEBREWARY.	23	Was bap marye daughter to Richard murthatt
ffEBREWARY.	28	Was bap Richard sonn to Nicolas browne
MARCH.	1	Was bap John sonn to Thomas ffothergill of Nubigin
MARCH.	4	Was bapt Jayms the sonn of henry fothergill as allso Ralfe the sonn of Christofer Allderson
MARCH.	8	Was bap margat daughter to John ffawcet of howceld
MARCH.	11	Was bap John the sonn of Thomas Knoustob
1668		as allso Sarah daughter to Richard breaks
APRILL.	5	Was bap mauball daughter to Henry handlay
APRILL.	12	Was bap Thomas sonn to william shawe as allso ezabell daughter to John hunter
MAY.	9	Was bap bri[d]ghat daughter to Michaell Tayler
JULY.	19	Was bap Richard sonn to John ffawcet
AGUST.	24	Was bap George sonn to John Bousfield
OCTOBER ye (68)	11[th]	Was baptised Thomas sone to Richard ffothergill the same day was Baptised Thomas sone to James ffawcet Alsoe was Baptised Christopher sone to Phillipp Bousfeild
OCTOBER ye 15th.		Was Baptised Anthony ffawcett sone to will[m] ffawcett of sandbed
NOUEM ye 5th.		Was Baptised Margerett daughter to Isack Bousfeild
DECEMBR ye 16th.		Was Baptised Margerett daughter to Robert Parkin Smith in ye street
JANUARY ye 30th		Was Baptised Henery sonne to Rodger Barben of Twone webster
ffEBRUARY the 2th.		Was Baptised Ann daughter to Robert Shawe of Tranihill the same day was Baptised Christopher sonne to John ffawcett of Tarne

MARCH. 7 Was Baptised John son to John Huetson wright
MARCH. 14 Was Baptised Richard and margret children to Thomas fawcet of Bleaflatt
MARCH. 21 Was Baptised Isabell Daughter to w^m ffothergill of streete
1669
APRILL. 25 Was Baptised Isabell Daughter of Henry Lawe
MAY the 23 Was Baptized George Sonn to George Clemison
the same day was Baptized Ann daughter to Ralph Alderson
JUNE. 13 Was Baptised Elin daughter to Thomas Dent of Bouderdail
JUNE. 18 Was Baptised James sonn of John ffawcett sonn of James of new *
JULY. 4 Was Baptised Richard son of Richard Breakes of Newbiggin
JULY. 7 Was Baptised william son of m^r Geo: ffothergill of Tarnehouse
JULY. 18 Was Baptised Ann Daughter of Henry Handley
AUGUST. 8 Was Baptised Elsabeth Daughter of Barnard Douer
AUGUST. 22 Was Baptised James son of John Tayler Ellergill
OCTOBER. 21 Was Baptised John son of michaell Tayler
NOUEMBER. 1 Was Baptised Thomas son of Tho: ffawcet of hole
NOUEMBER. 18 Was Baptised Ellin Daughter of Tho: Breakes
NOU. 25 Was Baptised margeret Daughter of John Blackburne
DECEMBER. 9 Was baptised Elsabeth Daughter of Richard whitehead
DECEMBER. 12 Was Baptised Edward son to John Hunter
DECEMBER. 23 Was Baptised Agnes Daughter of Hugh Blenkarne
DECEMBER. 28 Was Baptised mary Daughter of Robt. Handley
ffEBR. 1 Was Baptised John son of william shawe of Towne
the same day mary Daughter of Robt Ridding
ffEB. 10 Was Baptised Elin Daughter of Tho. ffawcet stouple
ffEB. 15 Was Baptised John son of John Haistwhitle scarsiks
1670 MARCH. 27 Was Baptised Sarah Daughter of Richard murthwaite
APRILL. 28 Was Baptised John son of John Birket of street
MAY. 15 Was Baptised Elin Daughter of Richard Bousfeild of Bouderdale
MAY. 22 Was Baptised mary Daughter of Robt. Hunter
MAY. 29 Was Baptised Robert son of John willson
JUNE. 1 Was Baptised John & margret children of Thomas Taylor
JUNE the 19 Was Baptised Margret daughter to
William Shaw off Crookes Beck, was Baptised the
same day Elsabeth daughter to Thomas ffawcett off streete
JUNE. 24 Was baptised Grace daughter to Richard ffallowfeild
JULLY. 3 Was baptised Mary daughter to Isack Bousffeild
allso the same day was baptised Elsabeth daughter
of John Petty off wesdaille
JULY. 30 Was baptised Richard and John
both suns off Henery law off wesdaille
AGUST. 7 Was Baptised Ellin daughter to Richard ffothergill
OCTOBER. 13 Was Baptised Mary daughter to Ralph Alderson of towne
OCTOBER. 20 Was Baptised margrat daughter to Robart Shaw trannahill
NOUEMBER. 13 Was Baptised Annas daughter to
Richard Simpson of bouberheade
NOUEMBER. 20 Was Baptissed Isabell daughter
to Thomas Middelton of dent
NOUEMBER. 24 Was baptissed Margrat daughter to
Roger Barben of Towne webster
Also the same day was Baptised Margrat daughter
to John ffawcet of nubegin Junior.
NOUEMBER. 25 Was Baptissed Robart sonne to
Robart Handlay of wesdaile
DECEMBER. 27 Was Baptissed William sonne to
Robart Parkin of streete smith

* Rest indistinct. Transcripts give "nubegin".

CHRISTNINGS.

DECEMBER the 29. Was Baptissed Robart son to Robart Turnner
JANUARY. 12 Was Baptissed Jennat daughter to Rouland Shearman
ffEBUARY. 7 Was Baptissed Ann daughter to Thomas ffothergill of nubegin
ffEBUARY. 12 Was Baptissed Robart sonne to Gylles Hall
ffEBUARY. 14 Was Baptissed Henery son to George ffothergill off Lowcome
1671
MARCH. 26 Was Baptissed Anthony son to Nicolas Broune
Also the same day mary daughter to George Ubanke
APRILL. 6 Was baptissed Thomas son to John Robinson of tranmore
APRILL. 9 Was Baptissed Issabell daughter to John Heutson
JUNE. 1 Was Baptissed Issabell daughter to Barnad douer
JUNE. 27 Was Baptissed James son to Richard Alderson
JULY. 9 Was Baptissed Issabell daughter to Henery Handlay
AWGUST. 15 Was baptissed Ellin daughter to John Hunter
SEPTEMBER. 7 Was Baptissed Adam son to Michaell Taylor
SEPTEMBER. 29 Was Baptissed William son to Richard ffallowfeild
OCTOBER. 22 Was Baptissed margrat daughter to George Clemyson
OCTOBER. 24 Was Baptissed Issabell daughter to John Pettey
NOUEMBER. 9 Was Baptissed George son to William ffothergill off the streete
NOUEMBER. 23 Was Baptissed Annas daughter to Thomas Taylor off Adamthwaite
DECEMBER. 7 Was Baptissed Michell sonn to John Knustub
DECEMBER. 10 Was baptissed Issabell daughter to Edward Willyamson milner of this mill
DECEMBER. 14 Was baptissed michell sonn to Heugh Blenkarne
JANUARY. 4 Was baptissed mary daughter to William Shawe of towne
ffEBRUARY 8 Was Baptissed Elsabeth daughter to John Hewetson Carpinter
ffEBRUARY 13 Was Baptissed margrat daughter to Richard Bousfeild of Bouderdaile
ffEBRUARY. 22 Was Baptissed Thomas son to John Robinson of Elergill
MARCH. 14 Was Baptissed Thomas son to Robart Huntter
Also the same day was Baptised John son To Thomas ffawcett off streete
1672 APRILL 4 Was Baptissed Thomas sonn to Rouland Shearman
MAY. 23 Was Baptised Anthony son to Anthony ffothergill of Adamthwaite
JULY. 14 Was Baptised Mary daughter to Cirstopher Alderson
AUGUST. 4 Was Baptissed John son to John Birkat
Also was Baptised the same day margaret daughter to John Wilson
AUGUST. 15 Was Baptissed Michell sonn to william Shaw of Ellergill
AUGUST. 22 Was baptised John son to Richard Breakes
AUGUST. 29 Was baptissed Henery son to William Whitfeild
SEP. 10 Was baptissed Ellinn daughter to Isack Bousfeild
SEP. 29 Was baptissed Michell son to Phillip Bousfeild of stenascu
OCTOBER. 17 Was baptised Margret daughter to John ffawcet of tarne
OCTOBER. 20 Was baptised ellin daughter to John Taylor of elergill
OCTOBER. 29 Was baptissed Mary daughter to John ffawcet of toune
NOUEMBER. 18 Was baptissed Elsabeth daughter to John Ouerend

1672 CHRISTNINGS

DECEMBER. 10 Was Baptised Jeffray and Rouland sonns
To Adam Shawe of bouderdaile
the same day stephen son to Richard Bouell of Rige
Also mary daughter to Thomas ffothergill of nubegin
DECEMBER. 11 Was Baptised Robart son to William Shawe
of the Crookesbeck
JANUARY. 1 Was baptissed Thomas sonn to Roger Barber webster
JANUARY. 3 Was baptissed Mary daughter to James mosse
MARCH. 9 Was baptissed Anthony son to George Perkin
MARCH. 18 Was baptissed Ralph son to William Milner
APRILL. 10 Was baptissed James son to George Perkin elder
1673 APRILL. 20 Was baptissed Abraham son to Thomas Haistwhitle
MAY. 8 Was baptissed Ellice daughter to Thomas Perkin of Ellerhill
Also the same day baptissed Issabell daughter to
James wilson of stenascah
MAY. 29 Was baptissed Abigall daughter to Richard murthwaite
also elsabeth daughter to edward Scaife
JULY. 28 Was baptissed Richard son to Richard Robinson of low loneing
Also was baptissed the same day John son to John
Hewetson off the midle off the toune
Also was baptissed John son to Richard Simpsson
Scoole master off bouber heade
AGUST. 26 Was Baptissed Robart son to Barnad Douer
SEP. 4 Was Baptissed Mary daughter to John Taylor off Backside
OCTOBER. 14 Was Baptissed Mary daughter to John Bladdes
OCTOBER. 15 Was Baptissed Mary daughter to Thomas Breeakes
OCTOBER. 19 Was Baptissed John son to William Greene cauldbeck
NOUEMBER. 18 Was Baptissed Elizabeth daughter to John ffawcett shoomakr
NOUEMBER. 23 Was Baptissed Cirstopher son to Ralph Alderson of towne
DECEMBER. 25 Was Baptissed Thomas sonne to Richard ffallowfeild
JANUARY. 1 Was Baptissed Ellice daughter to Robart Perkin of - - - - - -*
JANUARY. 13 Was Baptissed Elsabeth daughter to Stephen Chamberlaine
ffEBRUARY. 18 Was Baptised Issabell daughter to Robart Turner
MARCH. 11 Was Baptised Sibbell daughter to John Robinson of Elergill
MARCH. 13 Was Baptised mary daughter to Richard ffawcett
1674 MARCH. 26 Was Baptised John son to Henery Bousfeild
APRILL. 5 Was Baptised Sibbell daughter to Robart Hunter
MAY. 21 Was Baptised Jane daughter to Michell Taylor
MAY. 28 Was Baptised Issabell daughter to Richard Robinson of blaflat
MAY. 29 Was Baptised Heugh son to John Hunter
JULY. 29 Was Baptised Simond son to Thomas ffawcet of streetè
AUGUST. 2 Was Baptised John son to Richard Murthwaite
AUGUST. 9 Was Baptised Sarah daughter to Richard Bousfeild of bouderdaile
SEPT. 3 Was Baptised mary daughter to Heugh Blenckarne
SEPT. 17 Was Baptised michaell son to Richard Breakes
SEPT. 24 Was Baptised William son to Richard Whitehead
SEPT. 27 Was Baptised Robeart son to William Balife
OCTOBER. 22 Was Baptised Mary daughter to John Hewetson of townhead
OCTOBER. 31 Was Baptized John son to Stephen ffawcett of murthwaite
NOUEMBER. 15 Was Baptized Margaret daughter to John Robinson of tranmoore
NOUEMBER. 22 Was Baptized John son to John Ouerend
NOUEMBER. 26 Was Baptized elsabeth daughter to George Clemeyson
DECEM. 22 Was Baptized Ann daughter to John Hewetson of towne
JANUARY. 17 Was Baptized Thomas son to Edward willyamson milner
MARCH. 7 Was Baptized Sarah daughter to william Elyetson
MARCH. 16 Was Baptized margarett daughter to John Todd of Caudbeck
1675 MAY. 2 Was Baptized margaret daughter to Mathew Birckdaile
MAY. 9 Was Baptized Ann daughter to william Shawe toune
MAY. 21 Was Baptized Simond son to Isack Bousfield
DECEM. 5 Was Baptized Henery son to William Shaw of Crookesbeck
DECEM. 9 Was Baptized Ealsse daughter to John Taylor of backeside

* Indistinct; "streete," apparently. Transcripts have "smith".

1675 CHRISTNINGS

DECEM.	26	Was Baptized James son to willm Shawe of Stenerscugh
JANUARY.	1	Was Baptized George son to George Perkin of Lockholme
JANUARY.	13	Was Bap: George sonn to George Perkin of Stennerscugh
ffEB.	2	Was Bap. Christopher son to John Taylor of Ellergill
JANUARY.	15	Was Bap. mary daughter to Barnad Douer
MARCH.	5	Was Bap. mary daughter to Thomas ffothergill of brounber
MARCH.	9	Was Bap. Sarah daughter to Henery Bousfeild
1676 JUNE.	4	Was Bap. Thomas son to Richard Robinson of houkeld
JULY.	6	Was Bap. Henery sonn to Gyles Hall
JULY.	23	Was Bap. Elizabeth daughter to Thomas Taylor of Trannowhill
JULY.	25	Was Bap. Issabell daughter to John ffawcett
AUGUST.	24	Was Bap. Robart son to Henery Waller
SEPT.	9	Was Bap. Thomas son to John Adamtwaite of hill
SEPT.	24	Was Bap. Roger son to Roger barbar
SEPT.	28	Was Bap. Ellin daughter to Thomas ffothergill
NOUEM.	12	Was Bap. Henery son to Richard Simpson scoolmaistr
NOUEM.	30	Was Bap. James son to Robert Perkin smith
DECEM.	26	Was Bap. Elizabeth daughter to Nicolas Browne
JANUARY.	9	Was Bap. margarett daughter to Edward Scaiffe
ffEBRUARY.	8	Was Bap. Issabell daughter to Richard Rogerson
ffEBRUARY.	13	Was Bap Ellin daughter to Richard Bousfeild
ffEBRUARY.	18	Was Bap margarett daughter to Stephen ffawcett of murthwaite
ffEBRUARY.	22	Was Bap margarett daughter to henery ffothergill of bronbar
MARCH.	21	Was Bap. mary daughter to Richard Bouell
MARCH.	25	Was Bap William son to Thomas Knewstubb
1677 APRILL.	5	Was Bap myles son to John Robinson of Ellergill
MAY.	16	Was Bap. Robart son to William ffothergill of streete
JUNE.	8	Was Bap John son to Thomas Perkin of Ellerhill
JUNE.	14	Was Bap John son to Phillip Bousfeild of streetside
JULY.	9	Was Bap John son to mathew Birckdaile
JULY.	29	Was Bap Issabbell daughter to William Greene of Caudbecke
AUGUST.	19	Was Bap Robart sonn to John Ouerend
SEPT.	11	Was Bap John sonn to Christopher Punch
SEPT.	18	Was Bap John son to Henery Handlay
OCTOB.	7	Was Bap Issabell daughter to Richard ffothergill of lythside
NOUEMBER.	4	Was Bap John sonne to Thomas Robartson
NOUEMBER.	18	Was bap Elizabeth daughter to Robart Hunter
NOUEMBER.	21	Was Bap William sonne to Thomas ffothergill of brounbar
JANUARY.	13	Was Bap Heugh son to william Shawe of crokesbeck
ffEBRUARY.	17	Was Bap Thomas son to william Shawe of towne
ffEBRUARY.	28	Was Bap Richard son to Henery Waller
MARCH.	10	Was bap Anthony son to Richard Robinson of blaflat
MARCH.	14	Was Bap Simmond son to Vincent Bousfeild
MARCH.	17	Was Bap Elizabeth daughter to William Elyetson
1678 MAY.	21	Was Bap John son to Robart Hodgson
JUNE.	23	Was Bap Thomas son to william Adamthwaite of toune
JULY.	17	Was Bap Mary daughter to Anthony Wilson
JULY.	21	Was Bap Elizabeth daughter to John Robinson of Ellergill
AUGUST.	1	Was Bap Stephen son to Richard Breakes
AUGUST.	4	Was Bap Ann daughter to John Taylor of Ellergill
AUGUST.	25	Was Bap Agnas daughter to Thomas ffawcett* of nubegin the same day margrett daughter to John Taylor of backside
SEPT.	4	Was Bap Sarah daughter to Ralph Alderson of the toune

* Transcripts add "batter".

NOTE.—The next leaf (containing two pages) of the Register has been lost, but the missing entries, with the exception of those of 1862, are contained in the Transcripts, and are here introduced.

CHRISTNINGS.

(EXTRACTED FROM TRANSCRIPTS).

OCT. 6 Was Baptized Sarah daughter to Christopher Alderson
OCT. 10 Was Baptized William sonne to William Balife
DECEMBER. 19 Was Baptized William sonne to George Perkin of lowcome
JANUARY. 30 Was Baptized Thomas sonne to Stephen ffawcett of hole
ffEBRUARY. 9 Was Baptized Margrett daughter to Thomas Robinson smith
MARCH. 2 Was Baptized John sonne to John Hewetson of towne.
MARCH. 6 Was Baptized Sarah daughter to Richard Robinson of houkeld
MARCH. 16 Was Baptized Mary daughter to Richard Simpson
MARCH. 23 Was Baptized William sonne to William Greene of cauldbecke

1679 Christopher sonne to Richard Bousfield was Baptized JUNE. 8
Mary daughter to Stephen ffawcett was Baptized JULY. 8
Elizabeth daughter to Anthony Lowcoike of barbicke parish in the County of Yorkeshire was Baptized AUGUST. 7
Anthony son to Thomas dennies was Baptized AUGUST. 17
Ellin daughter to John Blades was Baptized AUGUST. 29
Christopher son to Richard Rogerson was Baptized AUGUST. 30
Betterasse daughter to George Whiteheade was Baptized SEP. 5
Issabell daughter to John mill was Baptized SEPTEMBER. 18
Anne daughter to Richard ffothergill was Baptized SEP. 28
James son to Robart Hodgson was Baptized NOUEMBER. 5
George son to John ffawcett was Baptized NOUEMBER. 20
Margrett daughter to John Birckett was Baptized NOUEM. 27
George son to George Hunter was Baptized DECEMBER. 11
Margrett daughter to Thomas Taylor was Baptized JANUARY. 13
Richard son to Thomas ffawcett hatter was Baptized JANUARY. 25
Elizabeth daughter to Henery ffothergill was Baptized JANUARY. 29
John son to Robart Riddin was Baptized ffEBRUARY. 5
Christopher son to Mr John Medcalfe was Baptized ffEB^r. 17
James son to Vincent Bousfeild was Baptized MARCH. 3

1680 Mary daughter to John Adamthwaite was Baptized APRILL. 1
Margrett daughter to Thomas Robartson was Baptized APRILL. 4
Issabell daughter to Stephen ffothergill was Baptized APRILL. 14
Robart son to Henery Handlay was Baptized APRILL. 25
Elizabeth daughter to M^ter George ffothergill was Baptized APRILL. 30
John son to Robart Robinson was Baptized MAY. 20
Michaell & Thomas sonnes to John Chamberlaine was Baptized JUNE. 16
Elizabeth daughter to Josep boorebanke was Baptized JUNE. 20
Issabell daughter to Richard Bouell was Baptized JUNE. 24
Jennat daughter to Robart Whitelocke was Baptized JULY. 16
Thomas son to Richard Chambarlaine was Baptized JULY. 18
Robart son to John Todd of weesdaile was Baptized AUGUST. 1
Margrett daughter to Thomas Rogerson was Baptized AUGUST. 29
Anne daughter to William Adamthwaite was Baptized OCTOBER. 7
Sarah daughter to Henry Waller was Baptized OCTOBER. 10
Author son to Henery Bousfeild was Baptized NOUEM. 16
Issabell daughter to Phillip Bousfeild was Baptized NOUEM. 17
Margrett daughter to George Whiteheade was Baptized NOUEMBER. 20

CHRISTNINGS.

(EXTRACTED FROM TRANSCRIPTS).

James son to Thomas Robinson was Baptized NOUEMBER. 23
Mary daughter to John Taylor of Ellergill was Baptized DECEMBER. 9
James son to Thomas ffothergill of brounber was Baptized DECEMBER. 16
Margrett daughter to Richard ffothergill of wandell was Baptized JANUARY. 4
Issabell daughter to John Hougill was Baptized JANUARY. 20
Thomas son to Richard Robinson of bleaflat was Baptized JANUARY. 30
Anthony son to George ffawcett of hole was Baptised FEBRUARY. 3
Thomas son to Robart Perkin was Baptized ffEBRUARY. 22
Peter & John sons to Richard Gyles was Baptized MARCH. 3
William son to John Robinson of Ellergill was Baptized MARCH. 10
Anne daughter to George ffawcett of stouphillyeate was Baptized MARCH. 24
Sarah daughter to Richard Rogerson was Baptized MARCH. 25
1681 James son to Thomas Perkin was Baptized APRILL. 23
Thomas son to niccolas Broune was Baptized MAY. 18
Issabell daughter to Mathew Birckdrile was Baptized JULY. 3
John son to Richard Powson of dubbs was Baptized JULY. 12
Margratt daughter to Robart Robinson was Baptized JULY. 24
John son to James Hall was Baptized JULY. 31
Thomas son George Perkin was Baptized SEPTEMBER. 4
Anne daughter to William Powson was Baptized SEPTEMBER. 13
John son to Richard Robinson of houkeld was Baptised OCTOBER. 3
Margreatt daughter to Richard Breakes was Baptized OCTOBER. 11
Issabell daughter to Robart Hodgson was Baptized OCTOBER. 25
Anne daughter to John Adamthwaite of hill was Baptized NOUEMBER. 10
The same day Jane daughter to John Chamberlaine was Baptized
Richard son to Richard ffothergill of lythside was Baptized NOUEM. 30
Mary daughter to John Birckett was Baptized JANUARY. 5
Margreatt daughter to John Powson was Baptized JANUARY. 12
Ellinor daughter to Richard Bouell was Baptized JANUARY. 17
Christopher son to Henery Handlay was Baptized JANUARY. 19
Robart son to Robert Hunter was Baptized ffEBRUARY. 16

(THE TRANSCRIPT FOR 1682 IS MISSING)

1683 William son to Thomas Rogerson was Baptized MARCH. 29
Ellin daughter to Thomas Hall of Uldaile was Baptized APRILL. 6
Richard son to Richard ffallowfeild was Baptized APRILL. 23
Margreat daughter to George Spooner was Baptized MAY. 3
Agnas daughter to James Hall was Baptized MAY. 17
Anne daughter to John Chamberlaine was Baptized JUNE. 3
John son to John Hougill was Baptized JUNE. 7
Phillise daughter to George Whiteheade was Baptized JULY. 1
Issabell daughter to Thomas Robinson smith was Baptized JULY. 13
Thomas son to Henery ffothergill was Baptized JULY. 19
John son to John Adamthwaite of hill was Baptized AUGUST. 16
*- - - - - - ter to John Birckett was Baptized SEPTEMBER. 6
*- - - - - - ter to William ffawcett of murthwaite was Baptized SEPTEMBER. 13

* Corner of Transcript torn. The next entry is that of SEPTEMBER 25, Ralph Milner, at which point the Register resumes.

1683 CHRISTNINGS.

Ralph son to william milner was Bap: SEPTEM 25
George son to James ffawcett of Crooks was Bap NOUEM 22
Issabell daughter to Richard ffothergill allis garthate was Bap DECEM 4
John son to Thomas ffothergill of brounbar was Bap DECEM 11
William son to James Adamthwaite was Bap ffEB 21
Issabell daughter to John Bousfeild scarsickes was Bap MARCH 9
Thomas son to Robart Hodgson was Bap MARCH 13
Mary daughter to stephen ffawcett of murthate was Bap MARCH 21
1684 Issabell daughter to George ffawcet was Bap APRILL 1
Richard son to william Shawe and John son to John
Robinson of Ellergill was Baptized APRILL 17
Issabell daughter to James dent was Baptized MAY 24
Christopher son to Richard Powson of dubs was Bap JUNE 3
Richard son to Thomas Rogerson of wandall was Bap JUNE 4
Thomas and John sonns to Richard Gyles was Bap JULY 24
Thomas son to Henery ffothergill of brounbar was Bap JULY 23
Robert & George sonns to Richard ffothergill
of lythside was Baptized JULY 29
margrat daughter to Richard Robinson of blaflat was Bap AUGUST 31
Richard son to mathew Birckdaile and margreat daughter
to Philip Bousfeild of streete was Baptized SEPTEM 14
Issabell daughter to Richard Bousfeild was Bap SEP 23
John son to John ffawcett of stennerscugh allso the same
day was Bap Elizabeth daughter to Thomas Robartson OCTOB 9
John son to Henery Bousfeild was Bap NOUEM 19
Stephen son to George ffawcett of grenside Bap NOUM 20
Christopher son to John Todd of weesdaile was Bap DECEM 16
Elizabeth daughter to Edward Bousfeild milner was Bap JANURY 11
Heugh son to william Shawe of Asfell was Baptizd JAN: 15
Elizabeth daughter to Thomas Robinson was Bap the same day
Mary daughter to John Chamberlaine of backside was Bap ffEB 12
Henery son to Thomas Hall of Uldaile was Bap MARCH 3
Simond son to Richard morland of adamthwaite Bap MAR 5
Mary daughter to John Robartson was Bap MARCH 12
1685 Sibbell daughter to Chrisopher Bousfeild was Bap APRIL 2 1685
William son to Richard Robinson of houkeld was Bap APR 29
Anne daughter to John Shawe of stennerscugh was Bap MAY 3
Robert son to William Shawe of Ellergill was Bap MAY 14
Stephen son to James dent of wray green was Bap MAY 28
Sarah daughter to John Adamthwaite was Bap JULY 19
Ellinor daughter to Richard Bouell was Bap AUGUST 6
Margrett daughter to Edward Willan was bap AUGUST 9
Elizabeth daughter to briam Birckbecke was Bap AUGUST 20
William son to William Adamthwaite of towne was Bap AUGUST 27
Robert son to John Handlay of wandell was Bap OCTOBER 1
Elizabeth daughter to Richard Rogerson was Bap OCTOB 22
Margreat daughter to Godfray milner was Bap NOUEM 19
Issabell daughter to James Perkin of greenside
and Richard son to Richard Chamberlaine was Bap JAN 21
Ellin daughter to Stephen ffothergill of nubegin and
Richard son to Richard Holme was Bap ffEB 16
Thomas son to thomas Rogerson was Bap ffEB 28
Issabell daughter to Anthony Knewstubb was Bap MARCH 11
John son to Thomas Adamthwaite of Adamthwaite was Bap MARCH 29

1686 CHRISTENINGS.

Issabell daughter to Agnas Taylor base begotten was Baptized	March.	29
Agnas daughter to George Spooner and margrett daughter to James ffawcett of crooks was Bap	April.	1
Thomas son to william Greene of caudbecke was Bap	April.	15
mabbell daughter to John Chamberlaine was Bap	April.	23
margrett daughter to George ffawcett of stouphill yeat was Bap	May.	25
margrett daughter to Robert Readman was Bap	June.	10
Ralph son to Ralph Alderson was Baptized	July.	3
John son to Henery Cautley was Baptised	July.	27
William son to John ffawcett of streete was Bap	August.	12
Mary daughter to Thomas ffawcett of cauldbecke was Bap	Aug.	19
Stephen son to Stephen dent of lythside was Baptizd	Sep.	2
William son to William Shawe of Asfell was Baptized	Sep.	7
John son William milner was Baptized	Octob.	26
Mary daughter to Thomas Perkin of Ellerhill was Bap	Nouem.	9
Mary daughter to Richard ffothergill of peares hill was Baptissed	Nouember.	16
Ellin daughter to William Shawe of streete was Bap	Nou.	25
Anthony son to Thomas ffothergill of brounbar Bap	Decem.	9
Beatrix daughter to william Powson Bap	Decem.	28
John son to Thomas Todd was Baptized	Decem.	30
John son to John Chamberlaine of nathat was Bap	Jan.	1
Anthony son to George Shawe and Agnas daughter to Christopher Bousfeild was Bap	Jan.	8
Mary daughter to Gilbart ffawcett of streete and Issabell daughter to ffrancis Blackbourne was Baptized	ffebreuary.	17
Elizabeth daughter to william ffawcett of murthwate and Issabell daughter to Thomas Robartson was Baptized	ffebreuary.	24
Issabell daughter to Robert Robinson was Bap	ffeb.	27
John son to Thomas Robinson smith was Bap	Mar:	17
1687 John son to Thomas Thompson was Bap	March.	31
Margrett daughter to John Robartson was Baptized	Aprill.	7
Margrett daughter to Robert Hodgson was Baptized	May.	10
Simon son to John Bousfeild of scarsickes was Bap	June.	3
Margrett daughter to George ffawcett of hole was Bap	July.	29
Jane daughter to Richard ffallowfeild Bap	Sep.	4
John son to william Hunter was Baptizd	Sep.	6
Jonathan son to Thomas Hall of uldaile was Bap	Sep.	8
Thomas son to Thomas Rogerson of tarne was Bap	Octob.	6
margreat daughter to John ffawcett tanner was Bap	Octo.	20
John son to Abraham Gouldington was Baptized	Decem.	8
Thomas son to Anthony knewstubb was Baptized	Decem.	15
Anthony son to John Shawe of stenascugh was Bap	Decem.	21
Margrett daughter to James dent of wraygreene Bap	Decem.	23
Thomas son to William Elyetson was Bap	Jan.	5
Margrat daughter to John Handlay was Bap	Jan.	6
Thomas son to Thomas Adamthwaite was Bap	Jan.	8
John son to John Todd of weesdaile was Bap	Jan.	26
Prudence daughter to Richard Robinson of low lonning was Bap	March.	14
stephen son to John Chamberlaine off greenside was Baptized	March.	15
Mary daughter to Henery ffothergill of brounbar was Baptized	March.	22

1688 CHRISTNINGS.

Elizabeth daughter to George ffothergill was Bap	APRIL.	12
Vincent son to William Shawe of streete and		
Issabell daughter to Henery Bousfeild was Bap	APRIL.	26
Margrett daughter to Robert Todd was Bap	APRIL.	27
Jane daughter to Richard Chamberlaine Bap	APRIL.	29
John son to Godfrey milner was Bap	MAY.	3
Richard son to Edward Willan was Bap	MAY.	6
Thomas son to John dent of bouderdaile was Bap	MAY.	11
Elizabeth daughter to James fawcett parke yeat Bap	MAY.	29
Mary daughter to Edward Bousfeild was Bap	JUNE.	4
Ellen daughter to Heugh Blenckarne was Bap	JUNE.	21
Anthony son to Henery Cautley was Bap	JUNE.	23
Thomas son to James Perkin was Bap	JULY.	18
Thomas son to John Chamberlaine of nathat Bap	JULY.	26
Thomas son to John Blackbourne Bap	OCTOB.	17
Michaell son to Richard Rogerson nathat was Bap	DECEM.	6
Issabell daughter to John Bousfeild scarsikes was Bap	JAN.	10
Issabell daughter to Robert Hougill was Bap	JAN.	17
John son to William Shawe of Asfell was Bap	FEB.	21
Ralph son to Simond Alderson was Bap	MARCH.	7
elizabeth daughter to mathew Scarbrough Bap	MAR.	9
margret daughter to Jonathan Alderson Bap	MAR.	21
1689 Anne daughter to Ralph Alderson was Bap	APRILL.	4
Thomas son to Henery ffothergill of brounbar and		
mary daughter to Thomas Taylor of bents Bap	APRIL.	25
Thomas son to George Whiteheade was Bap	APRIL.	28
Thomas son to John ffawcett and william son		
to Gilbart ffawcett and Richard son to		
william elyetson was Baptized	MAY.	2
George son to Stephen dent was Bap	MAY.	30
Anthony son to James ffawcett of crookes was Bap	JUNE.	20
Thomas son to Thomas Robartson was Bap	JULY.	18
Issabell daughter to James Townson was Bap	JULY.	25
John and Ellin son and daughter to		
George spooner was Baptized	AUGUST.	8
Anne daughter to Thomas Robinson smith		
was Baptized	NOUEMBER	5th
Sarah daughter to Richard Chamberlaine	NOUEM.	10
Richard son to John Chamberlaine of greenside		
was Baptized	NOUEMBER	16
margrett daughter to Thomas milner was Bap	NOUEM.	24
James son to Thomas Adamthwaite was Bap	DECEM.	15
Issabell daughter to Thomas Knewstubb Bap	DECEM.	16
Thomas son to ffrancis Blackbourne and Thomas		
son to John Rutson was Baptized	DECEM.	21
Thomas son to stephen ffothergill Bap	DECEM.	25
Anne daughter to Thomas Rogerson of weesdaile Bap	DECEM.	30
James son to Thomas ffawcett of towne Bap	JAN.	23
Issabell daughter to Thomas Todd was Baptized	ffEBRUARY.	13
1690 Issabell daughter to Thomas Rogerson of fell end was Bap	MARCH.	27
Richard son to William Greene was Baptized	APRIL.	17
John son to william Hewetson was Bap	APRILL.	24
Thomas son to John Shawe of stenerscugh Bap	MAY.	11
elsabeth daughter to John Bousfeild Bap	MAY.	16
Roger son to John Pinder was Baptized	MAY.	22
Thomas son to mathew Scarbrough and		
Henery son to Thomas Perkin was Bap	MAY.	29

1690 CHRISTNINGS.

Christopher son to Richard ffawcett Baptized	ffeb. 25	91*
Elizabeth daughter to Thomas Thompson Bap	June.	5
Ruth daughter to Thomas ffothergill was Bap	June.	17
Ellin daughter to Henery Cautley was Bap	June.	24
Mary daughter to Christopher Bousfeild Bap	June.	26
Agnas daughter to Thomas Cunnigam Bap	July.	15
Thomas son to Richard Morland was Bap	July.	24
Mary daughter to George ffawcett of hole Bap	Octo.	8
Mary daughter to Richard Robinson and Anne daughter to James ffawcett of greenside Bap	Octo.	14
Mary daughter to Jonathan Alderson Bap	Nou.	11
Mary daughter to Henery Bousfeild was Bap	Noum.	13
Anne daughter to Robert Todd was Bap	Decm.	4
Mary daughter to John Handlay was Bap	Decm.	6
Mary daughter to Richard ffallowfeild Bap	Jan.	1
John son to william ffawcet of murth waite was Baptized	October.	9
James son to William Hunter Bap	January.	27
Ellinor daughter to Edward Willan Bap	Mar.	1
William son to Robert Hougill was Bap	ffeb.	12
1691 Ralph son to Thomas milner was Bap	June.	2
Robert son to John ffawcett was Bap	June.	13
John son to stephen ffawcett weesdaile Bap	June.	23
Issabell daughter to Anthony Perkin was Bap	Sept.	29
James son to Thomas Robertson was Bap	Oct.	30
John son to John ffawcett Tanner Bap	Nouem.	27
Annas daughter to Godfrey milner was Bap	Decem.	25
Thomas son to Thomas ffawcett of towne Bap	Jan.	7
Elizabeth daughter to John Perkin Bap	April.	12
1692 Mary daughter to Richard powson was Bap	April.	21
John son to Oliver Waller was Bap	May.	3
Thomas son to Thomas milner was Bap	May.	12
Phillip son to Richard Bousfeild was Bap	May.	31
Mathew son to mathew Scarbrough was Bap	June.	8
Elizabeth daughter to Thomas Adamthwaite of Adamthwaite was Baptized	June.	9
Jonathan son to Jonathan Alderson Bap	Sep.	28
Ellin daughter to Robert Todd Bap	Noum.	17
mary daughter to Thomas Robinson smith Bap	Jan.	3
Elizabeth daughter to william Hewetson Bap	ffeb.	28
Henery son to James Townson Baptised	ffeb.	15*
Isabell daughter to Thomas ffawcett Bap	March.	16
Thomas son to Thomas wharton Bap	Mar.	19
1693 Richard son to Thomas Alderson Bap	April.	13
Robert son to George Whiteheade Bap	April.	16
Mary daughter to William Robertson Bap	May.	18
Alcie daughter to Thomas ffothergill Bap	June.	3
Henery son to George Townson Bap	June.	13
Phillip son to Thomas Rogerson Bap	August.	1
John son to Anthoy Pinder Bap	Sept.	6
Thomas son to John Knewstubb Bap	Sep.	20
Issabell daughter to Henery ffothergill of wandall was Baptized	Octob.	5
Michaell son to John Taylor Bap	Octob.	31
1694 Elizabeth daughter to Richard ffawcet off murthate and Simmond son to Tho. Adamtwhat Bap	Apr.	3

* After-insertions, and not in order of occurrence.

1694

William son to Thomas Robartson Bap	APRIL.	10
Margrett daughter to Robert ffawcett was Bap	APR.	19
Thomas son to Anthony Perkin was Bap	APR.	29
Richard son to James Clerkeson was Bap	MAY.	24
Isabell daughter to William Elyetson Bap	MAY.	31
William son to Thomas ffawcet Bap	JUNE.	2
Thomas son to Stephen dent was Bap	JUNE.	5
Isabell daughter to John ffawcett of streete Bap	AUGUST.	9
Elizabeth daughter to Richard fallowfeild Bap	AUG.	19
James son to Henery Knewstubb was Bap	SEP.	26
Robert son to James ffawcett was Bap	OCTO.	30
Simond son to John Bousfeild Bap	NOUEM.	15
Sarah daughter to Edward Willan of Wath Bap	NOUEM ye 29th	
Margaret daughter to Tho: Perkin of Eller Hill Bap	DECEMBER ye 4th	
Henery son to Stephen ffothergill of nubegin and Issabell daughter to John Robertson of bouber heade was Baptized	DECEEBER.	26
Margrett daughter to Anthony Pinder of the low lonning was Baptized	JAN:	9
John son to John Knewstubb Bap	JAN:	17
William son to Thomas milner Bap	JANUARY.	24
Issabell daughter to Godfrey milner Bap	JAN	26
Robert son to John Perkin smith Bap	JAN	31
James son to Thomas ffawcett smith Bap	fEB.	7
Jennat daughter to John Robinson of douingill was Baptised	ffEBRUARY.	13
William son to John Shawe of this towne was Baptized	ffEBRUARY.	28
Thomas son to William Greene Bap	MARCH.	20
William son to Anthony ffawcet of murthwaite was Bap	MARCH.	24
1695 George son to John Ubancke Bap	APRILL.	18
Stephen son to Abraham dent was Bap	MAY.	8
Elizabeth daughter to Thomas Shawe Bap	JUNE.	30
William son to Christopher Jackes Bap	JULY.	11
Ellinor daughter to Thomas Atkinson Bap	JULY.	18
Maudlin daugher to mathew Breakes Bap	AUG.	11
Richard son to stephen ffawcett of dubbs was Baptissed	AUGUST.	22
Anne daughter to James Dent of wraygreen was Baptissed	NOUEMBER.	28
Margrett daughter to John Baliffe Bap	JANUR.	4
Mary daughter to Henery ffothergill wandall Bap	JAN.	21
Thomas son to John Taylor of garthes was Baptissed	ffEBRUARY.	27
Nicolas son to Anthony Broune Bap	APRIL.	10
1696 Anne daughter to Richard Postelthate was Baptized	MAY.	10
John son to Thomas Rigge Bap	MAY.	12
Josep son to Richard Chamberlaine Bap	MAY.	28
mary daughter to william Elyetson Bap	JULY.	2
Issabell daughter to George Townson Bap	AUG.	10
Margrett daughter to Robart Hougill Bap	AUG.	1

1696 CHRISTNINGS.

William son to Anthony ffawcet of douingill and mary daughter to William ffawcett of foggegill was Baptized	AUGUST.	27
Sarah daughter to Henry Wharton Baptizd	OCTOBER.	6
Mary daughter to Richard ffawcett of galehead was Bap	OCT.	16
Issabell daughter to Thomas Adam thwaite of Adamthwaite Bap	OCTOB.	17
Elizabeth daughter to William morland was Baptized	NOUEM.	5
William son to William shaw of Asfeild was Baptizd	NOUEMBER.	10
James son to John Jackson and Thomas son to Robert ffawcett of hole was Baptized	NOUEMBER.	19
Elizabeth daughter to Richard ffawcett of mires was Baptized	NOUEMBER.	96
William son to John Shawe of hie stennerscugh was Baptized	DECEMBER.	10
Anne daughter to Thomas ffawcett Bap	JAN.	10
John son to Anthony ffawcett Bap	ffEB.	11
John and margrett childrin to Thomas Robinson of nubegin was Bap	MARCH.	8
Robert son to John Knewstubb and marye daughter to Hugh Blenckarn Bap	MARCH.	18
1697 Thomas son to William Wilson and mary daughter to John Hall Bap	APRILL.	1
Margrett daughter to Tho: Atkinson Bap	APIL.	8
Mary daughter to Anthony Perkin Bap	APRIL.	11
Sarah daughter to Thomas milner and George son to George whiteheade Bap	APRL.	20
Anne daughter to mathew Breakes Bap	MAY.	6
William son to John ffawcett of ome pot Bap	JUNE.	8
Elizabeth daughter to Anth. Pinder Bap	JUNE.	20
John son to John Balife was Bap	JULY.	8
Sarah daughter to Godfrey milner Bap	AUGUST.	13
Anne daughter to stephen ffawcett hole Bap	NOU.	30
Ellin daughter to John Ubancke Bap	NOUEM.	25
John son to Thomas ffawcett smith Bap	DECEM.	23
John son to Richard ffawcett galehead Bap	DECE.	27
John son to John Perkin smith Bap	JAN.	11
Anne and Margrett daughters to Anthony Broune was Baptissed	ffEBRUARY.	1
Edward son to John Richison Bap	ffEB.	17
1698 Ralph son to John Robinson nubegin Bap	APR.	22
Mary daughter to John Baliffe Bap	MAY.	12
Ralph son to Christopher Alderson Also mary daughter to George Cleasby Bap	MAY.	27
Jane daughter to Josep Shawe Bap	JUNE.	9
John son to John Shawe of towne was Bap	JUNE.	12
Thomas son to Anthony ffawcett douingil Bap	JUNE.	30
Christopher son to William Waller Bap	AUGUST.	9
Adam son to John Taylor was Bap	OCTOB.	8
mary daughter to stephen ffothergill Bap	OCTOB.	12

Thomas son to Richard Postelthat was Baptized	OCTOBER.	16
Agnas daughter to John Jackson Bap	OCTOB.	31
Mary daughter to William Morland Bap	DECEM.	25
Issabell daughter to John Bousfield scarsikes Bap	DECEM.	30
Issabell daughter to Thomas Atkinson was Bap	DECEM.	31
Thomas son to Anthony ffothergill and Mary daughter to John ffawcett was Bap	JANUARY.	17
Thomas son to William Shawe of Asfell Bap	ffEB.	7
Richard son to m^r^ter James michell was Baptized	MARCH.	2
John son to Thomas & Agnes Knewstub born	APRIL.20th 1698*	
		1699
Isaac son to John Baliffe Junior Bap	APRIL.	27
Richard son to Michaell Bouell was Bap	JUNE.	22
Hannah daughter to John Richison Bap	JULY.	11
Richard son to John Blades was Baptized	JULY.	21
Margrett daughter to William Elyetson Bap	SEP.	21
William son to Abraham Dent was Bap	NOUEM.	30
Margarett daughter to Chris. Alderson Bap	DECEM.	21
Alcie daughter to George Townson Bap	DECEM.	26
Issabell daughter to John Taylor Bap	DECEM.	27
Thomas son to William Waller Bap	JANUARY.	18
Lydea daughter to Thomas Milner Bap	JAN.	24
John son to John ffawcett of ome pot Bap	ffEB.	29
		1700
Margrett daughter to William Hewetson Bap	APRIL.	11
Anne daughter to Anthony Browne Bap	JUNE.	8
John son to Michaell Bouell was Bap	JUNE.	13
Thomas son to John ffawcett of Stenerscugh Bap	AUGUST	11
John son to James Richardson was Bap	SEP.	9
Phillip son to Michaell Bousfeild Bap	SEP.	26
George son to James ffawcett of greenside Bap	OCTOB.	1
Mary daughter to Thomas ffawcett smith Bap	OCTOB.	20
A daughter of mrter dawes heade borne	OCTOBER.	4
Ann daughter to mrter dawes heade Bap	OCTOBER.	31
Issabell daughter to John Handlay Bap	NOUEM.	12
Martha daughter to mrter James Michell was Baptized	NOUEMBER.	16
Was Baptized William son to Chris. Alderson	JANUARY.	19
Was Baptized John son to John Robinson	ffEB.	13
John son to William Morland was Bap	ffEB.	27
1701 Thomas son to John Taylor of mires Bap	MARCH.	27
Josep son to John Shawe of Towne was Bap	APRILL.	1
Mary daughter to Thomas Atkinson Bap	APRIL.	10
Thomas son to Richard fawcet of murthwaite Bap	APRILL.	13
Issabell daughter to Edmond Shawe was Bap	APRILL.	20
Anne daughter to William Shawe of Asfell Bap	JUNE.	28
John son to Anthony ffawcett was Bap	JULY.	19
Ruth daughter to William Elyetson was Bap	NOUEM.	23
Issabell daughter to Stephen Dent was Bap	DECEMBER.	4
A son of mrter dawes heade borne	DECEMBER.	24
John son of mrter dawes Heade Baptized	JANUARY.	22
Thomas son to Abraham dent Baptized	JANUARY.	24
Margrett daughter to Henery ffothergill Bap	ffEB.	26
1702 William son to John ffawcett of alme pot Bap	MARCH.	27
Also Susanah daughter to John ffawcett of Stephen Thomas and Sarah son and daughter to John Hall was Baptissed	MARCH.	28

* An after-insertion.

1702 CHRISTNINGS.

Anne daughter to James Richardson Bap	March.	29
John son to Thomas Atkinson Baptized	March.	31
Mary daughter to Thomas Hall and Hannah daughter to Christopher Alderson Bap	Aprill.	16
William son to William ffurnace Bap	May.	14
Sibbell daughter to michaell Bouell Bap	May.	20
Sarah daughter to Thomas ffothergill of clouds Bap	July.	2*
Ralph son to Godfrey milner was Bap	Octob.	1
John son to Anthony Broun Bap	Octob.	5
William sonn to Stephen ffawcett of hole Bap	Octob.	26
Mary daughter to John ffawcett Bap	Decem.	13
John son to John Baliffe was Bap	December.	27
Agnas daughter to John Blackbourne Bap	December.	29
Anne daughter to Richard Hunter Baptized	Jan.	2
Mary daughter to William Hunter Bap	March.	12
1703 Issabell daughter to Thomas dent was Bap	April.	27
Mary daughter to Roger Barbar Bap	May.	13
Issabell daughter to Robert ffawcett of hole Bap	May.	30
Margrett daughter to John Taylor of mires Bap	June.	7
Mary daughter to James Richardson Bap	Octob.	11
Ozwood son to John Robinson was Bap	Octob.	21
A daughter of m[r]ter dawes heade borne	Nouember.	3
Issabell daughter to m[r]ter dawes heade Bap	Nouem.	12
Elizabeth daughter of Henery ffothergill of Lockholme was Baptissed	December.	19
mathew son to John Birckdaile Bap	ffeb.	25
Agnas daughter to william ffurnace Bap	ffeb.	27
Thomas son to John Haistwhitle Bap	March.	7
1704 John son to Christopher Alderson Bap	April.	22
Anne daughter to Thomas milner Bap	April.	22
Stephen son to Thomas ffothergill of clouds Bap	May.	27
Mary daughter to John ffawcett of bridge Bap	Sep.	9
Henery son to John Handlay of garthes Bap	Sep.	19
Richard son to Michaell Bouell was Bap	Sep.	20
Mary daughter to Thomas Atkinson Bap	Octob.	20
Anthony son to Anthony ffawcett of douingill Bap	Nou.	4
Sarah daughter to John Blades Bap	Nouem.	16
Anne daughter to William Fothergill of Brownber Born	January y[e]	19th
Phillip son to Michaell Bousfeild Bap	March.	8
Thomas son to William Hewetson Bap	March.	13
1705 Issabell daughter to John Hewetson Bap.	Aprill.	1
Anne daughter to Henery ffothergill Senior Bap	Aprill.	15
Sarah daughter to Roger Barbar Bap	May.	22
Agnas daughter to Thomas Atkinson Bap	Aug.	27
Jane daughter to m[r]ter dawes Heade was Bap	Sep.	4
Thomas son to Thomas Winder was Bap	Sep.	6
Robert son to Thomas Hall was Bap.	Octobr.	17
George son to Henery ffothergill of Lockh[m] Bap	Decem[br].	30[th]
Jonathan son to Christopher Alderson Bap	January.	29
Elizabeth daughter to John ffawcett of Alme pot Bap	ffeb.	14
William son to James Richardson Baptized	ffeb.	17
1706 Issabell daughter to John ffawcet of lowcome Bap	Apr.	29
William son to Robert ffothergill of street Bap	May.	21
Issabell daughter to John Haistwhitle Bap	May.	22
Stephen son to John ffawcett of street Bap	July.	4
William son to Thomas Adamthwaite Bap	August.	4
the same day Margrett daughter to James Robinson		
Richard Break sun of Thomas Breaks Baptized	September second 1707	

1706 CHRISTNINGS.

Christopher son to John Punch was Bap	SEPTEMBER.	1
Rich^{d} son to william Hewetson Bap^{d}	SEPTEMBER.	9th
Thomas son to Anthony Broune was Bap	OCTOB.	15
Roger son to margrett Pinder was Bap	OCTOB.	29
Thomas son to John Shawe was Baptized	JANUARY.	6
Anne daughter to Roger Barbar Baptized	JANUARY.	19
Gilbert son to George Guy was Baptized	JAN.	28
Elsabeth daughter to John Hall Baptized	ffEB.	9
1707 James son of George & Eliz^{h} Burton Baptized	FEBRUARY.	18
Adam son to John Taylor of garthes Bap	MAY.	29
Margrett daughter to Richard Hunter Bap	MAY.	11
Mary daughter to John Richeson was Bap	AUGUST.	21
Robert son to michaell Bouell was Bap	AUGUST.	28
Margrett daughter to Robert ffothergill Bap	SEPTEM.	18
Issabell daughter to michell Bousfeild Bap	OCTOB.	26
William son to william Hunter Bap	OCTOBER.	30
Issabell daughter to Abraham dent Bap	NOUEM.	20
1708 Elizabeth daughter to Thomas Adamthwat Bap	ffEB.	26
dorathy daughter to Margrett Bircket Bap	MAY.	13
Richard son to Henery fothergill of Lockholme Baptized	JUNE.	15
James son to michaell Shaw Baptized	JUNE.	16
William son to Sarah fawcet Baptized	JUNE y^{e}	24
Richard son to Peter Giles was Baptized	JUNE.	19
Isabell daughter to Richard Todd was Baptized	JULY.	27
Thomas son to John fawcet of Blayflat was Baptized	AUG.	18
Issabell Daughter to John Punch was Baptized	OCTOBER.	10
Marey Daughter to Thomas fawcett of nabb was Bap	MARCH.	3
Stephen son to Sarah Ion was Baptized	MARCH.	7
Marey Daughter to John Hewetson was Bap	MARCH.	15
Richard son to George Gye was Baptized	MARCH.	15
1709 James son to stephen Dent of dubs Baptized	MARCH.	30
Robert son to Richard Hunter was Baptized	APRILL.	3
Margret Daughter to John Handlay was Baptized	MAY.	28
Agnas Daughter to George Moreland was Baptized	JUNE.	2
Henery son to Rodger Barber was Baptized	AUGUST.	14
Agnas Daughter to Thomas Adamthwaite was Bap	OCTOBER.	2
Ann Daughter to John ffawcet of needel house Bap	OCTOB.	4
Margret Daughter to Stephen fawcet of Newbegin Bap	OCTO:	16
Margret Daughter to Richard Tod was Baptized	NOVEMBER.	6
George son to George perkin Baptized	NOVEM.	21
Margret Daughter to James fawcett of street side Bap	DECEM.	1
George son to George parkin of Lockholme Bap	DECEM.	8
Issabell Daughter to James fawcet of stenerscugh bap	DECEM.	13
Martha Daughter to John Richardson of wesdaile Bap	DECEM.	25
Christopher son to John fawcet was Bap	JANNUARY.	5
John son to peter giles Bap	JANNUARY.	14
Michael son to Richard Shaw of studfold was baptized the same Day. John son to Michael Bousfield Baptized february the 5: Margrett and Mary daughters to Cristopher Alderson was Bap	MARCH.	2
Margrett Daughter to Michael Bovel was Bap	MARCH.	8
George son to Abraham Dent was Bap	MARCH.	16
1710 Marey Daughter to John fawcet of Alm pott Bap	MAY th	21
George son to Anthony parkin was Bap	MAY.	28
Elizabeth Daughter to William Adamthwaite Bap	JULY th	27

1577 WEDDYNGES 1577

JUNE	30	Was wedded Richard Robinson and Xpobell wharton newbygin
JULI	1	Was weded Xpofor wilkinson and Ellin ffawcit
OCTOBAr	6	Was weded willm heblethwat and margarett Vstarton Ristndall
	20	Was weded Cuthbartt swinbank and Alic baylye layt wif of James
JANEWARYE	26	Was weded willm pettye of Soulby
Ano Dni 1578		and Ellin layt wif of Robartt chambrlain
JUNE	29	Was weded willm Robarson and Janatt payCoke
JULI	6	Was weded willm shaw and Sybell huntar dawghtr of Cuth
	13	Was weded willm Chambarlaine and margarett ffothrgill
	13	Was weded myles payCoCk and Elizabeth ffothrgill
	13	Was weded also myghell Chambrlin and Xpobell Shaw daw to edw
	13	Was weded also Rogar ffawcit and maybell dawghtr John fothrgill
	17	Was weded herrye Swinbanke And Issaybell pkin dawghr to Roland
	20	Was weded Anthonye tayler and Ellin daughtr of gilbart ffothrgill
NOVEBAR	16	Was weded Robartt grene devingill & Issaybell ssawar of stodfowld
	23	Was wed giles pkin of Rystnedall & Issaybell pindar of newbygin
FAYBrEWArYE	25	Was weded Lanc shaw of the tranay hill and Ann dawghter of edward Tomson

1579		WEDDINGS
JULI	12	Was weded myghell wharton of wharton & maybell paycoke
AWGUST	23	Was weded John whythead of
An° Dni		flaykebrig & alic tayler
1580		
APPRELL	18	Was weded John Adamthwat and Ellin wharton of tebyheds
JUNE	14	Was wed John Coatlay of new bygin and Xpobell wharton
	22	Was weded Raynold grene of foggaygill & Elizabeth mosse
JULYE	3	Was wed willm Chambarlaine and margarett ffawcytt
	3	Was weded Thomas ffoth'gill and Janatt ffothergill
	3	Was weded Roger pind' of newbygin and Xpobell murthwat
	24	Was wed henrye Dentt & maybell Tomsonn tranahill
AWGUST	31	Was wed Thomas Shaw of Asfell & Issaybell Chamb'laine
NOVEMBA'	6	Was weded willm Cook off Locholme & ellin Rogarson
	6	Was wed willm Rogarson and Ellin Cook dawght' of giles
	27	Was wed John mayson and Janatt grene of Devingill
ffAYBREWARYE	7	Was wed Xpofor Adamthwat
An° Dni		and Ellin Dentt of Devingill
1581		
APPRELL	2	Was wed henrye shaw and margarett daught' of maythew Dent
	28	Was weded willm heblethwat and Janatt Chambarlaine
JUNE	25	Was weded willm harryson of Sowleby and Issaybell Swynbank of Locholme

1581		WEDDYNGS
Julye	2	Was weded Richard wharton of stoneaskew & mawde ffawcitt
	9	Was wed Raynold ffoth^{r}gill ottarkeld and margarett hunttar of bowb^{r}head
	16	Was wed george whythead and Issaybell ffoth^{r}gill of welssdall
	26	Was wed george wilson of Kyrke= bystayvin & Elizabeth ffoth^{r}gill
Awgust	27	Was wed John ffawcit blayflat and Janatt tayler of hartthead
	27	Was wed also Thomas walkar and mable walkar of newbygin
	27	Was wed James ffawcitt and Agness tayler of the hartthead
Octobar	8	Was weded Xpofor ffawcitt and Alic Collin to murthwat
Janewarye	21	Was weded Rainold ffoth^{r}gill of
An^{o} Dni		Ristnedall & Issaybell ffawcit
1582		
Maye	20	Was weded Rawff Awd^{r}son and Alic Chambarlaine
June	10	Was wed John wynn of Sedb^{r} and Alic Jackson
	17	Was weded Thomas ffoth^{r}gill of malearstang & mayble ffawcit
Julye	1	Was weded Steven Robinson eld^{r} and maybell paycok stodfowld
	1	Was weded also Steven Robinson yong^{r} and maybell Robinson
	8	Was wed Richard ffawcit of towne & margarett dawght^{r} of John todd
Septeb^{r}	23	Was weded george hawle welsdall and Ann dawght^{r} of george Dentt
	26	Was wed henrye garethwat and Ann shaw
Novebar	25	Was weded willm hunttar of bowbarhead & Issaybell paycok

1582		WEDDYNGS
FAYBREWA'Y	3	Was weded John thornburray
Ano Dni		of the Raine & margarett pindar
1583		
OCTOBAR	6	Was wed willm Vayray
		and Xpobell Bell
	13	Was wed Thomas Longhorne
		and Janatt tayler caldbeck
NOVEMBAR	10	Was wed Edward whythead
		and Sybell Busfeld
FAYB'EWARY	23	Wae weded willm weste and
Ano Dni		maybell Cooke of Locholme
1584		
JUNE	9	Was weded Raynold person
		& margarett ffawcit
	21	Was wed Robartt wallar
		& Issaybell parkin lochholme
	28	Was wed Jenkin ffawcit
		& Janatt wharton
		and Lanc murthwat &
		margarett hewatson orton
JULYE	22	Was wed Robartt Rogerson
		& Issaybell dawghtar
		of Richard pacok
OCTOBAR	11	Was wed James tayler &
		maybell ffoth'gill
	13	Was wed John walkar &
		Janatt Cowp of nathwat
JANEWARYE	17	Was wed myles holme
1585		& margarett maysonn
JUNE.	19	Was wed myles bowness
		& Issaybell gowldinton
JULYE	11	Was wed henrye Snawdon
		& Xpobell gowldinton
	25	Was wed myghell tayler
		& Issaybell walkar
	25	Was weded VinCentt Cook
		& Ellin paycok of stodfowld

Anº 1585		WEDDYNGS
OCTOBAR	3	Was weded Richard tayler & margarett tornear of Ristnedall
Anº Dni 1586		
APPRELL	7	Was wed henrye wharton of naytbye & Syble ffawcit
MAY	19	Was wed willm Colson and Agnes niColson Ristnedall
JULYE	17	Was wed Xpofor pkin Locholm & Issaybell Dentt
	17	Was wed Rowland Dentt and margarett parkin of Locholme
DECEBAR	1	Was wed Rawff Shaw strett and Sybell Sawar of stodfold
	22	Was wed Rainold ffoth^{r}gill and Dorrytye chambarlaine
FAYBREWARYE	26	Was weded John Robinson and margarett paycok dawght^{r} xpofor
Anº Dni 1587		
MAY.	8	Was wed Richard hodshon of Dentt & Issaybell handlay welsdall
JULYE.	2	Was wed willm holand and Ellin Cook layt wyf of vinCent
	20	Was wed willm gybson and Elizabeth wilkinson and Thomas peares and Issaybell Dentt dawghter of willm
AWGUST	17	Was wed Jenkin Bell and Agness Sawar of stodfowld
OCTOBAR	8	Was wed John Richardson & margarett edger of towne
1588		
MAYE	29	Was wed Robartt huntar and Sybell shaw of Asfell
JUNE	30	Was wed Richard Bell and Ann dawghter of miles busfeld
	30	Was weded John ffawcit of blackdobbs and maybell ffawCytt of Devingill

A^{no} D^{ni} 1588		WEDDYNGS
JULYE	7	Was weded georg ffoth^{r}gill and Ellin ffawcit locholm
	7	Was weded xpofor Rog^{r}son & Janatt grene of ellergill
AWGUST	11	Was wed Richard Dentt & Alic hawle welsdall
OCTOBAR	11	Was wed willm ffawcit and margarett pindar
An^{o} Dni 1589		
JUNE	11	Was wed Thomas murthat & Sybell holme newbygin
	15	Was wed Rainold ffoth^{r}gill & margarett shaw
JULYE	6	Was wed Thomas hynmar & Elizabeth ffothergill
SEPTEBAR	12	Was wed Lanc towneson & Alic Adamthwat
NOVEMBAR	2	Was wed maythew murthat & xpobell Todd
DECEMBAR	4	Was wed willm Cleasbye & Elizabeth Stewardson
	7	Was wed herrye ffawcitt & maybell Attkinson
FAYBREWARY	14	Was wed Robartt wilkinson & Ellin Rigg
An^{o} Dni 1590		
MARCH	30	Was wed John ffoth^{r}gill & margarett Awd^{r}son
JULI	19	Was wed Anthonye ffoth^{r}gill and margarett grene
	19	Was wed VinCentt Dentt and margarett busfeld
AWGUST	17	Was wed Edmond handlay & margarett ffoth^{r}gill
SEPTEBAR	6	Was wed Raynold grene & Sybell grene
OCTOBAR	4	Was wed myghell ffoth^{r}gill and margarett ffoth^{r}gill

1590 WEDDYNGS

DECEMBAR 16 Was weded Richard Yare and
margarett ffawcit of murthat

17 Was weded Thomas Yare and
margerye ffawcitt murthat

JANEWARYE 13 Was wed Thomas proctor and
1591 Annas heblethwat

JUNE. 2 Was wed Symond gye
and Issabell grene Devingill

13 Was wed myles Symson &
maybell Busfeld welsdall
the Same day James ward
& Elin busfeld of bowd^r^dall

JULYE 11 Was wed John todd and Dorryty
ffothergill of brownebar

AWGUST 29 Was wed Thomas tebbye &
Elizabeth grene of ellergill

29 Was wed Xpofor harryson and
margarett Awdarson nathat
and Xpofor Rog^r^son of Sowleby
& Ellin Rogerson of Vldall

SEPTB^r^ 8 Was wed Robartt shaw and
Elin shaw of Asfell

15 Was Steven pindar and
margaritt Adamthwat
Also the same day edward thorne
burray & Janatt Wilson

28 Was wed oswold Robinson
and margarett ffoth^r^gill

29 Was wed VinCentt ffoth^r^gill
& Issaybell busfeld

OCTOBAR 3 Was wed Cuthbartt Robinson
& margarett ffawcit

10 Was wed VinCentt tayler &
Ann ffoth^r^gill dawght^r^ of gilbartt

22 Was weded Lanc paycok &
margarett shaw of stoneaskew

1591		WEDDINGS
NOVEMBA^r^	8	Was weded James winttar & Alic Bell
JANEWARY	10	Was wed giles ffothrgill & margarett ffothergill
1592		
JUNE	20	Was wed myles ffothrgill & Janatt huntar And Thomas ffawcit & Alic ffawcit murthwat
JULLI	1	Edward Adamthwat & Xpobell Adamthwat
	15	Was wed george grene and Ellin grene
AWGUST	11	Was wed John todd & margarett shaw
1593		
JULYE	19	Was wed James pereson and Ellin shaw of malerstang
SEPTBr	8	Was wed Edward whithead & maybell pereson
1594		
JULYE	18	Was wed Edward Robarson & margarett swinbanke
AWGUST	11	Was wed myghell Longcak and Ellin powson
	15	Was wed herrye morland & Issaybell Sumpkin
SEPTEBr	14	Was wed myghell tayler And alic ffawcit
OCTOBAr	13	Was george ewbank and Issaybell Busfeld and Xpofor thorneburray & Ellin Ewbanke
	21	Was wed phillipp ffothrgill & Jane wynne
	22	Was wed Roger ward & Sybell Adamthwat
	29	Was weded pettar pindar & Sybell murthwat

		WEDDYNGS
1594 NOVEMBAr	26	Was weded hew shaw and Annas shaw
JANEWARY	26	Was wed willm heblethat and Aalic wildon
1595 MAY	6	Was weded Petter ffayntton and Essaybell Robinson
JUNE	22	Was weded Willm Dentt and xpobell Rogerson
JULY	6	Was weded Phillipp Darby and Alic Busfeld
		and willm ffuthergill and mabell ffawCytt
OCTOBER	7	Was weded John hewatson & Ellin Blertt was Thomas chesburne and grac blamyres
	15	Was weded John grene and Janat hawle
	23	Was weded Robart willmson and margrett adamthwat
NOUEMBAR	6	Was weded John hewatson & Janatt Pindar
1596 JUNE	14	Was weded Stepen busfeld & Elin busfeld
JULI	1	Was weded Richard whythead and Margrett adamthwat
	11	Was weded Lanc grene and Janatt ffothergill
AWGUST	28	Was weded Rowland Dentt and ffracys patrig
SEPTEMBER	9	Was weded hew haystwytle and essabell Bland
NOUEMBAR	6	Was weded Thomas ffawcyt and elin gowldinton
	28	Was weded Gorge murthwat and margrit Raykestro
JANEWARYE	11	Was weded Cuthbartt ffawcyt and elizabeth ffotergill
ffABREWARYE	6	Was weded John Cumstonne and Ann Swinbank but I know not whare
1598 JULY	2	Was weded henery ffothergill and margrett pinder
	2	Rowland ffuthergill and margrit ffawcyt
JULY	9	Was weded Edward huntter and Elizabeth Dent
SEPTEMBER	3	Was weded myles ffuthergill and Essabell shaw
ffAYBREWARY	17	Was weded Edward pindar and Issaybell Wharton
Ano Dni 1599 MAYE	28	Was weded Thomas ffawcit & Elizabeth parkin
JULLII	8	Was wed Anthonye morland & Ellin ffothrgill
	8	xpofor Todd & margayrett handlay the same day

1599		WEDINGS WEDDINGS
JULII	22	Was wedd VinCentt powson and xpobell pindar
SEPTEMBAR	2	Was weded Phillipp Grene to xpobell Cooke
OCTOBAR	22	Was wedid Thomas Robinsonn and mawbell Todd
JANEWARY. Ano Dni 1600	3	Was weded Rowland sponar and Annas pinder
MAY	15	Was weded Thomas Dennyson and Alice Swinbanke of Loucome

		WEDDINGS 1600
JUNE	1	Was wedded Myles ffothergill and Mabell Walker
	15	Was weddid John ffawcitt and Ellinge ffawcitt
JULY	6	Was wedded Richarde Hawle and Jannat ffawcitt
eadem di		Was wedded Richarde blande and Essabell Hawle
NOUEMBAR	9	Was wedded John Gray and Jannat Chambers
FABRUARIE Ano Dni 1601	2	Was wedded John Wharton and Issabell Shawe
APRELL Ano Dni 1601	4	Was wed John Adamthwat and Maybell ffoth^r^gill
JUNE	22	Was wedded Vincentt ffothergill & Ann Wilsonn
eadem di	22	Anthony Willsonn & mary Handley of th towne
NOUEMBER	24	Was wed Hewe shawe & Margaret paycoke & Lance shawe & margaret paycoke
DECEMBER	6	Was wed Rawffe Andersonn & Margaret Hawle
	11	Was wed Peter Pinder and Elizabeth ffothergill
1602		
JUNE	13	Was wed maythew pindar and Ann bovell
	27	Was wed herry bovell & Janat ffothergill
JULI	4	Was wed steven ffawcit & Ellin ffawcit
	18	Was wed herrye busfeld & margarett ewbank
JANEWA^r^Y	28	Was wed Anthonye pindar and Elizabeth sowarby
ffAYB^r^Y	26	Was wed henrye hayswytle And Janatt ffothergill

1603		WEDDINGS
June	26	Was wed Robartt ffawcyt & Janatt busfeld
Julii	10	Was wed xpoffor grene & Alic Busfeld
	10	Was wed maythe ffoth^{r}gill & maybell bland
	17	Was wed Robartt Adamson and Alic Busfeld
Awgust	3	Was wed Robartt Shaw and Sebell Busfeld
Sept	25	Was wed Richard Tayler and Janatt melner
Novem	3	Was wed Lanc Towneson and Elizabeth ffothergill
A^{no} Dni 1604		
Julii	11	Was wed Richard murthwat and Alic ffoth^{r}gill
Awgust	28	Was wed Robartt Rogerson and Ann handlay
Sept	10	Was wed willm whytlock and margaret grene
Novem	11	Was wed willm grene and Ann Walkar
Decem	21	Was wed Robartt Sympson and margarett Dentt
ffaybrew	2	Was wed Anthonye grene & Cayte powson
	9	Was wed John Adamthwat and sebell Busfeld
A^{no} Dni 1605		
June	2	Was wed Awth^{r} shaw & Janatt paycok
	8	Was wed Robartt hunttar and maybell ffawcyt
	23	Was wed Elizabeth hawle and Willm chambarlaine
Jullii	14	Was wed Olever thorneburray and Essaybell ffawcyt and Raynold pkin and Elizabeth Cooke and willm ffothergill and Issaybell ffoth^{r}gill
Octobar	13	Was wed george ewbank and Issaybell grene

WEDDINGS An° Dni 1605

Novem	5	Was wed Edward Cooke and Annas Rainoldsonn
ffaybrew	11	Was wed Edward ffawcyth and Elizabeth Wharton
An° Dni 1606	20	Was wed Robartt Waller and Elizabeth skayffe
June	15	Was wed Richard busfeld and Issaybell Wilson
	21	Was wed herry bartlatt and Annas symson
		Edward darby and ellin shaw
	30	Was wed Richard shaw & ellin hawle
		Anthonye grene and Issaybell ffawcyth
Jullii	6	James ffawcyth & ellin grene
		Was wed Roger shaw & Jane chambarlin
	16	Was wed John Crosby & Issaybell busfeld
Awgust	28	Was thomas bland & ellin Tayler
Septem	8	Was wed Anthony ffoth^{r}gill & mayry ffawcyth
Novem	2	Was wed James melner & Ann shaw
Novembar	20	Was wed Thomas shaw & margarett murthwat
An° Dni 1607	5	Was wed herry busfeld and Issaybell pkin
Jullii	12	Was wed James threlkeld and margarett grene
Septem	6	Was wed Robartt Benson and Elizabeth shaw
	29	Was wed Anthonye Robinson and xpobell grene
Novembar	22	Was wed Richard gye and Issaybell hawle
	30	Was wed Symond pindar and Annas sponor
ffaybrewa^{r}	4	Was wed Richard ffawcyth and annas bovell
An° Dni 1608		
Juli	9	Was nicolas murthat & ellin ffawcyt
	10	Wed James ffawcyt & margarett wharton
Awgust	4	Was wed Anthonye dentt and Janatt wilkinson
	28	Was wed Robartt wilson and Ann heblethwat

WEDINGS 1608

JANEWARY	26	Was wed myles ffothergill and
Ano 1609		margarytt Awdarson
JUNE	10	Was wed John shaw and
		Ann Wharton
	28	Was wed Richard ffoth'gill &
		Ellin ffawcyth
JULLI		Was wed xpoffor busfeld
		and Janatt Adamthwat
AWGUST	8	Was wed willm ffoth'gill &
		margarytt Tayler
NOVEM	25	myghell waller
		and Ann Adamthwat
Ano/Dni/		MAY 28 Was wed Thomas ffawcyth
1610		and Alic pkin
	31	Richard ffawcyth & Janatt ffawcyt
JUNE	10	James surgener & eales walkar
JULI	1	Was wed Edmond & Iassaybell dent
	8	Was wed willm grene & Issaybell busfeld
	10	Was xpoffor busfeld & Annas ffawcyt
	20	Was w Richard waller & margeritt Cooke
OCTOBAR	7	Was wed hew shaw & Issaybell ffawcyt
MAY	12	Was wed Richard Chambarlin & Ellic foth'gill
Ano Dni	20	Was wed James Cowtton & Elizabeth ffawcyt
1611		
JUNE	18	Was wed willm grene & Elizabeth busfeld
JULII	13	Was wed Roger murthwat & margerit shaw
SEPT	14	Was wed Edward ffawcit & Janatt ffawcyt
	8	Was wed Richard ffawcyt & margaryt moss
OCTOBAR	5	Was wed Rowland Adamthwat & Isaybell ffawcyt
ffABREW	8	Was wed oswold ewbanke & margaryt Tayler
Ano Dni		APRILL 30 Was wed John gowldinton & Janat Adathw
1612		
JULI	16	Was wed maythew dent & elizabeth grene
	23	Was wed Richard tayler & margaryt Ayray

WEDINGS Ano Dni 1612

SEPTEM BAR 24 Was wed Willm Cootts and Ellin ffawcyt
26 Was wed herry Coatlay and sebell paycok
27 Was wed Thomas walkar and sebell ffawcyt
1613
JUNE 6 Was wed pettar handlay and Ellin ffawcyth
26 Was wed hew ffoth[r]gill and margarit Robinson
JULLI 7 Was wed maythew busfeld and Elizabeth Atkinson
OCTOBAR 9 Was wed Richard powson and Alic bovell
NOVEM 10 Was wed herry handlay & Annas hunnttar
JANEWA[r]Y 6 Was wed pettar pindar and Ann ffothergill
ffAYBREW 10 Was wed Lanard grene and Janatt tayler
Ano Dni 1614 APPRELL 26 Was wed VinCent melner and Annas Jackson
JUNE 2 Was wed John hegdayle and Sebell ffawcyt
18 Was wed willm ffawcyt and margaritt Chambarlin
JULLI 6 Was wed Lanard peares & Jane bell
JANEWARY 14 Was wed Anthonye ffoth[r]gill & margarytt Robinson
Ano 1615
MAY 20 Was wed John grene & elizabeth niColson
31 Was wed Luke manares and Janat Inman
JUNE 3 Was wed maythew atkinson & bess Tayler
8 Anthony dentt & Janatt bovell
AWGUST 5 phillip busfeld & ellin ffoth[r]gill
OCTOB[r] 8 Was ormesyde * and Issaybell whythead
NOVEMB[r] 7 Was wed Robart mayson & maybell holland
15 Was * and ellic ffoth[r]gill
DECEMB[r] 2 Was wed willm Adamthat
26 & Janatt Cooke

henery Shaw

* Spaces left blank.

1616 WEDDINGS Ano/Dni/1616

MAY 2 Was wed herry ffothʳgill &
Annas pindar

20 Was wed Richard Rowth and
Janatt ffawcyt

JUNE 7 Was wed John handlay and mawdlin hawle

19 Was wed Robartt shaw & ellin ffothʳgill

27 Was wed Thomas hawll & elizabeth ffothʳgill

JULL 4 Was wed edmond handlay Issaybell ffothʳgill

1617 MAY 4 Was wed maythew breaks and
ellin Robinson

MAY 30 Was wed Anthonye ffothʳgill and
Ann dentt

JUNE 8 Was wed Rainowld ffawcyt and
Ann ffothergill

JULI 6 Was wed Thomas wilkinson and
margaritt walkar

AWGUST 6 Was wed Raynowld bovell & Janat pindar

18 Was wed John bovell and Issaybell Inman

NOVEM 8 Was wed John ffothʳgill & Issaybell shaw

JANEWARY 10 Was wed Rowland Tayler & margarit hanson

Anº Dni 1618 APRELL 30 Was wed George Chambarlin
and Annas Waller

JUNE 14 Was wed Anthony hegdall and Annas Cottlay

15 Was wed Lanc grene & elin shaw

JULI 6 Was wed Robartt Clark & Janatt grene

11 Was wed Anthony pindar & ellin ffothʳgill

NOVEM 16 Was wed willm shaw & Anne paycok

DEMB 4 Was wed John Chambʳlin & Ann huntar

1619 MAY 14 Was wed george handlay & Janat ffothʳgill

JUNE JUNE 19 Was wed herry Towneson &
Ellic ffawcyt

JULLII 8 Was wed John hewatson & maybell hunttar

OCTOBʳ 5 Was wed Thomas ffawcyt & Janatt dentt

16 Was wed Robartt Todd and Ann Cook

NOVEM 5 Was wed Thomas smartt & ellin ffothʳgill

DECEM 18 Was wed george ffothʳgill & margarit medcalff

ffABʳUAʳY 1 Was wed John pindar & Ann bovell

Anº 1620 APRELL 4 Was wed John ffawcyt & Annas shaw

MAY 10 Was wed ssaymewell ffawcyt and the
dawghter off Lanc ffawcyt

JULI 1 Was wed John parke & maybell busfeld
mortuus est

6 Was wed herry shaw & Ellic grene

14 Was wed willm ffawcyt & elizabeth Tayler

21 Was wed John shaw & Ellin ffothʳgill

WEDINGS Ano Dni 1620

JANEW ARY 10 Was wed Edward hewbanke
and margaryt tayler
18 Was wed herry bland
and Ann Bell
25 Was wed John walkar &
dorryty ffothrgill

Ano Dni 1621 MAY 18 Was wed John chambrlin
and mayrye shaw

Ano 1622 JANEWARY 18 Was wed Anthony Robinson
and margaritt ffawcyth
JUNE 13 Was wed harry Robinson
and Janatt Robinson
JULII 8 Was willm ewbank
and Ellin peares
AWGUST 10 Was wed John ffothrgill
and Ann (1) shaw
22 Was wed Richard bell
and Ann gowldinton
28 Was wed herry wharton
and Annas hawle
SEPTEM 4 Was wed hew ffothrgill
and Issaybell gowldinton
OCTOBAR 16 Was wed
myghell hawll & Annas Dentt

1623 WEDINGS

JULY 1 Rychard craiston & Janet winter
10 James Johnson & Janet garthwait
15 Wás wedded hew shawe & ellin Adamthwait
17 Was weded Rychard hunter & elizabethe futhergill
27 Was wed John loodman & An fawcet
FEBRUARIE 9 Was wed John Robinson & magdelain fawcet

1624 1624

MAY 19 Was wedded william hunter & margret haisthwitle
the same day Abraham bousphell & margret todd
and James dent and Essebell Cawtle
26 Was wedded John Chambrlain and ellin the
dowghter of Rowland sponner
29 Was wedded John Rychardson & margret hodgshon
NOVBR 25 Was wedded wylliam hugenson of soulby & margret
Adamthwait dowghter of John Adamthwait of lockholm
27 Was wedded william clemmeson & Janet Chambrelain

(1) Issaybell erased.

1625 WEDDINGS

May 28 Was wedded Rychard porter and ellise whithead
July 7 Was wedded John wharton of waithye
and margret bousfell
Agust 12 Was wedded william Rogerson
and Ann Chesburn
17 Was wedded philipp waller of yorke
and ezabell futhergill
Septr 10 Was weded peter Cawtle
and ezabell fawcet
October 21 Was wedded Robart sharpe of orton and
Sybell Shawe of ellergill
Januari 19 Was wedded oliver whitehead of orton
and elizabeth pinder
26 Was wedded John Atkinson of orton
and margret Robenson
Februari 14 Was wedded Thomas mosse of kirbie steven
and elizabeth todd
May 22 Was weded georg fawcet & magdelain fawcet
16 Was wedded Anthony pinder and mabell
1626 dowghter to Vincente futhergill
Awgust 30 Was weded thomas tomson of orton
& margret bousfell
Octobr 25 Was wedded Raynold holm of kirby steven
and mabell dowghter to Anthony wilson
Novebr 2 Was wedded Robart Shaw of Asfell and
mabell fothergill of brownber
18 Was wedded mychaell prockter and ellin bousphell
of mydelton at Sebber
Februari 6 Was wedded Rychard pinder & elizabeth Robinson
1627
July 5 Was weded Thomas dent and
magdelain haull
12 Was wedded Georg fawcet and
margret ffawcet
November 2 Was wedded Jeffray fawcet & magdelain fawcet
Januari 15 Was wedded Rychard powson & margret pinder
Februari 19 Was wedded Vincent powson & Janet bousfell
20 Was weded Symond bowsfell & ellin powson
1628
May 13 Was wedded John tomson and ellin haisthwitle
June 10 Was wedded Rychard fawcet of wandell banck
and ellin grene of grensyde

JUNE 18 Was wedded myles Bonskell of midelton
No dew for minister and margret dowghter to mychaell taylor
24 Was wedded Symond Alderson and margret bousfell
JULY 3 Was wedded John Knewstub & margret pearson
10 Was wedded Cuthbart hunter & margret futhergill
22 Was weded umphray gibson of lunds and mawbell dennyson
28 Was weded Rychard grene and Ann wilson
OCTOBER 9 Was wedded Raynold perkin and Annes simson
23 Was wedded wylliam Shaw & elsabeth Rogerson
30 Was wedded Abraham bousfell and ellin todd
NOVEMBER 27 Was wedded James pears & Janet Robinson
FEBRUARI 12 Was wedded Edward Adamthwait & eszabell futhergill of brownber
1629 14 Was wedded Cuthbart Robinson and margret futhergill
APRELL 26 Was wedded George (1) futhergill and ezabell waller
MAY 26 Was wedded James weaderhead of horton in Ribbelsdaill & marye dent
JUN 12 Was wedded Vincent Shaw & Janet futhergill
18 Was weded Christofer fawcet elsabeth Adamthwait
OCTOBER 18 Was wedded Thomas pkin and esszabell murthwait
NOVEMB^r 21 Was wedded John newton & ezabell adamthwait
1630
MAY 26 Was wedded georg winn of grisedaille and Jennett Rodgersonne
JUNE Was wedded Thomas favcett and Ellen ffothergill
JULII 2 Was wedded John pinder and Ellen fothergill
ffEBRIW 17 Was wedded Michell tod and Ann Green
1631
APRILL 30 Was wedded John haistwhitle and Ann ffawcett
JUNE 3 Was wedded gillbert fawcet and marye fawcet
JUNE 23 Was married John Alldersone and Elles Bousfeild
JULY 8 Was maried Anthony shaw and margat perkin
Was maried Renold Coke and sibbell Adamthwat no dew
OCTO^r 18 Was wedded Jaymes Atkinson and Elsabeth fawcet
Was weded Thomas haystewhitle and Ann Bousfeild
also Thomas Johnson and Ezabel perkin
Was wedded Henery shawe and Alzse Hunter

(1) Rychard erased.

1632

June	28	Was wedded Henery willinson and Ezabell faucet
June	30	Was wedded Thomas Robinson & Margat Bouell
Nou:	22	Was wedded Willm Wharton & Annas wharton
Janewary	28	Was weded Jaymes ffawcet and margat Atkinson
ffebryw	13	Was wedded Bartholemew sCafe and Ann dennyson
ffeb	26	Was wedded Thomas shawe and Elles shaw
1633 Aprill	22	Was wedded Jaymes simson & margat ffothergill
May	27	Was wedded Thomas Robinson & Sibbell Pouson
		Was wedded Thomas Townson & Elen bousfeld
June	2	Was wedded Jaymes fiawcet & Eles adamthwat
	3	Was weded Richard ffothergill & margat hunter
June	27	Was wedded william sanderson & mary ffothergill as allso Richard Todd & Isabell Bousfeild
July	4	Was wedded Michaell Bousfeild and Maubell ffawcet
		Also the same day was wedded John ffothergill and Issabell ffothergill
		Also Gerrerd Elyetson and Elsabeth Pouson
July	12	Was wedded John perkin and Elles ffawcet allso Jaymes Pacoke and Margat Pinder
July	26	Was weded william Johnson and Isabell lam * and no dews paid
ffeb	13	Was wedded william Rodgerson & Ellen murthwat
1634 May	30	Was wed stephen Green and Ezabell ffothergill
June	4	Was wed John Ubank and Maubell ffawcet
June	19	Was wed Richard branskill and Ezabell Willson
1635 Nouem	27	Was wedd Michaill Jackson and Ezabell willkinson
Aprill	9	Was wed Thomas Holme and Ellen Willson
Aprill	23	Was wed John Holme of sedber and An Pinder
May	3	Was wed Georg Murthat and Ellen ffawcet
June	5	Was wed Anthony bland and An Pinder
June	10	Wed Thomas Adamthwat and Ann Bousfeild
ffeb	11	Was wed Martin Willson and Margat shaw
1636		Was wed Richard shaw and Elles ffothergill
Agust	4	Was wed Christofer ffawcet and Elles Pacoke
1637 April	17	Was wed Anthony shaw and Maudlen Robinson
May	11	Was wed Thomas green and marye willson
		Was wed Gillbert ffawcet & Izabell perkin
Sept		Was wed Christofer bousfeild and Ellin ubank

* Indistinct—perhaps law.

1638

	Nov	4	Was wed william boure & Ellsabeth *
	Novem	9	Was wed John Heutson & Ellsabeth green
			Was wed Richard Gesslen & Ellen Taylor
	June	20	Was wed michell Chamberlain & Anas ffothergil
	Julie	3	Was wed Robert Balife and An Bovell
	Sep	13	Was wed Thom Cuningam & elsabeth Allderson
1639			Was wed Robart waller & Isabell Bousfeild
	May	28	Was wed Anthony Perkin & An Adamthwat
	June	20	*
	June	27	Was wed Edward pinder & Jennat ffothergill
	Jan	26	Was wed william ffawcet & An ffothergill
1640	May	11	Was wed Renold waller & Esabell Adamthwait
	May	26	Was wed stephen Bousfeild and sibbell Vbank
	July	9	Was wed Richard shaw & Jenet ffothergill
	1 Decem		Was wed Robart whitlock and Jenatt Willson
	ffeb	23	Was wed Thomas winn & Ezabell ffawcet
1641	May	17	Was wed Lanclot Hodshon & Ellen ffawcet
	June	8	Was wed Henery Pinder & Ellsabeth ffothergill
	June	24	Was wed will * & Ellen ffawcet
	July	10	Was wed John Shaw & Elen murthatt
	July	15	Was wed Thomas ffothergill & Ellsabeth hegdaile
	October	7	Was wed John Green and Izabell pinder
	November	10	Was wed Anthony shaw & Isabel Vbank
	Novem	25	Was wed Edward thornbrough and Elles ffothergill
			also George Chamberlaine & Ellsabeth wharton
Anº Dom	ffeb	19	Was wed Richard Haatan & Ezabell Turner
1642	April	30	Was wed Jaymes ffawcet & Elsabeth ffawcet
	May	6	Was wed Jaymes Tayler & margatt Vbank
	May	21	Was wed John Pettye & Ellsabeth ffawcet
	June	9	Was wed Robart Tod & Izabell Pinder
	Julye	2	Was wed William Whitehead & Ellsabeth fawcet
	Sep	22	Was wed Robart Tayler & Ellsabeth ffurnass
	Novem	29	Was wed Christofer Powson & Ann Green
	Janewary	26	Was wed William Adamthwat and Isabell Adamthwait
	Janewary	23	Was wed John ffawcet & Margratt Haule
	Janw	30	Was wed michaell Chamberlaine & Jaine fawcet
1643	Aprill	4	Was wed Richard Gouldinton and margarat Lam
	May	23	Was wed Jaymes Richardsone & Mary Pinder
	June	29	Was wed Thomas ffawcet & mary Handlay

* Spaces left blank.

	OCTOBER	26	Was wed Anthony Parkin & markatt willson
	NOUEMBER	2	Was wed John Waller & Jennat ffawcet
	ffEB		Was wed Anthony Shawe & Margatt ffawcet
			| mr ffawcet had the dews
1644	MAY	26	Was was wed Robart Handlay & Elen Gosslin
	JUNE	7	Was wed Thomas Robinson & Annas Green
	JUNE	11	Was wed Richard Powson & margatt whitehead as allso Abram Gouldinton & Annas winsten
	JUNE	27	Was wed Jaymes ffawcet & mary ffothergill
			| mr preston had the dews
	JULY	8	Was wed Jaymes ffawcet And sibbell Green
	NOVEM	7	Was wed Edward Bland & Margatt shaw
1645	JULY	12	Was wed Richard Hunter & Izabell ffawcet
		15	Was wed Thomas Adamthwait And Ellsabeth ffothergill
		24	Was wed George Alderson and Ellen perkin
	OCTOBr	28	Was wed Thomas Willson & margat hinemour
1646			as allso Archer Johnson & Agnas moore
	SEP	5	Was wed william ffawcet & Sarah pinder
	MARCH	12	Was wed John ffawcet & mary Green
1647	MAY	5	Was wed John Hunter and Mary Shaw
	MAY	12	Was wed Thomas Rigg and margat ffawcet
	MAY	26	Was wed Richard powson & Elsabeth whitehead
	JUNE	11	Was wed Jaymes ffawcett & margat shaw
		16	Was wed Richard shaw and Elsabeth smith
	NOVEMB	25	Was wed Christofer Jackson & sarah Handlay
1648	JUNE	6	Was wed stephn fothergil & maudlin ffawcet
	JUNE	60	Was wed Thomas thornbrough and Ellen Cheesbrough
	DECEMBER	21	Was wed Thomas deny and Jenet ffawcet
1649	MARCH	27	Was wed John Waastall and Isabell willkinson
	APRILL	26	Was wed Anthony ffothergill And Margatt Adamthwait
	JULY	4	Was wed John Adamthwait and Ann Richardson
1650	MAY	26	Was wed John Bew & Ellen Gouldinton
	OCTOBER	19	wed John Robinson and Marye Handlay
1651	JENEWARY	29	Was wed John Gouldinton and Jenett Couston
1652	JUNE	24	Was weded willyam Robinson Ann Adamthwaite
	JULY	1	Was wed Renold bouell & dorathy ffothergill
1652	OCTOBR	22	Wed Thomas Harrison & Margat Willison
1653	MAY	12	Was wed Stephn Chamberlan and Maubell Wilkinson

Anno dom. 1653

	June	29	Was wed Richard bouell and Sibbell ffothergill
	Jan	8	Was wed Thomas Atkinson and Elles ffawcet at kirby stephn by mr Willes
1654	Aprill	12	Was wed Isack Handlaw and Isabell Knoostob by Jaymes Cock at Kendall
1655	March		Was wed at Kirby stephn by mr Higgyson Jayms Willson and An ffawcet
	Aprill	29	Was wed at Kendal by Justiss Archer Abram Handlay and Ellen fawcet
	June	28	Was wed at apelbye by the maire at apellbye by Peter Rownson Peeter Cautly an An Handlay
	June	30	Was wed by the same man
1656			Tho ffothergill and margat green
	June	8	Was wed at Apelby by the maire Peter ffawcet And Mayry Pinder
	June the	24	Was wed Richard Robinson and Ann ffothergill by the maire of Ap
	July	25	Was wed Robart Shawe And Mary dodson at Kendall by Mr Archer
	November	29	Was wed Jaymes Rodgerson and Ellen Clarkson at Kendall by *
	ffebruary	8	Was wed John Knoostop & Ellen procter at Apellby by Justes Branthwait
1657	Aprill	25	Was wed Georg ffothergill and Margatt Allderson at Apelby by Justes Branthat
	Julye	9	Was wed John Shaw and Annas hesckat by Justess Branthwait
	October	14	Was wed Robart Hunter and Margrat ffothergill by mr dodson
	Decemb.	17	Was wed Richard breaks and
1658			Maudlen Bousfeild
	May	27	Was wed Henry Handlay
1659			And Jennat ffawcet
	June	14	Was wed John Heutson and Annas Adamthwait
	June	18	Was wed Robart dawson and Isabell Parkin
	July	6	Was wed Thomas benson And Ann Murthat

* Left blank.

1606

November 3 Was wed Edward Whitehead
as Ellsabeth Bovell
May 31 1606 Was wed John Adamthwat
and Elsabeth Alderson
June 20 Wes wed Ralfe Alderson
and Margat tod
Allso the same day Richard murthwait
and margat Vbanke
July 8 Was wed George Clemison and Izabell medop
1661 Aprill 27 Wed Richard Allderson & Mary perkin
June 6 Was wed Thomas thompson and margerett shawe
Sep 27 Was wed John ffawcet & elles ffothergill
1662 May 29 Was wed Thomas Tayler & Ellsabeth pinder
June 3 Was wed Jaymes ffawcet & Issabell Raine
June 12 } Was wed John blackburn & Ellsabeth Robinson
} as allso John Tayler & marie ffothergill
1663 April 20 Was wed Christofer Allderson
and Saraih perkin
Aprill 03 Was wed William Shawe and marye ffothergill
May 20 Was wed Thomas Haistwhitle
and margrat Allderson
Decembr 9 Was wed Robart parken & ellsabeth Adamthwait
ffeb 6 Was wed Henry ffothergill
1664 and Ezabell Thomson
May 12 Was wed william Robinso & Jenat waler
May 20 Was wed william ffawcet & Ellen ffothergill
June 23 Was wed Henry Handlay & ellen green
Aprill 17 Was wed Mr Christofer Jackson & Annas Tayler
1665 May 18 Was wed Robart Ridden & Elles ffawcet
June 1 Was wed Robart Handlay and
Margerat Ridman
Nouember 03 Was wed Charlles Willson & Margrat porter
Febery 9 Was wed Richard garthat
1666 and Ellen Rodgerson
Aprill 26 Was wed John huetson And
Ellsabeth Pacoke
May 18 Was wed John paulay and
mary Handlay
June 7 Was wed simond steuenson
and Mary Vbank
June 14 Was wed John Robinson and
Annas Cautley
June 28 Was wed Richard ffothergill and
Elles Procter
June 30 Was wed Henry Shawe and
margarat Adamthwait
Agust 15 Was wed Rodger barber
and dorathy Tomson

Anno dom 1667

	May	9	Was wed Nickalas brown & Ann pinder
	May	24	Was wed John Tayler and saraw Bousfeild
	May	28	Was wed Adam Shaw & Ann dent
	October	2	Was wed Jaymes bland and Elles fothergill
	October	23	Was wed Robart paulay and Annas Bousfeild
	Novemb	26	Was wed George bawsfeild & Isabell green
1668	May	21	Was wed Rouland Shearman and Ellen yellyetson
	May	28	Was wed henry lawe and Ann greene
	June	4	Was wed william ffothergill & margat shawe
	June	27	Was wed philipe Bousfeild & Isabell Ridden
	December ye	27th	Was weeded John ffawcett & Jane Robinson
	January ye 1668	28th	Was Maried Robert Pawley sone of will Powley and Jane Kenyon daughter to mr Roger Kenion vicar of orton allis ouerton
	ffebruary ye 2d (68)		Was maried Joseph winne of Grisdaile and Dorithy Taylor of this parish
1669	Aprill	22	Was maryed John Thistlethwaite of widdell and Mary Chamberlaine of this parish
	May	27	Was maryed John ffothergill & Mary Shaw
	May	31	Was maryed Rich: ffallowfield & Gilian warton
	June	10	Was maryed Rich: Bousfeild & Issabell millner
	June	17	Was maryed willm Shaw & Ann Todd of this towne the same day James Hall & Cibell Hunter
	June	24	Was maryed John Willson & Elsabeth Pinder
	September	9	Was maryed Thomas ffawcet & Elsabeth Alderson
	September	23	Was maryed Rich: Whitehead & Mary Parkin
	October	8	Was maryed Gilbert Guy & Mary Alderson
	November	25	Was marid Tho: Tayler & Elsabeth Adamthwaite
1670	ffeb	3	Was maryed Robt: Holme of Sedbergh parish and Elizabeth Hunter Asked in our Church and a lycence he brought from Mr mayor
	June	16	Was maryed John Heutson and Sarrah Todd
	June	23	Was maryed William Shaw and Ann Peacock
	July	5	Was maryed John Blades of the lunds of the parish of Aisgarth and Margret Parkin of this parish
	September	27	Was maried Thomas midelton off Dent and Elsabeth Meccay of this Parish
1671	May	4	Was maryed John Ouerend of the parish of Kirby steuen and Mary Greene of this parish
	June	29	Was maryed Anthony Peacock and Ann Todd Was maryed the same day Thomas Parkin and Mary Townson
	Nouember	16	Was maryed John Richison of the Parish off warcup and Ellin Shaw of this parish
1672	Aprill.	18	Was maried William Holme of witherslack and Cattrin Dobson of this parish
	May	2	Was maryed George Perkin and margrat Hunter

1672 WEDDINGS

MAY 28 Was maryed Edward Scaife and Ellice Powsson
JUNE 4 Was maryed John Taylor and Margreat Pearrson
JUNE 6 Was maryed William Milner and Issabell Hunter
was maryed the same day Richard Robinson & margret Powsson
JUNE 13 Was maryed George Perkin and Ann ffothergill
JUNE 20 Was maryed William Greene and margarett ffawcett
SEPTEMBER 17 Was maried John ffawcett and mary Chamberlaine
NOUEMBER 5 Was maried Mathew Birckdaile of smardaile
in the parish of Kirby steuen and Issabell
Hayton of this parish
ffEBRUARY 10 Was maryed Anthony Tompson off Ortton Parish
1673 and Jennat ffawcett of this parish
JUNE 5 Was maryed William Baliffe and Sibbell Shawe
JUNE 10 Was maryed Henery Bousfield and mary ffothergill
JUNE 12 Was maryed Richard Robinson and margaret perkin
JUNE 19 Was maryed John Pearson and Mary Rigge
JUNE 26 Was maryed William Elyetson and Ellin Bousfeild
OCTOBER 30 Was maried with A lycence mrer John Wilkinson
off the parish of hornebie in Yorkshire and Elizabeth
1674 warricke off the parish of Kirby Steuen
MAY 7 Was maried with A lycence mrer Christopher Pettey
of the parish of Ortton and Jane Kennion of the same parish
JUNE 11 Was married with A lycence Robert Shaw and Mary denney
JUNE 25 Was married John Todd and Sarah Elyetson
SEPTEM 12 Was married Milles Thiselthat of the parish
of Askerth and Margaret Whiteheade of this parish
NOUEMBER 12 Was maried George Potter of the parish of
Orton and Elizabeth Adamthwaite of this parish
NOUEMBER 26 Was married Phillip Greene and Margaret Harison
1675 MAY 6 Was married John mill and mary Shawe
JUNE 3 Was married Thomas ffothergill and Ann blades of Lunns
SEPT 16 Was married Henery Waller and Mary Todd
NOUEM 15 Was married Richard Rogerson and margarett Chamberlaine
JANUARY 17 Was married Rouland Shearman off the parish of
1676 Crosberauenswith and Gennat Adison of the same parish
APRILL 20 Was maryed John ffawcett and ellin Adamthwaite
APRILL 27 Was maryed George Barnot of the parish of orton
and ffranceas Nouble of this parish
MAY 11 Was maryed Henery ffothergill and dorathy ffothergill
SEP 14 Was maryed Thomas Robartson and Margarett Hunter
OCTOBER 5 Was maryed John Todd and margarett Balife
OCTOBER 26 Was married John Robinson and Barbary mayson
boath off the Parish of Aysgarth
NOUEM 30 Was married Richard ffothergill and mary Shawe
1677 MAY 17 Was married John ffawcett and Unicah Taylor
MAY 31 Was married John dawne of the parish of Arneclife
and mabbell Wilkinson of this parish
AUGUST 9 Was married Robart Taylor and Jennat Wilson
OCTOBER 30 Was maried Robart Coupland and margarat Greene
NOUEM 15 Was maried Thomas ffawcett and Elizabeth Rigge
ffEBRUARY 7 Was maried Robart Hodgson and mabbell Robinson
1678 APRILL 23 Was maried Thomas Robinson of this parish
and Elsabeth Waller of parish of Kirby Steuen

1678 WEDDINGS

May 7 Was maried William Clough and Issabell ffawcett
May 9 Was maried Richard ffothergill and Catrine westmerland
May 30 Was maried John Alderson and Ann ffawcett
June 8 Was maried with A lycence Lanclott dennison
and Ann Bindlesse both of the parish of Ortton
June 13 Was maried Stephen ffawcett and margrett Sanderson
August 13 Was maried John Powson and Ellin Robinson
August 22 Was maried George Harrison of the parish of
Kirby Steuen and Agnas denneys of this parish
Nouem 5 Was maried William Powson and Elizabeth Wilkin
Nouem 28 Was maried Stephen Robinson and Ellice darby

1679
Henery Sawelt of the parish of Kirby Steuen and margrett
Knewstubb of this parish was maried May ye 24th
Richard Chamberlaine and Sarah Bousfeild was maried June 17th
John Adamthwaite and margrett Pinder was maried June 19th
Robart Robinson and Ellin Cleasby was maried June 24th
mrer George ffothergill and margrett Birckbecke was marted June 26th
also stephen ffothergill and Issabell Cautley same day was maried the same day
John Swainson and Agnas Gibson was marid June 28
Gyles ffothergill and Jennat Atkinson was marid July 3
Robart Perkin and margrett Bousfeild was maried August 28
John Chamberlaine and Elizabeth ffawcett was maried Octob 17
John Haistwhitle of the parish of Kirby Steuen and
Jane Rogerson of this parish was maried Nouember 17
Robart Whitelocke and mary Parkin maried with A lycence Decem 30
Josep Boorebancke and Agnnas Scaife was maried ffeb 23
George ffawcett and ffrances Heskett was maried Aprill 16
1680
James Hall and Agnas Crosby was maried June 3
Richard Gyles and Anne Pinder was maried June 10
Richard Gouldington and Ellin Shearman was maried June 17
Richard Powson and margrett Gibson was maried June 24
Robart Perkin and margrett Waller was maried Octob 12
John Petty of the parish of Kirby Steuen and 1681
Agnas ffothergill of this parish was maried Aprill 4
Stephen ffothergill and Elizabeth ffothergill was maried May 7
John Robartson and Ellin Whiteheade was maried June 16
William Shawe and Sarah Shawe was maried June 30
John Bousfeld and Anne Hewetson was married with A lycence Decem 14
Richard ffallowfeild and Agnas Couert was maried June 8 1682
Thomas Hall of the parish of Sedbridge and Anne
Shawe of the parish of Ravinstondaile was maried June 12
George Spooner and Jennat Sawelt was maried June 15
William ffawcett and ellin ffaweett was maried the same day
John Shawe of this parish and Issabell moore of the parish
of askerth also was married the same day
William milner and margreat Parlour of the parish
of Kirby Stephen was maried Nouember 23

1683
James ffawcett and mary whitehead was mar: May 17
Thomas Robinson of the parish of Askerth and mabbell
Shawe of our parish was maried June 9
John Robinson of orton parish and Elizabeth Todd
of our parish was maried June 14
James dent and ellin ffawcett was maried June 28
William Shawe and margrett ffawcett was maried June 30
Thomas Rogerson and elsabeth ffothergill maried same day
Richard Holme of the parish of Askerth and
Elizabeth ffawcett of this parish maried July 10

1684 WEDDINGS

Christopher Bousfeild and Ann Swainson was maried	May	8
Edward Willan of the parish of crosbyrauenswuth and Sarah Perkin of this parish was maried	May	10
Thomas Todd and Jennat Perkin was maried	May	22
Henery Cautley and Sussana Prockter was maried	June	5
Gilbart ffawcett and margreat Hunter was maried	June	12
James Perkins and Alcie Knewstubb was maried	June	19
Godfreay milner and Isabell Shawe was maried	July	3
Stephen dent and Issabell Ubancke was maried		1685
also George Shawe and mary Todd maried	June	11
Robert Readman and Ellin Knewstubb was maried	June	22
John Chamberlaine and Anne murthwait was maried	July	2
George Perkin and mary fawcett was maried wth a licence	Mar:	20
		1686
William Elyetson and mary Bousfeild was maried	Aprill	22
Richard ffawcett and Issabell wilkinson was maried	May	15
William Hunter and mary Willan of lunns was maried	May	20
Thomas Thompson and Mary Slee was maried	May	25
James Townson and mary ffawcett was maried	June	17
		1687
Henery ffothergill and Anne Hunter was maried	Aprill	4th
Robert Todd and margrett Bousfeild maried	June	3
John Blackbourne and Agnas mosse was maried	June	21
Joseph Boorbancke and Jennat Bousfeild was maried	June	28
John dent of orton parish and Ellin ffawcett maried	July	5
James ffawcett and Sarah Adamthwaite was maried with A lycence	July	23
Henery ffawcett of the parish of Sedbridge and mary Adamthwaite this parish maried wth A lycence	August	18
Rouland Bowman of parish of Kirby steuen and dorathy Hegdaile of this psh maried	Nouem	8
William Richeson of the parish of Asbie and mary wilson of the same psh maried maried with A lycence	December	20
Robert Hougill and dorathy ffothergill maried	ffeb	23
Henery Hugison of the parish of Kirby stephen		1688
and margrat Swainson of this parish maried	Aprill	17
Thomas Shawe of the parish of Kirby stephn and mary whiteheade of this psh was maried	May	3
Jonathan Alderson and margratt Pinder maried	June	4
1689 Thomas milner and Anne Harrison was marid	Aprill	12
Thomas Knewstub and Issabell Townson mar:	Apr.	16
Thomas Cunnigam of the parish of Kirby Stephen and mary Shawe of this parish mar:	April	18
William Hewetson and Elizabeth Guddaile and Edward Powson and margrat Simpson marid	May	21
Thomas Hall and Issabell Hunter was mar:	May	27
James marson and margrett Robertson was marid	Janu:	9
John Baliffe and Issabell Shawe was mar:	Jan	30
Robert Todd and Agnas Spooner was mar:	ffeb	13
John Robinson and Anne Alderson was mar.	April	24
1690 James Rogerson and mary Shawe was maried	May	22
James Tennant of the parish of Sedbrig and margrett Alderson of this psh maried	May	27
Richard ffawcett and margrett Harrison maried	May	29
Anthony Perkin and Agnas mounsee maried	June	17

WEDDINGS 1691

	George Townson and Elizabeth ffothergill was maried	May	4th
	John Perkin and mary Tong was maried	May	19
	Thomas Knewstubb and Sarah murthwaite maried	May	28
	George Cleasby and Agnas forrest maried also Richard Bousfeild and Ellin Handlay maried	June	18
	Richard waller of the parish of musgraue and Elizabeth Adamthwaite of hill marid	Nouem	26
1692	James Townson and mary Cautley was marid	Aprill	28
	Thomas ffothergill and Ellin murthwaite was marid	May	5
	John Browne and Ellin Townson was mar:	May	14
	Richard Shawe and Jane Stewardson maried	May	26
	Thomas Alderson and Issabell ffawcet maried	June	16
	John Taylor and Jane Robinson of the pish of Kirby Stephen was maried with A lycence	October the	8
	Thomas Whiteheade of the parish of ortton and Issabell Knewstubb of this psh was maried with a lycence	Nouember	21
1693	John Knewstubb and mary Simpson mar:	May	1
	Robert ffawcett and Elizabeth Wilkinson mar:	May	8
	Regnold Robinson of crosby hill and margrett ffawcett of this psh was maried	June	19
	James Clerkson and Anne Alderson mar:	June	26
	John ffawcett and Elizabeth Thornborow maried at the meetting house	January	4
	mathew Breakes and margrett Robinson was maried	ffebruary	15
	Thomas Atkinson and mary Taylor mar:	Feb	17
1694	Anthony ffawcett and Elizabeth Hewetson of the parish of ortton was married	Aprill	13
	James Guy of psh of Askerth and Anne ffothergill of this psh was mar:	Apr.	17
	Stephen ffawcett and margrett Bousfeild was married	May	10
	Richard Broune and mary Thompson was maried	May	28
	Abraham dent and Issabell ffothergill maried	June	21
1695	Adam Bowes of the parish of Appelby and Elizabeth douer of this parish was maried	Aprill	18
	Anthony Browne and Elizabeth Knewstubb was maried	May	21
	Richard Postelthate and Allice morland was married	June	20
	Anthony ffawcett and mary Rogerson was married	October	31

Thesse are to certifie whom it may consarne that Henery wharton of the parish of Rauinston daile and Allice rapier of the parish of grinton were maried According to the cannons the 9 day of nouember 1695 by James moore Curate of muckor

WEDDINGS 1695

	Robert ffothergill and Sarah ffothergill of this towne was married *	January	30
1695	John Baliffe and dorathe Handlay was married	Aprill	16
	John Jackson and margrett Alderson was married	Aprill	20
	Robert ffawcett and mary pearson was married	May	5
	William Hewetson and Issabell Robinson was married Also John Hall and maudlin Thompson of the parish of Sedber was married	May	7
	Sammuell Tunstell of the parish of Kirckby Steuen and Elizabeth ffawcett of this pish mar.	Sep	10
	Henery Barbar and Agnas Todd was marr.	Octo	19
	Thomas Bainebridge of the pish of gains ford and mary Bousfeild was maried	Nouem	24
1697	Thomas Adamthwaite of Sedber parish and Sibbell Adamthwaite maried	May	6
	Josep Shawe of the parish of Kirckby stephen and Sarah Bousfeild was married Also John Richison and Issabell Bousfeld of the parish of Brough maried	May	26
	William Burah of the pish of whitinton and Agnes Taylor was married	May	31
	William Waller and Elizabeth Chamberlaine was married	July	29
1698	William ffawcett and Jennat Todd maried	July	30
1697	m^r^ter James michell and mary Adam thwaite was maried at the meeting housse * *	August	24
1699	James Richardson and margrett Shaw maried	June	8
	Richard Smith and Agnas Haiton of the parish of Shapp was maried	June	10
	James ffawcett and Sibbell Hunter maried	July	6
	George Thornborrow and Catrrine Wileson both of the parish of Orton was married	January	1
1700	John Hall of the parish of Appelby and margrett Thwaytes of the parish of Cresbyrauenswith was maried	Aprill the	1
	John Taylor and Elizabeth Hayton married	June	6
	Thomas Hall and Anne Shawe married	June	13
	Also William ffurnace of Crosbyrauenswith psh and Allice Wharton of this psh married the same day		
	John ffothergill and Issabbell ffothergill maried	July	4
	William Spooner of Kirby Stephen parish and Elizabeth Browne of our psh married	July	13
	michaell Bousfeild and elsabeth whithead was married	August	15
	Thomas waller and margrett ffothergill married * * *	ffeb	22
1701	Thomas ffothergill and mary ffothergill maried	July	15
1702	John Punch and mary Simpson married	Nouem	23
1703	William Hewetson and Jane Smith married	May	9
	John Robertson and Alleis docker married	October	5
1704	Humprey dauis of soulby and Anne Hewetson of our parish was married	June	22
	Thomas Knewstubb and margret Robertson maried	Aug	27

* Transcripts add—
"John Haistwhitle & dorathy Clerkson was married in the quaker way June 27

** 1699 "John Handlay and margrett ffawcett was married May 14

*** "Thomas Breackes and Margrett Blackburne was married July 10

MARRIAGES

1704	Henery Knewstubb and Elizabeth Goslin was married	October 19
1705	George Guy and Elizabeth Adamthwaite married	May 5
	Thomas Waller and margrat Blenckarne maried	May 30
	John Shawe of the parish of Kirckby stephen and margrat Bousfeild of our parish maried	June 14
	Robert ffothergill and mary Vbancke maried	June 21
	Thomas ffawcett of dent and margrett ffawcett of this parish was married	October 23
	James Robinson and Agnas ffawcett married	December 6
1706	Thomas Adamthwaite and Agnas Atkinson married	May 11
	John Richardson and Elizabeth Hewetsonn married	May 19
1707	peeter Gyles and Allis Guy was maried	July 3
	George ffawcett and mary Chamberlaine married	Octob 11
	Richard Todd and margarett Powson married	October 23
1708	Thomas ffawcett and mary Hewetson married	April 8
	John ffothergill and Jane Wilson married	Aprill 29
	William Hodgson and Isabell fawcet married	May 27
	George moreland and Ann fawcet married	June 3
	John Teasdell and Ann fothergill married	June 5
	Stepehn Dent And Ellsabeth Thompson married	June 19
	William Knewstub and Jane Thornber married	October 14
1709	James Willon and Ann foster of the parish of Askerth was married May the 5: Anthony parkins and Elizabeth Robertson was married June 2 Also James fawcet and Marey Harrison the same day	
1710	Thomas Robinson & Margrett fawcet married	June th 15
	James Hutchisson and Margrett Alderson married	July th 6

			BURIALLS
	1571		
	Novemba^{r}	15	Was buried Lancelote ffawcyt of murth whayt
	December	30	Was buried margreat vxo^{r} Lancelote grene
	Janwarye	23	Was buried Lancelote filis Abrahami tayle^{r}
	March	19	Was bur. Robart hawle
1572	Aprill	11	Was bur. Oliver whytheead
		16	Was bur. George filis willm Adamwhayt
	May	19	Was bur Bryam pinder
	Awgust	12	Was bur James paycok
	September	3	Was bur John Hawle
	December	12	Was bur Rowland dent
		20	Was bur margreat vxo^{r} Rychard Grene
	Janwarye	5	Was bur Elen Robinson
		23	Was bur Lanclot filis Expoferi wharton
		28	Was bur mylles filis Richardi ffothergill
	ffaybruarye	18	Was bur george dent senex
		23	Was bur Elen voxo^{r} Rogeri Grene
		25	Was bur willm ffawcett
	May	6	Was bur Jeffrey hablewhait
		15	Was buried Ann vxo^{r} Robarti ffothergill
		30	Was bur Grace vxo^{r} Stephani ffawcett
1576			
	December	30	Was buried margreat vxo^{r} Heneri bouell
	Januarye	8	Was bur Expofor bell
	Jannarye	18	Was buri sibell the wife of Henere swinba^{n}k
	Janwarye	26	Was bur Gyles cooke
	ffabruarye	6	Was buried Roland the sone of Vincent murthwhait
	Julye	10	Was bur Edward milner
1577	Aprill	26	Was buried Peter the sonee of Thomas fawcit
	Aprill	30	Was bur Margret the dowhter of Edward Thomsonne
	Maye	26	Was buried myles the sonne of Edward thomsonne
	Maye	26	Was bur Joan the Lait wife of gilbert ffawcitt
	Julye	31	Was bur Edward thomsonne
	Agust	11	Was bur mabell the wif of the saide Edward
	Agust	25	Was bur James Dente
	Agust	28	Was bur. An the wife of xpor torner
	October	1	Was bur merg^{a}rote the doughter of Robart todd
	October	3	Was bur Alice the doughter of xpor turner
	October	3	Was bur Cuthbertt fawcit
	October	19	Was bur Exable the wiefe of John pinder
	October	25	Was bur Henry Holme
	Nouemb^{r}	7	Was bur Symonnd the sone of John pider
	Nouember	8	Was bur Exable the wife of Anthonye ffuthergill

1577		BURYALLS.
Nouember	11	Was buried Elizabeth the doughter of Stephe futhergill.
December	3	Was bur mablee the doughter of Roger todd
December	18	Was bur. Thomas ffawcit
December	22	Was bur Cristablee the doughter of Abraha taylor
December	25	Was bur. Jhone the sone of James taylor
Janwarye	1	Was bur Cristablee the wife of Simod pinder
Janwarye	7	Was bur Alice the doughter of george turner
Janwarye	8	Was bur Joan the lait wiefe of gyles fawcit
Fabruarye	8	Was bur Nicolas futhergill
1578 Marche	25	Was bur xpor the sone of Stephen busfeild
Aprill	10	Was bur Sibill the *
Aprill	21	Was bur Abraham Taylor
Aprill	25	Was bur John nycolsone
June	17	Was bur Cristablee vxo[r] Robart Haull
July	26	Was bur Cristoper the sone of cuthbert swibank
Julye	27	Was bur xpor the son Thomas of Robinson
Septemb[r]	2	Was bur Thomas the sone of James ffawcit
Septemb[r]	9	Was bur xpor the sone of myles busfeld
Septemb[r]	10	Was bur Rowland holme
Septemb[r]	19	Was bur vswould perky
October	6	Was bur willm paicocke
October	9	Was bur mergarite the Doughter of John Robinsone
October	13	Was bur Alic the Doughter of Thomas grene
October	24	Was bur Cuthbart swinbanke
October	29	Was bur Richard grene
Nouember	8	Was bur James fawcit
Nouember	18	Was bur Helyen Layt doughter to henerye bouell
December	18	Was bur Richarde the sone of John robinsone
Decemb[r]	12	Was bur Izable the doughter of mathew paicok
Decemb[r]	18	Was bur margarit vxo[r] Roulay Adamtwhat
Janwary	3	Was bur Hewe the sone of John shawe
Jannarye	10	Was bur Cristablee the Doughter of george paicoke
Jannarye	11	Was bur margarit vxo[r] xpor whorton
Jannarye	14	Was bur willm fawcit
Jannarye	26	Was bur Cuthbert the Sone of Anthonye Swinbanke
Fabruarye	16	Was bur Joan the dough of oliuer paycoke
Marche	11	Was bur Joan vxo[r] John Shaw

* Left blank.

1579		BURYALLES 1579
APRILL	7	Was buried Siblee vxo[r] Edward Pinder
APRILL	16	Was bur. george fawcyte
APRILL	22	Was bur george the Sone of myles busfeilde
MAYE	8	Was bur Jhone the sone of cuthbert futhergill
MAYE	10	Was bur John walker
APRILL	9	Was bur margarite the Doughter of John haull
APRILL	14	Was bur Robart the sone of willm shawe
APRILL	14	Was bur An the doughter of henerye peares
APRILL	15	Was bur Elizabeth the wife of Richard Rogerson
APRILL	30	Was bur Christablee the Doughter of Richard bouell
MAYE	3	Was bur willm the sone of Richard Rogerson
MAYE	5	Was bur James the son of John Ewbanck
MAYE	26	Was bur Helyne the doughter of Richard wilson
MAYE	27	Was bur mergarit the wife of Simond taylor
AGUST	7	Was bur xpor turner
SEPTE	20	Was bur Edward Dent
NOVEMB	8	Was bur Anthony futhergill
JUNE	17	Was bur George Chamberline
JUNE	24	Was bur margarit the wife of willm Chamberlin
JULYE	3	Was bur willm the sone xpor adamtwait
AGUST	27	Was bur Roger todd
AGUST	29	Was bur Simonde the sone of a pore mn called myles Robinsone
SEPTEB	6	Was bur Helyn the wief of Stephen busfeld
SEPTEB[r]	21	Was bur Jhon todd
SEPTEB[r]	21	Was bur An the doughter of John perkyn
OCTOBER	7	Was bur Joane the wiefe of John Cautley
OCTOBER	24	Was bur Richard Rogerson
NOVEMB[r]	18	bur John the sone of willm Chamberline
NOVEMB[r]	28	Was bur Izabell the wiefe of henerye swinbank
DECEMB[r]	5	Was bur Joan the Doughter of John fawcit
DECEMB[r]	5	Was bur Izable the Doughter John Cawtleye
DECEMB[r]	12	Was bur mergarite the wife of John Robinson
JANWARYE	2	Was bur John the sone of adam fawcit
JANWARYE	13	Was bur george the sone of michell Chamberlin
FABRUARY	17	Was bur margarit the wife of Rowland wilson
FABRUARY	18	Was bur mathew Dent
FABRUARY	24	Was bur Izable the wiefe of Richard pacok
FABRUARY	24	Was bur mabele the wief of John futhergill
MARCH	22	Was bur Agness lait wife of nycolas futhergill
MARCH	23	Was bur Thomas Rogerson Dwellinge in sedber

BURYALLES 1580

NOVEMB[r]	29	Was buried Joan the wife of Reynold pearson
DECEMB[r]	7	Was buried Roland Dent
DECEMB[r]	31	Was bur. Izablee the wiefe of John fawcitt
JANWARY	1	Was bur mergarit the wiefe of willm hebletwait
JANWARY	7	Was bur willm Robinsonne
JANWARY	24	Was bur Henery futhergill lait sone to James futher
MARCH	10	Was bur Isable the doughter of Richard pynder
MARCH	15	Was bur willm Cowper
1581		
MAYE	16	Was bur Johne the Sone of Adam fawcit
JUNE	15	Was bur. Agness the wief of heneryе gartwait
SEPTEMB[r]	15	Was bur. Thomas the Sone of John futhergill
SEPTEMB[r]	23	Was bur margarit the wife of John futhergill
OCTOBER	17	Was bur Izable the doughter of Jhon handley
OCTOBER	18	Was bur mergarit the wife of Heugh shawe
OCTOBER	25	Was bur Ann the doughter of Richard wilson
NOUEBER	11	Was bur margarit supposed the doughter of willm fawcit and of Joan gouldington beton in the filthye sin of fornication
NOUEMBER	19	Was bur Agness the doughter of John haule
DECEB[r]	13	Was bur Cuthbert ffawcit
FAYBURARY	10	Was bur Edmond ffawcitt
MARCH	14	Was bur John ffawcitt
1582		
APRILL	7	Was bur Anthonye Dent
APRILL	24	Was bur Alice the wife of Gyles tailor
MAYE	11	Was bur Vincent the sone of John Cautley
MAYE	19	Was bur Richard the sone of Jhon cautley
JUNE	8	Was bur John Pinder
JULYE	8	Was bured the wief of John birkett
OCOBER	1	Was bur willm bouell
JANWARY	4	Was bur mable the wiefe of willm peares
JANWARY	30	Was bur Richarde cooke
FABRUARY	9	Was bur John the wiefe of willm grene
MARCH	19	Was bur Cristablee the wief of Robart todd
1583		
APRILL	12	Was bur george the sone of Anthonye futhergill
JUNE	23	Was bur xpor gouldington
NOUEMB[r]	17	Was bur mergarit the laite wife Alixander crosbi
DECEMB[r]	10	Was bur Agness lait wife of Thomas sawer
JANWARYE	20	Was bur Simond Taylor
FABRUARE	7	Was bur John the sone of Joan perking
MARCH	5	Was bur Elizabeth the laite wife of gyles cooke of locholm

1584 BURIALLES 1584

MAYE	4	Was buriede A pore weoma
MAYE	9	Was bur peter grene Sone of willm grene
JUNE	19	Was bur Richard fawcit
JUNE	30	Was bur Richard sone of John Robinson
JULY	17	Was bur Vswold futhergill
SEPTEB[r]	26	Was bur margarit the wife of Reynold futhergill
NOUEB[r]	30	Was bur Thomas ffawcitt
JANWARY	5	Was bur Joane Lait wif of James futhergill
JANWARY	22	Was bur Joane winter a poore weoma
NOUEBER	28	Was bur Jhon the sone of Richard futhergill
1585		
MAYE	27	Was bur margarit lait wief of James fawcit
OCTOBE[r]	1	Was bur Izablee the doughter of Jhon Robinsone
OCTOB[r]	18	Was bur Reynold the sone of Jhon pkyne
OCTOB	29	Was bur mare the doughter of John Birket
NOUEMB[r]	2	Was bur Sarah the doughter of gyles taylor
DECEMB[r]	18	Was bur willm grene
DECEMB[r]	26	Was bur Izablee daught[r] of gyles hawle
JANWARY	10	Was bur Stephaine busfeld
JANWARY	15	Was bur george Sone to Henerye Dentt
JANWARY	31	Was bur Edmonde fawcit
FABRUARY	24	Was bur Joan the wief of Thomas wilkynson
FABRUARY	26	Was bur margarit lait wiefe of Richard adath
MARCH	11	Was bur Edward grene
1586		
APRILL	20	Was bur Elizabeth the lait wife of John hedger
MAYE	17	Was bur Izable laite wife of James paycok
MAYE	29	Was bur george wilkinsone
JULYE	5	Was bur Lenoard Chamberline
JULY	17	Was bur Vincent cooke
FABRUA	11	Was bur hewge wilkinsone
MARCHE	21	Was bur Izable the lait doughter of Jaes taylor
1587		
MARCH	31	Was bur John futhergill
APRILL	4	Was bur mable the Doughter of Richard futher
APRILL	14	Was bur Izable the lait wife of John shearma
APRILL	28	Was bur Sible the lait wife of *
MAYE	13	Was bur mable the laite wife of oliuer whithead
JUNE	14	Was bur Cristable lait wief of Roulad Det
JUNE	14	Was bur Sible the laite doughter of Roland pacoke

* Left blank.

BURIALLES

JUNE	20	Was buried Anthonye Shawe
JUNE	20	Was bur. mergarit the wife of Jhon shawe
AGUST	4	Was bur An the doughter of willm Cooke
AGUST	5	Was bur henerye Shawe
AGUST	29	Was bur Alic the lait wife of george sumkin
SEPTEBAR	2	Was bur helyn the doughter of Robart fawcitt
SEPTEBAR	5	Was bur Joan the wife of John foirbys
SEPTEBAR	25	Waa bur Jhone Chapplelowe
SEPTEBAR	26	Was bur Ceceilbad yey[r] Lannc beyle doughter
OCTOBER	22	Was bur Joane the laite wief of James swinbank
OCTOBER	23	Was bur Izable Sponer a poore woman
OCTOBER	25	Was bur Cristable lait wife of Lanc boulyey
OCTOBER	26	Was bur henerye the sone of John Vbanke
NOUEMR[r]	1	Was bur Edward fawcitt
NOUEMBER	8	Was bur Em th laite wiefe of Cuthbert fawcit
NOUEMBER	16	Was buried Ezabeth lait wife of John raykestraw
NOUEMBR	19	Was bur Izable lait wife of Stephen Dent
NOUEMBER	26	Was bur margarit the wiefe of ovswould futhergill
NOUEMBER	30	Was bur Robert the sone of michell newton
DECEMBER	25	Was bur Joan the wief of Jhon bland
JANWARYE	2	Was bur James bell
JANWARYE	4	Was bur Richard the sone of gyles pkine
JANWARYE	24	Was bur angess tomson seruant to John Robinson
JANWARYE	26	Was bur margarit the wife of Richard bell
JANWARYE	28	Was bur Izable murthwait
JANWARYE	30	Was bur Richard habletwhait
FABRUARY	13	Was bur willm smartte
FABRUARY	16	Was bur Thomas futhergill
FABRUARY	18	Was bur margarit the wief of Rouland holme
FABRUARY	28	Was bur marye the doughter of stephen Dent
MARCH	4	Was bur Lenard winne
1588		
MARCH	27	Was bur Robarte the sone of willm adamtwhait
APRILL	13	Was bur agness doughter of gyles hawle
APRILL	24	Was bur Cristable the doughter of xpor busfeld
MAYE	27	Was bur John murthwait
MAYE	30	Was bur Elizabeth the lait wife of willm stones
MAYE	30	Was bur george the sone Raphe milner
JUNE	8	Was bur Jenat the lait wife of Thomas futher
JUNE	10	Was bureid John the Son of george haulle
JUNE	21	Was bur Cristable te wife of willm Richard son

1588		BURYALLES 1588
June	24	Was buried Alice the lait wief of willm fawcitt
July	15	Was bur Stephen Robinsone
Septeber	14	Was bur. John grene
October	21	Was bur mable the wife of myles futhergill
October	22	Was bur mable the wife of henery fawcit
October	27	Was bur Izable the wife of Thomas murthwait
Noueber	15	Was bur Izable the doughter of Thomas fawcitte
Noueber	25	Was bur mergarit the wife of Adam fawcitte
Deceber	8	Was bur Richard taylor
Decebar	10	Was bur Izable the wife of willm Smart
Janwary	27	Was bur Agness todd
Fabruary	14	Was bur Anthonye the Sone of James tailor
1589		
Marche	28	Was bur an the doughter of bertholomewe bouell
Aprill	23	Was bur Izable the wife of John handley
Maye	9	Was bur mergarit taffyne wh Dwelt at cadbecke
Agust	21	Was bur mr Huntur
October	29	Was bur John son to John handley
Noueber	10	Was bur mergarit vxor Lanc pinder
Deceber	3	Was bur Richard son to Robart Rogerson
Deceber	5	Was bur Elin vxor Roger fawcit
Deceber	6	Was bur Elizabeth wharton doughter to Richard
Jenwary	2	Was bur An the doughter to Reynould ffothergill
Jenwary	10	Was bur John hayswytle
Jenwary	11	Was bur Vincent son to Richard fothergill
Jenwary	28	Was bur Ane layte wife to gilbert pkinge
Jenwarye	29	Was bur willm son of Richard grene
Fabru	3	Was bur Richard ffuthergill
Fabrua	18	Was bur margarett vxor Richard taylor
March	15	Was bur Adam shaw
March	15	Was bur Elin the wife of maythew paycoke
1590		
March	28	Was bur Lanc taylor
Aprill	15	Was bur John the son to Richard holme
Aprill	3	Was buri John hartlaye
Aprill	30	Was bur Lenard the son of Thomas grene
Maye	30	Was bur myles ffothergill
June	5	Was bur margaritt ffothergill vxor Roger fothergill
June	12	Was bur Thomas wilkinson
June	15	Was bur xpor son of willm cleasbye
Septebr	3	Was bur gyles ffothergill
	3	Was bur Raynold Cowp
Septem	18	Was bur margaritt the doughter of James taylor
Noue	25	Was bur Janatt the doughter of hew shaw
Decemb	2	Was bur mawbe the doughter to Anthony fawcitt
Jennar	12	Was bur John Robinsone

BURIALLES 1590

JANWARY	13	Was buried An the wife of Robert gowldington
JANWARY	28	Was bur John Shaw
MARCH	18	Was bur george son willm Holland
MARCH	24	Was bur John smethsone
MARCH	28	Was bur John ffawcitte
APRILL	18	Was bur mable the doughter of anthonye taylor
APRILL	21	Was bur Elin the doughter to John hayswytle
JUNE	2	Was bur sebell vxo^r Edward pinder
JULYE	13	Was bur Eling vxo^r Thomas Rogerson
AGUST	2	Was bur henerye son to Richard busfeld
SEPTEBER	10	Was bur margarett vxo^r henery handley
SEPTEBER	12	Was bur uxo^r Thomas gowldington
SEPTEBER	14	Was bur Robart adamthwait
NOUEBER	17	Was bur Anthony futhergill
DECEBER	20	Was bur sebell vxo^r Rainold ffawcyt
DECEMB^r	24	Was bur margarit vxo^r xpor Robinson
FABRUARY	6	Was bur mathew sawer
MARCH	14	Was bur Elizabeth paicoke
MARCH	5	Was bur Robart todd
APPRELL	1	Was bur Essaybell Robinson
APRELL	3	Was bur John son to Richard wilson
1592		
APRILL	7	Was bur henerye shaw
APRILL	7	Was bur mergaritt layte wyfe to John Chamberlin
APRILL	15	Was bur Annis grene
	11	Was bur margarett barnes
MAYE	15	Was bur vxor Rouland paycok
JUNE	14	Was bur vxor willm Robinson
JULI		Elizabeth tebye
AYGUST	8	Was bur James ffawcitt
SEPTEBER	11	Was bur Dorryty todd
SEPTEB^r	28	Was bur Grac vxor Stephn futhergill
OCTOBER	14	Was bur Richard ffawcitt
NOUEMB^r	26	Was bur John ffuthergill
JANWARY	15	Was bur gilbert ffawcitt and John fawcit twenes and Em Sponer
MARCH	14	Was bur george Collinson and John colinson
1593		
MAYE	26	Was bur willm wharton
JUNE	22	Was bur margrett heblethat
SEPTEB^r	1	Was bur Ann ffawcyth
NOUEMB^r	27	Was bur Ellin Rogerson
NOUEMB^r	30	Was bur Peter futhergill
DECEMB^r	22	Was bur Anne vxor Cuthbert futhergill
JANWARY	10	Was bur Jannat xpor busfeld
FABRUAR	24	Was bur Anns vxor hew shaw
		Was bur John busfeld who was drowned

1594 BURYALLES 1593 ⋮ 1594

MARCH 4 Was buried Elizabeth adamthwait

1594

APRILL 16 Was bur. Reynold todd
APRILL 26 Was bur. Richard sonn to Thomas ffawcitt
AGUST 15 Was bur Cattran Cooke
24 Was bur Janatt hablethwat
SEPTEBER 15 Was bur. Stephen ffawcyth
OCTOBER 16 Was bur. Alic Shaw Doughter to henerye shaw
the same day Robartt wittons
NOUEBER 11 Was bur: Janat uxor george Dent
JANWARYE 8 Was bur margarit vxor John ffawcitt
JANWARYE 26 Was bur Ellin vxor Jhon adamthwait
FABRUARY 11 Was bur henery handley son to Robart handley
MARCH 24 Was bur myles hollme

1595

MAY 16 Was bur Janatt doughter to Robert hntur
MAY 17 Was bur mathew murthwat
JULY 5 Was bur Essabell grene doughter to edward
JULY 11 Was bur Robart ffawcytt and alies borrad of sedber
JULY 17 Was bur margaret doughter to James ffawcitt
AGUST 9 Was bur An the doughter to george ffothergill
AGUST 14 Was bur Essaybell the wyff of Roobart grene
SEPTEBER 6 Was bur margarit wife of xpor hawle
OCTOBAR 24 Was bur george heblethwait
OCTOBAR 31 Was bur willm peares and essaybell grene
NOVEBER 6 Was bur Roger fothergill
18 Was bur mathew murthat
26 Was bur myles futhergill
DECEBr 25 Was bur annas pkin
JANWAR 4 Was bur Vincent Coatley
MARCH 6 Was bur willm precat and Richard futhergill

1596

MARCH 20 Was bur xpor Robinson
JUNE 9 Was bur george hawle
JULI 1 Was bur henerye murthwait
8 Was bur Jon son to Lanc townson
AWGUST 3 Was bur Elizabeth doughter to Jahn bouell
4 Was bur the wif of michell murthwait
OCTOBER 3 Was bur Rowland Dentt
NOUEBER 8 Was bur Alice todd doughter of John todd
12 Was bur annas precat vxor John precat
20 Was bur John ward
DECEBER 6 Was bur Alic vxr ffawcyt
18 Was bur Sebell vxr James Dentt
JANWARY 10 Was bur Richard Todd
28 Was bur margaret vxor Vincentt Dentt

BURIALLES 1597

FABRU 17 Was buried vxer gilbartt fothergill
26 Was bur. Janatt peares
MARCH 11 Was bur. uxor John fothergill
1597 26 Was bur An dowghter to Robartt ffothergill
28 Was bur. Sonne to Thomas walkar
APRELL 4 Was bur. John Robinson the same day Jhon fawcyt
5 Was bur. Essabell vxor John hawle
7 Was bur. Essabell Richarde Cooke
8 Was bur. xpor ffothergill
25 Was bur. margaritt vxr willm ffawcitt
MAIE 1 Was bur Barttle Bouell Sonne to Richard
17 Was bur Stephen ffothergill
28 Was bur. Janat vxor xpor Busfeld
JUNE 2 Was bur. Richard todd
JULY 4 Was bur. peter ffainton
13 Was bur. george murthwat
AGUST 10 Was bur. edward son to lance shaw
SEPTEBr 8 Was bur. edward sonn to Lance shaw
17 Was bur John heblethwat
28 Was bur. maryon heblethwat
NOUEBr 8 Was bur. sebell ffawcit
17 Was bur. John heblethwat
28 Was bur. maryen heblethwat
NOUEBr 8 Was bur. sebell ffawcit
17 Was bur. Jannat vxer myles ffothergill
DECEBr 9 Was bur. Essabell todd
12 Was bur. henerye handley
28 Was bur. essaybell vxr Anthony ffawcyt
JANW 4 Was bur. Jhon Coatley
10 Was bur. Anthonye ffawcit
28 Was bur. xpor peares
FABRUA 7 Was bur. xpobell ffothergill
27 Was bur An vxor Thomas ffawcitt
MARCH 7 Was bur. margaritt Denic
1598
MARC 18 Was bur. Anthony Swinbanke
APRILL 25 Was bur margaritt vxor nicolas ffuthergill
MAY 2 Was bur Adam ffawcit
12 Was bur. margaritt heblethwait
JUNE 7 Was bur. Thomas peares
JUNE 28 Was bur. annas vxor xpor ffothergill
NOUEBEr 22 Was bur. mergarett vxor Richard murthwait
DECEMB 2 Was bur. Thomas Richardson
19 Was bur. mergerye vxor Anthony wharton
26 Was bur. James taylor
JANARY 7 Was bur. xpor Rogeson
9 Was bur Janat vxor Thomas Robinson

1598		BURYALLS
ffAYB^{r}EWARYE	8	Was buryed margarett huntta^{r} dawghter to willm huntar.
	19	Was buryed Janatt vx^{r} Steven Swinbanke
	23	Was buryed Ann dawghter to Anthonye Wharton
	28	Was buryed maythew Bell sonn of Jenkin bell
MARCH	4	Was buryed Steven Swinbanke
APPRELL	4	Was buryed vx^{r} John wildon
An^{o} Dni 1599	20	Was buryed Elizabeth daughter to Robartt Wilkinson
MAY	24	Was buryed Janatt peares
JULL	18	Was buryed Ann hunttar dawghter to edward and Richard pindar sonn to edward pindar
JULY	29	Was buryed John sonn to Richard Tayler
AWGUST	26	Was buryed Esabell Bovell
SEPTEMBER	15	Was buryed Thomas sonn to willm ffawcitt
OCTOBAR	1	Was buryed essaybell vx^{r} Anthoy pinder
	14	Was buryed vx^{r} Anthoney Wharton
	18	Was buryed myghell Todd
JANWERYE	10	Was buryed sebell hunter
ffAYBREWARYE	14	Was buryed Janatt vx^{r} George Chamberlin
MARCH	21	Was buryed Thomas ffothergill
An^{o} Dni 1600	28	Was buryed John Becke
APRELL	3	Was buryed Alic vx^{r} Lanc Townson George Grene

1600		BURYALES
MAY	18	Was buryed Richarde sonne to Thomas ffawcitt
	20	Was buryed Richarde sonne to Henery ffothergill
	25	Was buryed Ann Dawghter to to Vincent Powsonne
JULY	5	Was buryed Anthony Tayler
eadem		Was buryed vxor Vincentt ffothergill
	9	Was buryed Ellinge vxor Anthony Tayler
	20	Was buryed Christabell Daw ghter to Henery Swinbanke
	21	Was buryed Annas vxor John Walker
	22	Was buryed one childe of Anthony ffothergilles of Brownber
AUGUST	11	Was buried Richarde Gouldingto
SEPTEBER	8	Was buryed John Dentt
OCTOBER	6	Was buryed Stephen Bousfeld who was drowned
NOUEMBER	4	Was buried Willm sonne to Christopher Rogersonne
DECEMBr	6	W'as buried Jannatt holme
eadem di		was buried Anas huatsonne
	18	Was buried Willm Grene
JANWARIE	29	Was buried Ellis vxor Rawffe Andersonne
FABREWARIE	16	Was buried Margaritt Sawre
	19	Was buried Ellinge vxor Mathew Sawre
MARCH	17	Was buried Issabell vxor Roger pinder
		BURIALES 1601
APRELL	2	Was buried John Tayler
	12	Was buried Lannclot Grene
MAY	7	Was buryed Sebell vxr
Ano Dni 1601		Robartt ffothrgill
JUNE	7	Was bu Roger Pinder
JUNE	IX	Was buried a poore man
	XIX	Was buried Margarett daughter to Mathew Paycoke
	24	Was buried John ffawcitt
JULI	2	Was buried Richard sonn to Vincent ffothergill
	28	Was buried Hewe ffainton a poore man
SEPTEBAR	2	Was buried Henery Pinder
OCTOBER	25	Was buried a childe of Rouland Tayler
NOUEMBER	17	Was buried Margarett ffothergill & a childe of John Grenes
DECEBER	9	Was buried Margarett Haule
	23	Was buried Mathew son to George ffawcitt
JANWARY	26	Was buried Essabell vxr wm Huntur
	10	Was buried Mabell Rogersonn
FABRUARY	19	Was b. a childe of Petter Pinders
MARCH	6	Was b. Jane Waller
Ano Dni 1602	10	Was bur Henery Swinbanke
APRELL	5	Was bur Gabrell Holme

1602		BURYALLS
APPRELL	20	Was buryd vx^r xpoffor paycok
MAY	10	Was bur gilbartt ffoth^rgill
	28	Was buryed James baylay
JUNE	4	Was buryd Elizabeth pindar
AWGUST	15	Was bu John ffoth^rgill
	14	Was bu Elizabeth and Annas Adamthwat
SEPTEMBAR	24	Was bury a childe of Robart shaw
OCTOBAR	4	Was buryed vx^r Raynold Tod
	7	Was bu Richard sonn to John ffawcit
	20	Was bur Janatt holme
NOVEMBAR	1	Was buryd hew busfeld
	4	Was bu John ffawcyt
JANEWARY	6	Was Lewes proctor starved in the snow
ffAYBREWARY	2	Was bu margarett ffoth^rgill
MARCH	5	Was buryd margarett Tayler
	10	Was buryed willm bayleff
	12	Was bur Elizabeth pindar
Ano Dni 1603	24	Was buryed John pinder
APRELL	2	Was buryd Raynold swinbank
	25	Was buryed Roger ffawcyt
MAY	10	Was bury Elizabeth ffoth^rgill
	12	Was bury Alic vx^r John ffawcyth
	13	Was buryed george dent
	21	Was buryd margaret vx^r Lanc paycok
	28	Was buryed John busfeld
NOVEMBAR	12	Was bury Essaybell vx^r George Ewbanke
	19	Was bury Elizabeth barne
DECEMBAR	17	Was burryed xpoffor bell
	31	Was bur Elizabeth dawghter to John Adamthwat
ffAYBREWARY	11	Was buryed Alic vx^r willm holme
MARCH	8	Was buryed w^m son to georg ffoth^rgill
Ano Dni	14	Was buryed herry garethwat
1604 MAY	9	Was buryed Janat grene

1604		BURYALLS
JUNE	16	Was Buryed Ellic payCoke
	25	Was bury Essaybell vx^r Richard ffawcyth
	18	Was buryed xpoffor ffawcyth
JULII	28	Was bu Richard Bovell
AWG	7	Was buryed John ffothergill
SEPT	19	Was bured Richard ffothergill
	23	Was bu willm sonn to willm niColson
OCTOBAR	15	Was bu Thomas sonn to Thomas ffawcyth
NOVEB^r	4	Was buryd Elizabeth vx^r Edward hunttar
	28	Was buryed vx^r Lanard grene who was of aydge 100 yeares
DECEMB	3	Was bury mabell vx^r herry dentt
JANEWA^r	13	Was bury margaret vx^r hew shaw
ffAYB^rEW	20	Was buryed vx^r Lance murthwat
	26	Was bu^r Elizabeth dawghter to Rawfe Awd^rson
MARCH	9	Was buryd Janat Ward a poore woman
1605		
MAY	8	Was buryd John dawghte^r to John Todd
	14	Was buryed Janatt Adamthwat
JUNE	4	Was buryed Elizabeth Pindar
	27	Was buryed myghell shaw
JULI	22	Was buryed Richard ffoth^rgill
SEPT	27	Was bured Ellin vx^r Rowland Tayler
OCTOBA^r	12	Was buryed Janatt vx^r miles ffoth^rgill
NOVEM	8	Was buryd nicolas foth^rgill
	2	Vx^r giles perkin buryed
JANEW	1	Was buryed Ann ffothergill
	11	Was bueryd Rainold dentt
	18	Was buryed giles perkin
	25	Was buryd Lanc ffawcyth
	30	Was buryed Ann vx^r Richard pindar
ffABREW	1	Was buryed margarett ffoth^rgill Rff *
	5	Was buryed vx^r Lanc Shaw m *
	18	Was buryed xpoffor A *
	20	Was buryed Richard *
MARCH	4	Was buryed Maythe *
	14	
APPRELL		Ano/Dni/1606 was burye *
	20	Was buryed vx^r John *

* Rest of page gone.

Ano. Dni 1606		BURYALLS
MAY	24	Was buryed vx^r^ Edward dentt
JUNE	12	Was Ann vx^r^ Richard pindar
JULLII	6	Was buryd Annas Tayler
	16	Was bured Oswold dentt
	25	Was buryed x^r^ John grene
AWGUST	2	Was bured Richard Wharton
SEPTEM	26	Was vx^r^ John Adamthwat
NOVEM	3	Was buryed Janatt Robinson
	9	Was bured Ellin Waller
DECEM	19	Was bured a child oft John hewattson
ffAYBRRW	24	Was bured John sonn to steven dentt
An^o^ Dni APPRELL		
1607	24	Was buryed vx^r^ miles holme
	28	Was buryed Elizabeth Shaw
MAY	21	Was buryed John busfelde
JUNE	11	Was buryed Richard paycok
	28	Was buryed xpofor Rog^r^son
JULLY	1	Was buryed John Shaw son to Thomas
	2	Was buryed Maybell handlay vx^r^ John
	5	Was buryed Thomas ffoth^r^gill
	14	Was buryed Thomas hunttar son to
	16	Was buryed Jeffarray orwaine
AWGUST	7	Was buryed Janatt vx^r^ John Robinson
	15	Was buryed Issaybell vx^r^ w^m^ ffoth^r^gill
		26 Was buryed marye dawghter to giles Swinbanke
	30	Was buryed margarett vx^r^ VinCentt Coatlay off newbygin
		the same day was buryed John Robinson
SEPTEM	7	Was buryed Ellin Todd of Ristnedall towne
	10	Was buryed John dawght^r^ to steven Busfeld off Welsdall
		* Was buryed maybell vx^r^ Rainold Todd
		* Child off Anthonye grene
		* as buryed Anthonye ffawcyt devingill
		* as buryed Elin dentt daw to h dent
		* as buryed John ffawcyt
		* as buryed vx^r^ Roge^r^ wharton

* Rest of page gone.

BURYALLS

Janewary	1	Was buryed Rainold ffawcyt
	12	Was buryed Bartle bovell
	11	Was buryed John bovell
ffaybrew ary	4	Was buryed Richard pindar
	7	Was buryed Ellic Tayler
March	14	Was buryed John handlay
1608	29	Was buryed Edward ffawcyth
Aprell	2	Was buryed John hawle
	4	Was buryed Robartt grene
	9	Was bury Ann ffothrgill
	16	Was buryed John pkin
	17	Was buryed Thomas Rogerson
	30	Was buryed margarytt Todd
May	29	Was buryed Annas Bell daw to Rich
	31	Was buryed Elizabeth ffawcyt vxr Thomas
June	7	Was buryed Margarit dawghtr to Robart wilkinsonn
	14	Was buryed Caytheran Wharton vxr herry
	23	Was buryed Issaybell vxr pettar fainton
	29	Was buryed herry berttwell
Juli	10	Was buryed willm ffawcyth sonn to Thomas
Awgust	24	Was buryed Ann ffawcyt daw to geor
Septem	15	Was buryed vxr george ffothrgill of tarnhow
Novem	21	Was buryed vxr Rawff Shaw
Decem	18	Was buryed vxr xpofor Rogerson
Janewary	14	Was buryed vxr Roger Shaw Ann
	18	Was buryed hew shaw of Asfell
	31	Was buryed vxr Thomas murthwat
ffaybrew arye	23	Was buryed Richard murthwat
		Awgust 18 was bewryed vxr John ewbanke
Ano/Dni/ 1609		Decembar 22 was bew Abram dentt
		26 Was bewryd a child off James ward
Janewary	4	A Child off Willm grenes foggagill
	12	Was bewryed vxr willm dentt

1609		BURYALLS 1609
ffAYBREwARY	24	Was buryed Ellin parkin daw to Raynold
MARCH	7	Was buryed a child off John hegdayll
1610		Ano/Dni/ 1610
MAYE		MAY 25 Was buryed a child off Roger shawes
JUNE	10	Was bury vxr Lanc grene stoneaskew
JULLII	1	Was buryed Robartt ffawcyth
SEPTEM BAR	23	Was bury marye proctar
	15	Was buryed Robartt hawll
OCTOBAR	2	Was buryd a child Edward ffawcyth
NOVEMBr	15	Was buryed John Robinson brackinbar
	22	Was buryed herry shaw
JANEWARY	1	Was buryed vxr John Shaw strett
ffAYBrARY	4	Was buryd xpobell a pore woman
	11	& one Child of Thomas Cheseburgh
	15	Was buryed vxr John ffawcytt murthat
MARCH	17	Was buryed xpobell vxr mathew dent
1611		
APPRELL	10	Was buryed Lanc murthwat
MAY	10	Was buryed John grene
JUNE	8	Was buryed Richard Chambarlin
JULI	18	Was buryed vxr george heblethat
	28	Was buryed a child off Rawff Shaw
AWGUST	13	Was buryed vxr John ffothrgill
	20	Was buryed Issaybell grene
DECEM	24	Was buryed giles pkin
JANEWARY	2	Was buryed John Adamthat
	19	Was was buryd vxr John gegdayll
	25	Was buryed a child of vincent ffothrgill
ffAYBREW	13	Was buryed James ffawcyt
MARCH	5	Was buryed Thomas hayswytle
	20	Was buryed xpoffor busfeld
APRELL	5	Was buryed willm nelson
1612		
MAY	4	Was buryed vxr Anthony ffothrgill
	16	Was buryed Lanc pacok
JUNE	4	Was buryed Sebell paycok
	14	Was buryed herry ffothrgill
	18	Was buryed xpoffor busfeld

BURYALLS

AWGUST	3	Was buryed a child off John hewatson
	16	Was buryed vx^{r} myles paycok
	16	Was buryed Thomas ffawcyt drowned
SEPT	14	Was bewryed margaryt ffawcyt xff
OCTOB^{r}	10	Was bewryed xpoffor grame
NOVEM	14	Was buryed Robartt hunttar son to w^{m}
JANEWARY	6	Was bury a Child off a pore man John symson
	15	Was buryed vx^{r} John ffoth^{r}gill
	28	Was buryed Thomas Lowdar
ffAYB^{r}Y	26	Was buryed vx^{r} John pkin
	10	Was buryed herry shaw sonn to John shaw
MARCH	12	Was buryed James medcalff a pore child
1613		MARCH 10 Was buryed Janatt gowldiLton
AP^{r}ELL	28	Was buryed xpoffor paycok
MAY	4	Was buryed vx^{r} pettar pindar *
	11	Was buryed Rainold sonn to georg ffawcyt
	20	Was buryed vx^{r} pettar pindar
	26	Was buryed a Child off pettar pindar
AP^{r}ELL	6	Was buryed John dodsewrth
	26	Was buryed vx^{r} John Todd
MAY	8	Was buryed vx^{r} niColas murthat
	28	Was buryed herry skayff a poore yoth
JUNE	20	Was buryed vx^{r} xpoffor Adamthwat
AWGUST		28 Was buryed VinCentt Tayler
SEPT		8 Was buryed willm chambarlin
	15	Was buryed vx^{r} willm chambarlin
	26	Was buryed vx^{r} gilles hawle
OCTOBAR		4 Was buryed georg chambarlin
		8 Was buryed giles hawle
		And the wyf off Thomas ffoth^{r}gill
NOVEM	6	Was buryed vx^{r} george ffawcyt
DECEM	8	Was buryed willm holme
	18	Was buryed Janat Tompson
		A poore man his wyf
	20	Was buryed vx^{r} Anthony ffoth^{r}gill

* This entry appears to have been crossed out.

1613 BEWRYALLS

DECEMB^r 23 Was buryed A childe off Anthony ffoth^rgill
JANEWARY 6 Was buryed xpobell ffawcyt
28 Was buryed John ewbanke
ffAYBREW 14 Was buryed vx^r John ffawcyt
18 Was buryed vx^r Lanc grene
MARCH 6 Was buryed vx^r giles Tayler
18 Was buryed vx^r Anthony Swinbanke
1614 APRELL 10 Was buryed Janat Richardson
MAY 8 Was buryed vx^r Anthonye dentt
JULI 6 Was buryed John handlay
AWGUST 8 Was buryed herrye ffoth^rgill
OCTOB^r 9 Was buryed Thomas murthwat
15 Was buryed vx^r pettar grene
26 Was buryed Richard Chamb^rlin
NOVEMB^r 20 Was Elizabeth pindar
DECEM 4 Was buryed Richard Wilson
8 Was buryed Rowland ffoth^rgill
16 Was buryed John hayswittle
21 Was buryd Richard bovell
29 Was buryd Ellin busfeld
JANEW ARYE 3 Was buryed myghell waller
12 Was buryed Sebell ffawcyt
24 Was buryed vx^r herry bovell
29 Was buryed John bovell
ffAYB^rARY 9 Was buryed vx^r steven bell
13 Was buryed vx^r John Tayler
18 Was buryed Thomas ffawcyt
1615 28 Was buryed vx^r george shaw
SEPTEM 2 Was bured xpofor hawll & georg dentt
4 Was bured Richard Wilson
25 Was bured Rainold grene
OCTOB^r 9 Was bu vx^r Cuthbartt murthat
NOVEM 2 Was bured elyzabeth handlay
DECEM 9 vx^r Anthony ffoth^rgill
JANEWARY 26 Was bured John ffoth^rgill
ffAYB^rY 8 Was buryed myles busfeld
MARCH 4 Was buryed myles ffoth^rgill
20 Was buryed willm shaw

BEWRYALLS Ano. Dni 1616 March 27.

		Was buryed John Adamthwat
AP^{r}ELL	4	Was buryed pettar powson
	14	Was buryed Richard pindar
MAY	8	Was herrye * pind^{r} buryed
	20	Was bewryed vx^{r} barttle bovell
JUN	20	Was bur vx^{r} willm hunttar
JULI	4	Was bu vx^{r} John hayswyttle
	19	Was bured mayry hegdall
SEPT	28	Was bured vx^{r} John Todd
OCTOB^{r}	8	Was bured vx^{r} John bovell
NOVEM	18	Was bured xpofr Todd
DECEMB	6	Was bured xpofr busfeld
	15	Was bured maythew paycok
	18	Was bured margaryt Willson
MARCH	22	Was bured willm hunttar
1617	28	Was bured Janatt Taylor
APRELL	4	Was bured vx^{r} Jenkin bell
MAY	28	Was bewred maythew dentt
	29	Was buryed John Adamthat
OCTOBAR	4	Was bu Thomas horne
NOVEM	10	Was bur steven Robinson
25		Was buryed Robartt sonn to Lanc shaw
8	8	Was buryed maybell gowldinton
DECEM	6	Was buryed Rainold ffawcyt
JANEW ARY	16	Was bur Robartt shaw
	28	Was bur John ffawcyt
	29	Was buryed Richard Robinson
FAYB^{r}Y	6	Was bu Lanc shaw
	14	Was bur Janatt denison
	28	Was bu John Shaw
MARCH	8	Was bu vx^{r} John Chambarlin
ANO 1618	14	Was bu xpobell powlay
MARCH	26	Was bured Issaybell ffothrgill
	28	Was bur Janat Adamthwat
APRELL	4	Was buryed John pkin
	10	Was bur Anthony ffoth^{r}gill
	20	Was buryed vx^{r} Thomas grene and John busfeld
	27	Was bured Oswold Robinson
	28	Was buryed vx^{r} James Tayler
MAY	5	Was vx^{r} Richard ffawcyt buryd
	10	Was bur Richard busfeld
	25	Was bur Rainold Todd
JUNE	2	Was buryed Rich^{r}d Wilson and giles pkin
	10	Was buryed vx^{r} John Coatlay
AWGUST	26	Was buryed Olever paycok

* Symond crossed out.

BURYALLS 1618

SEPTM	26	Was buryed vx[r] Thomas ffawcyt
	28	Was buryed steven sonn to willm ffawcyt
OCTOBAR	2	Was bewryed steven ffawcyth
	8	Was buryed elizabeth ffawcyt
	16	Was buryed John grene
NOVEMB[r]	17	Was buryed vx[r] Symond busfell
DECEMB[r]	10	Was buryed John Adamthwat
	18	Was buryed vx[r] maythew paycok
JANEWARY	19	Was buryed Robartt Rogerson
ffAYB[r]EW	12	Was bewryed Robartt shaw
	25	Was buryed John Adamthwat eldest
Ano 1619	27	Was buryed James ffawcyt
APRELL	10	Was buryed John grene
MAY	6	Was buryed Jane bell
JUNE	13	Was buryed margaritt vx[r] steven pindr
AWGUST	8	Was bu Ambrose ffawcyt
	27	Was bu margarit ffawcyt
SEPT	9	Was bur Thomas Adamthwat
OCTOB[r]	10	Was bured Annas handlay
	14	Was bu xpobell shaw
DECEMB[r]	4	Was bu mayry handlay
	26	Was vx[r] Lanc Towneson
	28	Was buryd Richard bell
		a child off georg ewbanke
JANEWARY	14	Was myghell turnar
	22	Was bu Cuthbartt ffawcyt
ffAYB[r]Y	8	Was buryed myles ffoth[r]gill
Ano 1620	18	Was bured Janatt Robinson
APRELL	12	Was bured Janat hawle
	25	Was bu Elin ffawcyth
	29	Was buryd Richard ffoth[r]gill
MAY	10	Was bured Sebell Adamthwat
	14	Was buryed Rowland Adamthat
AWGUST	13	Was buryed vx[r] willm ffawcyt
SEPTEM	7	Was buryed Jenkin grene
DECEMB[r]	18	Was buryed willm Cook
JANEW[r]Y	17	Was buryed vx[r] John chamb[r]lin
ffAYB[r]	28	Was buryed myghell chambarlin
MARCH	4	Was buryed vx[r] w[m] bovell
1621		APRELL 3 Was buryed miles ffoth[r]gill

1621 BEWRYALLS

MAY	3	Was buryed vx[r] Jenkin ffawcyt and vx[r] olever paycok
	12	Was bur John berkhead
JUNE	10	Was bur Robartt Shaw
JULI	6	Was bured vx[r] John chamb[r]lin
AWGUST	5	Was bur vx[r] maythew busfeld
	6	Was buryed Rowland Adamthwat
	17	Was buryed Richard ffawcyth
SEPT	8	Was bured Alic Towneson
	10	Was bewred vx[r] John Richardson
	14	Was bured Anthonye Robinson
NOVEMB[r]	14	Was bured vx[r] Thomas ffoth[r]gill
	22	Was bured Thomas walkar
	28	Was bur Janatt mayson
	29	Was bured steven bell his son
DECEM	4	Was bured vx[r] VinCentt murthat
	28	Was bured a childe off george chamb[r]lin
JANEWARY	10	Was buryed vx[r] pettar pindar
	15	Was bured Vincentt murthwat
	18	Was bured vx[r] xpoffer powson
	24	Was bured vx[r] steven busfeld

1622 APRELL 23 Ano/Dni/ 1622
Was buryed Issaybell gowldinton
JUNE ffirst Symond busfel bur
2 Was ux[r] steven ffawcyt bur
a Child off John Taylores bur
AWGUST 10 Was herry niColson bur
16 Was bur Janatt Tayler
SEPTEM 16 Was bur vx[r] Robartt Wilkinson
OCTOBAR 28 Was bur herry Adamthat
NOVEMBAR 2 Was bu vx[r] willm grene
5 ellin gibson & maybell handlay
JANEWARY 2 Was bur Thomas denyson
8 Was bur Jenkin bell
13 Was burd Rainold greene
26 Was bur hew hayswyttle
28 Was bured vx[r] Anthony wilson
and tow cheldrin off the sayd Anthony
ffAYBREWARY 1 a child off lanard peares
3 Lanard peares was-buryed
8 Was bured Adam bell
16 Was bured vx[r] Lanc shaw
20 Was buryed ellic ffoth[r]gill
22 Was buryed Thomas ffothe[r]gill

1623 . BURIALLS

MAYE 14 Was Buried William Adamthwait
JUNE 4 Was buried Roger Murthwait
10 Was buried wyfe Robart fawcet
JULY 8 Was buried wyf of mychaell Shaw
13 Was buried wyfe of Edward Adamthwait
24 Was buried Steven Chamberlain
26 Was buried Essabell Sponer
27 Was buried margret Robinson
AGUST 23 Thomas gren buried
29 Was buried Rowland bell
30 Was buried Essabell pears
14 Was buried wyfe henrie Robinson
18 Was buried wyf Robart * Rogerson
SEPTR 3 Was buried William Rogerson
5 Was buried Rychard futhergill brownber
7 Was buried John Walker
10 Was buried Christopher fawcet
13 Was buried John fawcet
15 Was buried Steven futhergill
19 Was buried wyfe Raynold grene
21 Was buried thomas bland
27 Was buried James taylor
29 Was buried wyfe James taylor
OCTOBER 3 Was buried John goldington
7 Was buried georg Shawe
13 Was buried wyfe Christopher powson
17 Was buried wyfe of thomas pears
23 Was buried Robart handlowe
28 Was buried wyfe hew Shawe
NOVEMBR 5 Was buried wyfe John Chamberlain
7 Was buried 2 childer of Edward fawcet
20 Was buried 2 cripls
23 Was buried margret townson
JANNARI 13 Was buried wyfe william Rogerson
15 Was buried ellin handlowe
19 Was buried John Cheesbrough
FEBRUARY 3 Was buried wyfe Anthony Shaw
7 Was buried Raynold futhergill lowcom
8 Was buried Margret fawcet
10 Was buried John todd
13 Was buried wyfe henrie Shaw
18 Was buried R[a]ynold futhergill staneskew
20 Was buried John millner
24 Was buried a pour man
MARCH 1 Was buried ellin pears
3 Was buried wyfe Rychard barlay
1624 3 Was buried ellis futhergill
8 Was buried wyf cuthbart fawcet
APRELL 1 Was buried margret bell
9 Was buried mathew perkin
19 Was buried wyfe thomas fawcet murthwait
MAY 4 Was buried wyfe John fawcet wandilbank
5 Rowland ** dent was buried of nedlhous
8 Was buried Rychard bland
14 Was buried Margret dowghtr of georg fothergil
15 Was buried thomas son wylliam fawcet

* William crossed out "wyf Robart" substituted.
** Maythew crossed out.

1624		
MAY	15	Was buried a pour child was found dead
	19	Was buried the dowghtr of An hewetson
JUNE	16	Was buried An the dowghtr of georg fothergill
	29	Was buried Ezabell the wyfe of John ewbank
JULY	20	Was buried Elizabeth dowghtr of edward fawcet
AGUST	2	Was buried Anthonye pinder eldest
	6	Was buried John futhergill of nedlhouse
SEPTR	11	Was buried wyllyam habelthwait
	25	Was buried marie the dowghter of Gyles haull
OCTOBER	24	Was buried a pour mans wife
DECEMB	29	Was buried the wyfe of John Robinson
JANNARI	1	Was buried the wyfe of henrie garthwait
	3	Was buried John baylie .
	13	Was buried the wyfe wylliam Cooke
FEBRUARI	28	Was buried mychaell futhergill of bowdrdaill
MARCH	23	Was Buried 2 childr of william fawcets
1625		
MAYE	24	Was Buried henrye Robinson eldest
JULY	26	Was Buried Alliss dowghter to Rowland dent
AWGUST	17	Was buried Steven dent
OCTOBR	3	Was buried Rowland Sonn to Rychard taylor
JUN	9	Was buried marye dowghter to Gylles haull
NOVEBR	28	Was buried John ffuthergill son to Raynold futhergill of Ravenstondaill towne
JANUARIE	3	Was buried margret the wyfe of Raynold futhergill of stenerskew
	5	Was buried margret dowghtr to Robart todd
MARCH	14	Was buried Alles wyfe of mychaell Taylore of waingarthes
	15	Was buried Cuthbart Robinson
1626	19	Was buried margret dowghter to John hewetso
APRELL	19	Was buried Anthonye Son to Wylliam fawcet of murthwait
	30	Was buried the wyfe of Vincent powson
MAY	30	Was buried John Sonn to Rychard fawcet of nubegin
JUNE	21	Was buried the wyfe of Raynold parkin and the same day gilbart sonn to Robart fawcet of murthwait
JUNE	25	Was buried thomas son to Rychard fawcet of nubegin

June	29	Was buried Margret dowghter to henrye Cawtle of newbegin
July	4	Was buried Steven son to James fawcet of Ryssendaill towne
	10	Was buried margret Sister to Roger pinder
	23	Was buried Janet wyfe of Rychard bousfell
Agust	13	Was buried Thomas prockter of waingarthes
October	30	Was buried An wyfe of Robart handlowe of welesdaill
Novebr	18	Was buried ellin peares but no church dewtes had
Decebr	18	Was buried mabell the wyfe of Anthony pinder
Jannarie	14	Was buried mabell the dowghter of Anthony pinder
	24	Was buried John linslay
1627		
Aprell	2	Was buried Robart haull of wealsdaill
May	9	Was buried John hegdell of nedles
	17	Was buried henrye handlow of strete
June	1	Was buried George sonn to phillip Bousfell
	23	Was buried John Sonn to Rychard haull
July	17	Was buried the wyfe of mychaell Chamberlin
	19	Was buried the wyfe of William fawcet of brigg
Agust	27	Was buried Ezabell dowghtr to william Clemeson
Septr	28	Was buried Elizabeth Sponner
Novebr	9	Was buried a child of mathew pinders
	27	Was buried Ann dowghter to mychaell haull
Jannari	14	Was buried elizabeth dowghtr to Janet paycok
	16	Was buried An dowghtr to Robart Atkinson
	26	Was buried henry bovill of newbegin
Februari	19	Was buried margret the wyfe of Lanc fawcet
	24	Was buried myles paycok of stanescue
	28	Was buried mabell the wyfe of wylliam Shaw of tarnhous
March	12	Was buried mychaell Simson of the town
1628	27	Was buried margret the wyfe of Abraham Bousphell of Ellergill
Aprell	8	Was buried the wyfe of Rychard Goldington
	24	Was buried Christopher haull
Jun	1	Was buried Thomas Son to Rychard haull

BURIALLES

JULY	2	Was Buried Ezabell dowghter to James Johnson
AGUST	11	Was buried Annes dowghter to Steven fawcet
SEPTR	11	Was buried Ann dowghter to Rowland dent
OCTOBr	14	Was buried Lance Shaw of asfell
NOVEMBR	27	Was buried margret dowghter to Abraham handlowe
DECEMBR	29	Was buried wylliam powson
JANNARI	7	Was buried henrye bland of bowderlayll wathe
FEBRUARI	9	Was buried a pour boy of malastang
	26	Was buried Rychard Skayfe
MARCH	18	Was buried John beck but no deuties paied
1629	27	Was buried a child of William fawcets
	30	Was buried Janet dowghter to Rychard haull
MAY	30	Was buried margret wyfe of Roger baylie
JULY	18	Was buried henry son to John hodgeson
SEPTBr	3	Was buried georg son to John ewbank
	4	Was buried a child of Abraham bousfels
	26	Was buried Janet dowghtr Simod pindr
OCTOBR	10	Was buried a child of a tinklers received 9d.
NOVEMB	25	Was buried Robert Shawe of towne
DECEMBR	15	Was buried ezabell dawghter to phillip bousfeild
FEB	2	Was buried Elles wife to Henery Shaw
	10	Was buried Hewgh sonn to henery shaw
	02	Was buried John son to simond pinder
FEBREW	24	Was buried Richard green of greenside
MARCH	12	Was buried John sonn to michaell murthwait
1630		
	15	Was buried william Cooke
APRILL	23	Was buried ezabell fothergill of brownber
	29	Was buried elsabeth wife to thomas haiswitle
JUNE	12	Was buried Maubell wiff to william ffothergill of Lithside
JULY	9	Was buried sibbell wiffe to John hegdaell
	12	Was buried peter Robinson
SEPT	12	Was buried Ann daughter to Cuthbert hunter
	23	Was buried Ezabell the wiffe of edmond Shaw
OCTOB	18	Was buried Richard Bouell
		Was buried a child of henery Robinsons
NOVEM	21	Was buried the wiffe of thomas Adamthwait
DECEM	15	Was buried Gillbert ffawcet of murthwait
ffEB.	27	Was buried the wife of John fawcet
MARCH	17	Was buried stephen sonn to John pinder
	18	Was buried a sonn of henery whartons of steneska
MAY	27	Was buried Jenet shaw
JULY	4	Was buried Abram Handley
		Was buried doritie fothergill
SEPT	13	Was buried Elles wiffe to Richard powson
OCTOr	28	Was buried Anthony ffothergill of keldhead

Anno dom 1635

	MARCH	9	Was buried John Vbank
	MARCH	10	Was buried Thomas ffawcet
1636	MARCH	14	Was buried stephen Bell
	MARCH	19	Was buried Ellen willkinson
	MAY	21	Was buried Christofer ffawcet
1636	APRILL	9	Was buried Peter Powsonn
	APRILL	10	Was buried william ffawcet
	AP	11	Was buried william ffawcet smith
1636	APRILL	26	Was Buryed Jenkine ffawcet
	MAY	6	Was Buryed mathew ffothergill of Brownber
	MAY	13	Was buryed George Vbanke of Boutherdaile
	MAY	26	Was Buried Henery dent
	JUNE	8	Was Buried Thomas ffawcet of strete
	JUNE	18	Was Buried Maubell shawe
	JUNE	23	Was buried a child of Henery Robinsons
	JUNE	26	Was buried Mathew ffawcet
	JUNE	30	Was buried Elles Tayler
	JULY	11	Was buried Vinsent dent
	JULY	20	Was buried mary ffawcet
	JULY	22	Was buried Ealse hebelthat
	JULY	23	Was buried Maud ffawcet
	JULY	26	Was buried William Adamthwait
	AGUST	4	Was buried Elsabeth Brantwait
	AGUST	13	Was buried A Child of Anthony pinders
	AGUST	31	Was buried Cuthbert Rautlife
	SEPT	4	Was buried John wharton
	SEP	5	Was buried Izabell Shawe
	SEP	20	Was buried Ellsabeth pinder
	OCTOB	13	Was buried Anthony wharton
			all a child of Richard Birkets
	NOVEMB the	15	Was buried Heugh shaw
		22	Was buried william ffawcet
	DECEMB^r	2	Was buryed Margratt Todd wife to John Todd
		4	Was buryed Annas ffawcett wife to Geo: ffawcett
		9	Was buryed Issabell Birkbeck
		10	Was buried mathew pinder sonn to John
		15	Was buryed Ellen wife to Anthony pinder
		30	Was buryed * Handlay
	ffEB	22	Was buried vxor of Renold ffothergill
	MARCH	12	Was buried Ezabell ffothergill
1637	APR	24	Was buried Izabell ffawcet
	MAY	2	Was buried Margat ffawcet
	MAY	12	Was buried william ffawcet
	JUNE	13	Was buried Vinson wharton
	JUNE	25	Was buried Jenat Bousfeild
	JULY	11	Was buried Thomas Adamthwait
	JULY	16	Was buried Christofer ffothergill
	JEN	5	Was buried Charles Bousfeild
	JEN	8	Was buried william Gouldinton
	APR		Was buried Hew ffawcet
	APR	7	Was buried Margrat murthatt

* Blank space.

NOTE.—Between this page and the last there is a break of 5 years; a leaf probably has been lost.

Anno dom 1638

APRILL 14 Was buried John shaw
MAY 17 Was buried Ellen futhergill wife to Thom
17 Was buried Mychell Tod
17 Was buried Ann garthat
JUNE 13 Was buried vxor of John Robinson
JUNE 20 Was buried a child of a pore man
Was buried the wife of John Robinson
JULY 16 Was buried Jane dent
JULY 18 Was buried the wife of Henery Cautlay
AGUST 15 Was buried Mary the wife of Thomas Green
03 Was buried Jaymes Powson
SEP 25 Was buried maubell Hunter wife to Robert
26 Was buried Stephn ffothergill
OCTO 22 Was buried Janatt Bovell
25 Was buried a child of william Shaws Lancelott
NOUEM 25 Was buried mary wharton
28 Was buried * the wife of Jaymes ffawcet
DECEM 13 Was buried Annas Bland
DEC 15 Was buried vxor of Jaymes Pearson
JEN 20 Was buried Thomas Haull
23 Was buried George ffothergill
27 Was buried William Cooke
JEN 30 Was buried Georg Murthatt
FEB 2 Was buried william Green
FEB 17 Was buried George Pacok
MARCH 1 Was buried margat Adamthwait
16 Was buried Jenet wife to william adamthat
1639 MAY 9 Was buried Ellen wife to Lanslot green
24 Was buried mary ffawcet daught[r] to stephn
28 Was buried Georg ffawcet of douingill
JUNE 18 Was buried George Green
Was buried a Child of Jererd Ellyetson
25 Was buried Elsabeth willson
29 Was buried Sibbell pinder
JULY 15 Was buried Ellsabeth dent
JULY 24 Was buried Margat shaw wife to Anthony shaw
AGUST 7 Was buried Ellen wife to John Pinder
27 Was buried Agnas wife to Henery wharton
SEP 27 Was buried Henery wharton
SEP 28 Was buried Christofer wharton
OCTO 5 Was buried Richard wharton
26 Was buried Isabell wife to william ffawcet
NOV 1 Was buried John Heutson
28 Was buried Henery ffothergill
29 Was buried John Adamthwait
DEC 12 Was buried Gyles Parkin
14 Was buried Elsabeth daugter to michael Chamberlaine
DEC 27 Was buried dorathy Shawe
JAN 16 Was Buried Lenerd ffothergill
JAN 17 Was buried Ann ffothergill
JAN 22 Was buried Ellen wife to Thom ffawcet of wandall

	JAN	23	Was buried Elles ffuthergill
	FEB	6	Was buried Richard fawcet of wandall
	FEB	16	Was buried Richard wharton
1604	MAY	12	Was buried Heugh son to Robart shaw
			Was buried a child of John pearsons
	JULY	8	Was buried Ezabell denison
	AGUST	19	Was buried Edward Hunter
		24	Was buried Regnold Bell
			Was buried John ffawcet of wandal
	SEPT	18	Was buried mary Allderson
	OCTOB	9	Was buried margat daughter to Richard fothergill
		13	Was buried willam son to Richard fothergill
		18	Was bured Ezabell daugtr to John heutson
	NOVEM	23	Was buried Annas Pinder wif to simond
			Was buried John Handlay
	JANEW	12	Was bewried william elyettson
	JANEW	22	Was buried Annas Johnson
	JAN	27	Was buried An Perkin
	FEB	6	Was buried Gyles Handlay
	MARCH	9	Was buried Annas wife to George Chambrl
	APRIL	10	Was buried Thomas willson son to Richard
1641	MAY	7	W buried Elles denison wife to Thom
		24	Was buried Richard Alldersone
	JUNE	24	Was buried Jaymes ffawcet of tarne
	AGUST	20	Was buried michell Waller
		24	Was buried John ffothergill of chroksbeck
	SEPT	9	Was buried Ann Shaw
	OCTOB	11	Was buried Izabell Haull
		30	Was buried Edward Green
	NOVEM	21	Was buried Richard whithead
	DECEM	23	Was buried Christabell wife to philip grene
	DEC	26	Was buried vxor of Thomas ffawcet of street
	JANEW	4	Was buried Annas wif to Anthony Hegdail
	JAN	10	Was buried Eme birkitt wife to John birkit
	JAN	24	Was buried Agnas green wife to william
	MARCH	2	Was buried margat vxor of Jayms fawcet
		4	Was buried Jayms Pearson
	APRILL	2	Was buried Heugh Shaw of tranow hill
		11	Was buried Ellsabeth Johnson
	MAY	1	Was buried John ffawcet of murthat
	JUNE	3	Was buried Thomas ffawcet of wandaile
		12	Was buried Thomas ffothergill of Croksbeck
	JULY	6	Was buried Thomas Shaw son to John
	SEP	5	Was buried Marye daughter to John Hewtson
		10	Was buried Georg ffawcet
	OCTO	28	Was buried * Townson

* Left blank.

	ffEB	25	Was buried John Shaw
	MARCH	9	Was buried Margat tod
		12	Was buried Henery Gosslen
		24	Was buried stephn ffawcet of bridge as allso Janat Heutson
1643		25	Was buried William Ellyetson
			Was buried Thomas green son to wiliam
			Was buried Nickalas son to William Adamthwait no deus p
	MAY	31	Was buried John wharton
	JUNE	4	Was buried Ann ffawcet daughter to John
	JUNE	13	Was buried Richard bousfeilld and George Bousfeild sons to Phillip B.
		14	Was buried maubell wallker
	JULY	15	Was buried Ann Tod daughter to Robart tod
	SEP	29	Was buried Richard Powson of the mosse
	OCTOBR	26	Was buried a sonn of John Bouells
	NOV	11	Was buried Richard Goosslen
	DEC^{r}	15	Was buried Margatt Chamberlaine
	DEC^{r}	20	Was buried William Clemison
		25	Was buried Robart Shawe of Asfell
	ffEB	13	Was buried Gillbert Bleathorn no dews
		17	Was buried Ellen vxor Jaymes ffawcet of murthat
	ffEB	21	Was buried Rowland Tayler
1644	APRILL	6	Was buried William sonn to John ffawcet of murthat
		14	Was buried John Tod
	MAY	15	Was buried Ann Haiswhitle
			m^{r} tenard Rew(*) Townward
	JUNE	12	Was buried William ffothergill of Lithside
	AGUST	30	Was buried Vimson Powson
	OCTOB	4	Was buried Sary dodsonn
		25	Was buried Robart sonn to Lanclot Hodshon
	NOV	14	Was buried Robart flawcet of tarn hous
	DECR	2	Was buried Thomas Orton
		8	Was buried Peter Pinder
		16	Was buried Maude Powson
	JAN	4	Was buried Vinson ffothergill
		8	Was buried Jannatt Pacoke
		29	Was buried Anthony Robinson
	ffEB	3	Was buried maubell Adamthwait wife to John
	ffEB	4	Was buried margatt daughter to Richard ffothergill
			Was buried a child of Richard Powsons
	MARCH	24	Was buried a sonn of michell murthats
1644 (†)		03	Was buried Christabell murthat
	APRIL	5	Was buried stephn Bousfeild
		11	Was buried John Chamberlaine
		25	Was buried vxor of Anthony wharton
	MAY	7	Was buried vxor Rouland dent
	JUNE	6	Was buried a child of George Chamberlans
		15	Was buried margratt Shawe
	JULY	1	Was buried John son to Robart whitelock
		20	Was buried a daughter of michell murthatt
		30	Was buried Will ffawcet of tarne
	AGUST	5	Was buried the wife of George Green
	AGUST	9	Was buried Jean wife to Abram Handlay
	SEP	10	Was buried Ann wife to Renold ffawcet
		11	Was buried Elsabeth wife to Georg Cham
		18	Was buried Christopher ffawcet
		19	Was buried a child of Jeffray dents
		27	Was buried uxor of Edward pinder
	OCTOB		Was buried Marye Green daught to Tho grene

(*) An after-insertion and very cramped—perhaps Lenard Row
(†) For 1645

	OCTOBER	24	Was buried Issabell Hunter
	DECEM	16	Was buried Agnas denison
	JANEWARY	8	Was buried vxor of John Handley of wesdale
	JANEW	10	Was buried Adam son to John Tayler
		15	Was buried Richard Haull
		16	Was buried George ffawcet of street
	FEBRY	5	Was buried William ffawcet of murthwait
		12	Was buried a child of anthony pinders of crog (*)
	MARCH	19	Was buried Jaine wife to John Tayler
1646	APRILL	11	Was buried vxor of Lanclott Green
	MAY	02	Was buried maubell Adamthwait
		24	Was buried Ellen the wif of Robart Shawe
	JULY	3	Was buried Richard son to Christofer Powson
	AGUST	28	Was buried Henry Vbank
	SEPT	27	Was buried Robart Rodgerson
	DECEM	13	Was buried Anthony Willson
		29	Was buried vxor of Ralph Shaw
	JANEWARY	18	Was buried Richard son to Robart whitlock
		21	Was buried Izabell daughter to Robart Balife
	ffEBR	4	Was buried a Child of michall tods
	MARCH	14	Was buried John sonn to Jaymes ffawcet
1647		15	Was buried Ann tayler
	APRILL	8	Was buried William Adamthwait
		15	Was buried Ellen wife to Phillip Bousfeild
	MAY	8	Was buried mathew pinder
	JUNE	4	Was buried William Chamberlaine
		15	Was buried John Ridden
	JUNE	21	Was buried John huthison
	JULY	14	Was buried John shaw of town
		19	Was buried Thomas Townson son to henry
	AGUST	25	Was buried Heugh ffothergill
	OCTOBER	20	Was buried Renold Parkin
	NOVEMB	24	Was buried Richard ffawcet of Nubigin
	DECEM	29	Was buried Margat baylioy
	JANEW	5	Was buried John son to John Rodgerson
		10	Was buried Robart son to Robart whitlok
		14	Was buried Ann Waller wif to michell
	JANEW	28	Was buried Essabell Pinder
	FEB	16	Was buried Elles Taylor
	MARCH	3	Was buried Margatt ffothergill of brounber
		17	Was buried Joseph son to Richard Willson
1648	MAY	12	Was buried William Hunter
		13	Was buried a child of Henry Wilkinson
	MAY	21	Was buried a child of John ffawcets
	JUNE	26	Was buried Ralfe Shawe
	JULY	3	Was buried william huthison
		6	Was buried (**) Holl
		12	Was buried Thomas Robinson
	SEP	1	Was buried Edward thornbrew a solger
	SEL	12	Was buried wedow hayswitle
	SEP	17	Was buried a child of . . . . (†) ters
		20	Was buried Ann . . . . (†)
	NOVEM	21	Was buried An . . . . (†)

(*) Or Creg.
(**) Blank space.
(†) Portion of page gone.

NOVEM 4 Was buried a child of Edward blands
Was buried Henry fothergil of town
Was buried John bovell
Was buried Margat fothergill wedow of brounber
Was buried Grace ffothergill
DECEM 5 Was buried Thomas Parkin
Was buried Janat Gouldington wife to John Gouldington
Was buried Richard Greene son to willyam greene of caudbeck
Was buried mikill Bower
Was buried essbell greene daughter to Willyam grene of crosbanke these wer buried in NOUEMBER
DECEM 27 | Was buried the wife of John shaw of street unpaid dews
| as also John fothergill son to Thomas
JAN 29 Was buried william Bouell
Was buried a child of william Rodgersons
JAN 8 Was buried Elsabeth Green
JANEW 13 Was buried wedow Close
JANEW 14 Was buried Margat Chamberlaine
JAN 28 Was Buried a child of michaell Chamberlains
ffEB 1 Was Buried willyam son to Richard Rogerson
2 Was Buried Sybbell wife to Thomas Taylor
ffEB 11 Was Buried Elsabeth wife to willyam ffawcett of murthwait
ffEB 12 Was Buried A daughter of John Rogersons of studfold
ffEB 17 Was buried marye daughter to Thomas green
ffEB 18 Was buried George fawcet of murthatt
ffEB 19 Was buried Ann daughter to Anthony pinder
ffEB 24 Was buried Issabell ffothergill
MARCH 1 Was buried Robert son to George ffawcet
MARCH 5 Was buried Elles daught[r] to simond Alderson
MARCH 18 Was buried Ann Bouell
MARCH 22 Was buried a child of Thom Johnsons
APRILL 26 Was buried John scnn to John Laidman
1649 MAY 10 Was buried vxor Jayms ffawcett
11 Was buried michaell Haul
JUNE 30 Was buried William Chamberlaine son to michaell Chamb[r]
JULY 3 Was buried a child of william ffothergill
10 Was buried Christofer parkin
17 Was buried marye Robinson
19 Was buried a child of wedow Ridens
JULYE 24 Was buried Gyles Cooke
27 Was buried Richard son to Henry haull
SEPT 11 Was buried Annas uxor William Green
OCTOB 8 Was buried uxor Thomas ffawcet
NOVEM 25 Was buried Anthony pinder of hill
DECEM 14 Was buried mary daugtr to Anthony ffothergill
26 Was buried Elsabeth ffothergill
JANUARY 16 Was buried Robart Hunter
21 Was buried Cuthbert Hunter
22 Was buried Richard Hunter
24 Was buried Elles wife to Henry Townson
ffEB 11 Was buried stephn Bousfeild
11 as allso Ellen wife to Abram bousfeild
ffEB 23 Was buried margat Robinson
MARCH *.... buried Elsabeth Hunter
*.... buried Robert Green
1650 *...... m[r]ist[r] Corney
APRILL *....... ied Robart son to michael Tod
*....... ed Author son John Bousfeild

* Portion of page gone.

	May	3	Was buried Elles d. . . . to . . . .*
			Was buried elles fo . . . .* gil
		18	Was buried uxor of Robart A *. . . . . .
	June	18	Was buried John Green
	July	30	Was buried Anthony Green of gar . . . *
	Sep	12	Was buried vxor George ffothergill
	Octo	18	Was buried Thomas Robinson
	Sep	25	Was buried Peter Handlay
	Nouem	3	Was Buried Anthony Shawe
			Was buried a child of Christofer wharton
	Decem	31	Was buried will smith of brough
	Jan	15	Was buried Jannett Shaw of towne
	Jan	30	Was buried Margett denisonn
	ffeb	15	Was buried Ellen wife to George Alderson
1651	Aprill	26	Was buried George Townson
			Was buried Thomas murthat
			Was buried A child of Thomas ward
	June	27	Was buried michaell Taylor
			Was buried George Chamberlaine
	Agust	15	Was buried mabbell Branthwaite
	Agust	18	Was buried Issabell Greene
	Sep	1	Was buried a Child of Geo'g Heutsons
		23	Was buried vxor of Richard ffothergill
	Octo	24	Was buried a child of Robart tayler
	Nov		Was buried Thomas ffothergill
	Nov	25	Was buried Richard Branthwait
	Novem	27	Was buried vxor of Richard Tayler
	Dec	9	Was buried Agnas Townson
	Dec'r	27	Was Buried Thomas Dent of ye fells
	Janewary	13	Was buried vxor Henry ffothergill
	Jan	26	Was buried Margat todd of weesdale
	Jan	28	Was buried Margatt Robinson
	ffeb	29	Was buried Esabell ffawcet
	March	3	Was buried Thomas ffawcet of blaflat
1652	Aprill	23	Was buried a sonn to Thom Robinson
	June	2	Was buried Richard Bousfeild
	June	5	Was buried william wharton
			allso a daughter of Henry Robinson
	June	8	Was buried Thomas ffawcet of wandall
	June	13	Was buried Anthony Hegdaile
	June	25	Was buried Vincent dent wife
	Agust	26	Was buried Thomas Cautley
	Octo	6	Was buried vxor of Edward tay . . .*
	Decembr	30	Was buried Henry Bousfeild
	Janewary	1	Was buried Ezabell Green
		20	Was buried John hodshon
	March	25	Was buried Ann shawe
	Aprill	30	Was buried Georg p . . .* kin
	May	8	Was buried Ann baliff

* Illegible.

MAY	14	Was buried John pinder
JULY	4	Was buried Henry Cautlay
SEPTEMB	2	Was buried vxor of Richard fawcet
SEPT	6	Was buried vxor of William Shaw
OCT	2	Was buried vxor of Thomas Parkin
NOVEMB		Was buried Richard ffawcet of sandbed
NOVEMB		Was buried Annas Spooner
JANEW		Was buried Henry ffawcet of wandall
fEB	16	Was buried Janet wife to George handlay
fEB	18	Was buried william Green
MARCH	16	Was buried Else wife to Henry Shawe
MAY	19	Was buried Elles porter
MAY	26	Was buried dority Bouell
JUNE	20	Was buried vxor of John Rodgerson
JULY	9	Was buried Anthony Green
JULY	31	Was bap margat ffothergill
		Was buried Thomas millner
AGUST	13	Was buried William ffothergill
. . . .*	16	Was buried John sonne to Mr. Dodson
. . . .*	30	Was buried John Heutson
DECEMBER	11	Was buried Edward Adamthwait
DEC	14	Was buried George fawcet son to thom
DEC	15	Was buried a child of Richard pouson
JENEWARY	9	Was buried Anthony ffothergill of tranow hill
JENEW	12	Was buried vxor michell Bousfeild
JENEW	29	Was buried margat Cooke
ffEB	24	Was buried vxor of Thomas Green
ffEB	28	Was buried wedow whitehead buried
MARCH	6	Was buried mary daugh[r] to Tho green
APRILL	14	Was buried Thoamas Ellyetson
1655 MAY	16	Was buried Ellen Hutson

* Illegible.

Anno dom 1655

MAY Was buried Ellen Rodgerson
JUNE 9 Was buried Margat pender
JULY 22 Was buried mary pinder
AGUST 2 Was buried margat dent
SEPTEMBR 26 Was buried Elles wife to Tho Atkinso
OCTOBER 9 Was buried ould Elabeth Tayler
DECEMBR 6 Was buried Isabell Bouell
DECEMB 24 Was buried William whitelok and his wife
JANEWARY 1 Was buried vxor of Henry Boufell
JANEW 9 Was buried Michaell Chamberlaine
ffEB 12 Was buried Isabell wife to Lenard Adamthwait
MARCH 1 Was buried Isabell waller
MARCH 13 Was buried Isabell wharton
as allso Elsabeth wife to Georg ffothergill
MARCH 14 Was buried George ffothergill
1656 APRILL 9 Was buried Saraih Tayler
MAY 8 Was buried Isabell Bousfeild
JUNE 8 Was buried John Laidman
JUNE 15 Was buried Richard Pinder
JULY 5 Was buried An wife to William Robinson
14 Was buried a son of Anthones Shaws of stenerka
SEP 3 Was buried Edward Sanderson
JAN 21 Was buried Christofer powson of moss
FEBR 17 Was buried Ellsabeth Huetson wife to John
MARCH 11 Was buried a child of michell ffothergills of loucom
MARCH 14 Was buried Henry Bousfeild of scarsiks
15 Was buried Elen daught. to John ffawcet
22 Was buried Richard wharton
1657 Was buried steuen sonn to John ffawcet
JUNE 4 Was buried marye Haull
AGUST 6 Was buried John Adamthwat
NOVEMBR 7 Was buried Thomas Clemieson of lunns
NOV 15 Was buried John ffawcet of murthwait
NOUEMBR 18 Was buried Michaell prockter
DECEMBR 15 Was buried Michaell murthwait
JAN 6 Was buried vxor of John Bouell
ffEB 11 Was buried Jean shawe
ffEB 12 Was buried A child of Thomas ffothergill
ffEB 19 Was buried a child of John Hegdalls
ffEB 19 as allso a child of Robart ffawcet of tarn
FEB 22 Was buried Thomas Townson
MARCH 2 Was buried Thom burier
MAR 3 Was buried a daughter of George Chamberlain
MARCH 4 Was buried a daughter of Richard tods
MARCH 7 Was buried John shaw of wath
MARCH 11 Was buried Jenat Powson
21 Was buried william whitelock
1658 APRILL 7 Was buried Izabell Vbank
20 Was buried Phillip Green
APRILL 28 Was buried maubell shaw
MAY 1 Was buried Peter pinder
Was buried vxor John pinder

	MAY	15	Was buried Isabell Robinson
	MAY	19	Was buried Grace Cheesbrouh
	JUNE	14	Was buried Elsabeth wife to Henry pinder
	JULY	1	Was buried Ezabell waistall
	AGUST	12	Was buried Abram fothergill
	AGUST	02	Was buried Ellen wife to Robart Handlay
		27	Was buried wedow shawe of stenesca
	SEPTEMB	19	Was buried peter ffawcet
	SEP	20	Was buried Anthony parkin
	SEPT	28	Was buried elsabeth holme
	OCTOBER	1	Was buried Thomas Rigge
	NOUEMBER	3	Was buried Robart ffawcet of marthat
	DECEMB	4	Was buried saraih futhergill
	DEC	6	Was buried John shawe
	DEC	16	Was buried Jennat clemison
	DEC	29	Was buried Renold ffawcet
	FEB	8	Was buried a child of Thom Clemieson
	FEB	11	Was buried Richard son to peter fawcet
	FEB	23	Was buried simond Pinder
	APRILL	3	Was buried Elles ffawcet wedow
1659	APRILL	3	Was buryed Jaymes ffawcet of town
	APRILL	8	Was buried Thomas Willkinson
	MAY	29	Was buried marie wife to Thomas ffothergill
	JUNE	11	Was buried Isabell Bousfeild
	JULY	27	Was buried Marye powson
	AGUST	18	Was buried Henry Townson
	OCTOBER	2	Was buried Charles gibson
	JANEWARY	18	Was buried Ann wife to Peter pinder
	JANEWARY	24	Was buried vxor of Jaymes Millner
	JANEWARY	27	Was buried ellen Townson
	ffEBREWARY	5	Was buried Robart Green
1606	MARCH	1	Was buried Ann Heutson
	MARCH	02	Was buried Ellen prockter
	APRILL	6	Was buried sibbell ffawcet
	APRILL	23	Was buried marye ffothergill
	MAY	1	Was buried Thomas Perkin
	JULY	16	Was buried Richard Rigge
	NOVEMBR		Was buried 2 chilldren of Thom Dennis no dews paid
	NOVEMBER	19	Was buried maubell Robinson
	DECEMB	16	Was buried Thomas Robinson
	JANEWARY	6	Was buried Ann ffothergill
	JANEW	26	Was bured Ann ffawcet
	JAN	28	Was buried Michell ffothergill
	ffEB	13	Was buried Jaymes Millner
	ffEB	15	Was buried Richard ffothergill
	ffEB	23	Was buried Elles ffawcet
1661	MARCH	15	Was bured Thom ffawcet
	MARCH	16	Was buried John elyetson
			Was buried the wife of John ffawcet
	APRELL	2	Was buried Ellen Handlay*

* This entry is taken from page [138].

			1661
	APRILL	7	Was buried A daughter of William whithead
	APRILL	25	Was buried Christofer powson
	MAY	1	Was buried Cuthbert Robinson
	MAY	11	Was buried daughter to anthony shaw barntt
	MAY	17	Was buried an^{n}as daughter to Richard futhergill
	MAY	24	Was buried Elin daughter to abram gouldinton
	MAY	28	Was buried margre^{t} daughter to Thomas denye
	IUNE	23	Was buried Esabell daughter Christopher powson
	AGUST	7	Was buried Isabell denny
	AGUST	22	Was buried Agnas Gouldinton
	SEPT	4	Was buried George dodson
	OCTOBER	1	Was buried Izabell wife to John Neuton
	NOVEMBER	21	Was bured and the money he had 4s. 6d. was spent at his buriall
	DECEMBER	15	Was buried Elen wife to mathew breaks
	DEC^{r}	27	Was buried Thomas sonn to John sponner
	JAN	1	Was buried mary shaw daug to Robart
	JAN	3	Was buried Annas Winn
	ffEB	22	Was buried John son to Phillip bousfell
	MARCH	2	Was bured margat Hunter
	MARCH	3	Was bured vxor of Christofer fawcet
	MARCH	17	Was buried Richard ffawcet
	MARCH	18	Was burid willmam son to Hen^{y} garthat
1662	APRILL	13	Was buried Ezabell murthatt
	MAY	8	Was buried margrett wilkinson
	MAY	14	Was buried Richard ffothergill
	MAY	16	Was buried George Handlay allso a son of Christofer ffawcet oth tarn
	JUNE	29	Was buried Annas Green
	JULY	23	Was buried Thomas dent
	AGUST	8	Was buried Robart ffawcet of greenside
	AGUST	12	Was buried margat millner
	SEPTEMBR	6	Was buried vxor Henry Handlay
	OCTOBER	2	Was buried margat bowlan no dews
	OCTOBER	14	Was buried Henry ffothergill of crooksbeck no dews paid
	OCTOBR	17	Was buried John Rodgerson no dews
	NOVEMBER	8	Was buried Ann pinder no dews for . . . . .*
	NOVEMBER	17	Was buried m^{r} edmond Bra^{n}thwait nor this
	DECEMBER	1	Was buried Isabell parkin no dews p
	DECEBER	12	Was buried John Adamthwait the same day allso vxor of Henry Robinson
	JANEW		Was buried vxor of Anthony moreland
	JAN	31	Was bured Thomas ffawcet of neubigin
	ffEB	5	Was buried Izabell Tomsom
	ffEB	19	Was buried Janatt wife to Vinson Shawe
	MARCH	2	Was buried Gyles dent
	MARCH	10	Was bured Robart pinder
	MARCH	30	Was bured stepn ffawcet
1663	MAY	31	Was buried Ellen wife to stepn fawcet
	JUNE	9	Was buried Ellen Chamberlaine
	JULY	17	Was bured Isabell dent
	AGUST	9	Was buried margat murrthat
	AGUST	20	Was buried Robart willson

* Very indistinct; looks like ringster.

1663

	Sep	13	Was buried Thomas hayton
	Septem	18	Was buried william Tomson
	October	7	Was buried John pearsonn
	October	15	Was buried mairy shaw
	November	1	Was buried william green of crosbank
	Decemb	24	Was buried Jannat ffawcet
	Decem	25	Was buried Thomas spooner
	Janewarie	15	Was buried Christofer ffawcet
	Janewary	27	Was buried Robart sharp
	Jan	31	Was buried Thomas Tayler
1664	ffeb	29	Was buried John Gouldinton son to Richard
	May	8	Was buried william ffothergill of lowcom
	May	12	Was buried Vmp^{h}ery Gibson
	June	1	Was buried margat ffothergill
	June	2	Was buried vxor of Richard haistwitle
	June	28	Was buried Anthony ffothergill
	July	20	Was buried Thomas ffothergill
	July	28	Was buried Izabell Huntar
	Agust	4	Was buried Elsabeth willkinson
	Agust	28	Was buried John Gouldinton
	Agust	28	Was buried vxor of John birkitt
	Agust	29	Was buried a sonn of Anthony ffothergills
	Novembr	21	Was buried Elsabeth ffothergill
	November	26	Was buried a Child of Robart parkin
	Decem	18	Was buried John fawcet of murthat
			Was buried Isabell Robinson
	Janew	4	Was buried Ann Robinson of lunds
	Janew	7	Was buried vxor George Chamberlaine
	Janew	19	Was buried margrat Lawe wif to Henery
	Feb	10	Was buried Thomas Green
	Feb	27	Was buried Janat Robinson
	March	11	Was buried Ann ffothergill
1665		18	Was buried Henry Hesscatt
		19	Was bured Ellsabeth ffawcet
	Aprill	8	Was buried Ellsabeth Taylor wife to Robart
	May	26	Was buried Robart Rodgerson
	May	29	Was buried Elles Birket
			Was buried Robart son to Edward bland
	June	4	Was buried John Clemison
	Novem	6	Was buried Ellsabeth pinder
	Novem	24	Was bur Anthony son to steuen fothergill
	Decemb	6	Was bured Jaymes ffawcet
	Feb	28	Was bured vxor of John Allderson
	March	2	Was buried A sonn of willim shaw
	March	18	Was buried Elles murthat
1666	Aprill	6	Was buried Robart ffothergill
	Aprill	18	Was buried Ann Haistwitle
	July	3	Was buried Gillbert ffawcet
	Agust	5	Was buried Anthony sonn to Anthony ffothergill

			1666
			Was buried John pinder of howceld
			24 of Agust
	September	1	Was buried Janat fawcet
	Sept	4	Was buried A sonn of william gibsons
	September	7	Was buried Phillip Bousfeild
	December	27	Was buried Ellen bland
	ffebrewary	12	Was bured Edward ffawcet
	ffebrewary	18	Was buried A child of simsons maister
	March	11	Was buried John Robinson of dicks
1667	Aprill	2	Was buried Thomas Atkinson
	Aprill	10	Was buried William Robinson
	Aprill	14	Was buried John todd
	May	21	Was buried Ann ffothergill
	June	30	Was buried a poore womon
	July	28	Was buried John Neuton
	July	30	Was Buried Vinson shaw
	November	1	Was Buried Ellen Haull
	Novembr	13	Was buried Peter powson
	December	17	Was buried George Chamberlaine
	December	29	Was buried michell Bousfell
	Janewary	6	Was buried michell Todd of town
	Febrewary	14	Was buried A poor man of banton
1668	March	21	Was buried mary Bouell
	March	25	Was buried wedowe* ward of gars
	May	1	Was buried Ann Adamthwait
	May	4	Was buried Ann Robyson
	June	7	Was buried Isabell Routh
	June	9	Was buried Thomas Nickellson
	June	11	Was buried a child of Richard breaks
	June	26	Was buried Henry ffothergill son to Thomas
	July	4	Was buried A daughter of John birkit
	Agust	3	Was buried Thomas gibson
	October ye 1668	30th	Was Buried widdow wilkinson wife to John wilkinson of Crosbey
	Nouemr	15th	Was Buried Lanclott Shaw sone to wm shawe of Low stenerskew
	Nouemr ye	30th	Was buried Mathew Breaks of Nubegin
	Decembr ye	4th	Was buried A child of Richard Greenes ye Clockmaker
	ffebruary ye	2th	Was buried Marey Robinson of the Dikes
	ffebruary ye	10th	Was buried Richard Todd of weesdaile
	ffebruary ye	16th	Was buried simond Bousfeild of Scarside
	ffebruary	25	Was buryed Jonathan Dodson
	The same day		Margret Robinson widdow of Cuthbert Robinson
	March	5	Was buryed elsabeth servant to An Tod of this towne
	March	8	Was buryed Ann Daughter to James ffawcet of Bleaflat
	March	15	Was Buryed widdow Hall of vldall wife to Rich Hall
	March	19	Was buryed Thomas son to Christopher Alderson of Tiba heads smith
	March	30	Was buryed Henry Shaw of this towne
1669			and same day vxor anthony Robinson of Brownbar

* Transcript gives "Mabell ward widdow"

1669

MARCH 31 Was Buryed Thomas Harrison of Caudbeck
APRILL 4 Was Buryed A poore lasse borne in sedber Noe dues pd
APRILL 6 Was Buryed Agnes late wife of Henry ffothergill of Crooksbeck
MAY 5 Was Buryed George son of John Swainson of wandell
MAY 22 Was Buryed Elsabeth Daughter of Mr Geo: ffothergill Tarnhousse
JUNE 5 Was Buryed Margaret ffawcet of fell end
JUNE 12 Was buryed James Taylor of the wath
And A still borne Child of John pettyes of weesdale
JULY 19 Buryed a servant maid borne at Banton laied* at Newbiggen her Name Margaret wilkinson
AUGUST 3 Was Buried Richard Darby of bridgend
AUGUST 19 Was Buried Symond pinder
SEPTEMBER 8 Was buryed A boy of John Hastwhitles
SEPTEMBER 23 Was Buryed Richard powson of the loning
SEPTEMBER 24 Was buryed a still borne Child of Rowland shearemans
OCTOBER 20 Was Buryed willm willison
NOV 29 Was Buryed Henry Robinson of Newbiggen
DECEMBr 29 Was Buryed Sara Dodson
JANUARY 11 Was Buryed Elsabeth wife of John ffawcet of street
JANURY 18 Was buryed Jane wife to Richard willson
JANUARY 21 Was buryed Elin Shaw of scarsikes
JAN: 25 Was buryed Robt son of Giles Hall
ffEB 4 Was buryed widdow Riddin of low stenerskue
the same day A daughter of Roger metcalfes
ffEB 16 Was buryed Robert son of Tho: symson
ffEB 28 Was Buryed Richard Rogerson of street
1670 APRILL 4 Was Buryed Isabell Riding Daughter of Robt Riddin
APRILL 11 Was buryed John son of Christoper ffawcet of murthat
the same day Agnes Daughter of Hugh Blencarne
APRILL 30 Was Buryed Isabell Johnson of this towne
MARCH 18 Was Buryed James son of Robert ffawcet of street
JUNE 17 Was Buryed Sibbell wiffe of James Hall of wesdaile
JUNE 19 Was Buryed Ellin daughter of Richard Bousfeild
JUNE 25 Was Buryed grace daughter to Richard ffallowfield
JULY 20 Was Buryed Margret wife of Thomas Simpson
AUGUST 24 Was Buryed John Riddin
AUGUST 30 Was Buryed Richard sonne off Henery Hall
AUGUST 31 Was Buryed Ellin wife of James ffawcett
SEPTEMBER 13 Was Buryed Robart Balife
the same day was Buryed Ellin wife to John Tompson
SEPTEMBER 24 Was Buryed Mary daughter to Robart Hunter
the same day was Buryed John son to John Addeson
OCTOBER 16 Was buryed A still borne child of Thomas Robartsons
OCTOBER 26 Was Buryed A traueller which died at William ffawcetts of street his name Hodgson
JANUARY 2 Was Buried Issabell wiffe to Robart Todd
JANUARY 17 Was Buryed Lydea wife to A poore man
JANUARY 19 Was Buryed James Robartson
ffEBRUARY 4 Was Buryed Ann wife to Willm Shaw stenaska
ffEBRUARY 21 Was Buryed willm son to Mrter George ffothergill
MARCH 5 Was Buryed mary wife to Robart Shaw of tranahill
MARCH 6 Was Buryed James ffawcett of murthwaite Senior
MARCH 17 Was buryed Thomas Adamthwaite of Artelgarth
1671 APRILL 10 Was buryed James Peacoke
APRILL 14 Was buryed Thomas ffawcet of hole

* Perhaps lived.

BURYALLES

(Extracted from Transcripts).

	Aprill	22	Was Buryed Richard Taylor
			Allso the same day was Buryed John Haistwitle
	May	16	Was Buryed a Still born child of John Bousfields
	May	23	Was Buryed Margrat wife to Thomas Tompson
	June	17	Was Buryed Henery son to Thomas Hall
	July	16	Was Buryed Thomas Haistwitle
			Also was Buryed the same day Margrat daughter to John ffawcett of Nubegin Junior
	August	18	Was Buryed Edward Whortton
	August	19	Was Buryed Issabell wiffe to Gilbart ffawcett
	Septembr	18	Was Buryed William Hunter wife of Lunds
	September	30	Was Buryed Jennat wife to Richard ffawcett
	October	7	Was Buryed Ellin wife to Thomas ffawcett
	October	28	Was Buryed John ffothergill of stenasca
	October	29	Was Buryed Agnas wife to John Taylor
	October	31	Was Buryed A poore man his name Robart Wilkin
	December	20	Was Buryed John son to John Bousfeild
	December	29	Was Buryed James Robinson of towne end
	January	6	Was Buryed Abraham Handlay of ffell end
	ffebruary	17	Was Buryed Ann wife to Michell Todd
	ffebruary	20	Was Buryed William Shaw of Stenasca
	ffebruary	23	Was Buryed Thomas Greene
	ffebruary	24	Was Buryed Ellice wife to Cirstopher ffawcett
	March	11	Was Buryed John ffawcett of Nubegin
1672	Aprill	10	Was buryed Sarah Shawe of wath
	Aprill	15	Was buryed Thomas Taylor of towne heade
	Aprill	24	Was buryed John Handlay of wesdaile
	June	23	Was buryed a child of Richard ffothergill
	Agust	5	Was buryed John Alderson
	Sep:	16	Was buryed Sarah wife to Robart Shawe of malastange
	Octo:	7	Was buryed Ann Garthat
	Octo:	23	Was buryed Ann wiffe to Thomas Haistwhittle
	Nouem	24	Was buryed ffrancis wiffe to Robert Taylor
	Nouem	28	Was buryed Jennatt wife to Robart Whitelocke
	Jan.	10	Was buryed Richard Wilson
	Jan.	21	Was buryed Thomas ffothergill of brounebar
	Jan	22	Was buryed m[ter] Thomas Dodson
	Jan.	23	Was buryed michell Chamberlaine off nathat
	Jan.	24	Was buryed Ellice ffawcett off murthwaite
	Jan	29	Was buryed Jennat wife to Robart Atkinsson
	ffeb	7	Was buryed Phillip Taylor of murthwaite
	ffeb	10	Was Buryed Margarett wiffe to John ffawcet of murthwaite
	March	2	Was buryed Annas daughter to Cirstopher wharton
1673	Aprill	2	Was buryed Thomas Taylor of Adamthwaite
	Aprill	9	Was buryed Ralph sonne to William Milner
	Aprill	16	Was buryed William Rogerson
	Aprill	20	Was buryed Rouland son to Adam Shawe
	Aprill	21	Was buryed Agnas Whorton

Note.—There is a break in the Register from Aprill 14th, 1671, to April 29th, 1673; a page appears to have been lost as the Transcripts supply in full the missing portion

1673 BURYALLS

APRILL	29	Was buryed margarett wiffe to Richard ffothergill of needlehouse
MAY	17	Was buryed Ellin Shawe of the towne
MAY	22	Was buryed margarett Garthwaite
MAY	23	Was buryed Richard son to John ffawcett of nubegin
JULY	28	Was buryed Annas wife to John Swainson
SEP	3	Was buryed Abigall daughter to Richard Murthwaite
SEP	10	Was buryed George Peears
SEP	22	Was buryed Ann daughter to Robart Shawe
SEP	28	Was buryed Robart Atkisson
OCTOBER	19	Was buryed Peetter son to Isack Handlay
OCTOBER	22	Was buried Issabell wife to William Milner
NOUEMBER	10	Was buryed Margarett Willison
NOUEMBER	17	Was buryed Henry Coupland
DECEMBER	2	Was buryed Thomas sonn to Robart Shawe
		The same day was buryed Robart son to James ffawcett of murthwaite
DECEMBER	4	Was buryed Issabell wiffe to Robart Greene off nethergaithes
DECEMBER	24	Was buryed Richard Birkett
DECEMBER	28	Was buryed John son to John Hewetson of towne
JANUARY	9	Was buryed Peetter Pinder of weesdaile
ffEBRUARY	19	Was buryed Agnas Tompson of towne
ffEBRUARY	26	Was buryed William Shawe of stenaskah
ffEBRUARY	28	Was buryed Robart Whitlocke
MARCH	3	Was buryed Richard son to william ffothergill
MARCH	7	Was buryed Margarett wife of James ffawcet of wraygreene
MARCH	10	Was buryed Jennat wife of Thomas Robinson of nubegin
MARCH	15	Was buried Annas wife to John Pettey of wesdaile
1674 APRILL	6	Was buryed George ffothergill of Lockholme
APRIL	16	Was buryed Henery Lawe of wesdaile
APRIL	27	Was buryed Anthony Robinson off browenbar
MAY	4	Was buryed Issabell ffawcett off murthwaite
MAY	5	Was buryed Richard Haistwhitle of Lowcome
MAY	13	Was buryed Phillipp Adamthwaite of Artelgarth
MAY	19	Was buryed John son to Abraham Gouldington
JUNE	2	Was buryed Stephen ffawcett
JUNE	4	Was buryed Ann dobson and the same day hir grand-Child mary ffawcett was buryed
JUNE	6	Was buryed Bartholamew Scaife
JULY	12	Was buryed Edward Thorneborrow of Clouds
AUGUST	4	Was buryed Mary daughter to Thomas Breakes no dues paied
AUGUST	13	Was buryed mabbell ffothergill
AUGUST	17	Was buryed margaret wife to Robart Handlay
AUGUST	22	Was buryed mabbell Harison
AUGUST	25	Was buryed James son to John ffawcett of nubegin
AUGUST	27	Was buryed Elsabeth wiffe to John Petty elder
AUGUST	30	Was buryed maudlin wiffe to Stephen ffothergill
SEPTEM:	9	Was buryed Phillip son to Stephen Bousfeild of Longill
SEPTEM:	27	Was buryed Ann Shawe of Ellergill
OCTOBER	24	Was buryed Jeffraey son of Adam Shawe of malstang
NOUEM	11	Was buryed Jennat ffawcet of murthwaite
NOUEM	22	Was buryed Sarah wiffe to John Todd of weesdaile
		Was buryed the same day mary daughter to Heugh Blenckarne
DECEM	19	Was buryed Ellice daughter to John ffawcett of street side
DECEM	29	Was buryed James son of George Perkin elder
JANUARY	7	Was buryed Gilbart son to Robart ffawcet of Streete
JANUARY	24	Was buryed Robart ffawcett of malastang
ffEBRUARY	1	Was buryed mary wife to John ffothergill of wath
ffEBRUARY	11	Was buryed A poore man
ffEBRUARY	13	Was buryed margarett daughter to Robart Taylor

BURYALLS 1674

MARCH 9 Was buryed Issabell Adamthwaite of Adamthwaite
MARCH 21 Was buryed william Hunter of bouberheade
Was buryed George Chamberlaine the same day of nathat
1675 APRILL 28 Was buryed Elsabeth wiffe to Jarard Elyetson
MAY 2 Was buryed William son to Willlam Hunter of Lunns
MAY 4 Was buried Thomas Breakes
MAY 15 Was buryed Jarred Elyetson
MAY 16 Was buryed Jon Hewetson of touneheade
JULY 3 Was buryed Ealsse Rogerson
AUGUST 23 Was buryed John ffothergill of brounbar
SEPT 16 Was buryed Lanclot Peacocke
SEPT 25 Was buryed Issabell daughter to John Robinson of nubegin
SEPT 28 Was buryed Annas wife of Michell Hall
Was buryed the same day George Perkin
NOUEM: 7 Was buryed a child of John ffawcetts shoemaker unbaptized
NOUEM: 21 Was buryed margarett Hewetson
DECEM: 5 Was buryed mabbell wife to humpray Gibson
DECEM: 10 Was buryed Gyles ffothergill
JANUARY 20 Was buryed Elsabeth daughter to George Clemison
ffEB 1 Was buryed Henery ffothergill of Lockholme the
same day was buryed vincon son to Richard Shawe of streete
ffEB 18 Was buryed Annas daughter to John Birckct
MARCH 4 Was buryed John Taylor of garthes
MARCH 6 Was buryed Jane Chamberlaine of nathat
MARCH 8 Was buryed Sarah daughter to John Robinson of nubegin
MARCH 14 Was buryed Phillip Greene
1676 APRILL 27 Was buryed a child of A poore womans no dues paied
MAY 12 Was buryed A still borne of John ffawcets shomaker
MAY 16 Was buryed Issabell wife to George Clemyson
MAY 24 Was Buried m^rtris^ mary wife to m^rter^ Thomas dodson
JUNE 24 Was buryed Ellin* Chamberlaine
JULY 23 Was buryed Elsabeth wife to John Blackbourne
AUGUST 5 Was buryed Issabell daughter to John ffawcett
AUGUST 6 Was buryed mary wife to John ffawcett shoemaker
AUGUST 28 Was buryed Richard Robinson of nubegin
OCTOBER 1 Was buryed John ffawcett off Tarne
OCTOBER 11 Was buryed James ffawcett of nubegin
OCTOBER 30 Was buryed A still borne child of Richard Robinsons of blaflat
NOUEMBER 19 Was buryed m^rtris^ ffothergill† of Tarne housse
Was buryed the same day margarett daughter
To Richard Shawe of streete side
DECEMBER 13 Was buryed margarey Alderson of needlhouse
DECEMBER 23 Was buryed margarat Powson of dubbs
JANUARY 23 Was buryed James dent
ffEBRUARY 21 Was buryed margarett Greene of wainegarthes
MARCH 5 Was buryed Richard Hewetson of toune heade
MARCH 8 Was buryed Richard ffothergill of Tarn housse
MARCH 16 Was buryed Henery Jonson
1677 APRILL 2 Was buryed Anthony Bouell of Trannow hill
APRILL 4 Was buryed Ann Todd of nethergarthes
APRILL 6 Was buryed Issabell wiffe to Richard Hayton
APRILL 12 Was buryed Rachell daughter to William Gibson of Lunns
JUNE 10 Was buryed Richard Elyetson
JUNE 13 Was buryed Ellin wife to Richard Garthat
JUNE 15 Was buryed myles son to John Robinson of Ellergill
JUNE 18 Was buryed A still borne child of John mills

* Transcript adds "wife to George"
† " "wife to mter George"

BURYALLS 1677

	JULY	19	Was buryed Elsabeth ffawcett of murthwaite
	SEPT	11	Was buryed Anthony Shawe of hie stennerskugh
	SEPT	13	Was buryed Issabbell wife to Stephen Greene
	OCTOBER	12	Was buryed George ffawcett of stouphilyeate
	OCTOBER	22	Was buryed John Cautley of Nubegin
	OCTOBER	27	Was buryed Elsabeth Taylor of Toune heade
	NOUEM	11	Was buryed John Wharton of Greenside
	DECEM	5	Was buryed A still borne child of John Hewetsons
	DECEM	15	Was buryed Issabell daughter to Thomas Robinson of nubegin
			Was buryed the same day Sarah Wilson
	DECEM	20	Was buryed William Shawe of hie stennerskeugh
	DECEM	22	Was buryed James Peares
	JANUARY	8	Was buryed Jeffray Dent
	ffEB	14	Was buryed Elsabeth wife to Thomas ffawcet of streete side
1678	MARCH	31	Was buryed Elsabeth wiffe to Thomas ffuthergill tarnehouse
	MAY	21	Was buryed Robart Shawe of Trannow hill
			Was buryed the same day mary Pinder of weesdaile
			Also Issabell daughter to William Greene
	MAY	22	Was buryed A still borne child of Richard Rogersone
	MAY	28	Was buryed margrett daughter to Ralph milner
	JUNE	12	Was buryed Elsabeth Greene of this towne
	JUNE	29	Was buryed Elsabeth daughter to Barbery ffothergill
	JUNE	30	Was buryed A still borne child of John Bircketts
	JULY	5	Was buryed John Bircketts wiffe
	JULY	14	Was buryed Emmey daughter to John Petty of mallastang
	AUGUST	13	Was buryed Jennat wife to Thomas dennyes

Affidauits were lawfully made & brought to ye Curate of Rauenstondale parish that ye persons whose burials are here under Registred were wound up & buryed in nothing but wt was made of sheeps wool only according to an Act of Parliament to that purpose enacted

Ann	Bowson widdow of Nethergarths was buried	SEP:	9
Robert	Bland Taylor of weesdall was buryed	SEPT:	23
Issabell	ffawcet widdow of Ellerhill was buryed	OCTOBER	1
Robart	Shaw of douengill husbandman was buryed	OCTOBER	13
Anthony	Wilson yeoma: of Russendale town was buryed ye same day		
Mabbell	Gibson widdow of murthwaite was buryed	OCTOBER ye	22
John	ffawcett of mosse husbandman was buryed	OCTOBER	27
Sarah	Alderson daughter to Christopher was buryed	OCTOBER	28
Ann	wife to John Adamthwaite of hill was buryed	NOUEMBER	6
Sibbell	daughter to John Hunter was buryed	NOVEMBER	9
William	Shawe of Rauenstondale toune husbandman was buried	NOUEM:	14
John	wilson of the tarne taylor was buryed	NOUEMBER	25
margarett	wife to Richard Rowson of brackenbar	DECEM	14
A child	of Richard ffothergill of wandell unbaptized was buryed	DECEM	28
Ralph	Alderson of nathwaite husbandman was buried	JANUARY	6
Gyles	Hall of sprint gill husbandman was buried	JANUARY	8
Ellice	Adamthwaite of Adamthwaite was buried	JANUARY	26
Jennat	Pinder widdow was buried	JANUARY	27
Ellin	daughter to george ubanke was buried	MARCH	15
Sibbell	Atkinson widdow was buried	APRILL 25	1679
Henery	Townson husbandman was buried	APRILL 29	
Margrett	daughter to Thomas dent of Bouderdaile was buried	MAY	2
Ellin	daughter to John Robinson of nubegin was buried	MAY	26
mabbell	Shawe of Asfell widdow was buried	JUNE	3

BURYALLS 1679

Ann wife to Thomas Hall of uldaile was buried	July	11th
A poore woman hir name unknowne to us was buried	August	15th
John Blades of douengill was buryed	August	29
Betterasse wife to George Whiteheade was buried	September	5
Mary daughter to stephen ffawcett of murthwait buried	Sept	11
Mabbell wife to John Pearson was buried	October	16
Margrett wife to Robart Perkin smith was buried	Decem	29
Jennat Andrews was buried	January	14th
mary Cautley was buried	January	20
Thomas Townson was buried	January	29
mary Pinder was buried	January	31
Ellin wife to Heugh Blenckarne was buried	ffebruary	4
Agnas ffawcett of backside of wandall was buried.	ffebruary	6
James son to Vincent Bousfeild was buried	March	5
Margrett wife to Richard Gouldington was buried	March	19
1680 Thomas ffawcett husbandman was buried	March	26
John Thompson of dubs husbandman was buried	March	31
Isabell Todd of weesdaile widdow was buried	Aprill	15
Sarah daughter to Ralph milner was buried	Aprill	18
A Still Borne Child of John Powsons was buried	Aprill	19
John ffawcett of streete side husbandman was buried	May	19
Anthony ffothergill of Longill husbandman was buried	May	21
Thomas sonn to Henery ffothergill of tarnehouse was buried	May	23
Thomas son to stephen dent of lythside was buried	June	10
michell and Thomas sonns to John Chamberlaine was bur:	June	16
John sonne to Robart Robinson of Trannahill was buried	June	22
Jennat daughter to Robart Whitelocke was buried	July	16
Margrett wife to John Hegdaile was buried	July	21
Mary the wife of Robart Whitelocke was buried	July	23
Richard Whiteheade husbandman was buried	August	8
William son to Anthoy Shawe was buried	Septem	12
John Robinson of Nubegin elder was buried	October	14
Margrett Whitelocke was buried	October	21
Barnerd douer webster was buried	October	24
Ellice Shawe widdow was buried	Nouember	20
Mary daughter to Thomas Adamthwait of hill was buried	Decem	28
Thomas ffothergill of Tarne house husbandman was buried	ffeb	16
John Ouerend of greenside was buried	March	17
Henery Wilkinson husbandman was buried	March	21
John sonne to Richard Gyles was buried	April 11th	1681
mrter George ffothergill was buried	Aprill 27	
Elizabeth ffawcett of murthwaite widdow was buried	May	12
Robart Handlay of streete side husbandman was buried	May	17
Also the same day was buried Julian wife to Richard ffallowfeild		
John son to Thomas Breakes was buried	June	28
John son to James Hall was buried	September	13
Anthony shawe of douengill was buried	September	30
Heugh ffothergill of Long gill husbandman was buried	December	27
A Child of Richard Chamberlaines unpaptized was buried	Jan	7
Ellin Wilkinson of Nubegin was buried	January	9
Ellin daughter to Thomas Hall of Uldaile was buried	Jan:	16
Elizabeth Taylor of Cauldbecke widdow was buried	January	26
Christopher Handlay husbandman was buried	ffeberuary	11
Stephen Ouerend was buried	ffebreuary	14
Sibbell Robinson of Ellergill widdow was buried	March	5
George son to Stephen Chamberlane was buried	March	19
John Swainson* was buried	March	21

* Transcript adds—"of Wandaile"

BURYALLS 1682

	Elîin daughter to edward Bland was buried	March	24	
	Peter Cautley of nubegin was buried	March	25	1682
1682	Mary wife to John Todd of cauldbecke was buried	Aprill	5	
	Ellice daughter to Thomas Perkin of Ellerhill was buried	Aprill	11	
	Agnas daughter to John Birckett was buried	Aprill	13	
	John Greene of Cauldbecke was buried	May	1	day
	Ellin ffothergill widdow was buried	May	3	day
	John Knewstubb husbandman was buried	May	9	day
	Mary Robinson widdow was buried	May	10	day
	Margrett Atkinson was buried	May	19	
	Agnas Hodgson widdow was buried	May	21	
	Ellin wife to James Perkin was buried	May	22	
	Iffabel Shawe of Stennerscugh widdow was buried	May	24	
	Jeffery ffawcet of bridge was buried	June	9	
	Thomas son to George Perkin was buried	June	21	
	John ffawcett of nubegin was buried	July	19	
	Robart son to Robart Hunter was buried	July	23	
	Thomas Perkin of greenside was buried	July	26	
	Elsabeth breakes of nubegin widdow was buried	July	30	
	mabbel wife to Thomas ffawcett of backeside was buried	Septem	21	
	Margrett Alderson of nedlehouse was buried	September	23	
	Christopher Geldart was buried	October	22	
	Anthony Hegdaile was buried	October	25	
	Anne wife to George Perkin was buried	January	31	
	Christopher Rogerson was buried	ffebruary	12	
	John ffawcett of streete side was buried	ffebruary	23	
	Margreatt Blades widdow was buried	March	6	
	John son to Henery Bousfeild was buried	March	10	
	A still borne child of Richard Rogersons was bur:	March	11	
	Michaell Chamberlaine of nathat was buried	March	18	
	Also a still borne child of George ffawcetts was buried same day			
	William Whiteheade of lowcome was buried	March	22	
	George Hewetson was buried	March	25th	
1683	Thomas Robinson of tranmoore was bur:	March	29	
	Robart Perkin smith was buried	March	30	
	Richard son to Richard Alderson of needlehouse was buried	Aprill	3	
	Mary Alderson of needlhouse was buried	Aprill	14	
	Ellinor daughter to Richard Bouell was buried	April	21	
	A Still borne child of John Pratts was buried	July	16	
	Ellice Cumston was buried	August	1	
	dorathy morland was buried	August	3	
	Robart Handlay of wandell was buried	August	27	
	Lanclot Townson was buried	September	11	
	Agnas Taylor was buried	September	27	
	margreat Rogerson was buried	October	4	
	margreat wilson of Tarnhouse was buried	October	28	
	maudlin ffawcett was buried	Nouember	28	
	margreat Taylor of murthwaite was buried	Decem	3	
	Elizabeth Rogerson was buried	December	6	
	Roger Pinder was buried	December	10	
	Thomas Thorneborrow of Askgill was buried	Decem	11	
	Stephen Bousfeild of Long gill was buried	December	20	
	Edward Atkinson was buried	December	22	
	margrat wife to Ralph Alderson was buried	January	4	
	Anne Loadman of malastang widdow was buried	January	6	
	Issabell Greene of Cauldbecke widdow was buried	January	11	
	William Handlay of weesdaile was buried	January	26	
	Anne Hewetson of scarsickes was buried	ffebruary	6	

1683 BURYALLS

	Margratt wife to Simond Alderson was buried	ffEB	13
1684	A child of William Adamthwaite unbaptized was buried	MARCH	29
	Ellin ffothergill of weesdaile was buried	MARCH	31
	John ffawcett of murthwaite was buried	MAY	15
	Issabell daughter to James dent was bur:	MAY	31
	Richard son to Richard Shawe was buried	JUNE	2
	Mary wife to Henery Waller was buried	JUNE	13
	Anthony Peacocke was buried	JULY	1
	Elizabeth daughter to John Hegdaile was buried	JULY	2
	A still borne child of Richard Rogersons was buried	JULY	16
	Thomas son to Henery ffothergill of brounbar was burid	JULY	23
	Thomas son to Richard Gyles was buried	JULY	24
	William son to Richard Bouell was buried	SEPTEM	30
	Anne Rogerson of streete side was buried	OCTOBER	9
	Issabell darby widdow was buried	NOUEMBER	28
	George dennison was buried	DECEMBER	1
	Thomas Perkin was buried	DECEMBER	3
	Stephen ffawcett of murthwaite was burid	DECEM	7
	mary daughter of John Blackbourne was buried	DECEM	17
	John ffawcett of this towne was buried	JANUARY	6
	Ellinor wife to william elyetson was buried	JANUARY	14
	Thomas son to Robert Hodgson was buried	JAN	24
	margrett mosse of this Towne was buried	MARCH	19
1685	Mary daughter to Thomas ffothergill was buried	MARCH	30
	A child of Henery Cautleys was buried	APRILL	5
	A poore man was buried	MAY	26
	Issabell ffothergill of nubegin and dorathy ffothergill of brounbar were both buried	JUNE	1
	George Ubank of bouderdaile was buried	JUNE	7
	A child of george ffothergills of Adamthwait was bur:	JUNE	27
	John Taylor of this towne was buried	JULY	30
	John son to Thomas Tomson was buried	AUGUST	3
	Ellin Bousfeild of scarsikes widow was buried	OCTOBER	15
	Stephen ffothergill of lowcome was buried	OCTOBER	20
	Agnas daughter to George Cleasby was buried	NOUEM	5
	Anne murthwaite widdow of newbegin was bur:	NOUEM	20
	Stephen Greene was buried	JANUARY	3
	Richard ffothergill of needlehouse was buried	JANU:	18
	Thomas ffothergill of newbegin was buried	MARCH	20
1686	Issabell daughter to Annas Taylor was buried	MARCH	29
	Ralph milner was buried	APRILL	25
	A still born child of John Pratts was buried	MAY	11th
	Agnas wife to Abraham Gouldington was buried	MAY	24
	Agnas wiffe to Josep Boorebancke was buried	JUNE	9
	margreatt daughter to Robert Readman was buried	JUNE	11
	Robert son to William Shawe of streete was bur.	JUNE	21
	Issabell daughter to John Bousfeild was buried	JULY	3
	A still borne child of Stephen ffawcetts buried	JULY	6
	Margrett wife to Stephen ffawcett was buried	JULY	9
	Maudlen Shawe of douengill widdow was buried	AUGUST	8
	Thomas ffawcett of nubegin was buried	AUGUST	28
	william son to William Shawe of Asfell	SEP	12
	A child of Thomas Rogersons of felend unbaptized was buried	OCTOBER	24

BURIALS.

(EXTRACTED FROM TRANSCRIPTS)

(TRANSCRIPT FOR 1686 IS MISSING)

1687	Barbery ffothergill of nubegin was buried	APRILL	3
	Isabell wife of Edward Adamthwaite was buried	APRILL	30
	Beatrix daughter to William Powson was buried	MAY	1
	Henery Handlay was buried	MAY	12
	Robert Tayler was buried	MAY	31
	Elizabeth daughter to Edward Bousfeild was buried	JUNE	1
	Jane wife to William Robinson of nubegin was buried	JUNE	7
	John son to Thomas Todd of fell end was buried	JUNE	30
	A still borne Child of Richard Rogerson's was buried	AUGUST	16
	Mary Hunter was buried	SEPTEMBER	16
	William Glentton was buried	NOUEMBER	15
	Sisalah Taylor widdow was buried	JANUARY	7
	Simond son to John Bousfeild was buried	JANUARY	28
	Issabell Robinson of malastang was buried	JANUARY	30
	(TRANSCRIPT FOR 1688 IS MISSING.)		
1689	John Hunter of Bouberheade was buried	MARCH	28
	Anne Taylor of this towne was buried	APRILL	1
	ffrances Adamthwaite was buried	APRILL	15
	Mary ffawcett of nathat was buried	APRILL	30
	John Becke was buried	MAY	3
	John Dennison was buried	JUNE	5
	A poore mans child was buried	JUNE	14
	Anne Shawe was buried	JUNE	20
	Edward Adamthwaite and John Taylor was buried	JUNE	21
	A still borne child of George ffawcetts was buried	JUNE	28
	Ellin Shaw of wath widdow was buried	JUNE	29
	Richard Powson of Dubbs was buried	OCTOBER	24

NOTE.—Another leaf of the Register appears to have been lost, as a gap occurs between 24th Octr 1686 and Novr 11th 1689. Unfortunately the Transcripts for 1686 and 1688 are wanting; those for 1687 and 1689 (up to the date when the Register resumes) are given above.

1689 BURYALLS

	Mary wife to James Townson was buried	Nouem	11
	Sibbell wife to James ffawcett was buried	Decem	3
	Issabell wife to Thomas Knewstubb buried	Decem	16
	Issabell wife to ffrancis Blackbourne buried	December	21
	margrett Robinson of newbegin was buried	Decem	30
	Sibbell wife to william Balife was buried	Jan	28
	Anthony Pinder of wath and Thomas son to ffrancis Blackbourne was buried	ffeb	6
	Thomas Bland was buried	ffebruary	12
	John son to Ralph Alderson was Buried	March	18
1690	mary dawson of lunns was buried	May	25
	John son to William Shawe of malstang buried	June	20
	Margrett ffawcett of stouphilyeate was buried	July	16
	John Adamthwaite of Adamthwaite was buried	July	21
	Ann the wife of Adam Shawe was bur:	Aug	7
	A child of John Baliffes unbap. was bur	Aug	8
	mary wife to Richard Alderson was bur:	Aug	25
	A still borne child of George ffawcetts buried	Sep	16
	William darbby was buried	September	15
	Richard Bousfeild of boudrdaile was buried	Sep	24
	margrett wife to William Shawe buried	Octob	2
	A poore wommons child was buried no dues paide—hir name Mary Aire	Octob:	3
	Thomas son to Thomas Robertson was bur:	Octob	24
	A still borne child of James dents was bur:	Nouem	6
	Issabell daughter to John Balife buried	Nouem	26
	Margrett ffothergill of brounbar was bur:	Dec	4
	Ellin willan was buried	December	18
	A still borne child of William Robertson buried	Decem	28
	Ellin Rogerson of breckfoot buried	Jan	16
	Christopher Bousfeild of bouderdaile was buried	January	23
	Richard Robinson of blaflat was buried	ffeb	1
	Annas Rogerson was buried	ffeb	15
	margrett Peacoke and Thomas son to Robert Perkin was buried	ffebruary	16
	Jennat wife to Richard Shawe burid	ffeb.	18
	Margrett Perkin of streete buried	ffeb	19
	Elsabeth Atkin of lowcome bur:	ffeb.	26
	James son to Thomas Perkin bur:	Feb	28
	Josep Boorebancke was buried	March	3
	mathew Pinder was buried	March	7
	Phillip Bousfeild of streete buried	March	9
	John Taylor of murthwaite was buried	March	13
	John Hegdaile was buried	March	15
	John Alderson of hole was buried	March	18
	Margrett Taylor of wath widdow was buried	March	24
1691	Ralph son to Thomas Milner was burid	June	16
	Anne Shawe of stennerscugh was buried	June	18
	Margrett ffawcett of hole was buried	July	2
	William Gibson of lunds was buried	July	15
	Issabell wife to Thomas dent was buried	July	18
	Vincent son to William Shawe was burid	July	19
	Anne Peacocke of weesdaile was buried	July	30
	Thomas son to Robert Taylor buried	August	15

BURYALLS 1691

	A poore woman was buried	August	17
	Thomas ffawcett of alme pot was buried	August	28
	Thomas dennyes was buried	September	9
	Ellin wife to Christopher Bousfeild burid	Octob	14
	Edward Bousfeild was buried	Octob	21
	William ffawcett of douengill buried	Octob	25
	William Clemyson was buried	Nouember	1
	Thomas ffawcett of backeside and mary Bousfeild of hatters was buried	Nouember	20
	elsabeth wilson was buried	December	11th
	elsabeth dennison was buried	January	2
	William Robinson Junior was buried	Jan	3
	A still borne child of Henery Knewstubbs buried	Jan	3
	John Alderson and Anthony Pearson was buried the —	ffebruary	10
	John Bousfeild hatter was buried	ffebruary	26
	Issabell wife to George Bousfeild was bur:	March	4
1692	James ffawcett of Crookes was buried	April	4
	Robert son to Barnad douer was buried	April	12
	Jane ffothergill was buried	Aprill	19
	Jane daughter to George Whitheade bur:	May	11
	A still borne child of mathew Scarbrough bur	June	7
	Ellis Perkin of Ellerhill was buried	July	21
	Issabell daughter to Christopher Todd buried	Aug	6
	John morland was buried	August	7
	Rouland Shearman was burid	August	8
	Margrett Alderson of greenside burid	Sep:	6
	Elizabeth daughter to Henery Cautlay burid	Sep:	18
	Jonathan Alderson was Buried	Septem	21
	George Bousfeild of Pears hill buried	Octob.	28
	Sarah daughter to Ralph Alderson bur:	Noum	20
	Anne Pinder was buried	Nouember	28
	Issabell Chamberlaine was buried	Decem	1
	John Chamberlaine of greenside was buried	Decem	3
	Thomas Thompson of dubbs was buried	Decem	8
	Elsabeth wife to Stephen ffothergill was buried	Decem	16
	John ffawcett of bridge was buried	January	16
	Richard son to Richard Chamberlaine buried	ffeb:	13
	Richard Shawe of streete was buried	Mar:	25
1693	Ellin Shawe of Tranahill was bur:	April	16
	Mary daughter to Robert Riddin was burid	May	4
	William son to William Hunter was buried	May	5
	Margrett Pinder was buried	May	26
	Elizabeth daughter to Robert Hunter buried	May	21
	Ellin daughter to Edward willan buried	June	1
	Phillip Bousfeild of wath was buried	July	12
	Ellin wife to William Gibson of luns	July	19
	Margrett Haistwhitle widow was buried	July	19
	Elizabeth wife to William Powson buried	July	31
	Margrett Todd of nethergarthes burid	Sep	25
	Jennat Gouldington of this towne burid	Oct	23

Note.—Here another leaf has disappeared and there is no further entry until April 25th, 1698. All the missing entries, except those for 1693, are furnished by the transcripts.

BURIALS

(Extracted from Transcripts. Transcript for 1693 is Missing).

1694	Stephen Chamberlain was buried	March	25
	Issabell Bousfeild of bouderdaile was buried	Aprill	13
	John son to Anthony Pinder was buried	April	22
	Sarah wife to Thomas Knewstub and Ellin her daughter was buried	Aprill	27
	John Hegdaile junior was buried	May	3
	Thomas dennyes was buried	May	9
	Ellin wife to Abraham Handlay was buried	May	16
	A child of William ffawcetts was buried	May	30
	Robert Todd of our Towne was buried	June	6
	A Still borne child of James dawsons was buried	June	22
	Sarah wife to James dawson was buried	June	28
	A still borne child of mathew Scarbrug was buried	July	22
	George Spooner was buried	Agust	13
	Issabell Bousfeild widdow was buried	Agust	27
	Thomas son to William Greene was buried	Septem	13
	Issabell ffawcett widdow was buried	October	11
	Elizabeth wife to William Hewetson was buried	October	17
	Margrett Shawe was buried	Nouem	22
	Elizabeth wilson was buried	Nouem	24
	Agnas mill of our Towne was buried	Decem	26
	Elizabeth daughter to John Blackbourne was buried	December	27
	John Pearson was buried	December	28
	Thomas Haistwhitle was buried	January	1
	Mary daughter to Thomas ffothergill of brounbar was buried	Jan.	9
	John son to Thomas ffothergill was buried	Jan.	21
	Elizabeth daughter to Mary Ouerend was buried	Jan.	24
	Agnas wife to John Hewetson was buried	Jan.	30
	Henery Pinder was buried	ffebruary	6
	Mary Alderson of the hole was buried	ffebruary	16
	Elizabeth morland of Keldhead was buried	March	1
	Christopher Alderson was buried	March	12
	A still borne child of John Bircketts was buried	March	17
	Issabell Shawe of our Towne was buried	March	18
1695	Thomas Simpson was buried	Aprill	3
	Thomas Adamthwaite was buried	Aprill	11
	John Robinson of newbegin was buried	Aprill	22
	Richard ffothergill of dubbs was buried	Aprill	26
	Robert ffothergill of pears hill and Issabell mill was buried	June	7
	Thomas Todd of Tarnhouse was buried	July	8
	Agnas wife to John Shawe was buried	Agust	26
	James Perkins of lockholme was buried	September	28
	Mabbell Handlay of streete was buried	October	1
	Thomas son to Anthony Perkin was buried	December	25

BURIALS

(Extracted from Transcripts).

	James ffawcett of blayflat was buried	January	26
	Richard Garthwaite was buried	ffebruary	5
	Anne ffothergill of Stennerskugh was buried	ffebruary	11
	William son to Thomas ffawcett was buried	ffebruary	20
	Allice ffawcett of weesdaile was buried	ffebruary	13
	Thomas Benson was buried	March	3
	John son to Thomas Thompson was buried	March	4
	A still borne child of John Bircketts was buried	March	11
	Margrett wife to Richard Robinson was buried	March	20
	Also there was two buryalls in the quaker way Isaac Handlay & Simmond Alderson		
1696	Thomas son to Thomas Adamthwaite was buried	Aprill	2
	Margrett Robinson was buried	May	14
	Margrett Knewstubb was buried	June	6
	Margrett Bland was buired	June	11
	Simond Pinder was buried	July	7
	George son to James ffawcett was buried	July	13
	Edward Hunter was buried	August	7
	Issabell daughter to George Townson was buried	August	16
	Mary wife to William Hunter was buried	August	19
	James son to Robert Perkin was buried	Septem	4
	Anne Cautley was buried	Septem	7
	Mary daughter to Richard ffawcett was buried	Jan	1
	Sarah Scarbrough was buried	January	16
	John Parkin of malastang and James son to John Jackson was buried	January	17
	Robert Readman was buried	ffebruary	1
	Margrett Simpson was buried	ffebruary	15
	Issabell ffawcett was buried	ffebruary	18
	Sarah daughter to Edward Willan was buried	March	6
	Margrett wiffe to Thomas Robinson was buried	March	8
1697	Sarah wife to John Bousfeild was buried	Aprill	3
	Nicolas son to Anthony Broune was buried	May	20
	Sarah Alderson was buried	June	5
	Anne daughter to Thomas ffawcett was buried	July	2
	Margrett Blenckarne was buried	August	16
	John son to Thomas Robinson was buried	September	9
	John son to John Bailiffe was buried	October	12
	Sarah daughter to Christopher Todd was buried	October	24
	ffrances wife to Stephen Bouell was buried	Nouember	13
	Sarah wife to Christopher Wharton was buried	Nouember	24
	Margrett Perkin of lockholme was buried	Nouember	29
	Jennet wife to John ffothergill was buried	December	21
	Thomas Taylor was buried	December	28
	Robert son to Mary Ouerend was buried	January	15
	Anne & Margrett daughters to Anthony Broune was buried	ffebruary	3
	Issabell Cautlay was buried	March	24
1698	Anthony son to Robert ffothergill was buried	Aprill	11

Note.—The next entry is that of Adam Taylor, Aprill 25, where the Register resumes.

1698 BURYALLS

	Adam Taylor was buried	APRILL	25
	James birtle* of Sedbridge psh bur.	APRILL	30
	Issabell wife to Thomas Hall was bur.	MAY	4
	Hugh Blenckarne was buried	MAY	13
	Agnas wife to John Robinson buried	JUNE	20
	Nicolas Broune was buried	AUGUST	25
	Mabbell Thorneborrow was buried	SEP	14
	Mary Bird was buried	OCTOBER	9
	Adam son to John Taylor buried	OCTOBER	15
	A still borne child of Chris: Todd buried	NOUEM	5
	William ffawcett thriuer buried	DECEM	4
	mabbell dent of Bouderdaile was buried	JANUARY	3
	Margrett wife to John Taylor was buried	JANUARY	19
	A child of michell Shawes unBap buried	ffEB	28
	Issabell douer was buried	MARCH	21
	Phillip son to Richard Bousfeild buried	MARCH	23
1699	ffrancees milner was buried	APRILL	3
1699	William son to John ffawcett buried	APRILL	7
	Robert Riddin was buried	APRILL	14
	Robert Hougill was buried	APRILL	22
	Robert Wilson was buried	APRILL	23
	John ffawcett low loneing was buried	MAY	2
	mary wife to John Knewstub was buried	JUNE	11
	Henery Wharton was buried	JUNE	15
	Richard son to michaell Bouell buried	JUNE	27
	margret wife to Henery ffothergill buried	JULY	21
	Ann ffawcett of Greenside buried	AUGUST	1
	Christopher Waller was buried	SEP	13
	dorathy daughter to John Bircket buried	SEP	28
	Issabell Handlay and Mary daughter to George Cleasby was buried	OCTOB:	7
	margret wife to Richard Rogerson bur:	NOUEM	8
	John Handlay of Coldkeld was buried	NOUEMBER	27
	Thomas ffothergill of nubegin buried	DECEMBER	4
	Elizabeth daughter to Richard ffawcett of mires bur:	JANUARY	7
	Thomas Alderson of needlehouse was buried	JANUARY	21
	Thomas son to William Waller was buried	ffEBRUARY	5
	John Bousfeild of this towne was buried	ffEBRUARY	12
	mary daughter to Heugh Blenckarne buried	ffEBRUARY	15
	margrett daughter to Christopher Alderson bur:	ffEB	17
	John son to Stephen Bouell was buried	MARCH	3
	James ffawcett of blayflat was buried	MARCH	6
	John Jackson of our towne was bur:	MARCH	10
1700	Thomas ffawcett Smith was buried	APRILL	10
	Issabbell wife to mathew Birckdaile buried	APRILL	14
	John Bousfeild of Scarsikes buried	APRILL	26
	Ann ffawcett of stouphillyeat buried	MAY	5
	Gyles son to John Hall buried	MAY	24
	Stephen Bouell was buried	JUNE	2
	Thomas son to Richard Postelthat buried	JUNE	13
	Alice Riddin of elergill buried	AUGUST	17
	Vincent Bousfeild was buried	SEPTEMBER	28
	Elizabeth Bousfeild was buried	OCTOBER	21
	Robert son to Christopder Todd was buried	OCTOBER	26
	Ellin wife to John Lawe buried	OCTOBER	29

* Indistinct—perhaps Little.

1700 BURYALLS.

	m^r^tris mary wife to m^r^ter michell was buried	Nouember	19
	edmond dauie was buried	Nouember	21
	Timothy son to Richard Breackes bur	Nouem	22
	Gracie wife to Christopher Todd was buried	Nouember	24
	Richard son to Edward Willan was bur.	Decem	7
	Sibell Sharpe of Ellergill was buried	December	24
	James wilson of the bridge was buried	January	5
	Phillep son to michell Bousfeild buried	January	12
	William son to Christopher Alderson buried	January	20
	Thomas ffothergill of brounbar was buried	ffebruary	6
	William Adamthwaite was buried	ffebruary	11
1701	Anthony Robinson of blayflat and michell Breakes smith of newbegin was buried	April	1
	Mary Harrison was buried	Aprill	19
	mary dauther to Stephen ffawcett of hole bur:	Aprill	23
	Thomas son to John Taylor of mires bur.	Aprill	27
	George Cleasby was buried	May	22
	Mary daughter to Thomas Atkinson buried	June	3
	Ann ffothergill of Brounbar was buried	June	9
	Mary Taylor was buried	July	19
	Mary ouerend was buried	August	5
	John Bird of brounbar was buried	Sep	9
	Edmond son to John Baliffe was buried	Sep	23
	John Hewetson senior was buried	October	12
	Stephen ffothergill of wath bur.	Octob	22
	George son to George Bousfeild of uldaile bur:	Nouem	11
	Henery ffothergill of streete was buried	Nouem	27
	Thomas dent was buried	Nouember	28
	Mary daughter to William Greene buried	Nouem	29
	Ralph son to William Milner buried	Decem	20
	Margret Habber was buried	January	4
	John ffawcett of blayflat buried	January	8
	Anne ffawcett low loneing widdow buried	January	15
	John dent of bouderdaile buried	Jan	20
	Issabell Pearson of backside buried	ffebruary	24
	Margrett Coupland was buried	March	8
	Margrett daughter to Thomas Robinson buried	March	9
	william morland was buried	March	24
1702	margrett daughter to William Hewetson bur.	Aprill	13
	Robert ffothergill of this Towne buried	Aprill	15
	Issabell wife to William Hewetson buried	May	8
	A child of James Aldersons unbaptized buried	June	11
	Thomas son to Henery ffothergill of wandall bur:	June	27
	ellin daughter to George Spooner bur	July	6
	James son to John Taylor of elergill bur	Septem	17
	William Robertson was buried	October	21
	John son to William Greene buried	Nouem	21
	Thomas Robertson was buried	Nouember	23
	John son to John ffawcett and Issabell wife to John Ubanke was buried	Nouember	25
	Ruth wife to James ffawcett buried	Nouem	27
	William Greene was buried	Nouember	29
	Alcie ffothergill of dubs was buried	December	7
	Agnas wife to Thomas Knewstubb buried	January	29
	ffrancees wife to Thomas Taylor buried	ffeb	1
	ellin ffawcett of douingill buried	ffebruary	26

BURYALLS 1703

	Mary daughter to George Clemyson bur	APRILL	4
	Agnas Hall of weesdaile buried	APRILL	18
	Edward Bland of hoffe was buried	APRILL	29
	John Shawe of this towne was buried	MAY	3
	Issabell wife to William Clugh buried	JUNE	4
	ffillis daughter to George Whiteheade Bur	JUNE	30
	Anne ffothergill of lythside was buried	AUGUST	21
	Ellin Cautley was Buried was buried	OCTOBER	9
	Gracey Wilson was buried	OCTOBER	18
	Michall Taylor of garthes was bur	NOUEM	14
	Ellin Shearman was buried	DECEMBER	4
	margrett wife to m^r Thomas Waller buried	DECEM	27
	John Knewstubb of hie lonning burid	DECEMBER	28
	mary daughter to William Hewtson bur:	JANUARY	10
	Margratt denison was buried	JANUARY	11
	William wilson was buried	JANUARY	20
	Agnas Portter of brounbar buried	JANUARY	21
	Richard ffallowfeild was bur	JANUARY	24
	Henery son to James Townson bur	JAN	26
	George son to Stephen dent was buried	ffEBRUARY	9
	George Bousfeild of Uldaile buried	ffEBRUARY	10
	William Shawe of croosbecke buried	ffEBRUARY	17
	Richard ffawcett of galehead buried	ffEBRUARY	21
	Mary ffothergill of Trannahill buried	ffEBRUARY	25
	Elizabeth daughter to Henery ffothergill buried	MARCH	22
1704	Issabell Townson was buried	APRILL	1
	John son to Abraham Gouldinton buried	APRILL	24
	Ellin wife to Henery Knewstubb buried	MAY	24
	Mary daughter to Thomas ffawcett bur	MAY	23
	Anne wife to Thomas milner buried	MAY	27
	margrat daughter to Richard Hunter buried	JUNE	3
	Mary Shawe of crookesbecke was buried	AUGUST	15
	Robert Shawe of Asfell was buried	AUGUST	30
	Issabell ffothergill of Lockholme buried	OCTOB	3
	Mary daughter to Thomas Atkinson buried	DECEM	3
	Robert son to Gilbert ffawcett buried	JANUARY	17
	margrett wife to Anthony ffothergill buried	MARCH	8
	John Shawe of Stennerscugh was buried	MARCH	10
	Robert Shawe of Stennerscugh buried	MARCH	18
	Christopher wharton was buried	MARCH	19
1705	Elizabeth daughter to George ffothergill buried	APRILL	5
	Agnas Swainson was Buried	APRILL	10
	Ellis wife to Stephen Robinson Buried	APRILL	17
	m^rter dawes Heade was buried	MAY	19
	George ffawcett of Stouphill yeat bur	JULY	19
	Richard Bousfeild of wath buried	AUGUST	3
	Thomas son to John Knewstubb buried	AUGUST	4
	Henery son to George Townson buried	AUGUST	29
	m^tris Jane Head was buried	SEPTEMBER	4
	Thomas milner was buried	SEPTEMBER	16
	Margrett wife to John Todd buried	SEPTEMBER	24
	Thomas Adamthwaite of malastang buried	JANUARY	14
	Anne wife to Christopher Bousfeild buried	JANUARY	17
	Agnas daughter to John Blackbourne buried	JANUARY	24
1706	Thomas ffothergill of dubbs buried	APRILL	21
	Ellin douer was buried	MAY	3
	Thomas Waller was buried	JUNE	11

1706 BURYALLS

	Anthoney ffothergill of Adamthwaite buried	June	18
	Anne Chamberlaine was buried	Nouember	3
	John Powson of weesdaile buried	December	12
	Issabell Bousfeild of pears hill buried	January	10
	William son to William Waller buried	Jan	17
	Margrett wife to John Blades buried	January	19
	Issabell wife to Stephen dent buried	January	31
	William ffothergill of brounber was buried	ffebruary	18
1707	William Shawe of Asfell was buried	March	26
	Jennat wife to William Robinson buried	June	16
	Mary wife to Thomas Atkinson buried	August	12
	Elizabeth Whiteheade was buried	September	4
	Elizabeth wife to Thomas Robinson buried	September	15
	Agnas daughter to Thomas dent buried	September	17
	mabbell wife to John Shawe buried	October	26
	John Blackbourne was buried	Nouember	6
	Issabell daughter to William ffawcett buried	Nouem	8
	Henery Cautley was buried	December	13
	Agnas daughter to James Alderson buried	Decem	20
	George ffawcett of newbegin was buried	March	3
	John son to George Clemeyson was buried	March	6
	Sarah wife to John Taylor was buried	March	14
	Issabell Bousfeild of scarsikes was buried	March	23
1708	Allis wife to Thomas Robinson was buried	Aprill	1
	John son to John Hewetson was buried	Aprill	8
	Christopher Handlay was buried	Aprill	14
	John Robinson of nubegin was buried	Aprill	22
	Mary daughter to Richard Hunter buried	May	6
	Ellice daughter to George tounson buried	May	27
	William Balife of Toown was buried	May	28
	William Robinson of nubegin was buried	June	22
	James wilson of town was buried	July	2
	Marey fawcet of town was buried	the July	17
	Elizabeth Taylor of town was buried	August	11
	Robert fawcet of town was buried	September	28
	Stephen Robinson of Newbegin was buried	December	23
	Thomas Hunter of stenerscugh was buried	December	27
	Margaret ffothergill of tarnhouse buried	December	31
	John powson of weesdaile buried	March ye	4
1709	Sarah daughter to Michaell Knewstubb buried	May ye	10
	Issabell fawcet of Nuebigin was buried	May ye	22
	Issabell Taylor of Waine Gars was buried	July ye	5
	Margret wife of michaell Knewstub buried	July ye	14
	Issabell Daughter to thomas Robinson was buried	Sep	18
	Mis: Martha Mitchell was buried	September ye	23
	William ffothergill of Adamthwaite was buried	Sep:	24
	Marey Daughter to Henery Barber of town buried	Octo:	13
	Marey Blades was buried	ye 23 of November	
	Agnus Daughter to thomas Adamthwaite of town buried	12 Decemb	
	Ann Law of wesdaile was Buried	Jan the	11
	George son to george Clemeyison of Adamthwait was buried	Januwary the	18
	Margret Bovel was Buried	March the	8
1710	Agnus Adamthwait of town was Buried	March the	13
	George Clemey of town was Buried	April the	7

LIST OF SUBSCRIBERS.

Bell, Rev. Wm. R., Laithkirk Vicarage, Middleton-in-Teesdale.
Birkbeck, Robert, F.S.A., 20, Berkeley Square, London.
Bland, Miss, Highfield, Ben Rhydding.
Bousfield, Rev. Stephen, M.A., Sudbury, Derby.
Bousfield, Frederick, 21, Crowhurst Road, Brixton.
Bousfield, Harvey, The Mulberries, Great Crosby, Liverpool.
Brunskill, Stephen, Castle Meadows, Kendal.
Burra, Rev. Thos. Fawcett, M.A., Linton Vicarage, Maidstone.
Burra, Robert, Gate, Sedbergh.

Carter-Squire, Miss S. A., Catterick.
Carver, John, Greystoke, Hanger Hill, Ealing, London, W.

Dawson, Edw. Bousfeild, Aldcliffe Hall, Lancaster.
Day, Rev. H. G., M.A., 55, Denmark Villas, West Brighton.
Dixon, Wm., Causeway, Ravenstonedale.

Ferguson, The Worshipful Chancellor, F.S.A., Carlisle.
Fothergill, John, Brownber, Ravenstonedale.
Fothergill, John Wm., The Cottage, Ravenstonedale.
Fothergill, Richard, Ashley Bank, Ravenstonedale.
Fothergill, S. R., 71, Portland Place, London, W.
Fothergill, Watson, Mapperly Road, Nottingham.
Fothergill, Gerald, 29, Priory Road, Kilburn, N.W.
Fothergill, Miss, 27, Arboretum Road, Nottingham.

Greenbank, Richd. H., 49, S. Ruke's Road, Westbourne Park, W.

Hewetson, Mrs., Hwith, Ravenstonedale.
Hewetson, Miss, c/o Mrs. Thompson, Stobars Hall, Kirkby Stephen.

Lonsdale, The Rt. Hon. the Earl of, Lowther Castle, Penrith.

Magrath, Dr., Provost of Queen's Coll., Oxford.
Metcalfe, Edw. Parr, M.A., Rajahmundri, India.
Metcalfe-Gibson, Anthony, Coldbeck, Ravenstonedale.

Peacock, Rev. Wm., St. Luke's Vicarage, Darlington.

RIGG, MRS., Elm Bank, Appleby.
ROBINSON, JOHN, Ashfell, Ravenstonedale.
ROBINSON, WM., Greenbank, Sedbergh.
ROBINSON, ROBT., C.E., Beechwood, Darlington.

SEDGWICK, MISS, Thorns Hall, Sedbergh.
SWINGLEHURST, HENRY, Hincaster House, Milnthorpe.

THOMPSON, REV. WM., M.A., Guldrey Lodge, Sedbergh.
THOMPSON, MRS., Stobars Hall, Kirkby Stephen.
THOMPSON, MISS, The Croft, Kirkby Stephen.
THOMPSON, W. N., St. Bees.
TULLIE HOUSE FREE LIBRARY, Carlisle.

T. WILSON, PRINTER, KENDAL.

THE

RAVENSTONEDALE

PARISH REGISTERS.

TRANSCRIBED AND EDITED BY

THE REV. R. W. METCALFE, M.A.,

VICAR OF RAVENSTONEDALE.

VOL. II.–1710 TO 1780.

KENDAL:

T. WILSON, PRINTER, 28, HIGHGATE.

1894.

INTRODUCTION.

THE second Volume of the Ravenstonedale Registers is entitled "A Register Book of all Marriages, Births, Christnings, & Burials begining in the Year of our Lord Seventeen hundred and Ten—1710." It also bears the following in a different hand "Be it remembered that the fifty Pounds left to the Curacy of Ravenstondale by John Holme of Coldbeck Malster was laid out in the Purchase of the Messuage and Tenement commonly called and known by the name of Gateside in Dowbegin in the Parish of Sedbergh the Property of Thomas Ellis, together with four Hundred Pounds procured from Queen Anne's Bounty for Augmenting the Curacy of Ravenstondale aforesaid by M^{r}. Robert Toulmin of Gravel Lane, London." And on the last page, "Sept. 5 1828 Be it remembered that the £55 in the 3 per cents Consols formerly belonging to the Church of Ravenstonedale was sold out in April 1828 and vested in the Estate called Dubbs. J. Robinson, Minister, Richard Fothergill, W^{m}. Dawson." It measures 15 × 6 inches, contains 192 pages of parchment, is leather bound, and has had two brass clasps, but only one remains. Throughout the book each page is headed "Marriages," "Births & Christnings," or "Burials," as the case may be, very neatly written between red lines, the work, I think, of the Rev^{d}. Thos. Toulmin, the then Incumbent. Of the 192 pages, 27 have been set apart for Marriages, 100 for Births and Christnings, and 58 for Burials, but of these only 11, 87, and 51 have been used.

In 1753 the passing of Lord Hardwicke's Act necessitated a new book for Marriages, and Rose's Act in 1812, prescribing set forms of entry, rendered existing Registers unfitted for further use.

The third volume, containing Marriages only, dates from 1754 to 1812. Its dimensions are 11½ × 9½ inches with 188 pages of stout paper, each page has 28 lines ruled in red ink but no heading. The title page calls it "The Register Book of the Parish of Ravenstondale for Banns & Marriages Pursuant to an Act of Parliament taking Date March 25th 1754." It is bound in leather and on the back is stamped in gilt letters "The Register Book of the Parish of Ravenstonedale for Banns & Marriages." No Banns, however, are entered.

Amongst the "Births & Christnings" a few pages have been set apart, here and there, for the registration of "Dissent^{rs}. Child^{n}. born in Ravenstoned^{le}., given by the Parents." As these are entered in families, and not in order of time I have thought it best to defer their publication to vol. iii, where they will be found at the end of the Baptisms. The registration of the children of Non-conformists in the Church book may have been due to the tax on Births, Marriages, and Deaths ordered by William III's Act of 1694-95; or, possibly, to there being no Registers at the Presbyterian Chapel, none are extant older than 1777. The above mentioned tax, the Rev. H. Whitehead tells me, was never repealed but fell into disuse about 1710.

In this volume I have rigidly adhered to my rule of a letter for letter copy of the original. I have, however, released the printer from restrictions as to pages and lines, thus enabling the same type to be used throughout.

I have again made considerable use of the Diocesan Transcripts, and as will be seen, these furnish a great deal of valuable information not given in the original. Of these Transcripts from 1710 to 1780 (the period covered by vol. ii.) only one is missing, viz. that for 1711. "William Bayliffe parish Clarke" signs the Transcripts up to and including 1720. From 1721 to 1727 they are declared to be true copies "p. me Thos. Toulmin" in one or two he subscribes to "Vera hœc est copia Registrar.," or "Pub. Registrar.," as "Curate de Ravenstonedale." There is no minister's signature to the Transcript for 1728.* Mr. Toulmin was buried in August of that year, and the copy would be made in June or July of 1729, very probably before Mr. Mounsey's institution, as he did not take possession until October the 16th. The Churchwardens, however (and for the first time since 1673), attest the correctness of the copy, which seems to be in Mr. Mounsey's writing. Commencing with the Transcript for 1729 and for a period of half a century the extract (except that for 1730 which has no subscription) bears the familiar signature of "Robt. Mounsey, Min^{r}.", who sometimes adds "of the perpetual Curacy of Ravenstonedale." In each case the signatures of the Churchwardens are appended. In the Transcript dated May 1779 Mr. Mounsey copies the Marriages, but leaves the Baptisms and Burials to Mr. Taylor, whom it would seem failing health had compelled Mr. Mounsey to engage as assistant curate. The writing is very shaky and cramped, which prepares us for the entry amongst the Burials in the following March "The Rev^{d}.

---

* Old style, of course, viz. from Easter 1728 to Easter 1729, new style was adopted Jan. 1753.

M^{r}. Mounsey ag^{d} 84 and Minist^{r} of the Perpetual Curacy of Ravenstondale upwards of 50 years." Of the Transcript for 1779 I can find only a single sheet, containing Burials, written by Mr. Taylor but without his signature. The true extract for 1780 is certified "p. Jeff: Bowness Curate" the new Incumbent.

A few remarks on the posting up of the Registers may be of interest. The Rev. H. Whitehead, above mentioned, and a well known authority, after an examination of the first book is of opinion that to Henry Shaw, who wrote the memorandum on the title page, is due the credit of having been the first to commence the Ravenstonedale Registers in their present form. He thinks it very probable that Shaw during his tenure of office as parish clerk set about the copying upon parchment of the paper sheets then existing, himself taking the Burials and assigning the Baptisms and Marriages to some other hand. These parchments, added to as time went on, remained loose until 1710, when some one collected and stitched them together, without however having first arranged them in proper order. The last entry in Shaw's hand is the Baptism on "Agust" 24th, 1668, and he is buried in the March following. The Transcript for 1667, the only one signed by him, enables us to identify his handwriting. In a book of "Parish Accounts" there is a copy of an order of "y^{e}. four and twenty" dated 27th Feb. 1667 (1668 new style), containing the following "and we do Constitute and make Jonathan Dodson our Register during Pleasure, having special Confidence in M^{r}. Thomas Dodson his father and our minister, that he will see him keep the same in good order." Jonathan Dodson takes over the Church Register from Shaw, but does not survive him. His death must have been sudden, as he enters a Burial on Feby. 16th., 1668 (1669), and his own follows in his father's writing on Feby. 25th. On the death of his son Mr. Dodson continues the entries up to the Baptism on June 1st, 1670, when the handwriting is again changed. Mr. Dodson was buried Jan. 22, 1672 (1673) and was succeeded by Mr. Anth. Procter.

A memorandum (copy) in the Parish Book dated Oct. 23rd, 1673, says "The Four & Twenty men Chosen and from time to time Elected for the better management of the Publick Affairs and Concerns of the Parish of Ravenstonedale together with the approbation of Mr. Anthony Procter Clerck Curate of the parish of Ravenstonedale aforesaid according to ancient Custom hath made Choice and elected William Bayliff of Ravenstonedale town for their Register and Public Notary during pleasure, and the same day the said Mr. Anthony Procter did publicly swear him to keep the Register book of the said Parish faithfully and to do all other offices belonging the place and office of Register and Publick Notary within the said Parish during Pleasure as aforesaid."

The following extract is, perhaps, worth reproducing, it is taken from a copy of the original made by James Baylife circa 1738. "The form of y^{e}. oath, set down and appointed att all times hereafter by y^{e}. Jury to be ministred unto him that shall be appointed keeper of y^{e}. end book, and book of taxes & accounts wth. in y^{e}. L^{d}. shp. of Ravenstondale as followeth—

"You shall swear by God, y^{t}. to y^{e}. utmost of your power, you shall well and safely keep & preserve according to y^{e}. orders of this L^{d}. shp. set down in that behalf this y^{e}. parish end book comitted now to trust to you to keep by y^{e}. grand Jury, you shall allso register and write into this book al ends verdicts and orders in best manner y^{t}. you can, when and as they shall from time to time be committed and delivered unto you by Juries or arbiters and therwth. all shall deal truly and faithfully, likewise you shall register keep y^{e}. book of taxes, and accounts within this L^{d}. shp. well and truly in each respect as you can according to y^{e}. orders set down for that purpose, so God you help.

"W^{m}. Cooke being elected, nominated and appointed by y^{e}. Grand Jury of this L^{d}. shp. keeper of y^{e}. end book. and y^{e}. book of taxes and accounts of Constables &c. In open court had y^{e}. same books deliver'd to him by y^{e}. Jury, and y^{e}. afores^{d}. oath ministred unto him by y^{e}. clerk of y^{e}. court y^{e}. 24th of May 1584."

In my introduction to vol. i. it is stated that "W^{m}. Baylife parish clerk" signs the Transcripts from 1670 to 1720 inclusive. On May 28th, 1708 "W^{m}. Baylife of Toown was buried" and on a close inspection of the Register a change of handwriting is apparent in that month. There were therefore two consecutive parish clerks of the same name, the second being in all probability the "William sonne to William Baylife" who was baptized Oct. 10th, 1678, a relationship which may account for the great similarity in the handwriting. The son succeeds the father as Parish Clerk, and, excepting the Baptisms and Burials for 1710, posts up the entries until June 1721, when he gives place to Mr. Toulmin—his burial is recorded on Dec. 30th, 1756. Mr. Toulmin began the Baptisms and Burials in the new book, but at the end of the year left them to his clerk, entering only the Baptisms of his own children. The Burial entry of June 23rd, 1721, is the last written by W^{m}. Baylife, and once more Mr. Toulmin's copper-plate hand is before us, continuing to the end of 1723 (Feb. 1724). From this date up to the close of 1728 (Mar. 1729) the entries are in a hand which I am unable to identify. It is not Mr. Toulmin's, nor is it that of Mr. Shaw, the "Scoolmaster", for the obvious reason that it records their burial. On page 49 of the Marriages there will be seen a memorandum, which is in Mr. Mounsey's writing down to the date "1729"; the words "Whom may God bless . . . . . Blessings" are in another hand, somewhat resembling, but better written than the entries above mentioned. The Latin and Greek, the latter in well defined characters, with sundry flourishes of the pen are subscribed in very small letters by "Jn[an] Ud[ll] Clrk." I cannot find mention of any Jonathan Udall, only a John of that name, so possibly I have mis-read the signature, and it should be "Jh[on]."

Mr. Mounsey makes the entries during the whole of his incumbency, occasionally employing an assistant, perhaps Mr. Coulston the Schoolmaster.

The "Poor House" is first mentioned in 1748, in the Marriages. There is nothing obtainable from the Parish accounts to shew when it was instituted. In 1738, however, "y[e] four and twenty" distribute the Poor Rate; the name of each recipient is given, and the amount; in some cases the allowance is for board, in others for house rent. We may perhaps conclude from this that no Poor House was then in existence. This is the last detailed list given and the accounts in succeeding years are very much condensed, merely noting the balance handed over from the old to the new warden of each respective angle. In 1747 Mabel Robinson receives £3 0 3½ and "she yet wants an arrear of £3 6 8½." Was Mabel Robinson the Poor House matron? In 1755 the overseers pay Margaret Hewetson £3 3 11 "towards her next quarter Payment for y[e] Poor People" and "for Jacob Shaw two lads." In 1758 Mary Blackburn was in charge of "y[e] Poor People." Amongst these accounts is the following interesting entry in 1764, "to M[rs] Mounsey for mending the surpluse 34 years £0 5 0"!

It will be noticed in the Baptisms that Mr. Toulmin invariably gives the mother's Christian name. This, Mr. Whitehead informs me, is very early for this Diocese. In most parishes in this Diocese it did not become the practice to record the mother's name until about 1771.

With the commencement of the new Marriage Register in 1754 the signatures of the contracting parties were required, and the frequent occurrence of the (×) denoting "his" or "her mark," is at once noticeable. If this may be taken as a fair test of the educational status at that period it follows that 18 per cent of the male and 48 per cent of the female population were illiterates.

The heavy mortality evidenced in the record of Burials during the summer months of 1730 has already been referred to in vol. i. No further information is in my possession as to the nature of the epidemic.

I do not intend to continue the publication of the Ravenstonedale Parochial Registers beyond the year 1812, but I hope to include in the next vol. of this work the Registers of the Presbyterian Chapel, a transcript of which has been kindly placed at my disposal by Mr. Gerald Fothergill, one of my subscribers. Mr. Fothergill has also been good enough to copy for the same purpose the Ravenstonedale entries contained in the Digest or Index of the Quaker Registers kept at Devonshire House, the headquarters of the Society. The original Registers, both Non-conformist and Quaker, are preserved at Somerset House, but by a recent decision of the Registrar General they are no longer open to inspection, not even for literary purposes. The inclusion of these non-parochial Registers will make my publication as complete a record of "Byegone Ravenstonedale" as is possible.

NOTE.—In the following pages the mark † prefixed to an entry indicates that it is not to be found in the Transcripts, while the square brackets [T.] denote extracts from these documents.

RAVENSTONDALE

A

REGISTER-BOOK

OF ALL

MARRIAGES, BIRTHS, CHRISTNINGS &
BURIALS, BEGINING IN THE

YEAR OF OUR LORD

SEVENTEEN HUNDRED AND TEN

1710.

BIRTHS AND CHRISTNINGS.

1710.	
12th Sepber	Born Henry son of Hen : Fothergill of Lockholm
29th Sep.	Baptiz'd
	Born Anne Daughtr. of Mr. John Beck, Artlegarth
23rd Novr	Baptiz'd.
5th Novr	Born William, Son of George Fothergill, Tarnhouse
30th Novr	Baptiz'd
2d Jan :	Baptiz'd Isabel Daughter of George Moreland, Stoupelgate
14 : Dec :	Born.
13 : Feb :	Baptiz'd Mary natural Daughter to Christopher Alderson & Margaret Birkett
22 : Feb :	Baptiz'd John Son of Geo: & Elizabeth Guy
5 : March	Bap : James son of John & Margt Fawcett Blaeflat.
18 : March	Bap : Sarah Daughtr of Tho: & Mary Fawcett
7 : March	Born.
20 :	Bap : William son to James & Margt Hutcheson
18 :	Born.

1711.	
6 May	Bap : Henry Son to John punch of Backside
16 Aug	Mathew son to Richard Birtell Baptized
9 Sept	William son to William Adamthwaite Baptized
25 Octo	William son to John Hunter was Baptized
9 Octr	Born Issabell daughter to William Knewstubb
1 Novem	Issabel Daughter to William Knewstup Bap
2 Decem	Margrett Daughter to Anthoney parkin Baptized
7 Decem	John son to John Tayler of Garths Baptized
27 Decem	John son to George ffawcett of stenerscugh Bapd
16 Jann	George son to thomas Robinson Baptized
5 Feb	Jonathon son to James Hutchisson Bap :
20 March	Marey Daughter to James fawcet of street side Bap

BIRTHS AND CHRISTNINGS.

1712.

26 APRILL	Robert son to Thomas Hunter Baptized
4 MAY	Thomas son to John Richardson Baptized
18 SEPT	Abraham son to Abraham Dent Baptized
16th SEP	Born. John son of Tho. Tulmin Clerk &
5th OCT	Margaret his wife Baptiz'd
31 OCT	Ann Daughter to Richard Law Baptized
9 NOUEM	John son to Joseph Hanson Baptized
11 NOU	Ann Daughter to Peter Gyles Baptizd
14 NOUM	John son Richard Todd Baptizd
18 NOUM	George son to George Gye Baptized
7 DECEM	Ann Daughter to John Fawcet of Allmpot B:
1 JANNU	George son to George Moreland Baptized
26 FEB	John son to James Fawcett of Stenerscugh B:
1 MARCH	John son to Richard Birtell of Stenerscugh B.
	† Robt son of Thomas Breaks Bp. 10th of March 1712

1713.

12 APRILL	William son to Henery fothergill of Lockholme B.
25 APRILL	John son to John fawcet of Blaflat Baptized
7 MAY	Ann Daughter to Margret Birket Baptized
18 JUNE	Margaret daughter to John Blades Bap
16 JUNE	George son to Robert Fothergill Bap.
	JULY 9th Born Henery son to John Bousfield o' th' townhead
13 AUGUST	Henery son to John Bousfield of Town Head Bzd
24 SEPT	Edward son to Mr. John Beck Baptized
29 DECEM	Thomas son to George fawcett of stenerscugh Baptized
31 DECEM	Margret Daughter to william Adamthwaite B.

1714.

APRILL 6	Marey Daughter to stephen Dent of Dubs B.
13 APRILL	Issabell Daughter to John Taylor of wane gars
4 MAY	William son to Richard Wharton Bap
MAY 30	Thomas son to Richard Birtell Baptized
15 JUNE	Ann daughter to thomas fawcett of tranmore B.
16 JUNE	Issabell daughter to James Hutchison Bap.
2 JULY	William son to James fawcett of street side B.
4 JULY	Issabell daughter to Stephen Dent Bap.
11 JULY	Sibbel daughter to Anthony parkin Bapp.

BIRTHS AND CHRISTNINGS.

14 SEPT Issabell daughter to John parkin Baptized
26 SEPT Thomas son to Joseph Hanson of Newbegin Bap.
7 OCTO Thomas son to Richard fawcett of mollerstang B.
16 NOUM Marey Daughter to John Blades Bapized
peter son of peter Gyles Born OCTOBER the 14
OCTO 28 peter son of peter Giles Baptized
JAN 18 Margret daughter to John fawcett of Alm pott Baptized
FEB 7th Ann Daughter to ye Revd. Mr. Tolmin clerk and Margaret his wife Born
FEB 23d Baptiz'd.

1715.

Sarah daughter to *George Moreland Baptized APRILL 10th
FEBr ye 4 Thomas son of Thomas Dent born
MAY 26 Agnus Daughter to Richard fallofield Bap
JULY 5 John son to John Richardson Baptized
AUGUST 28 William son to George Cleasby Baptized
15 SEPT William son to Heugh Shaw Baptized
21st SEPTbr Thomas son to Henry Fothergill o' Lockholme Bd.
23 OCTO John son to thomas Robinson Baptized
29 OCTO William son to Hugh Balife Baptized
24 NOU John son to thomas Shearman Bap
18 DEC [T. 16] George son to stephen Dent of lyethside B.
1 JANN William son to John fawcett of Blaflatt B.

1716.

MARCH the 25 John son to Joseph Oglen By [T. omits "By"] & Elizabeth his wife. Both of the parish of Burton In the County of Westmorland Baptd
APRILL th 5 Jennatt daughter to John Spooner B.
29 AP. William son to James Whola Baptized
13 MAY Issabell daughter to Richard Birtell B.
15 MAY Thomas son to John Blades Baptized
11 JULY Margrett daughter to Joseph hanson B.
24 AUG [T. JULY] Ann daughter to James fawcett of Street side Baptized

---

* T. omits "Sarah d. to," which in the original occupies part of the line next above, and seems therefore to have escaped the copyist's notice.

1716 BIRTHS AND CHRISTNINGS.

5th Sept Philip son to James fawcett of high stenerscugh Baptized
4 Decem Thomas son to Michaell taylor Bap
Bap. 20 Ellice daughter to peter Giles Born 7th Decem
27 Decem Christopher son to Regnald Dixon Bapt.
Jann 20th Robert son to Richard fawcett Bap.
Jann 25 James son to John parkin of stenerscugh Bap
21 Feb Marey daughter to James Hutchison Bap
16 March Elizabeth daughter to Rodger Barber Bap
† 19 March Richard son to John Beck Baptized

1717.

May 16 Marey daughter to Anthony fawcett of Crooks Baptized.
May 19 Anthony son to stephen Dent Baptized
May 26 Marey daughter to thomas Shearman Bap.
May 19 [T. 27] Marey daughter to Richard falowfield Bap.
July 18 Ruth daughter to Margrett Birket Bap.
July 18 Margret daughter to George parkin Bap.
July 21 Ann daughter to Joseph Hanson Bapt.
Aug 27 Anthony son to George Moreland Bap.
Henery son to James fothergill of Stenerscugh Bap. 25th of December last 1716
Sep 1 John son to Wm Fawcett Schoolmr Born &
Sept 10 John son to Mr William fawcet Baptized
† Sept 11 James son to Mr. Magee Baptiz'd
Octo. 1 Elizabeth daughter to Richard Wharton B.
Sepr 28 Born a son of John & Ruth Bousfield o' th' Town head &
Octob. 10 Thomas son to John Bousfield Baptized
Octob. 6 Ann daughter to William Knewstubb Born Baptized November the 5 day.
Novem 7 Elinor daughter to George fawcet Bapt:
Novem 14 Marey daughter to Heugh Bayliffe Bapt.
Decembr 6th Robert son to ye Revd Mr. Toulmin Clerk and Margaret his wife Born And Baptiz'd the same Day.
12th Richard son to Richard & Ann Birtle Baptizd
Jann 23 James son to Hugh Shaw of Assfell Baptized
2 Feb Thomas son to James Whola Baptized
18th James son to Anthony Shaw of Ellergill Baptized

BIRTHS AND CHRISTNINGS.

MARCH 13 Robert son to John fawcett of Blaflat Baptized
16th Charles son to John Vdaal milner Baptized

1718.

MARCH 25 Marey daughter to Anthony parkin of lockholme B.
2 APRILL Marey daughter to thomas Alderson Bapt.
APRILL 23 Agnus daughter to thomas Blackbourn Bap.
MAY 1 Robert son to Michael taylor Baptized
JULY 27 Elizabeth daughter to John Blades Bap:
NOVEM the 9 Agnus daughter to thomas Robinson of tranmoore Baptized
George son to thomas fawcett of Brounber Baptized
NOVEMBER 10.
NOV: 27 Agnus daughter to William Jackson Bap.
† DECEMBER the 11 John son to William Shaw Baptized
DECEM 21 Thomas son to George parkin Bap.
21st John son to thomas Simpson of the parish
sedberige Baptized
JANN the 30 Henery son to Bichard Birtell Bapt.
22 MARCH Robert son to William Hougill Bap.

1719.

JUNE 23 Marey daughter to James fawcet of Low
Stenerscugh Baptized
JULY 7 James son to Anthony fawcet of Crooke B.
JULY 28 Issabel daughter to John Blackbourn B.
29 Richard son to Richard falowfield Baptized
AUG 11 Robert son to John Ridin Baptized
AUG 11 John son to Robert fawcet Bap.
AUG 12 Mathew son to Thomas Scarbrough B.
AUG 13 Thomas son to Thomas Rippan of Cocker-
meth Baptized.
Margret daughter to Mr. William fawcet
AUG 15 Born. Baptized the 21 day.
SEPT. 15 William son to Ann Ion Baptized
SEPT. 27 Sarah daughter to Joseph Hanson B.
OCTOB. 4 James son to Henry fothergill of Lock-
holme. Baptized
OCTOB 16 Thomas son to John fawcet of Blaflat B.
NOVEM 10 Ellice daughter to John Blades Bapt.

BIRTHS AND CHRISTNINGS.

NOVEM 29	John son to Robert Ratley Baptized
DECEM 6	Robert son to John Vdal Baptized
25th	George son to Anthony Shaw B. the same day Marey daughter to William Jackson. Baptized.
26th	Robert son to Hugh Shaw of Asfell B.
10 JANN	James son to James Whola Baptized
28th	John son to Michael Taylor Bapt.
3 MARCH	Ellice daughter to Ann Shaw Bapt.
19 MARCH	Agnus daughter to Wiliiam Blackbourn Bap
1720.	
7 APRILL	William son to Thomas Hunter Bapt.
AP: 15	Marey daughter to George Moreland B.
† APRIL 16	Richard son to Hugh Baylife Bap
28 APRL	Henery son to Richard Waler Bapt
10 MAY	John son to Thomas Blackbourn Bap.
MAY 24	George son to George parkins of Stenerscugh Baptized
JUNE 26	Marey daughter to Richard Birtel B:
3 JULY	Ann daughter to Anthony parkin B.
3 JULY	Richard son to Richard Chamberlain B.
19 JULY	James son to Richard Mitchel Bap
14 AUG	Isabell daughter to Rodger Beck B.
AUGUST 24	Thomas son to ye Revd. Mr. Toulmin Clerk and Margaret his wife Born—Baptized the 2d day of SEPTEMBER
4 SEPT	Sarah Daughter to John fawcet of Almpot Bap
SEPr 20th	Born Arthur son to John Bousfield
SEPT. 28th	Author son to John Bousfield of town head Baptized
	Henery son to Mathew Whitfield Baptized OCTOBER the 27
NOV. 5th	Dority daughter to William Hougill Bap.
9th	Ester daughter to James Linsay Bap.
NOV. 16	Sarah daughter to Thomas Shearman B
	Richard son to Mr. Thomas Robinson Baptized JANNUWARY the 3.
JANN the 26	Margret daughter to Robert petty B.
MARCH 9	Richard son Henry Baylife Bapt.

BIRTHS AND CHRISTNINGS.

MARCH 12 George son to George Whitelth Bapt.

1721.

JULY 30th Sarah wife of James Bayliffe o' Murthwaite (before a Quaker) Baptizd.

AUGt 20th William Son to Alexander Straughan A Card-maker & Jane his wife, Travellers Baptiz'd.

Sepr 27th Richard Son of Thomas & Eleanor Hunter Bp.

OCTr 4th John son of Richard & Agnes Mitchell Bpd Born SEPTr 24th 1721.

18th John an illegitimate child of Mary Atkinson

20th Mary Daughter of John & Margaret Fawcett

26th Mary Daughter of Thomas & Eliz. Bell Bpd.

Novr 9th Dorithy Daughter of Anth: & Isab. Fawçett

23rd John Son to Thomas Fawcett of Newbiggin Smith

DECr. 10th James Son to John & Anne [T. James] Udall o' th Garths Bpd

20th William Son o' thomas & Margt Robinson o' th' Freer-Bottom Baptized. Born Novr 28th 1721

FEB 3d Thomas son of Robt & Mary Fawcett o' Murtwhaite Baptiz'd.

9th John son o' Thomas & Eleanor Alderson o' Lockholme Baptiz'd

15th Elisabeth Daughter o' William & Mary Blackburne o' Newbiggin Bpd

22nd Ann Daughter of Richd & Ann Birtle o' th' Crossbank Baptiz'd

1722.

MARCH 27th Mary Daughter to George & Jane Cleasby Bapd

APR. 1st Richard son to Willm & Ann Howgill Bapd.

5th Michael Son to Michael & Jennet Taylor Bapd

6 James son to John & Elisabeth Redding Bapd

21 John son to James & Sarah Bayliffe o' Murthwaite Bpd

JUNE 17th Isabel Daughter to James & Frances Whaley

24th Agnes Daughter to Wm & Mary Jackson

AUG 9th Margaret Daughter to John & Mary Perkins [T. Parkin]

SEP 18th Sarah Daughtr to Richard & Tamar Fallowfield

BIRTHS AND CHRISTNINGS.

Octr 5th	Elisabeth Daughter to John & Mary Blades
Novr 13th	John son to Matthew & Mary Whitfield
22d	Elisabeth an illegitimate Daughter to Capstick & Mary Bayliffe Baptiz'd
29th	Hugh son of Hugh & Isabel Shaw
Jan 8th	Joseph son of Tho: & Margt Sheerman
Feb 2d	Thomas son of Richard & Ruth Fawcett.
7th	George son of Tho: Toulmin Clerk and Margaret his wife baptiz'd Born Jan 21st
12th	Joseph son of Henry & Elis. Fothergill
1723.	
Apr 4th	Elisabeth Daughter to Tho: & Isabel Fawcett of Newbign.
May 7th	William son of John & Ruth Bousfield Born
15	The said Wm was Baptiz'd
June 11th	John son of George & Ann Morland
30th	George son of George & Isabel Perkins
Augt 18th	Sarah Daughter of Tho: & Margt Scarborrow
Sep 28th	John son of John & Margt Todd Born
Octr. 17th	The Sd John was baptiz'd
Octr. 20th	Bridget Daughter of John & Anne Udal
Novr 5th	Mary Daughter of Tho: & Mary Law Born.
Decr 5th	Thomas son of William & Anne Howgill Baptizd
18	Mary Daughtr of George & Abigal Whitehead Bptd
Jan 22d	Thomas son of Thomas and Eliner Hunter Bptd
30th	Agnes Daughtr of Roger & Elisabeth Pinder Bd
Febr 13th	Elisabeth Daughter of Richd & Anne Birtle
1724.	
	† Mathw son of James Robinson born Febr 24th Bap March 6th 1724-5
April 3d	Robert Son of Anthony & Isabel Fawcett Bapd
9th	Mary Daughter of Rihard & Agnas Mitchel Bap
14th	Margaret Daughter of John & Sibbal Fawcet Bap
18th	Mary Daughtr of Richard & Mary Fothergill Bapd
28th	Jonathan son of Jonathan & mart Alderson Bap
May 28th	Isabell Dougtr of John & Mart Heuatson Bap
June 5th	Joseph son of Joseph & Mart Hanson Baptiz'd
5th	John Stubbs son of Jno & Mary Stubbs Baptd

BIRTHS AND CHRISTNINGS.

July 17th	Margaret Daugtr of Thos. & margaret Green Bap.
26th	James son of Matw & Mary Whitfield Bap.
September 12th	Mary Daugter of Jonn & Elizh Redding Bapd.
Octor 1st	John son of John & Jane Blackburne Bapd.
Novr 5th	Ruth Daugr of Richard & Ruth Fawcett bapd.
7th	Edmund son of James & Sarah Baylif Bad
13th	Margaret Daugtr of John Mart Fawcett Bapd
25th	Margaret Daughtr of John & Magret Todd Born [T. Dec 8th ye sd margt was Baptiz'd]
† Jan: 6th	James son of Thomas & Ann Perkin Born
March 4th	Allis Daugtr of Willm & Mary Jackson Bapd
11th	John son of Wilm & Mary Blackburn Bapd.
13th	Agnas Daugtr of James & Mary Fawcett Bapd
† 20th	Thomas son of Thos. & Mary Law Born
1725.	
Aprl 6th	John son of Joseph & Allis Udall Baptized.
25th	Debrah Daugtr of John & Mart Fawcet Bapd
25th	Thomas son of Robert & Anne Gibson [T.—of Peers hill] Bapd
June 23rd	Elizabeth Daugtr of John & Jane Fryer travellers bapd
24th	Thomas son of Anthony & Elizabeth Parkins [T.—of Lock-holme] Bd
July 13th	Benjamin & Sarah Son & Daughter of Thomas and Margaret Knewstubb Born.
August 24th	Mary Daugtr of George & Jennet Jackson Bapd
31st	Isabel Daughtr of Richard & Mary Fothergill Baptized 23 born
Sep 9th	William son of Rebecca Milner [T.—Widw] Baptized 6 born
19th	Mary Daugr of John & Sibbal Fawcett Bapd 5 Born
Novr 25	Samuel son of Mr Thos Toulmin Curat & Margt his Wife Baptized 16th Born.
Decr 9	Richard son of Matw & Mary Whitfield Bad.
Mar 7	Joseph son of Richd & Anne Birtle [T.—priv:] Bapd.
Novr 15th	Margaret Daugtr of Jonathan And Margaret Alderson Baptized

BIRTHS AND CHRISTNINGS.

1726.

APRIL 8th Ralph Stockdal an adult Person Bapd

17 John son of John & Anne Udall Bapd

MAY 5th Anne Daugtr of Geog & Anne Morland Bapd

JUNE 14th Ruth Daughtr of John & Jane Blackburne Bapd

JULY 3d John son of Thos & Elinor Hunter Bapd MAY 30th Born

JULY 10th Isabel Daugr of Michl & Janet Taylor Bapd

AUGt 18th George son of Janes [T.—James] & Mary Fawcett bad

30th Thomas an Illetimate Child of Elizth Adamthwait bd

SEP 14th Anthony son of Thos & Isabel Knewstubb Bapd—AUGt 29th ye sane Born

SEPr 27th Janes [T.—James] son of James & Sarah Bayliffe bapd—SEPr 1t the same Born

SEPr 20th Mary Daugr of John & Ruth Bousfield Born—28th Baptized

SEPr 14th Isabel Daugr of George & Isabel Parkins Born—29th Bapd

DECr 5th John son of Jno & Mary Huchinson Baptd

JANy 29th Thomas son of Joseph & Allis Udall Bapd

FEB 15th Margaret Daugr of Anty & Isabel Fawcett bapd

16th Abraham son of Stephen Margt Dent Born—Marh 9th the sane Baptd

MARh 2d John son of Roger & Elizh Pinder Born—30th the same Baptized

1727.

APRl 20th Mary Daugr of Wilm & Mary Blackburne bapd

23d Thomas son to John & Mary Perkin of Lockholm

MAY 4th Thomas son of Richd & Ruth Fawcett bapd.

6th Mary Daugr of Joseph & Anne Hunter Bapd

23d John son of Edward & Mary Robinson Bapd

23th Stephen son of Hugh & Isabel Shaw Bapd

30th Robert son of John & Margt Todd Born—JUNE 6th the same Baptd

JULY 11th Anne Daugr of Ralph & Anne Robinson [T.—of Dovingill] Bapd.

AUGt 1st Mary Daugr of Thos & Mary Fawcett [T.—o' th' Tarnhouse] Bapd

23d William an Ilegetnate son of Agnas Furnas Bapd

OCTr 10 Richard sun of Richd & Mary Fothergill [T.—o' th' Litheside] Bapd.

BIRTHS AND CHRISTNINGS.

Novr 5th Robert son of Thos & Marg^t Scarborough Bap
30 Mary Daug^r of John & Mary Parkins Bap^d
JAN^y 25 John son of George & Jennet Jackson Born—15th FEB^y the same Bapt^d.
FEB. 29 Ruth Daug^r of Willm & Mary Jackson Bap^d
MARCH 16 [T.—17] Isabel Daug^r of Mathew & Mary Whitfield Bap^d

1728.

APRIL 11th Agnas Daug^r of Elizabeth Harper Baptized
23 Margaret Daug^r of John & Rachel Richardson town Bap.
MAY 14 Richard son of John & Ma^rgaret Fawcett Blaflatt
MAY 16th William son of Willm & Alice Heskin Baptized
JUNE 11th Alice Daug^r of Willm & Ann Howgill Bap^d
14th Magdalen Daug^r of Soloman & Mary Constantine Bap.
20th Jane Daug^r of Michael & Jennet Taylor Bap.
27th Margaret Daug^r of Rich^d & Eliz^h Bovil Bap
JULY 2^d Elizabeth Daug^r of John & Mary Hutchinson
21th William son of John & Ann Udall Bap^d
25th Ruth Daug^r Anthony & Eliz^h Parkins Bap^d
AUG 14th Margaret Daug^r of ye Rev^d m^r Toulmin Deaseas^d and Mrs Margaret his wife Baptized
SEP 4th Agnas Daug^r of James & Marg^t Fawcett Bap^d
OCT^r 20 Margaret Daug^r of Joseph & Marg^t Hanson bap.
Novr 3^d Isabel Daug^r of Thos and Isabel Fawcett bap
19th John son of Jonathan & Marg^t Alderson Bap^d
DEC^r 15th Mary Daug^r of John and Jane [T.—Margaret] Blackburne bap
22^d Joshua illegitmate son of Richd Murthwaite & Margaret Pinder Bap
JAN 19th Agnas Daug^r of John & Marg^t Sanderson bap^d
FEB 13th Isabel Daug^r of Thos & Anne Fothergill Bapt^d
16th Sarah Daug^r of Hugh & Isabel Shaw bap

1729.

MAY 4th John son of Thom^s & Isabel Hastwhitle Bap^d
11th Ellian^r Daughter of Joseph & Allice Udall Bap^d
JUNE 1st Isabel Daught^r of John & Sibbal Fawcet B^d
1st Margaret Daught^r of Thos & Elian^r Hunter B^d
15th Sarah Daughter of Willm & Mary Blackurn B^d

BIRTHS AND CHRISTNINGS.

July 2d	Elizabth Daughtr of Rogr & Elizabth Pindar Bd
20th	George son of Christophr & Elizabth Marvil Bapd
20th	Margaret Daughtr of Willm & Margt Clemison Bd
Decemr 25th	George son of Anthony & Isabel Fawcet Baptd
Jan 22d	John son of Thoms & Isabel Whitehead Bapd
Feb 22d	Jennet Daughtr of solomn & Margt Constantine Bd

1730.

Ap 12th	Mary Daughter of John & Margaret Hewetson Bd
May 12th	Elizabeth Daughter of Richd & Sarah Fothergil Bap
June 4th	Isabel Daughter to Joseph &(1) Hunter Bapd
June 29th	Isabel Daughtr to John & Rachel Chamberlain Bd
July 2d	Thos son of Adam & Mary Bird Bapd
7th	Margaret Daughter to Willm & Mary Jackson Bd
Octob. 13th	Ruth Daughter to Richd & Margart Murthwait Bd
25th	George son to John & Anne Udale—Bapd
25	Dorathy Daughter to Thoms & Margaret Ion Bpd
Nov: 6th	Anne Daughter to Richd & Mary Fothergill Bd
Decem 3d	Agnes Daughter to John & Rachel Richardson Bd
6th	Was born Elizabeth Daughtr to the Revd Mr Mounsey
15th	& Mary his wife, & Baptized Decr: 15th
21st	Thos son to Willm & Mary Fawcet [T.—of Artlegarth] Bapd
Jan 28th	Anne Daughtr to James & Mary Fawcet Bd

1731.

May 14th	Stephen & Thoms 2 sons of Christophr & Eliz: Marvel [T. o' th' Wath] twins Bd
19th	Sarah Daughter to Thos & Mary Fawcet [T.—o' Stenneskeugh] Bapd
June 17th	Mary Daughter to John & Mary Coupld [T.—o' Caldbeck] Bd
July 4th	John son to John & Sibbal(2) [T.—Mary] Fawcet oth Back Side Bd
Augst 14th	John son to Thos & Frances Bayliff o' Murthw: Bapd
Sep. 24th	Mary Daughtr to Geo. & Mary Burton o' high Lane Bapd
Sep. 26th	Sarah Daughter to John & Jane Blackburn [T.—o' th' Town] Bd

(1) Christian name not given. T. has "Thomas & Anne."
(2) Originally "Mary."

BIRTHS AND CHRISTNINGS.

Sep. 30th Agnes * [T.—Isabel] daughter to Thos & Margaret Scarbrough Bap^{d}

Novemb^{r} 18 Anne Daughter to Sim^{n} & Elizabth Bousefield [T.— of Scarsikes] Bap^{d}

30th Was William son to Anthony & Jane Fawcet [T.—o' th' Crooks] Bap^{d}

Jan 13th Anne Daughter to Josep & Anne Hunter o' Wand^{l} B^{d}

March 18th Isabel Daughter to Rich^{d} & Mary Fawcet o' Dubs B^{d}

1732.

March 25th Was Isabel Daughter to Robt & Isabel Potter o' Fellend Bap^{d}

April 13th Elizabeth Daughter to Rich^{d} & Sarah Fothergill Bap^{d}

† May 17th John son of John & Marg^{t} Fawcet Townhead Born

Augst 13th Mary Daughter of Willm & Mary Jackson Bap^{d}

Augst 29th Isabella Daughter to Mr Thomas Coulston & Agnes his wife B^{d}

Septem^{r} 1st Mary Daughter to solom^{n} & Mary Constantine Bap^{d}

Sepr 10 George son to George & Jennet Jackson o' Fell-end Bap^{d}

Octob^{r} 4th Rich^{d} son to Mr Richd Mitchel & Agnes his wife o' Town end B^{d}

Decemb^{r} 7th Isabel Daughter to Jno & Mary Hutchinson [T.—o' Newbigin] Bap^{d}

25th Margaret Daughter to Jno & Mary Coupl^{d} o' Caldbeck B^{d}

Jan 1st Stephen son to Christoph^{r} & Elizabeth Marvel o' Wath Bap^{d}

9th Jonath^{n} son to Thom^{s} & Frances Bayliff o' murthw^{t} Bap^{d}

Jan 16th Mary Daughter to Rich^{d} & Mary Fothergill o' Lythside Bap^{d}

25th Elizabeth Daughter to Jno & Margaret Sanderson Bap^{d}

28th Margaret Daughter to George & Abigail Whitehead B^{d}

Febr 22^{d} Anne Daughter to Jno & Anne Udal [T.—o' Garrshill] Bap^{d}

27th Robt son to the Revd Mr Mounsey & Mary his wife was Born & the same Day Baptized.

March 15th George son to George & Margaret Perkin o' Lockholm Bap^{d}

16th Mary Daughter to Thomas & Agnes Stubbs o' Bowderdale B^{d}

1733.

Apr^{l} 26th Was Willm son to Henery & Elian^{r} Hunter Bap^{d}

---

* Originally "Isab^{l}."

BIRTHS AND CHRISTNINGS.

JUNE 6th — Margaret Daughter to John & Margaret murras [T.—o' Newbign] Bd

10th — Isabel Daughter to Willm & Mary Fawcet o'th High Lane Bapd

20th — James son to George & Mary Burton o' Greenside Bapd

AUGst 12th — Thomas son to Thoms & Margaret Metcalf o' Brounbr Bd

29th — George son to Thomas & Isabel Haistwhittle o' fellend Bd

SEPbr 6th — John son to John & Rachel Chamberlain o' steneskeugh Bd

18th — Agnes Daughter to Thomas & Margt Ion o' newbign Bd

OCTOBr 8th — Anne Daughter to Antho: & Elizabeth Robinson o' Brownbr Bd

13th — Anthony an illegitimate son to Agnes Meckow [T.— o' Brackenbr] Bapd

DECEMBr 14th — Sarah Daughter to Willm & Mary Fothergill o' fell end Bd

29th — William son to Richard & Agnes Mitchell o' Town Bap.

FEB 19th — Michael son of John & Sibbal Fawcet o' Backside Chrisd

24th — Margaret Daughter to Robt & Isabel Potter [T.—o' Sprintgill] Chrd

27th — Elizabeth Daughter to John & Mary Coupland o' Caldbeck Chrd

MARCH 5th — Thomas son to Joseph & Mary Chamberlain o' Adamthwt Chrd

10th — John son to Richard & Agnes Gregson o' Sandwath Chrd

1734.

APRIL 21st — James son to Jno & Rachel Richardson o' Town Chrd

MAY 2d — Margaret Daughter to Robt. & Elizabeth Bovel o' Newbign Chd

JUNE 9th — John son of John & Margaret Huetson Bapd

† 11th — Anne Daughter to Richd & Mary Fawcet Chrd

20th — Stephen son to Thomas & Faith Dent o' Sandbed Chrd

JULY 7th — John son to William & Anne Howgill Chrd

AUG 11th — Isabel Daughter to Ralph & Isabel Alderson o' Crooks Chrd

12 — Henery son to George & Margaret Perkins o' Lockholme Chd

25th — James son to Thomas & Margaret Metcalf [T.—o' stenneskeugh] Bd.

SEPTEMBr 20th — Isabel Daughter to John & Anne Alderson [T.—o' Cowbank] Chrd

BIRTHS AND CHRISTNINGS.

NOVEMBr 20th John son to Roger & Elizabeth Pindar o' high Lane Chrd

DECEMBr 5th Elizabeth Daughter to William & Barbara Hunter Chrd

8th Mary Daughter to Mr Thos Coulston & Ann his wife born & Baptd 19th

JAN 21st Phebe Daughter to Richd & Mary Fothergill o' Lytheside Chrd

23d Agnes Daughter to Richd & Sarah Fothergill o' Crosbanck Chrd

FEB 2d John son to John & Margaret Thompson [T.—o' Weesdall] Chrd

22d John son to Simon & Elizabeth Bousefield [T.—o' Scarsikes priv :] Chrd

25th Elizabeth Daughter to Richd & Margt Murthwait [T.—o' Low Lane] Chrd

MARCH 2d Isabel Daughter to George & Mary Burton [T.—o' Greenside] Chrd

1735.

MARCH 25th Elizabeth Daughter to Mathew & Isabel Constantine Chrd

APRIL 3d Mary * [T.—Elizabeth] Daughter to Solomn & Mary Constantine Chd

JUNE 16th John son to Thomas & Agnes Stubbs Chrd

26th William son to John & Margaret Sanderson Chrd

SEPTEMbr 15th Isabel Daughter to Anthony Robinson Bapd

Novbr 6th Thomas son to Thos & Isabel Haistwell Chd

15th Isabel Daughter to Thos & Faith Dent o' Sandbed Chd

27th John son to John & Mary Coupland o' Caldbeck Chd

DECber 20th Joseph son of John & Anne Udall Chd

JANry 31st George son to Richd & Agnes Gregson o' Sandwath Chd

FEBry 22d Christophr son to Christopher & Elizabeth Marvel Chd

26th John son to Christopher & Sarah Fawcet Chd

1736.

Apl 22d John son to Henery & Elianor Hunter Chd

MAY 25th Elizabeth Daughter to Jno. Fawcet o' sprintgill Chd

JUNE 2d Mary & Ruth Daughter—Twins of Robt. & Eliz. Bovel [T.—o' Newbign] Chd

---

* Originally written Elizabeth.

BIRTHS AND CHRISTNINGS.

JUNE 20th	John son to John & Rachel Richardson Chd
22d	Isabel Daughter to George & Margt Perkins Chd
JULY 11th	George son to Thomas & Margaret Metcalf Chd
AUG 15th	Jonathan son to Jno & Anne Alderson Chrd
SEPbr 8th	Anne Daughter to Willm. & Eliz. Fothergill o' Bridge Chd
12th	Jennet Daughter to Wm & Barbara Hunter Chrd
16th	Mary Daughter to Joseph & Isabel Hanson Chd
23d	Robt son to Mr Robt Mounsey Clerk & Mary his wife was born—& Bapd OCTOBr ye 7th
NOVbr 24th	John son to Antho. & Eliz. Robinson o' Newbign Chrd
DECbr 16th	Ephraim son to George & Isabel Jackson o' fellend Chd
28th	Agnes Daughter to Eliz. Adamthwait an Illegitimate child Chd
JAN 25th	James son to Thomas & Frances Bayliff Chrd
MARCH 6th	Richd son to Jno & Margaret Thompson [T.—o' Weesdal] Chrd
12th	Antho son to Antho & Frances Fothergill o' murthwt Chd

1737.

APRl 22d	Anne Daughter to Jno & Sibbal Fawcet o' Backside Chd
MAY 1st	George son to Miles & Eliz. Ayrey Chd
4th	Mary Daughter to Thos & Faith Dent o' Sandbed Chd
8th	Eliz. Daughter to Richd & Agnes Gregson Chrd
JUNE 7th	Mark son to Joseph & Anne Richardson o' Town Chd
30th	John son to Joseph & Mary Chamberlain Chrd
JULY 17th	Christophr son to Willm & Dinah Coupland Chrd
AUGst 26th	Isabel Daughter to Agnes Furnace an Illegitimate Child Chd
SEPber 27th	Margaret Daughter to Richd & Mary Fothergill o' Lythside Chrd
† OCTOr 16	Willm son of Thos & Agnes Stubbs Chrd
NOV. 9th	Mary Daughter to Richd & Mary Fawcet o' Dubs Chrd
DECber 18	Agnes Daughter to John & Mary Coupland Chrd
DEC 31	John son to Henery & Mary Fothergill o' Newbign Chrd
JANry 8th	Thomas son to John & Margaret Fawcet o' Town Bapzd
21th	Margaret Daughter to John & Margart Murras Bapzd
FEB 11th	Mary Daughter to Christophr & Sarah Fawcet Bapd
MAR 9th	Margt Daughter to John & Mar: Hewetson Sprintgill Bpd
20th	Elizabeth Daughter to Robt Potter o' Adamthwt Bd

BIRTHS AND CHRISTNINGS.

1738.

Apr^{l} 5th	Margar^{t} Daughter to Rich^{d} & Agnes Mitchel Ch^{d}
May 9th	Richard son to Thom^{s} & Marg^{t} Metcalf Bap^{d}
14th	Thomas son to Jno & Anne Alderson Chris^{d}
21st	John son to Jno & Mary Fawcet o' alm pot Chr^{d}
June 4th	John son to Chris. & Sarah Rennison Chr^{d}
June 7th	Elizabeth Daughter to Geo. & Mary Burton Chr^{d}
† 9th	James son of Thos & Isabel Fothergill of Brownb^{r} Born
July 27th	Stephen son to Thomas & Isabel Haistwhittle Chr^{d}
Sept^{ber} 21st	Hen^{ry} son to Henery & Elianor Hunter Bapt^{d}
Oct^{ber} 21st	Jane Daughter to James & Marg^{t} Hewetson B^{d}
Jan 16th	William son to Joseph & Sibbal Spooner Ch^{d}
30th	Mary Daughter to Antho: & Elizabth Robinson Ch^{d}
Feb. 25th	Richard Son to Robt & Sarah Fawcet Ch^{d}
March 10th	Anne Daughter to Rich^{d} & Agnes Gregson Bap^{d}
11th	Anne Daughter to Jno & Rachel Richardson Chr^{d}
15th	Mary Daughter to William & Marg^{t} Clemison Chr^{d}

1739.

Apr^{l} 1st	Was Margaret Daughter to Jno & Marg^{t} Thompson Chr^{d}
22nd	John son of Thomas & Margaret Ion Bap^{d}
28th	Isabel Daughter to Stephen & Margaret Dent o' Dovingill B^{d}
May 27th	Jennet Daughter to Joseph & Isabel Hanson Bap^{d}
June 24th	Hannah Daughter to Ralph & Isabel Alderson Bap^{d}
July 18th	William son to Simon & Elizabeth Bousefield Bap^{d}
22th	Jennet Daughter to John Shaw o' Stenneskeugh Chr^{d}
Augst 12th	Mary Daught^{r} to Christop^{r} & Sarah Fawcet Chr^{d}
30th	Margaret Daughter illegitimate of Alice Perkin Bap^{d}
Sep^{ber} 16th	Margaret Daughter to Thos & Marg^{t} Metcalf Chr^{d}
Nov^{ber} 11th	Joseph son to Thos & Marg^{t} Stubbs Chr^{d}
16th	Ruth Daughter to Mary Fawcet o' Intack B^{d}
Feb 22^{d}	Margaret Daughter to Rich^{d} & Sarah Fothergill o' Crosbank Ch^{d}
March 2^{d}	Elianor Daughter to Miles & Eliz: Lamb Chr^{d}
14th	Thomas son to Rich^{d} & Agnes Mitchel Chr^{d}
1740. 17th	Margaret Daughter to Jno & Mabel Fawcet Chr^{d}
April 24th	Margar^{t} Daughter to George Fawcet o' Murthw^{t} C^{d}

BIRTHS AND CHRISTNINGS.

APRIL 27th Sarah Daughter to Joseph & Mary Chamberln Chd
29th Richard son to Richd & Mary Fothergill o' Lythside Chrd
MAY 1st Isabel Daughter to Tho. & Frances Bayliff Chrd

1740.

3d Margt Daughter to Anthony Urwain Chrd
JUNE 4th Michael son to Robt. & Eliz. Bovel Chrisd
7th Was Anne Daughter to the Revd Mr Mounsey & Mary his wife born, & Bapd JUNE 17th
24th Mary Daughter to John & Barbary Atkinson Bd
JULY 8th Anne Daughter to John & Mary Birtel Chrd
11th Anne Daughter to Robt & Isabel Potter Chrd
23d Elizabth Daughtr to Mr Thos Coulston & Anne his wife Bapd
AUG 14th Thoms son to Robt & Mary Hunter sprintgill Chrd
21st Anne Daughter to Antho & Margart Morland Chrd
23d Margart Daughtr to Stephen & Margt Dent Dovingill Bd
31st Anne Daughtr to Solomn & Mary Constantine Bd
SEP 24th Ann Daughter to Geo: & Mary Burton Chrd
OCTOBr 9th Elizabeth Daughtr to Jos: & Sibbal Spooner Chd
† 18th Willm son of Thos & Isabel Fothergill of Brownbr born Bapd 22d
NOVber 8 John son to Mathew & Isabel Constantine Chd
FEB 15th Sarah Daughter to Hen: & Mary Fothergill Ch
23d Was John son to Richd & Frances Mounsey Chrisd—born JANrY ye 25th
MARCH 19th John son to Jacob & Mary Shaw o' Adamth'wt Ch
21st James son to John & Mary Ivison Bapd
22d Mary Daughter to John & Mary Fawcet Bd.

1741.

APRIL 9th Was James son to John Shaw o' Steneskeugh Chd
21st Rachel Daughtr to Jno & Rachel Richardson Chrd
28th Anne Daughter to John Murrace o' Newbign Chrd
MAY 9th Mary Daughter to Hen: & Eliant Hunter Chrd
JUNE 26th Michl son to Anthony & Eliz. Robinson Chrd
JULY 18th Isabel Daughter to Joseph & Isabel Hanson Chrd
SEPTEMbr 12th William son to James* & Margt Hewetson Chrd

* Changed from "Jno" to "James."

BIRTHS AND CHRISTNINGS.

Octobr 1st	Anne an illegitimate Child of Anne Porter Bd
Novbr 21st	Christophr son to Ralph & Isabl Alderson Chrd
Decber 19th	Hugh son to Richd & Isabel Bayliff Artlegarth Bd
26th	Henry son to Tho: & Margt Bousefield Bd
Jan 6th	John son to Mr Thos Coulston & Anne his wife Chrd
30th	Agnes Daughtr to Jno & Mabel Fawcet Chrd
Feb 18th	Thos son to Jno & Eliz Fawcet o' Backside Bd
March 3d	Thos son to Jno & Barbara Atkinson o' Caldbeck Chd
21st	Anto son to Geo: & Elianr Fawcet Chrd

1742.

June 17th	Was Mary Daughter to Jams & Mary Shaw Bd
26th	John son to John & Jane Aislop Chrisd
July 1st	John son to Anthony Urwin Chrd
26th	Anne Daughter to James & Anne Fawcet of Wath Cd
Augst 21st	Anne Daughtr to Stephn & Margt. Dent Chd
Sepber 6th	George son to Anthony & Margt Morland Chd
12th	Jams(1) [T.—Jo] son to Wm & Anne(1) [T.—Eliz.] Hutchinson Chrd
Octo. 17th	George son to Antho & Mabl Wooler Travelers Chrd
22d	Anne Daughtr to Richd & Mabl Nelson Chrd
23d	Elizabth Daugr to Robt & Mary Hunter Chd
Nov. 8th	Were two Daughter Twins to Thos. & Isabl Haistwell to wit Mary the elder & Elizabeth ye youngr Bapd
	The same day Isabel Daughter to John & Mary Birdal Bd
11th	William son to Thos & Isabel Fothergill Brounbr Bd
13th	William son to Jacob & Mary Shaw Chrd
14th	Christophr son to John & Mary Coupland Chrd
Decbr 30th	James son to Robt & Margt Fawcet Greenside Chrd
Jan 1st	Willm son to Tho & Frances Bayliff Chrd
23d	Margart Daughter to Willm. & Mary Hewetson Chrd
28th [T.--23]	Isl Daughter to John & Mary [T.—Margt] Fawcet Chrd

1743.

June 14th	Was Margart Daughtr to Willm & Agnes Adamthwait Cd
26th	Thos son of Jiffray & Eliz Hodgson Chrd
July 17th	Mary Daughr to Jno & Margt Murras Chrd

(1) These names appear to have been "Jo" & "Eliz."

BIRTHS AND CHRISTNINGS.

JULY 31st	Marg^{t} Daughter to Jno & Sarah* Fawcet Chr^{d}
AUGst 4th	Willm son to Joseph & Anne Hunter Chr^{d}
SEP^{ber} 4th	Mar. Daughter to Miles & Eliz Lamb Chr^{d}
NOV^{br} 14th	Jane Daughter to Rich^{d} & Jane Hewetson Chr^{d}
DEC^{br} 3^{d}	John son to John & Mabel Fawcet Chrd
11th	George son to James & Mary Shaw Chr^{d}
14th	Anne Daughter to Jno. Shaw Steneskeugh Chr^{d}
17th	John an illegitimate son of Isabel Fawcet Bap^{d}
26th	George son to Thos & Mary Fawcet Bowb^{r} h^{d} Chr^{d}
27th	John son to Geo: & Elin^{r} Fawcet Murthw^{t} Chr^{d}
30th	Marg^{t} Daught^{r} of Robt & Eliz. Britain Travel^{rs} B^{d}
JAN^{ry} 9th	George son to Ralph & Isab^{l} Alderson Chr^{d}
14th	James son to Joseph & Isab^{l} Hanson Chr^{d}
19th	Marg^{t} Daught^{t} to Antho & Eliz Robinson Chr^{d}
30th	John son to Jno & Anne Brown Chr^{d}
FEB^{r} 8th	Anne Daught^{r} to Joseph & Sibbal Spooner Chr^{d}
16th	John son to Robt Potter o' Adamthwait Chr^{d}

1744.

AP^{l} 13th	Was Marg^{t} Daugh^{r} to Jno & Bar: Atkinson Bap^{d}
MAY 28th	Agnes Daughter to Thos & Agnes Stubbs Bap first ith' N. Church
JUNE 1st	Antho son to James & Isab^{l} Fawcet [T.—Lockholme] Bap^{d}
JULY 16th	Stephen son to Antho Dent Lytheside B^{d}
AUGst 12th	Mary Daughter to Jno & Isab^{l} Robinson B^{d}
SEP^{r} 23^{d}	Anne Daughter to Jeoffrey & Marg^{t} Denny B^{d}
OCT^{r} 8th	Fawcet son to Robt & Mary Hunter Bap^{d}
13th	Joseph son to Chris: & Sar. Renaldson B^{d}
20th	W^{m} son to W^{m} & Agnes Adamthwaite B^{d}
21st	Miles son to Antho & Marg^{t} Morland B^{d}
26th	Robt son to Jos. & Mary Chamberlain B^{d}
DEC^{br} 6th	Ruth Daught^{r} to Thos & Marg^{t} Bousefield B^{d}
8th	James son to Jno & Mary* Fawcet B^{d}
15th	Eliz: Daughter to John Shaw Stenneskeugh B^{d}
24th	Anne Daught^{r} to W^{m} & Martha Milner Travellers B^{d}
27th	Robt son to Robt & Eliz Bovill Bap^{d}

* Originally written "Margt."

BIRTHS AND CHRISTNINGS.

Jan. 10th	Mary Daughter to Jno & Margt Stubbs Bd
28th	Isabl Daughr to James & Agnes Fawcet Bapd

1745.

March 28th	Was Eliz Daughtr to Wm & Temperance Hunter Bd
Apl 2d	Thos son to Thos & Margt Holme Bapd
14th	Thos son to Jacob & Mary Shaw Bd
21st	John son to John & Mary Elwood Bapd
May 5th	Antho. son Antho & Dor. Urwin Bapd
21st	John son to Robt & Margt Fawcet Greenside Bd
June 2d [T.—3d]	Mary Daugr to Jno & Anne Orton Bd
July 7th	John & Thos Twin sons to James & Margt Hewetson Bd
10th	Agnes Daughr to Josph & Frances Langhorne Bd
24th	John son to James & Margt Maggee Bapd born 4th
Augst 15th	Antho son to James & Mary Shaw Bd
19th	John son to John Robinson Dovingill Bapd
25th	Anne Daughtr to Mathw & Isabl Constantine Bapd
Sepber 6th	Thomas son to Jno & Mabel Fawcet Bapd
October 26th	Isabel Daughtr to Wm & Sar. Taylor Bapd
27th	Henry son to Willm & Alice Fothergill Crossbank Bd
30th	Anne Daughter to Wm & Anne Huttchison Bapd
Novber 6th	Richard son of Jno & Jane Aislop Bapd
17th	Anne Daughtr to James & Anne Fawcet Bd
Decber 10th	Jane illegitimate Daughter of Agnes Dover fellend Bd
31st	Faith Daughter of Thos & Faith Dent Bd
Janry 28th	Antho: son to Antho: & Eliz: Robinson Bapd
Feb 13th	Thoms son to Jno & Margt Thompson Bapd
19	Mathm son to Benjamn & Mary Judkin Bapd
March 6th	Jno son John & Mary Fawcet o' Murthwt Bapd
17th	Anthony son to Joseph & Sibbal Spooner Bapd

1746.

Aprl 2d	John son to Robt & Eliz. Fawcet Bapd
14th	Margt [T.—Mary] Daughtr to Joseph Hunter Bapd
15th	Isabl Daughtr to Anthony Dent Lytheside Bd
May 19th	Thos son to Stephen & Sarah Fothergill o' Lockholme Bd
June 7th	Willm son to Geo: & Elianr Fawcet Studfold Bd
17th	Antho: son to John & Mary Fawcet Dovingll. Bd

BIRTHS AND CHRISTNINGS.

July 13th	Anth° son to Jeofrey Denny Artlegarth Bd
20th	Thoms son to Richd & Jane Hewetson Bapd
29th	John son to Stephen Chamberln Bapd
Augst 25th	Willm son to Robt & Mary Hunter Bapd
Sepber 4th	Anne Daughtr to Jn° Robinson Dovingill Bapd
24th	Anth° son to Stephn & Margt Dent Dovingll Bd
Octobr 28th	Richard son to Jeofrey & Eliz. Hodgson Bapd
	Same Day Eliz Daughtr to Jn° & Anne Brown Bapd
Janry 23d	Richard son of Robt. & Eliz. Garnet Bapd
Febr 15th	John son of Michael Taylor Bd
March 15th	Anne & Mary Twin Daughters of Willm & Agnes Kitchin Bd
March 24th	Thomas son to Thos & Isabel Fothergill o' Brownbr Bd

1747.

April 3d	Was John son to James & Dorathy Perkins Bd
6th	Elizabth Daughter to James & Agnes Fawcet Bd
13th	Mary Daughter to Robt & Margt Fawcet Greensde Bd
May 17th	Joseph son to Joseph & Isabl Hanson Bapd
30th	Deborah Daughtr to Robt & Isabl Potter Bapd
June 10th	Rich son to John & Mary Birtel Bapd
July 30th	Barbary Daughter to John & Barbary Atkinson Bapd
Augst 4th	Ant° son to Ant° Urwin Bapd
15th	Richd son to Thos & Mary Fawcet Dovingill Bapd
Sepber 3d	Jn° son to Ant° & Margt Morland Bd
Octobr 27th	James son to John & Mabel Fawcet Bapd
Novbr 5th	John son to Richd & Eliz. Robinson Elmpot Bd
Decbr 3d	Hen: son of John & Isabl Robinson Stenkeugh Bd
19th	Anne Daughtr of Micl & Anne Taylr Newbign Bd
Janry 26th	Geo: son to Henry & Mary Fothergill Newbign Bd
28th	George son to Miles & Elizth Lamb Bapd
29th	Willm son to Anthony & Elizth Robinson Bapd
Febr 6th	Sibbella Daughter to Willm & Agnes Adamthwait Bd
10th	David son to James Richison o' Town Born

1748.

April 13th	Was William son to Thos & Margt Bousfield Town hd Bap
14th	Jacb son of Jacob & Mary Shaw Boutherdall Bapd

BIRTHS AND CHRISTNINGS.

APRIL 20th Henry son to Hen & Isab[l] Lickbarrow Bap[d]
JUNE 15th Margar[t] Daught[r] to Rob[t] & Eliz Fawcet Town B[d]
AUG[st] 14th Jn[o] son of W[m] & Temperance Hunter Bap[d]
17th W[m] son to William Taylor o' mirehouse [T.—Murthwait] Bap[d]
21st Mary Daughter to Rich[d] Gregson tranmire B[d]
OCTOB: 30th Eliz. Daughter to Jeofrey Denny Bapt[d]
NOV[br] 2d Anne Daughter to John & Anne Brown Bap[d]
NOV[br] 29th Jane Daughter to John & Eliz: Fothergill Bap[d]
DEC[br] 27th [T.—7th] Ma: [T.—Mar[t]] Daughter to Robt Garnett Bap[d]
JAN[ry] 16th Jonoth[n] son to Joseph & Hunter o' Wandal Bap[d]
FEB: 2d Mary Daughter to Tho[s] & Mary [T.—Marg[t]] Fawcet Dovingill B[d]
15th Mary Daughter to Joseph & Sibbal Spooner Bap[d]
† JAN 21st Joseph son to Jos & Sarah Breaks born

1749.

† APRIL 10th John son to John & Marg[t] Stubbs Bap[d]
APRIL 12th Was Edward son to Benjam[n] & Mary Judkin Bap[t]
25th Mary Daught[r] to Ralph & Isabel Alderson Bap[d]
29th Anne Daughter to Tho[s] & Isab[l] Fothergill Brownb[r] Bap[d] born 16th
JUNE 27th Isabel Daughter to W[m] & Marg[t] Shaw o' Steneskeugh Bap[d]
JULY 13th John son to Matthew & Isabel Wilkinson o' Newbig[n] Bap[d]
AUG[st] 26th Rich[d] son to John & Isabel Robinson Steneskeugh B[d]
SEP[ber] 17th George son to Geo: & Elian[r] Fawcet o' Studfold B[d]
23d Alice Daughter to Will[m] & Agnes Kitchin Bap[d]
OCTO[r] 23d { Ruth Daughter to Robt & Marg[t] Fawcet Greenside Bap[d]
Mar. [T.—Mar[t]] Daughter to Ant[o] & Marg[t] Morland Stoup-hill Yeat Bap[d] }
NOV[r] 2d Mary Daughter to John & Mabel Fawcet Bap[d]
DECEMB[r] 1st James son to William & Sarah Lynslay o' Town Bap[d]
JAN[ry] 3d Richard son to Richard & Jane Hewetson Bap[d]
17th William son to Michael & Mary Taylor Bap[d]
MARCH 15th Ruth Daughter to John & Eliz: Fawcet Backside Bap[d]
† MARCH 16th Thomas son of James & Agnes Fawcet B[d]

BIRTHS AND CHRISTNINGS.

1750.

April 4th	Was John son to John & Elizabeth Fothergill of Bowderdale Bapd
May 16th	Agnes Daughter to Thoms & Margt Bousefield Town hd Bd
	Same Day was Anne Daughter to Michael & Ann Taylor Bapd
19th	Robt son to Robt & Eliz: Fawcet of Town Bapd
June 22d	Thoms son to Richd & Mary Breaks Bapd
July 4th	Sarah Daughter to Richd & Margt Gregson Bapd
24th	Isabel Daughter to Mathw & Isabel Constantine Bapd
† 29th	Antho son to Jeofrey & Margt Denny Bapd
Augst 11th	Francis Daughtr to Thoms & Mary Wholay Bapd
12th	Edward son to Antho & Dorathy Urwin Bapd
Sepber 23d	Alice Daughter to Joseph & Sarah Breaks Bapd
28th	James son to Henry & Isabel Lickbarrow Bapd
Novr 3d	William son to Willm & Agnes Kitchin Bapd
Decr 1st	Thos son to Henry & Mary Fothergill Bapd
8th	Henry son to Edwd & Mary Beck of Artlegarth Bapd
14th	John son to William & Temperance Hunter Bapd
15th	Ralph son to Antho & Eliz: Robinson Bapd
Janry 20th	James son to William Taylor Bapd
Feb: 19th	John son to Thos & Isabella shaw Clappers Bapd
24th	Samuel Gill son to Benjamin & Mary Judkin Bapd
March 6th	Melleta Daughter to Jno & Eliz: Shaw Garrshill Bapd
8th	Anne Daughter to John & Anne Brown Town Bapd

1751.

March 28th	Was Thos son to John & Mary Dawson Greenside Bapd
May 22d	Hannah Daughter to Joseph & Anne Hunter Wandal Bapd
26th	William son to William & Margt Nelson Town Bapd
Augst 5th	Heugh* son to Miles & Eliz Lamb Bapd
17th	Wm* son to John & Mabel Fawcet Bapd
24th	Isabel Daughter to Willm & Margt Shaw Steneskeugh Bapd
Sepber 27th	Dorathy Daughter to Joseph & Isabel Hanson Bapd

---

* Both names indistinct in original and also in T.

BIRTHS AND CHRISTNINGS.

Octo^br^ 3^d^ [T.—1st] Ruth Daughter to Arthur & Marg^t^ Bousfield Born & Bap^d^ same day
Novr 8th W^m^ son to Ralph & Isabel Alderson Bap^d^
16th Robert son to John & Marg^t^ Haistwell Bap^d^
Dec^br^ 13th Isabel Daughter to James Perkins Greenside Bap^d^
23^d^ Thos son to Willm & *Hunter Sprintgill Bap^d^

1752.

Jan^ry^ 19th Isab^l^ Daught^r^ to Jos & Sibbal Spooner Bap^d^
† 16th Samuel son of Benjam^n^ and Mary Judkin Bap^d^
24th Robt son of Rich^d^ [T.—Robt] & Mary Breaks Bap^d^
† Feb 16th Thomas son of Willm and Mary Furnass Bap^d^
Feb 20 [T.—26] Jeremiah son to Thos & Jane Winder Wreygreen B^d^
March 6th Sibbal Daughter to Robt & Mary Hunter Street B^d^
April 9th George son to John & Isab^l^ Robinson Steneskeugh B^d^
Same Day Mary Daughter to W^m^ & Martha Thompson Bap^d^
11th George an Illegitimate son of Mary Coupland Town Bap^d^
30th Anne Daughter to Thos & Faith Dent Bap^d^
May 7th Agnes Daughter to Rich^d^ & Marg^t^ Gregson Bap^d^
10th Isab^l^ Daughter to Joseph & Sarah Breaks B^d^
20th George son to W^m^ & Mary Heblethwait Bap^d^
30th Robt son to Antho. & Sarah Dent Litheside Bap^d^
June 3^d^ John son to John & Mary Milner Bap^d^
4th William son to John & Alice Dent Bap^d^
6th Anne Daughter To Rich^d^ & Isab^l^ Taylor Bap^d^
July 20th Margar^t^ Daughter to Robt & Ruth Scarbrough B^d^
Sep^ber^ 17th Willm son to Jno & Marg^t^ Murrows Bap^d^
18th Isab^l^ Daughter to W^m^ & Temperance Hunter B^d^
Octo^br^ 2^d^ W^m^ son to Christop^r^ & Mary Mason Bap^d^
Novr 4th W^m^ son to Jno & Eliz: Fothergill Bowderd^le^ B^d^
20th John son to William & Isabella Milner Garrshill Bap^d^
24th Anth^o^ son to Anthony & Isabel Fawcet Town B^d^
30th [T.—20th] Thomas son to Henry & Isabel Lickbarrow B^d^
Dec^ber^ 6th Mary Daughter to James & Dorathy Perkins B^d^
26th [T.—22^d^] Agnes Daughter to John & Barbara Athinson B^d^

---

* Left blank, also blank in T.

BIRTHS AND CHRISTNINGS.

1753.

Jan^{ry} 24th	Jno son to Willm & Eliz Raw o' Newbig^{n} Bap^{d}
26th	James son to Thos & Mary Wholay Town Bap^{d}
Feb 8th	Geo: son to Geo: & Elin^{r} Fawcet Studfold Bap^{d}
April 15th	Anth^{o} son to Geo: & Isabel Shaw Murthw^{t} Bap^{d}
18th	Jno son to Christoph^{r} & Agnes Townson Springt^{ll} Bap^{b}
22^{d}	Willm son to Thos & Marg^{t} Bousfield Townhead Bap^{d}
May 12th	Anne Daughter to James & Mary Shaw Ell^{r}g^{ll} B^{d}
13th	Thomas son to John & Anne Brown Bap^{d}
16th	Elian^{r} Daughter to W^{m} & Isab Metcalf Backside Bap^{d}
17th	Thomas son to Willm & Marg^{t} Nelson Bap^{d}
July 4th	Sarah Daughter to Ant^{o} & Marg^{t} Morland Bap^{d}
8th	Thomas an Illegitimate Child of Marg^{t} Green Bap^{d}
Sep^{ber} 8th	Thos son to W^{m} & Martha Thompson B^{d}
19th	Thos son to James & Perkins Greenside Bap^{d}
Octo^{r} 7th	Ma: Daugh^{r} of Anthony Kirkbride of Backside Bap^{d}
15th	Michael son of Michael & Anne Taylor Bap^{d}
Novr 1st	Benjamin son to Rich^{d} & Ruth Shaw Town Bap^{d}
28th	Thos son to Willm Hunter Sprintgill Bap^{d}
Dec^{ber} 5th	Elizabth Daughter to Edwd & Mary Beck Artlegth B^{d}
15th	Sarah Daughter to Ralph & Isab^{l} Alderson Bap^{d}
19th	Mary Daughter to John & Marg^{t} Thompson Bap^{d}

1754.

Jan^{ry} 10th	Rich^{d} son of Thos & Isabel Wilson Bap^{d}
Feb 7th	Mary Daughter to W^{m} & Sarah Taylor B^{d}
15th	Mary Daughter to Rich^{d} & Jane Whitfield Bap^{d}
March 6th	Jane Daughter to Thos & Jane Windar Bap^{d}
	Same Day Agnes Daughter to W^{m} & Agnes Kitchin B^{d}
10th	John son to Arthur & Mag^{t} Bousfield Town Bap^{d}
20th	Mabel Daughter to John & Mabel Fawcet Town Bap^{d}
26th	Mathew son to Leon^{d} & Isabel Metcalf Bap^{d}
Ap 2^{d}	William An Illegitamate Son of Alice Knewstub Bap^{d}
9th	Thos son to Thos & Anne Preston Bap^{d}
16th	Thos son to James & Emmy Stubbs Town Bap^{d}
23^{d}	Anne Daughter to Thos & Mary Fawcet Bap^{d}
24th	Margaret Daughter to John & Isabel Robinson Bap^{d}

BIRTHS AND CHRISTNINGS.

May 18th Ma^{ry} Daughter to Geo: & Agnes Lamb Bap^{d}

June 6th Ruth an Illegitimate Daughter of Eliz: Adamthw^{t} B^{d}

July 14th Ma^{ry} Daughter to William & Mary Heblethwait Bap^{d}

Augst 27th Eliz: Daughter of Willm & Eliz: Shaw Bap^{d}

Sepr 7th Dorathy Daught^{r} of an unknown Wom^{n} brought to Nurse Fellend B^{d}

Novr 16th James son to August^{ne} & Anne Metcalf Town B^{d}

Decr 29th Joseph son to Benjam^{n} & Mary Judkin B^{d}

1755.

Jan^{ry} 2^{d} Elizabeth Daughter to Robert & Ruth Scarbrough* Bap^{d}

Jan^{ry} 17th John son to Thomas & Isabel Wilson Bap^{d}

24th Jane Daughter to Rich^{d} & Ruth Shaw Town B^{d}

Feb^{ry} 9th William son to Henry & Isabel Brunskel B^{d}

11th Thomas son to Thos & Marg^{t} Bousfield Town h^{d} Bap^{d}

March 1st Thos son to W^{m} & Eliz: Raw Town Bap^{d}

6th Willm son to Willm & Marg^{t} Hunter spr^{t} Gill B^{d} Wrey-

15th Mary Daughter to Math^{w} & Isab^{l} Wilkinson Newbig^{n}

Apr^{l} 2^{d} Antho son to Jno & Mary Birdal Bap^{d}

10th Eliz: Daughter to John & Alice Dent Bap^{d}

15th Agnes Daughter to Peter & Mag^{t} Hutchinson Bap^{d}

May 17th Agnes Daughter to Thomas & Mary Taylor Bap^{d}

24th Eliz. Daughter to Christop^{r} & Agnes Townson Bap^{d}

July 26th Thos son to Thom^{s} & Mary Fawcet Bap^{d}

borne Augst 15th [T.—17th] Eliz: Daughter to Arthur & Marg^{t} Bousfield Town Bap^{d} 29th

Sepb^{r} 4th Eliz Daughter to Ant^{o} & Eliz Robinson Bap^{d}

Decr 18th James son of James & Mary Shaw Ellerg^{ll} Bap^{d}

22^{d} Mary Daughter to Rich^{d} & Jane Whitfield Bap^{d}

28th Rich^{d} son to James & Emmy Stubbs Town Bap^{d}

1756.

Jan^{ry} 25th Was Mary Daughter to Francis & Anne Wholay Bap^{d}

same Day Eliz Daught^{r} of John & Anne Adamthw^{t} Bap^{d}

Feb 5th Isab^{l} Daughter to Steph^{n} & Ann Shaw born & Bap^{d} 12th and

Feb 29th Thom^{s} son of Isabel Stubbs wid^{w} Intack B^{d}

---

* Originally written "Murthwait."

BIRTHS AND CHRISTNINGS.

March 11th	Anthᵒ son of Thoms & Anne Preston Bapd
17th	Elianor Daughter to John & Isabel Banks Bapd
April 10th	Elth Daughter to Mathw & Ellin Whitfield Bapd
22d	John an Illegitamate son of Ellianr Fothergill murthwt Bd
May 2d	Eliz. Daughter to Richd & Jane Hewetson Artlegarth Bd
June 7th	Sarah Daughter to Willm & Sarah Taylor Bapd
10th	John son to Thos & Agnes Perkins Bapd
Ootobr 26th	Eliz. Daughter to Thoms & Mary Taylor Town Bapd
Novbr 22d	Tho. son to Thoms & Jane Winder Bapd
Decber 13th	Mary Daughtr to Michl & Anne Taylor Bapd
20th	Phebe Daughtr to Jno & Isabl Robinson Steneskeugh Bapd
21st	Thos son to Anto & Sarah Dent Litheside Bapd

1757.

† Janry 5th	Was Jno son to Richd & Jane Whitfield Bapd
[illegible] 16th	George son to Anto & Margt Morland Stouphill Yeat Bapd
28th	Ruth Daughtr to Wm & Agnes Kitchin Bapd
Noeb 3d	Jno son to Thos & Mary Fawcet Bapd
10th	Anne Daughter to Richd & Margt Howgill Bapd
[illegible] 12th	Thos son to Willm & Eliz: Shaw Bapd
March 16th	Mary Daughtr to Joseph & Sibbal Spooner Bapd
23d	Sarah Daughter to Richd & Ruth Shaw Bapd
24th	Richd son to John & Anne Brown Bapd
Apl 7th	Mary Daughter of Francis & Anne Whaley Bapd
17th	Geo: son of Rowland & Mary Postlethwait Bapd
May 5th	Anne Daughter to Wm & Temperance Hunter Bapd
June 3d	Anne Daughter to Wm & Margt Stubbs Town Bapd
12th	Thos son to Anthony & Margt Knewstub o' Hill Bapd
Augst 25th	John son of John & Barbary Atkinson Bapd
Octor 15th	Christiana Daughter to Thos & Magdalen Shaw Bapd
19th	James son of Willm & Margt Nelson Bapd
23d	Margt Daughtr of William & Eliz. Raw
Aovr 3d	Thos son of John & Elianor Haistwell fell-end Bapd
10th	John son of Jno & Anne Adamthwait fell-end Bapd
15th	Margaret Illegitimate Daughter of Agnes Fawcet widow Bapd
16th	Thos son of Robert and Ruth Scarborough of Low Lane

BIRTHS AND CHRISTNINGS.

Novr 17th Geo. son of James & Jane Fawcet Bapd
19th James son of Jno & Alice Dent Crooks Bapd
28th Thos son of Thos & Isabl Wilson Bapd
Decr 26th Mary Daughter of Richd & Eliz: Lindslay Bapd

1758.

Janry 18th Was Sarah Daughtr of Mathw & Elianor Whitfield Bapd
Same Day Fothergill son of Antho & Mary Metcalf Bapd
Feb 14th Jane Daughter of Thos Fothergill Bapd
April 15th Anthony son of Willm & Eliz Metcalf Bapd
May 31st Mary Daughter of Joshua & Mary Ewbank Lytheside Bapd
June 1st Hugh son of Stephen & Anne Shaw Town Bapd
6th Elizabeth Daughter of Thoms & Agnes Perkins Bapd
July 2d Richd son to James & Emmy Stubbs Town Bapd
Sepber 7th Margt Daughter of Christophr & Agnes Townson Bapd
Octor 14th Margt Daughter of Thos & Mary Fawcet
Decembr 13th [T.—18] Eliz. Daughter To Thoms & Jane Winder Wrey-green Bapd
19th Christopher son to Richd & Mary Willan Town Bapd

1759.

Janry 7th James son to William & Margt Nelson Town Bapd
14th Mary Daughter of Thos & Mary Taylor Town Bapd
26th Elizabeth Daugr of John & Ellianr Chamberlin Bapd
Febr 8th Edwd son of John & Margt Stubbs Bapd
27th Mary Daughter of Arthur & Margt Bousfield Bapd
March 1st Wm son of Antho & Margt Knewstubb Bapd
Apl 29th Ma Daughtr to Henry & Isabel Blackburn Bapd
July 26th Thos son to James & Mary Shaw Ellergill Bapd born June 11th
Augst 5th Sarah Daughtr to Richd & Ruth Shaw Town Bapd
9th Anne Daughtr to Geo: & Elizabth Udal Bapd
25th John son to Mr Wm* [T.—Thomas] Turner & Agns his wife Bapd
Septembr 26th Isabl Daughtr to James & Jane Fawcet Bapd
Octobr 1st Robt & Richd two illegitimate sons of Mary Coupland Youngr Bapd

---

* Originally "Thos."

BIRTHS AND CHRISTNINGS.

OCTOBr 18th Allon Fothergill son of Jno & Isabel Robinson Steneskeugh Bapd

Novr 28th James son of Mathw & Ellinr Whitfield Bapd

DECEMbr 15th Thomas son of Wm & Margt Hunter Sprintgill Bapd

16th Willm son of Francis & Ann Whaley Bapd

27th [T.—26] Mary Daughter of Wm & Margt Stubbs Bapd

31st James son of Anthony & Mary Metcalf Bapd

1760.

JANry 13th James Robinson illegitimate son of Isabl Fawcet Bapd

FEBr 7th Isabel Daughter of John & Elianor Haistwell Bapd

14th Thoms son of Willm & Agnes Kitchin Bapd

27th John son of John & Sarah Ward Bapd

28th Mary Daughter of John & Isabel Adamthwait Bapd

MARCH 23d [T.—3] John* [T.—James Braithwait] son of John & Eliz. Fawcet Town Bapd

24th Mary Daughter of Richd & Agnes Lambert Bapd

APRIL 30th Thomas son of Thomas & Agnes Perkins Bapd

MAY 24th Richd son of Michl & Anne Taylor Bapd

MAY 28th Wm son of Wm & Sarah Taylor Bapd

JULY 20th Ann Daughter of John & Margt Fawcet Bapd

SEPber 17 John son of John & Mary Thompson Bapd

18th Joseph son of John & Mary Birtal Bapd

OCTOr 2d Willm son of Wm & Sarah Lyndslay Bapd

8th John son of Jno & Alice Dent Bapd

13th Phebe Daughtr of Jno & Elianr Chamberlain Bapd

28th Eliz Daughter of Robt & Ruth Scarbrough Bapd

DECr 15th Edwd son of Christophr & Agnes Townson Bd

26th Thos son of Willm & Rachel Stubbs Bapd

1761.

JANry 3d Was Thos son of John & Mary Milner o' Greenside Bapd

FEB. 20th Mathew son of Mathew & Margt Constantine Bapd

APRl 20th John son of John & Eliz. Fawcet Bapd

APl 22d Jos son of Ths & Magdalen Shaw Bapd

23d James son of Anne Orton Bapd the name she went by here

---

* Originally "James Braithwait."

BIRTHS AND CHRISTNINGS.

May 12th Tho son of Thos: & Jane Winder Bapd
26th Tho. son of Thos: & Mary Tayler Bapd
† June 12th George son of James & Isabel Burton Baptd
Augst 19th Mary Daughr to Geo: & Eliz. Udal Bapd
Octor 28th Isabl Daughter of John Foster o' Hole Bapd
Novbr 2d Zilpah Daughter of John & Margt Stubbs o' Ashfield Bapd
19th Isabl Daughter of Anto & Agnes Hodgson o' Town Bapd
Same Day Anne Daughter of Stephen & Anne Shaw o' Town Bapd
Decbr 10th Margt Daughter to Richd & Ruth Shaw Bapd

1762.

Janry 2d Was James son of John & Elianr Haistwell Bapd
5th Hugh son of James & Mary Shaw Bapd
Feb 4th Mar. Daughter of Edmd & Sarah Waller Bapd
12th John son of Wm & Margt Stubbs Bapd
March 11th Thomas son of Mathew & Elizabeth Bell Lockholme Bd
13th Willm son of Thos & Mary Whoaley Bd
14th Anne Daughter to John & Isabel Banks Bd
May 9th John son to Wm & Margt Nelson Town Bapd
13th Jennet Illegitimate Daughter of Mary Constantine Bapd
31st Margt Daughter to James & Mary Shaw o' Ellergill Bapd
June 10th Sarah Daughtr to Wm & Agnes Kitchin Bapd
30th Margt Daughtr to Isaac & Anne Smith Bapd
July 15th Margt Daughter to Wm & Margt Witton Bapd
† Augst 14th Willm son to John & Isabl Robinson Steneskeugh Bapd
Sepber 5th George son of Wm & Eliz. Raw of Town Bapd
15th Richd son of Richd & Anne Cuningham Bapd
19 Anne Daughter of Francis & Anne Wholay Bapd
28th Sar. Daughtr of Thos Brown of Ridge End Bapd
Octobr 6th James son Of John & Anne Adamthwaite Bapd
Novr 16th [T.—10] Richd son of John & Mary Thompson Bapd

1763.

Janry 2d. Was Anne Daughter of Richd & Margt Howgill Bapd
11th A Child of Thos Preston Bapd [T.—named John]
Feb 5th Eliz. Daughter of John & Margt Fawcett Bapd
March 19th Willm son of James & Emmy Stubbs Bapd

BIRTHS AND CHRISTNINGS.

MARCH 30th Jonath^{n} son of Antho. & Eliz. Fothergill Bap^{d}
JUNE 8 James son of Stephen & Anne Shaw o' Town Bap^{d}
12th Marg^{t} Daughter of Rich^{d} & Sarah Thompson Bap^{d}
21st Isabel Daught^{r} of Thomas & Mary Fawcet Bap^{d}
22^{d} Agnes Daughter of Christop^{r} & Agnes Townson Bap^{d}
JULY 3^{d} Betty Daughter Michael & Marg^{t} Bovel Bap^{d}
JULY 7 Marg^{t} Daughter of Thom^{s} & Anne Armstrong Bap^{d}
SEP^{ber} 6th Eliz. Daught^{r} of Robt Udal of Steps Beck Bap^{d}
8th Sibb^{l} Daughter of W^{m} & Agnes Spooner Bap^{d}
OCTO^{r} 1st Geo. son of Geo. & Mary Perkins o' Crooks Bap^{d}
NOV^{r} 28th John son of Willm & Marg^{t} Stubbs Bap^{d}
DEC^{r} 2^{d} Marg^{t} Daught^{r} of John & Mary Milner Greenside B^{d}
14th Richard son of Thos & Magdalen Shaw Bap^{d}
28th Thos son of Thos & Mary Taylor Town Bap^{d}
30th Eliz. Daughter of Geo. & Martha Murthwait Bap^{d}

1764.

FEB. 16th Was Braithwait son of John & Eliz. Fawcet Greenside Bap^{d}
21st Robt son of Solom^{n} & Mary Constantine Bap^{d}
APRIL 28th [T.—26] James son of Willm & Marg^{t} Hunter Sprintgill Bap^{d}
MAY 18th Sarah Daught^{r} of Stephen & Anne Shaw Bap^{d}
JULY 10th Mary Daught^{r} of James & Anne Robinson Bap^{d}
12th Betty Daught^{r} of John Hebson Bap^{d}
AUGst 28th Mary Daught^{r} of Rich^{d} & Dorathy Shaw Town Bap^{d}
SEP^{br} 19th Mary Daught^{r} of Richd Shaw Hollin Hall Bap^{d}
22^{d} John son of John & Elian^{r} Haistwell Wreygreen Bap^{d}
1764 29th John son of Willm & Elian^{r} Atkinson Bap^{d}
OCTOB^{r} 2^{d} Thos son of Richd Metcalf Bap^{d}
8th Elis [T.—El^{r}] Daught^{r} of John & Isab^{l} Adamthwait Bap^{d}
17th Christop^{r} son of John & Judith Coupland Town Bap^{d}
NOV^{r} 26th Anne Daughter of Thos & Anne Armstrong Bap^{d}
DEC^{r} 6th Agnes Daught^{r} of Thos & Marg^{t} Garnet Bap^{d}
10th Robt son of Thos & Isab^{l} Wilson Bap^{d}
13th Martha Daughter of W^{m} & Marg^{t} Nelson Bap^{d}
21st Betty Daught^{r} of W^{m} & Marg^{t} Witton Bap^{d}
22^{d} John [T.—An^{y}] son of Anth^{o} & Eliz. Fothergill Bap^{d}

BIRTHS AND CHRISTNINGS.

1765.

Janry 4th	Was John son of Geo: & Eliz. Udall Bapd
14th	Mary Daughr of Edmund & Sarah Waller Bapd
19th	Ruth Daughtr of John & Anne Adamthwait Bapd
Feb 26th	Thos son of John & Agnes Foster Bapd
28th	Isabel Daughter of Miles & Agnes Birkbeck Bapd
March 30th	Ruth Daughter of Willm & Agnes Kitchin Bapd
Febry 8th	Anthony son of Anthony & Mary Metcalf Bapd
June 6th	Isabel Daughtr of Geo: & Mary Perkins Crooks Bapd
30th	Joseph son of Wm & Agnes Spooner Bapd
July 13th	James son of Wm & Rachel Stubbs Bapd
26th	Robt son of Geo & Martha Murthwait Bapd
Augst 31st	Esther Daughtr of Holmes & Esther Milner Bapd
Sepber 11th	Joh. son of John & Mary Thompson Bapd
14th	James son of Richd & Mary Willain Bapd
26th	William son of Richd & Anne Cunningham Bapd
Octobr 6th	Richd son of Richd & Agnes Lambert Bapd
Decbr 4th	Isabl Daughtr of Christopr Dobson Bapd

1766.

Janry 10th	Was Geo. son of Thos & Mary Tayler Bapd
16th	Mary Daughter of Anto & Agnes Hodgson Bapd
28th	Robt son of Fawcet & Anne Hunter Sprintgill Bapd
Mar 12th	Betty Daughtr of Geo: & Eliz: Udal o' Town Bapd
Aprl 16th	Agnes Daughter of James & Eliz: Fawcet o' Town Bapd
June 22d	Elizabth Daughter to John & Judith Coupland Bapd
Augst 16th	Ruth Daughtr to Willm & Margt Stubbs Bapd
28th	Sarah Daughtr to Robt & Ruth Scarbrough Bapd
26th	Robt & Wm Twin sons of Christor & Agnes Townson Bapd
31st	Margt Daughtr to Richd & Sarah Thompson Bapd
Octor 14th	Jno John son of Jos. & Anne Thompson Bd
Octor 26th	Margt Daughter of Wm & Margt Hunter Bapd
Novbr 4th	Willm son to John & Mary Milner Bapd
12th	James son of Jno & Agnes Foster o' Ridge End Bapd
13th	Abraham son of Wm & Margt Witton o' Newbign Bapd
16th	Ruth Daughtr of Thos & Isabl Fawcet o' Newbign Bapd
Decr 27th	Thomas son of Richd & Dorathy Shaw o' Town Bapd

BIRTHS AND CHRISTNINGS.

1767.

† March 18th Bap James son of John & Isabel Adamthwaite
Aprl 25th [T. 28] Was Elinr Daughtr of John & Elinr Haistwell Bapd
28th [T. 29th] Christophr son of Joseph & Jane Fothergill o' Garshill Bapd
30th Mary Daughtr of Jno Hebson o' Brackenbr Bapd
June 13th Joseph & Mary son & Daughter to Thos & Magdalen Shaw Bd
15th Betty Daughtr of Wm & Margt Hunter o' sprintgill Bapd
1767. July 16th Thos son of Mr John Robinson Schl Mastr & Isabl his wife Bapd
30th Betty Dar of Anto: & Ma: Fothergill o' Brownber Bapd
Sepber 26th Esther an illegitamate Child of Margt Stewerd in the Poor House Bapd
† 29th Robert son of Holmes & Esther Milner of Coldbeck Bapd
Octor 8th Henry son of Willm & Agnes Spooner o' Lockholme Bapd
Same Day Margt Daughtr of Willm & Margt Hewetson o' Town Bapd
Novbr 1st. Mally Daughtr of Elianr Fothergill o' Newbign Bapd
15th Nathan an Illegitamate son of Isabella Adamthwait Bapd

1768.

Jan 21st Was Geo. son of Geo. & Martha Murthwait Bap
26th Isabl Daughter of Geo. & Eliz Haistwell Bapd
Feb. 11th Isabl Daughtr of Jno & Sarah Shearman Bapd
12th Antho sun of Michl & Eliz. Robinson Bapd
13th Anne Daughr of Francis & Anne Whaley Bapd
March 12th Agnes Daughr of Thos & Mary Snawdon Bapd
May 12th Edmd son of Edmd & Sarah Waller Bapd
20th Mary Daughtr of Tho & Mary Taylor Bapd
30th John son of Thoms Thompson Bapd
June 17th Christopr son of Jno & Judith Coupland Bapd
21st Thos son of Jno & Margt Hunter Bapd
22d Thos son of Thos & Mary Haistwell Ellerhill Bapd
† Augst 22d Isabella Daughtr to John & Isabl Robinson stenesk gh Bapd
Augst 28th John son of Archibal & Mary Robinson Bapd
Octor 15th Thos son of Wm Taylor Bapd
Novbr 13th Edwd son of Geo. & Eliz. Udall

BIRTHS AND CHRISTNINGS.

DEC[r] 12th Anne Daught[r] of John & Mary Robinson Bap[d]
DEC 13th Marg[t] Daught[r] of Jos. & Anne Thompson Bap[d]
28th Jennet Illegitimate Daught[r] of Jane Taylor Bap[d]

1769.

JAN[ry] 21st Tho[s] son of W[m] & Marg[t] Stubbs o' Town Bap[d]
27 James son of Jn[o] & Mary Jackson o' Newbig[n] Bap[d]
Same Day Rich[d] son of Jno & Eliz. Hebson Bap[d].
MARY 10th Mary Daught[r] of Rob[t] & Ruth Scarbrough Low Lane Bap[d]
29th John son of Rich[d] & Eliz. Lindslay Bap[d]
30th Edm[d] son of Geo & Eliz. Udal Town Bap[d]
APR[l] 2[d] Anne Daughter of Anto. & Agnes Hodgson Bap[d]
6th Miles son of Rob[t] Garnet Bap[d]
20th Ma [T. Anne] Daught[r] of Rich[d] & Sarah Thompson Bap[d]
31st Hugh son of John & Sarah Shearman Bap[d]
MAY 21st Jane Daught[r] of Joseph & Jane Fothergill Garrshill Bap[d]
JUNE 15th Marg[t] Daught[r] of Anto. & Mary Fothergill Brownb[r] Bap[d]
AUG[st] 13th Bridg[t] Daught[r] of Jn[o] & Anne Adamthw[t] Bap[d]
18th Agnes Daught[r] of Mathew & Eliz. Scarbrough Bap[d] born JULY 31st
31st Thom[s] son of Isaac & Hannah Teasdal o' Caldbeck Bap[d]
OCTO[r] 5th Math[w] son of Anto. Birtal Bap[d]
8th Isab[l] Daught[r] of Geo. & Eliz. Haistwell Studfold Bap[d]
13th James son of Tho[s] & Eliz. Haistwell Ellerhill Bap[d]
25th Phinehas son of John & Marg[t] Stubbs Bap[d]
Same Day John son of Tho[s] & Jane Drybeck Bap[d]
28th Elian[r] Daughter of James & Jane Swainson Bap[d]

1770.

JAN[ry] 2[d] Was Naney Daught[r] to W[m] & Marg[t] Hewetson Bap[d]
11th Tho[s] son to Jn[o] & Mary Brown Bap[d]
19th Edw[d] son to W[m] & Mary Adamthwait Bap[d]
20th John son to Rich[d] & Dorathy Shaw o' Town Bap[d]
MARCH 15th Mary Daught[r] to Tho[s] Thompson Bap[d]
16th Peggy Daughter to Ant[o] & Isab[l] Urwin Bap[d]
Same Day Willy Illegitimate son to Jennet Hanson Bap[d]
26th James & Tho[s] Twin Sons to Francis & Anne Whaley Bap[d]

BIRTHS AND CHRISTNINGS.

July 8th	Jos. son to Willm & Rachel Stubbs Bapd
16th	Dorathy Daur to John & Judith Coupland Bapd
Augst 27th	Jos Illegitamate son of Eliz. Spooner Bapd
Sepr 25th	Joseph son of Anthony Spooner & his wife Bapd
29th	John son of Mathw & Mary Brown Bapd
Octor 15th	Stephn son of Mathw & Eliz. Scarbrough Bapd
18th	Tho. son of Antho & Mary Fothergill Bapd
Nov. 3d	Stepn son to Anto & Faith Dent Bapd
7th	John son of Richd Birtal & his wife Bapd
Dec. 5th	Wm son of John & Margt Howgill Bapd
† 10th	John son of John & Anne Murrace Bapd

1771.

Janry 15th	Was Mathw son of Edwd & Anne Metecalf [T. of Dovingill labourer, & Eliz. his wife] Bapd
28th	John an Illegitimate son of Isabl Fawcet [T. of Stepsbeck] Bapd
Feb 7th [T. 15]	Mart Daughtr of Mathw & Agnes Ward [T. of Litheside, Labourer] Bapd
9th [T. 17]	Margt Daughtr of Mr Jno Robinson & Eliz. his wife Bapd
	Same Day Edwd son of Wm & Jane Adamthwait [T. of Adamthwaite Yeon] Bapd
March 18	Thos son of Willm & Margt Witton [T. Thos son of William Witton Labourer & Margt his wife] Bapd
Apl 14th	Anne an Illegitimate Daughtr of Eliz Watson [T. spinster of Coldbeck] Bapd
17th	Anne Daughtr of Thos Hunter & his wife o' Wandal [T. husbandman] Bapd
May 7th	Mary Daughtr of Mathw & Margt Watson [T. of Brownber Farmer] Bapd
8th	Anne Daughtr of Chrisr Dobson [T. of Dubbs] & his wife Bapd
9th	Robt son of Richd & Anne Cuningham [T. of Bowberhead Chapmn] Bapd
June 2d	Anne Daughter of Thos & Eliz. Robinson Weesdl [T. of Garrs Carrier] Bapd

BIRTHS AND CHRISTNINGS.

† Sepr 16th	Isabel Daug^{r} to Robt. & Eliz. Hunter born & Bap^{d} Octo^{r} 22^{d} Bowb^{r} h^{d} *
Octo^{r} 4th	Biddy Daught^{r} of Geo: Udal & Eliz. his wife Innkeep^{r} Bap^{d}
22^{d}	Annas Daught^{r} of Anto Birtal & Eliz. his wife Labour^{r} Bap^{d}

1772.

Feb^{r} 11th	Was Betty Daugh^{r} of Wm Potter (Husb^{d}man) Bap^{d}
14th	Geo. son of Anto. & Mary Fawcet of Foggegill Bap^{d}
	Same Day Elizabth Daug^{r} of Mich^{l} Robinson B^{l}smith o' Street Bap^{d}
27th	Rich^{d} son of Thos Thompson Labourer Bap
April 22^{d}	Geo. son of Robt & Ruth Scarbrough o' low Lane Bap^{d}
May th 9th	Stephen son of John & Ann Fawcett
May 15th	Geo. son of Willm Fawcet o' fell End Bap^{d}
† 27th	Mary D. of John & Isabel Adamthwaite
Sep^{br} 15th	Agnes Daught^{r} to Geo. & Eliz. Haistwell Studfold Bap^{d}
Octo^{r} 8th	Ephraim son to Geo. & Mary Perkins Crooks Bap^{d}
10th	Anne Daught^{r} to John & Anne Murrace Bap^{d}
Novr 10th	Isabel Daught^{r} to Mr John Robinson & Isab^{l} his wife sch^{l} mas^{r} Bap^{d}
Decr 8th	Isab^{l} Daught^{r} to W^{m} & Rach^{l} Stubbs Carp^{r} Bap^{d}

1773.

March 8th	Jennet Daught^{r} of Ma. Brown Wid^{w} Rig End	Bap^{d}
Apr^{l} 17th	Betty Daught^{r} of Math^{w} & Agnes Ward	Bap^{d}
May 10th	Mary Illegitimate Daught^{r} of Ruth Proctor [T. Spinster]	Bap^{d}
15th	Jane Daught^{r} of Willm Adamthwait fellend	Bap^{d}
18th	Mary Daught^{r} of Edm^{d} Metcalf	Bap^{d}
20th	Betty Daug^{r} of John & Eliz. Spedding	Bap^{d}
June 4th	Harry son of Ant^{o} & Mary Fawcet Murtw^{e}	Bap^{d}
Jun 13th	Agnes Daught^{r} of Jno & Dinah Birtal	Bap^{d}
July 3^{d}	Joseph son of Jno & Sarah Shaw Weesdal	Bap^{d}
14th	Peggy Daught^{r} of Ant^{o} & Mary Fothergill Brounb^{r}	Bap^{d}
15th	Eliz. dau^{r} of Richd Birtal Lockholm [T. Farmer]	Bap^{d}

---

* "Bowbr hd" subsequently crossed out.

BIRTHS AND CHRISTNINGS.

JULY 30th Isabella Daughtr of Willm & Jane Fawcet [T. worcet-carrier] Bapd

AUGst 2d Jno son of Jno & Alice Perkins Caldbeck [T. farmer] Bapd

SEPBr 12th Chrisr son of James & Mary Waller [T. Innkeepr] Cdbeck Bapd

17th Peggy Daughr of Jno & Margt Dover [T. webster town] Bapd

21st Thos son of Thos Haistwell fell-end [T. farmer] Bapd

22d Peggy Daughtr of Isaac & Hannah Teasdal [T. Town, innkeeper] Bapd

OCTO 29th Alice Ion Spinr a Quaker aged 22 Bapd

30th Anne Daugr of Jno & Isabl Nelson [T. Husbandman] Bapd

NOVr 4th Thos son of Wm & Anne Potter [T. farmer] Bapd

5th Mary Daughr of Edwd & Sarah Whitehead [T. Farmer] Bapd

6th Jno son of Thos & Jane Drybeck [T. Town Carpentr] Bapd

DECbr 28th Anne Daugtr of Wm & Dorathy Nelson Town [T. Waller] Bapd

1774.

FEB 4th Was Robart son of Thos Hunter Wandal Bapd

10th Richd son of Geo. & Martha Murthwt Rig End Bapd

APl 11th Isabella Daug of Geo. & Eliz. Udal [T. o' Town] Bapd

14th John son of Jno Howgil Sandbed [T. Farmer] Bapd

30th Thos son of Wm & Margt Hewetson [T. Carpentr] Bapd

30th Thos son to Geo & Margt Hewetson [T. Thos son to Geo & Elizab Haistwell farmer Studfold] Bapd

MAY 2d Eliz. Daur of Mical Robinson Streetside [T. blksmith] Bapd

JUNE 19th Nanay Daur of John & Anne Adamthwt [T Carpr] Bapd

26th John son of Richd Atkinson [T. Daylabourer] Bapd

JULY 23d Thos son of Thos* & Eliz Hewetson [T. Town] Bapd

25th John son to Robt & Mary Thompson [T. Husbandman] Bapd

AUGst 28th Anne Daughr to James & Margt Fawcet [T. farmer] Bapd

SEPr 8th Margt Daughtr to Thos Thompson [T. farmer] Bapd

SEPr 12th Richd son to Robt & Eliz Hunter Bowbrhead [T. Drover] born Bap OCTOr 7th Bapd

13th Willm Illegitimate son of Eliz. Watson Bapd

---

* Originally "Geo."

BIRTHS AND CHRISTNINGS.

Sepr 24th	Joseph son to Antho^{y} & Mary Spooner [T. Taylor] Bap^{d}
Nov^{br} 8th	Isabel Daughter to Thos & Anne Ellietson Farm^{r} Bowderd^{le} Bap^{d}
Dec^{br} 2^{d}	Anne Daughter to Thos & Anne Rhumney Farm^{r} Dubbs Bap^{d}
8th	Eliz. Daught^{r} to Thos & Mellilet Thompson Daylabour^{r} Bap^{d}
27th	Margar^{t} Daught^{r} to Henry & Ruth Perkins Yeom^{n} [T. Lockholm] Bap^{d}

1775.

Jan 16th	Was Mary Daught^{r} to Geo & Isab^{l} Perkins Badger Bap^{d}
March 22^{d}	Eliz. Daught^{r} to Mathew & Mary Brown Taylor Bap^{d}
Apr^{l} 8th	Elian^{r} Daught^{r} to Thos & Anne Hunter Husb^{d}m^{n} Bap^{d}
30th	James son to W^{m} & Marg^{t} Stubbs Taylor Bap^{d}
May 7th	John son to Mathew & Agnes Ward Farm^{r} Bap^{d}
July 2^{d}	Peggy Daught^{r} to W^{m} & Anne Nelson o' Town Carpen^{r} Bap^{d}
10th	Joseph son to Robt & Eliz Chamberlain* Shoe mak^{r} Bap^{d}
12th	Mathew son to Wm Hunter [T. farmer] Bap^{d}
23^{d}	Willm son to Thos & Jane Wilson Caldbeck Innkeep^{r} Bap^{d}
30th	John son to Robt & Ruth Scarbrough Lowlane [T. yeom^{n}] Bap^{d}
Sept^{br} 2^{d}	James son to Ralph & Eliz Stockdall farmer Bap^{d}
3^{d}	Isabella Daught^{r} to John & Agnas Brunskill [T. clogg^{r}] Bap^{d}
15th	Ellian^{r} Daught^{r} to Antho^{y} & Mary Fawcet Murthw^{t} [T. farmer] Bap^{d}
26th	Edwd son to W^{m} & Dorathy Nelson Shop keep^{r} Bap^{d}
Octo^{br} 13th	Mathew son John & Dinah Birtell Farm^{r} Bap^{d}
18th	Peggy Daught^{r} to Anto & Faith Dent Yeo^{n} Bap^{d}
Dec^{br} 6th	Eliz. Daught^{r} to Willm & Elian^{r} Perkin of Tarn Farm^{r} Bap^{d}
16th	Peggy Daught^{r} to W^{m} & Anne Potter Farmer Bap^{d}

1776.

Feb 1st	Was Betty Daught^{r} to Jarret & Mary Robinson Farm^{r} Bap^{d}
15th	Rich^{d} son to Joseph & Anne Breaks Taylor Bap^{d}
20th	Anne Daughter to John & Marg^{t} Howgill Farmer Bap^{d}
30th	Hannah Daught^{r} to Anto & Peggy Birtell Husb^{d}man Bap^{d}

* Transcript gives "Taylor" instead of "Chamberlain."

BIRTHS AND CHRISTNINGS.

MARCH 2^{d}	Geo. son to John [T. & Marg^{t}] Robinson Farmer [T. milner] Bap^{d}
6th	Isab^{l} Daught^{r} to Willm & Mary Metcalf Day Labour^{r} Bap^{d}
APR^{l} 17th	Willm Illegitimate son to Isabella Adamthwaite [T.—of Newbig^{n}] Bap^{d}
18th	Isabella Daught^{r} to John & Isabella Nelson Farm^{r} Bap^{d}
19th	Anne Daught^{r} to Henry & Eliz. Fothergill, carrier Bap^{d}
26th	Elian^{r} & Agnes Twin Daughter to Willm & Fawcet Farm^{r} Bap^{d}
30th	Jane Daught^{r} to Thos & Eliz. Hewetson Artlegarth Joiner Bap^{d}
MAY 23^{d}	Hannah Daught^{r} to M^{r} & Mrs Williamson Excize Gager Bap^{d}
JUNE 3^{d}	W^{m} son to W^{m} & Rachel Stubbs Carp^{r} Bap^{d}
12th	Peggy Daught^{r} to Jno & Anne Morland Yeo^{n} Bap^{d}
JULY 2^{d}	John son to Anto & Mary Fothergill nigh Broun^{r} Yeo^{n} Bapt^{d}
JULY 20th	Anne Daug^{r} to Mr John & Isab^{l} Robinson Sch^{l}mas^{r} Bap^{d}
24th	Malley [T. Mary] Daug^{r} to Rich^{d} & Sarah [T. Mary] Thompson Farm^{r} Bap^{d}
AUGst 18th	Anto. son to Richd Birtell Daylabour^{r} [T. Farmer] Bap^{d}
SEP^{r} 25th	Mary Daug^{r} to John & Mary Robinson miln^{r} [T. Farmer] Bap^{d}
27th	Geo son to John & Marg^{t} Dover weav^{r} . Bap^{d}
OCTO^{r} 10th	Dorat^{y} Daught^{r} to Edwd & Bella Urwin Pension^{r} [T. from Governm^{t}] Bap^{d}
23^{d}	Agnes Daught^{r} to Geo & Eliz. Perkin Badg^{r} Bap^{d}
DEC^{r} 15th	Anne Daugh^{r} to Willm Ion Christn^{d} when ag^{d} 26 Bap^{d}
17th	Geo. son to Robt & Isabel* Fawcet Farm^{r} Bap^{d}
27th	Willm son to Mich^{l} & Agnes Robinson Bl^{k}smith Bap^{d}
29th	Geo. son to Anto & Mary Fawcet Murthw^{t} Farmer Bap^{d}

1777.

[T. JAN^{r} 6th	Marg^{t} Daughter to John Birtell day labourer & Dinah his wife born JAN 2^{d} & Bap^{d} JAN 6]
JAN^{ry} 6th	Was James & Thos twins to Thos & Jane Wilson Innkeep^{r} [T. at Caldbeck] Bap^{d}

* "Geo. & Eliz." crossed out.

BIRTHS AND CHRISTNINGS.

Feb 2^{d}	Mary Daught^{r} to John & Eliz. Speddy Shoemak^{r}	Bap^{d}
6th	Thos son to [T. Robt] Thomson Daylabourer	Bap^{d}
Feb 10th [T. 16]	Peggy [T. Marg^{t}] Daugh^{r} to James & Peggy Fawcet Farm^{r}	Bap^{d}
30th	Math^{w} son to Joseph & Anne Thompson Farmer	Bap^{d}
March 6th	Marg^{t} Daug^{r} to Robt & Mary Thompson Farm^{r}	Bap^{d}
10th	Lyddy Daught^{r} to W^{m} & Mary Metcalf Farm^{r}	Bap^{d}
Ap^{l} 12th	Sarah Daug^{r} to Robt & Marg^{t} Shaw born & bap^{d} Sep 3^{d} [T. born Ap 2^{d} & bap^{d} 12th] yeo^{n}	Bap^{d}
May 2^{d}	Isabella Daught^{r} to Henry & Ruth Perkin Yeo^{n} [T. born April 24th]	Bap^{d}
24th	Betty Daughter to W^{m} & Anne Nelson Join^{r}	Bap^{d}
25th	Anne Daught^{r} to Anto. & Agnes Birtal farm^{r}	Bap^{d}
June 5th	James son to Willm & Marg^{t} Stubbs Tayl^{r}	Bap^{d}
6th	John son to Math^{w} & Agnes Ward farm^{r}	Bap^{d}
18th [T. 15th]	Thos. son to Thos. & Anne Hunter yeom^{n}	Bap^{d}
28th	Willm Illegitimate son to Mary Adamthw^{t} serv^{t}	Bap^{d}
28th	Willm son to Thos & Melly Thompson daylabour^{r}	Bap^{d}
Augst 4th	Mary daught^{r} to Robt & Alice Chamberlain Shoemak^{r}	Bap^{d}
Sep^{br} 7th	Marg^{t} Daug^{r} to John Birtel farmer & Dinah his wife	Bap^{d}
13th	Anne Daug^{r} to Josua Hunter farm^{r} & Anne his wife	Bap^{d}
24th	Anto. son to John Morland Yeom^{n} & Anne his wife	Bap^{d}
25	Mary [T. Marg^{t}] Daug^{r} to Sarah & Harry Beck Badger	Bap^{d}
28th	Thos son to Mary & John Wilson smith	Bap^{d}
30th	Robt son to Willm Taylor Daylabour^{r} & Marg^{t} his wife	Bap^{d}
Octo^{r} 5th	John son to Mary & Richd Atkinson saxton	Bap^{d}
9th	Sarah Daught^{r} to Anne & Thos Metcalf Day labour^{r}	Bap^{d}
31st	Fanny Daug^{r} to Jane & James Bayliff farmer	Bap^{d}
Novr 8th	Christo^{r} son to Isabel & Thomas Rennison farmer	Bap^{d}
19th	John son to Elian^{r} & William Perkins farmer	Bap^{d}
26th	James son to Eliz. & Geo. Udal milner	Bap^{d}
27th	Anne Dau^{r} to Anne & Willm Spooner Taylor	Bap^{d}
28th	Marg^{t} Daug^{r} to Thos Nelson Carpent^{r} & Eliz. his wife	Bap^{d}
30th	Eliz. Dau^{r} to Ruth & Anto. Robinson smith	Bap^{d}
Decr 27th	Anne Daug^{r} to Marg^{t} & John Brunskill Clogg^{r}	Bap^{d}

BIRTHS AND CHRISTNINGS.

1778.

Jan^{ry} 5	Mary Dau^{r} an Illegitimate Child to Mary Clemison	Bap^{d}
9th	Sarah Dau^{r} to Marg^{t} & John Howgill farmer	Bap^{d}
13th	John son to Anne & Jos. Breaks Junr Tayler	Bap^{d}
Same Day	John son to Mary & John Murrace farm^{r}	Bap^{d}
March 5th	Mary Dau^{r} to Dorathy & Willm Nelson worset carrier	Bap^{d}
April 15th	John son to Mr John Baines surgeon & Hannah his wife	Bap^{d}
25th	Elian^{r} Dau^{r} to Henry Hunt^{r} Yeom^{n} & Anne his wife	Bap^{d}
May 2^{d}	W^{m} son to Mary & Anto. Fawcet Farmer Farm^{r}	Bap^{d}
3^{d}	Eliz. Daug^{r} to Agnes & Wm Fawcet Farmer	Bap^{d}
1778. 20th	Eliz. Illegitimate Daug^{r} to Dinah Scot serv^{t}	Bap^{d}
May 23^{d}	Marg^{t} [T. Mary] Daug^{r} to John Allon Farm^{r} born here & Isab^{l} his —	Bap^{d}
24th	Marg^{t} [T. Mary] Dau^{r} to Anne & John Haistwell Farmer	Bap^{d}
June 2^{d}	Robt son to Anne & Thos Dixon Yeo^{n} of Asby born here & Bap^{d}	
do. 12	Mathew son to Jane & Wm Adamthwaite Baptiz^{d}*	
do. 18	Jno son to Mary & Jno Metcalf Bapt^{d}*	
† do. 20	Thomas son to James & Mary Robinson of Scar	
Augt 2	Ann Daught^{r} Jarat [T. Jno] & Mary Robinson	
Sepb^{r} 6	Eliner Daug^{tr} to Ann & Wm Potter Bapt^{d}	
do. 17	Eliner Daug^{tr} to Mary & Wm Metcalf	
do. 19	Edward son to Bella Jno Nelson Bapt^{d}	
Octr 9	Elener Daug^{tr} to Isabel & Robt Fawcett	
do. 17	Matthew son to Jno & Jane Wilkinson	
[T.—do 26	Edwd son to John & Isabella Nelson]	

1779.

Jan. 10	Geo. son of Geo. & Betty Fawcett Wreygreen
do. 12	Thos son of Thos [T. & Melly] Thompson Bapt^{d}
do. 19	Jno son of James & Margret Fawcett Farmer
do. 22	Bella Daug^{tr} of Thos & Jane Wilson
do. 29	Jno son of W^{m} & Peggy Nelson
Feb^{r} 26	Aty Daug^{tr} of Jno & Ann Morland Yeom^{n}
March 20	Ruth D. of Jno & Ruth Chamberlain

* These two entries are dated Jany 12th & 18th in the T., and are so placed.

BIRTHS AND CHRISTNINGS.

APR^{l} 11 Jno son of W^{m} & Agness Dopherley Tramper
MAY 27 Jno son to Anthony Mary Fawcett
do. 28 Ruth Daug^{tr} to Henry & Ruth Perkin
do. 28 Jane Daug^{tr} to Betty & Thos Nelson Farm^{r}
JUNE 16 W^{m} son to Agnes Whithead illegitimate
do. 19 Isabella Daug^{tr} of Matthew & Agness Ward
do. 22 Joseph* [T. Jno] son to Jno & Mary Bell
JULY 14 Thos son to Geo. & Eliza Perkins
do. 31 James son to Jno & Mary Fawcett
AUG^{t} 7 Mary Daugt^{r} to Anthony & Ruth Robinson
do. 12 W^{m} son to W^{m} & Isabella Furnace
SEP^{t} 27 W^{m} son to Thos & Isabella Reyneson
do. 28 Benjamin son to Jane Shaw illegitimate
do. 29 Micael son to W^{m} & Marg^{t} Taylor
OCT^{r} 11 Thos son to Henery & Betty Fothergill
do. 29 Anthony son to Thos & Anne Hunter
NOV^{r} 2 Isabella Daug^{tr} to Jno & Margret Hunter
NOV^{r} 7 Deborah Daug^{tr} to Wm Agnes Shaw
do. 15 Jno son to Thos and Mellelet Thompson
DECM^{br} 6 Betty Daug^{tr} to Jno & Diana Birtell

1780.

JAN^{y} 9th Jno son to Eliz: Adamthwaite illegitimate
JAN^{y} 19 Thos son to W^{m} and Jane Fawcett
FEB^{y} 6 W^{m} son to Rich^{d} & Mary Bertale
do. 21 Elleanor Daug^{tr} to Geo: & Eliza: Fawcett
do. 27 Thos son to Thos & Nancy Wholley
MARCH 7 Mary Daug^{tr} to Henery & Ann Hunter
do. 12 Wm Shaw son to Jno & Isabella Robinson
13 Jno son to Michael & Nancy Robinson
19 Hannah Daug^{tr} to Thos & Hannah Parkinson
APRIL 5 Isabella Daug^{tr} to Robt & Marg^{t} Shaw
do. 7th **
do. 23rd Ann Daug^{tr} to Jno & Eliza: Stubbs
JUNE 8 John son to Marg^{t} Spooner illegitimate

* Originally entered "Jno."
** Left blank, no gap in T.

BIRTHS AND CHRISTNINGS.

do. 9	John son to John & Ann Hastwell
do. 20	Harry son to Jn° & Bella Nelson
do. 30	Sally daughter to Jn° & Ann Morland
July 2	Robt son to Wm & Mary Metcalf
July 8	Peggy daughter to Jn° & Mary Stubbs
† do. 27th	Agnes D. of Jn° & Ruth Chamberlain
Augt 4th	William son of John & Mary Milner of Ashfield
17th	William son of George Murthwaite of Rigend & Martha his wife
23d	Eliz. Daughter of James Fawcet of Sandbed & Margaret his wife
do.	Eliz. Daughter of George Hastewel of Studfold & Eliz. his wife
26th	Robert son of William Fawcet of Murthwaite & Agnes his wife
Sep 24th	Richard son of Wm Potter of Thornthwaite & Ann his wife
Oct 8th	William son of William Stubbs & Margaret his wife
Oct 13	Edward son of Henry Beck of Sandwath & Sarah his wife
21st	Ann Daughter of Joseph Thompson at Lane in Weesdale & Ann his wife
Nov. 18th	Sarah Daughter of Isaac Handley of Ravenstondale Town & Sybil his wife
Decembr 24th	John son of Eliz. Lambert Illegitimate
† 30th	James son of Mary Waller of Town

MARRIAGES.

1710.

10 FEB John Blades & Mary Robertson Married

1711. JULY 29 The Reverend Thomas Toulmin Clerke and Mrs Margaret Todd Married

AUGST 25 Thomas Adamthwaite & Isabel Baylife Married

OCTOB. 4 Regnald Dixon & Marey Bousfield Married

SEPT. 13 Richard Law and Issabel Todd Married

14 APRILL Joseph Hanson & Margrett Millner Married

23 FEB John Bousfeild & Ruth fothergill Married

1712. MAY 6 Michaell Knewstub & jane Lickbarrah Married

SEPT. 22 John Grainger of Kirby Stephen parish and Agnus Johnson of this parish Married

1713. 5 MAY Edward Chapmen of the Parish of Askwith and Mary jackson of this parrish Maried

7 MAY Richard fawcet & Mabbell Adamson Married

2 JUNE Richard fallofield & Tamar Mill Married

20 JAN John Shaw and Issabell Bousfield Maried

11 MARCH John Parkin & Marey Fawcet Maried

1714. 24 APRILL Thomas Garthwaite & Issabel Robertson Maried

29 APRILL William Baylife & Isabell Todd Married

6 MAY Hugh Shaw & Isabell Dent Married

22 MAY William Robinson & Jane Martindale Married

2 SEPT Anthony fothergill & Margrett Todd Married

2 DECEM George Cleasby & Jane Simpson Married

24 FEB George parkin & Issabell fawcett Married

1715. 24 APRILL Thomas Shearman & Margret taylor Married

JUNE 3 Mr William Fawcet and Marey Bousfield married

JUNE 4 James Whola & Frances Smith married

JUNE 3 [T. 5] John Dawson & Jane Medcoffe Married

NOUEM 24 James fothergill & Sarah wharton Married

1716. MAY [T. 17] James Mason of the parish of As * and Agnus Spooner of this parish

---

* Left blank, parishes not given in T.

MARRIAGES.

30 June	William Shaw & Issabell townson Married
3 Decem	Christopher Bousfield of dubs & Dority duckett Married
18 Decem	Thomas Willison of the parish of Ormside & Issabell fothergill Married with A Licsence
20 Decem	Walter Islip of the parish of Kirkby Stephen & Mary douer of this parish Mar.
Feb. 1	Anthony fawcett of Crooks & Issabell Howgill Married with a licence
1717. May 18	Anthony Shaw & Marey taylor Married
June 13	John Blackbourn & Sarah Robinson Married
June 26	Mr John Maggee & Ellinor townson Married
June 27	thomas Blackburn & Margrett Millner Married
July 11	Robert Breaks & Issabell fothergill Married
1717	
Novem 6	Joseph Moss & Issabell fawcet married
18 Feb	Thomas scarbrough & Margret fothergill married
1718 May 8	William parkin and Jane Chamberlain married
May 17	John Sidgswick & Elizabeth fawcett married
May 22	John Murthwate & Elizabeth Elyetson married
May 22	Richard Waler & Sarah Bousfeild married
May 22	Ralph Bousfield and Agnus Bousfield married
2 June	Thomas Coupland & Issabell Knewstubb married
3 June	William Hougill & Ann postelthwait maried
1 July	Thomas Broun & Elinor Bousfield married
26 August	Robert fawcett & Marey parkin married
1719 21 May	Ralph Milner & Marey Robinson married
25 May	Thomas Hunter & Elinor Shaw married
26 May	Mathew Whitfield & Marey fawcet married
1720 June 12	James Linsay & Marey Hunter married
June 23	John fothergill & Marey Adison married
Sept 1	John Robertson & Marey Robertson married
1721 May 28	Joseph Wederelth of the parish of Sedbridgh & Elizabeth Watson married
June 1	Thomas fothergill of Newbegin and Marey Fawcet of Street side married
21st	James Bayliffe o' Murtwhaite and Sarah Rogerson o' Russendale Town married

MARRIAGES.

JAN 1st John Sampson of Chester-le-Street in C. Durrahm & Joanna Bradley of Appleby in C. Westmrland married

1721

JULY ye 9th James Rogerson of Studfold in this Parish and Margaret Atkinson in ye Parish of Orton

1722

† MAY ye 13th Richard Fawcett of Greenside and Ruth Waller both o' this Parish married

† 15th Lancelot Shaw of Wharton-dykes & Jane Parkin of Steneskew married

28th John Todd & Margaret Haistwhittle both of ys Parish

JUNE 28th Robt Wilson of Midfeild in ye Parish of Orton and Mary Fawcett of Weesdale in this Parish

NOVr 8th Tho: Law & Mary Taylor both of this Parish

DECr 6th Roger Pinder & Elisabeth Hebson both of this Parish

JAN 1st John Adamtwhaite & Margery Henderson both of this Parish

1723.

MAY 4th Robt Gibson & Anne Halton both of this Parish

30 John Stubs of ye Parish of Orton and Mary Fawcett of this Parish married

31st John Hewetson & Margt Perkins both o' ys Prsh

JUNE 2d John Chamberlaine & Anne Adamtwhaite both of this Parish

4th John Perkins & Mary Clemyson both of this Parish

4th John Blackburne & Jane Fallowfield

OCTR 20th William Wilson & Anne Fawcett

DECr 28th James Fawcett & Agnes Robinson

FEBr 24th John Richardson of the Parish of Kendale & Anne Fawcett of this Parish

1724 MAY 2d James Fawcett & mary Parkins [T. Perkin] of ys Parish

28th John Socald of the Parish of Kirby stepn and Sarah Robinson of this Parish

28th George Jackson & Jannet Robinson boath of this Parish

JUNE 9th Joseph Udall & Aallis Fothergill boath of this Parish

OCTOBER 8 William Milner & Rebekah Rebanks boath of this Parish

15th Ralph Robinson & Anne Richardson boath of this Parish

MARRIAGES.

SEPTE^r^ 30th Richard Bac'hus of ye parish of Morland and Anne Shaw of this Parish

JANUARY 5th Thomas Ion of the Parish of Bongate and Margaret Robinson of this Parish

1725 MAY 28 Siman Bousfield & Isabel Atkinson of this Par.

APR^l^ 22 Leonard Harrison of the Parish of Appleby [T. Bongate] and Mary Rich^d^son of this Parish

MAY 11th Richard Fothergill [T. of Dubbs] & Mary Fothergill [T. of Coldbeck] of this p^h^

JUNE 3^d^ Gilbert Atkinson of the Parish of Orton and Isabel Dent of this Parish

FEB 22^d^ Thomas Fothergil & Eliner Eubank of y^s^ Par^h^

1726. MAY 14 Joseph Hunter & Anne Metcalf of this Par^h^

28th James Robinson & Jane Tenent of this parish

JUNE 2^d^ Richard Bovil & Elizabeth Dixon of this pa.

JUNE 2^d^ John Hutchinson & Mary Fothergill of this P.

8th Thomas Fawcet & Mary Wilson of this Parish

AUG 18th Anthony Fawcett & Prudance Robinson of y^s^ p.

DEC^r^ 5 Edward Robinson of ye Parish of Tunstal and Mary Knewstubb [T. Robertson] of this Parish

1727.

APRIL 4 William Dickinson & Elizabeth Huchinson of this Parish

22 Richard Wharton of Kirkby Stephen and Jane Thornbarrow of this Parish

MAY 25th Thomas Blackburne of y^s^ p. & Elizabeth Coulston of the Parish of Crosbygarret

JUNE 11th Solomon Constantine & Mary Spooner of this P.

SEPTEMBER 2^d^ John Chamberlaine & Rachel Waller [T. Walker] of y^s^ p.

DEC^r^ 27 John Blades & Agnas Attkinson of y^s^ parish

MAR^h^ 10 Thomas Hastwhittle & Isabel Dent of y^s^ Parish

† 14 Thos Fothergill & Anne Dent of this Parish

1728 JUNE 20 Michael Taylor of Crosby Garret and Isabel Atkinson of of this Parish

DEC^r^ 22 Richard Murthwaite & Margare [T. Margaret] Pinder of y^s^ Parish

1729 1729

JUNE 8. Thomas Fawcet & Anne Haistwhitle of this Parish

MARRIAGES.

† Mr. Robert Mounsey clerk was nominated Curate of the Parish Church of Ravenstondale & took Possession of the s^d^ Church Octob^r^ ye 16th 1729, whom may God prosper & always bless with ye choicest of his Blessings. hic & ubique. Amen.

Τω μονῳ θεω δοξῃ Per Jn^an^ Ud^ll^ Clrk

1730.

April 21st [T. 2nd] William Whitehead of the Parish of Ormside & Anne Fothergill of this Parish
May 5th William Fawcet & Mary Thompson of this P.
[T. June 11th John Coupland & Mary Morland of this Par. wed^d^]
Aug 26th George Burton & Mary Stubbs of this Parish

1731.

March 28th Adam Guy of Gastel & Mary Burton of this Par.
April 20th James Fothergill of mollerstang & Mary Perkin of y^s^ Par.
May 30th Richd Fawcet & Mary Hewetson of ys Parish
June 3^d^ Robt Potter & Isabel Fawcet of this Par:
6th Mathew Constantine & Isabel Bousefeild of y^s^ Par:
10th Simon' Bousefeild & Elizabeth Perkin of this Par:
Novemb^r^ 3rd Peter Giles & Anne Robinson of this Parish by Lic
Feb 8th George Park of Asby & Elizabeth Whitehead of y^s^ Par.

1732.

May 25th Were George Birkbeck & Mary Coatlay of y^s^ Parish m^d^
30th Robert Atkinson of the Parish of Orton & Isabel Dent of this Par. m^d^
30th Henery Hunter & Elian^r^ Knewstubb both of this Par: m^d^
31st Ralph Alderson & Isabel Morland both of this Parish m^d^
Feb 19th Anthony Robinson & Elizabeth Wharton of this Parish m^d^

1733.

April 26th Were Robt Bovel & Elizabeth Fothergill of y^s^ Par: w^d^
May 10th Richd Gregson & Agnes Morland of this Par: wed.
12th Ralph Stockdale & Isabel Fawcet of this Par: wed.
13th Joseph Chamberlain & Mary Hall of this Par: wed.
June 21st Willm Hunter & Barbara Foster of this Par: wed.

MARRIAGES.

Septembr 17th Thomas Dent o' Sandbed & Faith Richardson of this Par: wed

27th John Fawcet & Mary Fawcet of this Par: wed

Decembr 20th William Bell of Harker in the Par: of Rocklif in the County of Cumberland & Mary Wharton of Kirby Stephn wed

Feb 4th Joseph Hanson & Isabel Booth of this Parish wed

17th Thomas Fothergill of Brounber Senr in Ravenstondale & Margaret Holme of Dilliker were weded at Grayrig Chapel as appears by Certificate

1734.

May 4th Were John Thompson & Margt Todd of this Parh mard Lic.

June 22d Christopher Fawcet & Sarah Lancaster both of ye Parish wedd

1735.

April 30th John Bousefield in the Parish of Kirkby Stephen & Elizabeth Smith of this were wedded

May 15th Thomas Fawcet & Margaret Blackburn both of this Parish wedd

24th Mathew Birtell & Margaret [T. Agnes] Fawcet both of this Parish wedd

June 3d Thomas Fawcet & Mary Hewetson both of this Parish wedd

Novembr 29th Antho. Fothergill & Frances Bainbridge both of this Parish wedd Lic:

Feb 9th John Orton of the Parish of K. Stephen & Anne Parkin of this Par: wedd.

1736.

Apl 25th Miles Lamb & Elizabeth Ayrey both of ys Par: wed

Augst 26th Henry Knewstubb of New bond street in ye Par: of St George London & Sarah Hunter o' this Par: were wedded

Sepber 21st Thomas Hunter o' Great Strickland in the Par: of morld & Mary Robinson of this Par: wedd

22d Thomas Adamthwaite & Anne Ion both of this Par: wed

Jan 24th John Dent Batchlr & Margt Wharton widw both o' ys Par: wed Lic:

Feb 21st Henry Fothergill & Mary Ayrey both of ys Parish wedd

MARRIAGES.

1737.

Apr[l] 14th James Fawcet o' Midleton in the Par. o' K: Lonsdal & Isabel Banks o' this wed[d]

May 23d William Robinson & Mary Breaks both o' y[s] Par. wed

June 16th Christoph[r] Rennison o' Mollerstang & Sarah Hanson of this Par. wed[d]

30th John Perkin & Marg[t] Scarbrough both o' y[s] Par wed

Sep[ber] 15th Will[m] Handley of Garsdale & Mary Martindale o' this Par: wed

The same day were Joseph Hunter & Anne Whitwell both o' y[s] Par. wed

Novem 1st Anth[o]. Kearton of Oxnip in Swaledale in the County of York & Jennet Spooner of Greenside in y[s] Par. wed[d]

1738.

May 13th Were Jn[o] Atkinson of Garsdale in the Par. of Sedb[rg] & Anne Fawcet o' this wed[d]

The same Day were Rob[t] Hunter & Margar[t] Bovel both of this Par. wed

21st Rob[t] Fawcet & Sarah Wharton both of y[s] Par. wed

25th Thomas Robinson & Isabel Hewetson both of this Par. wed

The same Day were Ralph Dinsdal of Gale in the Par: of Aisgarth & Mary Steadman of this Par: wed[d]

June 1st John Hodgson of the Par: of Orton & Lydia Milner of y[s] wed

20th George Fawcet & Elianor Fawcet both of y[s] Par: wed

Aug[st] 13th James Hewetson & Marg[t] Bland both of this Par. wed[d]

Octob[r] 29th Joseph Spooner & Sibbal Parkin both of y[s] Par wed[d]

Nov[ber] 4th Robert Hunter & Mary Fawcet both of y[s] Par. wed[d]

Dec[ber] 21st Thomas Fawcet & Jeanet Swainson both o' y[s] Par: wed[d]

29th Rob[t] Fawcet & Anne Chamberlain both of y[s] Par. wed[d]

1739.

June 14th Were Thomas Birtell & Mary Blades both of y[s] Par wed

August 30th John Birtel & Mary Fawcet both of y[s] Par: wed[d]

Sep[ber] 3d Richard Robinson & Elizab[th] Fawcet both o' y[s] Par: wed

Octob[r] 23d Richard Fawcet of Crosshal in Sedberdge Par: & Eliz. Beck of y[s] wed[d]

MARRIAGES.

Feb 18th Thos Bousefield o' Townhead & Margaret Robinson both of this Parish wedd

The same Day were Jacob Shaw of Mollerstang in the Par. of Kir: Stephn & Mary Adamthwt of ys wedd

1740.

Apl 20th Was John Shaw of Grisdal in the Par: of Sedberdgh & Magart Howgill of this wed

Augst 14th John Ivyson & Mary Clemmison both of ys Par: wedd

Sepber 12th John Fawcet & Mary Fawcet both of this Parish wedd

1741.

May 10th Were Jno Shaw & Anne Hewetson both of ys Par. wedd

the same Day Mathw Scarbrough & Ruth Hewetson both of ys Par: wedd

27th James Fawcet & Anne Gyles both of this Par. wed

Octob 11th Richd Bayliff of Kaber in the Parish of Kirby Stephn & Isabel Beck of this Par. wedd

26th John Aislop & Jane Rennison both of ys Par wed

Decem 5th Willm Hutchinson & Anne Burton both of ys Par. wed

23d Willm Dickson & Sarah Morland both of ys Par. wed

28th Willm Hewetson & Agnes Blackburn both of ys Par. wed.

1742.

Aprl 18th Were Robt Garnard of Mansor in ye Par: of K. Lonsdale & Agnes Fallowfield o' ys Par. wed

July 26th Willm Adamthwait & Agnes Metcalf bo: of ys Par: wed

Aug 29th Thoms. Fawcet & Mary Birdale both of ys Par: wed

30th Thos Fawcet (aged 82) & Mary Scott bo: of this Par: wed

Novber 8th James Fothergill of Mollerstang in ye Par: of Kirkby Stephen & Sarah Fawcet of ys Par. wed

14th James Fawcet & Isabel Robinson both o' ys Par. wed

1743.

May 12th Were John Brown & Anne Atkinson both of this Parish wedd

17th John Collinson of the Parish of Crosbyravenswth & Anne Fothergill of ys Par. wed

Novber 17th William Kitchin & Agnes Jackson both o' ys Par wed

MARRIAGES.

Dec^{ber} 22^{d} Jeofrey Denison & Marg^{t} Brunschill both of ye Par: wed

26th John Elwood & Mary Whitehead both o' this Par: wed

27th James Fawcet & Agnes Robinson both o' this Par: wed

Feb^{r} 6th Robt Shaw & Marg^{t} Fawcet both o' this Par: wed^{d}

7th Miles Chambers of the Parish of Kendal & Mary Fawcet of this Parish wed^{d}

Mar. 22^{d} John Stubbs & Marg^{t} Stubbs both of ye Par: wed^{d}

1744.

May 21st Were Thos Elliotson & Mary Dixon both o' ye Par: wed^{d}

June 16th Michael Taylor & Sarah Lancaster both o' ye Par. first ith' n: Chur. w^{d}

20th Wm Hewetson & Eliz. Fallowfield both o' ye Par. wed^{d}

23^{d} Michael Break & Roseamond Hutchinson both o' ye Par. wed

Novr 17th William Taylor & Sar: Lancaster both o' ye Par. wed^{d}

1745.

May 15th Were James Regnaldson of the Par. of K. Stephen & Anne Birtell of this wed^{d}

24th Stephen Fothergill & Sarah Bowman both o' ye Par. w^{d}

June 1st Robert Fawcet & Eliz. Atkinson both o' ye Par. wed^{d}

July 2^{d} Thos Kirkbride of ye Par. of K. Stephen & Margaret Fawcet of this wed^{d}

Nov^{ber} 7th James Perkins & Dorathy Fawcet both o' ye Parish marr^{d}

Dec^{ber} 24th Thos Robinson & Anne Shaw both o' ye Parish mar^{d}

1746.

April 3^{d} Were Richard Elliotson & Marg^{t} Fothergill both of this Parish marr^{d}

June 1st Henry Lickbarrow & Isabel Wholey both o' this Par. mar^{d}

9th John Robertson of Orton Par: & Ruth Fawcet of this mar^{d}

17th John Fawcet & Mary Shaw both of this Parish marr^{d}

Augst 3^{d} Christoph^{r} Stubbs of Ormside Par: & Jane Fothergill of Stainmore in the Par: of Brough mar^{d}

Jany 5th Richd Winter of Tebay in Orton Parish and Mary Bowness of Bolton in ye Par. of Morl^{d} mar^{d}

8th Michael Knewstubb & Eliz. Rogerson both of ye Par: mar^{d}.

MARRIAGES.

1747.

APRIL 29th Were Miles Hutchison & Isab^l Haistwell both of this Par: married

AUG^st 17th Richd Chamberlain & Marg^t Law both of Parish marr^d

24th Christoph^r Mason of Dent in the Parish of Sedbergh & Mary Blackburn of this wed^d

DEC^r 31st [T. 32] Antho Brown & Sarah Fallowfield both of this Par. w^d

1748.

APRIL 26th Were John Fothergill & Eliz. Sowerby both of this Parish wedded

MAY 1st Leonard Burton of Dent in the Parish of Sedberdg & Martha Hewetson of this Parish wedded

2^d John Dawson & Mary Shaw both of this Par. wed^d

AUG^st 22^d Mathew Breaks & Anne Bousefield both of this Parish (& in the Poorhouse, a Paralitick Man & an old wom.) wedded

NOV^ber 13th William Adamthwait & Marg^t Whitfield both of ye Par: wed

1749.

APRIL 9th Were William Furnace & Mary Perkins both of ye Par. wed

27th Robt Howgill & Mary Fawcet both of this Parish wed

MAY 6th Thos Wholay & Mary Coupland both of ye Par: wed^d

17th Richard Breaks & Mary Shearman both of ye Par. wed^d

18th John Holme & Mary Beck both of this Parish wed^d

JUNE 26th Willm Lindslay & Sarah Hutchison both of this Parish wed^d

DECEM^r 2^d Christopher Bousefield & Eliz. Knewstubb both of this Par: wed^d

19th John Hastewell & Marg^t Shaw both of this Parish wed^d

1750.

APRIL 16th Thom^s Shaw of Mallerstang in the Parish of Kirkby Stephen & Isabel Shaw of this wed^d

MAY 19th Thom^s Gibson of Park in the parish of Orton & Margar^t Perkins of this Par: wed^d

20th Thomas Knewstubb and Mary Fawcet both of this Parish wed^d

JULY 2 John Shaw & Elizabeth Hutchison both of ye Par: wed^d

MARRIAGES.

Novr 17th John Law of Garsdale in the Paris of Sedbergh & Mary Fawcet of y^{e}

Decr 27th Arthur Bousfield & Margaret Bovell both of this Par. wed^{d}

March 4th William Nelson & Margaret Stubbs both of this Parish wed^{d}

1751.

April 26th William Shaw of Mallerstang in the Parish of K: Stephen & Agnes Furnace of this married

May 13th James Hillburn of the Par: of Aisgarth Yorkshire & Isabel Bousefield of ye Par: mar^{d}

May 14th William Thompson & Martha Fawcet both of Parish wedded

29th John Dent & Alice Blades both of this Parish married

July 7th John Milner in the Parish of Burgh & Mary Robinson of this Mar^{d}

Sep^{ber} 30th Henry Brunskill & Isabel Blackburn both of this Par. wed^{d}

Octo^{r} 27th Willm Raw & Eliz. Ion both of this Parish wed^{d}

30th Willm Milner & Isabella Coulston both of this Par. mar^{d}

Novr 2^{d} George Shaw & Isabel Perkins both of this Par. wed^{d}

5th George Fawcet & Alice Perkins both of this Par. wed^{d}

1752.

Jany 4th Robert Scarbrough & Ruth Murthwait both of Par. wed^{d}

May 19th Thos Morland & Elianor Shaw both of this par. wed^{d}

20th Christop^{r} Townson in the par: of Sedbergh & Agnes Sanderson of this wed^{d}

Octob^{r} 16th Augustin Metcalf & Anne Fawcet both of this Parish wed^{d}

Nov^{ber} 1st Thomas Garthwait & Grace Branthwait both of this Parish wed^{d}

1753.

Feby 22^{d} Thomas Wilson & Isabel Fawcet both o' ye Par. wed^{d}

April 26th Richd Whitfield & Jane Sockdale both o' ye Parish wed^{d}

May 20th John Adamthwait & Isabel Keasly both of ye Par. wed

July 17th [T. 11] Richd Shaw & Ruth Blackburn both o' ye Par· wed

Octo. 14th Thomas Preston & Anne Perkins both o' ye Par. w^{d}

21st Peter Hutchison & Marg^{t} Green both o' ye Par. wed.

1754.

†Feby 21st William Shaw & Elizabeth Pindar both of this Par. wed^{d}

MARRIAGES.

* This Entry made in the Form, or to the Effect Following that is to say—

Stephen Dent of the Parish of } Ravenstondale
And Sarah Scarrbrough of the s[d] Parish of }

were married in this Church by Banns first published pursuant to Act of Parliament with Consent of Parents &c.

this 21st Day of MAY 1754

by Me Rob[t] Mounsey Cur.

This Marriage was solemnized between us } Stephen Dent
} Sarah Dent

In the Presence of us

John Perkins }
Rich[d] Murthwaite }

13 JULY 1754. Thomas Taylor & Mary Stubbs (×) by Banns (f.a.)
Witnesses, Row[d] Postlethwaite, Rob[t] Halton

19 NOV. 1754. Mathew Constantine of the Moss in the p. of Sedbergh & Marg[t] Fawcet (×) by Banns (f.a.)
Witnesses, Anthony ffawcett, James Fawcett

13 JAN. 1755. Thomas Shaw (×) & Magdalin Constantine (×) both of Murthwaite by Banns (f.a.)
Witnesses, Solomon Constantine (×) Nathan Morland

5 APRIL 1755. Francis Whaley of Tarnhouse & Anne Fothergill of Dubbs by Banns (f.a., c.p.)
Witnesses, William Whaley, Richard Fothergill

8 APRIL 1755. John Adamthwaite of the Town & Anne Udall (×) of Step's beck by Banns (f.a.)
Witnesses, Tho[s] Robinson, Robt Halton

13 APRIL 1755. Thomas Stubbs (×) of Town & Isabel Hewetson (×) of Intack by Banns (f.a.)
Witnesses, Rob[t] Mounsey, Tho[s] Robinson

22 APRIL 1755. John Chamberlain of Lockholme & Elianer Udal of Cowbank by Banns (f.a.)
Witnesses, John Chamberlain (×), Joseph Udall

---

* NOTE. With the above entry commences the third of the Register Books, containing Marriages only. As a sample of the form then in use I have reproduced the entry in full, but in those following I have thought it desirable to omit unnecessary repetition.

Except where otherwise stated the officiant is "Robt Mounsey, Min[r]" and the contracting parties described as being "of this parish." The (×) is an abbreviation for "his" or "her mark"; (f.a.) "of full age," and (c.p.) "with consent of parents."

MARRIAGES.

2 May 1755. Mathew Whitfield (×) of Bowberhead & Elianor Mason (×) of same place by Banns (f.a.)
Witnesses, Rich[d] Shaw, John Coppand

19 May 1755. Richard Lindslay of Shaw Mire & Elizabeth Lambert (×) of Tarn house by Banns (f.a.)
Witnesses, James Linsay, George Whitwell

5 July 1755. Philip Waller (×) of Hartlay in p. of Kirkby Stephen & Alice Foxcroft (×) by Banns (f.a.)
Witnesses, Richard Lindsay, William Harrop

7 Sep 1755. John Banks of Tarn & Isabel Fothergill of Murthwait by Licence (f.a.)
Witnesses, Thomas Fothergill, John Cautley

15 Oct. 1755. Thomas Perkins of Streetside & Agnes Pindar (×) of high Lane by Licence (f.a., c.p.)
Witnesses, Rog[r] Pindar (×), John Perkins (×), Henry Perkins

20 Oct 1755. John Elliotson of Scarsikes & Isabel Dent of Sandbed by Banns (c.p.)
Witnesses, Robert Mounsey, John Fothergill

29 Oct 1755. Rob[t] Thompson of Kirkby Stephen & Sarah Pindar of High Lane by Licence (f.a.)
Witnesses, John Taylor, John Pinder, Robert Mounsey

14 Dec 1755. Solomon Constantine (×) & Mary Hunter (×) both of Town by Banns (f.a.)
Witnesses, Anthony Fawcett, Thomas Robinson

2 Feb 1756. James Burton of Town & Isabel Hunter (×) of Intack by Banns (f.a.)
Witnesses, Anthony Fawcett, George fawcett

16 May 1756. Rich[d] Howgill of Crossbank & Margaret Metcalf (×) near the same place by Banns (c.p.)
Witnesses, W[m] Fothergill, John Coupland

16 May 1756. James Bird of the Town & p. of Kirkby Stephen & Anne Howgill (×) of Crossbank by Banns (c.p.)
Witnesses, W[m] Fothergill, John Coupland

2 June 1756. Anthony Knewstubb of Hill in the Low Lane & Margaret Clemison of Adamthwait by Banns (c.p.)
Witnesses, Tho[s] Knewstupp, William Clemeson, John Pinder

MARRIAGES.

20 June 1756. John Stubbs of Newbigan & Margaret Wilson of Frear Bottom by Licence (f.a.)
Witnesses, Thos Robinson, John Cowpland, Robt Mounsey, Henry Perkins

21 Aug. 1756. William Stubbs (×) of Lockholm & Margaret Coupland (×) of Town by Banns (c.p.)
Witnesses, John Stubbs, William Fawcett

1 Sep 1756. James Fawcet of Lytheside & Jane Dawson (×) of Bowberhead by Banns (f.a.)
Witnesses, Joshua Ewbanke, Anthony ffawcett

10 Nov. 1756. John Perkins & Mary Perkins both of Town by Licence (f.a.)
Witnesses, James Perkins, Robt Mounsey

20 Nov. 1756. Richard Renison (×) & Jane Metcalf (×) both of Newhouse by Banns (f.a.)
Witnesses, Thos Winder, John Sidgswick

22 Nov. 1756. Peter Handlay (×) of Town & Sarah Shearman (×) of Weesdal by Licence
Witnesses, Thomas Elyetson, John Shearman

27 Nov. 1756. Richard Lambert (×) & Agnes Dent (×) both of Bowberhead by Banns (c.p.)
Witnesses, Jacob Renison (×), Isabel Perkins, Ann Mounsey

16 Feb 1757. Anthony Metcalf of Adamthwait & Mary Fothergill of Newbign by Licence (f.a.)
Witnesses, Thos Winder, Ths Fawcett

3 May 1757. Richd Backhouse in p. of Sedbergh & Elizabeth Constantine (×) by Banns (c.p., f.a.)
Witnesses, Mathew Constantine, John Parrington

5 Sep 1757. Miles Hutchison of Newbigan & Isabel Coatlay (×) of Greenside by Banns (f.a.)
Witnesses, Robertt Fawcett, William Rudd.

5 Sep 1757. Martin Wilson of Lambrig in p. of Kendal Batchlr & Margaret Fothergill of Lythside singlewomn by License (c.p.)
Witnesses, Joshua Ewbanke, Robertt Fawcett, James Fawcett

MARRIAGES.

6 Oct. 1757. Holmes Milner singleman & Esther Newton (×) singlewoman both of Ashfell by Licence (f.a.)

Witnesses, John fawcet, George Fawcett

25 Oct 1757 John Haistwell of Alder Hill singleman & Elianer Fothergill of Murthwait singlewoman by License (f.a.)

Witnesses, Jn° Beck, John Banks.

3 Nov. 1757 John Shaw of p. of Kirkby Stephen & Sarah Bird (×) by Banns (f.a.)

Witnesses, Richard Shaw, Jane Fothergill

15 Nov 1757 John Tarlton (×) & Agnes Adamthwait (×) both of Town by Banns (f.a.)

Witnesses, John Fawcett, James Robinson

11 Feb 1758 James Beetham of Meaburn in p. of Crosby Ravensworth & Mary Bousfield of Caldbeck by Banns (c.p., f.a.)

Witnesses, Anthony Fothergill, John Bousfield

12 Ap. 1758 Joseph Parker (×) & Alice Knewstubb (×) by Banns (f.a.)

Witnesses, Thos Robinson, Geo. Udal

18 Ap. 1758 John Fawcet & Margaret Dalton (×) by Banns (f.a.)

Witnesses, Anthony Fawcett, John Fawcett

13 May 1758 Henry Law of Weesdal & Eizabeth Birtell (×) of Banks by Banns (f.a.)

Witnesses, John Todd, Richrd Bitelle

28 May 1758 Robert Collinson of Nether Stavely in the County of West^{d} & Diocese of Chester yeom^{n} & Elizabeth Murthwaite spinster by Licence (c.p.)

Witnesses, Robt Murthwaite, Ri Murthwaite

23 Sep. 1758 Isaiah Fothergill of p. of Kirkby Stephen & Marg^{t} Todd (×) by Banns (f.a.)

Witnesses, Thos Robinson, John Fawcett

30 Sep. 1758 Richard Willan of Shap Schoolmaster & Mary Elmes spinster by Licence (f.a.)

Witnesses, Robert Graham, Hannah Perkins

11 Nov 1758 William Witton the younger of Ridge End & Margaret Bowness of new Intack in p. of Crosby Ravensworth by Banns (the man with consent of Parents, the woman of full age)

Witnesses, Will. Witton, Thos Robinson

MARRIAGES.

16 Nov. 1758 Edward Beck & Isabel Robinson (×) both of Artlegarth by Banns (f.a.)
Witnesses, Jn°. Beck, Henry Perkins

12 Feb. 1759 Robert Todd & Elizabeth Giles both of Weesdal by Banns (f.a.)
Witnesses, Thomas Robertson, John Todd.

27 Feb. 1759 John Atkinson of p. of Ormside & Marg[t] Perkins (×) by Banns (c.p.)
Witnesses, George fawcett, William Atkinson

29 Ap. 1759 Thomas Fawcet of Becks & Mary Robinson (×) of Bowberhead by Banns (f.a.)
Witnesses, William Robinson, Tho[s] Robinson

21 May [T. March] 1759 Richard Birdall & Hannah Perkins both of Town by Banns (f.a.)
Witnesses, James Perkins, Isabella Perkins

21 May 1759 John Thompson of p. of Morrington [T. Mirrington] & Thermutas Richardson (×) by Banns (f.a.)
Witnesses, James Perkins, Iasbella Perkins

22 May 1759 John Ward (×) & Sarah Ward (×) both of Bowberhead by Banns (f.a.)
Witnesses, Tho[s] Parkin, John Coupland.

24 Dec. 1759 Rich[d] Hugginson of Mallerstang in p. of Kirkby Stephen & Ann Gregson by Banns (c.p.)
Witnesses, Richard Gregson, Benj[n] Judkin

24 Dec. 1759 Anthony Hodgson (×) & Agnes Fawcet (×) by Banns (f.a.)
Witnesses, Benj[n] Judkin, Thomas Taylor

29 Jan. 1760 Will[m] Stubbs & Rachel Armstrong (×) by Banns (f.a.)
Witnesses, William Shaw, W[m] Nelson

29 Jan. 1760 Joseph Udal of Cowbank & Alice Perkins of Moss by Banns (f.a.)
Witnesses, Rob[t] Scarbrough, Stephen Dent

11 Feb. 1760 John Thompson of high Lane & Mary Fawcet of Weesdal by Banns (f.a.)
Witnesses, John Hewetson (×), Joseph Udal

MARRIAGES.

22 MAY 1760 Thomas Alderson of Newbig[n] & Elizabeth Hutchison of Brownber by Licence (f.a.)
Witnesses, Tho[s] Fothergill, Eliz. Fothergill (×)

†5 JULY 1760 Robert Slack of Dockar in p. of Kendal & Sarah Shaw (×) of Steneskeugh spinster by Licence (f.a.)
Witnesses, Isaac Wilson, Tho[s]. Wilson

6 OCT 1760 William Fawcet (×) & Mary Robinson (×) both of Tranmire by Banns (f.a.)
Witnesses, Thomas Brown, Anthony Metcalf

17 OCT. 1760 Richard Allen of Town & Agnes Dawson (×) of Bowberhead by Banns (f.a.)
Witnesses, John Dawson, Thomas Taylor

13 NOV. 1760 Thomas Robinson of p. of Orton & Elizabeth Gregson of this p. were married in the p. church of Orton by Banns (f.a.) by Rob[t] Mounsey min.
Witnesses, Richard Gregson, Robert Todd

2 FEB 1761 Richard Thompson of Blasterfield in p. of Crosby Ravensworth & Sarah Shaw by Banns (f.a.)
Witnesses, John Thompson, Tho[s]. Udal.

28 MARCH 1761 Mathew Bell of Soulby in p. of Kirkby Stephen yeom[n] & Elizabeth Fothergill spinster by Licence (c.p.)
Witnesses, Rich[d] Fothergill, John Waller

31 MARCH 1761 James Shaw of Ashfield [T. Ashfell] Yeom[n] & Mary Coulston of Waingarrs spinster by Banns (f.a.)
Witnesses, William Shaw, William Milner

19 AP 1761 Isaac Smith (×) & Anne Brown (×) widow by Banns (f.a.)
Witnesses, James Richardson, Tho[s]. Robinson, Richard Shaw, Benj[n] Judkin

23 MAY 1762 W[m] Raw (×) & Elizabeth Langstaff (×) by Banns (c.p.)
Witnesses, James Richardson, Simon Nickal [T. Nicols]

5 JUNE 1762 George Perkins (×) of Crooks & Mary [T. Eliz.] Shaw (×) of Ellergill by Banns (c.p.)
Witnesses, Tho[s] Fawcett, Anthony Shaw, Thomas parkins, George Shaw

MARRIAGES.

16 June 1762 James Robinson (×) of Lockholme & Anne Whitehead by Banns (f.a.)
Witnesses, George Udal, Simon Nickal

17 June 1762 Thomas Whitehead of Kellet in p. of Orton & Mary Atkinson by Banns (c.p.)
Witnesses, William Whitehead, John Robertson

10 July 1762 Michael Bovell & Margarat Fothergill spinster by Licence (c.p.)
Witnesses, Rob[t] Bovell, Rich[d]. Fothergill.

13 July 1762 William Brunskill (×) of p. of Kirkby Stephen & Anne Robinson (×) by Banns (f.a.)
Witnesses, James Richardson, Wharton Brunskill

5 Ap. 1763 John Ernest of p. of Crosbygarret & Ann Fawcet by Banns (f.a.)
Witnesses, James Allen, John Fawcett

23 May 1763 William Spooner of Caldbeck & Agnes Wilkinson (×) of Weesdal (f.a.)
Witnesses, Robart Todd, Eliz. Spooner (×)

16 June 1763 Mathew Thompson of p. of K[y] Stephen singleman, & Mary Bovell of Newbigan spinster by Licence (c.p.)
Witnesses, Rich. Bovell, John Thompson

16 June 1763 John Coupland (×) wid[w] & Judith Huggison (×) both of Town by Banns (f.a.)
Witnesses, James Richardson, John Alderson

2 July 1763 John Shearman of Weesdal & Sarah Shaw (×) of Caldbeck by Banns (f.a.)
Witnesses, Stephen Shaw, Richard Breaks

13 July 1763 Georg Murthwait of Parrock Moor and Martha Peacock (×) of Rig End by Banns (f.a.)
Witnesses, William Atkinson, John Foster

1 Aug 1763 Thomas Hanson of p. of Greenwich co. of Kent & diocese of Rochester Gentln & Anne Hanson spinstr. by Licence (f.a.)
Witnesses, George Spedding, William Dixon

11 Oct 1763 John Tunstall of Dovingill & Jennet Shaw (×) of Steneskeugh by Banns (f.a.)
Witnesses, Thomas Fawcett, Nancy Mounsey

MARRIAGES.

14 Nov.	1763	Richd. Shaw & Dorathy Dalton (×) by Banns (f.a.) Witnesses, Joshua Ewbanke, Edward Beck.
22 Feb.	1764	Thos. Garnett of Weesdal & Margaret Adamthwait of Newbigan by Banns (c.p.) Witnesses, Robert Garnett, Robert Todd
23 Feb	1764	Fawcet Hunter yeomn & Anne Robinson spinster by Licence (c.p.) Witnesses, John Robinson, Robert Hunter
21 Ap.	1764	Joseph Bowyer Brass pounder[1] & Margaret Fothergil Spinster by Licence (f.a., c.p.) Witnesses, John Fothergill, G. Holme
24 Ap.	1764	Thomas Clemmet of p. of Asby & Elianor Lamb (×) by Banns (f.a., c.p.) Witnesses, Miles Lamb (×) John Lamb
10 May	1764	Richard Hunter & Elianor Hewetson by Banns (c.p., f.a.) Witnesses, Thos. Taylor, Thos Hunter
[2] 11 Aug	1765	Thomas Fawcet of Town Singleman & Isabel Regnaldson of Caldbeck singlewoman by Licence (f.a.) Witnesses, Jno. Stubbs, Ricd Taylor (×)
9 June	1764	John Coats & Margaret Winder [T. Pindar] by Banns (c.p.) Witnesses, William Milner, Thos Birtall
8 Ap	1765	Isaac Relf and Ann Chamberlain by Banns (f.a.) Witnesses, John Milner, John Chamberlain
11 May	1765	John Hunter & Margaret Dent by Banns (c.p.) Witnesses, Stephen Dent, Thomas Hunter
22 July	1765	Michael Breaks & Mary Heblethwait (×) by Banns (f.a.) Witnesses, Mathew Constantine, Isaac Relph
14 Aug	1765	William Hunter & Mary Broadburry (×) by Banns (f.a.) Witnesses, John Bradberry, Miles Birkbek
8 Sep	1765	John Hunter & Ann Haistwel by Banns (f.a.) Witnesses, Henry Knewstub, George Hastwell
13 Jan	1766	Mathew Constantine & Isabel Stubbs (×) by Banns (f.a.) Witnesses, John Constantine, William Fawcett.

(1) founder (?)

(2) The year has been subsequently changed from 1764 to 1765. In the Transcript the entry bears the later date, and is placed below that of 22d July 1765.

MARRIAGES.

16 Jan. 1765 Hugh Shaw & Jane Wharton by Banns (f.a.)
Witnesses, James Richardson, Thomas Taylor

30 Ap. 1765 William Campbell of p. of K^{y} Stephen & Jennet Metcalf (×) by Banns (f.a.)
Witnesses, John Haygarth, Thos Taylor

1 May 1766 John Robinson of Street & Mary Perkin (×) by Banns (f.a.)
Witnesses, James Parkin, Anthony Robinson

17 June 1766 Joseph Thompson & Anne Birtell (×) by Banns (c.p.)
Witnesses, John Thompson (×) Mat Bertel

1 July 1766 Thomas Swinbank (×) of Garsdale in p. of Sedbergh C^{o} of York & Diocese of Chester, Mason & alice Handley (×) spinster by Licence (f.a.)
Witnesses, Rich^{d}. Fothergill, Thos. Fothergill

13 July 1766 John Udal yeom^{n} & Isabel Hewetson spinster by Licence (c.p., f.a.)
Witnesses, Robt. Hewetson, Thos Udal

27 Sep 1766 John Robinson & Isabel Shaw by Licence (c.p.) by William Fawcett, curate [T. Curate of Kirkby Stephen]
Witnesses, Henry Bousfield, Georg Fawcett

18 Oct. 1766 John Fothergill of Brownber & Mary Robinson of Lytheside by Licence (c.p.)
Witnesses, Jno. Robinson, William Elyetson

21 Oct. 1766 Willm. Metcalf & Elizabeth Blades (×) by Banns (f.a.)
Witnesses, Thos Birtell, John Dent

24 Feb 1767 George Haistwell & Elizabth Hemsley by Banns (f.a.)
Witnesses, John Hull, Thomas Hastwell

2 Mar 1767 Robt. Wilkinson of p. of Sedbergh and Mary Robinson (×) by Banns (f.a.)
Witnesses, William Simm, John Robinson

7 May 1767 William Metcalf (×) of p. of K^{y} Stephen & Jane Dawson (×) by Banns (f.a.)
Witnesses, John Dawson, John Breaks.

16 May 1767 Thomas Jackson of the p. of Asby & Elizabeth Shaw (×) by Banns (c.p.)
Witnesses, John Shaw, Geo: Jackson

MARRIAGES.

19 MAY 1767 Thomas Fothergill & Mary Dixon by Banns (f.a., c.p.)
Witnesses, Francis Whaley, Richard Dixon

19 MAY 1767 Thomas Relph of Seberham C° Cumberland singleman & Elianer Fothergill of Dubbs singlewoman by Licence (f.a.)
Witnesses, Francis Whaley, Tho[s] Relph

20 JULY 1767. James [T. Tho[s]] Hodgson (×) & Hannah Tebay (×) by Banns (f.a.)
Witnesses, Isaac Relph, John Chamberlain

20 OCT. 1767. Thomas Snowdon & Mary Kitchen (×) by Banns (c.p.)
Witnesses, William Kitchin, John Snowdon (×)

7 MAY 1768. Thomas Hewetson of Ellergill singleman & Isabel Shaw of Town singlewoman by Licence (c.p.)
Witnesses, Ja[s] [T. Jn°] Collinson, John Shaw

7 MAY 1768. John Beck of Artlegarth & Anne Shaw of Town by Banns (c.p.)
Witnesses, Edward Beck, John Hewetson

25 MAY 1768. James Swainson & Jane Hewetson by Banns (f.a.)
Witnesses, Anthony Shaw, Thomas Fawcett

22 JUNE 1768. Matthew Scarbrough, widower & Elizabeth Woof (×) of Greystoke C° Cumberland widow by Licence (f.a.)
Witnesses, John Perkins, Mary Mounsey

20 JULY 1768. Rob[t] Garnet & Ann Cock of p. of Orton by Banns (f.a.)
Witnesses, Tho[s] Fothergill, Tho[s] Taylor

3 SEP. 1768. William Potter & Anne Denison (×) by Banns (f.a.)
Witnesses, Anthony Fothergill, Robert Hutchinson

17 SEP. 1768. George Fawcet & Isabel Birtell (×) by Banns (f.a.)
Witnesses, Thomas Fawcet, John Birtell (×)

24 SEP. 1768. Edw[d] Metcalf (×) of p. of Sedbergh & Anne Constantine (×) by Banns (f.a.)
Witnesses, Mathew Constantine, Andrew M[c]millan

27 SEP 1768. Edw[d] Hebson, & Rachel Borrowdale (×) both of Brackenber by Licence (f.a.)
Witnesses, Miles Lamb (×) John Bowman (×)

6 OCT. 1768. John Hewetson of Lockholme foot & Isabel Elliotson of Wath by Licence (f.a.)
Witnesses, Matt. Robinson, Anne Gibson (×)

MARRIAGES.

12 Nov. 1768. Richard Birtel & Isabel Robinson (×) by Banns (c.p.)
Witnesses, John Birtal (×), Francis Robinson (×)

17 Nov. 1768. Anthony Spooner (×) & Mary Ward (×) by Banns (f.a.)
Witnesses, Thos Fothergill, Christopher Gregson

1 Ap. 1769. Anthony Dent of Dovingill & Faithy Dent of Sandbed by Licence (c.p.)
Witnesses, Stephen Dent, Thomas Hewetson.

17 Ap. 1769. Antho. Urwin (×) & Isabel Hanson (×) by Banns (f.a.)
Witnesses, James Hanson, Thos Fawcett

15 May 1769. James Moor (×) & Agnes Woof (×) by Banns (f.a.)
Witnesses, James Gosling, Benjn Judkin

12 Sep. 1769. Mathew Brown (×) & Mary Hewetson (×) by Banns (f.a., c.p.)
Witnesses, *

19 Sep. 1769. Ellick Scythe (×) & Mary Backhouse (×) by Banns (f.a.)
Witnesses, James Fawcett, John Fawcett

16 Oct. 1769. Edwd Burrow & Ruth Adamthwait (×) by Banns (f.a.)
Witnesses, Thos Adamthwait (×) John Adamthwait

30 Oct. 1769. Mathew Ward (×) & Agnes Lambert (×) by Banns (f.a.)
Witnesses, James Dent, Joshua Ewbank

11 Nov. 1769. James Hanson of p. of Crosby Ravensworth & Dorathy Steadman (×) by Banns (c.p.)
Witnesses, Thos Steadman, Thomas Fawcett

8 March 1770. William Elyetson of Browfoot & Agnes Robinson of Steneskeugh batchlr & singlewoman by Licence (c.p.)
Witnesses, Richard Dixon, Robt Bovell

14 Ap. 1770. Richd Hewetson & Ann Dixon by Banns (c.p.)
Witnesses, Richard Dixon, Richard Hewetson

7 May 1770. John Murray in p. of Kirkbythure & Anne Murray (×) by Banns (f.a.)
Witnesses, *

30 Dec 1770.** John Birtal (×) & Dinah Helton (×) by Banns (c.p.)
Witnesses, Mathew Birtel, George Fawcett

---

* No Signatures.

** This date, both in original and in Transcript, has been changed from 1 Jan. 1771.

MARRIAGES.

24 JAN. 1771. James Capstick [T. 54] of Dent in p. of Sedbergh & Mary Constantine [T. 56] (×) by Banns (f.a.)
Witnesses, Anthony Fawcett, Christopher Mason

27 AP. 1771. Edw[d] Whitehead (×) [T. of Wandal Husbandm[n] 65] & Sarah Chamberlain (×) [T. of Studfold, spinster 28] by Banns (f.a.)
Witnesses, Jonathan Alderson, Benj[n] Judkin

30 AP. 1771. John Fawcet [T. of Wrey Green, Husbandman 26] & Anne Hunter (×) [T. of Brigg, Spinster 24] by Banns (c.p)
Witnesses, Stephen Fawcett, Thoma Fawcett

12 MAY 1771. Anthony Fawcet [T. of Foggigill, Husbandm[n] 25] & Mary Hunter [T. of Brigg Spinst[r] 26] by Licence (c.p.)
Witnesses, George Hastwell, John Fawcett

15 MAY 1771. John Todd [T. Yeom[n] 40] and Isabel Perkins (×) [T. Spinster 36] by Banns (f.a.)
Witnesses, Thomas parkins, Robert Todd

1 SEP. 1771. Will[m] Fawcett [T. Day Labourer 22] & Agnes Whitehead [T. Spinst[r] 25] by Banns (f.a.)
Witnesses, Ch[r] Gray, Fawcett Hunter

12 OCT. 1771. Mathew Brunskill of Gaisgill Row in p. of Orton [T. Batchl[r] about 26] & Margaret Atkinson of Coldbeck [T. Spinster 20] by Licence [T. with consent of John Atkinson Father of s[d] Margaret]
Witnesses, John Atkinson, Steph[n] Brunskill

19 NOV. 1771. John Nelson (22) [T. of Coldbeck, waller] & Isabel Smith 20) (×) [T. of the Hole, Spinst[r]] by Banns [T. with Consent of Th: Smith, Father of s[d]. Mabel]
Witnesses, Georg (?) Smeth, John Kendall

26 JAN. 1772. John Wilson of p. of Kirkby Lonsdale singleman & Hannah Hunter singlewoman by Licence (c.p.)
Witnesses, Isaac Relph, Edmund Wilson

6 FEB. 1772. Joshua Hunter [T. Serv[t]man] & Anne Adamthwaite (×) [T. Serv[t] woman] by Licence (c.p.)
Witnesses, Rich[d] Fothergill, James Fawcett

8 JUNE 1772. George Perkin (33) yeom[n] of p. of K[y] Stephen & Isabel Fawcet (27) by Banns
Witnesses, George Robinson, Ant. Knewstupp

MARRIAGES.

22 JUNE 1772. John Spedding (27) [T. Shoemaker] & Elizabeth Denison (23) (×) [T. Spinst[r] 22] by Banns
Witnesses, Edmund Wilson, Joseph Hanson

2 JULY 1772. Edm[d] Metcalf (26) (×) [T. Day Labourer] & Anne Kitchin (25) [T. Spinster] by Banns
Witnesses, Thomas Snowden, William Kitchen

5 SEP 1772. Rob[t] Thompson (23) [T. Farmer 22] & Mary Birtell (22) (×) [T. Spinst[r]] by Banns
Witnesses, Mathew Bertel, Joseph Thompson

21 SEP 1772. Will[m] Fawcet (39) of Lockholme Batchl[r] [T. & Farmer] & Jane Waddington [T. Spinst[r]] (21) of Kiln Mire spinster by Licence
Witnesses, James Hutchinson, Richard Winter

7 OCT 1772. John Dover (23) [T. weaver] & Margaret Wilson (30) (×) [T. Spinster] by Banns
Witnesses, Edmund Wilson, Anthony Fawcett, Benj[n] Judkin

26 DEC. 1772. Chris[r] Coupland (52) [T. Farmer] & Allice Howgill (44) (×) [T. Spinster] by Banns
Witnesses, W[m] Howgill (×), John Fawcett

21 FEB. 1773. John Hewetson & Mary Ewbank, yeom[n] & spinst[r] by Licence (c.p.)
Witnesses, Rob[t] Hewetson, Joshua Ewbank

20 MAR 1773. Michael Knewstubb (20) batchl[r] & Ruth Chamberlain (23) Spinst[r] by Licence
Witnesses, John Chamberlain, Isaac Relph

3 AP 1773. John Perkins, Carpenter, [T. 48] & Alice Nelson (×) spinster [T. 34] by Licence (f.a.)
Witnesses, William Nelson, Hannah Birtel (×)

27 AP 1773. William Nelson (26) waller & Dorathy Shaw (34) widow by Banns
Witnesses, John Dalton, John Nelson

23 SEP 1773. Stephen Brunskill (24) of p. of Orton & Sarah Hewetson (21) (×) by Banns
Witnesses, John Hewetson, Robertt Murry

MARRIAGES.

21 Nov. 1773. Rob[t] Chamberlain (28) [T. Shoemaker] & Alice Ion (21) [T. Spinster] by Banns
Witnesses, Jonathan Alderson, John Brunskill

6 Feb 1774. Hen[y] Perkins (39) & Ruth Bousfield (29) by Licence
Witnesses, Tho[s] Bousfield, Henry Beck

1 Mar 1774. Matthew Robinson (40) of Thring gill in p. of K[y] Stephen & Mary Shaw (30) of Steneskeugh by Licence
Witnesses, John Shaw, John Thompson

11 May 1774. Thomas Hunter (49) & Anne Morland (33) (×) by Banns
Witnesses, John Morland, Richard Dixon

26 Sep 1774. Will[m] Nelson (23) [T. Carpenter] & Anne Gibson (25) [T. Spinster] by Banns
Witnesses, Benj[n] Judkin, Isaac Teasdale

19 Oct 1774. Thomas Thompson (21) [T. Day Labourer] & Melly Shaw (23) (×) [T. Spinst[r]] by Banns
Witnesses, James Waller, James Hewartson

22 Nov. 1774. John Shaw (37) [T. Batchl[r]] & Elizabeth Coulston (33) by Licence
Witnesses, William Milner, Robert Shaw

25 Dec 1774. James Taylor (22) & Agnes Barnet (24) (×) by Banns
Witnesses, Mathew Wilkinson, William Taylor (×)

16 Jan 1775. Rob[t] Howgill (55) & Anne Hayton (25) (×) by Banns
Witnesses, John Howgill, Rich[d] Howgill

16 Feb 1775. John Heblethwaite (27) [T. Shoemaker] & Hannah Teasdal (33) [T. Widow] by Banns
Witnesses, John Stubbs, Bryan Heblethwaite, John Fawcett, Matthew Harrison

11 May 1775. Will[m] Metcalf (26) [T. Day Labourer] & Mary Chamley (29) [T. Spinst[r]] by Banns
Witnesses, John Heblethwaite, Alex[der] Nowell, Thomas Shaw

13 May 1775. John Morland (26) Batchl[r] & Anne Dent (23) spinst[r] by Licence
Witnesses, Richard Dixon, Stephen Dent, Henry Robinson

23 May 1775. Rob[t] Campbell, (26) [T. Schoolmaster] & Isabel Chamberlain (22) [T. Spinster] by Licence
Witnesses, Henry Law, James Hewitson, George Hastwel, John Heblethwaite

MARRIAGES.

25 MAY 1775. Dawson Buck (25) (×) Batchl^{r} & Anne Fawcet (36) (×) [T. Widow] by Licence
Witnesses, Wm Ion (×), Thomas Hewetson

8 JUNE 1775. Thomas Hewetson (28) Joiner & Elizth Perkins (32) (×) Spinst^{r} by Licence
Witnesses, Henry Perkins, Richard Hewetson

1 JULY 1775. John Murthwait (39) [T. Batchl^{r}] & Elizth Perkins (31) Spinst^{r} by Banns
Witnesses, Robt Murthwaite, John Hewetson

18 SEP 1775. Edwd Urwin (25) [T. Pensioner at Chelsy] & Isabella Adamthwaite (26) (×) [T. Spinst^{r}] by Banns
Witnesses, John Dawson, William Morros

23 [T. 22] JAN 1776. Wm Hutchinson (29) [T. Carrier] & Nancy Hewetson (31) [T. Spinst^{r}] by Banns
Witnesses, John Hewetson, Robert Hutchison

10 AP. 1776. James Hewetson (28) & Anne Spooner (30) (×) by Banns
Witnesses, James Clogston, John Spedding, John Milner

11 MAY 1776. James Bayliff (38) (×) of p. of Orton & Jane Fothergill (24) (×) by Banns
Witnesses, James Waller, John Spedding, John Robinson

23 MAY 1776. Robt Shaw (35) [T. Yeom^{n}] & Margar^{t} Robinson (22) by Licence
Witnesses, Henry Robinson, Thos Williamson

2 JULY 1776. John Fawcett ( )* of Gate in p. of Sedbergh singleman & Elizabeth Morland (27) (×) of Stouphill Gate Spinst^{r} by Licence
Witnesses, John Morland, Leon^{d} Haygarth

6 OCT. 1776. Robt Fawcett (23) of Wreygreen Batchl^{r} & Isabel Haistwell (×) of Ellerhill spinst^{r} by Licence (c.p.)
Witnesses, John Hastwell, Anthony Fawcett

28 OCT 1776. Anto^{ny} Birtell (21) [Day Labourer] & Agnes Hutchison (22) [T. Servt] by Banns
Witnesses, George Fawcett, Miles Hutchison (×)

9 NOV. 1776. Henry Beck (26) [T. badg^{r}] & Sarah Gregson (26) [T. Spinst^{r}] by Banns
Witnesses, Richard Grgson, Edward Beck

---

* Indistinct. T. gives 31.

MARRIAGES.

12 Nov. 1776. Thomas Rennison (38) [T. farmer] & Isabel Hutchison (31) (×) [T. Spinr] by Banns

Witnesses, Robert Hutchinson, Anthony Fothergill

13 Nov 1776. Wm Taylor (23) (×) [T. Day Labourer] & Margt Robinson (19)* (×) [T. Spinr] by Banns (c.p.)

Witnesses, Willm Nelson junr, Edward Borrow

16 Dec 1776. James Buck (34) [T. Servt man] & Anne Ion (26) [T. Spinr] by Licence

Witnesses, Robt Chamberlain, Matthew Wilkinson

7 Jan 1777. [T. Mr] John Baines (24) [T. Surgeon] of Lockholme & Hannah Chamberlain (20) [T. Spinr] by Licence

Witnesses, John Chamberlain, Thos Udal

7 Jan 1777. John Wilson (22) [T. husbandn] & Mary Perkins (24) [T. Spinr] by Banns

Witnesses, John Parkin, Richard Wilson

4 Feb. 1777. Thomas Hewetson (22) [T. batchlr] of Lockholme & Sarah Walker (23) [T. Millianr] of Town Spinstr by Licence

Witnesses, John Heblethwaite, Nancy Mounsey

18 Mar 1777. James Hewetson (25) of Lockholme [T. mercer] Batchlr & Margaret Richardson (20) of Town [T. mantil maker] Spinstr by Licence with consent of her brother Willm Richardson her guardian

Witnesses, Wm Richardson, Wm Bousfield

15 Ap 1777. John Haistwell (26) (×) [T. farmer] of Murthwaite & Anne Rennison (20) (×) [T. servt maid] of Sprintgill by Banns

Witnesses, Christophr Rennison (×), Fawcett Hunter

16 Ap 1777. Henry Hunter (38) of Rowhey Bridge Batchlr & Anne Shaw (23) of Ellergill spinstr by Licence

Witnesses, Thomas Fawcett, George Shaw

21 Ap 1777. John Gibson (28) [T. gentlen] of the p. of Crosby Ravensworth & Ruth Bousfield (25) [T. Spinr] by Licence

Witnesses, Arthur Bousfield, Geo. Gibson

22 Ap 1777. Thomas Nelson (22) Carpenter & Elizth Armstrong (25) [T. Spinr] by Banns

Witnesses, William Nelson, Thos. Wilson

---

* The age has been altered subsequently from 22 (?) to 19. T. has 19.

MARRIAGES.

3 JUNE 1777. John Machell (57) of p. of Kirkby Kendal, Butcher & Margaret Bovall (43) Spinst^r by Licence

Witnesses, George Robinson, Richard Hewetson

6 JULY 1777. John Allen (36) of p. of Bondgate singleman & Isabel Dent (31) of Lythside singlewoman by Licence

Witnesses, Stephen Dent, Nancy Mounsey

12 JULY 1777. John Chamberlain (30) [T. yeo^n] of Greenside, singleman & Anne Bousfield (23) of Rig-end singlewoman by Licence

Witnesses, James Somerville, Isabella Somerville, Richd Bousfield

7 OCT. 1777. Thomas Adamthwaite (23) serv^t man & Anne Fawcet (23) (×) [T. of Bleaflat Singlewoman] by Banns

Witnesses, George Fawcett, Thos. Perkins

13 NOV. 1777. Thomas Bateman (29) of p. of Skelton, Cumb^d, yeom^n & Agnes Winder (29) (×) spinst^r by Licence

Witnesses, Thomas Rumney, Nansey Mounsey

1 DEC. 1777. George Fawcett (28) [T. batchl^r] & Elizabeth Fawcett (20) (×) [T. Servt maid] by Banns by W. Adamthwaite, curate

Witnesses, James Fawcett, Anthony Fawcett, William Fawcett

2 DEC 1777. James Robinson, (22) [T. of Town] smith & Mary Hewetson (24) [T. of Lockholme] Spinst^r by Banns

Witnesses, William Adamthwaite, Thos. Robinson, Robt. Hewetson

7 DEC. 1777. John Stubbs (21) [T. batchl^r] Tayl^r & Mary Milner (23) (×) [T. Greenside] Spinst^r by Banns

Witnesses, John Milner, Matthew Wilkinson, Ann Todd

30 DEC. 1777. Thomas Udal (45) [T. batchl^r] farm^r & Isabella Burton (28) spinst^r by Banns

Witnesses, Robert Robinson, John Heblethwaite

26 JAN 1778. Willm Furnace (20) & Isabel Metcaff (23) (×) by Banns

Witnesses, Robert Hutchinson, Richard Furnace, Mathew Wilkinson

MARRIAGES.

* 16 Ap 1779. John Bell (19) & Mary Thompson (26) by Licence
Witnesses, Thomas Fawcett, William Shaw

2 May 1779. Thomas Whaley (22) & Nancy Adamthwaite (22) (×)
Witnesses, James Whaley, Henry Robinson

6 June 1779. Robt Hutchinson (35) & Ann Brunskill (24) (×) by Banns
Witnesses, John Hellethwaite, Matthew Wilkinson

24 July 1779. Joseph Hunter (84) (×) & Mary Adamthwaite (26) (×) both of Tarn House by Licence
Witnesses, george fothergill, James Waller

17 Oct 1779. Jno Stubbs (23) & Elizabeth Winder (20) by Banns by Wm Taylor curate
Witnesses, Thos Wilson, Matthew Wilkinson

20 Oct 1779. Isaac Handley (21) & Sybil Hunter (27) by Licence by Wm Taylor curate
Witnesses, Fawcett Hunter, George Shaw

20 Dec 1779. Robt Dawson (23) (×) & Marg^{t} Longstaff (28) (×) by Wm Taylor curate
Witnesses, John Dawson, Matthew Wilkinson, John Fothergill, Jane Dawson

16 Feb. 1780. John Milner (27) & Mary Cunningham (23) by Licence by Wm Taylor curate
Witnesses, William Milner, John Shaw, R^{d} Cunningham, Ann Bird

14 Mar 1780. Wm Bousfield (26) & Isabella Shaw (23) by Licence by Wm Taylor curate
Witnesses, Stephen Shaw, Henery Bousfield

9 Ap. 1780. Wm Alderson of p. of K^{y} Stephen & Mary Adamthwaite (×) by Wm Taylor Curate (f.a.)
Witnesses, Henry Robinson, John Stubbs, Edward Stubbs

9 May 1780. Thos Fothergill & Betty Shaw by Wm Taylor (f.a.)
Witnesses, William Shaw, Thos Shaw

† 9 May Wm Hewetson & Martha Burton p^{r} Wm Taylor curate (f.a., c.p.)
Witnesses, Thos Udal, John Shaw

---

* There appears to be no Marriage Transcript for 1779.

MARRIAGES.

20 MAY 1780. Thos Kirkbride (×) of p. of Autheret, Cumbd, & Jane Shaw pr Licence by Wm Taylor curate (f.a., c. of friends)
Witnesses, Ralph fothergill, John Robinson

24 MAY 1780. Michael Middleton of p. of Ky Stephen & Ellianor Dent (×) by Banns by Wm Taylor curate (f.a., c.p.)
Witnesses, William Dent, John Hugginson

17 JUNE 1780. James Hill of Dent in p. of Sedbergh & Mary Breaks (×) by Licence by Wm Taylor curate (f.a., c.p.)
Witnesses, Joseph Cragg, Charles Hill, Richard Breaks

7 AUG 1780. Robt Parkinson & Mary Woofingdale (×) by Banns by Jeff: Bowness, ministr (c.p.)
Witnesses, John Overend, Robert Thwaits

26 SEP 1780. Thomas Parkin & Ann Perkins by Licence by Jeff: Bowness, ministr of Ravenstonedale (f.a., c. of friends)
Witnesses, John Todd, Richrd Brlel [T. Birtle]

17 OCT 1780. Richd Wilcock of p. of Burton & Deborah Fawcet by Banns by Jeff: Bowness Minister
Witnesses, Matthew Wilkinson, James Willcock

16 DEC. 1780. Richd Furnass & Eliz. Rennison (×) by Banns by Jeff: Bowness Minister
Witnesses, Joseph Birtel, William Furnass

BURIALS.

1710. 13th April	Anne Todd of the Town Buried
3 June	Mary Daughter to Chri. Alderson B.
15 July	Lucy Moreland of Lockholm B.
27th	Stephen Fawcett of Newbiggin B.
14: Augt	Richard Chamberlaine of Needless B.
14th	Anne Wife to Wm Hunter of Steneskew B.
13 Novr	Ralph Alderson of Greenside Buried
3 Decemr	John Fawcett of Lockholm B.
24 Feb	John Bailiffe of Mortwhaite B.
6 March	Margaret Fothergill of Lockholme Widw B.
18th	Isabel Peers of Townhead Spinster Buried
1711. 21	William son of James & Margaret Hutcheson B.
25	Margaret Fawcett wife to Ricd Fawcett of Mortwhaite B.
29	Margaret Robinson of Blaeflatt widw B.
2 April	Stephn Dent of Sandbed Buried
5	Margaret Spooner of Greenside Widow B.
24 Aprill	Agnes Thompson was Buried
26 Aprill	Richard Rogerson son of thomas Rogerson B:
25 June	Richard Giles of Wesdaile Buried
2 July	Ellin wife of William perkin Buried
6 July	Jane wife of William Dixon Buried
20 July	John Taylor of Mires Buried
26 Sept	Marey Medcalfe of Greenside Buried
11 Decem	Issabell Blamire of high Loneing Buried
2 Jann.	William son to William Adamthwaite Buried
15 Feb:	Issabell wife of Richard fawcett of newbigin B.
8 March	Marey Daughter to John Nelson Buried
13 March	Ellsabeth Vbank of Lythside Buried
1712. 30 March	John punch of Backside Burried
10 April	John son to John Punch Burried
13 Aprill	Christopher son to John Punch Burried
26 Aprill	Elizabeth wife to Thomas Hunter Burried
28 May	Robert son to James Alderson was Buried
13 June	Robert Hodgson of town Buried

BURIALS.

27 Aug:	John Simpson was Buried
5 Sept.	Marey fothergill of Brownber was Buried
15 Sept	Mr James Mitchel of Lockholme Buried
14 Sept.	John Hewetson of hill was Buried
24 Sept.	William Whitfield Buried
1 Octo:	Sarah ffothergill of Lockholme Buried
5 Octo:	Robert son to George Whited [T. Whitelth] Buried
18 Octo:	Anthony son to John Shaw Buried
17 Nov.	John son to Richard Todd Buried
4 Dece	Mathew Birdall Buried
14 Dece	Abraham Bousfield of town head Buried
27 Jan:	Margret fawcet of Newbegin Buried
2 Feb.	Ellinor Knewstubb of Greenside Buried
19 March	Margret wife of Robert Hunter Buried
† 6 Aprill	John son to James Robinson of twoun Buried
1713. 16 Aprill	Abraham Bousfield of Nabb Buried
17 Aprill	Agnus wife of James Robinson Buried
1 May	Mabbell Chamberlaine of Newbegin Buried
25 May	Richard fawcett of Backside Buried
16 July	Grace pinder Buried
20 Sept	John Birket of Street Buried
13 Oct.	Christopher Bousfield of wandaile B.
18 Octo.	Marey Wilson of townhead B.
13 Nou	Elizabeth Daughter to Henery Fothergill of Loukholme was Buried
18 Noue	Richard Alderson Buried
5 Decem	Margret daughter to Henery Fothergill of Loukholme Buried
13 Jann	Marey pouson of Brackinber Buried
22 Jann	Marey Daughter to William Hunter Buried
29 Jann	Sarah wife of Anthony fothergill Buried
Feb th 6	Margret Daughter to William Adamthwaite B.
1714. 27 March	William fothergill of tarne house Buried
1 Aprill	Marey Dau [T. Dave] of the town Buried
29 Aprill	Thomas Rogerson of the town Buried
13 May	John son to George fawcet of stenerscugh B.
31 May	Thomas Burton Buried

BURIALS.

15 JUNE Annas Bounas Buried
1 JULY Marey Dent Buried
15 JULY Sarah Waller of the town head Buried
9 SEPT. Margrett wife of John Adamthwaite Buried
24 OCTO William Milner of Assfell Buried
30 OCTO. Ellinnor Elyetson of Scarsikes Buried
7 DECEM Issabell fawcet of Newbegin Buried
12 FEB. Issabell daughter to John Taylor Buried
1715. 17 MAR Dority daughter to Michael Knewstubb B.
† 15 MAR Ellinnor powson of Weesdaile Buried
† 13 APRILL Jamer Clarkon of Ellerhill Buried
28 APRILL Agnus Bland seruant att alm pott Buried
21 JUNE Francees Adamthwaite Buried
23 JUNE Richard Gouldington Buried
14 AUGUST Robert son to John Knewstubb Buried
4 OCTOB: Marey daughter to thomas fawcett Buried
8 OCTOB: Marey wife of Ralph Alderson Buried
1 NOUEM Issabell Mounce of this town Buried
21 NOUEM James fawcett of newbegin Buried
24 NOU Ann daughter to thomas Shaw Buried
26 NOU Jennatt fothergill of this town Buried
3 DECEM James fawcett of stenerscugh Buried
5 DECEM Isabell wife of Richard Hunter Buried
10 DECE[r] James Robinson of stenerscugh Buried
1715. 27 DECEM Ellinor wife of John fawcett Buried
14 JANN George son to stephen Dent Buried
23 JANN Thomas son to thomas shaw Buried
22 MARCH Margrett wife to Richard todd Buried
1716. 26 APRILL John son to John Hewtson Buried
2 JUNE Marey Moss of this town Buried
21 JULY Ellinor wife of John Briham Buried
3 AUGU William Shaw of Streett Buried
4 AUG. Richard Murthwaite Buried
3 SEP[t] Margrett daughter to Joseph Hanson Buried
8 SEP[t] Sarah daughter to John Briham of Mollerstang Buried
OCTOB. the 20. Robert Hunter Buried
6 NOUEM Sarah wife to John hewetson Buried

BURIALS.

17 NOVEM Marey wife to Giles Hall Buried
20 NOVEM Richard fawcett of Murthwaite Buried
5 DECEM John taylor of ellergill Buried
JANNU 7 Marey wife to Regnald Dixon Buried
FEB: 2 Henery Bousfield of townehead Buried
† APRILL 19 Christopher taylor of Elergill Buried
1717. JUNE [T. APRIL] 19 Annas wife to thomas Dent Buried
Elizabeth wife to John Murthwaite the same Day Buried
JUNE 11 John hall of Murthwate Buried
JUNE 13 Regnald Dixon Buried
JUNE 15 Ann daughter to Rodger Barber Buried
JUNE 16 Thomas son to William Robinson Buried
JULY 6 thomas Dent of weesdale Buried
AUGU th 9 Margret Milner of Asfell Buried
AUG 31 Jennat fawcet of sprintgill Buried
SEPT 18 thomas parkin of Adamthwaite Buried
SEPT 22 Richard Kendall Buried
SEPT. 23 Ann Giles & Margrett Murthwaite Buried
OCTOB: 24 Agnus wife to Robert fawcet of Murthwate B.
NOVEM 8 Thomas falowfield Buried
NOVEM 13 Abraham Dent Buried
Nov 17 Ellsabeth Bousfeild of scarsikes Buried
11 JANN James powson Buried
11 JANN Thomas Hastwhitell of greenside Buried
18th George fawcett of low Stenerscugh Buried
25th Richard son to Richard Birtell Buried
30th Margret daughter to Richard Robinson Buried
FEB 11th Ellice Birket of street Buried
MARCH 8th Ellice Robertson of high stenerscugh Buried
1717. 22 MARCH Ruth daughter to William Elyetson Buried
1718. 8 APRILL Dority daughter to Margaret Birket Buried
13 APRILL Richard fawcett of Newbegin Buried
14 APRILL Richard Clarkson Buried
13 MAY Marey wife to George parkin Buried
2 [T. 1] JULY Cristopher son to Regnald Dixon Buried
23 JULY Thomas son to John fawcet of blaflat B.
AUGUST 9th Elizabeth daughter to John Blades Buried

BURIALS.

12 OCTOB:	Thomas son to John Hall Buried
NOVEM the 12	George son to thomas fawcet of Brounber Buried
NOVEM 17	Henery son to Richard Breaks Buried
24th	John Robinson of town buried
DECEM 3	Agnus daughter to William Jackson B.
26th	Margret Willson of this town Buried
JANRY 4th	Agnus daughter to Richard fothergill of Orton buried
the 23d	Mathew scarbrough Buried
25	George whitelth Buried
MARCH 16	Henery son to Richard Birtell B.
1719.	
MARCH 31	Michael Chamberlaine Buried
6 APRILL	Sarah Shaw of Ashfell Buried
13 APRILL	John son to John Milner Buried
24 APRILL	Marey fothergill of lythside B.
25 APRILL	Sarah Ellyetson of scarsikes B.
9 MAY	Elinor Gouldington Buried
16 MAY	Thomas son to Robert fawcet B.
JULY 26	Margret Johnson Buried
AUG. 22	Grerge fothergill of Newbegin B.
SEPT 2	Mrs Marey fawcet Buried
SEPT 8	James fawcet of Murthwaite B.
DECEM 6	John son to John Whitfield Buried
DECEM 8	John son to Joseph Hanson Buried
FEB 27	Issabell Bird of Newbegin B.
same day	James Moss of the town head B.
21 MARCH	Ellizabeth fawcet of this town B.
1720.	
29 MAR	Issabell daughter to Marey fawcet B.
2 APRILL	Richard Fothergill of lithside B.
1720.	John Law Buried APRILL the 28
24 MAY	Margret parkins of stenerscugh Buried
JUNE 25	Annas daughter to Godfrey Milner Buried
JULY 3	Richard Chamberlaine Buried
	Maudlen Breaks Buried SEPT 24th
NOVEM 14	Dority daughter to William Hougill Buried
	Ann Bousfield Buried NOVEMBER 30th

BURIALS.

DECEM the 17 Stephen fawcet of Weesdaile Buried
JANN 8 Elice Giles of Weesdaile Buried
JANN 31 William perkins of Assfell Buried
JANN 31 Ann daughter to Richard Hunter Buried
FEB. 13 Thomas Hall of Streetside buried
FEB. 27 Henry fothergill of Wath Buried
MARCH 2 Elutheria [T. Lutheria] Ubanck Buried
MARCH 8 John son to John Baylife of Murthwait Buried
13th George son to George parkin of stenerscugh B.

1721

21 APRILL Thomas son to Thomas Millner Buried
27 APRILL Marey Wife to John fawcet of street side B.
MAY 12th Edward son to Mr George Briggs Buried
MAY 16 Elizabeth Hunter Buried
MAY 24 Sarah Milner Buried
MAY 24 Mabell Chamberlain Buried
JUNE 23 Isabell Daughter to William Hunter of Wandale Buried
JULY 21st Barbary Morland (Buried)
27th Mabbel Hodshon o' th' Town-End (buried)
AUGt 18th Sarah wife to Jno Blackburne Weavr Bd
19th Alice Perkin o' Greenside Bd
SEPr 13th Eleanor Bousfield o' th' Wath Widw Bd
OCTr 19th John an illegitimate child of Mary Atkinson
25th Thomas Taylor o' th' Bents Buried
NOVr 20th Margaret wife to Tho. Blackburn o' Newbiggn Bd
24th Henry Perkin of Adamthwaite Buried
DECr 31st Wm son to Wm Hunter o' th' Street Buried
JAN 2d Margaret Daughter to Elis. Taylor o' Weesdale Bd
9th William Ellietson o' th' Scarsikes Buried
14th Elsabeth Edmonson o'th' Waingarrs buried
30th Mary Fothergill of Adamtwhaite Widw Brd
1721 FEB 4th Wm Hunter o' Russendale-Town buried

1722

MARCH 31st Anne Daughter to Matthew & Margt Breaks Brd
APR. 6th Sarah Chamberlaine o' Wandale buried
15th Agnes Robinson Widow buried
18th John Whitfield of Ellerhill Buried

BURIALS.

Apr. 21st	Sarah Wife to Edward Willan Brd.
May 10th	Uzwood Robinson o' Dovengill Brd.
15th	John son to Thomas Fawcett of Newbiggin Smith Buried
June 15th	Mary Bousfeild alias Mary Hunter o' Newbiggin
July 4th	Margaret Green of Coutbeck Widow
Sepr 7th	Agnes Fothergill o' th' Peers-hill Widow
Octr 7th	Thomas son to Anth. & Mary Fawcett o' Dovingill
19th	Robert Petty o' th' Intack
Novr 23rd	Elisabeth Fawcett o' th' Gailehead Widow
Decr 30th	Margt Fawcett of Orton Parish Widow
Jan 12th	Jane Bousfeild of Bouderdale Widw
Feb 3d	Thomas son to Richard & Ruth Fawcett
7th	Richard Waller of Russendale Town
10th	John son of Thomas & Mary Fawcett o' Wath
1723. March 30th	Anne Hall Widow Buried
Apr. 3d	John & Isabel son and Daughter of John & Elisabeth Fawcett of Newbign
12th	Thomas son of John & Mary Blades
25th	William son of Anth. & Mary Fawcett
May 2d	Frances Fawcett of Newbiggin Widow
14th	Edwd Willan of Bouberhead
June 2d	William son of Tho: & Margt Robinson
19th	John son of George & Anne Morland
July 9th	Elisabeth Adamtwhaite Widow
21st	Thomas son of Joseph & Margt Hanson
Novr 12th	Philip son of Michael & Elis. Bousfield
18th	Isabel wife of James Fawcett of Artlegarth
26th	Richd Rogerson of Lockholme foot
1723. Decr 12th	Stephen Sponner of Greenside
14th	Thomas Fothergill of Lockholme
Feb. 1st	Anne Brown Widow
7th	John Hewetson Senr of Lockholme foot
1724. April 5th	Anne Busfield [T. Spinster] of Scarsike Buried
May 4th	John Overend Taylor Buried
23d	Margaret Fothergill Spnr Brd.
June 7th	Joseph son of Thos & Margt Shearman
25th	John Adamthwaite Junr of Artlegarth

BURIALS.

July 25 — Michaiel Bouil Marchant of London
Augt 1st — Mary Daught^{r} of Rich^{d} & Mary Fother^{l} Lithside
7th — Mary Bousfeld of tounend widdow
Sepr 6th — Margrett Fawcett spinst^{r} of needless
22^{d} — Mary Mill of Toun widdow
Octr 2^{d} — William Pouson of Nether garths
11th — James son of Mathew & Mary Whitfield
Novr 13th — Anne Handley of wandall spinster
Feb. 12th — William Fawcett of Foggey gill
12th — Jacob son of Henry & Mar^{t} Haward of Selsi^{d}
Mar 19th — Thomas Shaw [T. Batchl^{r}] of Crookes Beck
1725. Mar^{h} 28th — George Clemmison of Adamthwaite
Apr^{l} 19th — Agnas Daug^{r} of James & Mary Fawcett
May 21st — John son of John & Eliz^{h} winter botta^{m} of Dunninton in Yorkshire Buried
June 3^{d} — John Adamthwaite of Artlelegarth
26th — Agnas Doug^{r} of John & mar^{t} Milner
28th — Thos Shaw of Bouberhead
July 15th — Benjamin & Sarah son & Daug^{r} to Thos & Marg^{t} Knewstubb
Sepr 3^{d} — William Milner of Toun
Octr 23 — Margaret Hastwhittle widdow
Decr 2^{d} — John son of M^{r} [T. John] Maggee
23^{d} — Mary Fawcett of Blaflatt widow
Jan 7th — Michael Parlor Batchler
25 — Thomas Morland Batchler
1726. Apr^{l} 6th — Elz^{h} Renton widow Buried
18th — Margaret Doug^{r} of Robt & Eliz^{h} Petty
23^{d} — John son of John & Martha Knewstubb
26th — Mr [T. W^{m}] Fawcett Scoolmaster Buried
May 12th — John Ridding of Town
July 1st — Thomas Breaks of Nubiggin
16th — Agnas Doug^{r} of John & Marg^{t} Milner
28th — Sarah Waller widow
31st — Margaret Wife of John Fawcett Elmpot
Augt 10th — Elizabeth Wife Thos Rogerson
29th — John Fawcett of Newhouse

BURIALS.

Aug[t] 30th Ellinor Fawcett of Foggy gill widow
Sep[r] 7th James son of Tho[s] & Marg[t] Ion
Dec[r] 8 John son of John & Mary Huchinson
24 William son of John & Ruth Bousfeild
Jan[y] 2[d] Christopher Todd [T. Widower] Buried
11th Sarah Fawcett Spinster of Ashfell
12th Elizabeth wife of Rob[t] Fawcett town
Feb 6th Elizabeth Robinson of Dovingill widow
1727. April 14th John Stubbs of Town Buried
18th Stephen Chamberlaine Batchlor
27th Allice Taylor Spinster
June 10th John Chamberlaine of Wandall
18th Agnas wife of Henry Barber
28th Mary Fawcett widow
29th Margarett Blackburne Spinster
July 9th Elizabeth Postletwhaite Spinster
13th Elliner wife of Tho[s] Fothergill murtw[t]
Aug[t] 9th Mary Fawcett of Crooks widow
Sep[r] 27th Thomas Hewetson Batchlor
Oct[r] 19th Joseph son of Joseph & Mar[t] Hanson
Nov[r] 16th John Todd Jun[r] of Cowbank
27th Eliner Blades spinster
Dec[r] 7th M[r] Robert Bovil sumtime of London
30th Richard Fawcett widower
31st Jennet Bourbank widow
Jan[y] 27th William Dixon Widower
27th Anne Clerkson Widow
Mar[h] 16th Elizabeth wife of George Burton
1728. Apr[l] 7th [T. 4th] Roger Barber of Town Buried
May 17th Thomas Robinson Blacksmith
June 29 Isabel Daug[r] of Rich[d] & Isabel Law
July 2[d] Margaret Robinson spinster
Aug[t] 10th y[e] Rav[d]. M[r] Tho[s] Toulmin Curate
10th Eliner Daug[r] of George & Mary Fawcett
22[d] Mary Daug[r] of Rich[d] & Eliner Heuatson
28th John Pinder of High Lane
Oct[r] 10th Isabel Fawcett Spinster

BURIALS.

Novr 19th	Mary wife of Richd Brown
Decr 5th	Jane wife of Thos Whithead Collior
21st	James Fawcett of Townhead
Jan 7th	John Taylor of Backsid
Feb 22^{d}	Richard Hunter of Bowberhead
Mar^{h} 2^{d}	Henry Barber of Townhead
9th	Mary Wife of Robt Fawcett of Adam^{te}

1729.

1729. April 2^{d}	Mary wife of Anthony Shaw B^{d}
3^{d}	George Fothergill of Tarn house Bur^{d}
May 14th	Margaret wife of Joseph Hanson Bur^{d}
20th	James Fothergill of Brownber Bnr^{d}
June 15th*	Sarah Daughter of Willm & Mary Blackburn B^{d}
July 4th	Richard Pindar B^{d}
Augst 26th	Thomas Perkin of Greenside Bur^{d}
Sept. 14th	Elian^{r} Daught^{r} of Rich^{d} & Mary Fothergill Dubs B^{d}
25th	Ralph Robinson of Dovingill B^{d}
Octob 12th	Margaret Daugthter of Thos. & Elian^{r} [T. Margaret] Hunter B^{d}
Nov. 23	Jane wife of William Robinson B^{d}
Jan 21st	Gilbert Fawcet Bur^{d}
25th	Agnes Cleaseby of Artlegarth wid^{w} B^{d}
30th	Agnes Daught^{r} of Thom^{s} Whitehead B^{d}
Feb 16th	Agnes wife of John Blackburn Bur^{d}
21st	Thomas Hunter of Sprintgill Bur^{d}
March 1st	Sarah Fawcet of Town Bur^{d}
3^{d}	Richd Beetham of Orton Parish B^{d}
9th	Francis Blackburn o' Town B^{d}
10th	Mary Elliotson Spinster B^{d}
1729. March 15th	Isabel wife of John Coupland B^{d}
19th	Isabel wife of Anthony Fothergill o' Murthwait B^{d}
22	John Fawcett of Crossbank B^{d}

1730.

April 3^{d}	Thomas Robinson of Nether-Garrs was bur^{d}

* T. has Augt 5, and places the entry below July 4th.

BURIALS.

APR. 14th Mary Shaw of Ellergill widdow Bd
15th Thoms Robertson of Stenneskeugh Burd
19th Margaret Daughter of Joseph Hanson
MAY 29th Richard Postlethwait of Crossbanks Burd
JUNE 8th John Morland of Keld-head Batchlr Burd
12th William son to Robt & Mary Fothergill o' street Bd
14th Mary wife of Robt Fothergill o' street Burd
14th James son to John & Margaret Fawcet o' Bleaflat Bd
22 Thos son to John & Margaret [T. Isabel] Fawcet [T. Shaw] o' Town Bd
JULY 2d Isabel Daughter to Antho & Agnes Knewstup o' Hill Bd
5th Mary Shaw of Stenneskeugh Widw Bd
5th Thos & Richard Two sons of Jno & Margart Fawcet Bd
6th Isabel Daughter to Jno & Rachel Chamberlain Bd
6th Richd son of Peter Giles of Weasdal Bd
9th Jonathn son to Christophr & Isabel Alderson Bd
10th Mary wife of James Dawson of Artlegarth Bd
10th Mary Daughter to Richd & Alice Breaks Bd
14th John Todd of Weasdal Burd
18th Isabel wife of George Perkin o' Crooks [T. Lockholme] Burd
19th Robt Robinson of Greenside Bd
22d Margaret Petty of Mollerstang Burd
22d George son of Anthony & Isabel Fawcet Bd
24th Margaret Daughter of Willm & Mary Jackson Bd
29th Michael son to Jane Fothergill o' Brounber Bd
AUGst 2d Richard Powson of Brackenbr Burd
3d George Morland o' stouphill-yeat Bd
3d Esther Preston of Greenside spinster Bd
4th Jno son to Roger & Elizabeth Pindar o' high Lane Bd
5th Willm son to Antho. & Isabel Fawcet o' stenneskeugh Bd
17th Isabel wife of George Perkin o' Lockholme Bd
25th Richd son to Richd & Mary Fothergill o' th Lytheside Bd
SEPTEMBr 1st Robt Coupland of Crooks beck Bd
27th Isabel wife of Hugh Shaw of Asfell Bd
NOVEMBr 1st Elizabeth Robinson of Newbign widow Burd
8th James Townson of Artlegarth Bd

BURIALS.

Novembr 16th	Mary Daughter of Thomas & Anne Alderson Bd
Decembr 1st]T. 2]	Mary Daughter to John & Elizabth Fawcet Bd
3d [T. 1st]	John son to Michael Bovell Bd
12th	Mary Daughter to Jame [T. James] & Jane Robinson Bd
Feb 4th	Ruth wife to Richd Fawcet o' Dubbs Burd
5th	Stephen Fawcet of Newbigan Burd
7th	Richd Fawcet of Newbign Bd
11th	Margaret Daughter to James & Sibbal Fawcet Bd

1731.

April 16th	Agnes wife of Anthony Knewstup o'th Hill Bd
May 20th	Anne Danghter to Willm & Mary Jackson [T. o' Stennerskeugh] Bd
June 2d	Alice Postlethwait of Crossbank Widow Burd
19th	Margaret Daughter To George Perkin o' Crooks
Augst 3d	Isabel Shaw of Tranmire spinstr Burd
23d	Elizabeth wife of Jno Chamberlain [T. Senr, o' stenes-keugh] Burd
Septembr 12th	George Townson of Greenside Burd
Novembr 16th	Stephen son to Christophr & Elizabeth Marvel [T. o' Wath] Bd
23d	Mabel Fawcet of Newbigan widow Bd
24th	Anne Barber o'th Town widow Burd
Decembr 2d	Stephen Dent o' Lytheside Burd
14th	Thos son to Christopher & Elizabeth Marvel [T. o' th' Wath] Bd
30th	Mabel Fawcet of Newbign widow Burd
Jan. 9th	Sibbal wife of Thoms. Adamthwait [T. of Adamthwait] Burd
10th	John Colston o' th' Fell End in the Par. of Cros-Gart at Rus. Bd
17th	James son to George Burton o' high Lane Bd
28th	Anne Law of Weesdale spinster Bd
Feb. 10th	Lancelot Hunter of Wandal Bd
16th	Richard Dixon of Casaway-End nigh Newbign Bd

1732.

April 22d	Anthony Murrow poor man was Burd

BURIALS.

May 9th	William Hunter o' Street widow^{r} Bur^{d}
Augst 27th	Elizabeth Daughter of Willm & Mary Blackburn Bur^{d}
Septemb^{r} 4th	Mabel Jakes or Handlay Bur^{d}
26th	Margaret Morland widow of Keldhead Bur^{d}
Octob^{r} 31st	John Fothergill of Brounber Bur^{d}
Novemb^{r} 5th	James Dent o'th' Town Batchl^{r} Bur^{d}
11th	Mary Robertson widow of Caldbeck Bur^{d}
1732. Novemb^{r} 18th	Thomas Fothergill o' Murthwait Bur^{d}
Decemb^{r} 18th	Thomas Robinson of Sandwath Bur^{d}
24th	Jane Fothergill of Brounber widow B^{d}
Jan^{ry} 18th	George Murthwait of Rigg-end Batchl^{r} B^{d}
26th	George Perkin the eldest o' Lockholm Bur^{d}
30th	Isabel Langhorne of Ashfield Spinster Bur^{d}
Feb^{ry} 2^{d}	Mary Shaw o' th' Town Widow Bur^{d}
4th	Anne Morland of Stouphill Yeat Widow B^{d}
6th	Elizabeth Wife of John Fawcet o' Adamthw^{t} B^{d}
11th	Elian^{r} Wife of John Magee Dissenting minist^{r} B^{d}
13th	John Chamberlain of Stenneskeugh widow^{r} B^{d}
March 2^{d}	Isabel Fothergill of Brounber Widow Bur^{d}

1733.

May 4th	Was Charles Udall of Garrshill widow^{r} Bur^{d}
25th	Stephen Dent o' Sandbed Bur^{d}
29th	Sarah Powson of Greenside widow Bur^{d}
June 13th	Isabel wife of Thomas Fawcet o' newbig^{n} B^{d}
July 6th [T. 2^{d}]	Marg^{t} Todd of Cowbank widow Bur^{d}
Augst 19th	Isabel Dent o' Sandbed widow Bur^{d}
Octob^{r} 2^{d}	Elian^{r} Robinson o' Town poor widow B^{d}
Novem^{br} 21st	George son to Geo: & Margar^{t} Perkins o' Lockholme B^{d}
Decem^{br} 28th	Agnes Daughter of Rich^{d} & Agnes Mitchel o' Town B^{d}
30th	Willm Fawcet o' fell end B^{d}
Jan. 3^{d}	Susanna Coatlay widow B^{d}
14th	John Bousefield o' Caldbeck Batchl^{r} B^{d}
24th	Isabel Daughter to Rich^{d} & Mary Fawcet o' Dubbs B^{d}
Feb 24th	Eli^{r}. wife of John Fawcet o' newbig^{n} Bur^{d}

1734.

May 4th	Was Marg^{t} Daughter to John & Mary Blades Bur^{d}

BURIALS.

May 16th	Elizabeth wife of Thos Blackburn o' $newbig^{n}$ B^{d}
June 15th	Mary Bousefield o' Town head widow bur^{d}
July 18th	Alice Daughter to Peter Giles o' weesdal $spinst^{r}$ B^{d}
Aug^{st} 5th	$Elian^{r}$ wife of Isaack Handlay [T. o' Fellend] Bur^{d}
18th	Henery Bousefield son of Jno & Ruth Bousefield o' Town-head $Batchl^{r}$ B^{d}
$Octob^{r}$ 1st	Ruth Daughter to John & Isabel Fothergill [T. o' Brown-ber] Bur^{d}
$Novemb^{r}$ 23^{d}	Agnes wife of Anthony Perkin [T. o' town] B^{d}
23^{d}	$Thom^{s}$ Fawcet o' Stouphill Yeat [T. $Batchl^{r}$] B^{d}
$Decemb^{r}$ 3^{d}	$Marg^{t}$ Dent o' Lytheside widow B^{d}
9th	Thomas Scarrbrough o'th' Moss [T. o' Dubbs] Bur^{d}
† Jann 10th	James Dent o' Wrey Green Bur^{d}
March 10th	Elizabeth Hall o' fell end spinster Bur^{d}
13th	George son of Mrs Margaret Toulmin widow B^{d}
March 22^{d}	Robert son to the Revd Mr Mounsey [T. Clrk] & Mary his wife B^{d} aged 2 years

1735.

April 1st	Elizabeth Bousefield o' Scarsikes spinster Bur^{d}
3^{d}	Elianor Dent o' Wrey Green widow Bur^{d}
May 19th	Elianor Fothergill o' Russendale Town spinster B^{d}
22	John Shaw o' Ellergill B^{d}
Aug^{st} 31st	Thomas Fawcet o' Lockholme B^{d}
Sep^{br} 5th	Jane Whitehead o' Town widow B^{d}
15th	Isabel Daughter to $Anth^{o}$. Robinson o' $newbig^{n}$ B^{d}
Dec^{ber} 30th	Dorathy Howgill o' Town widow Bur^{d}
Jan^{ry} 17th	John Fothergill o' Coldkeld Bur^{d}
Feb. 8th	George son to $Rich^{d}$ & Agnes Gregson B^{d}
27th	$Christoph^{r}$ Marvel o' Wath Dy^{r} B^{d}
March 2^{d}	Margaret wife of Math. Breaks o' $Newbig^{n}$ B^{d}

1736.

Apr^{l} 22^{d}	Isabel wife of $Thom^{s}$ $Adamthw^{t}$ o' $murthw^{t}$ B^{d}
May 10th	Stephen Fothergill o' Green head $Newbig^{n}$ B^{d}
22^{d}	Michael Bousefield o' Brunt hill B^{d}
30th	Geo. Morland o' stouphill Yeat $Batchl^{r}$ B^{d}
June 8th	Elizabeth wife of Antho. Pindar o' Low lane B^{d}

BURIALS.

JUNE 15th Timothy Breaks o' Coatgill Orton Parish [T. at this Church] Bd

JULY 3d {Thomas son to Robt. & Anne Hall Bd
{John Hutchinson o' Newbign Burd

9th Christophr alderson o' Cowbank Burd

29th Jennet Spooner widow o' Greenside Burd

AUGst 8th Anne wife of Joseph Hunter o' Wandal Burd

SEPber 14th Barbary wife of Willm Hunter Burd

15th Jane wife of Jno Fothergill o' Newbigan Burd

NOVEMbr 4th Margaret Fawcet o' Fell-End widow Burd

17th Gyles Fothergill o' Town Burd

23d Richd. Robinson o' Row-foot Burd

DECbr 22d Richd. Hunter o' Bowberhead Bd

25th Agnes Daughter of Richd & Agnes Mitchell o' Town Bd

MARCH 13th Robt. Fothergill o' Lytheside Batchlr Burd

1737.

APRl 4th Jennet Daughter to Willm Hunter o' Bowberhead Bd

8th Isabel Law o' Town Burd

JULY 1st George Son to Thoms. & Margart. Metcalf Burd

12th Mary wife of Robt. Fawcet o' fell end Burd

SEPber 9th Joseph Richardson of Town Land Ld. Burd

27th Roger Barber o' Town Widowr. Burd aged 98

Novber 4th Thomas Bousefield o' Clouds Batchlr Burd

25th Sibbal wife of Jno. Fawcet o' Backside Burd

30th Elizabeth Coulston of Garrshill widow Burd

JAN. 14th Thomas son of John & Margaret Fawcet Burd

1737. JANry 22d Mary Elliotson o' Scarsikes widow Burd

FEB. 6th Agnes Fallowfield o' Town widow Burd

16th Mary Daughter of Christophr. Fawcet Burd

MARCH 23d [T. 22] John Fawcet o' Alm-Pot [T. Widowr] Burd

1738.

APRIL 2d Was Margaret Fawcet o' Crooks spinster Burd

MAY 9th John Shaw o' Town Burd

16th Margaret Daughter to Richd. & Agnes Mitchel Burd

JUNE 20th Abigill wife to George Whitehead o' Town Burd

JULY 21st Anne Knewstubb o' Low Lane Spin. Burd

BURIALS.

July 25th Margt. Fawcet o' Newbigan Widow Burd
26th Robt. Hall o' Fell End Burd
Septembr 15th Henery Fothergill o' Newbign. Batchlr. Burd
Novemberber 4th Mary wife of Jno. Robertson o' Coldbeck Burd
5th Jennet wife of Michael Taylor Burd
21st Mary Fawcet Spinster o' Murthwt. Burd
27th Margaret Simpson o' Town Spinstr. Burd
Decemberber 6th Margaret Hodgson Spinster Burd
10th James Fawcet o' Mireous Burd
18th John Blackburn o' newbign. widowr. Bd
Jan: 21st Sarah Fothergill o' Townhead Spinstr. Burd
30th Agnes Daughtr to Jno. & Mary Coupland Burd
Feb 3d James Fawcet o' Greenside Burd Aged 80
17th John Coulston o' Garr's hill Batchlr. Burd

1739.

Mar 25th Was Isabel Clemmison o' Town Spinstr. Burd
Apl. 9th Anne Hall widow the youngr. o' Fell end Burd
July 1st Isabel wife of Simon Bousefield Burd
Augst 6th George Whitehead o' Town widowr. Burd
25th Mabel Fawcet o' Greenside Spinster Buried
27th James Fothergill o' Lockholme Batchlr Burd. agd 19
Sepber 24th James Fawcet o' Intack Burd
Novber 7th Margaret wife of Antho. Fothergill o' Brounbr Burd
27th Ruth Daughter to Mary Fawcet o' Intack Burd
Decemberber 27th Mary Perkin widow o' Fell-End Burd
Janry 3d Margart. Bell spinster o' Town Burd
13th Anthony ffawcet o' Fell-End Burd
28th Michael Bovel o' Newbigan Widowr. Burd
Feb 6th Thoms. Adamthwait of Adamthwt. Widowr. Bd

1740.

Aprl 24th Was Thomas son to Thos. & Marg: Metcalf Burd
May 12th Agnes wife to Richd. Gregson Burd
Augst 17th Anne wife of Thos. Fawcet o' Garr's Burd
31st Jane wife of Wm. Hewetson o' Artlegarth Bd
† Sepber 28th Richard Law of Weesdal Burd
Octobr 22d Mary Townson Widow Burd

BURIALS.

Nov 7 James son to Thos. & Marg^{t}. Fothergill B^{d}
9th Anthony Perkins o' Town Bur^{d}
Dec^{ber} 10th Willm. Fawcet o' fell end Bur^{d}
Jan: 21st Anne Fothergill widow o' Dubbs Bur^{d}
Feb: 9th Ralph son to Jno. Milner o' Ashfell Batch. B^{d}
11th Robt. Fawcet widower o' street Bur^{d}
23^{d} Sarah Daught^{r} to Hen: & Mary Fothergill B^{d}
March 8th John son to Margaret [T. Isabel] Law o' Weesdal B^{d}
9th Mary Bousefield o' fell-end spinst^{r}. B^{d}
21st William Fallowfield o' Town widow^{r}. B^{d}

1741.

March 27th Was Richard Todd o' Weesdal Bur^{d}
July 12th Thomas son to Thom^{s}. & Marg^{t}. Metcalf Bur^{d}
27th Eliz. Daughter to W^{m}. Hunter o' Bowberhead Bur^{d}
Augst 11th Isabel Daught^{r} to Godfrey Milner Bur^{d}
Nov^{br} 14th Elian^{r}. Bousefield o' scarsikes spinst^{r}. Bur^{d}
22 Isabel Law o' Weesdal Widow Bur^{d}
29th Rich^{d}. Fothergill o' Lithe Side Bur^{d}
Decem^{br} 23^{d} Elizabeth Daught^{r} to Jno. & Marg^{t}. Sanderson B^{d}
Feb. 25th Elianor Breaks of Newbigan Bur^{d}
26th Mary wife of Thom^{s}. Fawcet Bur^{d}
27th Godfrey Milner o' Town Bur^{d}
28th Margar^{t}. Fawcet of Greens^{de} Wid. B^{d}
March 5th Anth^{o}. Pindar o' Low Lane Bur^{d} Ag. 88
11th Th^{s}. Lamb o' Weesdal Bur^{d}
15th Anne Chamberlain o' Greenside Bur^{d}

1742.

Apr^{l} 13th Was Dorathy wife of W^{m}. Adamthwait B^{d}
14th Mathew Breaks o' steneskeugh Widow^{r}. Bur^{d}
May 7th Henry Knewstup o' Tarn house Bur^{d}
22^{d} Mary Daughter of Anne Orton Bur^{d}
June 7th Robert Gibson of Peer's Hill Bur^{d}
1742. July 14th Isabella Walker a stranger Bur^{d}
18th Robt. Fawcet o' Murthwaite Bur^{d}
Sep^{ber} 18th Anth^{o}. son to George Perkins Bur^{d}
Nov^{ber} 28th Mary Daughter to Thos. Haistwell B^{d}

BURIALS.

Dec^{ber} 14th John son to Richard Gregson Bur^{d}
Jan. 11th James Alderson o' Greenside Bur^{d}
21st Willm. son to James Fawcet o' street i'th Fell-end B^{d}
Feb. 8th Elizabth. Daught^{r} to Thos. Haistwell Bur^{d}
March 13th Anthony Perkins o' Lockholme Bur^{d}
24th Anne Beck o' Artlegarth Spin^{r}. Bur^{d}

1743.

March 30th Was John Milner o' Russendale Town Batch. B^{d}
Apr^{l} 6th Thomas son to Jno. & Anne Alderson Bur^{d}
8th Anne Hall o' Wandal widow Bur^{d}
11th Ma: Daughter to Thos. & Isab^{l}. Haistwell Bur^{d}
17th John Fawcet from Garsdal widow^{r}. Bur^{d}
25th Elizabth. Daughter to John & Mary Coupland B^{d}
May 8th John Fawcet of Newbigan [T. Widow^{r}] Bur^{d}
June 14th Mabel Fawcet widow Newbig^{n}
July 26th Mary Bainbridge o' Mazon Wath Bur^{d}
Augst 2^{d} Thos. Shearman of Weesdal Bur^{d}
Sep^{br} 14th Elizabeth Townson widow Bur^{d}
Jan^{ry} 3^{d} John Haistwitle o' Newbig^{n}. Widow^{r}. B^{d}
14th Anne Daught^{r} to John Shaw Sten: B^{d}
15th Willm. Fawcet o' Bleaflat Bur^{d}
17th Marg^{t}. Breaks widow Bur^{d}
Feby 4th John Ewbank o' Bowderdale foot Bur^{d}
19th Mar^{t}. Shaw Wid^{w} Bur^{d}
March 6th Thos. Rogerson Townhead Bur^{d}

1744.

May 26th Was Eliz. Bousefield wid^{w}. Bur^{d}
June 17th Marg^{t}. Robertson widow Bur^{d}
26th A Daugh^{r}. of Stephen Fawcet o' fell end Bur^{d}
July 13th Jonathan Alderson o' th' Town Bur^{d}
Augst 18th Mary Fawcet o' the Fell-End Wid^{w}. Bur^{d}
Sepr 17th Marg^{t}. wife of John Milner Ashfield Bur^{d}
Octr 6th Eliz. Morland Spinster Bur^{d}
25th Isabel Rogerson Spinster Bur^{d}
31st [T. 30th] Anth^{o}. son to James & Isab^{l}. Fawcet Bur^{d}
Novr 6th Thomas Sewell o' Town Bur^{d}

BURIALS.

DEC^{r} 5th	John Robertson o' Caldbeck Bur^{d}
FEB. 15th	Isabel Milner o' th' Town Bur^{d}
25th	Isabel Alderson widow Fellend Bur^{d}
MARCH 15th	John Beck Elder Apoth. o' Artlegarth Bur^{d}

1745.

AP^{l} 7th	Was Robert Shaw o' Mollerstang Bur^{d}
MAY 3^{d}	James Robinson o' th' Town Bur^{d}
19th	John son of John Blackburn o' th' Town Bur^{d}
JUNE 13th	Robt. Fawcet o' Greenside Bur^{d}
18th	Mary Daught^{r} to Jno. & Anne Orton Bur^{d}
21st	Anth^{o}. son to Antho. & Dor. Urwin Bur^{d}
29th	Alice wife of Rich^{d}. Breaks Bur^{d}
AUGst 29th	John son of Jno. Robinson Bur^{d}
SEP^{ber} 14th	Eliz. Pindar widow Bur^{d}
OCT^{ber} 22^{d}	Willm. son of Hugh Bayliff Bur^{d}
23^{d}	George Ewbank o' Bowberdale Foot Bur^{d}
NOV^{ber} 12th	Alice wife of Wm Fothergill Crossbank Bur^{d}
22^{d}	Elian^{r}. Dent Wid^{w}. Bowderdale Bur^{d}
DECEM^{br} 8th	[T. 1st] Mary wife of Jno. Perkin o' mollerstang Bur^{d}
12th	John Fawcet of Adamthwait Bur^{d}
JAN^{ry} 7th	John Murthwaite o' Ridge End Bur^{d}
8th	Thos. Adamthwaite Steps beck Bur^{d}
10th	Marg^{t}. Robinson o' freer bottom widow Bur^{d}
13th	Thomas Shaw o' Steneskeugh Bur^{d}
26th	John Robinson o' freer Bottom Bur^{d}
29th	Joseph Birdell o' Steneskeugh Bur^{d}
FEB. 27th	Isabel wife of Jame [T. James] Fawcet o' Lockholme Bur^{d}
MARCH 10th	Marg. Clemmison of Adamthw^{t}. wid^{w}. Bur^{d}
16th	Marg^{t}. Breaks spinster Bur^{d}

1746.

APRIL 16th	Was Marg^{t}. Hayton spinst^{r}. Bur^{d}
22^{d}	Elizabeth Taylor widow Bur^{d}
MAY 14th	George son of Anto: & Jennet Kerton B^{d}
15th	Elizabeth Beck widow Bur^{d}
16th	Anthony Knewstubb o' Hill Bur^{d}
17th	Elizabeth Daughter of Mary Burton Bur^{d}

BURIALS.

May 17th	Jane wife of John Taylor Burd
30th	Richard Robinson of Artlegarth Burd
31st	Margaret Clemmison of Town Burd
June 7th	Jane wife of Michl. Knewstubb of Lockholm Bd
July 4th	Anne Daughter to John Birtel [T. Burton] o' th' Town Burd
Augst 2d	James Hewetson of Artlegarth Burd
12th	Prudence wife Antho. Fawcet o'th' Town Burd
30th	Isabel Fothergill of Greenhd. widow Burd
Sepber 13th	Jno. son of Miles Lamb Burd
† Octobr 12th	Simon Bousefield of Backside Burd
[T. Sepber] 19th	John Shaw of Town Burd
Novber 2d	Sarah Rogerson Spinster Burd
4th	Anne wife of Thos. Robinson of Town Burd
March 6th	William son of Jane Robinson of Town Burd
15th	Jno. son to John Milner Ashfield Burd

1747.

Aprl 18th	Was Eliz: Daughter to James & Margt. Fawcet Burd
20th	Isabel Hodgson o' Bleaflat widow Burd
22d	Mary Daughter of Jane Robinson of Town Burd
May 20th	Thomas son of Thoms. Coupland Burd
July 16th	Richd. son to Sarah Fawcet Widw. Burd
20th	John son to Wm. & Tempernce. Hunter Burd
Augst 2d	Isabella Daughtr to Geo: & Margt. Perkins Burd
Sepbr 25th	A son of Jeofrey Denny Burd
Octobr 25th	{ John Perkins of Steneskeugh Burd
	{ Same Day Richd. Beck of Caldbeck Batchr. Burd
Novbr 13th	Robt. Fothergill of Streetside [T. Street] Widowr. Burd
Decbr 28th	Sarah Daughtr of Jno & Jane Blackburn Burd
31st	Margt. Fawcet of Bouberhead Spinstr. Burd
Jan 18th	James Udall of Steppsbeck burd
Jan 25th	Willm. son to Robt. & Mary Hunter o' Sprintgill Burd
Feb. 1st	Isabel wife to Robt. Breaks Newbign. Burd
11th	John Taylor of Stepsbeck Burd
March 24th	Jane wife of John Blackburn o' Townhead Burd

1748.

March 28th	Was Thoms. Blackburn o' Newbign. Burd

BURIALS.

April 30th	Thoms. son to Thos. & Isabl. Fothergill o' Brounbr. Burd
Augst 24th	Jane Robinson o' th' Town Burd
Decber 5th	Thomas Fawcet of Street Burd
10th	Peter Gyles of Weesdal Burd
January 20th	Mary Daughter of Wm. & Mary Jackson Burd
28th	Thomas son to Robt. & Mary Hunter o' Sprintgill Burd
Feb 9th	Michael Knewstub o' Lockholme Burd
19th	Thomas Coupland o' Town Burd
21st	Sibbal wife of James Fawcet o' Street Burd
22d	Alice Daughter of Wm. & Mary Jackson Burd
March 20th	Elianor Fothergill widow Burd

1749.

March 31st	Was Robt. Fawcet o' Town head Burd
May 1st	Jane Daughter to Jno. & Eliz. Fothergill Burd
3d	Elizabeth Knewstubb widow Burd
June 17th	James Ridden o' Town Batchlr. Burd
28th	Isabel Daughter to Wm. & Margt. Shaw Burd
July 13th	Hugh Bayliff of Town head Burd
Novr 6th	Alice Daughter of Wm. & Agnes Kitchen
Decemr 3d	William Coupland of Town Batchlr. Burd
Feb 5th	Anne Fawcet o' Murthwait spinster Burd
10th	Mary Hutchison widow of Newbign. Burd
20th	Eliz. wife of Mathew Metcafl Burd
23d	Thomas Robinson of Bleaflat Burd
March 18th	Richard Breaks of Newbiggn. Widower Burd

1750.

May 14th	George Perkins of Crooks widower Burd
June 25th	William Fawcet of Streetside Batchlr. Burd
Augst 11th	Mathew Breaks of the Fell end Burd
Septemr 20th	Jane wife of William Knewstubb of Low Lane Burd
Octobr 1st	Isabel wife of Willm. Bayliff of Town Burd
Decber 3d	Mary Daughter of Isabel Bayliff of Townhead Burd
Janry 21st	John Whitehead of Ridge End Burd
27th	Anne Fawcet of Newbign. widow Burd
29th	John Fothergill of Newbign. widowr. Burd
Feb 3d	Elizabeth Daughter to Richd. & Margt. Murthwait Burd

BURIALS.

FEB 20th Joshua son to Rich^{d}. & Margar^{t}. Murthwait Bur^{d}
MARCH 10th William son to Thom^{s}. & Marg^{t}. Bousefield Townhead Bur^{d}
15th Margaret wife of Thomas Fothergill Brownber Bur^{d}

1751.

MAY 1st Was Mary wife of William Jackson Street Bur^{d}
8th John son to Jno. & Mary Dawson Bur^{d}
28th John son to Willm. & Temperance Hunter Bur^{d}
JUNE 16th James Fawcet of Street Buried
23^{d} Richard Birdall of Steneskeugh Bur^{d}
SEPT^{ber} 26th John Bousfield of Wath Batchl^{r}. Bur^{d}
28th Thomas Bayliff of Sprintgill Bur^{d}
OCTOB^{r} 26th Thos. Green of Town Bur^{d}
DEC^{r} 23^{d} Miles son to Anth^{o}. & Marg^{t}. Morland Stouphillyeat Bur^{d}

1752.

JAN^{ry} 16th Wm Jackson of Street Widow^{r}. Buried
APR^{l} 22^{d} George Fothergill Lytheside Batchl^{r}. Bur^{d}
27th Mary Daughter to Rich^{d}. & Anne Cunningham B^{d}
MAY 10th Robt. son to John & Marg^{t}. Hastwell Bur^{d}
JUNE 19th Anne Daughter to Rich^{d}. & Isab^{l}. Taylor Bur^{d}
JULY 19th Sarah wife of Anthony Brown Bur^{d}
1752. AUGst 2^{d} James Fawcet of Newbig^{n}. Bur^{d}
6th Robt. Shaw of Ashfell Batchl^{r}. Bur^{d}
SEP^{ber} 24th [T. 2^{d}] Margaret Robinson widow Bur^{d}
OCTOB^{r} 17th Thomas Metcalf of Town Bur^{d}
NOV^{ber} 6th Robt. Milner of Ashfield Batchl^{r}. Bur^{d}
18th Thomas Fothergill of Murthwait Bur^{d}
26th Mary wife of William Furnace Bur^{d}
DEC^{br} 13th Deborah Fawcet Spinster Bur^{d}

1753.

JAN^{ry} 2^{d} Elizabeth wife of W^{m}. Beetham Bur^{d}
28th Margaret Birtell Spinster Bur^{d}
FEB. 3^{d} William Hewetson of Town Bur^{d}
27th James Fothergill of Steneskeugh
MARCH 11th James son of Thomas Robinson Town Bur^{d}
19th Mary wife of Rich^{d}. Fothergill o' Dubs B^{d}
APRIL 18th George son to W^{m}. & Mary Heblethwaite Bur^{d}

BURIALS.

April 27th Henry Fothergill o' Lockholme Burd
May 10th Margaret Jackson widow Burd agd 92
13th Isabel wife of Thos. Shaw Burd
16th Anne Daughter to Willm. Beetham Burd
June 17th Willm. son to John & Mabel Fawcet Burd
20th Tho. [T. John] son of Christopher Coupland Burd
26th John son of Wm. & Mary Blackburn Burd
July 8th Isabel wife of Mathw. Constantine from Moss in Sed. Par. Bd
23d Margt. Daughter to Anto. & Margt. Urwin Burd
Augst 6th Mary Fothergill of Lockholme Widow Burd
Octobr 9th Robt. [T. Geo.] Murthwait of Turra [T. Parrack] moor widowr Burd
14th Thomas son to Richd. & Mary Breaks Burd
18th Robt. son to Richd. & Mary Breaks Burd
Decembr 12th Isabl. Daughter of Thoms. Shaw
Same Day Thomas son of Willm. Hunter Sprintgill Burd

1754.

Janry 26th Benjamin son to Richd. & Ruth Shaw Burd
28th Thomas Bowerbank Burd
30th John Fawcet from Wharton Hall in Kir. Par. Bd
March 12th John son to Arthur & Margt. Bousfield Town Burd
May 2d Eliz. Perkins widow Lockholm Burd
16th Isabel Alderson widow Hole Burd
26th Geo. Lamb Newbign. Buried
June 30th Michael Shaw Scarsikes Burd
July 6th Willm. son of Joseph & Isabl. Hanson Burd
14th Stephen Fothergill Lockholm Burd
Augst 10th James Richardson of Crooksbeck Burd
22d Thomas Fawcet of Newbign. Burd
Sepr 6th Margt. Fawcet from Kirkby Stephn. widw. Bd
Novr 17th Jennet wife of Thoms. Fawcet Burd
20th Jennet Shearman Spinster Weesdal Burd
30th Isabel Daughter to Joseph & Sarah Breaks Bd
Decbr 2d Margt. Daugtr to Richd. & Mary Breaks Burd
27th Thos. son to Joseph & Mary Chamberlain Burd

BURIALS.

1755.

Janry 20th	Mary wife of Mathew Whitfield Bowbr. hd. Burd
Feby 4th	Margt. Fawcet from Wharton Dykes spinr. Burd
15th	William Heblethwait of Newbign. Burd
March 3d	Roseamond wife of Michael Breaks newbign. Burd
6th	Margt. Fawcet widw. Newbign. Burd
15th	Richd. Backhouse of Artlegarth Burd
20th	Anne Daughter to Meleta Shaw high Lane Burd
31st	Mary wife of Solomon Constantine Burd
April 6th	Stephen Dent of Town Buried
23d	Peter Giles of Weesdal Burd
May 3d	Thos. Fawcet of Greenhead Newbign. Burd
8th	Mary Fawcet widow of Greenhead Newbign. Buried
June 1st	Margart. Railton Spinster Burd
2d	Margt. Todd of Town Widw. Burd
9th	Jane Daughter to Richd. & Jane Hewetson Burd
Augst 17th	John Spooner of Greenside Burd
Sepbr 30th	Margaret wife of Jacob Scarf from K. Stephen Burd
Octobr 2d [T. 3d]	Margaret wife of John Perkins Moss Burd
Novr 2d	Mary wife of Edwd. Beck Burd
6th	Agnes Daughter of John & Mabel Fawcet Burd
14th	Thos. Stubbs younger Townhead Burd
18th	A Child of Benjamn. & Mary Judkin Burd
Decbr 2d	Mary Burton o' Greenside Buried
6th [T. 12th]	Mary Fawcet o' Town widow Burd
10th	Agnas wife of John Udal Weesdal Burd
	Same Day a Child of John Udal Burd
15th	A Child of Willm. & Margt. Nelson Burd

1756.

Janry 10th	Was Richard Son of Mary Fothergill Litheside Burd
18th	Margt. wife of Willm. Adamthwait Streetside Bd
19th	Mabel Daughtr. of John & Mabel Fawcet Burd
25th	Anne Daughter of Solomon Constantine Burd
27th	Mary Daughter of Francis & Anne Wholay Burd
30th	Mary Daugr. of Christopr. & Sarah Fawcet Bridge Bd
Feb 3d	Jennet Daughtr. of Solomn. Constantine Burd

BURIALS.

5th John son to Christop^{r}. & Sarah Fawcet Bridge Bur^{d}

10th Elizabeth Daught^{r}. of Meleta Shaw Bur^{d}

20th Eliz. wife of Miles Hutchinson Bur^{d}

25th [T. 23] John Blades of Tarnhouse Bur^{d}

MARCH 12th A Child of Jno. Nelson of Streetside Bur^{d}

21st Mary Handlaÿ o' Town Spinster Bur^{d}

APR^{l} 30th John son of Elian^{r}. Fothergill Murthw^{t}. Bur^{d}

MAY 8th Mary wife of John Shaw Steneskeugh Bur^{d}

13th Thos. son to Thos. & Mary Fawcet Bur^{d}

JUNE 11th Robt. Postlethwait of Greenside Bur^{d}

17th Roger Pindar of high Lane Bur^{d}

23^{d} Mary Dixon of Newbig^{n}. wid^{w}. Bur^{d}

† JULY 2^{d} Geo: son to Ant^{o}. & Marg^{t}. Morland Bur^{d}

* 19th William Adamthwaite of Adamthwaite Bur^{d}

AUGst 1st A Child of Willm. Adamthwaite Bur^{d}

DECEM^{r} 14th James Lindsay of Shawmire Bur^{d}

30th Willm. Bayliff of Town Bur^{d}

1757.

† JAN^{ry} 8th Was Isabel Wilson Spinster Bur^{d}

† 31st Michael Bovel of Newbig^{n}. Batchl^{r}. Bur^{d}

† MARCH 4th Thomas Stubbs of Town Bur^{d}

26th John son of Agnes Stubbs [T. Widow] of Town Bur^{d}

MAY 17th Marg^{t}. [T. Mary] Daughter of Math^{w}. & Marg^{t}. Constantine Bur^{d}

28th Mabel wife of John Fawcet of Town Bur^{d}

JULY 24th Mary Daught^{r}. of the Rev^{d}. M^{r}. Mounsey & Mary his wife Bur^{d}

AUGst 5th Isabel Wilson Spinster Bur^{d}

SEP^{ber} 4th M^{r}. Thos. Coulston schoolmaster Bur^{d}

15th Mary Birket Spinster Bur^{d}

NOV^{r} 29th Alice Fothergill of Tarnhouse wid. Bur^{d}

DEC^{r} 20th Rich^{d}. Brown of Townhead Bur^{d}

26th Mary Denny Bur^{d}

---

* T. places this entry under June 19th.

BURIALS.

1758.

March 12th Was Isabel Bayliff of Town wid. Burd
13th Richd. Elliotson of Wath Burd
April 18th Elianr. Wife of Thomas Brown Burd
30th Anne Breaks of Newbign. widow Burd
24th Mary Daughter of Robt. & Mary Hunter Sprintgill Burd
Same Day Geo. son of Anthony & Margt. Morland Burd
July 30th Mary wife of Thomas Birtell Burd
Augst 12th Geo. Perkins Elder of Lockholme Burd
26th Isabel Dent Widow from Coatgill in Orton Parish Burd Agd 90 yrs
Sepber 3d Sarah Daughtr. of Richd. & Ruth Shaw Town Burd
Octor 8th Jno. son of John & Margt. Haistwell Burd
16th [T. 15th] A Child of John & Margt. Haistwell Burd
Novr 12th Elianr. Daughter of George & Margt. Perkins Lockholme head Burd
16th A Child of William & Temperance Hunter Burd
18th John Elliotson of Wath Burd
Decembr 6th Elizabth. wife of John Hunter Tarnhouse Burd

1759.

Janry 28th Was Margt. wife of Antho. Morland Stouphill Burd
Febry 17th John Bousfield of Caldbeck Burd
20th Eliz. Daughtr. of Robt. and Ruth Scarbrough Burd
Mar 3d Elianr. wife of Thos. Alderson Burd
March 4th Isabl. wife of Thos. Knewstup Hill Burd
7th Willm. son of Anthony & Margt. Knewstup Hill Burd
9th Thos. Knewstup of Hill Burd
30th Ruth Daughter of John & Eliz: Fawcet Town Burd
Same Day Elizabeth Murthwait of Brownber Burd
Apl 21st Isabel Shaw of Town widow Burd
27th Richard Fawcet of Beck Weesdal Burd
May 26th Willm. son to John & Isabel Fothergill Brownber Burd
Same Day Mary Daughter to Richd. & Mary Breaks Burd
Septembr 14th Willm. Knewstub of Low Lane Burd

1760.

March 8th Was Henry son to James & Eliz. Fawcet Town Burd

BURIALS.

May 28th James Perkins of Town Burd
Augst 28th Heugh Shaw of Ashfell Burd
Sepbr 14th A Child of Antho. & Agnes Hodgson Burd
15th James son of John & Margt. Atkinson Burd
Novr 26th John Coupland of Celdhead Batchlr. Burd
29th Isabl. wife of Ralf Stockdal from Wharton dikes Burd
Decr 8th Thomas Richardson of Sandbed Burd
16th Mary Knewstub of Moss Spinstr. Burd
30th Robt. son of Mary Coupland the youngr. Burd

1761.

Feb 8th Was Joseph Udal of Cowbank Burd
24th Isabel Whitfield wid. Burd
24th Richd. son of Mary Coupland the youngr. Burd
Apl 20th Eliz. Wife of Wm. Raw Town Burd
22d Anne Backhouse widow Burd
May 4th Cateran Doway Travelr. Burd
6th Margt. wife of Anthony Knewstup o' Hill Burd
June 14th [T. 4th] Anthony Fothergill Elder o' Brownber Burd
Augst 13th Mary Birket from the poor house Burd
Octor 18th Mary wife of Jno. Coupland Burd
24th Margt. Tennant Burd
Novr 2d Isabel Haistwell o' Litheside widow Burd
13th Dorathy wife of Chrisr. Bousfield o' Dubs Burd
19th John Fothergill of Brownber Burd
24th Mary Yare of Brackenbr. widow Burd

1762.

Feb 27th Was Thos. son of Thos. & Mary Taylor Burd
March 17th John Hunter Widwr. Tarnhouse Burd
Aprl 16th Elizabeth Haistwell of Newbign. Spinster Burd
May 3d Willm. Blackburn o' Newbign. Burd
15th Tamar Fallowfield widw. Burd
1762. May 22d Martha Perkin of Town Widow Burd
July 11th Ruth Daughter of Wm. & Agnes Kitchin Burd
Same Day William Clemison of Town Burd
19th Anne Birtall widow Burd
Sepber 14th Geo. Perkins Lockholme Burd

BURIALS.

1763.

JANry 14th — Was Simon Nicols of Town Batchlr. Burd
28th — A Child of Thos. Preston Burd
FEB. 2d — Margt. Shearman Weesdal Widw. Burd
6th — Mr. John Beck Apothry. Town Burd
11th — James Richardson Batchlr. Town Burd
13th — John Milner of Ashfell Burd
MARCH 30th — A child of Richd. & Hannah Birtell Burd
Apl 2d — Zilpah Daughtr. of Jno. & Margt. Stubbs Burd
19th — William Fawcet o' Tranmire Burd
MAY 30th — Mary wife of Miles Chambers o' Town Burd
JUNE 6th — Thomas Garthwait o' Lytheside Burd
JULY 30th [T. 20th] Edmd. son of Edmd. & Sarah Waller Burd
OCTOr 23d — Isal. Swainson Widw. Burd

1764.

JAN 8th — Was James son of Richd. & Agnes Lambert Burd
10th — Thos. Winder o' Fell-End Burd
12th — Mary [T. Margt.] Daughtr. of Margt. Elliotson o' Wath Burd
MARCH 4th — Isabel Robinson of Bleaflat widow Burd
12th — Alice Bland widow Burd
27th — Ruth wife of Mathew Scarbrough of Garrs Burd
31st — Elizabeth Beck of Town Widow Burd
APRIL 14th — Eliz. Daughter of Willm. & Margaret Witton Burd
22d — Eliz. Daughter of Robt. & Ruth Scarbrough Burd
MAY 30th — Betty Daughtr. of Michael & Margt. Bovell Burd
JULY 16th — Mar. wife of Jno. Slee Burd
SEPr 24th — Wm. son of Holmes & Esther Milner Burd
† OCTOr 6th — Eln. wife of * Backside Burd
DECEMr 16th — Isabel wife of Thos. Haistwell Fell-end Burd
20th — John Fawcet of Dovingill Burd

1765.

JANry 12th — Was Thos. Dent of Sandbed Burd
28th — Agnes Stubbs widow Burd
FEB. 4th — Christopher Bousfield o' Town Burd

---

* Left blank.

BURIALS.

April 2d	Michael Taylor of Stepsbeck Burd
May 20th	Isabel Milner Traveler Burd
June 2d	Agnes Daughtr. of Thos. Garnet Burd
Augst 4th	Richd. Green Batchlr. Burd
10th	Frances wife of James Whaley Burd
Octobr 18th	Agnes wife of Robt. Garnet Burd
Same Day	Christopr. son of Mary Willain Burd
Novbr 2d	John son of Mary Willain Burd
10th	Chrisr. son of John & Judy Coupland Burd
28th	Richd. Chamberlain of Adamthwait Burd
Decbr 2d	Anne Daughter of Francis & Anne Whaley Burd
8th	Sarah wife of Wm. Lindslay Burd
17th	Mary Daughtr. of Richd. & Dorathy Shaw Burd

1766.

Janry 20th	Was Alice Udal widw. o' Cowbank Burd
Feb. 3d	Margt. wife of John Thompson Burd
10th	James Stubbs o' Town Burd
15th	Isabel wife of Willm. Metcalf Burd
21st	Anto. Brown widowr. Burd
28d	Mary Daughter of Richd. & Margt. Gregson
March 8th	Eliz. Fothergill widw. of Lockholm Burd
11th	Thos. son of Isabel Elliotson of wath Burd
16th	Thos. Fothergill of Foggegill Burd
29th	Robt. Bovell of Newbign. Burd
April 5th	Solomon Constantine Bowderdale foot Burd
	Same Day Margt. Daughtr. of Jno. Thompson Burd
9th	Thomas Robinson of Bleaflat Batchlr. Burd
July 28th	John Shaw of Town Burd
Augst 6th	Anne Hutchison of Town Burd
8th	Sicily wife of Jno. Knewstubb o' Town Burd
Septber 7th	William Dixon of Causway End Burd
Octor 20th	Robt. son of Christopr. & Agnes Townson Burd

1767.

Jan 28th	Was John Knewstubb from Poor House Burd
Feby 8th	Anthony Fawcet o' Lockholm Burd
17th	John Perkin Breckonbr. Burd

BURIALS.

March 6th	Agnes Stubbs of Town Spinstr. Burd
May 2d	Elianr. wife of Wm. Atkinson o' Caldbeck Burd
Sepbr 23d [T. 1st]	Margt. Shaw of Town Widw. Burd
Decbr 6th	John Hewetson of Townhead Burd

1768.

Feb. 7th	Sarah Fothergill widw. o' Newbign. Burd
March 30th	Isabl. Perkins spinstr. of Moss Burd
Aprl 17th	Richd. Rennison of Stone House fell end Burd
30th	Richd. Lambert of Litheside Burd
† July 18th	Sarah Fothergill widw. of Steneskeugh Burd
Augst 28th	Mary Fothergill Spinstr. Newbign. Burd
Novr 31st	Margt. wife of Richd. Murthwaite Low Lane Burd
Decr 3d	Mary Hemsly widow Studfold Burd

1769.

April 2d	Was Mary Linslay widow Burd
May 30th	William Spooner [T. o' Newbign.] Batchlr. Burd
Augst 16th	Margt. Green [T. o' Town] Widw Burd
Sepber 26th	Mathw. Metcalf Widowr. Burd
Octo. 2d	Willm. Kitchin o' fellend Burd
23d	Margt. Daughtr. of Anto. & Mary Fothergill Brownbr. Burd
Nov. 20th	Margt. Daughtr. of Jno. & Margt. Robinson Schoolmr. Ash-fell Burd
Decr 16th	Stephen Chamberlain o' Greenside Burd

1770.

Jan 20th	John Fawcet of Townhead Burd
Janry 26th	Was Mary Daughtr. of Jane Winder spinstr. Burd
	Same Day A son of Stephn. Fawcet Fell end Batchlr. Burd
March 20th	Thos. Fothergill o' Lock home head Batchlr. Burd
March 26th	Mart. Metcalf Spinstr. Fell-end Burd
Aprl 19th	Thos. son of Mr. John & Isbl. * Robinson Schoolmastr. Burd
20th	Mary Perkins o' Town widow Burd
May 12th	Margaret Elliotson Brounbr. spinstr. Burd
† 13th	Margt. Elliotson spinsr. Brownber Burd
June 27th	John Banks o' Fell-End Burd

* "Margt." altered to "Isabl."; "Isabl." in T.

BURIALS.

July 16th John Orton of Poor House Burd

Augst 28th Hannah wife of Richd. Shaw Burd

Same Day Elinr. Daughtr. of Hen. & Mary Fothergl. Burd

Sepr 3d Mary wife of John Perkins [T. o' Caldbeck] Burd

15th Anne Daughtr. of Geo. & Eliz. Perkins Burd

18th Geo. Perkins of Lockholme head Burd

Octor 12th James son of James & Mary Shaw Burd

1771.

Janry 10th Was James son of Richd. & Isl. Taylor [T. of Townend aged 22] Burd

19th Dorathy Witton widw. [T. of Wm. Witton late of Newbign. aged 78] Burd

28th John Chamberlain of Lockholme [T. Yeomn. aged 86] Burd

Feby 10th Edmd. son of Edmd. & Sarah Waller [T. Shoemaker aged 3] Burd

March 12th [T. 10th] John Udal of Cowbank [T. Worsted Carrier aged 48] Burd

21st Willm. Fothergill o' Tarn house Batchlr. [T. aged 60] Burd

* May 10th Micl. son of Thos. & Isabl. Wilson Burd

Sepber 12th Mary Birkbeck widow Newbign. Burd aged 72

14th John Gibson of Coldbeck Grocer aged 34 [T. 31] Burd

16th Edmund Waller o' Town Shoemaker aged 46 Burd

20th Sarah Fawcet spinster o' Newbign. aged 60 Burd

Octor 2d Anne Fothergill widow o' Murthwt. aged 74 Burd

6 Anne wife of Edwd. [T. Edmund] Metcalf Street aged 22

1772.

Feb 1st Isabl. Daughter of Anto. & Agnes Hodgson aged 11 Burd

17th Thos. Elliotson of Scarsikes Yeomn. aged 84 Burd

25th Isabl. Coupland widow o' fellend aged 82 Burd

March 5th John Shaw o' Steneskeugh widowr. yeon agd 68 Burd

Apl 30th Mary Daughter of Richd. Gregson Carpenr. agd 24 [T. 25] Burd

Sepbr 22d Rachel Richardson widw. agd 68 Burd

29th John Pinder o' High Lane Batchlr. aged 42 Burd

Octobr 27th [T. 22d] Anto. Perkin Batchlr. aged 20 Burd

---

* T. has "Michl. son of Thos. Wilson, Blacksmith & Isl. his wife of Crossbank aged 13."

BURIALS.

1773.

Jan 4th	Richard Shaw o' Town Shopkeepr. aged 74 Burd
March 8th	Mrs Toulmin widow o' Town aged 84 Burd
Apl 5th	Mary wife of Robt. Howgill aged 67 Burd
May 20th	John Gill of weesdal, Badger aged 43 Burd
June 14th	Isabl. Fothergill widw. Brownbr. aged 78 Burd
July 12th	Mary Robinson widw. Artlegarth agd 63 Burd
Augst 21st	Christr. son of Richd. & Margt. Gregson [T. Batchlr.] agd 21 Burd
22d	Sibbel wife of Joseph Spooner aged 59 Burd
Sepr 19th	Margt. wife of Thos. Bousefield [T. Yeomn.] Townhd. agd 55 Burd
20th	Jno. Jackson Farmr. at Brownbr. aged 42 Burd
Novr 12th	Thos. Elliotson Scar sikes [T. yeomn.] aged 84 Burd
Decr 16th	John Perkins o' Moss [T. yeomn] agd 86 B.
18th	Mary wife of Joseph Chamberlain agd 62 Burd

1774.

Janry 7th	Was Sarah wife of Peter Handlay Town agd 58 Bd
8th	John Fothergill Batchlr. Streetside aged 22 Burd
21st	John Coatlay [T. Greenside] Batchlr. aged 88 Burd
Feb. 6th	A Child of a Travelling womn. aged 5 Burd
9th	Anto. Morland Widowr. stouphl. yeat agd 56 Burd
26th	John Fawcet Par. Clrk agd 61 Burd
Apl 12th	Margt. wife of Jno. Fawcet Clk. agd 53 Burd
May 2d	Anne Daugr. of James & Margt. Fawcet agd 2 Burd
12th	Margt. Daughtr. of Jno. Murras Newbign. Infant Burd
Octobr 2d	Isaac Teesdal o' Town Innkeepr. aged 38* Burd
Novr 10th	Eliz. wife of Simon Bousfield agd 72 Burd

1775.

March 20th	Was Wm. son of Willm. Fothergill o' street aged 8 years Burd
April 16	Mary Daughtr. of Geo. & Isabl. Perkins Inft. Burd
June 3d	Anne Daughtr. of [T. Mr.] John Robinson Schl.masr. Inft. Burd
July 25th	James Whaley from Coatly aged 84 Burd

* The second digit is indistinct. T. has 38.

BURIALS.

AUG^st^ 3^d^ Isabel wife of Edwd. Beck, Artlegarth ag^d^ 46 Bur^d^
OCTO^r^ 1st Mat^w^. son Math^w^. Whitfeild aged 15 Bur^d^
25th Rachel Chamberlain wid^w^. o' Lockholm Aged 78 Bur^d^
30th James son to Willm. & Marg^t^. Stubbs o' Town Aged 2 Bur^d^
NOV^r^ 4th Anne wife of John Adamthwaite Carp^r^. o' Street Aged 58 Bur^d^
9th Bridget Daught^r^. of John Adamthwait o' Street Ag^d^ 10 Bur^d^
DEC^br^ 14th Marg^t^. wife of John Fawcet wid^w^. o' Town Ag^d^ 84 Bur^d^

1776.

JAN^ry^ 4th Was Marg^t^. Clemison widow from Chap^l^. in Orton Par. aged 78 years Bur^d^
FEB^ry^ 2^d^ John son to Math^w^. & Agnas Ward Ag^d^ 6 Bur^d^
MARCH 4th Anne Gyles Wid^w^. Aged 86 Bur^d^
12th Anne wife of Thos. Metcalf ag^d^ 34 [T. 36] Bur^d^
21st John Haistwell o' Studdfold aged 58 Bur^d^
27th John Atkinson o' Caldbeck Aged 76 Bur^d^
29th Mary Constantine o' Town [T. Spin^r^. aged 48 Bur^d^]
APR^l^ 3^d^ Alice Daught^r^. of Joseph & Alice Udal ag^d^ 10 Bur^d^
9th Agnes Chamberlain widow ag^d^ 94 Bur^d^
17th Agnes Kitchin wid^w^. ag^d^ 56 Bur^d^
MAY 2^d^ Edwd. son to Edw. & Ruth Burrow Infant Bur^d^
3^d^ Peter Handlay widower o' Town Ag^d^ 74 Bur^d^
JUNE 16th Sarah wife of Ant^o^. Dent Lithside aged 56 Bur^d^
JULY 16th James Shaw o' Elergill aged 57 Bur^d^
AUG^st^ 18th Mary Blackburn widow aged 68 Bur^d^
SEP^r^ 3^d^ Eliz. wife of Thomas Robinson ag^d^ 43 [T. 46] Bur^d^
14th John Holme of Caldbeck Malster aged 72 Bur^d^
OCTO^r^ 3^d^ William Shaw o' Ashfield ag^d^ 64 Bur^d^
30th Marg^t^. Hewetson widow ag^d^ 85 Bur^d^
NOV^r^ 3^d^ Isabella Daught^r^. to Edwd. Isabel Urwin Ag^d^ 2 Bur^d^
15th Willm. son to John & Mary Fothergill Brownber Ag^d^ 8 Bur^d^
22^d^ Geo. Fawcet o' wrey-green ag^d^ 68 Bur^d^

1777.

† 1777. JAN^ry^ 7th Anne Tunsdall from Mallerstang Ag^d^ 48 B^d^
† 30th Joseph Chamberlain widow^r^ aged 72 B^d^
† Same Day John Fawcett Batchl^r^. Ag^d^ 36 B^d^
† MAY 25 John Murray o' Newbig^n^. Ag^d^ 71 B^d^

BURIALS.

† May 26th Mary Bovell o' Newbig^{n}. Ag^{d} 40 Bur^{d}

† 28th Rachel wife to Rich^{d}. Gibson fıom Coatly Ag^{d} 46 Bur^{d}

June 29th [T. Thos.] A Child of Rich^{d}. Birtel Inf^{t}. Ag^{d} 2 Bur^{d}

July 6th Edwd. Burry Shoemaker Ag^{d} 36 [T. 42] Bur^{d}

20th Mary Daug^{r}. to Will. & Sarah Taylor Ag^{d} 23 Bur^{d}

Augst 2^{d} Isab^{l}. Dau. to W^{m}. & Sarah Taylor Ag^{d} 32 Bur^{d}

13th John son to John Murrace Ag^{d} 6 Bur^{d}

Sep^{br} 1st John Murthwaite o' Ridg [T. Moor] Side Ag^{d} 41 Bur^{d}

Oct^{br} 15th Thos. Shaw son to Dora^{ty}. Nelson Ag^{d} 10 Bur^{d}

Nov^{br} 15th A child of Hen. & Eliz. Fothergill Ag^{d} 4 Bur^{d}

21st Isab^{l}. Dau^{r}. to Geo. & Eliz. Udal Ag^{d} 6 Bur^{d}

22^{d} A child of Hen. & El. Foth^{r}gill Ag^{d} 2 [T. 10] Bur^{d}

Dec^{br} 13th [T. Thos.] A Child of Thos. Fothergill Dubbs Ag^{d} 2 [T. 8] Bur^{d}

14th Thos. Alderson o' Newbig^{n}. Ag^{d} 88 Bur^{d}

30th Eliz. wife of Rich^{d}. Robinson o' Bleaflat Ag^{d} 56 [T. 62] Bur^{d}

1778.

1778. Jany 12th Anne wife of Rich^{d}. Cunningham Bowb^{r}head Ag^{d} 42 Bur^{d}

31st Jan wife of Leon^{d}. Metcalf Aged 36 Bur^{d}

Feb. 22^{d} Nancy Daug^{r}. to Sarah Waller wid^{w}. from Kend^{l}. ag^{d} 15 Bur^{d}

Augt 17 Ann Daughter to Stephen & Marg^{t}. Dent Ag^{d} 31

† Octr 17 Matthew son to Jno. & Jane Wilkinson infant

do. 23 [T. 29] Anthony Dent of Lythe-side aged 61

Octr 26 Stephen Dent Dovingill aged 83

Novr 5 Jno. Milner Greenside aged 26

Decem^{br} 2 [T. 14] Sally Daught^{r}. of Stephen & Ann Shaw ag^{d} 14

Buried 1779.

Jan 13 Jno. Fawcett of Mid-Town aged 82

Feby 2 Thos. Brown late of Rig-end ag^{d} 99

do. 26 Mary wife of Robt. Hunter fellend Ag^{d} 66

May 9th Thos. Perkins of Stouphilgate Ag^{d} 52

May 18th Mary Fallowfield of Town Ag^{d} 88

do. 30th Thos. Fawcett Stenerscah ag^{d} 70

June 28th Mary Burton from Dent Ag^{d} 70

July 18 A child of Sarah Robinsons Greenside

do 27 Allice wife to Robt. Chamberlain

BURIALS.

Sept 23	Jno.* son to Thos. & Ann Metcalf
Octr 28	Henery Brunskill [T. aged 66]
Novr 25	Sarah** Mackledow Penrith [T. Aged 84]
do. 26	Mabel Robinson Ag^d 84
do. 28	Peggy Dent Ag^d 91
Decr 12	James Orton Ag^d 18
do. 15	Edwd. Whitehead Kelleth [T. aged 64]
do. 25	Mary Fawcett Ag^d 84
do. 26	Mary Holmes ag^d 76

1780.

Jany 22	Ruth Bousfield Ag^d 89
do. 23	Thos. Perkins Ag^d 21
do. 28	Mary Elliardson Ag^d 78
Feby 27	Rich^d. Fallowfield Ag^d 60
March 29	The Rev^d. M^r. Mounsey Ag^d 84 and Minst^r. of the Perpetual Curacy of Ravenstondale upwards of Fifty years
April 25	Jno. Fawcett Dovengill 80
†	About the same time died the the Wife to Robt. Howgill of Adamthwaite
May 20th	Anthony Fawcett of Town 75
do. 22	Isabella Hutchinson ag^d 77
June 5th	Michael Breaks Ag^d 74
do. 18th	Eliza: Todd of Work-house
do. 30th	Ellianor Hunter ag^d 93
July 3rd	Eliza: Wife to Geo: Perkins Ag^d 26
Augt 22^d	William son of George & Martha Murthwaite of Rig-end aged 5 weeks
Sep 3^d	Rich^d. son of Thos. & Magdalen Shaw his wife [T. 18]
do.	William son of Jno. Milner of Ashfield [T. Ashfell] & Mary his wife [T. aged 5 weeks]
8th	William Sanderson of Clouds [T. Aged 27]
22^d	Thomas Wilson of Low Stannerskugh [T. Aged 58]
Novemb^r 24th	Alice wife of John Parkin of Coldbeck [T. Aged 52]
Decemb^r 5th	Robert Murthwaite of Parrock Moor [T. aged 67]
30th	James Waller of Town [T. aged 40]

* Afterwards crossed out. T. has "Jno."
** Originally "Peggy."

LIST OF SUBSCRIBERS.

Bell, Rev. Wm. R., Laithkirk Vicarage, Middleton-in-Teesdale
Bousfield, Rev. Stephen, M.A., Sudbury, Derby.
Bousfield, Frederick, 31, Crowhurst Road, Brixton.
Bousfield, Harvey, The Mullberries, Great Crosby, Liverpool.
Brunskill, Stephen, Castle Meadows, Kendal.
Burra, Rev. Thos. Fawcett, M.A., Linton Vicarage, Maidstone
Burra, Robert, Gate, Sedbergh.

Carter-Squire, Miss S. A., Catterick.
Carver, John, Greystoke, Hanger Hill, Ealing, London, W.
Crisp, F. A., Grove Park, Denmark Hill, London, S.E.

Dawson, Edw. Bousfield, Aldcliffe Hall, Lancaster.
Day, Rev. H. G., M.A., 55, Denmark Villas, West Brighton.
Dixon, Wm., Causeway, Ravenstonedale.

Ferguson, The Worshipful Chancellor, F.S.A., Carlisle.
Fothergill, John, Brownber, Ravenstonedale.
Fothergill, John Wm., The Cottage, Brownber, Ravenstonedale.
Fothergill, Richard, Ashley Bank, Ravenstonedale.
Fothergill, S. R., 71, Portland Place, London, W.
Fothergill, Watson, Mapperly Road, Nottingham.
Fothergill, Gerald, 29, Priory Park, Kilburn. N.W.
Fothergill, Miss, 27, Arboretum Road, Nottingham.
Furness, William, Senr., 17, Woodbine Street, Moss Side, Manchester.

Greenbank, Richard H., 49, S. Luke's Road, Westbourne Park, W.

Hewetson, Mrs., 8, S. James's Terrace, Regents Park, London.
Hewetson, Miss, Finnich Malise, Drymen, N.B.
Hovenden, Robert, F.S.A., Heathcote, Park Hill Road, Croydon.

Langhorne, Miss, Lowther Street, Penrith.
Lonsdale, The Right Hon. the Earl of, Lowther Castle, Penrith.

MAGRATH, DR., Provost of Queen's College, Oxford.
MARSHALL, G. W., F.S.A., Rouge Croix, Heralds College, London, E.C.
METCALFE, E. P., M.A., Rajahmundri, India.
METCALFE-GIBSON, ANTHONY, Coldbeck, Ravenstonedale.

RENNINSON, MISS JANE, 78, Wellington Street, Moss Side, Manchester.
ROBINSON, JOHN, Ashfell, Ravenstonedale.
ROBINSON, ROBT. C. E., Beechwood, Darlington.
ROBINSON, WM., Greenbank, Sedbergh.

SAVORY, SIR JOSEPH, Bart., M.P., Buckhurst Park, Ascot.
SEDGWICK, MISS, Thorns Hall, Sedbergh.
SMITH, CHAS. E., 35, The Park, Sharples, Bolton-le-Moors.
SWINGLEHURST, HENRY, Hincaster House, Milnthorpe.

THOMPSON, REV. WM., M.A., Guldrey Lodge, Sedbergh.
THOMPSON, MRS., Stobars Hall, Kirkby Stephen.
THOMPSON, MISS, The Croft, Kirkby Stephen.
THOMPSON, W. N., St. Bees.
TULLIE HOUSE FREE LIBRARY, Carlisle.

WOODS, SIR ALBERT W., Garter, College of Arms, London. E.C.

——

THE

RAVENSTONEDALE

PARISH REGISTERS.

TRANSCRIBED AND EDITED BY

THE REV. R. W. METCALFE, M.A.

VICAR OF RAVENSTONEDALE.

VOL. III.—1781 TO 1812.

KENDAL :

T. WILSON, PRINTER, 28, HIGHGATE.

1894.

INTRODUCTION

THE Ravenstonedale Parish registers from 1780 to 1812 possess few features worthy of remark. The entries are mostly in the handwriting of the incumbent "Jeff: Bowness" who signs the Transcripts up to and including 1809; Thomas Moss "assistant Curate" those for 1810 and 1811; and the last is subscribed by John Robinson "minister" who writes a long and elaborately constructed verifying clause. The Transcripts for 1795 and 1804 are wanting.

The Births and Baptisms of "Dissent^n. Child^rn.," which in the Register are entered here and there in groups of families, have been collected, and will be found on p. 38 in the same order as in the original.

I give a list of Ravenstonedale Incumbents and Grammar School Masters gathered from the Episcopal Registers; also the names of the Churchwardens mentioned in the Transcripts; and I have also written short notes on the Presbyterian and Quaker Registers.

It has been suggested to me that an index would greatly enhance the usefulness of these printed Registers; but the addition of an index would considerably increase the cost of publication, and as the demand would be very small I have reluctantly decided not to incur further expenditure.

My task is now completed. It remains but to thank all those who have assisted me in my undertaking; Mr. Bowman for unlimited access to Diocesan records contained in the Bishop's Registry; Mr. Gerald Fothergill for the loan of his Chapel Transcript, and for copying the Quaker entries at Devonshire House for this publication; Canon Sherwen, Rector of Deane; Rev^d. G. M. Gorham, Vicar of Masham; Rev^d. J. Moden, Vicar of Well; M^r. Geo. Watson of Penrith for searches made in answer to my enquiries; Mr. Fothergill of Brownber and Mr. Metcalfe-Gibson of Coldbeck for the loan of old Parish Papers, &c. The Rev^d. H. Whitehead of Lanercost Priory has taken the greatest interest in this work, and his wide experience has been invaluable in points involving doubt and difficulty. To my publisher, Mr. Wilson, I am much indebted for making enquiries and obtaining information concerning County Records, and also to his compositor for the care he exercised in setting up his type—a task by no means easy owing to the many restrictions I imposed upon him.

RAVENSTONEDALE INCUMBENTS.

The following list of Incumbents is compiled from the Episcopal Registers commencing 1561. Until the middle of the present century the benefice was a perpetual Curacy, and therefore the Incumbents were licensed only and not instituted. In the earlier Registers the licensing of Curates does not appear to have been of sufficient importance to be entered in the records; and this probably accounts for the very meagre information to be gleaned from them as regards the Curates of Ravenstonedale. I have gone very carefully through these Registers, and I do not think that any entry relating to my predecessors has escaped me. I give the results of my search; the marginal number gives the page of the Register on which the entry appears.

Anthony Carlton.

44 Ordination 7 July 1572. Deacons—Anthony Carlton p. of Penrith dioc. Carl. aged 23.

47 Ordination 25 Dec. 1572. Priests—Anthony Carlton p. of Ravenstondal. Carl. dioc. aged 24 "*ad titulum &c*" of Thomas Carlton of Carlton Co. Cumb^d^. gentleman "*in villa de Penreth.*"

There is no mention, Mr. Watson tells me, of this Anthony Carlton in the Penrith Registers, which, however, do not commence until the year 1556, or 7 years after his birth, nor does his name occur in the pedigrees of the Carltons of Carlton Hall. He may have been a younger son and therefore not entered. The mother of Anthony was perhaps, "Anne wife of M^r^. Thomas bur. 1558" [Penrith Registers].

Thomas Hunter.

76 Thomas Hunter p. Ravenstondale. Carl. dioc. literate aged 24 ordained deacon 10 June 1576.

77 Thomas Hunter p. Ravenstondale Carl. dioc. aged 24 ordained priest 9 Sep. 1576.

Hunter was very probably a native of the parish—born some 19 years before the commencement of the Registers. Judging from the earliest entries and the note on the fourth page it seems that when Hunter took over charge he found no proper Register Book in use, so after collecting all the loose slips he could find, he commenced a regular record of Baptisms, Weddings, and Burials, in the new book referred to in the note.* At any rate a regular system of registration began in 1577, and this was the year following Hunter's ordination.

"Mr. Huntur" was buried Aug. 21. 1589.

Thomas Dodson.

Thomas Dodgson, literate, ordained deacon, 23rd May 1624.

There is no direct evidence to show who were the Incumbents between the death of Hunter in 1589, and the arrival of Thomas Dodson. Perhaps Mr. Calvert (Baptisms 1594), and Mr. Benson (Baptisms 1619—1622), filled the gap. The first Dodson entry is dated Novr. 1628, when his daughter Grace was baptized. An old account book, the property of Giles Cooke, now in the possession of Mr. Fothergill, of Brownber, states that in 1636, Mr. Tho: Dodson and Tho: Perkin rented the portion of the Ravenstonedale Parks, called the Wheatfields, for £32 per annum; the total rental of the Parks being at that time £112. According to Calamy he was ejected for nonconformity in 1662, but afterwards conformed, and as he is mentioned in the Parish Book as being Minister in 1664, he must have conformed almost immediately after his ejectment. The Parish Book mentions him as one of "ye four & twenty" in 1667, representing the Town angle. His son Jonathan was appointed "Register" in 1667-8 (vide Introduction vol II).

Mr. Dodson was buried 22 Jan. 1672-3.

Anthony Procter.

Thomas Dodson was succeeded by Anthony Procter, but there is no record in the Episcopal Register to show when the latter was licensed to Ravenstonedale. As already stated (Introduction vol. I) Procter signs the Transcripts for 1673 and 1677 as "minister" and "curate" respectively. The parish book speaks of him as being "curate" on Octr. 23rd 1673. He remained here

* Mr. Whitehead is doubtful about Hunter having written the note. He thinks it was written by the transcriber who made the parchment copy, and that it was he who collected all the loose entries "that could be found."

until he became Rector of Deane, where there is the following entry in the Register "Anthony Proctor Rector of Deane was instituted the nineteenth day of March 1689 and inducted the 26th day of the same moneth." This agrees with an entry to the same effect in the Episcopal Register. Canon Sherwen the present Rector of Deane has kindly sent me the following extracts.

"Mrs Proctor buried 22 day Aprill 1701"

"Buried An: Dom: 1702 Anthony Proctor July 23"

"Buried An: Dom: 1705 March 29th Mr. Anthony Proctor Rector of Deane."

Anthony appears to have been a favourite name in the Procter family, and this makes it a difficult matter to trace the antecedents of the particular Anthony who was curate of Ravenstonedale. The Preachers' Licenses List for 1672, in the Record Office, has the following entry under date of 20th Novr. "Licence to Anthony Procter, Mr. of Arts of Kirby Massard in the Co: of York, presbyterian." The Masham Register says that in 1651 "Mr. Anthony Prockter was Curate under Mr. Christopher Lancaster, who had obtruded himself into the Living (to the exclusion of the Revd. Benjamin Brown, the rightful Vicar) July 12. 1649" In the year following, Lancaster left Masham and Kirkby Malzeard, and Procter "intruded under the hand and seale from Mr. Brown, vicar of Kirkby," with the consent of the "fower and twentye." In 1655 "Mr. Prockter did leave Masham and goe to the Vicaridge of Well", an adjacent parish. In the Well Register he is described as a "Nonconformist," and is stated to have been "dispossessed" in 1662, when Wm. Stead a previous Vicar was "restored by the Bartholomew Act." From this date I can find no trace of him until he takes out the licence to preach in 1672. In the year following he becomes Curate of Ravenstonedale, presented doubtless by the Presbyterian patron, Lord Wharton. In a very old book of accounts at Masham Church certain sums (6d., 2s., and 1s., 3d.) are stated to have been spent "in charges when Mr. Prockter preach't" there in 1673, 1675, and 1676 respectively. From this Procter seems to have occasionally visited the scene of his former labours after he became minister at Ravenstonedale. The Carlisle Episcopal Register mentions that on March 16. 1678 Anthy. Procter "from the Durham diocese" was ordained deacon. If this was the

Ravenstonedale Procter it shews that considerable laxity prevailed at that period in ministers holding benefices without having been episcopally ordained.

The Torre M.S. in a list of the Incumbents of Linton-in-Craven (a rectory of two medieties) gives the death of John Procter, Rector of the first mediety, in 1508; also the resignation of Anthony Procter of the second mediety in 1570, and of the first at some date (not given) between 1602 and 1615. These, possibly, were the forefather of the subject of this note.

Another "Anthony Procter A.B." is mentioned in the Episcopal Register as having been licensed to the Ky. Stephen Free Grammar School 29 May 1691, ordained deacon Feb. 1891-2, priest 24 Dec. 1693 and licensed to Greystoke. Probably he was the "Mr. Anthony Procter" who according to the Ky. Stephen Register "was wedd to Mrs. Mary Solly 1702 June 4."

THOMAS HUNTER.

222. Thomas Hunter, priest, licensed Curate of Ravenstonedale, 2 June 1691.

233. Thomas Hunter instituted to Croglin on the death of George Sandrson, nominated by Philip Lord Wharton, 2nd August 1691.

ARTHUR TEMPEST.

253. 23rd May 1692. Arthur Tempest A.B. licensed Curate of Ravenstonedale.

JOHN WRIGHT.

284. 7th Feb. 1693-4. John Wright A.B. licensed to Ravenstondale, alias Russendale.

JOHN DALTON.

339. John Dalton Coll. Regin. Oxon. ordained deacon 22 Dec. 1695, and licensed Curate of Appleby.

352. John Dalton A.B. Coll. Regin. Oxon. and Curate of Ravenstondale ordained priest 20th May 1697 and licensed to Ravenstondale.

John Dalton succeeded Anthony Procter as Rector of Dean on Aug. 24th, 1705, presented by Thomas Lord Wharton.

THOMAS TOULMIN.

116. Thomas Tolmin Curate of Ravenstondale ordained priest 19th May 1706 and on 21st. May 1706 licensed to Ravenstondale.

Close to the south door of the Church on the east side of the path there is a headstone with the following inscription, "In memory of | The Rev^d. Thos. Toulmin | Minister in Ravenstondale | 24 years who died the 8th day of | August 1728 aged 52 years | Also of Margaret his wife who | died the 4th day of March 1773 | aged 84 years—They were both interred in the | Quire on the east side of the | Communion Table | Also of Mr. John Toulmin their eldest son who died the 11th day | of July 1783 aged 70 years"

ROBERT MOUNSEY.

9. Mr. Robert Mounsey ordained priest, 21st Sep. 1735.

September 22nd 1735. Robert Mounsey Clerk admitted and licensed Curate of Russendale or Ravenstonedale upon the nomination of Robt. Lowther.

47 13th March 1738. Richard Fothergill a literate person was licensed to be Parish Clarke of Ravenstonedale in the dioc. of Carl. upon the nomination of Robert Mounsey Clerk Curate there.

63 Wm Adamthwaite a literate person ordained deacon and nominated to be assistant Curate to the Rev^d. Robert Mounsey Curate of Ravenstonedale 31st. Aug. 1777.

In the Chancel there is a mural brass tablet in memory of the Mounsey family—"Near this place | are deposited the mortal remains of the Rev^d. Robert Mounsey Cl. (51 years minister of | this Parish) who departed this life 29th March 1780 in the | 84th year of his age: and of Mary his widow | who died 23^d. March 1786 in the 85th year of her age | Also | of Mary their daughter who died in the year 1755 Æt. 32 | And | of Robert their son, who died in his infancy."

It was during Mounsey's long incumbency that the tower, and afterwards the Church, were rebuilt, the former in 1738, the latter in 1744. The only description of the old Church that I can find is that contained in Bishop Nicolson's primary visitation in 1703, published by our Archæological and Antiquarian Society. In the year 1709, as I gather from an old (Churchwarden's) memorandum book, certain repairs were required for the steeple, and payments were made to a smith, a "glasner" and "tow plumers". In October 1737 a vestry meeting decided "to erect a steeple on the middle of the west end of the Church 11 ft. square inside, and 15 yds. high............ .....an arch betwixt the Church and steeple as at present only the said arch to be lessened in proportion to the said new steeple, to be made of the old arch stones... ....and unanimously to lay aside all thoughts and conclusions about or anyway relating to repairing the said Church till the money arising by the brief (now obtain'd) was all come into the Trustees' hands." In January following a petition was sent to the Bishop praying for a Faculty to pull down and rebuild the steeple, because "a considerable part of it is fallen to the ground and the rest of it is so very ruinous that the whole of it must be taken down and rebuilt." The Faculty was decreed on the 19th of the May succeeding. The plans, contracts, receipts, &c., are still extant in the parish chest. The contractor for pulling down the old steeple was "to take all the old windas and arch next the Church downe with Great Care and Lay them each winda by it selfe and the arch by it self and to Leave none of the foundations Laying but all to be Laid above ground" Care was to be taken in the pulling down "that no stones faw on to the Church Leads to dow Damadg and to be puld down with all speed." In the accounts there are two items "for pulling down part of the Church wall and walling up again." The work, including the hanging of the bells, appears to have been completed by the spring of 1739. The Brief brought in £321 : 14 : 4, and the cost of the steeple was £264 : 3 : 5¾, leaving a balance of about £57 in hand. Unfortunately there are no records relating to the rebuilding of the Church, but the Faculty issued on Novr. 20th, 1742, and the building was finished in 1744.

The above extracts establish conclusively the relative ages of tower and Church as they now stand. But on the north side of the present building are what tradition affirms to be the foundations of the former edifice. The tower, it is said, stood alone on pillars, on the west side of the footpath which passed between it and the Church, and from inspection of the ground this would appear to have been the case. But this does not correspond with the description as given in the resolution of the Vestry. It follows, apparently, that either the proposed site of the new tower was subsequently altered and moved southwards, and then the Church built up to it, or these foundations are the remains of a structure more ancient still than the Church visited by the Bishop in 1703, and demolished in

1742. In the "Articles of Agreement" between the Trustees and the Contractors for the removal of all the old lime, sand, &c., which are dated the 17th Jany. 1738-9, it is stipulated amongst other things that the contractors are "to level 18 inches below the off take of the steeple on the south side to the corner of the Church porch." This proves, I think, that the old Church occupied the same site as the new.

JEFFREY BOWNESS.

8 15th Sepr. 1768. Jefferey Bowness Clerk was admitted and licensed Curate of the Chapel of Mallerstang nominated by the Earl of Thanet.

84 July 26th 1780. Jeffrey Bowness was admitted and licensed to the Parish Church of Ravenstonedale on the nomination of Sir James Lowther.

The Revd. Jeffrey Bowness Incumbent Curate of Ravenstonedale and Mallerstang was buried at Ravenstonedale April 16th. 1813 aged 80 by Thomas Moss Assistant Curate.

JOHN ROBINSON.

225 June 4th. 1796. John Robinson a literate person licensed to the Free Grammar School at Ravenstonedale on the nomination of the Trustees.

316 24th June 1813. John Robinson D.D. licensed to the perpetual curacy of Ravenstonedale vacant by the death of Jeffrey Bowness on the nomination of Rt. Hon. William Earl of Lonsdale.

In the Burial Register on March 11th 1813 John Robinson signs as "Curate of Mallerstang."

159 20th. Sep. 1833. John Robinson clerk resigned the perpetual curacy of Ravenstonedale.*

THOMAS MOSS.

159 24th Sep. 1833. Thomas Moss admitted and licensed to the perpetual Curacy of Ravenstonedale vacant by the resignation of John Robinson on the presentation of the Earl of Lonsdale.

WILLIAM CHARLES KENDALL.

313 3rd Aug. 1842. Wm. Chas. Kendall admitted and licensed to the perp. curacy of Ravenstonedale vacant by the death of Thomas Moss.

471 20th Dec 1848. Wm. C. Kendall resigned.

* The following is on a foot stone in the Chancel of Clifton Church—
I. Robinson D.D. Rector 1840.

William Yarker.

477 14th June 1849. William Yarker was admitted and licensed to the perp. curacy of Ravenstonedale vacant by the resignation of Wm. Chas. Kendall.

The Revd. William Yarker, Vicar of this Parish, was buried April 30th. 1871 aged 61 years by James Simpson Rural Dean of Kirkby Stephen.

Ismay Barnes

12th July 1871. Ismay Barnes was admitted and instituted to the Vicarage, Ravenstonedale vacant by the death of William Yarker.

George Atkinson

26th. May 1873. George Atkinson was admitted and instituted to the Vicarage of Ravenstonedale vacant by the death of Ismay Barnes.

Robert Weston Metcalfe.

7th. Decr. 1888. Robert Weston Metcalfe was admitted and instituted to the Vicarage of Ravenstonedale vacant by the resignation of George Atkinson.

CHURCHWARDENS.

The year given is that for which the return was made; the signatures would be affixed from April to July of the year following.

1673 Tho. Dennyes. Anthony ffothergill. Thomas Perkin.

1728 Heny. ffothergill. Thomas Hunter.

1729 Heny. ffothergill. Richard Todd.

1730 No Signatures.

1731 Richd. Todd. James Richardson.

1732 Richd. Todd. John Robertson.

1733 Richd. Todd. Rob. ffawcett. John Robinson. George Moreland.

1734 Thomas Dent. Richd. Todd. Georg Perkins. John Spooner.

1735 Richd. Todd. John Spooner.

1736 Richd. Todd, John Spooner, James Bayliff, Richd. Hewetson.

1737 James Bayliff. Thomas Green. Simon Bousfield (x). Edw. Beck. Richd. Todd. Jno, Beck. John Spooner. John Robinson.

1738 Robt. Bovell, Edw. Beck, James Rogerson, Simon Bousefield (x).

1739 Will: Hewetson, James Rogerson, John Orton, John Shearman.

1740 Will: Hewetson. John Spooner.

1741 John Spooner, John Robertson, James Bayliff, William Clemeson.

1742 John blackburn, John Spooner, William Adamthwait, John Shearman.
1743 Rich[d]. Bovell, John blackburn, Robert Potter.
1744 John Atkinson. Jn[o]. Blackburn. Ja: Bayliff. Tho: Fothergill.
1745 Thos. ffawcett. Jas. Bayliff. Simon Bousefield (x). John blackburn.
1746 Thos. ffawcett. Robertt Fawcett. Simon Bousefield (x). Robert Potter.
1747 John Bousfield, Joseph Hunter, John Shearman, Edw[d]. Beck.
1748 John Bousfield, John Holme, Jn[o]. Blackburn, Simon Bousfield.
1749 John Holme, John Blackburn, Arthur Bousfield, Simon Bousfield.
1750 John Fawcett, Rich[d]. Breaks, John Shearman, Richard Hewetson.
1751 Simon Bousfield, William Howgill, Richard Breaks, John Shearman.
1752 Will[m]. Howgill, Edw. Beck, Geo. Robinson, Simon Bousfield.
1753 James Bayliff, Rich[d]. Murthwaite, Edw[d]. Beck, Rich[d]. Gregson.
1754 Rich[d]. Murthwaite, John Blackburn, Thomas Fothergill, Edw. Beck.
1755 John Coupland, John Milner, John Holmes, Tho. Fothergill.
1756 Jas. Bayliff, Thos. Fothergill, John Coupland, Ro[t]. Mounsey Jun[r].
1757 Jas. Bayliff, John Bowness, George Udal.
1758 Anth[y]. Knewstupp, Geo. Udale, John Coupland.
1759 John Hastwell, Thomas Fawcett, William Shaw, John Coupland.
1760 Will[m]. Shaw, Tho[s]. fawcett, Geo. Udale, John Coupland.
1761 Rich[d]. Robinson, Joseph Atkinson, John Hastwell, Will[m]. Shaw.
1762 Tho[s]. Brown, Ri: Murthwaite, John Hunter.
1763 Rich[d]. Murthwaite, John Shearman, Tho[s]. Hunter, Geo: Fothergill (x).
1764 R[d]. Cunningham, Ant. Knewstupp, Tho[s]. Fothergill, Thomas Fothergill.
1765 Rich[d]. Murthwaite, Anth. Dent, Rob[t]. Hunter, Tho[s]. Fothergill.
1766 R[d]. Cunningham, Thos. Fothergill, John Shearman, James Parkin.
1767 Thos. Fothergill, John Shearman, Tho[s]. Hunter, george fthergill.
1768 Ri: Murthwaite, Ch[t]. Knewstupp, Fawcett Hunter, george fothergill.
1769 Anth[y]. Knewstupp, Wm. Shaw, george fothergill, W[m]. Hunter.
1770 John Holme, Stephen Dent, george fothergill.
1771 John Holme, Arthur Bousfield.
1772 Arthur Bousfield, Fawcett Hunter, Thomas Atkinson.
1773 George Fothergill, James Shaw, John Milner, Fawcett Hunter.
1774 george fothergill, James Shaw, W[m]. Shaw, John Milner.
1775 george fothergill, John Milner, John Hunter, Stephen Dent.
1776 george fothergill, John Milner, W[m]. Shaw, Rich[d]. Shaw.

1777 George Fothergill, Heny. Bousfield, Richd. Shaw, thomas metcalf.
1778 Wm. Shaw, George Fothergill, Heny. Robinson, Geo. Hastwell.
1779 No signatures.
1780 Wm. Shaw, George Hastwell, George Fothergill.
1783 Heny. Beck, John Richardson.
1784 Arthur Bousfield.
1785 Wm. Shaw. Thos. Hunter.
1786 Thos. Hunter, Geo. Hastwell, Wm. Shaw.
1788 Wm. Shaw, Thos. Hastwell.
1789 Joseph Fothergill, Michl. Bovell.
1790 Thos. Hastwel, John Richardson.
1791 Thos. Fothergill.
1793 John Richardson, Thos. Milner.
1794 Isaac Handley.
1797 Heny. Beck.
1798 Heny. Beck, Heny. Robinson.
1799 Heny. Robinson.
1800 Fawcett Hunter, Thos. Scarborough.
1801 Richd. Dixon.
1802 Richd. Dixon, Sept. Robinson, Thos. Scarborough, Thos. Hunter.
1803 John Parkin, Richd. Fothergill, Isaac Handley, Thos. Knewstup.
1805 Robt. Hunter, Thos. Scarborough, Wm. Furnass, John Fawcett.
1806 Thos. Scarborough, Anthy. Hunter, Wm. Furnass, Isaac Handley.
1807 Robt. Hunter, Richd. Beck, Geo. Thexton, John Parkin.
1808 John Parkin, Richard Beck, George Thexton, Robert Hunter.
1809 Edmund Hodgson, Richd. Dixon, Michl. Bovell, Robt. Wilson.
1810 Geo: Fawcett, John Parkin, Thos. Milner, Richd. Fothergill.
1811 Thos. Milner, Wm. Dawson, Wm. Morros, Charles Hastwell.
1812 Thos. Milner, Wm. Dawson, Anthy. Priston, Richd. Potter.

MASTERS OF THE FREE GRAMMAR SCHOOL.

608 June 4. 1677. John Metcalf was admitted Master of the Free School of Ravenstonedale Co. Westm'land dioc. Carl. having first subscribed the Articles and the Declaration required of him by law.

3 James Calvert A.B., ord. deacon 15 Mar. 1684. "James Calvert A.B. licensed to teach School at Ravenstondale hath subscribed &c.

In witness whereof I have hereunto sett my hand and seal this 23rd. Sepr. Anno Dni. 1684. (signed) Tho: Carliol." James Calvert A.B. Dioc. Carl. ord. priest 24 Feb. 1688.

205 Whereas the ffree Grammar School in ye Town of Ravenstondale in the County of Westmrland is become destitute of a Schoolmaster for the said school by the departure of Mr. Myles Hodgson late schoolmaster there I Abraham ffothergill of Chancery lane in the County of Middlesex Gen. Doe nominate & appoint and hereby place Mr. Thomas Barber Schoolemr. of the said schoole. Witnesse my hand and seale the thirtieth day of June in ye second yeare of ye Raigne of our Soveraign Ld. & Lady King William and Queen Mary Annoq. Dni 1690.

Signed Sealed & Delivered
in the pr.sense of
R. Belwood. Abr. ffothergill (l.s.)
John Comins.

Tho. Barber, literate, licensed 1st. Aug. 1690 having first made Declaration &c.

289 Matthew Rudd, literate, 18th Sepr. 1694 licensed to the Free Grammar School at Ravenstondale.

400 24th May 1700. Robt. Shaw A.B. licensed Master of the F.G.S. at Ravenstondale. Robt. Shaw A.B. ord. deac. 27th May 1700.

19 James Moore A.B. licensed F.G.S. at Ravenstondale 1702 Sep. 7. Ord. deac. 10 May 1703.

58 Marmaduke Holme A.B. 10 March 1703 licensed F.G.S. Ravenstondale.

148 William Fawcett A.B. 8 Sep. 1707 licensed F.G.S. Ravenstondale.

626 13 July 1726. Edw. Holmes A.B. of Sedbergh licensed F.G.S. Ravenstondale, nominated by 12 Trustees.

702 1 July 1728. Thomas Coulston licensed F.G.S. Ravenstondale.

285 4 July 1759. Thos. Robertson a literate person licensed F.G.S. Ravenstondale on nomination of Trustees, subscribed &c.

330 Sep. 7. 1764. James Sedgwick, literate, licensed F.G.S. Ravenstondale nom. by Trustees, subscribed &c.

345 Aug. 14 1767. John Robinson, a literate person, &c. &c.

225 June 4th 1796. John Robinson, a literate person &c. &c.

TERRIER 1704.

The following is the oldest Ravenstonedale Terrier. It is printed at pp. 204-5 of Bishop Nicolson's Miscellany Accounts of the Diocese among the "Terriers of the Glebe Lands, &c., as given in at my Primary Visitation in the month of May, 1704" (p. 159). The original is in the Bishop's Registry with the other Ravenstonedale Terriers, but we have no duplicate in the Church Safe, and a copy may be of interest. I give it literatim :—

To the R^{t}. Rev^{d}. Father in God William (by Divine Permission) L^{d}. Bishop of Carlisle.

We your Ld.ships most dutiful Servants the Minister & Churchwardens of the Parish of Ravenstondale according to y^{r} Ld.ships command do present y^{r} Ld.ship with this full Terrier of the Glebe & other Endowments of our Church.

1st. A Mansion house wth a Barn & Stable & Garden belonging to it, Land of about five Acres of the yearly value of five pounds.

2^{d}. The summ of five pounds & one shilling pay'd yearly out of Blatarn in the Parish of Warcopp & given to the Church by M^{r}. William Morland, Parson of Graystock.

3^{d}. The Summ of Eight pounds pay'd yearly by the R^{t}. Honble. the L^{d}. Wharton which is all his Ld. ship thinks due out of the Tiths.

4th. All the Tiths of Corn, Wool & Lamb & the Oblations at Easter are pay'd to the R^{t}. Honble. the L^{d}. Wharton to the value of an hundred pounds yearly.

We humbly thank y^{r} L^{d}. ship for that great care y^{r} L^{d}. ship shews for the Security of that Little which at present we have and shall ever pray for y^{r} L^{d}. ship long continuance over us.

Y^{r} L^{dships}
Most Obedient
sons & servants
Jo: Dalton Curate

Michael Bovell, Mathew Breaks, Stephen Dentt, Thomas Dent.
Churchwardens.

PRESBYTERIAN REGISTERS.

These with all other non-parochial Registers were called in by Act of Parliament in the year 1840, and are now deposited at Somerset House. For the purpose of this work application was made to the Registrar General for permission to make copies of these and also of the Quaker Registers, but it was refused on the ground that there was no accommodation at Somerset House for transcribers, nor was there a sufficient staff of clerks to superintend such work. Fortunately, however, some few years ago one of my subscribers (Mr. Gerald Fothergill) had made a copy of the Chapel Registers for his own use, and this copy he has very kindly placed at my disposal. He wishes me to say in reference to it that "it is not intended to be a letter for letter copy, but only an index to show the contents of the book; and owing to the cramped space and bad light afforded him, some slight and unimportant errors may have crept in."

The entries, it will be noted, date only from the year 1775. From the absence of any pre-existing Chapel records I am inclined to think that the Presbyterian Births and Baptisms were entered in the Church Register, on pages specially set apart for them (vide pp. 38 to 50).

As to the date of the building of the Presbyterian (now Congregational) Chapel there has always been much uncertainty, but there is little doubt that it resulted from the labours of a "Mr." Christopher Jackson who is said to have been ejected from the Rectory of Crosby Garret, an adjoining parish, in 1662, because of his refusal to accept the Act of Uniformity.

Calamy (Nonconformists' Memorial—Palmer's Edition vol II p. 495) thus refers to him. "Crossby *on the Hill.* Mr. Christopher Jackson, of Magd. Col. Camb. He was born at *Leeds* designed for trade, and put out an apprentice: but his friends observing his bookishness took him from his trade and sent him to *Cambridge*, where he studied under Mr. Joseph Hill. He was a very pious man, of an holy life and competent learning. He was turned out somewhere in *Yorkshire*, and afterwards in this place. He lived meanly upon a little estate in the parish of *Ravistondale*, sometimes preaching occasionally. Some ministers, who had conformed, once telling him that he had a bare coat, he made answer 'if it was bare, it was not turned.'"

The Tutor of Magdalen College has been good enough to send me the following extract from the Matriculation Register:—

"Junii 22 1652. Christopherus Jackson filius Thomæ de Leedes in comitatu Eboracensi annum agens vigesimum primum e scholâ ibidem Leodiensi admissus est Pensionarius, Tutore Mro. Hill."

There is, however, no further trace of his having been admitted to a Scholarship or Fellowship at Magdalen.

The University Registrar informs me that a Christopher Jackson of Magdalen College took his B.A. in 1655, but does not appear to have proceeded to any higher degree.

The Episcopal Registers both at Carlisle and York contain no entries of the Commonwealth period, consequently there is no record of Jackson's ordination, that is, presuming he did receive episcopal ordination. In my search through the Carlisle records I found that Edmund Mauleverer was instituted to the Rectory of Crosby Garrett Dec. 10th 1636, on the death of Richard ffallowfield on the nomination of Philip Musgrave, Bart. Again Edmund Maulinerer, Rector of Crosby Garret, is mentioned as being a Commissioner in the 13th year of Charles II (viz. 1662); and also on Oct. 22nd 1663 Edmund Maulverer, Rector, surrenders Crosby Garrett to Bishop Stern, and is succeeded by Thomas Denton.

Very probably Maulverer was deprived of his benefice by the Cromwellians under the Sequestration Act of 1643, and Lord Wharton in 1655, or subsequently, may have appointed his protege Jackson to the vacancy. On the Restoration in 1660 all deprived Incumbents were restored to their benefices, and Jackson being an "usurper" or "intruder," as the Parliamentarian nominees were termed, would have to vacate to make room for Mauleverer who was still living, and in this sense he may be said to have been ejected, but it does not appear to have been altogether 'for conscience sake.' He had no opportunity of shewing that he preferred to vacate the benefice rather than accept the Act of Uniformity, which did not come into operation until two years after his ejection.

The Ravenstonedale Parish Register states that Mr. Christopher Jackson and Annas Tayler were married April 17, 1664. This is the only mention of his name I can find in any local record.*

* "Chroferus Jackson dioc. Cestrien. ord. p. 1634." (Episcopal Register). This, possibly, was some relative.

Mr. Dawson, one of the Trustees, has very kindly sent for my perusa the oldest documents the Chapel possesses. The first is an indenture, tripartite, dated the 18th of August 1693 between (i) George Parkin of Lowcome, yeoman, (ii) Thos. Fothergill of Brownbarr, yeoman, and (iii) Peter Pinder of the Borough of Southwark, gentleman; Wm. Milner of Assefell; Chrisr. Todd, of the Nethergarths; Thos. Knewstubb of the Dubbs; Jas. Perkin, of Greenside; Richd. Hunter, of Bowbarhead; Robt. Fothergill and Geo. Murthwaite both of Wath; and Heny. Cautley, of Greenside, yeomen. In the previous year George Parkin had purchased from Richd. Wharton, of Waitby, gentleman, the "firehouse" called by the name of the new chamber, with a peat house at the south end thereof, and one barn, one cowhouse, one stable, one close called the High Gills, and one half of a pasture called the great pasture, and one half of all that Close called the Gales and the garden in it, and one half of the Lilly Garth, with all edifices &c., &c., for the sum of three score and thirteen pounds. By a deed dated the 17th August 1693 George Perkin mortgages the above to Thos. Fothergill for the sum of £100, with the proviso that if the said George Perkin should pay to the above named Thos. Fothergill, the sum of £100, before the 17th August 1696, then the mortgage deed should be void; and if not, then the property should pass to Thos. Fothergill in trust for Peter Pinder and the others above mentioned, who had provided the purchase money. The "proffitts" of the estate were to be paid by Thos. Fothergill and George Perkin to Timothy Punshon, Clerk, and his successors during the time he continued to be the licensed minister to preach or officiate as a Minister at the house of the said George Perkin situate in the town of Ravenstondale the same being a licensed place for that purpose by law, or at any other licensed place in Ravenstonedale. It was provided further that if it should at any time happen that such licensed preachers should be legally authorised to preach in the public churches, and accept of the public maintenance and encouragement of this kingdom without such conformity as is now required by law, or that this present liberty for the preaching of Dissenting Ministers shall be taken away, then the same Trustees shall yearly employ such profits for the encouragement for the faithful and powerful preaching of the gospel in Ravenstonedale aforesaid, according to the direction and with the approbation of the nine trustees abovenamed.

"Philip Lord Wharton gave by his will* the sum of £100, the interest thereof to go for the benefit of Mr. Timothy Punchen the then dissenting

* This Lord Wharton died Feby. 4th, 1694; the benefaction would be made during his lifetime.

minister and his successors for ever; the same to be laid out in the purchase of land as soon as might be convenient. Accordingly in the year 1693 the sum was laid out in a mortgage in Ravenstonedale, with a declaration of trust that the same should endure for the benefit of the minister; the mortgage to be renewed every three years according to the custom of the said manor." (Nicolson and Burn, vol. 1, pp. 523-4).

On March 7th 1736 a similar indenture was executed by (i) John Parkin, of Low Stainerscugh, (ii) Wm. Robinson, of High Stainerscugh, and (iii) Thos. Knewstub, Godfrey Milner, John Shaw, James Robinson, of Ravenstondale Town; James Alderson, of Whole; John Hewitson, of Lowcome; Richd. Hewitson, of Alergill; Rob. Hunter, of Bowberhead; and Wm. Shaw, of Artlegarth, all yeomen; by which indenture the mortgage now amounting to £128 6s. 8d. was secured upon the following property previously purchased by John Parkin from Jonathan Alderson, of Ravenstondale Town, yeoman, for the sum of £330, viz; a Messuage & Tenement lying at the Townhead,* to wit, one dwelling house, barn, stable, and peat house & a garth, one close called Hill with a little bottom adjoining same, one close called Low New Close, together with land lying on the Town Croft adjoining the ground late Madam Atkinson's on the east side (and other closes and lands which is since sold of) with all edifices &c.

About this time differences arose between the Minister and the Trustees, which resulted in a trial "James Richie, Clerk, Plaintiff, *versus* John Perkin and others, Defendants" in the Lord Chancellor's Court, the 8th July, 1741. A copy of the order thereon is preserved in the Orton Church Chest, and has been kindly forwarded to me for perusal by the Vicar, the Revd. Edwd. Holme. It consists of six pages of closely written foolscap, and is somewhat dilapidated at the folds.

The Plaintiff, it seems, was called by the major part of the contributing members of the Congregation on or about the 9th Sep. 1733; but before the expiration of a year from that date a number of the Trustees found fault with their Minister's doctrine, alleging it was contrary to that of Calvin and to the Westminster Confession of Faith. They accordingly withheld his stipend, withdrew their subscriptions and in the end evicted him and his section of the congregation from the Meeting House. In his suit Plaintiff sought to recover the several sums due to him, and also the rightful possession of the Meeting House. In this he was successful, his opponents being thoroughly discomfited.

* The date stone on the house is—"I.A. 1715."

The Order is very valuable, because it determines beyond all doubt the age of the present building. In his Bill the Plaintiff states, "that within the Parish of Ravenstonedale in the County of Westmorland there is, & for 40 years last past & upwards hath been, a Congregation for religious worship of the Protestant Dissenters called Presbyterians and a place for their meetings & worship was duly certified, registered and recorded according to the Act of Toleration made in the 1st year of the Reign of K.W. & Q.M. ....that the place whereon the Meeting House is built & the Garth thereto adjoining called the Meeting House Garth was a piece of Ground purchased of Richard Hewitson about 13 years ago for £6 out of the common stock,..... ....that after such purchase the said congregation by voluntary subscription & by the contributions of Dissenters in the neighbourhood built the said Meeting House & laid out in the said building & seating the same about £200...............that the said House was built in 1726 & the same on or about the 10th of April 1727 was duly registered & recorded in the public sessions at Appleby as a Meeting House for the said Dissenters."

On the back of the 1736 deed are the names of the Trustees from time to time appointed to fill existing vacancies, and as they may be of interest to their descendants I give the list.

1738. A majority of the survivors of above nine viz.—John Hewetson, Wm. Shaw, Richd. Hewetson, Robt. Hunter, James Robinson appoint Thomas Shaw.

March 4th, 1756. Survivors, Richd. Hewtson, Wm. Shaw, and Robt. Hunter elect Robt. Hewtson and John Hewtson, both of Lockholme foot; Heny. Hewtson, of Streetside; Thos. Knewstub, of High Stenerskew; and Thos. Robinson, of Scarr.

Feb. 19th, 1778. Survivors, Wm. Shaw, Thos. Robinson, John Hewetson, Robt. Hewetson, and John Hewetson elect Christr. Coupland of or near Crossbank, and Robt. Todd of Greenside "being credible persons and of Calvinistic principles."

May 19th 1784. Subscribers, John Hewetson, Robt. Hewetson, John Hewetson, and Robt. Todd elect John Shaw, of Artlegarth; Richd. Hewetson, of Ellergill; John Hewetson, of Crook's Beck, and Richd. Hewetson, of Newbyginn, credible persons, &c.

Dec. 10th 1793. Subscribers, John Hewetson, of Ellergill; John Hewetson, of Lowkholm foot; Richd. Hewetson, of Ellergill; Richd. Hewetson, of Greenside; John Hewetson, of Lowkholm; appoint Thos. Morland, of

Russendale Town; John Chamberlane, of Greenside; W^{m}. Fawcet, of Newbiggin; and Robt. Hewetson, of Lowkholm; credible persons, &c.

June 3rd, 1805. The surviving trustees (the names are not given) appoint the Rev^{d}. John Hill in the room of John Hewetson, Elergill, deceased.

March 22nd 1810. Subscribers, John Chamberlain, of Greenside; Rich^{d}. Hewetson, of Greenside; Robt. Hewetson, of Ashfull; being a "mager" part, elect Chris^{r}. Bousfield, of Weasdale; Joseph Udale, of Cowbank; Robt. Hewetson, of Lockholm foot; Benjmen Hewetson, of Green; credible persons &c.

Sep. 9th, 1813. Majority of survivors, John Chamberlain, Benj. Hewetson, Joseph Udale, Robt. Hewetson nominate Thos. Robinson, Thos. Ireland, and Thos. Hunter.

Novr. 16. 1826. Survivors, Benjn. Hewetson, Joseph Udale, Robt. Hewetson, Thos. Robinson, Robert Hewetson and Thos. Hunter nominate Stephen Chamberlain and John Beck.

There is also a third indenture, dated June 1st 1805, between W^{m}. Elyetson of Scarsikes, Esquire, and John Hewetson, of Streetside, yeoman. W^{m}. Elyetson in consideration of the sum of £32 sells to John Hewetson "all that customary Housestead and Garth adjoining upon each other fronting to the Town street and adjoining backwards to the Burial ground of the Dissenting Meeting House there holden under the R^{t}. Hon. W^{m}. Viscount Lowther, by payment of the yearly old rent one penny, late the property of Anthony ffawcett, deceased, and now in the possession of William Elyetson, together with all rights, &c. &c."

The house was subsequently pulled down in order to extend the burial ground.

Further information relating to the Chapel and its ministers will be found in Nightingale's Lancashire Nonconformity pp. 309 to 318.

In a recent letter on this subject the Rev^{d}. Bryan Dale, of Bradford, says, "Oct. 8. 1691. Lord Wharton certified 'a new house adjoining to Smarber Hall in Swaledale (Low Row) to be set apart for a public meeting house for Protestant Dissenters'. And it is probable that about the same time a similar place was certified at Ravenstonedale. The Sessions Rolls for Westmorland would show whether this was the case."

Although the Ravenstonedale Presbyterians would find a powerful protector in Lord Wharton, it is not likely that they would venture to build any special place of worship before the Toleration Act of 1689. The indenture of 1693 speaks of the minister officiating at the licensed house of George Perkin, from which we may, I think, conclude there was no chapel then existing. The Church Register states that a marriage took place "at the meeting house" on Jany. 4 1693-4, and again on Aug. 24 1697 —but this would be George Perkin's licensed house. The Toleration Act required that Dissenting places of Worship should be certified to the Bishop of the diocese, or to the Archdeacon, or to the Justices of the Peace at their Quarter Sessions, to be registered. Our Diocesan Registrar tells me he has no such list at Carlisle; and I have carefully gone through the Orders of the Quarter Sessions without finding any mention either of the licensed house, or of the Chapel built in 1726.

Nicolson and Burn (i, 524) quote the following additional benefactions towards the endowment of the Chapel, "One Mr. Pindár, a dissenting minister at London, gave to the said meeting house £30. John Thomson of Kirkby-Stephen, hosier, £20. Isabel Langhorn £6. James and Mary Fawcet £20. George Murthwaite, £10. All which sums have been laid out in the purchase of lands. There was also £100 in money, contributed by Christopher Todd and others; £20 of which hath been lost, and the rest is let out at interest by the Trustees."

I have received every assistance from the Chapel Authorities in my endeavour to ascertain its early history. My thanks are due to the Rev^{d}. Charles Illingworth, the present minister, for his kind co-operation; and especially to Mr. Edwd. B. Dawson, Aldcliffe Hall, Lancaster, for the loan of all the old deeds, &c., belonging to the Chapel, from which I have been enabled to extract a considerable portion of the above information.

SOCIETY OF FRIENDS.

The original Registers of the Society of Friends like those of the Presbyterians are deposited at Somerset House, and are closed to public inspection. The Friends in 1838, throughout the country refused to part with their Registers, though they were temporarily taken to London for inspection by the Commissioners, who say (p. 12): "We saw enough of their state and condition to testify that they exhibit an admirable specimen of the state to which order and precision can be carried in the classification and arrangement of records of this description." Mr. S. Burn, however, in his history of Parish Registers (p. 234) states that "the Friends' registers, arranged and indexed, were in 1840 deposited at Somerset House."*

Certified copies of these registers with the entries arranged alphabetically may be consulted at the Society's Central Office, Devonshire House, on payment of certain fees; and it was from this source that, through the kindness of Mr. Gerald Fothergill, the Ravenstonedale entries were extracted for this publication. The Ravenstonedale records are included in those of the "Westmorland Quarterly Meetings," a list embracing portions of the adjacent counties of Cumberland, Lancashire, and Yorkshire.

Through the courtesy of Mr. Jas. Harrison, the custodian, I have had free access to a copy of this Westmorland Register kept at the Meeting House, Kendal, and this has been of great assistance to me in revising the proofs.

As stated in the Commissioners' Report, above referred to, the Friends' registers are a model of order and precision, but, unfortunately, in the earlier entries the place of residence is not always given, only the Monthly Meeting to which the parties belonged. Brigflatts in the adjoining parish of Sedbergh seems to have been the local headquarters of the Society, since most, if not all, of the Ravenstonedale Meeting entries are described as being also of the "Sedbergh M.M."† Where the residence column is left blank there is nothing to show whether the entry refers to a Ravenstonedale

*Revd. H. Whitehead on "Ravenstonedale Registers."

† Over the porch of the Brigflatt's Meeting house there is a date stone "Anno Do: 1675." George Fox preached there in 1677.

or a Sedbergh member. On this account, therefore, some Ravenstonedale entries may have escaped me.* Again, it is quite possible that in transcribing the originals the compilers of the index may have failed to discriminate between Murthwaite (Ravenstonedale) and Marthwaite (Sedbergh).

On the fly-leaf of the Kendal copy there is a memorandum that the Birth register ranges from 1635† to 1837; the first convert being Elizabeth Hooton in 1647; the earliest marriage, John Spooner and Ann his wife 9th of 12th mo. 1654; the earliest burial, Grace dt. of Robert Teasdale of Temple Sowerby bur. 5th of 6th. 1655.

Mr. John Handley of Brigflatts has very kindly furnished me with the following particulars concerning the early Ravenstonedale Friends, gathered from papers in his possession. He can find no record to show that George Fox, the founder of the Society, was ever in Ravenstonedale, although several of the inhabitants became his followers at the time of his first visit to the North in 1652. They may have met him either at Sedbergh, where he preached from a bench under the Yew Tree in the Church yard, or at Great Strickland. Amongst the early Ravenstonedale members were John Pinder of Wath, and Richard Wilson. For the first 50 years the meetings were held in private houses. The Friends being so scattered, those living in Weasdale and at Wath, the north-west corner of the parish, with those from the neighbourhood of Orton, would meet at Wath; those in Fell-end, Mallerstang, and Grisedale would assemble at the house of Anthony and Mary Robinson at Dovingill in Fell-end, the southern extremity—where, according to the minutes of the Sedbergh Monthly Meeting, a meeting for all the Friends of Ravenstonedale, Sedbergh, and Dent was held in 1677.

By a deed dated the 10th of July 1705, Anthony Robinson conveyed to Robert Rogerson of Ravenstonedale his house at Cat-keld,‡ "formerly called Smiddy, as it is newly erected and built" and half-an-acre of land for the building of a Meeting house, which is the one now in existence near the old Toll Gate; and in 1720 Robert Rogerson then of Whingill in the Parish of Kirkby Stephen conveyed it to Ralph Alderson of Narthwaite. At the first recorded meeting held in it in 1709 the 24th of 5th mo., it was agreed that they must have a stable, and Anthony Robinson (£2), Richd. Clarkson (10s.), Richard Adamthwait (5s.), Robert Rogerson (10s.), John Rogerson (10s.), Thomas (2s.) and George (10s.) Thornburrow, Ralph

* Vide Note p. 116.

† This must be incorrectly quoted, unless it be the birth date of some convert.

‡ There is no such place now known as Cat-keld.

Alderson (wood worth 15s.), and Isabel Clarkson (2s. 6d.) at once promised subscriptions towards it. Meetings were held regularly at Catkeld until about the beginning of the present century, when nearly all the Ravenstonedale Friends were residing in the immediate neighbourhood of Narthwaite, a hamlet about 3 or 4 miles nearer Sedbergh. This being a more convenient centre a room was fitted up for a Meeting house, in which meetings have been held from about 1790 up to the present time.

By another deed bearing date April 16th 1718, Anthony Pindar of Brigflatts (previously of Ravenstonedale) conveyed to William Tyson also of Brigflatts, cordwainer, in trust and for the use of the people called Quakers for a particular burying place for their dead a piece of ground, 23 yards in length and 13 in breadth, situate at Wath, at the southwest corner of the close called Parrock Moor. It is clear that Wath had been the burial ground long before this, as Anthony Pinder was admitted a tenant in 1710 under a deed from James Clarkson by Richard Baynes, Steward. It was afterwards conveyed to Ralph Alderson. The burial ground still remains walled off from the close, but all trace of interments has now disappeared. The same may be said of the burial ground at Catkeld, while the old Meeting-house itself is fast falling into decay and there are, I believe, but two members of the Society now living in the Parish.

Comparatively speaking the Ravenstonedale Friends suffered little from the persecution of the times. Yet it is said that within a period of 17 years at the commencement of the present century goods to the amount of £1,021 were taken from the few Friends of the Sedbergh Monthly Meeting, of which Ravenstonedale formed a part. Seizure consisted of a variety of things—cows, calves, sheep, geese, hay, corn, barley, malt, shoes and stockings. Joseph Handley who had a small farm at Wandale in this parish had a fat cow and 3 "stirks" taken at one time—for his objecting to military service.

Chancellor Ferguson's "Early Cumberland and Westmorland Friends" contains as an appendix local extracts from Besse's "Sufferings of the People called Quakers," from which I gather the following:—

In 1660 John Fothergill (? of Ravenstonedale) was imprisoned fourteen months for his conscientious refusal to pay tithes (p. 180).

In 1678 "an account" was presented to Parliament "of the names of such persons who are no Papists but Protestant Dissenters and distinguished by the name of Quakers, and have been prosecuted upon the Statutes of 23 and 28 of Elizabeth made against Popish Recusants, and

Levies made for the Yearly Profits of their Lands thereupon made by the Sheriff's Bayliffs of the said County by process out of the Exchequer for the year 1677." In this list appear James Clarkson, John Pinder and Anthony Robinson, all of Ravenstondale. Yearly val. of lands seized £1 : 19 : 4 val. of goods levied £4 : 12 : 0. And again, Richard Clarkson, Anthony Pinder, and Thomas Fawcett, all of Ravenstondale, had their goods seized to the value of £1 : 1 : 4 by Exchequer Process in 1677 and 1678. (p. 200)

In the Parish Book there is a memorandum on the subject of the appropriation of the seats in the new church in 1746. It appears that two seats near the door had been allotted to Thomas Thornborough, and two to Thomas Close; but they, being Quakers, refused to pay for the said seats the sum of £1 : 4 : 4 which had been assessed. Thereupon the Rev[d]. M[r]. George Fothergill, Fellow of Queen's Coll., Oxford, purchased them for the poor and lame people of the parish.

Alice Burton, of Dent, who in 1717 married Ralph Alderson, of Narthwaite, was a noted minister, and travelled as a preacher long before her marriage. In 1720 accompanied by Eleanor Moore she visited meetings in Ireland, which occupied them five months. In Dec. 1722 the same two spent a couple of months in Cumberland, after which Alice remained at home for nearly five years. In the early part of 1732 she visited the American Colonies, where she stayed over 2 years, the name of her companion is not known. In 1736, and again in 1743, she attended the half yearly meetings at Dublin. She died at Narthwaite on the 15th Aug. 1766 aged 88.

John, son of the above named Ralph and Alice, was a minister about 12 years, dating from 1740. In the course of his ministry he visited the whole of England, and was staying at the house of his friend Thomas Jackson, in London, when he died about midnight on the 26th April 1764, aged 43. He was interred in Bunhill Fields on the 30th, after a large and solemn meeting at Devonshire House, held for that purpose.

While on a recent visit to Brigflatts I had the privilege of perusing the minute book of the Ravenstonedale Meeting. It begins in the year 1709, and contains little beyond the election of a representative to attend the Monthly Meeting at Sedbergh. Here and there at rare intervals mention is made of some member offending against the rules of the Society. He is thereupon interviewed by certain influential members deputed by the meeting to "deal with him." The deputies report to the next meeting the result of their efforts, which were generally effectual—but, occasionally, the offender is pronounced incorrigible and forthwith formally expelled.

The following extracts shew the care exercised to prevent marriages with outsiders—

"Preparative Meeting 28 10th 1718. Some account is brought that Sarah Rogerson bears company with a young man of a differing Perswation Respecting Religion on ye account of marrige. This meeting apoints Ralph Alderson and Thomas Thornburrow to deal with her, and give account to ye next meeting." "Preparative Meeting 25. 11th. 1718. Ralph Alderson and Thomas Thornburrow have had an opportunity with Sarah Rogerson and according to her account she is clear upon ye said account at present."

The admonition Sarah received from her elders seems to have had only a temporary effect, if "the young man of a differing persuasion" was James Baylife, of Murthwaite, who married Sarah Rogerson on the 21st June 1721 in the Parish Church, and had his bride baptised at the same place on the 30th of the month following (vide Church Register). For her apostasy she was disowned by the Society, but a few years before her death she rejoined the Quakers, and was engaged in writing a paper giving her reasons and stating how the change in her views had been brought about, when she was seized with small-pox and died suddenly in 1730. Her husband survived her 36 years, and although interred in the Quaker burial ground he does not seem to have changed his views, being described as a non-member.

This case of small-pox gives a clue to the nature of the epidemic which carried off so many in Ravenstonedale in July 1730.

Mr. John Handley, of Brigflatts, has rendered me most valuable help in connection with the Friends' Registers, and my thanks are due to him, and also to Mr. James Harrison, of Kendal, for free and unlimited access to all Registers and Deeds in their custody.

BIRTHS AND CHRISTNINGS.

BAPTIZED.	1781.
MARCH 4th	Margaret Daughter of William Adamthwaite of Adamthwaite & Jane his wife.
† do. 9th	Ann D. of William Hewetson of Town & Martha his wife.
APRIL 4th	Jno. Robinson son of Fawcet Hunter of Sprint Gill & Ann his wife.
8th	William son of Thos. Nelson* of Town & Margaret his wife.
13th	James son of Wm. Alderson of Lytheside & Mary his wife.
23d	Richard son of James Hill of Newbegin & Mary his wife.
28th	Anthony son of Anthony Fawcet of Murthwaite & Mary his wife.
29th	Thos. son of James Bayliff of High Stennerskugh & Jane his wife.
MAY 10	John son of Anthony Robinson of Town & Ruth his wife.
1781. JUNE 5th	Baptized Ann Daughter of Anthony Dent of Dovingill & Faithy his wife.
9th	Bap. Thomas son of Wm. Bousfield [T. of Town] & Bella his wife.
12th	Bap. Margaret D. of Thomas Kirkbride of Bleaflat & Jane his wife.
27th	Agnes Daughter of Wm. Spooner of Weesdall & Margt. [T. Agnes] his wife.
JULY 4th	Gardus son of Jonathan [T. Winder] of Newbegin & his wife.
16th	Wm. son of John Milner of Ashfell & Mary his wife.
SEP. 14th	George son of Thomas Parkin of Flass and Ann his wife.
28th	Liddy Daughter of John Howgill of Adamthwaite & Margaret his wife.

* "Wm. Stubbs" crossed out. "Thos. Nelson" in T.

BIRTHS AND CHRISTNINGS.

SEP 16th	William son of Richard Dixon of Cawsey End & Isabella his wife.
OCT. 26th	Isabel Daughter of William Furnass of Cross Bank & Isabel his wife.
NOV. 10th	Mary Daughter of Robert Thompson of Sandbed & Mary his wife.
do. 15th	Sarah Daughter of Wm. Shaw of Wandal & Agnes his wife.
DECEMBr 1st	Mary Daughter of Thos. Shaw of Ellergill & Mary his wife.
do. 2d	John son of Eliz. Bellas Illegit.
do.	John son of Math. Hunter of Town & Eliz. his wife.
12th	Mary Daughter of John Morland of Stople Gate & Ann his wife.

1781. BAPTIZED.

DECEMBr 15th	John son of Robert Dawson of High Lane & Margaret his wife
do.	Mary Daughter of Thomas Thompson of Bents & Melly his wife
1782. † JAN 27th	Born Eliz. D. of Jno. & Ruth Chamberlain
FEB 1st	Henry son of William Hewetson of Town & Margt. his wife
do. 17th	Robert son of John Wilkinson of Coldbeck & Jane his wife
do. 27th	Joseph(1) & Agnes Children of Jno. Spedding of Town & Eliz. his wife
28th	(2) Wm. John, Edmund & George Children of Edmund Metcalf deceased late of Newhouse & Ann his widow.
MARCH 10th	James son of John Stubbs of Town & Eliz. his wife.
16th	Ann Daughter of Isabel Constantine Illegitimate.
do.	Eliz. Daughter of Robert Hutchinson of Newbegin & Ann his wife.
17th	Margaret Daughter of Willm. Taylor of Coldbeck & Margt. his wife.
MARCH 29	William son of Thomas Shaw of High Lane & Ann his wife.
APRIL 9th	James son of Geo. Murthwaite of Parrock Moor & Martha his wife
MAY 15	Eliz. Daughter of Eliz. Watson Illegitimate

---

(1) T. omits "Joseph &."
(2) T. omits "Wm. John, Edmund &" and has "George son of Isabel Metcalf of Newhouse, widow."

BIRTHS AND CHRISTNINGS.

1782. May 23d John son of Geo. Parkin of Town & Margaret his wife
26th Mary Daughter of James Taylor of Adamthwaite & Agnes his wife
June 1st Isabella D. of John Milner of Ashfield & Mary his wife
22d Peter S. of Isaac Handley of Town & Sibyl his wife
28th Richard S. of Henry Beck of Sandwath & Sarah his wife
† 30th Thos. son of Joseph Breeks of Hill & Ann his wife
July 7th Isabel D. of John Robinson of Wath & [T. Ann] his wife
13th Margaret D. of Wm. Bousfield of Town & Bella his wife
14th Thomas son of John Shaw of Artlegarth & Eliz. his wife.
23d Jane D. of John Petty of Wharton & Margt. his wife
Augt 3d John son of John Murrow of Newbegin & Ann* his wife
do. 10th Eliz. Daughter Thos. Hewetson of Hill & Eliz. his wife
† do. 17th of Richd. Birtle of & Isabel his wife
Sep. 15th [T. 17th] Wm. son of Jno. Nelson & Isabel his wife.
do. 27th Wm. son of Wm. Nelson of Town & Dorothy his wife
Oct. 19th Jane Daughter of Jas. Hill of Newbegin & Mary his wife
1782. Oct. 27 Isabel Daughter of John Wilson of Low Stennerskugh & Mary his wife
Nov. 3d Christr. son of John Hastewell of Piperhole & Ann his wife
do. Isabel D. of Robert Metcalf of Newbegin & Agnes his wife
do. 24 William son of James Fawcet of Murthwaite & Margt. his wife
do. Isabel Daughter of Willm. Brunskill & Ann his wife
do. Ann Daughter of Ann Banks Illegitimate
Nov. 29th Margaret Daughter of William Eleotson of Scarsykes & Agnes his wife born the 27 Day of March
Decembr 21st Ann Daughter of William Fawcet of Murthwaite & Agnes his wife

1783.

1783. Jan 17 Mary Daughter [T. Mathew son] of Anthony Birtle of Low Stennerskugh & Mary his wife
do. 23d William son of William Metcalf of Town & Mary his wife
do. Susan [T. Margt.] Daughter of Thomas Kirkbride [T. of Bleaflat] & Jane his wife

* "Mary" crossed out.

BIRTHS AND CHRISTNINGS.

do. 26 William son of Thomas Stubbs of Town & Isabel his wife
do. 31st John son of Joseph Birtle of Artlegarth & Jennet his wife
FEB 8th Margt. Daughter of Thos. Hunter of Fellend & Ann his wife
do. 15th Abraham son of Thos. Hastewell of Fell end & Mary(1) his wife
do. 16th James son of Mathew Hunter of Town & Elizabeth his wife
1783. MARCH 1st Ann Daughter of Richd. Atkinson of Town & Mary his wife
MAY 2d Alice(2) [T. Margt.] Daughter of Robert Shaw of Coldkeld & Margt. his wife
JULY 5th Margt. D. of Henry & Agnes [T. Isabel] Bousfield
JULY 9 Thomas son of John Morland of Stoophill Gate & Ann his wife
do. 25 Margaret D. of Mic. Robinson of Street & Agnes his wife
AUGt 4 . Isabel D. of Thos. Nelson of Town & Eliz. his wife
SEP 13th Eliz. Daughtr. of Geo. Fawcet of Wreagreen & Eliz. his wife
do. 18 Agnes D. of Henry Perkins of Lockholme & Ruth his wife
do. 20 Thos. son of James Morland of Town & Isabel
OCT 2(3) his wife
OCT 12 James son of Math. Ward of Dubbs & Agnes his wife
do. James son Jno. Stubbs of Town & Eliz. his wife. Pauper
do. Wm. son of John Nelson of Edis . & Isabel his wife
do. 26 Susanna Daughter of Thos. Kirkbride of Bleaflat & Jane his wife
Nov. 9th Eliz. Daughter of Robert Dawson of Freer Bottom & Margaret [T. Isabel] his wife
do. 25th Jacob son of Christr. Rennison of Townhead & Agnes his wife
do. 30th Sarah D. of Thos. Thompson of Brackenber & Ann his wife
DECEMBr 4th Eliz. D. of Thos. Shaw of High Lane & Ann his wife
1783. DECEM 10th [T. 15] Isabel Daughter of John Taylor of Adamthwaite & Hannah his wife.
do. 27 Sarah Daughter of Richard Parkin of Bowberhead & Isabel(4) his wife.
do. 31st John son of John Milner of Ashfield & Mary his wife

BAPTIZED 1784.

JAN 6 Peggy Daughter of Joseph Udal of Weesdale & Allis his wife

---

(1) Blank in T.
(2) "Isabel" scratched out.
(3) T. omits "Oct 2."
(4) Blank in T.

BIRTHS AND CHRISTNINGS.

† JAN 6	Thos. S. of Mic. Knewstubb & Eliz. his wife
JAN 17th	Eliz. Daughter of Mr. John Robinson Schoolmaster & Isabel his wife
JAN 25	Hannah D. of Wm. Gibson and Elizabeth his wife
do. 31st	Deborah Daughter of Robert Raw of Uldal & Ann his wife
FEB 12	Rachel Daughtr. of James Udal of Lockholme & Eleanor his wife
do.	Nanny Daughter of Wm. Eleotson of Scarsykes & Agnes his wife
do. 29th	Wm. son of Elizabeth Burton Illegit: Paup.
MAR 9	Born(1) Mary(2) D. of Jno. Chamberlain of Greenside & Ann(2) his wife
MAR 27	Jane Daughter of John Crosthwaite of Intake & [T. Agnes] his wife
AP. 7th	Mary Daughter of John Stubbs of Town & Mary his wife
24th	Alice Daughter of John Howgill of Adamthwaite & Margt. his wife
MAY 1st	Henry son of Willm. Hewetson of Banks & Martha his wife
MAY 6th	Sarah Daughter of Henry Hunter of Roathy Bridge & Ann his wife
16th	Margaret Daughter John Brunskill of Town & Agnes his wife
1784. JUNE 27	Ann Daughter of John Birtle of Dovingill & Dinah his wife
AUGt 3d	Peter S. of Robert Hutchinson of Newbegin & Ann his wife
do. 8th	Robert s. of Robt. Thompson of Sandbed & Mary his wife
do. 25th	Ann D. of Robert Chamberlain of Town & Mary his wife
SEP. 10	John son of William Furnace of High Stannerskugh & Isabel his wife
do. 26	Isabel Daughter of John Wilkinson of Coldbeck & Jane his wife
OCT 16th	Thomas son of Henry Bousfield of Town & Agnes his wife
do. 26th	Mally Daughter of James Hill of Newbegin & Mary his wife
do. 27th	[T. Mary Daughter] of Geo. Parkin of Town & Margt. his wife
do. 28th	John son of Jane Taylor

(1) "Born" omitted in T.
(2) Originally "Ruth" in both places. T. has "Mary" and "Ann."

BIRTHS AND CHRISTNINGS.

† Oct 29th	Anthony son of Thomas Wharton of Gilber & Margt. his wife, late Shaw

Baptized 1785.

Jan 16	Rachel D. of Thomas Stubbs of Town & Isabel his wife
do.	Ann D. of Richard Furnace of Crosbank & Eliz. his wife
Mar 1st	Stephen son of Thos. Fawcet of Foggy Gill & Ann his wife
do.	[T. Ann] Daughter of John Morland & Ann his wife
April 10th	Margaret D. of Wm Brunskill of Wandale & [T. Ann] his wife
do.	Math. son of Joseph Birtle of Lytheside & Jennet his wife
do. 16th	Sarah D. of Thomas Rennison of Tranmire & Isabel his wife
17th	Jonathon son of Robert Fothergill & Mary his wife
1785. May 15	Robert son of Robert Metcalf and Agnes his wife
do.	Thomas son of James Taylor of Wandale & [T. Isabel] his wife
26th	Joseph son of Thos. Thompson of Newbegin & Melly his wife
June 5th	Stephen son of William Bousfield of Town and Isabel his wife
do. 12th	Richd. son of Wm. Hewetson of Town & Margt.* his wife
do. 14th	Margt. Daughtr. of John Fawcet of Greenside & Alice his wife
do. 22d	Thomas son Thos. Metcalf of Browfoot & Ann his wife
July 10th	William [T. 19th Thomas] son of Wm. Potter & Ann his wife
Augt 14	Thomas son of Anth. Preston of Bowderdale & Isabel his wife
Sep 3d	Jonathon son of John Shaw of Brounber & [T. Mary] his wife
Oct. 10th	Mary Daughter of John Warcop of Newbegin & Ann his wife
Nov. 20th P:	James son of John Bell Dancing Master & Mary his wife
do.	Ann Daughter of Thomas Alderson & [T. Isabel] his wife

Baptized 1786.

** Jan 8th	Thomas son of John Crossthwaite of Intake & his wife
do. 18th P	Thomas son of John Hastewell of Low Stannerskugh & Ann his wife
do. 22d	Thomas son of James Udal of Crossbank & Eleanor his wife
do. 28th	Robert son of Thomas Shaw of Newbegin & Ann his wife

* "Isabel" crossed out. "Margaret" in T.
** There seems to be no T. of Baptisms for 1786.

BIRTHS AND CHRISTNINGS.

1786. Feb. 3d William son of Thomas Nelson of Town & Elizabeth his wife

do. 12th William son of John Nelson of Town & Jane his wife

do. 26th George son of George Parkin of Town & Margaret his wife

Mar 4th Edward son of Robert Raw of Ulgill in the parish of Sedbergh & Ann his wife

do. 23d John son of Henery Beck of Sandwath & Sarah his wife

Apr. William son of Wm. Preston of Tranmire and his wife

Apr. Sarah Daughter of John Taylor of Adamthwaite & Hannah his wife

May 6 Mary D. of Isaac Handley of Town & Sibyl his wife

May Isabel Daughter of Richd. Furnace of Low Stannerskugh & Eliz. his wife

do. 20th Ralph son of Mic: Robinson of Town & Ann his wife

May 23 Mary D. of Math. Haygarth of Murthwaite & Margt. his wife

June 18 Thos. son of John Shaw of Weesdale & Eliz. his wife

July 6 John son of Thomas Perkins of Flass & Ann his wife (late Perkins)

July 23d Elizabeth Daughter of John Nelson of Edes & Isabel his wife (late Smith)

July 30 Ann Daughter of Willm. Metcalf of Town Labourer & Mary his wife (late Chambley)

Augt 6 Jane Daughter of Robt. Fawcet of Street Taylor & Eleanor his wife (late Hastewel)

do. Thos. son of John Moister of Street Labourer & Ann his wife (late Hutchinson)

Sep. 8th Richard son of Robert Thompson of Low Stannerskugh & Mary his wife (late Birtel)

do. 9th Margaret D. of Thos. Thompson of Newbegin & Melly his wife (late Shaw)

Oct. 5 Sarah D. of Robert Chamberlain Shoe Maker & Mary his wife (late Rennison)

do. 8th Ann D. of Richd. Brown of Rig-end & Margt. his wife (late Metcalf)

1786. Nov. 12 Robert son of John Howgill of Crossbank & Margt. his wife (late Rennison)

do. 14th Isabel D. of Alderson Illegit.

BIRTHS AND CHRISTNINGS.

1786. Nov 20th Christopher son of James Hill Cowper & Mary his wife (late Breeks

BAPTIZED 1787.

JAN 11th Eliz. Daughter of John Morland of Stoophill Gate & Ann his wife (late Dent

do. Mary Daughter of John Birtle [T. Labourer] of Dovingill & Dinah his wife (late Helton

JAN 20th John son of Anthony Preston [T. Farmer] of Bowderdale & Isabel his wife (late Overend

JAN 27th John son of John Wharton of Coldbeck Innkeeper & Mary his wife late Gibson

FEB. 11th Robert son of Robert Hutchinson [T. Farmer] of Newbegin & Ann his wife (late Brunskill

MAR: 3 Thos. son of Wm. Furnace [T. Farmer] of High Stannerskugh & Isabel his wife (late Metcalf

MAR. 13th Ann D. of Henry Hunter [T. Yeomn.] of Street & Ann his wife (late Shaw

MAR. 18th Margt. D. of Robert Dawson [T. Farmer] of Fell-head & Margt. his wife (late Longstaff

APRIL 17th [T. Thos.] son of Thos. Alderson [T. Farmer] of Rig-end [T. and Isabel his wife late Farrer]

do. 18th Deborah Daug. of Thos. Fawcett [T. Labourer] of Greenslack & Ann his wife (late Hastwell

do. 19th Isabel Daughter of Thos. Fawcet of Hill & Margt. his wife late Burton

do. 22d Richd. son of John Wilson [T. Blacksmith] of Elmpot & Mary his wife late Parkin

† MAY 9th John son of John Fothergilll of Greenside & Sarah his wife (late Parkin

MAY 27th Born MAY 14 Christr. s. of Richd. Dixon of Cawsey End [T. Yeoman] & Isabella his wife (late Rudd

do. 29th Ann D. of Robert Hunter of Street & Eliz. his wife (late Bowness

1787. JUNE 17th John s. of Willm. Bousfield of Town and Isabel his wife (late Shaw.

do. 23d Richd. s. of Willm. Gibson of Wath [T. Farmer] & Eliz. his wife (late Kirkbride.

BIRTHS AND CHRISTNINGS.

July 1st — Isabel D. of Thos. Stubbs of Town [T. Carpinter] & Isabel his wife (late Metcalf.

do. 15th — Eleanor D. of Robert Metcalf [T. Farmer] of Greenside & Agnes his wife (late Richardson.

do. 15th — Dorathy D. of Anthony Robinson Innkeeper & Ruth his wife (late Harbet.

† Augt — ·of John Shaw of Wreagreen & Eleanor his wife late Adger.

Oct 30 — Ann D. of Robt. Fawcett of Streetside Taylor & Eleanor his wife late Hastwell.

Nov 18th — Stephen son of Christopher Fawcett of Foggygill & Margt. his wife (late Foster.

do. — Eliner* Daughter of John Warcop Taylor & Ann his wife (late Winder.

Dec 9th — William son [T. Sarah Daughter] of John Taylor [T. Farmer] of Clouds & Hannah his wife late Addison

do. 16th — Mary Daughter of Joseph Birtle of Bleaflat & Jennet his wife late Constantine.

1788. Jan 18 — born Isabel Howgill Daughter of Ann Howgill Illegetmet.

1788. **Baptized.**

Jan 10 — James & Willm. sons of Henry Hebden Shoe Maker [T. Cordwainer] & Eliz. his wife (late Fothergill.

Feb 9th — Isabel Daughter of Robert Raw of Murthwaite & Ann his wife (late Banks.

do. 17th — Wm. son of Thos. Thompson of Newbegin Pauper [T. Labourer] & Melly his wife (late Shaw.

do. 25th — Christr. son of James Hill Cooper & Mary his wife (late Breeks.

Mar 28 — Thos. & Ann son & Daughter of Thomas Shaw [T. Innkeeper] of Newbegin & Ann his wife [T. late Todd]

do. 29 — Thos. son of William Hewetson Carpinter & Margt. his wife (late Waddington.

1788. April 26 — John son of Mic. Knewstub [T. Yeoman] & Eliz. his wife (late Beck.

---

* Originally "Ann" as in T.

BIRTHS AND CHRISTNINGS.

June 22d	Isabel Daughter of Wm. Parkin [T. Farmer] & Eleanor his wife (late Banks).
do. 25th	Richd. son of John Noble Innkeeper & Agnes his wife (late Potter.
do. 29th	Mary D. of Agnes Stubbs illegit. P. [T. Paup.]
† July 18th	William son of Jno. Hastwel Pauper & Ann his wife (late Rennison.
do. 27th [T. 21st]	Isabel Daughter of Wm. Shaw [T. Innkeeper] & Agnes his wife late Raw.
do.	John son of Willm. Fawcett Butcher & Eleanor his wife late Hunter.
† Augt 1st	John son of William Fawcett, and Sarah his wife late Hewetson.
Augt 3d	Isaac son of Richd. Teasdale [T. Farmer] of Low Lane & Dinah his wife (late
Augt 10th	John son of Willm. Morros [T. Farmer] of Brownber & Jane his wife late Dawson.
do. 17th	Eliz. Daughter of John Brunskill Clogger & Agnes his wife (late Rowlandson.
do. 20	Isabel Daughter of John Morland [T. Yeoman] of Stoop-hillgate & Ann his wife late Dent
Sep. 15th	Eliz. Daughter of Jno. Wilkinson Mason & Jane his wife (late
do. do.	[T. William s.] of William Fawcet [T. Farmer] & Agnes his wife [T. late Whitehead]
Oct 8th	Christr. son of Henry Beck [T. Yeoman] of Artlegarth & Sarah his wife late Gregson.
do. 12	Isabel Daughter of John Shaw Labourer & Eliz. his wife late Peacock.
do. 14	Eliz. Margt. Daughter of Mr. John Robinson Schoolmaster & Isabel his wife [T. late Shaw]
do. 26	Mary Daughter of James Whaley Taylor & Mary his wife (late Tweedal.
Nov. 7th	Willm. son of Anth. Preston [T. Farmer] of Bowderdale & Isabel his wife (late Overend.
do. 9th	Bap. Edwd. Allison from America at the age of [T. aged 9 years]

BIRTHS AND CHRISTNINGS.

Nov. 9th Baptized James Allison from America at the age of [T. aged 7 years]

Dec. 13th Thomas son of John Kirkbride [T. Farmer] of Lockholme & Margaret his wife (late Earnest.

1789. Baptized.

Feb 10th Mary Daughter of John Nelson Waller and Isabel his wife (late Smith.

do. 11th Mary Daughter of Robert Hunter of Streetside [T. Yeoman] & Eliz. his wife late Bowness.

do. Eleanor Daughter of Thos. Fawcett of Green Slack [T. Farmer] & Ann his wife (late Hastwell.

March 11th Eliz. D. of Robert Dawson of Freerbottom [T. Farmer] & Margt. his wife (late Longstaff.

Mar. 22 Agnes Daughter of Thos. Stubbs [T. of Town] Carpinter & Isabel his wife (late Metcalf.

do. Mary Daughter of Richd. Fawcett [T. of Town] weaver & Eliz. his wife (late [T. Dobson]

April 4 Eliz. Daughter of Robert Chamberlain Shoe Maker [T. Cordwainer] & Mary his wife (late Rennison.

do. 11th [T. Mary] Daughter of Robert Thompson of Low Stannerskugh [T. Farmer] & Mary his wife (late Birtle.

do. 20th Dinah Daughter of John Birtle of Clouds [T. Farmer] & Dinah his wife late [T. Helton] Pauper

May 3d Henry son of Wm. Brunskill [T. of Wandale, Yeoman] and Ann his wife (late Fawcett.

do. 10th Anthony son of Willm. Gibson of Wath [T. Farmer] & Eliz. his wife (late Kirkbride.

do. 21st Robert son of Isaac Handley of Town [T. Yeoman] & Sibyl his wife (late Hunter.

† do. 30th Thos. son of Mary of Town

June 7th Margaret Daughter of Richard Brown of Rig End [T. Farmer] & Margt. his wife (late Metcalf.

do. John son of Wm. Bousfield of Lockholme [T. Farmer] & Isabel his wife (late Shaw.

Sep 6th Alice Daughter of James Simpson Paup. Dealer in Pots & Jennet his wife (late Taylor.

BIRTHS AND CHRISTNINGS.

SEP. 12 Richd. son of Willm. Furnass of High Stannerskugh & Isabel his wife (late Metcalf.

1789. OCT 15th Richard son of Richard Birtle Labourer & Isabel his wife (late [T. Robinson]

do. Isabel Daughter of Anth. Birtle Labourer & Mary [T. Margt.] his wife (late [T. Hutchinson]

NOV. 21st John s. of John Kirkbride [T. Farmer] & Margt. his wife [T. late Earnest]

DEC. 1st Sarah Daughter of Ruth Kitchen Ill.

do. 5th Mary D. of John Stubbs Shoe Maker [T. Cordwainer] & Isabel his wife (late Fawcett.

1790.

FEB. 6th Richard son of Thos. Alderson of Rigg End & Isabel his wife (late Farrer.

do. 21st John son of Ann Richardson Illegit.

do. 24 Isabel Daughter of Jonathon Metcalf of Beck Stones & Eliz. his wife (late Graham.

do. 27 Uzzi son of Mic. Robinson Black Smith & Agnes his wife late [T. Hemsley]

MAR 18th Willm. son of John Noble Innkeeper & Agnes his wife (late Potter.

APRIL 9th Margt. Daughter of Robt. Metcalf of Greenside & Agnes his wife (late Richardson.

do. 28th Agnes Daughter of Richd Furnass* & Eliz. his wife late Rennison.

do. 30th Margt. Daughter of Mic. Knewstup [T. of Kilnmire] & Eliz. his wife (late Beck.

MAY 25 Margt. Daughter of Joseph Birtle P. of Bleaflat [T. Paup.] & Jennet his wife (Constantine.

JUNE 22d John son of Robert Raw of Tarn & Ann his wife (late Banks.

do. 20th [T. 23d] Edward son of William Shaw Innkeeper & Agnes his wife (late Raw.

do. 26th Anthony son of Robert Dent of Sandbed & Mary his wife (late Holme.

---

* "Birtle" crossed out. T. has "Furnass."

BIRTHS AND CHRISTNINGS.

JUNE 27th Sarah D. of Thos. Shaw Innkeeper & Ann his wife (late Todd.

JULY 1st Ann Daughter* of Thos. Thompson [T. Labourer] of Town & Melly his wife late Shaw P.

AUGt 10th Mary Daughter of Thos. Taylor [T. Labourer] of Town & Eliz. his wife (late Spooner.

1790. AUGt 15th Jane Daughter of Robert Dawson of Freerbottom & Margt. his wife (late Longstaff.

do. 16th Ann Daughter of Eliz. Adamthwaite Illegit. P.

do. 20th Anna Maria D. of James Fawcett P. of Greenslack & his wife (late

SEP 1st Thos son of Joseph Shaw of Town & Isabel his wife (late Fothergill.

NOV. 9th Jennet D. of Richd. Tunstall of Crossbank & Isabella his wife (late Robinson.

DECEM 27th Thos. son of John Nelson of Brackenber & Isabel his wife (late Smith.

1791.

JAN 1st Willm. son of Willm. Gibson of Wath & Elizabeth his wife (late Kirkbride.

do. 8th James Fawcett son of Robt. Hunter of Streetside & Eliz. his wife (late Bowness.

do. 20th Leonard [T. John] son of Anthony Preston of Bowderdale & Isabel his wife (late Overend.

MAR 19th George son of John Morland of Stoophill Gate & Ann his wife (late Dent.

do. 20th Jane Daughter of William Fothergill of Bleaflat & Jennet his wife (late Hutchinson.

APRIL 19th William son of Mr. John Robinson Schoolmaster & Isabella his wife (late Shaw.

do. 20th Elizabeth [T. Ann] Daughter of Isaac Handley of Town & Sibyl his wife (late Hunter.

do. 26th Elizh. Daughter of James Hill of Newbegin Cooper & Mary his wife (late Breaks.

---

* "Jos. son" crossed out. T. has "Ann."

BIRTHS AND CHRISTNINGS.

May 1st Thomas son of William Murros of Brounber & Jane his wife (late Dawson.

do. 8th Eliz. Daughter of William Brunskill of Wandale & Ann his wife (late Fawcett.

June 9th [T. Anthony son] of Richard Birtle of Crooks & Isabel his wife (late .

1791. June 10th John son of John Taylor of Adamthwaite & Hannah his wife (late Addison.

July 1st Thomas son of Robt. Fawcet Tayler of Street & Eleanor his wife (Hastwell.

Augt 24th John son of John Wilson of Elmpot Blacksmith & Mary his wife (late Parkin.

Augt 28th Robert son of John Warcop Taylor & Ann his wife (late Winder.

Septem 7th Mary Daughter of Geo.* Whitehead of Kelleth & Ruth his wife (late Fawcett.

Sep 24 Ann Daughter of William Potter of Green & Ann his wife (late Dennison.

Oct. 23d William son of Thos. Stubbs Carpinter & Isabel his wife (late Metcalf.

Nov 12th John son of Robert Fawcett of Ellerhill & Isabel his wife (Hastwel.

do. 20th John son of Thos. Milner Mason & Mary his wife (late Knewstup.

Decem 4 Sarah Daughter of Thos. Alderson of Rig-End & Isabel his wife (late Farrer.

do. 29th Isabel Daughter of John Birtle of Weesdale & Sibyl his wife (late Spooner.

1792.

Mar. 17th William son of John Hutchinson of Lytheside & Alice his wife (late Fothergill.

do. 18th Mary Daughter of Willm. Fawcett of Town Butcher & Eleanor his wife (late Hunter.

do. 24 Frances Daughter of Robert Hutchinson of Newbegin & Ann his wife (late Brunskill.

---

* "Thos." crossed out. T. has "George."

BIRTHS AND CHRISTNINGS.

1792. BAPTIZED.

APRIL 8th	Eliz. Daughter of Richd. Fawcett weaver & Eliz. his wife (late Dobson.
do. 10th	Eliz. Daughter of John Shaw of Town & Elizabeth his wife (late Peacock Pauper P.
do. 12th	Ann Daughter of Ja'. Simpson Tinker & Jennet his wife (late Taylor Paup.
do.' 22d	Margaret Daughter of Jonathon Fothergill of Coldbeck & Mary his wife late Richardson.
do. 29th	Robert son of Robert Dawson of Freerbottom & Margt. his wife late Longstaff.
do. do.	Mary Daughter of Fawcett Hunter of Waingarth & Ann his wife (late Robinson.
MAY 20th	Mary Daughter of Ann Richardson Illegi: Pauper.
do. 26th	Peter son of Thos. Shaw of Greenside & Ann his wife (late Todd.
JUNE 24	Agnes Daughter of Robert Metcalf Innkeeper & Agnes his wife (late Richardson.
JULY 1st	Robert son of Jonathan Metcalf of Beckstones & Eliz. his wife (late Graham.
do. 8th	Thos. son of William Shaw of Street & Agnes his wife (late Raw.
AUGt 19th	Ann Daughter of James Whaley Innkeeper at Coldbeck & Mary his wife (late Tweedal.
do. 28th	John son of John Morland of Stoophill Gate & Ann his wife (late Dent.
OCT 4th	Hugh son of William Furnass of High Stannerskugh & Isabel his wife (late Metcalf.
OCT. 21st	Eliz. Daughter of Robert Chamberlain & Mary his wife (late Rennison.
OCT. 28th	Rachel Daughter of John Stubbs P. [T. of Town] & Isabel his wife (late Fawcett)

1792. BAPTIZED.

NOV. 12th	Henry son of Michael Knewstupp and Elizabeth his wife (late Beck.
do. 13th	Isabel Daughter of Robert Hunter of Streetside & Eliz. his wife (late Bowness.

BIRTHS AND CHRISTNINGS.

Nov. 30th	Margaret Daughter of Henry Beck of Artlegarth & Sarah his wife (late Gregson.
Decem 15th	William son of Robert Raw of Tarn & Ann his wife (late Banks.
do. 26th	Margaret Daughter of Joseph Shaw of Town & Isabel his wife (late Fothergill.
1793.	
Feb. 15th	Mary Daughter of Willm. Winder of Scar and Nancy his wife (late Guy.
Mar. 23d	John son of Thos. Fawcett of Greenslack & Ann his wife (late Hastwell.
do. 26th	Jonathan son of Willm. Brunskill of Wandal & Ann his wife (late Fawcett.
do. 27th	Thos. son of Thos. Airey Cowper & Mary his wife (late Ireland.
April 1st	Anthony son of Anthony Preston of Bowderdale & Isabel his wife (late Overend.
do. 15th	James [T. Robert] son of Robert Fawcett Tailor & Eleanor his wife (late Hastwell.
May 4th	Eleanor Daughter of Jas. Haygarth Innkeeper & Mary his wife (late Rennison.
do. 31st	Agnes Daughter of William Fothergill of Bleaflat & Jennet his wife (late Hutchinson.
June 1st	William son of William Gibson of Wath & Eliz. his wife (late Kirkbride.
1793. Baptized.	
July 21st	Mary Daughter of Richd. Brown of Rigend & Margt. his wife (late Metcalf.
do. 22d	John son of Ralph Milner of Bowderdale & [T. Eliz.] his wife (late Elyetson.
do. 25th	Mathew son of Hanah Birtle of Town illegitimate Paup.
Augt 30	Richd. son of John Birtle of Greenside and Sybil his wife (late Spooner.
Sep. 14th	Benjamin son of Thos. Thompson of Town & Melly his wife (Shaw Pauper.
do. 28th	Elizabeth Daughter of Thomas Hunter of Elmpot and Ann his wife (late Hutchinson.

BIRTHS AND CHRISTNINGS.

Oct. 12th William son John Stubbs of Backlane & Isabel his wife Paup. (late Fawcett.

Nov. 8th Baptized Eliz. Daughter of Thomas Alderson of Rigend & [T. Margt.] his wife (late Farrer.

Decem 26th Baptized Thos. son of Thos. Milner of Greenside & Mary his wife (late Knewstup.

1794.

Feb 21st George son of George Parkin of Town Cordwainer and Margaret his wife (late Tweedal.

April 4th Ann Daughter of John Thompson of Crooksbeck & Margt. his wife (late Hunter.

April 5th Mary Daughter of Robert Shaw of Low Stannerskugh & Margt. his wife (late Robinson.

do. 17th Margaret Daughter of Thomas Knewstupp of Hill & Nancy his wife (late Hebblethwaite.

1794. Baptized.

June 11th Jeffery son of Henry Hebden Cordwainer & Eliz. his wife (late Fothergill.

Augt 14th Margt. Daughter of Willm. Murros of Greenside & Jane his wife (late Dawson.

do. 17th Margt. Bousfield Daughter of Edmund Hodgson of Backlane & Elizabeth his wife (late Bousfield.

do. 18th [T. Elizabeth] Daughter of Richard Fawcett weaver & Eliz. his wife (late Dobson.

do. 20th [T. Jane] Daughter of Willm. Winder of High Lane & Nancy his wife (late Guy.

do. 23d Thos. son of Thos. Shaw of Greenside & Ann his wife (late Todd.

Sepbr 17th Robt. son of John Warcop of Town Tailor & Ann his wife (late Winder.

Oct 5th George son of William Shaw of Street & Agnes his wife (late Raw.

do. 7th William son of James Haygarth Innkeeper & Mary his wife (late Rennison.

Nov. 5 Barbara Daughter of Jonathan Metcalf of Beck Stones & Eliz. his wife (late Graham.

BIRTHS AND CHRISTNINGS.

Nov. 5 — Thomas son of Stephen Dent of Townhead and Mary his wife (late Turner.

do. 9th — Agnes Daughter of Jonathan Ward of Brownber & Agnes his wife (late Thornborrow.

* 1795.

Jan 18 — Margaret Daughter of James Hill of Newbegin and Mary his wife (late Breeks.

do. — William son of Geo. Fawcett of Murthwaite & Sarah his wife (late Whitfield.

Feb. 1st — Born & baptized Jeffery Bowness son of Robert Hunter of Streetside and Elizabeth his wife (late Bowness.

Feb. 7th — Richard Illegitime son of Eliz. Atkinson.

March 27th — Eliz. Daughter of Thomas Airey Cooper and Mary his wife (late Ireland.

Baptized.

April 11th — Michael son of John Nelson of Lowlane and Isabel his wife (late Smith.

May 8th — Ann Daughter of Robt. Fawcett Tailor and Eleanor his wife (late Hastwell.

do. do. — Mary Daughter of James Fawcett of Newhouse and (late

** do. 20th — son of Robert Fawcet of Streetside

June 3d — Eleanor, Daughter of Robt. Raw of Tarn & Ann his wife (late Banks.

do. 8th — Eliz. Daughter of Richd. Furnass of Bleaflat & Eliz. his wife (late Rennison.

do. 14th — John son of John Rennison of Lytheside & Eliz. his wife (late

do. 19th — Isabel Daughter of Thomas Alderson of Rigend & Isabel his wife (late Farrer.

do. 21st — Miles son of John Morland of Stoophillgate & Ann his wife (late Dent.

July 26th — Agnes Daughter of Thomas Knewstupp of Hill & Agnes his wife (late Heblethwaite.

---

* The Transcript for 1795 is missing.
** This entry subsequently crossed out.

BIRTHS AND CHRISTNINGS.

JULY 26th of James Fawcett of Newbegin & Mary his wife (late

AUGt 1st James son of Robert Dent of Sandbed & Mary his wife (late Holme.

AUGt 8th Ann Daughter of George Alderson of Tarnhouse & Isabel his wife (late Adamthwaite.

SEPt 7th Elizabeth Daughter of Charles Hastwell of Ellerhill & Deborah his wife (late Dixon.

do. 28th Anne Daughter of Anthony Preston of Bowderdale & Isabel his wife (late Overend.

do. do. Agnes Daughter of Thomas Hunter of Bowberhead & Ann his wife (late Hutchinson.

OCT. 4th Ann Daughter of Robert Metcalf of Bleaflat & Agnes his wife (late Richardson.

1795. BAPTIZED.

OCT. 25th Mary Daughter of James Haygarth of Town Innkeeper & Mary his wife late Rennison.

DECr 7th William son of Thos. Taylor of Town & Elizabeth his wife (late Spooner.

DECr 17th Richard illegitimate Child of Margaret Atkinson of Town.

do. 25th Margaret Daughter of John Thompson of Crooksbeck & Margaret his wife (late Hunter.

1796.

JAN 17th Isabella Daughter of Thos. Milner of Greenside & Mary his wife (late Knewstupp.

FEB 3d [T. John] son of John Petty of Town & [T. Eliz.] his wife (late Fothergill.

MAR. 15 Henry son of William Brunskill of Wandale & Ann his wife (late Fawcett.

† do. 19th Anthony son of Stephen Dent of Dovingill & Margaret his wife (late Parkin.

do. 20th Math. son of George Caygill of Hegdale Lane & [T. Isabel] his wife (late

do. 28 Ann Daughter of James Rennison of Studfold & Hannah his wife (late Harrison

BIRTHS AND CHRISTNINGS.

April 20th	Henry son of James Fothergill of Lockholme & Margt. his wife (late Thompson.
June 24th	Eleanor Daughter of Thos. Hastwell of Foggygill & Phœbe his wife (late Chamberlane.
Sep 6th	Margt. Daughter of Robt. Wilson of Weesdale & Isabel his wife (late Shearman.
do. 29th	Mary Daughter of Thos. Hunter of Bowberhead & Ann his wife (late Hutchinson.

Baptized.

Oct. 16th	Thomas son of Septimus Robinson of Town & Rachel his wife (late Atkinson.
do. 29th	Anthony son of Thos. Knewstupp of Low Lane [T. of Hill] & Ann his wife (late Heblethwaite.
do. 30th	Richd. son of Richard Jackson of Brownber & Sarah his wife (late Bousfield.
Nov 23d	Born & baptized Robert son of Robt. Hunter of Streetside & Elizabeth his wife (late Bowness.
†	of Thos. Stubbs of Town Carpinter & Isabel his wife (late Metcalf.
Decem 7th	William son of George Jackson of Weesdale & his wife (late Stewardson.
	of John Shaw of Town and Elizabeth his wife (late Peacock.
1797.	Stephen son of Robt. Hutchinson and Ann his wife, late Brunskill.
† Feb 10th	Jonathan son of William Alderson of Wandale & Eliz. his wife (late Shaw.
Mar 28th	Ann Daughter of William Winder of High Lane & Nancy his wife (late Guy.
April 10th	Margaret Daughter of Mary Dent [T. of Town] Illegitimate
May 1st	Richd. son of John Birtle of Tranmire & Sybil his wife (late Spooner.
do. 10th	Eleanor Daughter of Robt. Fawcett of Streetside Tailor & Eleanor his wife (late Hastwel.
do. 17th	Uzwald son of Thos. Airey Cooper & Mary his wife (late Ireland.

BIRTHS AND CHRISTNINGS.

JUNE 17th — John son of James Mkinsey & Mary his wife (late Hodgson.

do. — Mary Daughter of Thomas Shaw of Greenside & Ann his wife (late Todd.

* † JULY 16 — John son of James M'Kinsey Tinker and Mary his wife (late Hodgson.

1797. BAPTIZED.

JULY 31 — Henry son of Stephen Dent of Dovingill & Margt. his wife (late Parkin [T. Perkins].

AUGt 6th — Mary Daughter of William Murros of Greenside & Jane his wife (late Dawson.

AUGt 21st — John son of William Shaw of Street & Agnes his wife (late Raw.

AUGt 25th — Robert son of Robt. Raw of Tarn & Ann his wife (late Banks.

SEP. 20th — Math. Son of Geo. Fawcett of Narthwaite and Sarah his wife (late Whitfield.

OCT. 27th — John son of Charles Hastwel of Ellerhill [T. Ellergill] & Dorathy his wife (late Dixon.

do. — Eliz. Daughter of Jonathan Metcalf Innkeeper & Eliz. his wife (late Graham.

Baptized OCTr 28th, Born 13th of OCTr — Agnes Daur. of the Revd. John Robinson, School-master & Mary his wife (late Raisbeck.

NOV. 19th — Thos. son of Thos. Parkinson of Intack & Agnes his wife late Hodgson.

DECEM 7th — Jane Daughter of James Fawcett of Newbegin & his wife late

do. — Thos. son of Thos. Taylor of Town & Eliz. his wife (late Spooner.

1798.

JAN 17th — Jane Daughter of Thos. Alderson of Low Stannerskugh & Isabel his wife late Farrer.

FEB 4th — Martin son of Robt. Wilson of Weesdale & Isabel his wife late Shearman.

1798. MAR 28 — Thos. son of Thos. Ireland Cordwainer & Ann his wife (late Hutchinson.

---

* Subsequently crossed out.

BIRTHS AND CHRISTNINGS.

APRIL 12 — William son of James Haygarth of Town & Mary his wife (late Rennison.

MAY 1st — James son of George & Margaret Jackson of Weesdale & (late Stewardson.

do. 2d — Elizabeth Daughter of Robert Hunter of Streetside & Elizabeth his wife (late Bowness.

do. 9th — [T. Mary Daughter] of William & Elizabeth Alderson of Wandale (late Shaw.

MAY 18th — Jane Daughter of Thomas Fawcett of Greenslack & Ann his wife (late Hastwel.

AUG 6th — John son of Thos. Airey of Town Cooper & Mary his wife (late Ireland.

SEP 14th — Agnes Daughter of Agnes Birtle of Adamthwaite Illegitimate.

do. 29th — Agnes Daughter of Thos. Hunter of Bowberhead & Ann his wife (late Hutchinson.

DECEMr 18 — Margt. Daughter of Thos. Harrison of Bowderdale & Mary his wife (late Barnett.

DECr. 19th — Henry Son of the Revd. John Robinson, Schoolmaster, and Mary his wife (late Raisbeck.

do. 30th — Ann Daughter of Richard Fawcett Weaver & [T. Elizabeth] his wife late [T. Dobson]

1799.

JAN. 6th — Eliz. Daughter of John Udal Miller & Ann his wife (late Birtle.

do. 9th — Thos. & Agnes Twins to Willm. & Ann* Winder of High Lane.

1799. JAN 26th — Faithy Daughter of Stephen Dent of Dovingill & Margt. his wife (late Parkin.

FEB. 23d — Isabel Daughter of Robt. Fawcett of Streetside & Eleanor his wife late Hastwell.

MAR 6th — Elizabeth [T. Ann] Daughter of Robt. Raw of Tarn & Ann his wife (late Banks.

APRIL 17th — Margt. Daughter of Stephen Hunter of Bowberhead & Ruth his wife late Perkin.

---

* T. has "Ann his wife (late Guy."

BIRTHS AND CHRISTNINGS.

APRIL 23d John son of Wm. Furnass of Lockholme & Margt. his wife late Fothergill.

do. John son of Agnes Thompson of Sprintgill Illegitimate.

MAY 25th Margaret Daughter of John Hunter of Sprintgill & Mary his wife (late Wilson.

do. 26th Eliz. Daughter of Jno. Fawcett from Manchester & Ann his wife (late Shaw.

JUNE 1st Joseph son of John Birtle of Weesdale & Sibyll his wife (late Spooner.

JUNE 20th George son of Ann Nelson of Lowlane Illegit.

JULY 10th James son of Robt. Fothergill of Studfold & Eliz. his wife late Pearson.

† AUG 25 John son of James Hill of Newbiggin cooper & Mary his wife, late Breaks.

AUGt 25 Stephen son of Wm. Brunskill of Wandale & Ann his wife (late Fawcett.

do. 31st Margt. Daughter of John Fawcett of Greenside & Alice his wife (late Udal.

OCT 7th Isabel Daughter of Thos. Ireland Cordwainer & Ann his wife (late Hutchinson.

[T. do. 29th] Thos. son of Mathew Brown Tailor & Jennet his wife (late Birtle.

Nov 27th Joseph son of Henry Hugginson of Lytheside & Isabel his wife late Dodd.

do. 29th Robert son of George Fawcett of Coldkeld [T. Coldbeck] & Sarah his wife (late Harrison.

1799. DEC 2d Benjamin Son of Sarah Morland of Stoophill Gate.

do. 3d Agnes Daughter of Charles Hastwel of Ellerhill & Dorothy his wife (late Dixon.

Baptized DECr 6, Born Novr 27 } Henry, Son of the Revd. John Robinson, Schoolmaster, and Mary his wife (late Raisbeck.

do. 22 Elizabeth Daughter of Thos. Parkinson of Intake & Agnes his wife (late Hodgson.

do. 26th Ann Daughter of Richard Dixon of Cawsey End & Isabel his wife (late Rudd.

† DECEM 28 Eliz. Daughter of Jno. Udal & Ann his wife late Birtle.

BIRTHS AND CHRISTNINGS.

1800.

JAN 18th	Sarah Daughter of Robert Wilson of Weesdale & Isabel his wife late Shearman.
FEB. 1st	Isabel Daughter of Robt. Chamberlain Cordwainer & Mary his wife late Rennison.
do. 2d	John son of Eliz. Coupling Illegit.
do. 16th	George son of Richard Shaw Intake & Mary his wife (late Parkinson.
FEB 25	Mary Daughter of Septimus Robinson Cooper & Rachel his wife late Atkinson.
APRIL 1st	Agnes Daughter of Stephen Hunter of Bowberhead & Ruth his wife (late Perkins.
†	of James Robinson of Newbegin & his wife late
† APRIL 27th	Margaret Daughter of Thos. Shaw of Greenside & Ann his wife (late Todd.
1800. MAY 23d	Isabel Daughter of Thomas Airey Cooper & Mary his wife (late Ireland.
JUNE 29	Thomas son of Robt. Raw of Tarn & Ann his wife (late Banks.
do.	Mary Daughter of Jonathon Metcalf Innkeeper & Elizabeth his wife late Graham.
JULY 27th	Alice Daughter of Robert Hunter of Streetside & Elizabeth his wife (late Bowness.
*	of William Winder of High Lane & Nancy his wife late Guy.
OCT. 7th	Mary Daughter of Mathew Hunter of Murthwaite & Jane his wife (late Perkins.
do. 14th	Edward son of Thos. Brunskill of Fell End & Nanny his wife (late
NOV. 1st	Sarah Daughter of Thomas Harrison of Bowderdale & Mary his wife (late Barnet.
do. 4th	Ruth Daughter of Stephen Dent of Dovingill & Margt. his wife (late Perkins.

* This entry subsequently crossed out, also entered and crossed out in T.

BIRTHS AND CHRISTNINGS.

DECEMBr 15th Thos. son of Richd. Fawcett of Brackenber weaver & [T. Elizabeth] his wife late [T. Dobson]

do. 21st Margaret Daughter of Jno. Kirkbride of High Stannerskuth & Margaret his wife (late Earnest.

1801. JAN 25th Ruth Daughter of Thomas Milner of Greenside & Mary his wife (late Knewstupp.

FEB 6th Agnes Daughter of John Udal Miller & Ann his wife (late Birtle.

1801. MAY 8th Sarah Daughter of Thos. Hunter of Bouberhead & Ann his wife (late Hutchinson.

JUNE 30th Christopher son of Thos. Fawcett of Greenslack & Ann his wife late Hastwell.

JULY 1st Margaret Daughter of William Winder of High Lane & Nancy his wife late Guy.

JULY 1st Born and baptized Robert son of the Revd. John Robinson Schoolmaster and Mary his wife (late Raisbeck.

† DECr 11th Parkin* son of John & Sarah** Fothergill Greenside Yeoman.

OCT. 20th Jane Daughter of Robt. Wilson of Weesdale & Isabel his wife late Shearman.

NOV. 1st Ruth Daughter of Stephen Hunter of Lockholme & Ruth his wife (late Perkins.

NOV. 7th John son of Jno. Birtle of Lane in Weesdale & Sibyl his wife (late Spooner.

DECEMBr. 17th Mary Daughter of Robert Fawcett of Streetside Tailor & Eleanor his wife (late Hastwell.

do. 20th Thomas son of Thomas Thompson Cordwainer & Margaret his wife (late Thompson.

1802. JAN 14th Simon son of Christr. Alderson of Tarn House & Agnes his wife (late Wilson.

FEB. 4th Ann D. of Mathew Hunter [T. of Murthwaite] & Jane his wife [T. late Perkins]

FEB 25th Thos. son of John Murthwaite of Parrockmoor & his wife late Graham.

---

* Septimus crossed out.
** Margaret crossed out.

BIRTHS AND CHRISTNINGS.

MAR 7th Mary Daughter of John Dixon [T. of Town] & Eleanor his wife late Ewin.

do. 17th Sarah Daughter of James Rennison of Bouberhead & Hannah his wife (late Harrison.

1802. MAR 21st Math. son of John Hunter of Bouberhead & Ann his wife (late Rennison.

APR. 18th Eliz. Daughter of Thos. Ireland of Town Cordwainer & Ann his wife (late Hutchinson.

JULY 4th Agnes Daughter of Henry Hugginson of Lytheside & Isabel his wife (late Dodd.

do. 5th George son of Jno. Udal Miller & Ann his wife (late Birtle.

Richd. son of Thomas Airey Cooper & Mary his wife (late Ireland.

SEP 26 Mary Daughter of Thos. Parkinson of Intake & Agnes his wife late Hodgson.

do. Ann Daughter of Joseph Hunter of Wandale & Isabel his wife (late Wilson.

NOVEMBr 28th Bella Daughter of Jno. Ellis of Brounber & [T. Bella] his wife (late

DECEM 5th Ann Daughter of Robert Savage of Potlands & Isabel his wife [T. late Robinson]

do. 11th James son of Wm. Brunskill of Wandale & Ann his wife (late Fawcett.

do. 12th Ann Daughter of Mathew Broun [T. Taylor] of Tranmire & Jennet his wife (late Birtle.

do. 23d Willm. son of Thos. & Margaret Thompson [T. William son of Thos. Thompson of Town & Margaret his wife late Thompson.]

do. 26th Jonathan son of Jonathan Metcalf of Town Innkeeper & Eliz. his wife (late Graham.

do. 31st Ruth Daughter of Stephen Dent of Dovingill & Margaret his wife (late Perkins.

† 1803. FEB. 21. 1803. Thos. son of Agnes Thompson Illigitimate.

1803. JAN 29th Ann Daughter of John Kirkbride of High Stannerskugh & Margt. his wife (late Earnest.

FEB. 21st John & Isabel twins of Thomas Taylor of Town & Elizabeth his wife (late Spooner.

BIRTHS AND CHRISTNINGS.

MAR. 4th Agnes Daughter of Thomas Shaw of Greenside & Ann his wife (late Todd.

Born FEB. 3d Baptized FEB. 26th Mary Daughter of the Rev. John Robinson Schoolmaster and of Mary his wife (late Raisbeck.

APRIL 1st Margaret Daughter of Thos. Wharton of Waitby & Isabella his wife late Milner.

APRIL 2d Isabel Daughter of Thomas Harrison of Bowderdale & Mary his wife (late Barnet.

do. 15th John son of Robert Wilson of Weesdale & Isabel his wife late Shearman.

MAY 22d [T. 23d] William son of Thos. Theckston of Backside & Eliz. his wife late Fawcett.

do. 23d Ruth Daughter of William Adamthwaite of Sprintgill & Mary his wife (late Knewstup.

do. 29th John son of James Mkinsey of Town & Mary his wife (late Hodgson.

do. 30th Agnes Daughter of Thos. Robinson of Cawtley & Margaret his wife late Hall.

1803. JULY 3d Robert son of Richard Hastwel of Newbegin & [T. Isabel] his wife (late Richardson.

do. do. Agnes Daughter of George Robinson of Garrs & Ann his wife late Stewardson.

AUGt 14th Elizabeth Daughter of James Lindsay of Lockholme & Agnes his wife late Hall.

SEPTEM 4th John son of Edward Beck of Dubbs & Mary his wife (late Morland.

OCT [T. Mary Daughter] of George Jackson of Brounber & Margaret his wife late Stewardson.

Nov 9th William* son of Mathew Hunter of Tranmire & Jane his wife (late Perkins.

† NOVEMbr 11th John son of Math. Hunter **

[T. do. 11th] John son of Stephen Hunter of Lockholme & Ruth his wife (late Perkins.

Nov 26 Eliz. Daughter of John Hunter of Murthwaite & Ann his wife late Rennison.

---

* Originally "John". "William" in T.
** "John s. of Math. Hunter" struck out

BIRTHS AND CHRISTNINGS.

Nov. 27 Margaret Daughter of Jn°. Emmerson & his wife late

Decem 4th Ann Daughter of John Metcalf of Coldkeld & his wife late Blades.

Decem 18th Margaret Daughter of Thos. Hunter of Bowberhead & Ann his wife (late Hutchinson.

1804. Jan 11th Thos. son of Christr. Rennison of Newbegin & Isabel his wife late Fawcett.

Feb 11th Margaret Daughter of Stephen Dent of Dovingill & Margt. his wife late Perkins.

do. 12 Isabel Daughter of Thos. Clayton of Crossbank & his wife (late Eglin.

* 1804. Baptized.

Mar. 16 Ann & Mary twins Daughters of Jn°. Airey of Wandale & Ann his wife late Hunter.

Mar. 21st Thomas son of Michael Taylor of Broughfoot & Eliz. his wife late Whitehead.

Mar. 25 John son of Thos. Airey of Town & Mary his wife (late Ireland.

do. 28th James son of William Winder of High Lane & Nancy his wife Late Guy.

do. 29th Ann Daughter of William Watson of Town and Mary his wife late Nelson.

April 19th Ann Daughter of Richard Fawcett of Brackenber and Elizabeth his wife (late Dobson.

June 3d Robert son of Mathew Thompson of Low Stannerskuth & Ann his wife (late Martindale.

Septr 16 James son of Richard Hastwell of Newbegin and Mary his wife late Richardson.

Sep 17 Sarah Daughter of Henry & Isabel Hugginson.

Septr 20 James son of Thomas Cowper of Newbegin and Mary his wife late

Nov. 11th Joseph son of Thomas Relph of Town & Margaret his wife late Robinson.

Nov. 24th James son of Thos. Ireland Cordwainer & Ann his wife late Hutchinson.

---

* Transcript for 1804 is missing.

BIRTHS AND CHRISTNINGS.

DECEMB^r^ 1st Jane Daughter of Mathew Broune Taylor & Jennet his wife late Birtle.

1804. DECEMB^r^ 3^d^ Mary & Marg^t^. twins Daughters of Joseph & Isabel Hunter Wandale.

do. 4th Agnes Daughter of Jno. & Ann Udal.

do. 21st Eliz. Daughter of John Murthwaite of Parock Moor & Mabel his wife (late Graham.

Born Nov. 18, Baptized DEC. 2 Isabella, Daughter of the Rev. John Robinson Schoolmaster and of Mary his wife late Raisbeck.

1805. JAN 5th Mary Daughter of Thomas Harrison of Bowderdale & Mary his wife (late Barnet.

MAY 12 Ann Daughter of Edward Beck of Dubbs & Mary his wife (Morland.

JUNE 16 George son of Thomas Theckston of Backside & Elizabeth his wife (late Fawcett.

JULY 3^d^ Margaret Daughter of George Robinson of Gars & Ann his wife late Stewardson.

JULY 14th John son of Joseph Stubbs of Newbegin and his wife late Parkinson.

SEP. 15th Edward son of Thomas Clayton of Crossbank and Mary his wife late Eglin.

OCT. 2^d^ [T. Frances] Daughter of Thomas Steel of street & Sarah his wife late Hugginson.

OCT. 15th Elizabeth Daughter of Mathew Hunter of Tranmire & Jane his wife (late Perkins.

OCT. 15th John son of John Hunter of Murthwaite & Ann his wife late Rennison.

1805. OCT. 16 [T. Eliz. Daughter] of Robert Murthwaite and Ann his wife late Nelson.

DEC^mbr^ 6 Melly Daughter of Thomas Thompson [T. of Fellend] and Margeret his wife (late Hunter.

DECEM^br^ 12 Margeret Daughter of Robert Wilson of Weesdale and Isabel his wife late Shearman.

1806. JAN^ry^ 21 Henry son of Stephen Hunter of Lockholme and Ruth his wife late Perkins.

MARCH 7th Ann Daughter of John Ellis of Brounber and Mary his wife late Braithwaite.

BIRTHS AND CHRISTNINGS.

MARCH 23d Matthew and Sarah Children of Anthony Taylor of Friarbottom & Bridget his wife late [T. Willan]

† JAN 27 Wm. son of Chrisr. Rennison of Newbiggin & Isabel his wife (late Fawcett.

MAR. 27th Isabella Daughter of Michael Taylor of Browfoot & Eliz. his wife late Whitehead.

APRIL 8 Richard son of James Lindsley of Studfold and Agnes his wife Late Hall.

JUNE 1st James son of George Thackstone of Weesdale and Agness his wife late Wharton.

JUNE 29th William Nelson son of William Watson of Town Miner & Mary his wife (late Nelson.

Born MAY 31, Baptized JUNE 8, John, son of the Rev. John Robinson, Schoolmaster, and of Mary his wife (late Raisbeck.

AUGst 19th Sarah Daughter of Thomas Fawcett of Greenslack and Ann his wife late Hastwell.

do. 30 Margt. Daughter of William Fawcett Taylor & Ann his wife (late Wharton.

1806. OCT 23d Isabella Daughter of Will: Edrington & Mary his wife (late Nelson.

do. 26th Alice Daughter of Thos. Parkinson of Intake & Agnes his wife late Hodgson.

NOV. 10th Jno. son of Mathew Thompson of Burnthill & Ann his wife late Martindale.

DECEM 28 Jane Daughter of Willm. Winder of High Lane & Nancy his wife late Guy.

1807. JAN 10th William son of Christr. Rennison of Newbegin & Isabel his wife (late Fawcett.

[T. do.] Isabella Daughter of Charles Hastwel of Ellerhill & Dorothy his wife late Dixon.

JAN 23d Sarah Daughter of Jane Hill [T. of Newbiggin] Illigitimate.

MAR 15 Jonathan son of Jonathan Metcalf of Town Innkeeper & Eliz. his wife (late Graham.

APRIL 9th Willm. son of William Potter of Lytheside and Agnes his wife late Brown.

BIRTHS AND CHRISTNINGS.

† MAY 20th John Fawcett son of Anth. Fawcett of Artlegarth &* wife.

APRIL 10th William son of Thos. Airey Cowper & Mary his wife late Ireland.

APRIL 10th Mary Ann** Daughter of Thos. Robinson Scar Cordwainer & Mary his wife late Thompson.

APRIL 12 Isabella Daughter of Mathew Hunter of Tranmer & Jane his wife late Perkins.

† APRIL 13 Sarah Daughter of Richard Beck of Sandwath and of Margaret his wife (late Hewetson.

1807. JUN 1st Ann Daughter of Wm.*** Hunter of Adamthwaite & Mary his wife late Robinson.

SEP. 13th Thos. son of Thomas Harrison of Bowderdale & Mary his wife late Barnett.

do. Thos. [T. Eliz. Daughter] son of Thos. Thackstone of Sprintgill & Eliz. his wife late Fawcett.

AUGUST 16th Margaret Daughter of Ann Dent of Town Illegitimate.

AUGt 30th Eleanor Daughter of Miles Turner of Marthwait & Eliz. his wife late Parkin.

OCT. 8th Richard son of Thos. Haward of the Township of Natland & Ann his wife (late Haward.

NOV. 1st Robt. son of William Furness of Town & Isabella his wife late Wilkinson.

do. 15th William son of James Stewardson of Brownber & Margaret his wife (late Hodgson.

DECEMBr 8th Jno. son of William Watson of Town & Mary his wife late Nelson.

1808. JANUARY 18th William son of Christr. Alderson & Agnes his wife late Wilson.

FEB 25 James son of James Fawcett & Nancy his wife (late Relph.

MARCH 4th Isabel Daughter of Richard Robinson of lythside and Margaret his wife late Morland.

1808. MACH 4th Margaret Daughter of Sarah Thomson Illegitimate.

APRILL 8th Ann Daughter of Robert Murthwaite of Nubegin and Ann his wife Late Nelson.

---

* Indistirct, looks like "Ehrz." perhaps "Eliz."

** "Anna Maria" originally. T. has "Anna Maria."

*** "Mathew" originally. T. has "William."

BIRTHS AND CHRISTNINGS.

APRILL 8th Thomas son of William Sidgwick of Ashfield & Jane his wife (late Taylor.

APRILL 17th Thomas son of George Hall of Artlegarth and Mary his wife late Allen.

MAY 22 Ruth, Daughter of Thomas Relph Carrier and of Margaret his wife (late Robinson).

Born APRIL 14, Baptized MAY 22, Elizabeth, Daughter of the Rev. John Robinson Schoolmaster, and of Mary his wife (late Raisbeck).

JULY 19th John son of Richard Fothergill of Greenside Lane and Mary his wife (late Jackson.

JULY 31st Edmund son of Mic. Taylor of Browfoot and Eliz. his wife late Whitehead.

do. do. Mary Daughter of Thomas Wilson of High Stannerskugh and Ann his wife (late Taylor.

† AGUST 7 Marey Daughter of James Haygarth and Marey his wife (late Reminson Town head Laborar.

1808. SEPTEMBER 25th Joseph son of John Hunter of Gate and Ann his wife (Late Rennison.

do. do. Martha Daughter of John Murthwaite of Parrockmoor and Mable his wife (Late Peacock.

do. 27th Robert son of Robert Fawcett of Dovingill and Eleanar his wife (Late Hastwell.

do. do. Isable Daughter of Thomas Hunter of Bowberhead and Ann his wife (Late Hutchinson.

† OCT 12th Peggy Daughter of Thos. Clayton of Crosbank & Mary his wife late Eglin.

do. 16th Mary Daughter of Thomas Dixon of Nateby and Isable wife (Late Hewetson.

NOV 14th Hannah Daughter of Thomas Parkinson of Intake and Agnes his wife (Late Hodgson.

DECEMBr 13th Margaret Daughter of Annas [T. Agnes] Thomson Illegitimate.

1809. FEB 14th George son of George Thaxton of Weesdale and Agnes his wife late Wharton.

APRIL 2d Henry son of Richard Beck of Sandwarth and Margaret his wife (Late Hewetson.

BIRTHS AND CHRISTNINGS.

do. 8th — Richard son of Robert Wilson of Weesdale and Isable his wife (Late Shearman.

June 28th — William son of James Hunter of Coldbeck and Mary his wife (Late Whitehead.

1809. Sepbr 2d — Thomas son of Stephen Hunter and Ruth his wife (late Parkin.

Decembr 15 — James son of Thomas Fawcett of Greenside and Elizabeth his wife (late

July 8 — Margaret Daughter of James and Nancy Fawcett Tailor Town.

Decembr 23d — Mary Daughter of Richard Fothergill of Greenside and Mary his wife (Late Jackson.

do. 28th — Jno. son of Richard Robinson of Lithside and Margaret his wife (Late Morland.

1810.

Born Dec 2 1809, Baptized Jan 6 1810 William Richardson, son of the Rev. John Robinson, Schoolmaster, and of Mary his wife (late Raisbeck.

Jan. 21st — Mary Daughter of William Watson of Town, Miner and Mary his wife (Late Nelson.

do. 24th — Ann Daughter of Thomas Taylor of Town and Elizabeth his wife (late Spooner.

March 4 — Jane Daughter of John Hunter of freerbottom and Bouth [T. Jane] late [T. Booth] his wife.

do. 9th — Margaret Daughter of James Hayarth of Town and Mary his wife (late Rennison.

Mar. 10th — Humphrey son of Thos. Smith of Bleaflat & Margaret his wife (late Addison.

1810. May 11th — Henry son of David Alderson of Needlehouse and Eleanor his wife (late Hunter.

June 23 — Ann Daughter of Thomas Wilson of High Stannerskugh & Ann his wife (late Taylor.

do. do. — Michael son of William Adamthwaite* of Coldbeck & Polly his wife (late Knewstupp.

---

* Originaly "Hunter". T. has "Hunter."

BIRTHS AND CHRISTNINGS.

JUNE 24	Thomas son* of Miles Turner of Bleaflat & Eliz. his wife (late Parkin.
do. do.	Isabel Daughter of John Udal of Coldbeck and Ann his wife (Late Birtle.
JUNE 30th	Elizabeth Daughter of Christopher Alderson of Tarnhouse and Ann his wife (Late Wilson.
do. do.	Isabel Daughter of Mary Birtle Illegitimate.
JULY 18th	Hannah Daughter of Sarah Taylor Illegitinmate.
do. 22d	Robert son of William Furnass of Banks and Elizabeth his wife late Blencarn.
SEP: 9	James son of Matthew Thompson of Stannerskugh and Ann his wife late Martindale.
OCT: 4th	Mary Daughter of Edward Beck of Dubbs and Mary his wife (Late Morland.
1810. OCTOBER 14th	Ann Daughter of Richard Potter of Studfold & Eleanor his wife (late Fawcett.
do. 16th	Nahomi Daughter of Richard Fawcett of Brackenbar & Frances his wife (late Dobson.
NOV. 10th	Nanny Daughter of Michael Taylor of Browfoot and Elizabeth his wife (Late Whitehead.
do. 15th	John son of Mathew Hunter of Tranmire and Jane his wife (Late Parkin.
DECbr 16th	Chrisd. Isabella Daughter of Robert Murthwaite and Ann his wife late Nelson.
1811.	
JAN 22d	Richard son of James Birtle of Street & Mary his wife late Thompson.
JAN 24	William son of Thomas Parkinson [T. Parkin] of Inntack & Agnes his wife late Hodgson.
do. 24th	Thomas son of John Herd of Greenside Lane and Nancy his wife late Whitehead.
FEB. 14th	Thomas son of Margt. Allen, Illegitimate.
FEB. 20th	John, son of John Dawson of Stannerskugh and Margt. his wife late Nicholson.

* Originally "Elizabeth daughter." T. has "Elizabeth daughter."

BIRTHS AND CHRISTNINGS.

FEB: 24th John son of Joseph Thompson of Town & Sarah his wife (late Metcalfe.

MAR: 1st Thomas son of Anthony Wharton of Stannersksugh & Eleanour his wife (late Alderson.

APRIL 4th William son of Bell Parkin of Murthwaite & Ann his wife late Hunter.

† Baptized APRIL 5, born JAN. 27, Henry son of Stephen Dent of Dovengill and of Margaret his wife (late Perkins.

1811. Born MAY 22, Baptized JUNE 2, Matthew Wilkinson, son of the Rev. John Robinson, Schoolmaster, and of Mary his wife (late Raisbeck.

JUNE 30th William son of Richard* Furnass of Stannerskugh & of Mary his wife (late Whalley.

JULY 6th Mary Daughter of Geo: Robinson of Gars & of Ann his wife (late Stewardson.

JULY 7th Ann Daughter of James Fawcett of Town & of Nancy his wife (late Relph.

JULY 10th [T. 9th] Jane Daughter of James Stewardson of Weesdale & of Margret his wife (late Hodgson.

JULY 17 Mary Daughter of Richard Beck of Sandwath and of Margaret his wife (late Hewetson baptized.

JULY 26 Ann Daughter of John Ellis of Newbiggin, & of Mary his wife (late Braithwate.

do. 26 Eleanor Daughter of John Ellis of Newbiggin & of Mary his wife (late Braithwate.

AUGUST 15th Robert, son of John Atkinson of Weesdale & of Alice his wife (late Hodgson.

do. 18 George son of John Murthwaite of Parrock Moor & of Mable his wife (late Graham.

SEP 22d Ann Daughter of William Potter of Lytheside & of Agnes his wife (late Brown.

do. 29th John son of Thomas Kirkbride of Weesdale & of Mary his wife (late Clayton.

† OCTr 13 Benjn. son of Benjn. Hewetson of Green.

---

* "William" crossed out. T. has "Richard."

BIRTHS AND CHRISTNINGS.

Nov. 3rd William son of Richard Potter, of Studfold & of Eleanor his wife (late Fawcett.

1811. Nov. 10th Mary Daughter of Wm. Hetherington of Newbiggin, & of Isable his wife (late Nelson) Baptized.

Dec. 1 Mary Daughter of Nancy Clayton of Crossbank, illegitimate.

Dec. 21 Mary Daughter of James Hunter of Coldbeck, & of Mary his wife (late Whitehead) Baptized.

1812.

Jan: 6th Sarah, Daughter of Richard Fothergill of Greenside, & of Mary his wife (late Jackson).

Jan: 11th Isabel Daughter of Thos. Hunter of Bowberhead, & of Ann his wife (late Hutchinson).

Jan: 12 Baptized Jane & Sarah Daughters of Christopher Renniscn of Newbiggin & of Isabel his wife (late Fawcett).

Feb: 23rd Matthew son of Elizabeth Brown of Rigg End (illegitimate).

March 5 Margret Daughter of Miles Turner of Bleaflat, & of Elizabeth his wife (late Parkin).

March 23rd George son of Eliz: Sedgwick of Burnt Hill (illegitimate).

April 12 Thomas, son of Thomas Wilson of Stannerskugh & of Ann his wife (late Taylor).

April 21 George son of William Adamthwait of Coldbeck, & of Mary his wife (late Knewstupp).

May 25 John son of Michael Taylor of Bowderdale, & of Elizabeth his wife (late Whitehead).

June 1st Thomas son of Eleanor Rennison of Townhead, Illegitimate.

June 7th Martha Daughter of Joseph Hunter of Wandale, & of Isabel his wife (late Wilson).

June 24th Anthony, son of John Udal of Coldbeck Mill, & of Ann his wife (late Birtle).

June 26 John son of George Fothergill of Dovingill, & of Isabel his wife (late Coates).

1812. June 26th Deborah Daughter of Eleanor Fawcett of Greenslack Illegitimate.

BIRTHS AND CHRISTNINGS.

JUNE 28th James son of William Furnass of Banks and of Elizabeth his wife late Blenkarn.

AUGUST 16th Eleanor Daughter of Bell Parkin of Adamthwaite, & of Nancy his wife late Hunter.

AUGUST 30th Richard son of William Dixon of Coldkeld, and of Alice his wife (late Shaw).

AUGUST 30th Richard & John sons of Richd. Moyster of Backside and of Ann his wife (late Spooner.

SEP. 6th William son of David Alderson of Needlehouse and of Eleanor his wife (late Hunter).

NOV. 1st Mary Daughter of John Todd of Crooks and of Isabel his wife (late Adamthwaite).

NOV: 2nd Robert son of James Birtle of Burnt Hill and of Mary his wife (late Thompson).

NOV: 15 Matthew son of James Haygarth of Town & of Mary his wife (late Rennison.

DECr 6 Eleanor Daughter of Richard Potter of Studfold & of Eleanor his wife (late Fawcett.

DEC. 27th James son of Anthony Wharton of Ellergill and of Eleanor his wife late Alderson.

1813. † FEBy 19 Mary the daughter of Benjn. Hewetson Green and his wife Peggy late Wilson.

BIRTHS AND CHRISTNINGS.

DISSENTrs. CHILDrn. BORN IN RAVENSTONDle. GIVEN IN BY THEIR PARENTS.

APRl 9th 1738. A Daughter of Thos. & Isabel Fothergill of Brownber was born.

Jane Daughter to Thos. & Isabel Fothergill Baptized.

JUNE 8th James son to Thos. & Isabel Fothergill of Brounber was born & bapd 11th JUNE 1740.

FEBy 22 1735. Wm. son of Wm. & Anne Florigill born.

Agnes Lawful Daughter to Mr. Thos. & Isabl. Collier born NOVEMBr 5th 1745 & bapt. in sd month.

David Lawful son to Mr. Thos. & Isabl. Collier born 19th MAY & Bapd JUNE 1st 1747.

Thos. Lawful son to the Parents above sd. born 4th or 5th of Aprl. & bapt. 16th of sd. month 1752.

this was given in by a Note.

MAY 30th 1767. Edwd. son of John & Mary Gill Born.

MAY 2d 1775. Thos. son to Willm. & Agnas Elliotson, Scarsikes born given in by the Fathr.

John son of James & Elizth. Fawcett, Greenside born 3d Day of FEB 1752 given in by the Fathr.

BIRTHS AND CHRISTNINGS.

(Of Dissenters' Children).

John son of Isaac & Anne Relf born March 5th 1766.

Sarah Daughtr. of Isaac & Anne Relf born July 18 1767.

Stepn. son of Isaac & Anne Relf born July 21st 1769.

Nanny Daughter of Isaac & Anne Relf born Decr 17th 1771.

Ruth Daughr. of Isaac & Anne Relf born Decr 9 1774.

given in by the Fathr.

John son of Robt. & Mary Murthwait bapd May 9th 1730.*

Eliz: Daughter to Robt. & Mary Murthwait Bapd Feb 22nd 1731.*

Geo: son to Robt. & Mary Murthwait Bapd Feby 12th 1740.

given by the Fathr.

Feby 15th 1726.	Was Thos. son to Richd. & Mary Fothergill, Dubs born.
Augst 1st 1730.	Anne Daughtr. to Richd. & Mary Fothergill, Dubs born.
Decr 15th 1732.	Elianr. Daughr. to Richd. & Mary Fothergill, Dubs born.
Sepr 6th 1734.	Mary Daugr. to Richd. & Mary Fothergill, Dubs born.
Octr 29th 1736.	Henry son to Richd. & Mary Fothergill, Dubs born.

Decr 3d 1742.	Elianor Daughter of John & Eliz. Hewetson Ellergill born.
Jan 4th 1744.	Richd. son of John & Eliz. Hewetson Ellergll. born.
Apl 15th 1747.	Thos. son of John & Eliz. Hewetson Ellergill born.
March 25th 1752.	Sarah Daughter of John & Eliz. Hewetson Ellergll born.
May 9th 1755.	Henry son of John & Eliz. Hewetson Ellergll. Born.
Sep 5th 1757.	Isabl. Daugter of Jno. & Eliz. Hewetson Ellergll. Born.
June 27th 1761.	John son of Jno. & Eliz. Hewetson born.
Feb 12th 1763.	James son of Jno. & Eliz. Hewetson born.

givn in by the Far.

---

* These two dates are doubtful, perhaps 1736 and 1751.

BIRTHS AND CHRISTNINGS.

(Of Dissenters' Children).

Anne Daughr. of Thos. & Ann Robinson born O. S. Novr 2d 1746.
Agnes Daughr. of Thos. & Eliz. Robinson born O. S. Jan 6th 1750.
James son of Thos. & Eliz. Robinson born Octr 21st 1752.
Mary Daughr. of Thos. & Eliz. Robinson born Feb 4th 1754.
James son of Thos. & Eliz. Robinson born Feb 4th 1756.

Sepber 23d 1742. Was Mary Daughtr. to Wm. & Sarah Dixon born.
May 14th 1744. Richd. son to Wm. & Sarah Dixon born.
Apl 7th 1746. Anne Daughtr. of Wm. & Mary Dixon born.

Feby 5th 1764. John son Richd. & Mary Willan born.

Thomas son to Anthony fothergill of Brounber was Born ye 21 of July in 1708.

John son to Anthony fothergill of Brounber was Jannuwary 26 In 1713.

Robert son of Anthony fothergill of Brounber was Born the first of July in 1715.

Margaret Daughter to Anthony fothergill of Brounber was Born ye 31 of March in 1718.

William son to Anthony fothergill of Brounber was born the 21 Day of December in 1719.

Ruth Daughter to Anthony Fothergill of Brounber was born ye. 29th of June 1722 being St. Peter's Day.

Mary Daughter of Anthony Fothergill born the 27th of March baptized 1st of April 1735.

Anne Daughter of Roger & Anne Barber Born Augt. 22d 1724.

{ Octr 12th 1711. A Son of James & Jane Fothergill of Brownber Born.
{ 22nd Thomas son of James & Jane Fothergill Baptiz'd.
{ Jany 27th 1713. A son of James & Jane Fothergill Born.
{ Feby 6th Michael son of James & Jane Fothergill Baptiz'd.
{ Jany 20th 1716. A Daughter of James & Jane Fothergill Born.
{ 28th Ann Daughter of James & Jane Fothergill Baptiz'd.

BIRTHS AND CHRISTNINGS.

(Of Dissenters' Children).

{Jan^y^ 9th 1719. A Son of James & Jane Fothergill Born.
{ 18th William son of James & Jane Fothergill Baptiz'd.

{July 20th 1722. A Daughter of James & Jane Fothergill Born.
{ 30th Margaret Daughter of James & Jane Foth^r^gill Baptiz'd.

Margaret Daughter of Thomas Fothergill of Brounber the elder born ye 23^d^ of March 1734/5. Bap^d^. y^e^. 3^d^ of April 1735.

Robt. son of John & Mary Hewetson of Lockholm born April 29 17775.
Joshua son of John & Mary Hewetson born 6th of June 1777.
given in by the Father.

Thos. son to Thos. & Marg^t^. Fothergill the Eld^r^. born 2^d^ Feb & bap^d^ the 8th 1741.

George son of Richard & Margaret Murthwait born 15th January 1732 & Bap^d^ 25th.

A Register of the Births of John Milner of Ashfel's children—

1711. July 8th Margaret Daughter of John & Marg^t^. Milner Born.
1712. Novr 30th Ralph son of John & Margaret Milner Born.
1714. March 12th Robert son of John & Marg^t^. Milner Born.
1717. Octr 4th W^m^. son of John & Marg^t^. Milner Born.
1720. June 29th John son of John & Marg^t^. Milner Born.
1722. Decr 28th Holmes son of John & Marg^t^. Milner Born.
1724. April 9th Agnes Daughter of John & Marg^t^. Milner Born.

Births of Dissenters Childr^n^.

1743/4. Feb 16th Anne Daughter to Steph^n^. & Agnes Chamberlain Greenside born.
July 24th 1749. Ruth Daughter to Stephen & Agnes Chamberlain born.

Jan^ry^ 27th 1766. Robt. son of Rich^d^. Bousfield Low Lane born.

BIRTHS AND CHRISTNINGS.

(OF DISSENTERS' CHILDREN).

Thos. son of Richd. Hunter o' fell end born FEB 6th 1765.
Elinr. Daughtr. of Richd. Hunter o' fell end born JUNE 24th 1767.

1741-2. MARCH 9th Was Thomas son to Mathw. & Ruth Scarbrough of Gars born.
MAY 10th 1743. Margaret Daughter to Mathw. & Ruth Scarbrough of Gars born.
1744-5 FEBY 14th John son to Mathw. & Ruth Scarbrough of Gars born.
OCTOBr 12th 1746. Mathew son to Mathw. & Ruth Scarbrough of Gars Born.
Isabel Daughtr. to Mathw. & Ruth Scarbrough born 14th MARCH 1747.
Ruth Daughter to Matt. & Ruth Scarbrough born 8th FEB. 1749.
Sarah Daughtr. to Mathw. & Ruth Scarbrough born 8th FEB 1752.
Robert son to Mathew & Ruth Scarbrough born 23d APRIL 1755.

FEB. 23d 1743. Isabel Daughtr. to Robt. & Mary Hewetson Lockolme Born.
JANY 2d 1745. Anne Daughter to Robt. & Mary Hewetson o' Lockholme Born.
JANY 12th 1747. Sarah Daughter to Robt. & Mary Hewetson of Lockholme born.
MARCH 3d 1748-9. Mary Daughter to Robt. & Mary Hewetson of Lockholme born.
John son to Robt. & Mary Hewetson of Lockholme born.
1752. MARCH 22d Thos. son to Robt. & Mary Hewetson Lockholme born.
MAY 30th 1761. Betty Daughtr. to Robt. & Mary Hewetson born.
FEB 18th 1763. Lydia Daughtr. to Robt. & Mary Hewetson born.

AUG 4th 1743. Margt.* Daughter to Geo. & Marg. Perkins Lockholm head Bapd.
JULY 16th 1745. Elianor Daughter to Geo. & Margt. Perkins Lockholme head Born.
SEP. 21st 1747. Mary Daughr. to Geo: & Margt. Perkins Lockholme head Born.

---

* Or perhaps "Mary"; it appears to have been "Elizabeth" originally.

BIRTHS AND CHRISTNINGS.

(Of Dissenters' Children).

Sep. 26th 1749. Anne Daugh^{r}. to Geo: & Marg^{t}. Perkins Lockholme head Born.

Dec^{br} 18th 1751. Anthony son to Geo. & Marg^{t}. Perkins Lockholme head Born.

July 4th 1770. Was Thos. son of John & Isabel Hewetson of Lockholm Foot Born.

Jan 31st 1773. Was born W^{m}. son to John & Isabel Hewetson of Lockholm Foot born.

Novemb^{r} 5th 1742. Isabel Daughter to John & Anne Shaw of Town Born.

Feb. 24th 1745. Anne Daughter to John & Anne Shaw of Town Born.

June 11th 1754. Peter son to Peter & Elizabeth Giles born & Bap^{d} 27th.

Octo^{r} 16th 1742. Was John son to John & Anne Hewetson of Murthwait Born.

Octob^{r} 22^{d} 1745. Sibal Daughter to John & Anne Hewetson Murthwait Born.

Augst 13th 1748. James son to John & Anne Hewetson Murthwait Born.

May 20th 1751. Robt. son to John & Anne Hewetson Murthw^{t}. Bap^{d}.

June 28th 1769. Anne Daughter of John & Isabel Hewetson of Lockholm Foot born. Given in by the Fa^{r}.

Decr 25th 1753. Was Alice Daught^{r} to John & Agnes Udal born.

Octo^{r} 17th 1755. Mary Daugther of Rich^{d}. & Mary Breaks born.

Feby 18th 1758. Marg^{t}. Daughter of Rich^{d}. & Mary Breaks born. given in by Father.

Aug 1st 1759. Born Peggy Daughter of John & Mary Thompson.

Mar. 8th 1761. Born George son of John & Mary Thompson.

May 14th 1778. Born Joseph son of Isaac Relph of Town weaver & Ann his wife (late Chamberlain.

BIRTHS AND CHRISTNINGS.

(Of Dissenters' Children).

July 17th 1767. Sarah Daughter of Isaac Relph of Town weaver & Ann his wife late Chamberlain.

July 22 1769. Stephen son of Isaac Relph of Town weaver & Ann his wife late Chamberlain.

Decem 11 1771. Agnes Daughter of Isaac Relph of Town weaver & Ann his wife late Chamberlain.

Augt. 24 1780. Nancy Daughter of Isaac Relph of Town weaver & Ann his wife late Chamberlain.

Oct. 14 1783. Thos. son of Isaac Relph of Town weaver & Ann his wife late Chamberlain.

Oct. 29 1788.* Eliz. Relph Daughter of Isaac Relph weaver & Ann his wife late Chamberlain.

1802. April 20th Born Jno. son of Thomas Fawcett Couper & Susanna** his wife late Hill Baptized May 9th 1802.

A Register of the Births & Baptisms of James & Anne Richardson's childer of Ravenstondale Town Merchant as follows—

Isabel Daughter to James & Anne Richardson born Novembr 1st 1743 & Bapd Novr 8th.

Willm. son to James & Anne Richardson born Novembr 8th 1746 & Baptd Novr 25th.

David son to James & Anne Richardson born Feb 10th 1747-8 & bapd 11th Feb.

Francis Daughter to James & Anne Richardson born Decr 28th 1749 & Bapd Jan 2d.

James son of James & Anne Richardson born May 2d 1754 & Bapd May 9th.

John & Thomas Twin sons to James & Anne Richardson born Decembr 16th 1758 & baptizd Janry 2d 1759.

Anne Daughter to James & Anne Richardson born 18th June 1761 & Bapd the 25th.

Mary Daughtr. of James & Anne Richardson born Septr 12th & Bapd 21st 1763.

---

* Or perhaps 1787.
** Originally "Charlotte."

BIRTHS AND CHRISTNINGS.

(OF DISSENTERS' CHILDREN).

OCTOBr 1st 1758. Isaac son to Peter & Sarah Handlay Town Born.

MARCH 3d Isabl. Daughtr. to John & Alice* Perkin Caldbeck born.
Thomas. son of John & Isabel Adamthwait born APRl 30th 1754.
Anne Daughter to John & Isabel Adamthwait born 24th JUNE 1757.
Mary D.
Mary Daughr. of Jno. & Mary Gill born FEB 12th 1765.
William son of Richard & Margaret Elliotson of Browfoot at Wath born 27th MAY (old stile) 1746.
Mary Daughter of Richd. & Margaret Elliotson of Browfoot at Wath born DECEMBr 20th 1748.
Thomas son of John & Isabel Elliotson of Wath born AUGst 6th 1758.
Willm. son of William Robinson born MARCH 6th 1747.

John son of James & Eliz. Fawcet born FEB. 3d 1752.
Henry son of James & Eliz. Fawcet born OCTOr 6th 1754.
Margt. Daughtr. of James & Eliz. Fawcet born MAY 7th 1757.
Henry son of James & Eliz. Fawcet born OCTOr 7th 1760.

APRIL 27th 1751. Was Margt. Daughtr. to Thos. & Mary Knewstup born.
DECEMBr 27th 1752. Michael son to Thos. & Mary Knewstup born.
JANry 23d 1755. Sibal Daughtr. to Thos. & Mary Knewstup born.
FEB. 16th 1759. Mary Daughtr. to Thos. & Mary Knewstup born.

APRl 12th 1748. John son of John & Margt. Stubbs born.

MARCH 13th 1757. Anne Daughter to John & Mary Perkins born.
MAY 24th 1758. Thomas son to Jno. Mary Perkins born.

1769. APl 16th John son of Thos. & Isabel Hewetson Town born Given in by the Fathr.

---

* Indistinct.

BIRTHS AND CHRISTNINGS.

(OF DISSENTERS' CHILDREN).

FEB 16th 1771. Rich^{d}. son of Thos. & Isab^{l}. Hewetson Town born Given in by the Fath^{r}.

MAY 22^{d} 1773. Thos. son of Thos. & Isab^{l}. Hewetson o' Town born Given in by the Fath^{r}.

MAY 29th 1775. Willm. son of Thos. & Isab^{l}. Hewetson o' Town born Given in by the Fath^{r}.

NOVEMB^{r} 22^{d} 1748. Agnes Daught^{r}. to Rich^{d}. & Marg^{t}. Chamberlain born.
AUGst 4th 1750. Rich^{d}. son of Rich^{d}. & Marg^{t}. Chamberlain born.
JAN^{ry} 29th 1752. Isab^{l}. Daught^{r}. to Rich^{d}. & Marg^{t}. Chamberlain born.
JAN^{ry} 30th 1754. Anne Daughter to Rich^{d}. & Marg^{t}. Chamberlain born.
MARCH 3^{d} 1758. John son to Rich^{d}. & Marg^{t}. Chamberlain born.
MARCH 7th 1760. Ruth Daught^{r}. to Rich^{d}. & Marg^{t}. Chamberlain born.

Henry son of John & Ann Hunter of Greenside born AUGst 8th 1766.
Thos. son of John & Ann Hunter Greenside born.

Peter son of Peter & Eliz. Giles of Weesdal born JUNE 11th 1754.
Anne Daughter of Robt. & Eliz. Todd of Weesdal born Nov^{ber} 23^{d} 1759.

John son of John & Mary Dawson born FEB^{y} 3^{d} 1748.
Melly Daught^{r}. of John & Mary Dawson born 6 MAY 1755.
Robt. son of John & Mary Dawson born 11th Novr 1757.
Jane Daught^{r}. of John & Mary Dawson born 13th FEB 1760.
} Given in by the Fath^{r}.

Anne Dau^{r}. to W^{m}. Fawcet worset Carrier born FEB 6th given by ye Fath^{r}.

25th MARCH 1758. John son of Holmes & Esther Milner Bap^{d}.
Marg^{t}. Daught^{r}. of Holmes & Esther Milner born MAY 21st 1763. Given in by M^{r}. Jno. Milner Grand father at Ashfell.

AP^{l} 8th 1777. Mary Daugh^{r}. to Willm. & Nanny Elliotson Scarsikes giv^{n} in by the Fath^{r}.

BIRTHS AND CHRISTNINGS.

(Of Dissenters' Children).

Agnes Daught^{r}. of Thos. & Jane Drybeck Town Born June 17th 1764.

Given in by the Fath^{r}.

Richard son of Henry & Anne Hewetson of Streetside born Augst 5th & Bap. 25th 1747.

Willm. son of Hen. & Ann Hewetson Ap^{l} 7th Bap^{d} 17th 1749.

John son of Hen. & Ann Hewetson born March 18th Bap^{d} 29th 1753.

Henry son of Hen^{y}. & Ann Hewetson born Dec^{br} 19th Bap^{d} 22^{d} 1754.

Elian^{r}. Daught^{r}. of Hen. & Ann Hewetson born June 4th Bap 12th 1758.

Isabel Daught^{r}. of Hen. & Ann Hewetson born Novr. 7 Bap 13th 1760.

Jos. & James sons of Henry & Ann Hewetson Bap Nov. 7th 62.

Benjam^{n}. & Ann son & Daught^{r}. to Hen. & Ann Hewetson born March 13th 1766.

David son to Hen. & Anne Hewetson street born Octo^{r} 25th 1767.

Robt. son to Hen. & Anne Hewetson born Sep^{tr} 16th 1770.

Joseph son of Joseph & Alice Udal born Sep^{br} 24th 1760.
of Jo^{s}. & Alice Udal born

Giv^{n} in by the Fath^{r}. { Thomas son to John & Isab^{l}. Hewetson o' Lockholme Foot Born 7th July 1775.
Benjam^{n}. young^{r} son to John & Isab^{l}. Hewetson of Lockolm foot born Octob^{r} 10th 1776. }

1769. Ap^{l} 23^{d} John son of Jno. & Anne Beck Town End Born Given in by the Fa^{r}.

July 1st 1768. Mary Daught^{r}. of Thos. & Mary Fothergill of Dubbs born.

July 14th 1769. Rich^{d}. son of Thos. & Mary Fothergill o' Dubbs born.

Feb. 28th 1773. W^{m}. son of Tho. & Mary Fothergill o' Dubs born.

Sep^{br} 9th 1777. Was Betty Daug^{r}. to W^{m}. & Nancy Huthison born given in by the Fath^{r}.

BIRTHS AND CHRISTNINGS.

Dissenters.

1784. Feb. 5th Bap. Ebenezer son of the Revd. Jas. Sommervile & his wife Born 11th of Decembr 1783.

Decem 10th 1785. Mary Daughter of Thomas & Mary Milner of Green Baptized.

Decembr 27th 1785. Born Edward son of Mic. Knewstubb & Eliz. his wife (late Beck).

Dec. 10th 1785. Born Ann D. of John Chamberlain of Greenside & Ann his wife.

May 9th 1787. Born John son of John Fothergill of Greenside & Sarah his wife.

Nov. 5th Born Margaret Daughter of Thos. Milner of Town & Mary his wife (late Knewstup).

Dec. 17th Born Stephen son of John Chamberlain of Greenside & Ann his wife late Bousfield.

1788. Nov. Born Eliz. Daughter of Isaac Relph weaver & Ann his wife late Chamberlain.

April 10 1788. Baptized Eleanor D. of Eleanor Gibbon of Smardal Hall Born March 11th.

1789. Oct 31 Born Sybil Daughter of Thos. Milner of Town & Mary his wife late Knewstup.

1790. May 20 Born Isabel & Hannah Twins D. of John Chamberlain of Greenside & Ann his wife late Bousfield.

Augt 12 Born Richard son of Christr. Bousfield of Weasdale & Sarah his wife (late Wilson.

Born.

1791. March 30th Born James son of John Fothergill of Greenside & Sarah his wife (late Parkin.

1771. Sep 25th Ann Daughter of Richard Hewetson of Beckstones & Ann his wife (late Dixon.

Oct 18th 1775. Sarah Daughter of Richd. Hewetson & Ann his wife (late Dixon.

Oct. 13th 1778. Henry son of Richd. Hewetson & Ann his wife (late Dixon.

July 15th 1781. Eleanor Daughter of Richd. Hewetson & Ann his wif (late Dixon.

BIRTHS AND CHRISTNINGS.

(Of Dissenters' Children).

Augt 2^d^ 1785. Mary Daughter of Rich^d^. Hewetson & Ann his wife (late Dixon.

1782. Nov 22^d^ James son of Jno. Guy of Town & Isabel his wife (late Chamberlain.

Jan. 27 1787. Richard son of John Guy of Town & Isabel his wife (late Chamberlain.

Feb. 17th 1787. John son of Jno. Guy of Town & Isabel his wife (late Chamberlain.

May 1st 1789. Willm. son of John Guy of Town & Isabel his wife (late Chamberlain.

Nov. 15 1791. Thos. son of Jno. Guy of Town & Isabel his wife (late Chamberlain.

1797. Augt 29th Henry son of Jno. Guy of Town & Isabel his wife (late Chamberlain.

Nov 12th 1799. Henry son of John Hewetson of Street & Mary his wife late Smith.

April 14th 1798. Rich^d^. son of John Chamberlain of Greenside & Ann his wife late Bousfield.

Sep. 5th 1797. Robert son of John Chamberlain of Greenside & Ann his wife late Bousfield.

Jan. 31st 1797. Born Ann Daughter of Thos. Hunter of & Ann his wife (late Taylor.

July 6th 1798. Born Eleanor Daughter of Thomas Hunter of Town & Ann his wife (late Taylor.

Jan 27th 1801. Born Henry Hewetson son of Thos. Hunter of Coldbeck & Ann his wife (late Taylor.

Mar. 10 1805. Born John son of Richard Hewetson of Ellergill & Elizabeth his wife late Robinson.

Feb 16th 1805. John son of Ann Thompson Illegitimate.

Feb. 21st 1803. Thos. son of Agness Thompson of Newbegin Illegitimate.

Augt 20th 1800. William son of James Haygarth of Town & Mary his wife late Rennison.

1803. Jo^s^. son of James Haygarth of Town & Mary his wife (late Rennison.

1806. March 14th Born Elizabeth Hewetson Daughter of Richard Hewetson of Ellergill & Elizabeth his wife late Robinson.

BIRTHS AND CHRISTNININGS.

(Of Dissenters' Children).

Born.

June 29th 1802. Isable Todd.

June 26th 1803. John Todd.

July 13th 1804. Ann Todd.

April 25th 1806. Thomas Todd.

October 16th 1809. Robert Todd.

March 30th 1811. Richard Todd.

Children of John Todd of Crooks & of Isabel his wife (late Adamthwaite.

Dissenters' Children, as given in by their Parents.

Children of John and Ann Rennison, of Ravenstonedale Townhead.

1785. Dec. 24 Born Jacob Rennison.

1787. July 1 Born Eleanor Rennison.

1789. Feb. 26 Born Benjamin Rennison.

1791. Feb. 7 Born Ann Rennison.

1793. May 31 Born John Rennison.

1796. April 9 Born Mary Rennison.

1800. July 6 Born James Rennison.

Children, as given in by their Mother.

Children of Thomas and Sarah Steel of Stennerskugh.

1807. May 29 Born Tamar Steel.

1809. April 5 Born Thomas Steel.

MARRIAGES.

1781. Jan. 30 Miles Hutchinson, & Isabel Ireland of the p. of Kirkby Stephen by Licence (f.a.)
Witness, John Fothergill.

1781. Feb. 4 Mathew Hunter & Elizabeth Brunskill by Licence (f.a.)
Witnesses, Thos. Bousfield, John Brunskill.

1781. May 27 Thos. Shaw & Ann Todd by Licence (f.a.)
Witnesses, John Heblethwaite, William Morros, John Stubbs.

1781. June 17 John Petty of the p. of Kirkby Stephen & Margaret Fawcet by Licence.
Witnesses, Thos. Bousfield, Robert Petty, John Fawcett.

1781. July 3 Thomas Wilson of the p. of Orton & Isabel Hewetson by Banns.
Witnesses, John Hewetson, Robert Farrer.

1781. Oct. 4 Stephen Dent & Margaret Bowyer by Licence (f.a.)
Witnesses, Thos. Fothergill, John Heblethwaite, Richard Holme.

1781. Nov. 11 John Shaw (×) & Eliz. Peacock (×) by Banns.
Witnesses, Isaac Handley, Robt. Chamberlain.

1781. Dec. 1 Thomas Shaw & Mary Head by Banns.
Witnesses, Wm. Rudde, Henry Hunter, george Shaw.

1781. Dec. 9 John Guy & Isabella Campbell by Banns.
Witnesses, John Milner, John Milner.

1781. Dec. 10 William Stephenson of Bolton in p. of Morland & Elizabeth Bellas (×) by Banns.
Witnesses, Matthew Wilkinson, George Parkin.

1781. Dec. 10 Richard Robinson & Margaret Shaw (×) by Banns.
Witnesses, John Robinson, James Shaw.

1782. Jan. 13 William Brunskill (×) & Ann Fawcet by Banns.
Witnesses, James Fawcett, Christopher Fawcett.

Note.—Except where otherwise stated the officiating Minister is "Jeff: Bowness."

MARRIAGES.

1782.	Feb. 12	Christopher Moss of the p. of Crosby Ravensworth & Phœbe Robinson by Licence (f.a.) Witnesses, Henry Robinson, Rich[d]. Robinson, Eliz. Bowness.
1782.	Ap. 16	Thomas Taylor of the p. of Sedbergh & Mary Birkbeck by Banns. Witnesses, Thomas Knewstupp, John Taylor.
1782.	May 18	John Udall & Agnes Rennison (×) by Banns. Witnesses, Richard Furnass, Jams Udall.
1782.	July 15	Joseph Birtle & Jennet Constantine (×) by Banns. Witnesses, John Constantine, Richard Birtell.
1782.	July 23	Robert Metcalf (×) & Agnes Richardson (×) by Banns. Witnesses, Rich[d]. Hewetson, Tho[s]. Wilson.
1782.	Sep. 29	Thomas Stubbs & Isabel Metcalf (×) by Banns. Witnesses, James Stubbs, Matthew Hunter.
1782.	Oct. 7	James Morland & Isabel Hewetson by Licence (f.a.) Witnesses, John Dickinson, Mary Bousfield, John Shaw.
1782.	Oct. 12	James Udal of the p. of Sedbergh & Eleanor Fawcet (×) by Banns. Witnesses, George Fawcett, John Udal (×).
1783.	Jan 25	Christopher Taylor of the p. of Sedbergh & Isabel Morland by Licence. Witnesses, John Taylor, Nancy Mounsey, Ann Hewetson.
1783.	Feb. 10	John Moister of the p. of Sedbergh & Ann Hutchinson (×) by Banns. Witness, Elizabeth Bowness.
1783.	Feb. 25	Henry Bousfield & Agnes Burton (×) by Licence. Witnesses, Matthew Wilkinson, Eliz. Bowness.
1783.	Ap. 27	John Taylor & Hannah Addison by Banns. Witnesses, Matthew Wilkinson, William Addison.
1783.	May 25	Michael Knewstubb & Elizabeth Beck (×) by Banns. Witnesses, Rob[t]. Bovell, John Beck.
1783.	Sep. 29	Christopher Rennison & Agnes Fawcet (×) by Banns. Witnesses, John Fawcett, Elizabeth Hewetson.

3[d] Duty on Marriages took Place 2[d] of October 1783.

1783.	Oct. 5	Robert Raw of the p. of Sedbergh & Ann Banks by Banns. Witnesses, Rich[d]. Robinson, Thomas Hastwell.

MARRIAGES.

1783. DEC. 8 Thomas Robinson & Margaret Hunter (×) by Banns.
Witnesses, Robert Todd, Isabel Overend (×).

1783. DEC. 28 Geo. Close (×) of the Chapelry of Mukar in the p. of Grinton & Isabel Fawcet by Banns.
Witnesses, James Close, James Fawcett.

1784. MAY 2 Robert Chamberlain & Mary Rennison (×) by Banns.
Witnesses, Isaac Handley, Matthew Wilkinson.

1784. MAY 10 Robert Fothergill & Mary Beck by Banns.
Witnesses, Henry Beck, Ralph fothergill.

1784. JUNE 8 Thomas Wharton of the p. of Kirkby Stephen & Margaret Shaw by Licence.
Witnesses, george Shaw, Henry Hunter, Eliz. Bowness.

1784. JUNE 15 Richard Brown (×) & Marg[t]. Metcalf (×) by Banns.
Witnesses, thomas metcalf, Jn[o]. Warcopp (×).

1784. OCT. 28 Thomas Milner & Mary Knewstubb (×) by Licence.
Witnesses, William Milner, Sally Scouler.

1784. NOV. 16 Thomas Knewstupp & Ann Fothergill by Banns.
Witnesses, Tho[s]. Holme, Tho[s]. Taylor.

1784. DEC. 12 John Warcop (×) & Ann Winder (×) by Banns.
Witnesses, Math. Brown (×), Matthew Wilkinson.

1784. DEC. 27 Thomas Fawcet & Ann Hastwel (×) by Banns.
Witnesses, Christopher Fawcett, Thomas Hastwell.

1785. FEB. 8 John Fawcet & Alice Udal by Banns.
Witnesses, John Heblethwaite, Stephen Dent.

1785. MAR. 6 W[m]. Preston (×) & Mary Clayton (×) by Banns.
Witnesses, Anthony Preston, Anthony Fawcett.

1785. AP. 3 John Nellson & Jane Stainton by Banns.
Witnesses, thomas nelson, Jn[o]. Wilkinson.

1785. AP. 26 Anthony Preston & Isabel Overend (×) by Banns.
Witnesses, George Shaw, Henry Beck.

1785. MAY 3 Mathew Haygarth & Margaret Hewetson by Banns.
Witnesses, John Hewetson, George Haygarth.

1785. JUNE 2 John Stubbs of the p. of K[y]. Stephen & Alice Coupland (×) by Licence.
Witness, John Heblethwaite.

1785. JUNE 28 John Chamberlain & Mary Waller by Banns.
Witnesses, Richard Chamberlain, John Robinson.

MARRIAGES.

1785. JULY 11 Anthony Fothergill & Frances Whaley (×) by Banns.
Witnesses, James Whaley, John Fothergill, Jonathan Fothergill.

1785. SEP. 1 Edmund Hodgson of the p. of St. Marylebone & Elizabeth Bousfield by Licence.
Witness, Arthur Bousfield.

1785. OCT. 10 Michael Winskill & Rebecca Moor (×) by Banns.
Witness, Rodger Moor (×).

1786. JAN. 11 Miles Lamb (×) & Isabel Farrer (×) by Banns.
Witnesses, Thomas Fothergill, Betty Fothergill.

1786. FEB. 21 Robert Murray of the p. of Warcop & Alice Chamberlain by Licence.
Witnesses, Richard Richardson, Phebe Chamberlain, John Fothergill.

1786. FEB. 28 William Fawcet & Sarah Hewetson by Banns.
Witnesses, John Hewetson, Anthony Fawcett.

1786. AP. 4 Robert Fawcett & Eleanor Hastewel (×) by Banns.
Witnesses, Thomas Hastwell, William Fawcett, John Parkin, Hugh Haygarth.

1786. AP. 17 Henry Hebden & Elizabeth Fothergill (×) by Banns.
Witnesses, thomas metcalf, Geff. Fothergill.

1786. MAY 14 Christ[r]. Fawcett & Margaret Foster (×) by Banns.
Witnesses, Thomas Hastwell, Henry Hunter.

1786. JUNE 10 William Fawcett & Eleanor Hunter by Banns.
Witnesses, Rob[t]. Hunter, John Hunter.

1786. JUNE 20 Tho[s]. Fawcett (×) & Margaret Burton (×) by Banns.
Witnesses, Thomas Knewstupp, Ann Knewstupp.

1786. SEP. 10 John Stubbs & Isabel Fawcet (×) by Banns.
Witnesses, James Stubbs, Mary Fawcett.

1786. SEP. 5 Robert Hunter & Elizabeth Bowness by Licence.
Witness, Rob[t]. Bowness.

1786. SEP. 29 George Alderson & Isabel Adamthwaite (×) by Banns.
Witnesses, James Alderson, Daivd Alderson.

1786. NOV. 12 Thomas Hastwell & Phœbe Chamberlain by Banns.
Witnesses, James Hastwell, Agnes Bousfield.

1787. AP. 30 William Morros & Jane Dawson by Banns.
Witnesses, Nathan Adamthwaite, Richard Thompson.

MARRIAGES.

1787. JUNE 3 George Whitehead of the p. of Orton & Ruth Fawcett by Licence.
Witnesses, John Wharton, John Fawcett.

1787. DEC. 10 Nathan Adamthwaite & Eliz. Murthwaite by Banns.
Witnesses, Robert Murthwaite, Mary Collinson.

1788. AUG. 3 James Whaley & Mary Tweedal (×) by Banns.
Witnesses, Isaac Handley, Fawcett Hunter.

1788. AUG. 5 James Simpson (×) of the p. of Ulverston in co. of Lancaster & Jennet Taylor (×) by Banns.
Witnesses, John Noble, Mary Hodgen.

1788. SEP. 5 Thoˢ. Shaw of the Chapelry of Barnerdcastle in the p. of Gainforth & Isabella Birkbeck by Banns.
Witnesses, John Stubbs, John Elwood.

1788. OCT. 20 John Gibbons (×) of p. of Appleby & Mary Hebblethwaite (×) by Banns.
Witnesses, John Fawcett, John Howe.

1788. OCT. 26 Samuel Relph of p. of Kʸ. Lonsdale & Agnes Bousfield by Licence.
Witnesses, Thomas Bousfield, Henry Perkins.

1788. OCT. 27 Edward Gibson (×) & Mary Birtle (×) by Banns.
Witnesses, James Birtle, (×) Agnes Birtle (×).

1788. DEC. 30 John Shaw of the p. of Kʸ. Stephen & Dorothy Haygarth (×) by Banns.
Witnesses, Thoˢ. Miller, Matthew Wilkinson.

1789. FEB. 23 John Varey (×) of the p. of Sedbergh & Mary Lodge (×) by Banns.
Witnesses, John Ayrey, John Wilkinson.

1789. SEP. 20 Richard Tunstall & Isabella Robinson by Licence.
Witnesses, Thomas Scarborough, Mary Bousfield, Hugh Shaw.

1790. AP. 26 Thomas Taylor (×) & Elizabeth Spooner (×) by Banns.
Witnesses, Thomas Adamthwaite, Henry Robinson.

1790. AUG. 26 Joseph Shaw & Isabel Fothergill by Banns.
Witnesses, John Shaw (×), John Tarlington (×).

1790. SEP. 28 Jonathan Fothergill of the p. of Kʸ. Stephen & Agnes Fothergill (×) by Licence.
Witnesses, Robert Atkinson, Giffrey Fothergill, Henry Hebdon.

MARRIAGES.

1790. Oct. 18 Jeremy Taylor of the p. of Asby & Ann Hewetson by Banns.
Witnesses, James Hoggart, Benjn. Hewetson.

1791. Mar. 6 John Hunter & Mary Wilson by Licence.
Witnesses, James Hunter, Edward Wilson, Margret Hunter, John Stubbs.

1791. Ap. 13 John Williamson of the p. of K^{y}. Stephen & Elizabeth Metcalf (×) by Licence.
Witnesses, Anthony Metcalfe, John Warton.

1791. June 13 John Birtle (×) & Sibyl Spooner (×) by Banns by James Fothergill [T. Jeff: Bowness] Off^{g}. Minister.
Witnesses, William Spooner, Richard Birtel.

1791. Sep. 29 David Hewetson of the p. of K^{y}. Stephen & Mary Fothergill by Licence.
Witnesses, Rich^{d}. Dixon, Benjn. Hewetson, John Hewetson.

1792. Jan. 24 Robert Sheraton of the p. of Houghton in the Co. of Durham & Isabel Robinson by Licence.
Witnesses, Mary Fothergill, Henry Robinson, John ffothergill.

1792. June 16 Thomas Airey & Mary Ireland by Banns.
Witnesses, William Airey, John Fothergill.

1792. June 25 Robert Kirk of the p. of Aisgarth & Sibyl Richmond (×) by Banns.
Witnesses, Mich^{l}. Bovell, Matthew Wilkinson.

1792. Sep. 4 James Haygarth & Mary Rennison by Licence.
Witnesses, Christopher Rennison, William Haygarth.

1792. Sep. 10 Joseph Rennison & Eleanor Metcalf (×) by Banns.
Witnesses, Robt. Bowness, Matthew Wilkinson.

1792. Nov. 25 William Winder (×) & Nancy Guy (×) by Banns.
Witnesses, John Guy, John Milner.

1793. Feb. 12 David Hewetson of the p. of K^{y}. Stephen & Sarah Skouler by Licence.
Witnesses, Ann Hewetson, Fawcett Hunter, Benjn. Hewetson.

1793. Feb. 12 Thomas Knewstupp & Ann Hebblethwaite by Banns.
Witnesses, Anthony Metcalfe, James Whaley.

MARRIAGES.

1793. May 15 John Thompson & Margaret Hunter by Banns.
Witnesses, Thomas Ireland, James Hunter.

1793. May 19 William Urwin (×) of the p. of Kendal & Mary Atkinson (×) by Banns.
Witnesses, William Fothergill, James Whaley.

1793. May 22 Henry Dodgson of the p. of Brough & Sarah Coats (×) by Licence.
Witnesses, Thomas Sturdy, Nanny Devis (×).

1793. June 17 Thomas Hunter & Ann Hutchinson (×) by Licence.
Witnesses, Adam Hutchinson, John Hunter.

1793. Aug. 16 Thos. Ash (×) & Mary Procter (×) by Banns.
Witnesses, Robt. Bowness, William Raw.

1793. Oct. 19 Robert Hunter & Ann Smith by Licence.
Witnesses, Ann Hunter (×), John Nelson.

1794. Jan. 20 Stephen Dent & Mary Turner by Licence.
Witnesses, William Howgill, Robert Bowness, John Fawcett.

1794. Ap. 29 William Furnass & Elizabeth Fothergill by Banns.
Witnesses, Richard Furnass, John Fothergill.

1794. Sep. 29 James Udal & Ann Hewetson by Banns.
Witnesses, Benjamin Hewetson, John Udal, Peggy Morland.

1794. Dec. 7 George Fawcett & Sarah Whitfield by Banns.
Witnesses, Robert Udal, William Dawson.

1795. Jan. 1 Robert Deighton of the p. of K^{y}. Lonsdale & Margaret Thompson by Banns.
Witnesses, Thomas Thompson, W^{m}. Dawson.

1795. May 11 James Rennison & Hannah Harrison (×) by Banns.
Witnesses, John Rennison, Aggnes Harrison.

1795. May 24 Stephen Dent & Margaret Perkins by Licence.
Witnesses, John Morland, Isabella Perkins, Peggy Morland, Stephen Hunter.

1795. July 5 George Perkin of the p. of K^{y}. Stephen & Isabel Atkinson by Licence.
Witnesses, Robt. Bowness, John Wilkinson.

1795. Sep. 22 Isaac Hodgson & Ann Hunter by Licence by Robt. Bowness, Curate.
Witnesses, W^{m}. Dawson, Jno. Cooper.

MARRIAGES.

1795. Dec. 1 John Robinson (x) & Mary Fawcett by Banns.
Witnesses, Thomas Adamthwaite, Isable Adamthwaite, John Guy.

1796. Jan 5 Mathew Brown (x) & Jennet Birtle (x) by Banns.
Witnesses, John Udall, John Rennison.

1796. Jan. 17 James Fothergill (x) & Margaret Thompson (x) by Banns by Robt. Bowness, Curate.
Witnesses, James Hunter, John Thompson.

1796. Mar. 21 Ralph Ion & Elizabeth Potter by Banns by Robt. Bowness, Curate.
Witnesses, Joseph Chamberlain, John Wilkinson.

1796. Ap. 12 Robert Hewetson & Bridget Richardson by Banns.
Witnesses, Robert Hewetson, * Hewetson, Joseph Udal.

1796. May 1 James McKinzie (x) of the p. of Wigton & Mary Hodgson by Banns.
Witnesses, Thomas Clarkson, Ellisabeth Robinson.

1796. June 17 Robert Wilson & Isabel Shearman by Licence.
Witnesses, Isaac Handley, Margre Shearman, Stephen Shaw.

1796. Aug. 22 John Foster of the p. of Sedbergh & Mary Haygarth by Banns.
Witnesses, Wm. Inman, John Booth.

1796. Nov. 29 James Martin & Ann Thompson by Banns, by Robt. Bowness, Curate.
Witnesses, Wm. Dawson, John Robinson.

1796. Nov. 29 Thomas Hunter & Ann Taylor by Banns, by Robt. Bowness, Curate.
Witnesses, Richd. Dixon, John Hewetson, John Udal.

1797. Feb. 20 James Udal (x) & Isabel Stubbs (x) by Banns.
Witnesses, William Stubbs, John Wilkinson.

1797. Feb. 23 William Inman of the p. of Sedbergh & Sarah Shaw by Licence.
Witnesses, Mary Elyetson, Mabel Inman, Isabel Shaw, John Wallas, Henry Robinson.

---

* Illegible.

MARRIAGES.

1797. Mar. 20 John Cooper & Ann Fawcett by Banns.
Witnesses, Isabel fawcett, Thomas Robinson.

1797. Ap. 10 John Robinson Schoolmaster & Mary Raisbeck by Banns.
Witnesses, John Stubbs, John Wilkinson.

1797. May 29 John Warcopp (×) & Mary Dent (×) by Banns by Robt. Bowness, Curate.
Witnesses, John Wilson, James Hunter.

1797. May 30 William Slee of the p. of Longmarton & Mary Fothergill by Banns.
Witnesses, Dan. Simpson, Henry Fothergill.

1797. June 20 Thomas Ireland & Ann Hutchinson by Banns.
Witnesses, Isabell fawcett, George Scarborough.

1797. June 26 John Farrah (×) of the p. of St. Mary's in Kingston upon Hull & Mary Chamberlain (×) by Licence.
Witnesses, Joseph Chamberlain, Agnes Buck.

1797. Nov. 14 John Airey of the p. of Sedbergh & Ann Hunter by Licence.
Witnesses, Joshua Hunter, Joseph Hunter.

1797. Nov. 19 John Udal (×) & Ann Birtle (×) by Banns.
Witnesses, Anthony Birtell, Edmund Udal (×).

1797. Nov. 27 Anthony Lambert of the p. of Sedbergh & Ann Broun by Banns.
Witnesses, Wm. Dawson, John harper.

1798. Mar. 1 William Furnass (×) & Margaret Fothergill (×) by Banns.
Witnesses, Ralph fothergill, John Wilkinson.

1798. Mar. 5 John Warcop (×) & Ann Wharton (×) by Banns.
Witnesses, Robert Chamberlain, John Wilkinson.

1798. May 9 Stephen Hunter & Ruth Perkins by Banns.
Witnesses, James Hunter, Bella Perkins, Stephen Dent.

1798. Dec. 16 John Hewetson & Mary Smith by Banns.
Witnesses, Nancy Richardson, Jane Taylor, Henry Hewetson, John Hill.

1799. Feb. 26 Robert Fothergill & Elizabeth Pearson by Banns.
Witnesses, Wm. Dawson, Mark Stalker, Edward Adamthwaite.

1799. May 6 Benjamin Hewetson & Isabella Perkin by Banns.
Witnesses, James Udal, Stephen Hunter.

MARRIAGES.

1799. June 8 George Lambert of the p. of Sedbergh & Agnes Fawcett (×) by Banns.
Witnesses, John Hunter, William Fawcett.

1799. July 3 James Hastwell & Ann Hunter by Licence.
Witnesses, Matthew Hunter, George Fawcett.

1799. July 23 George Fawcett & Sarah Harrison by Banns.
Witnesses, George Fawcett, James hastwell.

1799. Nov. 11 John Murthwaite & Mable Graham (×) by Banns.
Witnesses, George Murthwaite, Mary Collinson, Robert Murthwaite.

1799. Nov. 14 William Hall (×) & Margaret Thompson by Banns.
Witnesses, Matthew thompson, John Wilkinson.

1799. Nov. 21 George Fawcett & Catherine Toping (×) of the p. of K^{y}. Stephen by Banns.
Witnesses, W^{m}. Dawson, John Wilkinson.

1800. May 20 Mathew Hunter & Jane Perkins by Banns.
Witnesses, Joseph Hunter, Eleanor Hunter.

1800. June 3 Thos. Theckston of the p. of Sedbergh & Eliz. Fawcett by Banns.
Witnesses, George Theckston, John Ellis.

* 1800. Aug. 19 Thomas Fawcett & Susanna Esther Hill by Banns.
Witnesses,

1801. Feb. 10 Thomas Coatesworth of the p. of Haughton & Isabel Shaw by Licence.
Witnesses, Henry Robinson, Aley Shaw, Thos. Sowerby.

1801. May 11 Adam Robinson (×) & Elizabeth Watson (×) by Banns.
Witnesses, W^{m}. Dawson, Jo^{s}. Shaw.

1801. June 22 Thomas Thompson & Margaret Thompson by Banns.
Witnesses, Thos. Ireland, Mary Rennison.

1801. July 18 Thomas Fawcett of the p. of Grinton in Co. of York & Nanny Alderson (×) by Licence.
Witnesses, John Fawsett, Christopher Alderson.

1801. Sep. 1 John Hunter & Ann Rennison (×) by Banns.
Witnesses, James Hunter, John Rennison.

---

* This marriage is also entered in the older Register, where "John Hill," and "William Fawcett" sign as witnesses. Probably the proper Register had been mislaid at the time of the Marriage.

MARRIAGES.

1801. Sep. 22 Joseph Hunter & Isabella Wilson by Banns.
Witnesses, James Wilson, Nancy Arey.

1801. Oct. 10 Christopher Alderson & Agnes Wilson by Licence, by Geo: Bowness Curate (pro tempore).
Witnesses, Thomas Fawcett, John Hunter.

1801. Nov. 23 Richard Moister (×) of the p. of Sedbergh & Agnes Spooner (×) by Banns.
Witnesses, John Wilkinson, Isabella Wilkinson.

1801. Dec. 1 James Robinson of the p. of Kirkby Lonsdale & Elizabeth Robinson (×) by Banns.
Witnesses, Rich[d]. Guy, John Guy.

1802. Jan. 2 John Wharton of the p. of K[y]. Stephen & Isabella Milner by Licence.
Witnesses, John Milner Senior, Rich[d]. Dixon, W[m]. Dawson.

1802. Jan. 19 Robert Savage of the p. of Orton & Isabel Robinson by Banns.
Witnesses, George Robinson, W[m]. Burry, Jane Thompson.

1802. Mar. 2 Christopher Taylor of the p. of Sedbergh & Eleanor Fawcett by Banns.
Witnesses, Richard * John Grisdale.

1802. Mar. 7 John Dixon of the p. of Bongate & Eleanor Ewin (×) by Licence.
Witnesses, John Ewin, Robert Ewin.

1802. Mar. 24 John Todd & Isabel Adamthwaite by Banns.
Witnesses, George Parkin, Richard Hewetson.

1802. June 15 William Adamthwaite & Mary Knewstupp by Banns.
Witnesses, Edward Knewstupp, Ruth Chamberlain.

1802. Dec. 21 Michael Steel & Mary Graham by Banns.
Witnesses, Thomas Scarborough, John Wilkinson.

1802. Dec. 27 William Bayles of the p. of Gainforth & Sarah Hewetson by Licence.
Witnesses, Rich[d]. Hewetson, Eleanor Hewetson.

1803. Jan. 4 Edward Handley of the p. of Sedbergh & Eleanor Fawcett by Banns.
Witnesses, Thomas Hastwell, Geo. Lambert.

---

* Illegible. Transcriph has "Bouth."

MARRIAGES.

1803. FEB. 19 James Lindsay & Nanny Hall (×) by Banns.
Witnesses, george Hewetson, William Hall.

1803. FEB. 21 Joseph Thompson & Mary Rennison by Banns.
Witnesses, W^{m}. Dawson, Geo. Fawcett.

1803. MAR. 8 Christopher Rennison & Isabel Fawcett by Banns.
Witnesses, Susannah Fawcet, Ruth Chamberlain, Thomas Fawcett.

1803. AP. 19 Edward Beck & Mary Moreland by Licence.
Witnesses, Anthony Morland, Peggy Morland, William Dixon, Ann Dent, Anthony Hunter.

1803. JUNE 13 Anthony Birtle & Ann Fothergill (×) by Banns.
Witnesses, James Birtel, John Wilson.

1803. OCT. 2 William Watson & Mary Nelson by Banns.
Witnesses, Jacob Tallentire, George Sayer.

1803. NOV. 14 Thomas Steel & Sarah Hugginson (×) by Banns.
Witnesses, Joseph Atkinson, John Wilkinson.

1804. MAY 28 Thos. Robinson & Mary Thompson by Banns.
Witnesses, W. Dawson, Eleanor Hewetson, Robert Robinson.

1804. JUNE 5 Thcmas Relph & Margaret Robinson (×) by Banns.
Witnesses, Septimus Parkns Udal, John Wilkinson.

1804. JUNE 5 Joseph Dent (×) & Elizabeth Steadman (×) by Banns.
Witnesses, Ralph Lonsdale, John Emerson.

1804. JUNE 19 Richard Hewetson & Elizabeth Robinson by Licence.
Witnesses, Michael Robinson, Richard Hewetson.

1804. JUNE 25 John McMinnies of the p. of Lancaster & Eleanor Hewetson by Licence.
Witnesses, Rich^{d}. Dixon, Rich^{d}. Hewetson.

1804. JULY 2 Mathew Birtle of the p. of Sedbergh & Ann Cowper by Banns.
Witnesses, Henry Shaw, John Wilkinson.

1804. JULY 3 Anthony Fawcett & Elizabeth Fothergill by Licence.
Witnesses, Rich^{d}. Hewetson, James Fothergill.

1804. SEP. 11 William Turner & Ruth Whitehead by Banns.
Witnesses, Thomas Hunter, Anthony Metcalfe.

MARRIAGES.

1804. Sep. 17 William Fawcett (×) of the p. of Tinmouth & Ann Wharton by Licence.
Witnesses, Wm. Dawson, Joseph Chamberlain.

1804. Sep. 24 Thomas Fawcett & Elizabeth Wilkinson by Licence.
Witnesses, John Robinson, John Wilkinson.

1804. Nov. 14 John Thompson & Alice Dent (×) by Banns.
Witnesses, Wm. Raine, Robert Thompson.

1804. Nov. 30 William Dixon & Alice Shaw by Licence.
Witnesses, John Wharton, Henry Robinson, Richd. Dixon.

1804. Dec. 24 William Potter & Agnes Brown (×) by Banns.
Witnesses, Richard Potter, John Wilkinson.

1804. Dec. 25 Robert Murthwaite & Ann Nelson by Banns.
Witnesses, George murthwaite, Edward Nelson.

1805. May 1 Robert Hewetson & Eleanor Hunter (×) by Banns.
Witnesses, Joseph Udale, John Hewetson.

1805. July 8 Edmund Whitehead of the p. of Orton & Mary Hewetson by Licence.
Witnesses, John Hewetson, Michael Taylor.

1805. Aug. 12 Rodger Moister of the p. of Sedbergh & Ann Fawcett by Banns.
Witnesses, Tomas Jockson, John Wilkinson.

1805. Sep. 25 George Hall & Mary Allen (×) by Banns.
Witnesses, Thomas Allen, Benj. Hewetson.

1806. May 24 Wm. Mackreth of Strickland kettle & Bella Furness (×) by Banns.
Witnesses, William Furnass, Isabella Wilkinson.

1806. Aug. 25 Richard Beck & Margaret Hewetson by Licence.
Witnesses, Henry Beck, Robert Hewetson.

1806. Oct. 15 Jeffery Fothergill & Mary Coates by Banns.
Witnesses, Thomas Kirkbride, Henry Robinson.

1806. Dec. 23 William Furness & Isabella Wilkinson by Banns.
Witnesses, John Robinson, Jon. Wilkinson.

1806. Dec. 31 Richard Robinson & Margaret Morland by Licence.
Witnesses, John Morland, Anthony Morland.

1807. May 5 Miles Turner (×) & Elizabeth Parkin (×) by Licence.
Witnesses, Wm. Dawson, Jno. Wilkinson.

MARRIAGES.

1807. JULY 5 James Fawcett (x) & Nancy Relph by Licence.
Witnesses, Thomas Relph, John Wilkinson.

1807. NOV. 9 David Alderson (x) & Eleanor Hunter by Banns.
Witnesses, Richard Alderson, Mary Hunter, James Wilson.

1807. NOV. 17 Richard Fothergill & Mary Jackson of the p. of Asby by Licence.
Witnesses, Thos. Jackson, Mary Fothergill, William Fothergill.

1808. MARCH 31 Thomas Dixon of the p. of Ky. Stephen & Isabel Hewetson by Licence.
Witnesses, Robert Hewetson, Mary Petty.

1808. DEC. 26 George Fairclough of the p. of Liverpool & Elizabeth Margaret Robinson by Licence.
Witnesses, * Valentine, Sarah Jackson.

1809. JAN. 14 Jno. Perkins of the p. of Hayton & Elizabeth Alderson by Banns.
Witnesses, Esther Dent, Richard Wilson.

1809. JAN 15 Henry Nelson & Susanna Kirkbride by Banns.
Witnesses, Ralph fothergill, Edward Wilkinson.

1809. MAR. 5 Michael Smith & Peggy Udal by Licence, by John Robinson Officiatg. Mintister.
Witnesses, Mary Emmerson, Peter Handley.

1809. MAY 1 Bell Parkin & Nancy Hunter by Banns.
Witnesses, Anthony Wharton, John Parkin.

1809. JUNE 24 Thomas Fawcett of the p. of Dent & Margaret Elyetson by Licence.
Witnesses, Henry Robinson, Michaell Bovell.

1809. JULY 3 Joseph Breaks & Nancy Shaw (x) by Banns.
Witnesses, James F. Hunter, Jno. Wilkinson, William Shaw.

† 1809. JULY 17 Mark Watson of the p. of Middleton & Eleanor Fawcett Rennison by Licence.
Witnesses, Thomas Robson, Wm. Watson, Mary Handley.

1810. FEB. 13 James Birtle & Mary Thompson by Banns.
Witnesses, Joseph Thompson, John Thomson.

---

* Illegible.

MARRIAGES.

1810. Feb. 19 Richard Potter & Eleanor Fawcett (×) of the p. of Garsdale by Banns.
Witnesses, William Potter, Jn°. Wilkinson.

1810. Ap. 9 William Furnass & Elizabeth Blenkhorn by Banns.
Witnesses, Richard Furnass, Jn°. Wilkinson, Isabella Blenkhorn.

1810. May 30 Joseph Thompson (×), & Sarah Metcalf (×) of the p. of Asby by Banns.
Witnesses, Wm. Dawson, John Metcalf.

1810. Nov. 14 Thomas Kirkbride & Mary Clayton by Banns.
Witnesses, John Clyton, Jane Canby (×).

1811. Jan. 9 Richard Furnass of Shap & Mary Whaley by Banns.
Witnesses, James Hunter, John Knewstubb.

1811. May 23 John Clarkson of the p. of West Witton & Mary Fothergill by Licence.
Witnesses, Nancy Ellyetson, Richd. Fothergill.

1811. July 17 William Callon of the p. of Kendal & Sarah Braithwaite by Licence.
Witnesses, William Braithwaite, John Beck.

1811. Sep. 21 John Alderson of the p. of Muker & Sarah Hunter by Licence.
Witnesses, David Alderson (×), Ann Hunter, Robt. Hunter.

1812. July 13 William Shaw & Margaret Benn by Banns by Jn°. Fawcett Assistent Curate.
Witnesses, Robt. Herd (×), James Hunter.

1812. Oct. 22 John Fothergill & Elizabeth Stephenson by Banns.
Witnesses, Edwd. Hoggarth, James Fothergill, Jeffery Hebdon.

1812. Oct. 26 Richard Thompson of the p. of Ky. Stephen Batchelor & Mary Elyetson Spinster by Licence.
Witnesses, Nancy Ellyetson, Margaret Sheraton, Margaret Fawcett, Thos. Fawcett.

BURIALS.

1781.

JAN. 7th	William Howgill of Lane agd 90.
FEB. 17th	Joseph Hunter of Tarnhouse.
MARCH 5th	Thos. Fawcett of Greenside.
do. 20th.	Eliz. wife of Thos. Fothergill of Brounber.
do. 27th	Isabel Fawcet of Burnthill.
APRIL 10th [T. 5th]	Isabel Handson of Garshill.
do. 12th	[T. Margaret] Daughter of Wm. Spooner.

* BURIED.

AUGt. 17th	William son of Jno. Milner of Ashfield & Mary his wife.
18th	William son of Mr. Jno. Robinson of Ashfield & Isabel his wife.
SEP. 27th	Sarah wife of Jno. Dockerah of Dubbs.
OCT. 12th	Jane Daughter of Wm. Adamthwaite of Adamthwaite & Jane his wife.
do. 31st	John Dockerah of Dubbs.
Nov. 13th	John son of Eliz. Lambert Illegitimate.
† do. 16th	
DECEM. 9th	Elizabeth wife of Richard Alderson of hole.

1782.

† FEB. 1st	
MARCH 22d	Margaret Daughter of Richd. Thompson of Hill & Sarah his wife [T. aged 13 years].
25th	Thomas son of William Elliotson of Scarsykes & Agnes his wife [T. aged 3 years].

---

* About a quarter of a page left blank. No blank in T.

BURIALS.

April 13th	William son of Wm. Stubbs of Townhead & Margaret his wife [T. 1 year].
18th	James son of John Stubbs & Eliz. his wife [T. aged 1 year].
May 2d	Robt. Johnstone a Traveller [T. aged 80].
7th	William s. of Thos. Nelson of Town [T. an Infant].

1782. Buried.

May 23	John son of Margt. Spooner [T. of Newbegin, an Infant].
July 19	John Birtle of Artlegarth [T. aged 70].
† 21st	Jane D. of John Petty of Wharton.
24th	Isabel Dent of Dovingill [T. aged 27].
Sep. 25th	Margaret Elliotson of Broughfoot [T. of Scarsykes] Aged 75.
Oct. 1st	Mathew Whitfield of Low Lane Aged 88.

1783.	1783.
Feb. 1st	Thomas Fothergill of Brounber Aged 72.
do. 8th	James Hewetson of Newbegin Aged 50.
Mar. 26	Ann Richardson a Pauper Aged 86.
do. 27th	Mary Ewbank of Crooks beck Aged 50.
June 15	Margt. Petty of Wharton Aged 26.
† 21st	Margt. Ion a Pauper Aged 80.
23d	Eliz. Fothergill of Scarsykes [T. aged 50].
July 3d	Mary Maiden a Pauper removed from Brough.
do. 16th	John Toulmin of Town Agd 70.
do. 20th	Eliz. Hewetson a Pauper Agd. 85.
do. 22d	Ann Robinson of Scar Agd 36.
† Sep. 22d	Simon Bousfield of Gars Aged 89.
Nov. 22d	Anthony Robinson of Garshill aged 76 A Pauper.
do. 27	Jacob Rennison an Infant.

1783. Buried.

Decem. 13	Fothergill Metcalf [T. of Brownber] Aged 25.
do. 14	Margaret wife of William Stubbs a Pauper Aged 51.
do. 21st	Mary Urwin a Pauper Agd 10.
do. 27	James Shaw of Garshill Aged 66.

BURIALS.

1784.

JAN. 1st	Ruth Procter of Garshill Aged 45 Paup.
FEB. 13	Robert Hunter of Town Aged 74.
do. 15	Anth. Fawcet of Street Agd. 42.
do. 28th	Willm. Fothergill of Lockholme Aged 71.
APRIL 1st	Margt. Robinson of Greenside [T. aged 68].
APRIL 3d	Richd. Bovel of Newbegin Aged 78.
do. 11th	Richard Robinson of Bleaflat Agd 70.
SEP. 12	John Adamthwaite of Fell end Aged 26.
do. 19th	Margt. Metcalf [T. a Pauper] Aged 86.
OCT. 1st	Margt. wife of Martin Wilson Aged 46.
do. 4th	Edward Beck of Artlegarth Aged 73.
do.	Thos. Richardson of Dubbs agd 72.
do. 28th	William Fawcett of Wreagreen Aged 82.
NOV. 16	Thomas Robinson of Scar Agd 77.

BURIED.	1785.
JAN. 6th	Richard Fothergill of Lockholme Aged 76.
do. 17th	Robt. Todd of Greenside aged 57.
FEB. 15	Henry Hunter of Fell End Agd 75.
do. 16	Sarah Breeks of Newbegin Agd. 79.
MAY 1st	Margaret Dent of Dovingill Aged 82.
do. 4th	Eleanor Fawcet of Wreagreen Aged 75.
do. 8th	John Robinson of Garshill Aged 84.
do. 14th	Isabel Fothergill of Brounber Aged 73.
do. 15th	Jeffrey Lodge of Coldbeck Aged 57.
JULY [T. 5th]	Dorothy Urwin of Newbegin Aged 79.
SEP. 3d	Mary Fothergill of Lytheside Aged 81.
do. 5th	Christr. Fawcet of Cawtley Aged 75.
do. 9th	Eliz. Hewetson of Newbegin Aged 41.
OCT. 23d	Sarah wife of Joseph Breeks of Newbegin Aged 76.

1786.

JAN. [T. 5]	Barbara Daughter of Willm. Spooner of Weesdale Aged 14.
JAN. [T. 16]	Mary wife of Anthony Metcalf Aged 50.
MAR. 4	Mary Fothergill of Foggy gill Aged 89.
do. 5	George Shaw of Studfold Ag. 67.
do. 12	Thomas Hanson of Coldbeck Ag. [T. 75].

BURIALS.

1786. BURIED.

APRIL [T. 5] Peggy Daughter of John & Alice Fawcet [T. an Infant].
APRIL 30 Willm. Stubbs Taylor Aged 50.
† MAY 10 Daughter of Mark Richardson P.
JULY 1st Isabel Wilson Widow Agd 57.
JULY 6 Isabel* Kirkbride [T. of Wandale] Agd 67.
JULY 23d William Preston Taylor Ag. 22.
JULY 24 Edward Stubbs Taylor Ag. 27
OCT. 25 Mary wife of Robert Fothergill [T. of Studfold] Aged 27.
NOV. 15 Thos. [T. son of Geo:] Hastewell Aged 12.
do. 16th Margt. [T. Daughter of Thos.] Thompson an Infant.
do. 21st Thos. Cherry Aged 18.
DECEMBR. 21st Allan Robinson of Highstannerskugh Aged 27.

1787.

JAN. 20th Eliz. D. of Mr. [T. John] Robinson [T. Schoolmaster] of Ashfield & Isabel his wife Aged 3** years.
JAN. 26th Joshua Ewbank of Crooks [T. Yeoman] Aged 57.

MAY 18th Richd. Murthwaite of Low Lane [T. Yeoman] Aged 82.
JUNE 20th Richd. Hewetson of Artlegarth [T. Carpinter] agd 37.
do. 24 Margt. Robinson of Bleaflat [T. Spinster] Agd 59.
JULY 3d John Hastewel of Foggygill [T. Labourer] Agd. 57.
do. Jane Wilson of Murthwaite [T. Spinster] Agd 28.
do. 12th Richd. Scarbrough of Low Lane [T. Surgeon] Agd 24.
AUGt [T. 6th] Margt. Gegson [T. wife of Richd.] of Sandwath Agd 75.
OCT. 20th Thos. son of Wm. Hewetson Carpinter [T. aged 12].
do. 29th Wm. Haygarth of Newbegin [T. Yeoman] Aged 59.
† NOV. 16 Richard Hewetson of Artlegarth.
† DEC. 14 Margaret Murrow aged 75.

* Originally "Elizabeth." "Isabel" in T.
** Or, perhaps "8."

BURIALS.

1788. BURIED.

FEB. 10th	Nancy wife of Thos. Knewstupp [T. aged 38 years].
do. 15th	Francis Dinsdal [T. of Fellend] Pauper 80.
MARCH 5th	Thos. Dent of Gars Aged 86.
do. 26	A child [T. Isabel, Daughter] of Richd. Furnass.
APRIL 5th	Faithy Dent of Stoophill Gate [T. aged 70].
JULY 2d	Eliz. Fawcett of Town Agd 72.
AUGt 8	John Fawcett of Town Agd 19.
OCT. 2	Mary Gosling of Fell end [T. aged 52].
do. 18th	Mary Birtle of Fell end Agd 76 P.
do. 19	William son of Henry Hebden [T. an Infant].
NOV. 2d	Joseph Breeks Taylor Agd 79.
do.	Margt. Dennison [T. of Town] Aged 80 P.

1789.

JAN. 1st	Thos. son of Thos. Shaw Innkeeper Aged six months.
do. 5th	Henry Perkins of Lockholme Agd 54.
do. 7th	James son of Henry Hebden Aged 1 year.
do. 10th	Mary Taylor of Town Aged 85 Pau.
[T. FEB. 4th	Robert] son of John Thompson Aged 14 Paup.
MARCH 28th	Richard Atkinson of Town [T. Labourer] Aged 48 P.
MAY 4th	Sarah Scarbrough of Low Lane Agd 22.
do. 6th	Agnes Drybeck of Town Agd 28 P.
do. 10th	Wm. Metcalf of Beckstones [T. Farmer] Agd 72.
JUNE 12th	Ann Coulston of Waingarth [T. Widow] Agd 74.
do.	Isabel Urwin Pauper [T. aged 48].
JULY 13th	Margt. Hastwell Pauper Agd 74.
do. 20th	Wm. son of Thos. Thompson an Infant.
do. 27th	Thos. Fawcett of Town [T. Labourer] Aged 75.
do. 31st	A Child of Agnes Stubbs Illegit.
AUGt. 5th	The Revd. Anthony Shaw Aged 43.
do. 10th	Miles Lamb of Intack [T. Labourer] Aged 75.
do. 18th	Ann Watson [T. a Servant] Aged 19 [T. 18] Paup.
do. 24th	Edward Cherry of Bleaflat [T. Farmer] Aged 59.
OCT. 13th	Isabel Fawcett Paup. Aged 57.
do. 30th	William Hunter of Sprint Gill [T. Yeoman] Agd 70.

BURIALS.

Nov. 5th John Fawcett of Adamthwaite Agd 57.
1789. Nov. 6th Dorothy wife of Mark Richardson P. [T. aged 48].
do. 26 John Thompson [T. of Town] P. Aged 87.

1790. Buried.

Feb. 2d Betty Daughter of Christr. Rennison of Town Aged 3 years.
do. 9th John s. of John Kirkbride Aged 4 months.
March [T. 1st] Thomas Hastwel Agd 87 yrs.
March [T. 5th] John Hastwel Paup. Aged 37.
March [T. 15th] George son of Geo. Parkin Agd 4.
March [T. 30th] Martha Thompson Aged 75 P.
April 21st Mary Fothergill of Dubbs Agd 47.
May 1st Anthony Hodgson Aged 70 Paup.
do. 16th Agnes Daughter of Thos. Stubbs an Infant.
do. 17th Thos. Fothergill of Dubbs Aged 63.
do. 21st Eliz. Daughter Robert Chamberlain an Infant.
do. 23d John Robinson of Stannerskugh Agd 68.
June 29 Esther Milner of Longgill Agd 57.
July 3d Margt. D. of Joseph Fothergill of Lockholme & Jane his wife Agd 18.
do. 9th Isabel Armstrong Aged 86.
do. 12th [T. 10th] son of John Fothergill of Greenside yr 1.
Augt. 7 Sarah Daughter of Ruth Kitchen an Infant.
do. 14th Ann Metcalf of New House Paup.
do. 22d Mary D. of Robt. Scarbrough [T. of Low lane] Agd 21.
do. Agnes Furnass Aged 88 Paup.
do. 25 John Dent of Garshill Aged 70.
Sep. 25 Stephen Fawcett of Wreagreen Aged 84.
Oct. 4th William Thompson of Town Aged 63.
do. John Drybeck of Townhead Aged 18.
Nov. 3d Agnes D. of Henry & Ruth Perkins Aged 7.
do. 30 [T. William son] of Thos. Stubbs of Town Aged 2.

1791.

Jan. 7 Leonard Metcalf of Town 65.
Feb. 6th Thos. son of John Shearman Aged 24.

BURIALS.

1791. Buried.

Feb. 17th	Richd. Fothergill of Dubbs Aged 22.
do. 24th	Peter son of Robert Hutchinson of Newbegin Aged 6 years.
do. 26th	Mathew Birtle of Town aged 84.
do.	Agnes D. of Richd. Furnass an Infant.
March 8th	John Alderson of Studfold Aged 85.
April 7	Jane Felton of Newbegin Agd 67.
do. 12th	Sarah Fothergill of Dubbs Agd 18.
do. 19th	Sarah Dixon of Causey end Agd 76.
May 14th	Anth. Urwin of Town Agd 83 P.
do. 20th	Revd. Thos. Fothergill of Lockholme Agd 27.
June 1st	Mary Fawcett of Newbegin Pauper Aged 83.
Augt. 15	Eliz. Robinson of Scar Aged 72.
Sep. 30	Thos. Shaw of Street Aged 30 Paup.
Oct. 20th	Margaret Scarbrough of Low Lane Aged 39.
Decembr. 3d	George Fothergill of Tarnhouse Aged 78.
do. 31st	Elizabeth Hunter of Elmpot Agd 20.

1792.

Jan. 1st	John Dent of Turnpike Gate Agd 83.
do. 2d	Richard Alderson of th' Hole Agd 88.
Jan. 16th	William Fothergill of Dubbs Agd 18.
do. 17th	Sarah Fothergill of Lockholme Agd 84.
do. 31st	Matthew Constantine of Town Agd 83 P.
Feb. 1st	Jarret Robinson of Greenside Agd 62.
do. 23d	John Ward of Town Taylor Agd 24 Pauper.
do. 25th	Eleanor Fawcett of Schoolhouse Agd 16.
March 1st	Thos. Wilson of Elmpot Aged 14.
do. 4th	Jane Hewetson of Hill Agd 72.
do. 10th	Mary [T. wife of David] Hewetson of Kirkby Stephen Aged 24.
do. do.	John Thompson of Rigend Agd 24.
April 13	John Taylor of Town Agd 7 Pau.

1792. Buried.

April 15th	Frances Daughter of Robt. Hutchinson of Newbegin an Infant [T. aged 1 year].

BURIALS.

APRIL 17th Eliz. Daughter of John Shaw of Town an Infant Pauper.
do. 22d [T. 23d] Jonathan Alderson of Studfold Aged 55.
do. 24th Richd. Gregson of Artlegarth Agd 85.
do. 26th Mathew Metcalf of Backside Agd 32.
MAY 2d Ann Daughter of Eliz. Adamthwaite Illegit. Pauper [T. an Infant].
MAY 11th John Milner of Greenside Agd 70.
do. 26th Joseph Birtle of Lytheside Agd 30 [T. Pauper].
JUNE 5th Thos. Shaw of Town Aged 6 Pauper.
do. 18th Willm. son of Mr. John Robinson Schoolmaster [T. Infant].
JULY 8th Margaret Hastwell of Bleaflat Agd 15 [T. Paup].
† do. 19th Longhorn of Appleby an Infant.
AUGt. 9th Eliz. Fawcett of Townhead Agd 63.
do. 11th Jane Taylor of Bridge End Agd 45 Pau.
SEP. 7th Henry Fawcett of Townhead Agd 33 [T. 32].
NOV. 4th Mary Dennison of Waingarth Agd 48.
do. 12th Elizabeth [T. wife of Michael] Knewstupp of Agd 38.
DECEM. 2d Isabel Bousfield of Lockholme Agd 36.
do. 23d Mary an illegitimate Child of Ann Richardson P.
do. 28th Sarah Dent of Townhead Aged 69.
do. 29th Robert son of John Warcop [T. an Infant] Agd 2 yrs.

1793.

JAN. 16th Mary Brown of Tranmire Agd 61.
FEB. 11th Faithy Parkin of Rigend Aged 72 Pau.
do. Christian Shaw of Townhead Agd 37 Pau.
FEB. 26th Hugh son of William Furnass of High Stannerskugh & Isabel his wife (Infant.
do. William Taylor of Town Agd 75 Pau:
APRIL 18th Isabel wife of Wm. Furnass Aged 37.

1793. BURIED.

MAY 25th Margt. [T. Mary] Daughter of Thos. Hewetson of Hill & Eliz. his wife Aged 14 years.
do, 28th Richd. Thompson of Newbegin Agd 58.
JUNE 1st Thos. son of Mic. Knewstupp Ag 9.
do. 7th Agnes Archer of Ashfell Agd 73.

BURIALS.

JULY 6th	John Chamberlain of Lockholme Agd 58.
do.	Mary Fawcett of Town Agd 80 P.
AUG. 1st	Joseph Shearman of Weesdale Agd 20.
do. 6th	Hugh Shearman of Weesdale Agd 24.
do. 19th	Sarah Shearman of Weesdale Agd 70.
do. 20	Eliz. Bovell of Back Lane Agd 89.
OCT. 6th	Mary Fawcett of Fell End Agd 84.
NOV. 13	Richd. Cunningham of Bowberhead Agd 71.

1794.

JAN. 10th	Sarah Ward of Newbegin Aged 64.
do. 26th	Eliz. Robinson of Newbegin Agd 82.
FEB. 1st	George Fawcett of Town Agd 50.
do. 12th	Eliz. Grainger of Coldbeck P. Agd 84.
MAR. 10th	Richd Hunter of Elmpot Agd 72.
MAR. 11th	Hannah Robinson of Town Agd 75.
MAR. 20th	Ruth Chamberlain of Town Agd 34.
[T. do. 27th]	Mathew Wilkinson Parish Clerk Agd 68.
APRIL 9th	A Child of Wm. Potter's Artlegarth.
do. 23d	Joseph Udal of Weesdale Agd [T. 30].
MAY 1st	Isabel Fawcett of Town Agd 56.
JUNE 29th	Anthony Dent of Sandbed Agd 4.
JULY 7th	Margt. Dent of Dovingill Agd 18.
AUGt. 13th	John Coupland of Town Paup. Agd 95.
NOV. 26	Stephen Dent of Townhead Aged 60.
DEC. 16	Wm. Alderson of Needlehouse Aged 62.
do. 18	John Shaw of Low Stannerskugh Agd 59 [T. 60].
do. 26th	Holmes Milner of Longill Aged 73 [T. 63].
do. 28th	William Haygarth of Town an Infant.

1795.

JAN. 16	Mary Wilson of Fell End Aged 43.
do.	John Dawson of Town Aged 70.
do. 28th	Ann Shaw of Town Aged 67.
1795. FEB. 8th	Richard illegitimate son of Eliz. Atkinson.
do. 25th	Margaret wife of Richd. Howgill Agd 69.
do. 28th	Joseph Spooner of Newbegin Agd 24.

BURIALS.

Mar. 7th	Margaret Fothergill of Town Agd 70.
April 2d	Robert Scarbrough of Lowlane Agd 68.
April 15th	Robt. Udal of Weesledale Agd 20.
April 30th	Elizabeth Adamthwaite of Town Agd 32.
May 3d	Thomas Whitehead of Town Agd 5.
May 12th	Thomas Robinson of Weesledale Agd 75.
do.	Nanny Bouch of Garshill Aged 63.
June 3d	Peggy Chamberlain of Town Agd 76.
do. 8th	Eliz. Daughtr. of Richd. Furnass of Bleaflat an Infant.
July 14th	Sarah Fothergill of Lockholme Agd 89.
Aug. 4th	George Parkin of Town Agd 50.
do. 12th	Ann Daughter of George Alderson an Infant.
do. 15th	of Robert Chamberlain an Infant.
Octr. 24th	Sarah Beck of Artlegarth Agd 45.
Novr. 3d	Eleanor Hunter of Greenside Agd 91.
Decr. 18th	William Stubbs of Town Agd 58.

1796.

Jan. 3d	Margaret Hewetson of Town Agd 81.
do. 31st	Bobt. [T. Robt.] Warcopp of Town an Infant.
Feb. 8th	Ann Warcopp of Town Agd 41.
do. 10th	Barbara Robinson of Tarnhous Agd 87.
do. 23d	Ruth Scarborough of Lowlane Agd 65.
do. 29th	Eliz. Alderson of Newbegin Agd 67.
† Mar. 5th	son of John & Eliz. Shaw of Town.
do. 24th	John Thompson of Crooksbeck Agd 29.
Apr. 11th	Mary Thompson of Sprintgill Agd 20.
May 30th	Robt. Fawcett of Coldkeld Aged 43.
July 23d	Thos. Murros of Greenside Agd 5.
do. 28th	Margt. Atkinson of Town Agd 24.
Augt. 31st	Isabel Robinson of Dovingill Agd 75.

Buried.

Nov. 8th	Mathew Graham of Low Dovingill Aged 80.
Decr. 8th [T. 4th]	Agnes Birtle of Town 86.
do. 12th	Mary Fawcett of Town Aged 55.
do. 26th	John Son of Ths. Stubs Carpinter 5.

BURIALS.

1797.

Feb. 24th	Alice Fawcett of Sandwath Aged 75.
do. 26th	Mary Shaw of Ellergill Aged 81.
Mar. 29th	Leonard son of Anthony Preston Aged 6.
April 15th	Thos. Hunter of Bridge Aged 19.
do. 25th	James Taylor of Beckstones Aged 46.
do. 30th	Isabel Furnass of Lockholme Aged 80.
May 1st	Ruth Parkin of Coldbeck Aged 68.
do. 3d	Wm. Whaley of Coldbeck Tailor Aged 35.
do. 28th	Jeffery Bowness Son of Robt.. Hunter & Eliz. his wife (Streetside Aged 2.
June 1st	George son of John Gibbins of Appleby & Mary his wife Aged 3 years.
July 2d	Mary Warcop of Town Agd 34.
do.	Thomas Murthwaite of Parrot moor Agd 20.
Nov. 2d	Mary Fawcett of Fellend Aged 45.

1798.

Jan. 18th	Barbara Atkinson of Coldbeck Agd 80.
Jan. 31st	Jno. Robinson of Town Aged 82.
Feb. 13th	The Revd. Robert Bowness Curate of Ravenstondale & Mallerstang Aged 26 years.
do. 27th	Anth. Metcalf of Brounber Agd 62.
April 5	Agnes Furnass of Lockholme Agd 49.
do. 10th	Richd. Murthwaite of Parrot Moor 24.
do. 12	Henry son of Stephen* & Margt. Dent [T. an Infant].
14	John Shaw of Town Pauper Agd 57.
15th	Jonathan son of Wm. & Eliz. Alderson [T. Infant].
17	Jas. son of Thos. & Isabel Stubbs Agd 4.
27	Miles son of John & Ann** Morland of Stoophill Gate [T. an Infant].
1798. May 3d	Jeffery Dennison of Garshill [T: Waingarth] 73.
do. 9th	Robt. Howgill of Adamthwaite 79.
do. 16	Ann Daughter of Jno. & Sarah Fothergill of Greenside Infant.
21st	Margaret Bovell of Newbegin 58.

* Originally "Anth." T. has "Stephen."
** Originally "Isabel." T. has "Ann."

BURIALS.

JUNE 4th Mary Milner Greenside [T. widow] Agd 77.
do. 17th Eliz. Shaw of Town [T. Widow] Agd 58.
do. 29th Ann Fothergill of Waingarth Agd 71.
JULY 31st Isabel Preston of Bowderdale Aged 40.
SEP. 21st Martha Murthwaite of Parrot Moor Aged 61.
John Howgill of Town Aged 24.

1799.

JAN. 6th Anthony Fothergill of Foggy Gill Aged 62.
JAN. 21st Ann Hanson of Coldbeck Aged 81.
FEB. 11th Henry Robinson of Schoolhouse an Infant.
do. 14th Eleanor Potter of Green Agd 20 yrs.
do. 20 John Hunter of Gars Agd 77 yrs.
do. 27th George Warriner of Weesdale Agd 90.
MAR. 12th Joseph Fothergill of Lockholme Agd 76.
APRIL 13th Eliz. Bovell of Newbegin Agd 90.
do. 19th Alice Dent Mallerstang Agd 79.
do. 27th Hannah Dawson of Town Agd 40.
MAY 22d Mary Dawson of Town Widow Agd 75. [T. 77].
† do. 27th Mic. Taylor of Town Pauper Agd 77.
AUGt. 17th Margt. Parkin of Town Pauper Agd 49.
1799. Nov. 10th A Child of Richard Fawcett [T. Weaver].
do. 29th Mary Dent of Tounhead Widw. Agd 45 [T. 44].

1800.

FEB. 21st Robert Shaw of Low Stannerskugh Ag 62.
MAR. 16th Mary Robinson from Kendal Agd 72.
do. 17th Jane Winder of Newbegin Widow 81.
do. 22d Wm. Urwin of Bowberhead Agd 60.
APRIL 2d Jno. Alderson of Tarnhouse Agd 24.
do. 28th Margaret Hall of Crossbank Agd 23.
do. 29th Arthur Bousfield of Back Lane Agd 79.
do. 30th Sarah Rennison of Coldbeck Agd 81.
MAY 9th Benjamin Morland [T. Robinson] an Infant.
do. 16th Grace Robinson of Townhead Ag. 60.
do. 19th Mary Murthwaite of Weesdale Place Aged 87.
AUGt. 10th Simon Alderson [T. of Tarnhouse] Aged 14.

BURIALS.

SEPTEM. 25th	William Robinson Dancing Master 65.
do. 10th	Henry Fothergill of Artlegarth Agd 60.
OCT. 7th	Joseph Son of Mark Stalker of Bleaflat.
do. 21st	Ann Adamthwaite of Coldbeck Agd 20.
NOV. 5th	John Furnass of Town an Infant.
do. 15th	Mary Hebblethwaite of Town Agd 91.
do. 22d	Ruth Daughter of Stephen Dent of Dovingill & Margt. his wife an Infant.
DECEM. 4th	Jno. M'Kinsey of Town Agd 3.
do. 13th	Richd. Jackson of Brounber Agd 51.

1801.

JAN. 15th	Thos Preston of Town Aged 67.
do. 18th	Agnes Taylor of Beckstones Agd 52.
do. 23d	Thos. Parkin of Flass Aged 82.
do. 24	John son of Thomas Airey Cooper an Infant.
FEB. 13th	Isabel Wilkinson of School house [T. aged 75].
do. 17th	Agnes Tounson of Stannerskugh Aged 75.
APRIL 17th	Mary Shaw of Waingarth Aged 66.
MAY 28th	Mary Stubbs from Reeth Agd [T. 79].

1801. BURIED.

JUNE 28th	Agnes Chamberlain of Town Agd 82.
do. 29th	Willm. Turner of Newbegin Agd 80.
SEPTEMBR. 15th	Agnes Ward of Coldbeck 58.
[T. SEPTEMBER 18th]	Agnes Udal an Infant.
do. 20th	Elizabeth Metcalfe of Town 78.
do. 25th	Agnes Clogson of Coldbeck 82.
NOVEM. 1st	Eliz. Atkinson of Bleaflat Agd 32.
DECEMBR. 10th	Margaret Daughter of Robert Wilson of Weesdale Agd 5.

1802.

JAN. 6th	Mary Beck of Artlegarth Agd 24.
do.	Elizabeth Chamberlain of Town Agd 62 [T. 33].
do. 8th	Thos. Thompson of Town an Infant.
FEB. 27	Thos. Fothergill of Brownber Aged 94.
MAR. 10th	Eliz. Furnas of Banks Agd 33.
do. 30th	Eliz. Robinson of Coldbeck Agd 21.

BURIALS.

APRIL 24th Melly Dawson of Town Agd 48.
MAY 21st [T. 27th] Margt. Fothergill of Town Agd 69.
AUGt. 8th Isabel Brunskill Widow of Town Agd 84.
DECEMr 1st Isabel Constantine of Rig end 78.
do. 5th Richard Lindsey of Intake Agd 71.
do. 25th William Lindsey of Newbegin 75.

1803.

JAN. 11th John Perkins of burnt Hill Agd 75.
do. 24 Christr. Townson of Stannerskugh Agd 74.
FEB. 2d Anthony Urwin of Coldbeck Aged 55.
FEB. 23d William Milner of Ashfield Agd 85.
do. 24 Agnes Daughter of Thos. Stubbs Agd 14.
do. 27th Isabel Fawcett of Town Aged 80.
MAR. 15th [T. 5th] George Robinson of Frier bottom Aged 93.
† MAR. 24 Ann Taylor of Town Aged 82.
1803. APRIL 3d Thos. Fawcett of fellend Aged 84.
do. 6th Anth. Fawcett of Town Aged [T. 50].
MAY 2d Christopher Rennison of Town Aged 88.
MAY 18 John Fothergill of Asby Mill 73.
do. 19th Thos. Fawcett of Newbegin 60.
MAY [T. 3d] William Haygarth of Kirkby Stephen Aged [T. 29].
AUGt. 28th Eleanor Whitfield of Newbegin 83.
SEPTEM. 4th Edward Beck of Artlegarth Agd 22.
NOV. 27 George Udal of Weesdale Agd [T. 29].

1804.

FEB. 18 1804. Buried Mary Robinson of Town.
MAR. 2d Robert Howgill of Intack 18.
do. 21st Isabel Laycock of Waingarth 74.
do. 25th Mary Urwin of Town Aged 61.
APRIL Alice Udal of Weesdale Aged 64.
MAY 18th Ann Buck of Streetside Ag. 72.
AUGt. 27th Margaret Hunter Fellend Aged 23.
do. 30 Robert Dent Fellend Aged
DEC. 25 Mary Robinson.

BURIALS.

1805.

1st JAN. Mary Turner of Newbegin 83.
FEB. 5th Margt. Murros Aged 60.
do. Mary Thompson Aged 46.
MARCH Agnes Capstick Aged 30.
Math. Scarborow 85.
APRIL 7th Jno. Wilson of Fell end 49.
do. 14th Isabel Banks Aged 80.
do. 21st Ann Fawcett Pauper 85.
do. 28 Margt. Hunter Widow 64.
JUNE 1st Anthony son of Jno. Fothergill 8.

1805. BURIED.

JULY 18th Thomas Hastwel of Town Agd 69.
SEPTbr. 13 Isabel Birtle of Lockholme Head 45.
OCT. 5th William Spooner of Weesdale [T. aged 26].
OCT. 7th James Fawcett of Town Agd 77.
John Shearman of Weesdale Aged 90.
NOVEMbr. 3d Hugh Shaw of Town Aged 83.
Novbr. 16 Richard Howgill of Town Aged 84.
DECEMbr. 15 Thos. Fawcett of Town Aged 63.

1806.

JANry. 25 Margaret Johnson of Langdal Aged 84.
[T. do. 31st] Anthony Dent of Town Aged 59.
Dorothy Perkins of Town Aged 84.
Martha Birtle of Lockholme Head Aged 40.
A Child of John Ellis [T. of Brownber].
† Sarah Taylor of Town Aged 80.
[T. JUNE 20th A Child of Thos.] Fawcett of Fellend [T. of Greenslack Aged 3 years.
JULY 8 Stephen Shaw of Town Aged 78.
JULY 20th Mary Haygarth of Town Agd 10.
AUGUST 20 Thomas Stubbs of Town Aged 10.
do. 28th Elizabeth Scarborough Aged 70.
DECEM. 16th [T. 10th] James son of Thos. Ireland of Town Cordwainer [T. an Infant].

BURIALS.

1807.

JAN. 12th Margaret Machel of Newbegin Aged 72.
FEB: 9th Eleanor Parkin [T. of Murthwaite] Aged 50.
do: 15th Jno. Stubbs [T. of Town] an Infant.
APRIL 7th Ann Daughter of Thos. Relph [T. Infant].
do: 9th George Fawcett of Town 79.
do. 24th Jas. Martin of Cross Gates 35.
1807. APRIL 24th Jas. Udal of Cleapan [T. Clapham] Aged 37.
MAY 26th Geo. Hall Daughter an Infant.
JUNE 11th Jas. Bell of Town Aged 22.
JULY 6th Ann Shaw of Greenside 19.
AUGUST 2d Joshua Hunter of Wandale 58.
do. 6th Jno. Tarleton [T. Tarlington] Aged 84.
do. 29th Ann Dent of Town Aged 26 [T. 23].
SEPr. 8th Ruth Parkin [T. of Dovingill] Aged 62.
do. 29th George Hastwell of Town 74
DECEMr. 29th Elizabeth Todd Aged 85.

1808.

FEB. 8th Eleanor Hastwell of felend Aged 78.
MARCH 17th Nanny Smith of Bleaflat Aged 5.
do. 29th John Todd of Crooks Aged 84.
do. 30th Eleanor Hunter of Brig Aged 33.
APRIL 19th Geo. Hall Son an Infant.
do. 27th Judith Coupling [T. Coupland] Agged 76.
JUNE 3d George Farrer of Rig End 20.
do. 3d [T. 4th] Margaret Fawcet of Fell End Aged 70.
do. 25th Thomas Bousfield of Town 99 [T. 89]
Nov. 10th Thomas Potter Aged 35.
do. 21st John Brunskill of Wandale 24.

1809.

JUNE 15th Eliz. Fothergill [T. of Artlegarth] aged 60.
JUNE 22d Ann Hunter of Bridge Aged 70.
AUGst. 17 William Shaw of Newbegin aged 80.
SEPbr. 12th Peter Handley [T. of Town] aged 27 years.

BURIALS.

Octr. 14th	Thomas Rennison [T. of Bowberhead] Aged 72.
do. 20th	Jno. Winder Infant.
do. 21st	Mary Thompson Aged 28.
do. 31st	Marg^t. Robinson Aged 74.
Nov. 9th	Jno. Hall an Infant.
do. 9th	Jane Drybeck [T. of Town] Aged 70.

1810.

Jenuary 8th	Mary Hamilton Aged 4.
Febr^y. 27th	John Hunter Aged 74.
do. 28th	Will: Howgill of Adamthwaite Ag^d 83.
March 5th	James Swainson Aged 67.
do. 11th	James Fawcett Aged 46.
Feb. 27	Mary Fawcett of Artlegarth Aged 88.
	April 4th Ann Morros of Newbegin Ag^d 68.
do.	Elizabeth Hunter of Weesdale 50.
May 15th	Isabel Robinson late of Stannerskugh 84.
do. 18th	Ann Thompson of Waitby 31.
June 20	Jennet Fawcett of Fell end 80.
July 18th	George E. Lyon late from Jamaica a Scholar at this School Aged 10 years.
do. 29th	Matthew Ward of Bowber Head aged 69 years.
Septem. 18th	William Brunskill of Wandale 57.
Decr. 6th	Elizabeth Fawcett of Holme Pot aged 75.
December 9th	William Spooner of Weesdale Aged 72.
Decem^br. 18	Agnes Hodgson of Cold Beck Aged 72.

1811.

Feb. 26th	Ruth Scarborough of Brackenber Aged 62.
March 5th	Eliz. Alderson of Tarn House An Infant.
do. 10th	Ant^y. Knewstupp of High Lane Aged 84.
do. 13th	Eliz. Handley of Town Aged 19.
do. 27th	Jno. Fawcett of Town Ag^d 22.
do. 27th	Elizabeth Adamthwaite [T. of Town] 55.
April 18th	Jno. Robinson Hunter [T. of Dovingill] Ag^d 30.
May 15th	Ann Hunter of Dovingill aged 64.
May 18th	Emma Stubbs of Gars Hill aged 81.

BURIALS.

JUNE 1st	Mary Robinson of Beck Stones ag^{d} 39.
JUNE 7th	Mary Hill of Newbiggin aged 55.
JUNE 28th	Rich^{d}. Robinson of Litheside aged 62.
JULY 5th	Mary Fothergill of Brownber aged 67.
NOV. 12th	Joseph Rennison of Town aged 67.
DEC. 13th	Thos. Shaw of Nateby aged 67.
14th	Eliz. Parkin of Greenside aged 89.
25th	Jane Shaw of Garths Hill aged 79.
25	Thomas Thompson of Newbiggin ag^{d} 67.

1812.

JAN. 5	Jane Stewardson of Weesdale; an Infant.
FEB. 2nd	Marg^{t}. Robinson of Gars; aged 6.
do. 4	Agnes Thompson of Newbygin ag^{d} 33.
do. 7	Elizabeth Shaw of Newbiggin ag^{d} 82.
FEB. 14	William Furnace of Town aged 84 [T. 74].
FEB. 21st	Hugh Shaw of Gars Hill aged 50.
do. 22^{d}	Isabella Ireland of Town aged 12.
do. 26	Matthew Scarborough of Lowlane aged 65.
MARCH 6th	Ann Taylor of Town aged 2.
APRIL 23	Robert Fawcett of Murthwaite aged 13.
MAY 1st	George Steel of Stannerskugh aged 1.
do. 2nd [T. 4th]	Ann Bousfield of Ashfell aged 40.
do. 10th	Ann Beck of Dubbs aged 7.
JUNE 24th [T. 4th]	Thomas Knewstupp of Hill aged 55.
JULY 8th	William Laycock of Orton aged 84.
AUG: 16th	Marg^{t}. Thornborrow of Narthwaite aged 79.
SEP: 13th	Marg^{t}. Kirkbride of Stannerskugh aged 44.
SEP: 13th	Ann Hastwell of Town aged 55.
OCT: 5th	Rev^{d}. John Beck of Artlegarth aged 26.
NOV: 7th	Eliz. Watson of Rigg End aged 70.
NOV. 21st	Mary Milner of Ashfell aged 56.
DEC. 1st	Matthew Brown of Moss aged 64.
3	William Taylor of Lytheside aged 37.
18	Joseph Udal of Weesdale aged 77.

REGISTERS

OF THE

PRESBYTERIAN CHAPEL

RAVENSTONEDALE

1775 TO 1837.

CONTENTS OF THE REGISTER BOOK OF THE INDEPENDENT CHAPEL AT RAVENSTONEDALE.

List of Church Members in 1790.

John & Isabella Hewetson of Lowkholm Foot.

Wm. Hewetson, Banks.

John & Ann Chamberlain, Greenside.

Thomas & Isabella Udale, Newbiggin.

(PRESBYTERIAN).

List of Church Members in 1790.

Anthony & Fanny Fothergill, Crossbank.
Elizabeth Hewetson, Ellergill.
John Todd, Low Stennerskew.
Thomas & Elenor Morland, Town Head.
Mary Fawcett, Town.
Mathew Medcalf ,,
Betty Fawcett ,,
Peggy Chamberlain ,,
Joseph & Alice Udal, Weasdale.
Isabella Udal, Weasdale.
Sarah Fawcett, Artlegarth.
Betty Todd, Greenside.
Peggy Beck.*
Eleanor Chamberlain, Lockholm or Town.
Margaret Fothergill, Greenside.
Ann Chamberlain, Town.
Margaret Hewetson ,,
W^{m}. & Jinny Fawcett, Coldcreek.
Richard Hewetson, Beckstone.
Betty Robinson, Town.
Margaret Parkin, Lockholme Head.
John Dent, Turnpike.
Ann Hewetson, K. Stephen.
Thomas Hodgson, Orton.
Betty Fothergill made member 1791.

Names of Catechumens in 1793.

Charlotte Brisbane niece of the Hon: Lady Maxwell.
Sussannah Hill child of John Hill, Minister.
Ruth, Nancy, Betty, & Mally children of John Chamberlain of Greenside.
Eleanor child of Richard Hewetson of Newbiggin.
Nancy Fawcett & Thomas Fawcett children of William Fawcett of Coldbeck.
Ann child of John Brunskill of Greenside.
Henry child of Richard Hewetson of Newbiggin.
Henry child of W^{m}. Hewetson of Banks.
John child of William Hewetson of the Hole.

---

* Or perhaps "Buck."

(PRESBYTERIAN).

Baptisms.

Robert Elderson son of John Hewetson baptized 1775.

1775. Edward son of John Beck bap. 1775.

Ruth Daughter of Isaac Relph bap. 1775.

Jacob son of Eleanor Reynoldson Needle House bap 1775.

Isabel Daughter of John Perkin Coldbeck bap 1775.

John son of John Hunter of Fell End bap 1775.

At Stainton Hannah Daughter of Rob. Kirkenham of Crabtree House bap 1775.

George son of Geo. Broun of Kirkby Stephen, bap 1775.

John son of Matthew Slinger Coldbeck bap 1775.

1776. Baptisms 1776.

Sarah daughter of Richard Hewetson of Newbigging.

Robert son of M^r^. Campbell, Fell End.

Elizabeth dt. of William Broun of Orton.

Anthony son of Anthony Lambert.

William son of Joseph Udal.

Benjamin son of John Hewetson, Senior of Lockholme.

1777. Baptisms 1777.

John son of Richard Bell at Crosby.

Joseph son of Isaac Relph.

Mary Daughter of William Elyetson of Scarsykes.

Ann dt. of Thomas Fothergill Dubbs at home.

John son of William Brown at Orton.

Agnes dt. of Peter Strafford.

Betty dt. of William Hutchinson.

William son of John Fothergill of Brounber.

Mary dt. of Robert Tait at Natham near Kendal.

Joseph son of John Giffard of Hutton.

Jacob son of Robert Kirkham of Kendal.

1778. Baptisms 1778.

Isabel dt. of Thomas Adamthwait.

Robert son of Thomas Hewetson of Kendal.

James son of James Aberden at Kendal.

Nancy dt. of William Faucett of Crossbank.

(PRESBYTERIAN).

Baptisms.

Betty dt. of Matthew Slinger at Cottardale.
Bailif son of George Broun of Kirkby Stephen.
Ann dt. of John Beck of Town.
Joseph son of David Mackay, of Segswick, Stainton.
Mary dt. of John Hewetson Junr. Lockholme.
Thomas son of James Robinson of Scar.
1778. Henry son of Richard Hewetson of Newbiggin.
Alice dt. of Thomas Udal of Loukeholme.

1779. ### Baptisms 1779.

Edmund son of William Broun of Orton.
Ruth dt. of John Chamberlain of Greenside.
April 25. At Chanelkirk Church in Scotland Alexander son to Alexander Clapperton at Hill as also
May 2. At same place Adam son of Adam Dickson at Airhouse.
John son of James Hewetson of Town.
James son of James Taylor of Burkie.
Mary dt. of Anthony Lambert of Colbey.
Septimus Perkin son of Joseph Udal of Wesdale.
Gilbert son of James Aberdeen of Kendal.
James son of George Atkinson at Scar.
Mary dt. of William Hutchinson in Smardale.
John son of Revd. Mr. Prattman at Cottherstone.
William son of John Fothergill at home.

1780. ### Baptisms 1780.

William son of Thomas Hewetson of Kendal.
Thomas son of William Fawcett of Crossbank.
Peggy dt. of Matthew Slinger of Cottardale.
John son of Peter Strafford.
Joseph son of Thomas Udal of Loukeholme.
Isabel dt. of William Eyletson of Scarsykes.
Robert son of James Robinson of Scarr.
Ann dt. of James Hewetson of Town at home.
11 o'clock at night, when new born very weak.
Agnes dt. of John Chamberlain of Greenside.

(PRESBYTERIAN).

Baptisms.

Richard son of John Hewetson junior of Loukeholme.
James son of William Broun of Orton.
Isabella dt. of Geo. Broun of Kirkby Stephen.

1781. ### Baptisms 1781.

John son of George Atkinson of Scarr.
Ann dt. of Will Hewetson of Town.
Jane dt. of John Armstrong at Newhouse near Brough.
Elizabeth dt. of Robert Broun of Kirkby Stephen.
Helen dt. of Richard Hewetson of Newbiggin.
Robert son of James Robinson of Scarr.
Isabella dt. of William Hutchinson of Smardale.
Two children at Kilmaronack.
One child at Anderstoun, by Glasglow.
These three while in Scotland this year.

1782. ### Baptisms 1782.

John son of David Mackay of Segswick, Kendal.
Mary dt. of Thomas Hewetson of Kendal.
Elizabeth dt. of John Chamberlain, Greenside.
John son of Thomas Udal Newbiggin.
Four boys at Kilmaronack.
William son of William Brown, Coldbeck.
Joseph son of Mr. Prattman of Cotherstone.
Margaret dt. of William Elyetson of Scarsykes.
James son of John Guy, Town.

1783. ### Baptisms 1783.

Robert son of James Robinson, Scarr.
John son of John Hewetson, Junior Loukholme.
Thomas son of James Morland.
Betty dt. of Thomas & Isabel Wilson at Ellergill.
Janet dt. of Robert Broun of Kirkby Stephen.

1784. ### Baptisms 1784.

Ebenzor son of Mr Somervin, Minister at Ravenstonedale.
A Daughter of William Elyetson of Scarsykes.
Mary dt. of John Chamberlain of Greenside.

(PRESBYTERIAN).

Baptisms.

Isabel dt. William Broun, Coldbeck.
Henry son of William Hewetson of Banks.
James son of James Robinson of Scarr.
Leonard son of Thomas Udal.
Eleanor Faucett Robinson.

1790. Baptisms 1790.

John son of John & Alice Faucett, Greenside.
James son of John & Alice Faucett, Greenside.
Richard son of Christopher Bousfield, Midfield.
Nancy dt. of John & Mary Hewetson, Loukeholme.

Baptisms 1791.

1791. Mary dt. of William Broun of Sedberg.

1792. 1792.

Ruth dt. of John & Mary Hewetson of Lockholme.
John son of Christopher & Sarah Bousfield, Midfield.

1793. Baptisms 1793.

Ann dt. of David & Sarah Hewetson.
Elizabeth dt. of John & Alice Faucett, Greenside.

1794. Baptisms 1794.

Thomas son of John & Mary Hewetson, Loukeholme.
Robert son of Christopher & Sarah Bousfield, Midfield.
Isabella dt. of James & Ann Udal.

1795. Baptism 1795.

Betty dt. of William Broun.

1796. Baptisms 1796.

Peggy dt. of James & Ann Udal.
Thomas son of John & Alice Faucett, Weasdale.
Benjamin son of John & Mary Hewetson, Greenside.
William son of Sarah & Christopher Bousfield, Lockholme.

1797. Baptisms 1797.

Ann dt. of Thomas & Ann* Newbiggin.

---

* "Hunter" appears to be omitted.

(PRESBYTERIAN).

BAPTISMS.

Richard son of David & Sarah Hewetson.
Agnes dt. of William Broun.

1798. BAPTISMS 1798.

Eubank son of John & Mary Hewetson, Lockholme.
Joseph Robert son of James & Ann Udal.
Elleanor dt. of Thomas & Ann Hunter, Town.
Agnes dt. of John & Ann Stockdale, Weasdale.

1799. BAPTISMS 1799.

Margaret dt. of John & Alice Faucett, Greenside.
Henry son of John & Mary Hewetson, Streetside.
Nanny dt. of Christopher & Sarah Bousfield, Midfield.

1800. BAPTISMS 1800.

Betty dt. of John & Mary Hewetson, Lockholme.
Isabella dt. of David & Sarah Hewetson.
William son of Thomas & Sussanna Faucett.
John Hewetson son of James & Ann Udal, Cautley.
Nelly dt. of John & Ann Stockdale, Weasdale.

1810. BAPTISMS 1801.

Henry Hewetson Hunter, son of Thomas & Ann Hunter, Town.
William son of John & Mary Hewetson, Streetside.

1802. BAPTISMS 1802.

Ann dt. of Christopher Bousfield of Midfield.
John son of Thomas & Sussanna Faucett.
Isabella dt. of John & Isabella Tod.
Robert son of David & Sarah Hewetson.

1803. BAPTISMS 1803.

Sally dt. of James & Ann Udal, Cautley.
George son of John & Anne Stockdale, Weasdale.
John son of John & Isabella Tod.

1804. BAPTISMS 1804.

Hannah dt. of Hugh & Rebecca Watson, Weasdale.
Jane dt. of Thomas & Sussannah Faucett.

(PRESBYTERIAN).

BAPTISMS.

Ann dt. of John & Isabella Todd.
John son of Thomas & Ann Hunter, Coldbeck.
Robert son of James Broun.

BAPTISMS 1805.

1805. Emma dt. of John & Jane Hill, Dustin Hill.
John son of Richard & Betty Hewetson, Ellergill.
George son of James & Ann Udal.
Robert son of James & Sarah Richardson, Dent.
Nanny dt. of William & Ann Nelson.

1806. BAPTISMS 1806.

Mary dt. of Thomas & Ann Hunter, Coldbeck.
Emma dt. of Thomas & Sussanna Batty.
Elizabeth dt. of Richard & Betty Hewetson of Ellergill.
Thomas son of John & Isabel Tod, Stainskew.
Henry son of Thomas & Sussannah Faucett.
Mary dt. of Thomas & Ann Coldbeck.
John son of John & Mary Hewetson, Streetside.

1807. BAPTISMS 1807.

Thomas son of John & Mary Hewetson, Streetside.
John son of Robert & Elenor Hewetson, Lockholme.
Mary dt. of William & Ann Nelson.
Margaret dt. of John & Ann Stockdale, Weasdale.
James son of James & Ann Udal, Clapham.

1808. BAPTISMS 1808.

Isabella dt. of Christopher & Isabella Burgenson, Newbiggin.
Jane dt. of William & Mary Coile.
Elizabeth dt. of Thomas & Sussannah Faucett.
Ellen dt. of Richard & Peggy Battey.
Robert son of John & Isabella Tod.

1809. BAPTISM 1809.

Sarah dt. of David & Sarah Hewetson.

(CONGREGATIONAL).

1811. BAPTISMS 1811.

Richard son of John & Isabella Todd, Bracks* Beck.

Benjamin son of Benjamin & Margaret Hewetson, Green.

1812. BAPTISMS 1812.

Robert son of Thomas & Eliz Faucett, Greenside.

Robert son of Thomas & Mary Lang, Sandford.

Mary dt. of Benjamin & Margaret Hewetson, Green.

1813. BAPTISMS 1813.

Agnes Sanderson.

Lancelot son of Robert & Bridget Hewetson, Claylands.

1814. BAPTISM 1814.

Mily son of Thomas & Elizabeth Fawcett, Green.

1815. BAPTISM 1815.

Milly dt. of Joseph & Sarah Thompson, Wandale.

1817. BAPTISM 1817.

Clement son of Thomas & Elisabeth Faucett.

BAPTISM 1818.

1818. Richard son of Helen Faucett.

Thomas son of John & Mary Jaques.

Eliza Holmes dt. of Rev. R. H. Bonner & Sarah his wife.

Ephraim son of John & Isabella Todd.

Richard Wright dt. of John & Ann Farraday, Kirkby Stephen.

1819. BAPTISMS 1819.

John son of John & Mary Beck of Dubbs.

John Robinson son of John & Mary Jaques.

1820. BAPTISMS 1820.

Ann dt. of John & Mary Beck of Dubbs.

Sarah Hamilton Bonner dt. of Rev. R. H. Bonner & Sarah his wife.

BAPTISM.

Robert son of John and Mary Beck, Dubbs.

---

* Perhaps "Crooks Beck."

(CONGREGATIONAL).

Baptisms.

John Beck of Dubbs has generously given a pound to the Minister at the Baptism of each of his children.

Isabella dt. of John & Mary Jaques of Town.

1823. Baptisms 1823.

John James Bonner son of R. H. Bonner & Sarah his wife.

Edward son of John & Mary Beck of Dubbs.

1824. Baptism 1824.

James son of John & Mary Buck, Lockeholme.

1825. Baptism 1825.

Benjamin Holme Bonner son of R. H. Bonner & Sarah his wife.

Sophia Robinson dt. of Philip & Betty Robinson, Appleby.

1826. Baptism 1826.

Henry son of John & Mary Beck, Dubbs.

Ann dt. Richard and Mary Hewetson of the Hole.

Ann dt. of John & Mary Buck, Lockholme.

1830. Baptism 1830.

Isabella dt. of Annas Birtle.

Brian Bell son of Elizabeth Davis, born 1829.

1831. Baptism 1831.

Ruth dt. of Ewbank & Ruth Hewetson.

1832. Baptism 1832.

Isabella dt. of Elizabeth Davis born 1832.

1828. William son of Rev. R. Hamilton Bonner & Sarah his wife born 1828.

1831. Dorathy Lee dt. of Rev. R. H. Bonner born 1829.

1835. Baptism 1835.

John Birtle son of Agnes Birtle of Farground.

Baptism 1837.

1837. Thomas Andrew Fraser son of Rev. Robert H. Bonner born 1831.

Ann Hamilton dt. of Rev. R. H. Bonner born 1833 & Sarah his wife.

(PRESBYTERIAN).

Burials.

1776.

Peter Handley.
Elizabeth Bousfield.

1777.

Robert Hunter of Bowberhead aged 67 son of Richard Hunter, a great man in Rissendale &c.
Mary Breaks.
Isabel Fawcett.
Isabell Coupland.
Joseph Knewstubb.
Robert Hunter.

1778.

Mary Fawcett.

1779.

Mary Perkin.
William Shaw of Artlegarth.

1780.

Mrs. Sarah Hewetson.
Died James Hewetson very suddenly, only a few hours after his young child & both burried in the same coffin; this is inserted as a most alarming providence.
Mary Elyetson.
Abergail Chamberlain aged 89.
Thomas Taylor aged 91 years 10 months.
Mrs. Knewstubb aged 80 years.

1781.

Sarah Robinson.
Agnes Foster.

(PRESBYTERIAN).

Burials.

1782.

No burials this year.

1783.

Henry Hewetson of Street.

Elizabeth Fothergill.

Ann Robinson.

Christopher Coupland.

1784.

John Bell.

Thomas Robinson.

Robert Todd.

1813.

Elizabeth Chamberlain of Greenside.

(CONGREGATIONAL).

1817.

M^rs^. Margaret Hewetson of Town.

1818.

Richard Wright Esquire of K. Stephen interred in the burying ground aged 76.

Thomas son of John & Mary Jaques, aged 9 months.

1821.

Sarah Hamilton Bonner, aged 7 months, she was a lovely child & only tasted of the cup of Life & put by dowbtless perceiving it to be a bitter draught. Vita est brevis sed æternitas est longa.

1822.

M^rs^. Isabell Udal of Cross Bank, aged 79.

Henry Hewetson Hunter buried in 1821 at K. Stephen.

William Fawcett grandson of the late Rev. John Hill.

1823.

At Lockholme Fanny Richardson, a poor Lunatic.

Elizabeth Hewetson of Town, a Grocer.

At Greenside John Chamberlain.

At Greenside Margaret Knewstubb.

(CONGREGATIONAL).

BURIALS.

At Gate House, Dent, M^{rs}. Agnes Elyetson, Widow of late W^{m}. Elyetson of Scarsykes aged 78.

At Claylands Bridget wife of Robert Hewetson aged 52.

Anne daughter of Richard Fawcett of High Lane.

1824.

Mary Hewetson of Town.

Ann wife of John Rennison of Town.

1825.

Mary Hewetson widow of John Hewetson of Crooksbeck.

1830.

Elizabeth widow of Rev. John Hill.

Henry Hewetson of Kendal died 1832.

Benjamin Hewetson of Kendal died 1832

1833.

John Beck of Dubbs.

Isabella Guy widow of late John Guy carrier to Kendal.

Ruth wife of Eubank Hewetson of Coldbeck.

REGISTER OF THE

SOCIETY OF FRIENDS

CONTAINING THE RAVENSTONEDALE ENTRIES,

EXTRACTED FROM THE INDEX KEPT AT THE

SOCIETY'S CENTRAL OFFICE, DEVONSHIRE HOUSE.

(SOCIETY OF FRIENDS).

Births.

1655	6	24	Elizabeth dt. of George Alderson of R.M.
1657	7	29	Ann dt. of George Alderson of R.M.
1672	4	26	Robert son of Robert & Ann Atkinson R.M.
1684	4	28	Elizabeth dt. of Richard & Mary Adamthwaite R.M.
1687	6	29	Margaret dt. of Richard Adamthwaite R.M.
1692	2	1	Anne dt. of Simon Alderson R.M.
1694	8	5	Elizabeth dt. of Simon Alderson R.M.
1717	12	4	Simon son of Ralph Alderson R.M.
1719	6	23	William son of Ralph Alderson R.M.
1721	8	22	John son of Ralph Alderson born at Ravenstonedale.
1724	9	1	Agnes dt. of Ralph Alderson R.M.
1761	9	1	Ralph son of John & Alice Alderson R.M.
1762	9	1	Ralph son of John & Alice Alderson R.M.
1763	9	24	Richard son of John & Alice Alderson R.M.
1777	4	13	Mary dt. of James & Ann Buck husbandman of Nathwaite psh. of Ravenstonedale West[d]. N.M.
1779	5	30	Agnes dt. of James & Ann Buck husbandman of Narthwaite psh. of Ravenstonedale West[d]. N.M.
1781	5	13	Alice dt. of James & Ann Buck of Ravenstonedale S[t]. West[d]. N.M.
1784	2	13	Elizabeth dt. of James & Ann Buck of Street psh. of Ravenstonedale West[d].
1785	7	15	Margaret dt. of James & Ann Buck husbandman of Street psh. of Ravenstonedale West[d].
1789	4	29	Thomas son of James & Ann Buck husbandman of Street psh. of Ravenstonedale West[d].
1791	12	1	William son of James & Ann Buck husbandman of Street psh. of Ravenstonedale West[d].

Note.—R.M.—Ravenstonedale Meeting. N.M.—Non-member.

(SOCIETY OF FRIENDS).

Births.

1795 2 6 John son of James & Ann Buck husbandman of Street psh. of Ravenstonedale West^{d}.

1821 9 22 James son of Thomas & Ruth Buck husbandman of Low Stenaskew psh. of Ravenstonedale West^{d}.

1824 11 1 William son of Thomas & Ruth Buck husbandman Weesdale psh. of Ravenstonedale West^{d}. N.M.

1827 11 6 Margaret dt. of Thomas & Ruth Buck husbandman Weesdale psh. of Ravenstonedale West^{d}. N.M.

1833 2 19 William son of John & Mary Buck husbandman of Lockholme psh. of Ravenstonedale West^{d}. N.M.

1662 9 25 James son of Richard Clerkson of R.M.

1664 7 9 James son of Richard Clerkson of R.M.

1667 4 10 Isabell dt. of Richard Clerkson of R.M.

1668 10 29 Dorothy dt. of Richard Clerkson of R.M.

1672 6 22 Elizabeth dt. of Richard Clerkson of R.M.

1677 11 16 John son of Richard Clerkson of R.M.

1676 6 2 Maudlin or Maydlee dt. of James Dent R.M.

1677 7 9 Thomas son of James Dent of R.M.

1659 6 1 John son of William Fawcet R.M.

1662 12 12 Gilbert son of Robert Fawcet R.M.

1662 3 6 Mary dt. of William Fawcett R.M.

1665 3 7 Anthony son of William Fawcett R.M.

1668 8 2 James son of William Fawcett R.M.

1671 9 13 Elianor dt. of Robert Fawcett R.M.

1663 1 17 Isaac son of Joseph Handley R.M.

1664 7 17 Isaac son of Joseph Handley

1667 10 15 Elianor dt. of Joseph Handley of R.M.

1693 3 2 Joseph son of Isaac Handley of R.M.

1694 8 13 Philip son of Isaac Handley of R.M.

1697 3 7 Mary dt. of Isaac Hanlay of R.M.

1699 6 19 John son of Isaac Hanlay of R.M.

1702 4 19 Peter son of Isaac Hanlay of R.M.

1736 1 3 Isaac son of John Handley R.M.

1738 10 7 Eleanor dt. of John Handley R.M.

1766 1 16 John son of Isaac & Mary Handley R.M.

1767 8 8 Ann dt. of Isaac & Mary Handley R.M.

(SOCIETY OF FRIENDS).

Births.

1769 3 2 Thomas son of Isaac & Mary Handley R.M.

1770 9 1 Mary dt. of Isaac & Mary Handley R.M.

1772 11 12 Joseph son of Isaac & Mary Handley R.M.

1774 4 29 Eleanor dt. of Isaac & Mary Handley R.M.

1777 3 31 Margaret dt. of Isaac & Mary Handley husbandman of Narthwaite psh. of Ravenstonedale West[d]. R.M.

1794 11 10 Elizabeth dt. of Robert & Ann Hunter of Mourthwaite p: of Ravenstonedale, Cordwainer N.M.

1797 5 23 John son of Robert & Ann Hunter of Morthwaite psh. of Ravenstonedale West[d]. Cordwainer N.M.

1798 1 12 Isaac son of John & Margaret Handley husbandman of Narthwaite psh. of Ravenstonedale West[d].

1798 5 22 Eleanor dt. of Robert & Ann Hunter of Morthwaite psh. of Ravenstonedale West[d]. Cordwainer N.M.

1799 3 1 John son of John & Margaret Handley husbandman of Narthwaite psh. of Ravenstonedale West[d].

1800 6 17 Mary dt. of John & Margaret Handley husbandman of Narthwaite psh. of Ravenstonedale West[d].

1801 4 21 John son of Robert & Ann Hunter Cordwainer of Narthwaite psh. of Ravenstonedale West[d]. N.M.

1802 2 9 William son of John & Margaret Handley Farmer Narthwaite psh. of Ravenstonedale West[d].

1803 4 4 Isabella dt. of Robert & Ann Hunter Cordwainer Narthwaite psh. of Ravenstonedale West[d]. N.M

1803 5 3 Thomas son of John & Margaret Handley husbandman Narthwaite psh. of Ravenstonedale West[d].

1805 7 29 Thomas son of John & Margaret Handley husbandman Narthwaite psh. of Ravenstonedale West[d].

1810 8 31 Isaac son of Joseph & Ann Handley husbandman of Wandle psh. of Ravenstonedale West[d].

1812 2 2 Mary dt. of Joseph & Ann Handley husbandman of Wandle psh. of Ravenstonedale West[d].

1813 9 16 Ann dt. of Joseph & Ann Handley husbandman of Wandale psh. of Ravenstonedale West[d].

1815 4 25 Jane dt. of Joseph & Ann Handley husbandman of Wandale psh. of Ravenstonedale West[d].

(SOCIETY OF FRIENDS).

Baptisms.

1816	7	3	Eleanor dt. of Joseph & Ann Handley husbandman of Wandale psh. of Ravenstondale West[d].
1818	10	11	Margaret dt. of Joseph & Ann Handley husbandman of Wandale psh. of Ravenstonedale West[d].
1820	4	2	Agnes dt. of Joseph & Ann Handley yeoman of Wandale psh. of Ravenstonedale West[d].
1821	8	17	Simon son of James & Alice Hunter husbandman of Needlehouse psh. of Ravenstonedale West[d].
1821	12	9	Alice dt. of Joseph & Ann Handley husbandman of Wansdale psh. of Ravenstonedale West[d].
1750	7	2	Ann dt. of William & Agnes Ion of R.M.
1752	2	17	Alice dt. of William & Agnes Ion of R.M.
1758	12	15	Mary dt. of William & Agnes Ion of R.M.
1763	4	29	John son of William & Agnes Ion of R.M.
1770	8	4	Ralph son of William & Agnes Ion of R.M.
1756	7	20	Philip son of Anthoney & Isabel Kirkbride of R.M.
1759	6	15	Mary dt. of Anthoney & Isabel Kirkbride of R.M.
1757	5	9 or 2	Frances dt. of Henry & Isabel Lickbarrow of R.M.
1760	3	24	Isabel dt. of Henry & Isabel Lickbarrow of R.M.
1762	12	22	Mary dt. of Henry & Isabel Lickbarrow of R.M.
1765	5	25	Margaret dt. of Henry & Isabel Lickbarrow
1768	10	6	Joshua son of Joshua & Agnes Leighton of R.M.
1668	7	28	Richard son of Edward Newby of R.M.
1650	2	x	Mary dt. of John Pinder of R.M.
1652	7	x	Sarah dt. of John Pinder of R.M.
1653	7	25	Sarah dt. of John Pinder of R.M.
1656	10	x	Temperance dt. of John Pinder of R.M.
1657	12	4	John son of Anthony Pinder of R.M.
1659	4	7	Mary dt. of Anthony Pinder of R.M.
1667	11	10	John son of William Perkin of R.M.
1664	9	25	Abigail son of Richard Pinder of R.M.
1665	9	18	Jonathan son of Anthony Pinder of R.M.
1666	8	8	Bridget dt. of Richard Pinder of R.M.
1668	8	18	John son of Richard Pinder of R.M.
1671	12	9	Joseph son of Richard Pinder of R.M.
1679	9	19	Rachell dt. of Thomas Pratt of R.M.

(SOCIETY OF FRIENDS).

Baptisms.

1681 10 2 or 1681 2 10 Rebecca dt. of Thomas Pratt of R.M.
1657 9 5 Isabell dt. of James Rogerson of R.M.
1659 12 2 Isabell dt. of Reynold Rowell of R.M.
1659 7 23 John son of James Rogerson of R.M.
166? 3 3 Robert son of James Rogerson of R.M.
1662 12 18 James son of James Rogerson of R.M.
1684 5 14 Isabell dt. of John Rogerson.
1686 11 5 Margaret dt. of John Rogerson, Stredfold*
1689 10 3 Mary dt. of John Rogerson of R.M.
1692 5 9 James son of John Rogerson of R.M.
1695 7 13 Sarah dt. of John Rogerson of R.M.
1699 5 x Ann Daughter of John Rogerson of R.M.
1725 6 5 Isabel dt. of Robert Rogerson of R.M.
1661 10 16 Rachel dt. of Michael Scaife of R.M.
1663 8 28 Sarah dt. of Michael Scaife of R.M.
1664 1 3 Jacob son of Michael Scaife of R.M.
1668 10 8 Mary dt. of William Scaife of R.M.
1669 2 2 Margaret dt. of John Shaw of R.M.
1670 7 4 Barbary dt. of William Scaife of R.M.
1671 10 16 Isabell dt. of Edmund Shawe of R.M.
1671 10 22 Elizabeth dt. of John Shaw of R.M.
1673 9 30 John son of William Skaife of R.M.
1674 1 25 Isabell dt. of John Shaw of R.M.
1676 9 26 John son of John Shaw of R.M.
1677 2 22 John son of James Skaiffe of R.M.
1682 7 13 Elizabeth dt. of John Salkeld of R.M.
1683 8 31 Joseph dt. of James & Mary Scaife of R.M.
1685 11 26 Anne dt. of James & Mary Scaife of R.M.
1687 9 29 Abigail dt of James Skaiff.
1768 4 8 Ann dt. of Edward & Eleanor Smith of R.M.
1770 8 26 John son of Thomas & Mary Snowdon of R.M.
1770 11 8 John son of Edward & Eleanor Smith of R.M.
1773 4 13 Elizabeth dt. of Edward & Eleanor Smith of R.M.
1775 8 16 Michael son of Edward & Eleanor Smith.

---

* "Studfold" is doubtless meant.

(SOCIETY OF FRIENDS).

Baptisms.

1778 4 14 Isaac son of Edward & Eleanor Smith Cordwainer Ravenstonedale psh. of Ravenstonedale West[d].

1780 10 17 Rebekah dt. of Edward & Eleanor Smith Cordwainer o Backside psh. of Ravenstonedale West[d].

1783 4 16 Stephen son of Edward & Eleanor Smith Cordwainer o Backside psh. of Ravenstonedale West[d].

1667 3 9 Elizabeth dt. of Thomas Tompson of R.M.

1669 9 15 or 1 15 Sarah dt. of Thomas Tompson of R.M.

1671 8 28 John son of Thomas Thomas Tompson of R.M.

1733 11 7 Thomas son of Thomas Thornborrow.

1735 7 16 Simon son of Thomas Thornborrow of Nathwaite.

1834 5 19 Samuel son of Robert and Agnes Thompson Farmer of Needlehouse psh. of Ravenstonedale West[d]. N.M.

1836 7 9 Aaron son of Robert and Agnes Thompson Farmer of Needlehouse psh. of Ravenstonedale West[d]. N.M.

1651 3 x Mary dt. of Thomas & Elizabeth Winn of Ravenstonedale or Grisdal Meeting.

1654 1 11 Robert son of Richard Wilson of R.M.

1658 11 6 or 6 11 Peter son of Richard Wilson of R.M.

1663 4 x Thomas son of Thomas & Elizabeth Winne Grisedale & of R.M.

1661 8 27 Thomas son of Richard & Katherine Wilson R.M.

1664 12 17 Richard son of Richard & Katherine Wilson.

1667 6 25 Elizabeth dt. of Richard & Katherine Wilson R.M.

1670 6 18 Samuel son of Edmond Winn Grisedale and R.M.

1685 8 21 Agnas dt. of Edmond & Agnes Winn.

1686 8 21 Agnes dt. Edmond & Agnes Winne his first Wife R.M.

1685 9 12 Joseph son of John & Margaret Winne R.M.

(SOCIETY OF FRIENDS).

Marriages.

1683 7 14 Richard Adamthwaite of Lowcombe to Mary Middleton married at Rich[d]. Adamthwaite's house

1745 3 12 William son of Ralph Alderson of Ravenstonedale to Mary Dover at Lamrigge.

1717 3 8 Ralph Alderson, Nathwaite Ravenstonedale Co. West[d]. Yeoman to Alice Burton spinster dt. of W[m]. Burton of Scalegill foot in Kirthwaite in Dent at Loaning in Dent.

1717 12 13 Margaret Adamthwaite, spinster, dt. of Richard & Mary Adamthwaite of Lockholme, Ravenstonedale to William Alderson married at Street, Co. West[d].

1717 12 13 William Alderson son of Robert & Sarah of Smeedy Holme in Swaledale to Margaret Adamthwaite spinster dt. of Rich[d]. & Mary of Lockholme at Street Co. West[d].

1723 3 30 Ann Alderson of Nathwaite in Ravenstonedale to Thomas Thornborrow of Orton at Street, Co. West[d].

1731 4 30 Elizabeth Alderson of Nathwaite, Ravenstonedale spinster Michael Ackrigg of Grizedale at Street, Co. West[d].

1765 5 1 William son of Ralph & Alice Alderson of Ravenstonedale to Rachel Stewartson at Grayrigge.

1777 5 5 Elizabeth dt. of Thomas & Mary Buck of Dent, Co. York to John Thompson of Nathwaite at Ravenstonedale.

1800 8 27 Agnes dt. of James & Ann Buck of Ravenstonedale to Michael Smith of Kidderminster at Brigflats.

1809 5 31 Alice dt. of James & Ann Buck of Ravenstonedale to James Hunter of High Hall in Dent at Leyet.

1819 12 22 Elizabeth dt. of James & Ann Buck of Street in Ravenstonedale to James Hunter of Apperset at Aysgarth.

1705 10 4 Elizabeth dt. of Richard Clerkson of Ravenstonedale to Thomas Mason of Stonehouse in Dent at Ant[y]. Robinson's house in Ravenstonedale.

(SOCIETY OF FRIENDS).

Marriages.

1711 6 2 Isabell Clerkson of Studfold in Ravenstonedale to Edward Thompson of Sedbergh at Ravenstonedale.

1717 1 28 Thomas Close of Grisdale, Sedbergh, yeoman to Margaret Rogerson at Street in Ravenstonedale.

1744 3 31 Margaret Close of Studfold in Ravenstonedale to John Thistlethwaite at Street in Ravenstonedale.

1675 3 9 James Dent to Mary Winn at Ravenstonedale.

1709 5 7 James son of Thomas Fawscett of Backside in Ravenstonedale to Rachell Hewertson of Penrith at Penrith.

1709 5 7 Rachell dt. of John Hewetson of Penrith to James Fawscett of Ravenstonedale at Penrith.

1730 2 23 or 7 23 John son of William & Elizabeth Hodgson & Mary Rogerson at Street in Ravenstonedale.

1734 3 9 John Handley of Nathwaite in Ravenstonedale, Husbandman & Ann Fothergill, Frostrow at Brigflatts.

1765 4 3 Isaac son of John & Ann Handley of Backside Co. West[d]. to Mary Buck at Layet in Dent.

1762 5 13 Elinor dt. of John & Ann Handley of Backside in Ravenstonedale to Edward Smith at Ravenstonedale.

1797 3 30 John Handley, Yeoman, son of Isaac & Mary Handley of Narthwaite Psh. of Ravenstonedale to Margaret Hunter at Brigflats.

1797 6 13 Ann Handley dt. of Isaac & Mary Handley of Narthwaite Psh. of Ravenstonedale to Richard Rawlinson of Beetham Hall.

1799 5 9 Ellinor Handley dt. of Isaac & Mary of Narthwaite in Ravenstonedale Co. West[d]. to John Hunter son of John & Ann Hunter of Heblethwaite in Sedbergh at Brigflatts.

1809 10 4 Joseph Handley of Wandal in Ravenstonedale son of Isaac & Mary Handley of Nathwaite in Ravenstonedale to Ann Hunter dt. of John & Ann Hunter of High Hall in Dent at Leyet.

1794 12 1 Mary dt. of Isaac & Mary Handley of Narthwaite Co. West[d]. to Richard Sill, Sedbergh, at Ravenstonedale.

(SOCIETY OF FRIENDS).

Marriages.

1834 5 6 William of Brigflatts, farmer son of John & Margaret Handley of Nathwaite Co. West^d. to Isabella Garlick at Brigflats.

1834 12 9 Mary dt. of Joseph & Ann Handley of Ravenstonedale to James Seddon of Liverpool at Brigflats.

1735 8 9 John Jackson of Preston Patrick, Haberdasher & Isabel Thornburrow of Studfold at Street.

1779 1 8 Mary dt. of William & Agnes Ion of Nathwaite in Ravenstonedale to Anthony Thistlethwaite of Dent at Street in Ravenstonedale.

1788 1 5 John Ion of Leayet in Dent p. of Sedbergh, Cordwainer son of W^m. & Agnes Ion of Narthwaite in Ravenstonedale & Elizabeth Greenwood of Liniker at Brigflats.

1794 3 31 W^m. Jackson of Derry in p. of Sedbergh joiner & widower son of W^m. & Esther Jackson of Crosdalebeck p. of Sedbergh & Mary Kirkbride dt. of Anthony & Isabel of Ravenstonedale at Ravenstonedale.

1675 4 1 John Knewstubb & Sibell Shaw at Ravenstonedale.

1705 10 4 Thomas Mason of Stonehouse in Dent & Elizabeth Clerkson at Ant^y. Robinson's house in Ravenstonedale.

1686 3 6 Sarah Pinder of Warth in Ravenstonedale & John Atkinson of Frostray at Brigflats.

1681 3 11 Mary dt. of John Pinder of Ravenstonedale to James Skaife of Ravenstonedale at Ant^y. Pinder's house at Wath.

1717 1 28 Margaret dt. of John & Sibill Rogerson of Studfold in Ravenstonedale & Thomas Close of Grisdale at Street.

1719 1 24 Isabell Rogerson, spinster, dt. of John & Sibill of Studfold in Ravenstonedale to George Thornburrgh of Langdale at Street in Ravenstonedale.

1730 2 or 7 23 Mary Rogerson, spinster, dt. of John & Sibill of Studfold & John Hodgson at Street in Ravenstonedale.

1675 4 1 Margaret Story & John Knewstub at Ravenstonedale.

1681 3 11 James Skaife of Ravenstonedale & Mary Pinder of Ravenstonedale at Ant^y. Pinder's house, Wath.

(SOCIETY OF FRIENDS).

Marriages.

1762 5 13 Edward son of Henry & Isabel Smith of Harding p. of Morland & Elinor Handley of Ravenstonedale.

1794 12 1 Richard Sill of Sedbergh, Grocer, son of Ric: & Mary of Kendal & Mary Handley dt. of Isaac & Mary at Ravenstonedale.

1795 10 28 Isabel dt. of Edward & Elinor Smith of Backside in Ravenstonedale & Stephen Binks of Warrington at Ravenstonedale.

1797 4 17 Elizabeth dt. of Edward & Eliner Smith of Ravenstonedale & Ric[d]. Graham.

1800 8 27 Michael Smith of Kidderminster co: Worc: son of Edward & Elinor Smith of Ravenstonedale & Agnes Buck at Brigflats.

1711 6 2 Edward Thompson of Sedbergh & Isabel Clerkson of Studfold in Ravenstonedale.

1735 8 9 Isabel Thornburrow of Studfold in Ravenstonedale widow, & John Jackson of Preston Patrick at Street in Ravenstonedale.

1744 3 31 John son of W[m]. & Alice Thistlethwaite of Harbergill in Kirthwaite & Margaret Close at Street in Ravenstonedale.

1723 3 30 James Thornborrow of Orton & Ann Alderson of Naithwaite at Street in Ravenstonedale.

1719 1 24 Geo: Thornburrgh of Langdale, p. of Orton, yeoman & Isabel Rogerson at Street, in Ravenstonedale.

1777 5 5 John Thompson of Nathwaite, husbandman, son of Thomas & Agnes Thompson of Dent & Eliz. Buck at Ravenstonedale.

1779 1 8 Anthony Thisththwaite of Dent son of Ric. & Elizabeth of Harbourgill in Dent & Mary Ion at Street, in Ravenstonedale.

(SOCIETY OF FRIENDS).

Burials.

DIED.			BURIED.			
			1695	4	x	Simon Alderson of Nathwaite at Sedbergh.
1714	4	25	1714	4	27	Agnes Alderson of Nathwaite at Sedbergh.
1766	1	15				James Baylieff age of Murthwait N.M.
1780	1	26	1780	1	29	Agnes Blaimire age 74, parent, of Narthwaite Co. West[d]. dt. of Ann at Catceld.
1788	5	6	1788	5	8	Isaac Blamire age 85 of Narthwaite at Cat-Celd.
1785	6	18	1785	6	20	Thomas Buck age 81 of Narthwaite Psh of Ravenstonedale husbandman at Cat-eld N.M.
1800	3	31	1800	4	3	James Buck age 57 of Street, Psh. of Ravenstonedale husbandman at Catceld.
1805	4	27	1805	4	30	Ann Buck age 54 of Dovingill in Ravenstonedale at Cat-keld.
1820	3	23	1820	3	26	Rowland Bownas age 77 of Eller Hill at Brigflatts.
1777	4	24	1777	4	27	Margaret Close age 90 of Stodfold Co. West[d]. widow of Thomas at Cat-keld.
1708	6	25	1708	6	26	Thomas Fawcett of Murthwaite.
1781	1	17	1781	1	28	Deborah Fawcett age 67 of Ravenstonedale, Wife of Stephen, husbandman at Cat-Celd N.M.
1790	9	15	1790	9	19	Mary Gosling age 56 of Narthwaite Co. West[d]. at Catkeld.
			1695	3	24	Isaac Handley, Bridge.
			1704	3	7	Abraham Handley of Mourthwate.
			1712	1	11	Magdalene Hall of Murthwaite.
1750	10	1	1750	10	4	Isaac Handley at Ravenstone Dale.
1759	5	24	1759	5	27	Joseph Handlay at Ravenston Dale.

(SOCIETY OF FRIENDS).

Burials.

Died.			Buried.			
1777	7	8	1777	7	9	Isaac Handley age 41 of Nathwaite Co. West[d]. husbandman at Cat-Celd.
1777	7	16	1777	7	18	Margaret Handley age 15 wks. dt. of Isaac & Mary at Cat-Celd.
1802	5	27	1802	5	29	John Hunter age 1 yr. of Narthwaite, Ravenstonedale son of Robert & Ann at Stramongate in Kendal N.M.
1804	1	30	1804	2	1	Thomas Handley age 8 mos. of Narthwaite in Ravenstonedale son of John & Margaret at Cat-keld.
1813	10	1	1813	10	4	Mary Handley age 77 of Narthwaite, widow at Catkeld.
1815	5	2	1815	5	4	Ann Hunter age 11 mos. of Hall Intack p. of Sedbergh dt. of Robert & Ann at Catkeld N.M.
1830	11	25	1830	11	28	Edward Hunter age 22 of Hall Intack p. of Sedbergh N.M.
1836	3	26	1836	3	29	Ann Handley age 22 dt. of Joseph, a farmer, of Wandale at Brigflats.
1836	6	1	1836	6	5	Robert Hunter age 62 of Bridge at Catkeld N.M.
1798	2	15	1798	2	18	Agnes Ion age 73 of Narthwaite in Ravenstonedale wife of William at Catkeld.
1808	6	25	1808	6	27	William Ion age 94 of Studfold in Ravenstonedale at Cat-keld N.M.
1828	7	9	1828	7	12	Mary Jackson age 69 of Narthwaite Psh. of Ravenstonedale at Brigflats.
			1677	5	15	Sibill Knewstubb wife of John.
			1678	6	15	Dorathy Knewstubb dt. of John.
1833	8	15	1833	8	18	Philip Kirkbride age 77 of Narthwaite in Ravenstonedale yeoman son of Antony of Molerstang at Brigflats.
1789	1	17	1789	1	20	Henry Lickbarrow age 40 of Fawcett Bank in Cautley at Catkeld.

(SOCIETY OF FRIENDS).

Burials.

DIED.			BURIED.			
1711	6	12	1711	6	14	Anthony Robinson of Dovengill.
1743	3	8	1743	3	10	Sibel Rogerson at Ravenstonedale.
1791	5	5	1791	5	5	John Smith age 20 of Backside Psh. of Ravenstonedale at Catkeld.
1791	5	3	1791	5	5	John Smith age 20 of Backside Psh. of Ravenstonedale at Catkeld.
1795	11	26	1795	11	29	Eleanor Smith age 57 of Backside wife of Edward at Catkeld.
1734	6	6	1734	6	8	Tho[s]. Thornborrow Jun[r]. of Nathwaite son of Thomas
1763	1	10	1763	1	12	Tho. Thornborrow at Ravenstonedale.
1785	10	6	1785	10	9	Ann Thornborrow age 88 of Narthwaite Co. West[d]. at Catkeld.

(SOCIETY OF FRIENDS).

A Register of the Births, Marriages, & Burials of the People called Quakers Belonging to the Quarterly Meeting of Westmoreland from 1649 to 1776 inclusive.*

Marriages.

1656	9	11	Anthony Pinder and Jane Clerkson were marryed, Ravenstondale &c.
1659	25	1	Reynold Rowell** & Elizabeth his wife were marryed Ravenstondale &c.
1663	3	3	Joseph Handley & Isabell Holme were marryed Ravenstondale &c.
1666	24	4	Simon Harker & Isabell Skaife were marryed Ravenstondale &c.
1666			Thomas Tompson & Mary Dent were marryed in ye 4 mo.
1667	22	4	William Perkin & Elizabeth Groasdale were marryed Ravenstondale &c.
1667	6	8	William Skaife & Isabell Askell were marryed.
1668	3	3	Edmond Shawe & Margaret Ffawcet were marryed Ravenstondale &c.
1668	10		John Shawe & Agnes Groasdale were marryed.
1668	24		Thomas Moore of Newbiggin and Margaret Aray were marryed.
1669	27	4	Christopher Rogerson & Elizabeth Winn were marryed, Ravenstondale &c.
1675	9	3	James Dent & Mary Winn were married, Ravenstondale &c.
1675	1	4	John Knewstub & Sibill Shaw were married.
1676	17	1	James Skaife & Agnes Harker were married, Ravenstondale &c.

* After the preceding pages had passed through the press I was shown the above Register, through the courtesy of Mr. Handley of Brigflatts. These supplemental entries are, I find, contained in the Digest, excepting one or two, but are described as being of the "Sedbergh M.M." only, and so had escaped me. The Births are identical with the previous list and are therefore not repeated.

** An error on the part of the transcribers, no doubt "Bouell" (=Bovell) is meant.

(SOCIETY OF FRIENDS).

Marriages.

1681 11 3 James Skaife & Mary Pinder the dt. of John Pinder both of Ravenstondale took each other in Marriage in the presence of many witnesses in the house of Anthony Pinder at Wath.

1683 14 7 Richard Adamthwaite of Lowcome & Mary Middleton took each other in Marriage at the house of Richard Adamthwaite in the presence of many witnesses..

1686 6 3 John Atkinson son of Edward Atkinson of the Side in the parish of Sedbergh and County of Yorke and Sarah Pinder of the Warth in Ravenstondale in County of West[d]. took each other in marriage in the public meeting-house at Brigflatts.

1705 4 10 Thomas Mason of Stonehouse and Elizabeth dt. of Richard Clerkson of Ravenstonedale marryed at a public meeting at Antho. Robinson's in Ravenstondale.

1709 7 5 James Fawcett of Ravenstondale [D. son of Thomas, Backside] & Rachel Hewetson of Penrith marryed at Penrith.

1744 31 3 John Thistlethwaite & Margaret Close were married at Ravenstondale.

1762 13 5 Edw[d]. Smith & Eleanor Handley were marryed at Ravenstondale.

The old method of keeping the Register ends here. The new one directed by the yearly Meeting in London beginning with the year 1777.

(SOCIETY OF FRIENDS).

Burials.

1659 3 2 John Skaife of Blackeside [D. Blacksike] was buryed, Ravenstondale.

1660 2 John Skaife was buryed in ye 2d motb, Ravenstondale.

1661 16 2 Mary dt. of Anthony Pinder was buryed, Ravenstondale.

1664 11 3 James son of Richard Clerkson was buryed Ravenstondale.

1666 23 4 William son of Michael Askall was buryed Ravenstondale.

1668 20 11 George Alderson dyed about 20th Ravenstondale.

1669 18 11 Margaret Chamberlaine dyed Ravenstondale.

1670 18 6 Mary wife of John Winn dyed Ravenstondale.

1671 22 10 Elizabeth Creusdale was buried Ravenstondale.

1671 [D. 1679] 18 6 Agnes wife of Jeoffrey Atkinson was buryed Ravenstondale.

1673 15 5 Mary the wife of Tho: Fawcet was buried Ravenstondale.

26 9 Richard Fawcet was buried.

27 12 Mabell the wife of John Skaife was buried.

1674 3 1 John Handley was buried Ravenstondale.

1675 4 William Addamthwaite was buried in the third week of the fourth month Ravenstondale.

1676 4 Ellen Adamthwaite was buried in the third week of the fourth month Ravenstondale.

1677 1 3 Agnes the wife of James Skaife was buried, Ravenstondale.

15 5 Sibill the wife of Jno. Knewstubbe was buryed.

1678 15 6 Dorothy the dt. of John Knewstubbe was buryed, Ravenstondale.

Elizabeth the wife of Robert Parkin in the latter end of the 6th mo.

10 Elizabeth the wife of William Adamtht. was buried in the 10th month.

1681 20 6 John Petty was buried, Ravenstondale.

28 9 Mary the dt. of James Fawcett was buried.

(SOCIETY OF FRIENDS).

Burials.

1682	29	7	Robert Dent was buried the 29th of the 7th month.*
	9	10	Richard Dawson [D. of Grisedale] was buried the ninth day of the 10th month.
	16	9	Isabel the wife of Reginold Bouell was buryed the 16th of the ninth month.
	11	12	Michaell Ayskell was buried the eleventh day of the twelfth month.
	3	1	Margaret Adamthwaite was buried the 3rd day of the 1st month 1682-3.
1683	29	2	Anne dt. of James Fawcett was buried Ravenstondale.
	29	4	Peter Denison of Kirkby Steven was buried.
	26	9	Rebecca dt. of Isaac Handley was buried.
	8	10	John Winne, Grisdale, was buried.
1684	23	9	Isabel wife of James Clarkson was buried, Ravenstondale.
1685	18	9	Jonathan son of Anthony Pinder was buried Ravenstondale.
1686	27	8	Agnes wife of Edmond Winne buried Ravenstondale.
	19	1	Agnes wife of George Mason buried.
1687	1	3	Thomas Shaw buried, Ravenstondale.
1692	21	12	Agnes Chamberlayn buryed, Ravenstondale.
1695	24	3	Isaac Hanley of Bridge, Ravenstondale.
		4	Simon Alderson of Nathwaite
	10	1	Elizabeth Prat.
1697	31	3	James Fawcet, of Riggside, Ravenstondale.
1704	7	3	Abraham Hanley, of Mourthwaite, Ravenstondale.
1706		10	Mary Fawcett of Riggside buryed, Ravenstondale.
1707		7	Margaret Fawcett Dyed, Ravenstondale.
1708	26	6	Thos. Fawcett of Murtht. was Buryed, Ravenstondale.
1709	28	11	Isabell Rogerson dyed & buryed ye 31st Ravenstondale.
1709	28	8	Eleanor wife of Anthony Robinson buryed Ravenstondale.
	12	12	Richard Clarkson buryed.
	31	11	Isabel wife of James Rogerson of Whinfell [D. Whingill].
1711	31	3	William Shaw of Mollerstang buryed, Ravenstondale.
	14	6	Anthony Robinson of Dovengill buryed.

* No place of residence is given for this group of Burials, but the names seem to belong to Ravenstonedale.

(SOCIETY OF FRIENDS).

Burials.

1712	5	8	Isabell Perkings buryed, Ravenstondale.
	11	1	Magdalene Hall of Marthwaite buryed.
1713	10	9	George Shaw Buryed Ravenstondale.
1714	27	4	Agnes Alderson of Marthwaite [D. Nathwaite] was buried Ravenstondale.
1721	2	11	Edward Shaw of Murthwaite [D. Marthwaite] buried Ravenstondale.
	21 [D. 20]	1	Margaret Shaw his widdow buried.
1722	28 [D. 20]	3	Anne Dennison dyed Aged 105, Ravenstondale.
1730	8	7	Sarah Bayliff buryed, Ravenstondale.
1731		10	Edward Thompson buryed, Ravenstondale.
1732	5	3	Dorathy Hastwell buryed, Ravenstondale.
1736	24	4	Mary Shearman was buried, Ravenstondale.
1739 [D. 1738]	20	4	Isabel Rogerson Buried 1758,[*] Ravenstondale.
	23	5	Ann Close was Buried.
1743	10	3	Sibill Rogerson was buried at Ravenstondale.
1749	27	12	William Addison, Ravenstondale.
1749	27	12	Willm. Addison was Buryed at Ravenstondale.
1750	4	10	Isaac Handley was burryed at Ravenstondale.
1755	23	11	Adam Walker Ravenstondale.[**]
1758	5	5	John Seubby [D. Sealby] was buryed at Ravenstondale.
1759	27	5	Joseph Handley was Buried at Ravenstondale.
1763	12	1	Thomas Thornborrow was buryed at Ravenstondale.
1764	30	4	John Alderson died on a visit to Friends in the South, was buryed at London.
1766	24	1	Mary wife of John Hodgson was buryed, Ravenstondale.
	2	2	Philip Handley [D. Hindley] was buried.
	18	8	Alice wife of Ralph Alderson was buried.
1767	4	10	Isabella Jackson was buried, Ravenstondale.
1768	2	4	Ann wife of John Handley was buried, Ravenstondale.
1770	13	5	John Handley was buried, Ravenstondale.
	5	6	Thomas Close was buried.
1771	3	4	Mary Fawcett was buried, Ravenstondale.

* Evidently an error for 1738.
** This entry does not appear to be in the Digest.

(SOCIETY OF FRIENDS).

Burials.

1772	29	1	Ralph Alderson was buried, Ravenstondale.
1773	14	7	Simon Alderson was buried, Ravenstondale.

The old method of keeping the Register ends here. The new one directed by the yearly Meeting in London beginning with the year 1777.

ERRATA.—FRIENDS' REGISTERS.

Pages 106, 107, 108, for "Baptisms" read "Births."
Page 107, 10th entry from bottom read "John son of James & Mary Skaiffe."
Page 111, 3rd line from bottom, strike out the Marriage entry between Margaret Story & John Knewstub.

LIST OF SUBSCRIBERS.

Bell, Rev. Wm. R., Laithkirk Vicarage, Middleton-in-Teesdale.
Bousfield, Rev. Stephen, M.A., Sudbury, Derby.
Bousfield, Frederick, 31, Crowhurst road, Brixton.
Bousfield, Harvey, The Mullberries, Great Crosby, Liverpool.
Brunskill, Stephen, Castle Meadows, Kendal.
Burra, Rev. Thos. Fawcett, M.A., Linton Vicarage, Maidstone.
Burra, Robert, Gate, Sedbergh.

Carter-Squire, Miss S. A., Catterick.
Carver, John, Greystoke, Hanger Hill, Ealing, London, W.
Crisp, F. A., Grove Park, Denmark Hill, London, S.E.

Dawson, Edw. Bousfield, Aldcliffe Hall, Lancaster.
Day, Rev. H. G., M.A., 55, Denmark Villas, West Brighton.
Dixon, Wm., Causeway, Ravenstonedale.

Ferguson, The Worshipful Chancellor, F.S.A., Carlisle.
Fothergill, John, Brownber, Ravenstonedale.
Fothergill, John Wm., The Cottage, Brownber, Ravenstonedale.
Fothergill, Richard, Ashley Bank, Ravenstonedale.
Fothergill, S. R., 71, Portland Place, London, W.
Fothergill, Watson, Mapperly Road, Nottingham.
Fothergill, Gerald, 29, Priory Park, Kilburn, N.W.
Fothergill, Miss, 27, Arboretum road, Nottingham.
Furness, William, Senr., 17, Woodbine Street, Moss Side, Manchester.

Greenbank, Richard H., 49, S. Luke's Road, Westbourne Park, W.

Hewetson, Mrs., 8, S. James's Terrace, Regents Park, London.
Hewetson, Miss, Finnich Malise, Drymen, N.B.
Hovenden, Robert, F.S.A., Heathcote, Park Hill Road, Croydon.

Langhorne, Miss, Lowther Street, Penrith.
Lonsdale, The Right Hon. the Earl of, Lowther Castle, Penrith.

MAGRATH, DR., Provost of Queen's College, Oxford.
MARSHALL, G. W., F.S.A., Rouge Croix, Heralds College, London, E.C.
METCALFE, E. P., M.A., Rajahmundri, India.
METCALFE-GIBSON, ANTHONY, Coldbeck, Ravenstonedale.

RENNISON, MISS JANE, 78, Wellington Street, Moss Side, Manchester.
ROBINSON, JOHN, Ashfell, Ravenstonedale.
ROBINSON, ROBT., C. E., Beechwood, Darlington.
ROBINSON, WM., Greenbank, Sedbergh.

SAVORY, SIR JOSEPH Bart., M.P., Buckhurst Park, Ascot.
SEDGWICK, MISS, Thorns Hall, Sedbergh.
SMITH, CHAS. E., 35, The Park, Sharples, Bolton-le-Moors.
SWINGLEHURST, HENRY, Hincaster House, Milnthorpe.

THOMPSON, REV. WM., M.A., Guldrey Lodge, Sedbergh.
THOMPSON, MRS., Stobars Hall, Kirkby Stephen.
THOMPSON, MISS, The Croft, Kirkby Stephen.
THOMPSON, W. N., St. Bees.
TULLIE HOUSE FREE LIBRARY, Carlisle.

WOODS, SIR ALBERT W., Garter, College of Arms, London, E.C.

Lightning Source UK Ltd.
Milton Keynes UK
UKHW022149270722
406481UK00003B/120